U0905098

THE GERMAN CIVIL CODE

BY CHUNG HUI WANG

德国民法典

王宠惠英译本

戴永盛　校勘

中国政法大学出版社

2019・北京

图书在版编目（CIP）数据

德国民法典:王宠惠英译本/戴永盛校勘. —北京:中国政法大学出版社,2019. 12
ISBN　978-7-5620-7585-1

Ⅰ.①德…　Ⅱ.①戴…　Ⅲ.①民法—法典—德国　Ⅳ.①D951.63

中国版本图书馆CIP数据核字(2017)第255823号

出 版 者　中国政法大学出版社

地　　址　北京市海淀区西土城路 25 号

邮寄地址　北京 100088 信箱 8034 分箱　邮编 100088

网　　址　http://www.cuplpress.com (网络实名：中国政法大学出版社)

电　　话　010-58908437(编辑室)　58908334(邮购部)

承　　印　北京中科印刷有限公司

开　　本　710mm×1000mm　1/16

印　　张　43.25

字　　数　780 千字

版　　次　2019 年 12 月第 1 版

印　　次　2019 年 12 月第 1 次印刷

定　　价　198.00 元

THE

GERMAN CIVIL CODE.

TRANSLATED AND ANNOTATED,

WITH AN

HISTORICAL INTRODUCTION AND APPENDICES.

BY

CHUNG HUI WANG, D. C. L.,

Member of the Internationale Vereinigung für vergleichende Rechtswissenschaft und Volkswirtschaftslehre zu Berlin;

Member of the Société de Legislation Comparée, &c.

LONDON:

STEVENS AND SONS, LIMITED,

119 & 120, CHANCERY LANE,

Law Publishers.

1907.

TO

THE FACULTY OF THE

LAW SCHOOL

OF

YALE UNIVERSITY

This Work

IS BY PERMISSION

Dedicated

AS A

TOKEN OF RESPECT AND ESTEEM.

王寵惠，字亮疇，祖籍廣東東莞，生於一八八一年十月十日。一八九五年考入北洋大學堂法科，一九〇〇年獲中國第一張大學畢業文憑（欽字第壹號）。一九〇五年獲美國耶魯大學法學博士學位。一九〇七年在英國倫敦出版『德國民法典』英譯本，為『德國民法典』的首位英譯者。辛亥革命後被推為副議長。歷任南京臨時政府外交總長、司法總長，北洋政府教育總長、國務總理，國民政府司法院院長、外交部長等職。曾任海牙常設國際法庭正法官多年。參與制定聯合國憲章。一九四八年當選中央研究院院士。被譽為民國第一位法學家。一九五八年三月十五日病逝於臺北。

PREFACE.

THE new Civil Code for the German Empire (*Bürgerliches Gesetzbuch für das Deutsche Reich*) received the Imperial sanction on August 18th, 1896, and came into effect on January 1st, 1900. Four French, one Spanish, one Italian, and two Japanese translations have thus far come to my notice, and possibly there may be translations into other languages. The present translator himself hopes to bring out a Chinese rendering at no distant date. No English translation has as yet appeared, and consequently the work has not received the attention which it deserves in the English-speaking countries [(a)].

The need for an English translation is, however, undeniable. Unlike the *Code Napoléon*, the German Civil Code is the most carefully worded and scientifically arranged code extant, representing no less than twenty-two years of careful study and research by the most eminent German jurists. The late Professor Maitland referred to it (in his *Political Theories in the Middle Ages*, p. xvii.) as being "the most carefully considered statement of a nation's laws that the world has ever seen", while Dr. A. Pearce Higgins speaks of it as being "a standing object-lesson to all States that are looking forward in the future to a scheme of codification" [(b)]. This monumental work of German intellect deserves, therefore, if not a prominent place, at least some place in English legal literature.

Nor is the German Code of mere academic interest to the English-speaking peoples. Both England and America are closely connected with Germany—the former commercially, by its proximity to the Continent; the latter socially, by the

(a) The Yale University Law School is, so far as I know, the only law school in the United States which gives regular instruction in the German Civil Code.

(b) See his able article on "The Making of the German Civil Code" in the *Journal of the Society of Comparative Legislation*, New Series, No. XIII.

great influx of German immigrants in recent years. In this age of international intercourse, cases involving the conflict of laws come up from time to time, and it is not an uncommon thing for an English or American Court to be called upon to decide a question of German law. To place in the hands of English-speaking lawyers a reliable rendering of the Code is my object in undertaking this task. How far this object has been attained will depend upon the judgment of the profession.

I have taken great pains to make the translation as faithful as possible, and have, in more than one instance, sacrificed style to accuracy. The condensed statement of the text needs elucidation even to the Germans themselves, while the different sections are so mutually dependent that it is difficult, if not impossible, fully to comprehend the meaning of one without reference to some other section or sections. Consequently, such annotations and cross-references have, wherever necessary, been added as would conduce to a proper appreciation of the text, care having been taken not to make the book unwieldy. During the progress of this work an important change has been made in the plan as originally conceived. In order to put the fundamental principles of German civil law in clearer light before English-speaking lawyers, I thought it advisable to emphasize the salient points of similarity and dissimilarity between the German Civil Code and the corresponding rules of English law. The attempt was finally given up, though not without hesitation, and in spite of the fact that much time and labour had already been spent in this direction. The reasons are threefold. First, those who take an interest in the study of this Code may be safely presumed to have already a good knowledge of English law, and they can, therefore, compare their own system of law with that of the Germans in a much better way than one to whom both German and English are acquired languages. Secondly, the timely appearance of the proposed codification of the English civil law (*Das bürgerliche Recht Englands auf Grundlage einer Kodification*) and of Dr. Schuster's admirable work on "The Principles of German Civil Law", renders the task of comparing the two legal systems comparatively easy. Lastly, the change was due to an earnest desire to reduce the book to as convenient a size as possible.

Among the numerous works consulted may be especially mentioned the following: H. Dernburg's *Das bürgerliche Recht des deutschen Reichs und Preussens*, 6 vols. ; Ed. Heilfron's *Lehrbuch des bürgerlichen Rechts*, 4 vols.; F. Endemann's *Lehrbuch des bürgerlichen Rechts*, 3 vols.; K. Cosack's *Lehrbuch des deutschen bürgerlichen Rechts*, 2 vols.; G. Planck's *Bürgerliches Gesetzbuch mit Einführungs-gesetz*, 6 vols.; J. v. *Staudinger's Kommentar zum bürgerlichen Gesetzbuch*, 6 vols.; and L. Enneccerus and H. O. Lehmann's *Das bürgerliche Recht*, 2 vols. Among the different editions of the Code which I have made use of are those by H. Rosenthal, A. Achilles, W. and F. Brandis, O. Fisher and W. Henle. I have also derived much help from the various translations in different language. To all these authors, commentators and translators, I gladly acknowledge my indebtedness, but to do one am I under deeper obligation for the rendering of some of the technical terms and expressions than to my former teacher, Prof. E. V. RAYNOLDS, D.C.L., of the Yale Law School. It is he who has revealed to me the scientific value of comparative law, and who has, above all, taught me that the study of law is not merely a profession, but is a science in the truest sense of the word. Grateful acknowledgment is also due to A. S. GAYE, Esq., M. A., Barrister-at-Law, for reading over the manuscripts and for valuable suggestions and corrections which have safeguarded me from falling into many a serious mistake; and to Dr. E. J. SCHUSTER for his personal advice, and specially for his kindness in permitting me to adopt many of the technical terms which he has so ably translated. Finally, I desire to express my sincere thanks to my former teacher, J. BROMLEY EAMES, Esq., M.A., B.C. L., Barrister-at-Law, for encouragement in various ways, and to my honoured friend, Dr. FELIX MEYER, Justice of the Prussian Supreme Court of Judicature, whose profound learning in comparative law has always been my admiration.

If this edition of the German Civil Code creates among the English-speaking peoples an interest, however slight, in the study of comparative law, the labour which I have bestowed on this work will be amply repaid.

C. H. W.

CHARLOTTENBURG, BERLIN.
August 1st, 1907.

TABLE OF CONTENTS.

FIRST BOOK.
General Principles.

SECOND BOOK.
Law of Obligations.

THIRD BOOK.
Law of Things.

FOURTH BOOK.
Family Law.

FIFTH BOOK.
Law of Inheritance.

APPENDIX A.
INTRODUCTORY ACT TO THE CIVIL CODE.

APPENDIX B.

APPENDIX C.

APPENDIX D.

HISTORICAL INTRODUCTION.

To the Germans the enactment of a civil code for the whole Empire is of the greatest importance, when the pre-existing legal circumstances are taken into consideration. In 1495 the Roman law was "received" in Germany as the common law of the land. "The Roman law as 'received', though in theory Justinian, was in practice the law that had been elaborated by a long race of Italian commentators and glossators. This 'reception' also was only as a supplement to the local customary law; 'it came to the aid of particularism'. Whole departments of law affecting the every-day life of the people—family law, land law, marriage, succession—were for centuries largely governed by old Germanic customs as they had been transformed by feudal influences. It was in the law of obligations that Roman law exerted its greatest influence. The local customs, however, after the reception required to be proved as such, while the Courts took judicial notice of the Roman common law, and as proof was often difficult, the chief Germanic survivals came from those customs which had been reduced to writing." According to the informations furnished to the Reichstag by the Imperial Office of Justice, the division of the Empire from a juridical standpoint was as follows:

(1) In the heart of Germany lies an immense territory extending from the Alps to the Baltic Sea, from the River Weser to the River Elbe, and from the Black Forest to Bohemia, and containing a population of 16, 500, 000. This region was subject to the *Gemeines Recht*, *i.e.*, the Roman common law as received in 1459, and numerous ancient local laws, urban laws, privileges and statutes.

(2) In Prussia, with a population of 21, 200, 000, the Prussian Code of 1794 (*Das allgemeine Landrecht für die Königlich-preussichen*

Staaten) prevailed.

(3) In the Rhine Provinces, 6, 700, 000 of the inhabitants were subject to the *Code Napoléon* of 1804, and 1, 700, 000 to the *Badisches Landrecht* of 1809.

(4) In Saxony, containing a population of 3, 500, 000 the *Sächsisches bürgerliches Gesetzbuch* of 1863 was in force.

(5) In Schleswig-Holstein, with a population of 15, 000, the Danish law of 1683 obtained.

(6) A small district in Bavaria, having a population of not more than 2, 500, was subject to the *Österreichisches allgemeines bürgerliches Gesetzbuch* of 1811.

Of these laws, some were written in German, some in French, some in Greek, some in Latin, and some in Danish. To add to the complexity, each of these systems was subject to change by local laws and customs. The situation was vividly depicted by Herr Nieberding, Secretary of the Office of Justice (Session of February 3, 1896), when he said: "What confidence can people have in their rights when they find, as is often the case, that the law of succession is totally different in two contiguous places? Here the wife inherits; there she has no rights of succession whatsoever; here the brothers and sisters of full blood and half-brothers and half-sisters on the father's side are admitted on equal terms; a few steps away their rights differ completely." Such was the legal condition in Germany prior to the adoption of the Civil Code. That such an anomalous state of things could have been tolerated for so long a time is a legal mystery which remains to be solved.

The Germans were not, however, slow in realising the necessity as well as the importance of the unification of civil legislation. Even as early as the beginning of the last century and not long after the formation of the German Confederation by the Congress of Vienna, a movement was on foot to enact a code for the whole Confederation. This gave rise to the celebrated dispute between Thibaut and Savigny, and it was then that the latter founded the "historical school" for which he has ever since been famous. Savigny contended with much force andability that the time was not yet ripe for Germany to receive a code, and that a nation's laws could be truly improved not so much by artificial means—by *Gesetzesrecht* (*i.e.*, enacted laws) —as by the spontaneous growth of legal ideas—by *Volksrecht* and *Juristenrecht* (*i.e.*, customary laws and legal principles as enunciated by the jurisconsults and the tribunals). The final triumph of the "historical school" checked for a time the progress of the movement for codification.

Another serious difficulty to be encountered was the constitutionality of such an undertaking, there being no central organ in the newly-formed Confederation competent to legislate for the whole Union. However, popular sentiment grew stronger and stronger in favour of legal unification as time went on, and finally found expression in the project for the new Constitution of 1849, Art. XIII (59) of which declares *inter alia* commercial law, bills of exchange, criminal law, and civil procedure to be subject to federal regulation. Unfortunately, the project did not go beyond the stage of an official draft, and the only result was the adoption of a Commercial Code and a Law on Bills of Exchange. These were originally enacted as *State* laws by each of the States individually, and it was not until after the establishment of the North German Confederation in 1867 that they became *Federal* laws. In 1862 a conference representing ten States met at Dresden to draft a uniform Code of Obligations which was completed after four years' work, but was never adopted. The Constitution of 1867, Art. XIII. (4), declared the law of obligations to be within the competence of the Federal Legislature, and this provision was without any extension reproduced in the new Constitution of April 16, 1871. The federal legislative power was subsequently enlarged by successive amendments adopted in 1872 and 1873, and the amendment of December 12, 1873, finally conferred full powers on the *Reichstag* to legislate on all matters relating to civil law.

In February of the following year, in pursuance of this amendment, the *Bundesrat* nominated a commission of five, officially known as the *Vorkommission*, to fix the plan of the work and the method of procedure. The plan recommended by the commission was that the task should be entrusted to a commission, and that each of the main divisions of the proposed Code should be allotted to a single member, whose work, when once completed, should form the basis of deliberation and modification by all the commissioners sitting together. The mode of procedure having been approved of by the *Bundesrat*, a commission of eleven members—jurisconsults, professors and magistrates—was appointed on July 2 of the same year (1874), under the chairmanship of Dr. Pape, Privy Councillor and President of the Imperial Supreme Court of Commerce. The common law element was represented by a distinguished Romanist (Windscheid) and an eminent Germanist (Roth); three members represented the regions subject to the Prussian Code; two, those subject to the Code *Napoléon*; while Bavaria, Wurttemberg, Prussia and Saxony were each represented by one member on the commission. The allotment of the work was as follows: To Gebhard was entrusted the General Part; Kübel, the Law of Obligations (he, however, died before the completion of his work, and the commission relied upon the Dresden Draft of 1866); Johow, the Law of Things; Planck, the Family Law; and von Schmitt, the Law of Inheritance. After thirteen years of labour and discussion, a project, known as the "First Project", was submitted to the Imperial Chancellor on December 27, 1887, who in turn transmitted it to the *Bundesrat*. In order to submit it to a thorough examination by the whole nation, the project was published in the following year, together with five volumes of "Motive" (one for each look), containing a summary of the existing laws and the various reasons which led to their adoption or repudiation.

As had been expected, the publication of the project gave rise to bitter criticism on all sides. The Germanists, headed by the distinguished jurist, Dr. Gierke, charged the codifiers with having sacrificed the national laws by giving too much predominance to the Roman law; the Socialists objected to the Code on the ground that it was too favourable to the capitalists, and detrimental to the interests of the labouring class. Another objection, by no means a slightone, was based on the fact that the commission was composed of doctrinaires and officials only; that the commercial, agricultural and industrial interests were entirely neglected; and that the draft was couched in obscure language unintelligible to the lay mind. To pacify the popular dissatisfaction, the *Bundesrat*, on December 4, 1890, appointed a new extra-parliamentary commission of twenty-two members to revise the project. The commission was composed of practical men, selected from among various classes of people; four of the former members were, however, retained in order not to break the thread of the Work. The commission began to sit in April, 1891, and each part of the new draft was published as soon as it was completed, so that the revisers might he in touch with public opinion. In March, 1895, the draft was finished; but in view of the public criticism which had arisen in the meantime, it was again thoroughly revised, whence its name: "The Second Project: Second Version", or, "The Second Revised Project". In the following October it was presented to the *Bundesrat*, which referred it to its Committee of Justice. Another revision took place. The Sixth Book on Private International Law was struck out, and in lieu thereof certain provisions were drawn up and embodied in the Introductory Act. In January, 1896, this "Third Project", together with an official Memorandum (*Denkschrift zum Entwurfe eines bürgerlichen Gesetzbuches*), was transmitted to the *Reichstag* for its consideration.

It was here that the draft passed through its most severe ordeal. After having been subjected to a general discussion, it was laid before a committee of twenty-one members in which all the political parties were represented. The Committee held, altogether, fifty-three meetings, and on June 12 it presented its report to the House. On June 27 the second reading took place.

The debates were lengthy and animated; but the order, the dignity, the patriotism with which they were conducted were also significant. The only important amendment was that to 1305, fixing the age of twenty-one instead of twenty-five as the age at which a person is permitted to marry without parental consent. The deliberation chiefly centred on the following topics:

(1) Interdiction of persons on account of habitual drunkenness (6), six speakers taking part in the discussion.
(2) The juristic personality of associations (21), eight speakers.
(3) The avoidance of juristic acts which are contrary to law, or *contra bonps mores* (309), eight speakers.
(4) The liability for damage caused by animals (833), twelve speakers.
(5) The liability for damage caused by game (835), thirty speakers.
(6) The responsibility of public officers (889), eight speakers.
(7) Civil marriage (1303), fourteen speakers.
(8) Consent of parent to marriage (1305), nine speakers.
(9) Insanity as a ground for divorce (1569), eleven speakers.
(10) Parental power (1089*et seq.*), nine speakers.

(11) Holograph wills (2231), ten speakers.

The principal speakers were: Lenzmann, Stadhagen, von Cuny, Bachem, Planck, Enneccerius, Niderding, Dziembowski, von Buchca, von Stumm, Frohme, Rickert Bebel and Auer.

After the third reading the Bill passed the *Reichstag* on July 1, the *Bundesrat* on July 4, and received the Imperial sanction on August 18, 1896. It was formally promulgated on the 24th of the month, and on January 1, 1900, it came into effect. Thus for the first time in the history of Germany there came into being a *German* Civil Code, in the truest sense of the term, which obtains throughout the length and breadth of the Empire [(a)].

(*a*) It may not be out of place to emphasize the fact—very often overlooked by foreign readers—that the Civil Code does not cover the whole field of German private law. Dr. Schuster (Principles of German Civil Law, p. 5) has truly remarked: "In order to find out the law on any given point, it is not sufficient to refer to the provisions of the BGB and HGB." (these are the usual German abbreviations for the Civil and Commercial Codes respectively) "or of any other Imperial statute that may be applicable to the matter in hand, but that in each case it must be ascertained: (1) whether the subject of the inquiry is one on which the State law, including the AG (*i.e.*, *Ausführungsgesetz*) of the particular State, contains any supplementary provisions; (2) whether any Imperial customary law affects the particular subject; (3) whether, in the event of the subject being one which may be affected by State law, any local customary law relating thereto is in existence. These circumstances alone make it clear that the BGB did not, either in intention or in effect, reduce the whole of German law into one compact mass."

GERMAN CIVIL CODE.

WE, **WILLIAM**, by the Grace of God, German Emperor, King of Prussia, &c., decree in the name of the Empire, with the consent of the Federal Council and the Imperial Parliament, as follows:

FIRST BOOK.
General Principles.

FIRST SECTION.
PERSONS.

FIRST TITLE.
Natural Persons.

1. The legal capacity [(a)] of a human being begins with the completion of birth [(b)].

2. Majority begins with the completion of the twenty-first year of age.

3. A minor who has completed his eighteenth year of age may be declared

---

(*a*) *I.e.*, the capacity to have rights, in contradistinction to the disposing capacity (see 104 *et seq.*), *i.e.*, the capacity to enter into juristic acts.

(*b*) However, the maxim *infans conceptus pro jam nato habetur* is admitted by the Code, a child *en ventre sa mère* being capable of having certain rights in matters of succession. See 1923.

of full age by order of the Guardianship Court [c].

By the declaration of majority the minor acquires the legal status of a person of full age.

4. The declaration of majority is permissible only if the minor gives his approval.

If the minor is under parental power, the approval of the parent [d] is also necessary, unless he has neither the care of the person nor of the property of the child. For a minor widow the approval of the parent is not necessary.

5. The declaration of majority should issue only if it will promote the welfare of the minor.

6. A person may be interdicted [e]:

(1) if in consequence of insanity or feeble-mindedness he is unable to manage his affairs [f];

(2) if by prodigality he exposes, himself or his family to the danger of want;

(3) if in consequence of habitual drunkenness he is unable to manage his affairs, or exposes himself or his family to the danger of want, or endangers the safety of others.

The interdiction shall be revoked if the cause for the interdiction disappears.

7. A person [g] who resides habitually in a place establishes his domicile in that place.

Domicile may exist simultaneously in several places.

Domicile is lost if, with the intention of abandoning it, residence is discontinued.

(c) This corresponds to the *emancipatio* of the Roman Law.

(d) Usually the father, but sometimes the mother. See 1684.

(e) This provision applies to minors as well as to persons of full age. The District Court has jurisdiction in such matters.

(f) Incapacity to manage *certain* kinds of affairs is not a sufficient ground for interdiction.

(g) This applies only to natural persons. For juristic persons, see 24, 80.

8. A person who is incapable of disposing [(h)] or is limited in disposing capacity [(i)], may neither establish nor abandon a domicile without the consent of his statutory agent.

9. A person in military service has his domicile in the place where he is stationed. In the case of a person whose command has no home station, the last home station of the command is deemed to be the place of his domicile.

These provisions do not apply to persons in military service who are serving only their compulsory term of military service, or who may not establish a separate domicile [(k)].

10. A wife takes the domicile of her husband. If the husband establishes a domicile in a place in a foreign country to which the wife does not follow and is not bound to follow him, the wife does not take his domicile.

So long as the husband has no domicile or the wife does not take his domicile, the wife may have a separate domicile.

11. A legitimate child takes the domicile of the father [(l)], an illegitimate child the domicile of the mother, an adopted child the domicile of the adoptor. The child retains his domicile until he legally abandons it [(m)].

A legitimation or adoption not taking place until after the child has attained his majority does not affect the domicile of the child.

12. If the right to the use of a name by a person entitled to it [(n)] is disputed by another, or if the interest of the person entitled is injured by the fact that another uses the same name without authority, then the person entitled may demand from the other abatement of the injury [(o)]. If a continuance of the injury is to be apprehended, he may apply for an injunction.

(*h*) 104.

(*i*) 114.

(*k*) *I.e.*, without the consent of the statutory agent. 8.

(*l*) No matter whether he exercises the parental power or not.

(*m*) He cannot do so without the consent of his statutory agent (8) until he has attained majority.

(*n*) This provision applies to natural as well as juristic persons.

(*o*) The wrongdoer is also liable to pay damages in certain cases. See 823.

13. A person who has disappeared may, subject to the conditions provided for by 14 to 17, be declared dead by means of public summons.

14. The declaration of death may be made, if for ten years no news has been received that the missing person is alive. It cannot be made before the close of the year in which the missing person would have completed his thirty-first year of age (p).

A missing person who would have completed his seventieth year of age may be declared dead, if for five years no news has been received that he is alive.

The periods of ten and five years respectively begin to run from the close of the last year in which the missing person was reported to be still alive.

15. A person who, as a member of an armed force (q), has taken part in a war, has been missed during the war, and has not since been heard of, may be declared dead, if three years have elapsed since the conclusion of peace. If no conclusion of peace has taken place, the three years begin to run from the close of the year in which the war was brought to an end.

A person who accompanies an armed force in the capacity of official or servant, or as a volunteer, is also deemed to be a member of an armed force.

16. If a vessel shall have been lost during a sea voyage, any person who was on board at the time, and who has been missing since the loss of the vessel, may be declared dead, if one year has elapsed since the loss.

The loss of the vessel is presumed if she has not arrived at her place of destination, or, if she had no fixed destination, has not returned, and if

(a) in case of voyages within the Baltic Sea, one year;

(b) in case of voyages within other European waters, including all parts of the Mediterranean, the Black Sea, and the Sea of Azov, two years;

(c) in case of voyages extending beyond European waters Three years have elapsed since the beginning of the voyage. If news has been received of the vessel, the expiration of that period is necessary which would have had to elapse if the vessel had taken her departure from the place

(p) This provision does not apply to the cases provided for by 15—17.

(q) Whether of the Empire or of a foreign power makes no difference.

where she was last reported to be.

17. If a person has been in peril of his life in circumstances [r] other than those specified in 15, 16, and has never thereafter been reported alive, he may be declared dead if three years have elapsed since the occurrence whereby the peril of life arose.

18. The declaration of death establishes the presumption [s] that the missing person died at the date fixed in the judicial decree for declaration of death.

Unless the ascertained facts indicate some other date, death is presumed to have occurred:

(a) in the cases provided for by 14, at the date at which the declaration of death could first lawfully be made;

(b) in the cases provided for by 15, at the date at which peace was concluded, or at the close of the year in which the war was brought to an end;

(c) in the cases provided for by 16, at the date at which the vessel was lost or is presumed to have been lost;

(d) in the cases provided for by 17, at the date at which the occurrence took place.

If the time of death is fixed only as a certain day, death is deemed to have taken place at the end of that day.

19. So long as the declaration of death has not been made, the missing person is presumed to have lived up to the date which, according to 18, par. 2, is presumed to be the date of death in the absence of any other indication from the ascertained facts; the provision of 18, par. 3, applies *mutatis mutandis*.

20. If several persons have perished in a common peril, it is presumed [t] that they died simultaneously.

(r) *E.g.*, fire, explosion, railway accident, &c.

(s) This presumption is rebuttable.

(t) The presumption is rebuttable.

SECOND TITLE.
Juristic Persons.

I. Associations.

1. *General Provisions.*

21. An association whose object is not the carrying on of an economic enterprise [(u)], acquires juristic personality by registration in the register of associations of the competent District Court.

22. An association whose object is the carrying on of an economic enterprise acquires juristic personality, in the absence of special provisions of Imperial law, by grant from the State. The power to make such grant belongs to the State in whose territory the association has its seat [(x)].

23. An association whose seat is not in any State may, in the absence of special provisions of Imperial law, be granted juristic personality by resolution of the Federal Council.

24. Unless it is otherwise provided, the place when the affairs of an association are managed is deemed to be its seat [(y)].

25. The constitution of an association having juristic personality, so far as it does not depend upon the following provisions, is determined by the articles of the association.

26. The association must have a directorate. The directorate may consist of several persons.

(*u*) The term "economic enterprise" (*wirtschaftlicher Geschäftsbetrieb*) is almost incapable of definition. It has a broader meaning than the more familiar term "commercial enterprise", as it also includes any enterprise which is carried on not for pecuniary profits, but for the mere convenience of its members, as, *e.g.*, the students' co-operative societies of some of the American universities. This term is discussed at great length in the French official translation of the Code (p. 23), and the references contained therein. See Bibliography, Appendix B.

(*x*) Associations which have not acquired juristic personality are treated as partnerships. 54.

(*y*) This corresponds to the "domicile" of a natural person.

The directorate represents the association in judicial proceedings and in all other affairs; it is in the position of a statutory agent [(z)]. The extent of its representative authority, as against third persons [(a)], may be limited by the articles.

27. The appointment of the directors is effected by resolution carried at a members meeting [(b)].

The appointment is revocable at any time, without prejudice to any claim for agreed compensation. The revocability may be limited by the articles to the case where a grave reason for the revocation exists; such reasons are, *e.g.*, gross breach of duty, or incapacity for the proper management of business.

The provisions of 664 to 670, applicable to mandate, apply, *mutatis mutandis*, to the management of affairs by the directorate.

28. If the directorate consists of several persons, the carrying of their resolutions is regulated by the provisions of 32, 34, applicable to resolutions of the members of the association [(c)].

If a declaration of intention is required to be served upon an association, it is sufficient if it be served upon one of the directors.

29. If a requisite quorum of directors cannot be formed, the District Court in whose district the association has its seat shall, in urgent cases and upon the application of an interested party [(d)], appoint temporary directors to act for the time being.

30. It may be provided by the articles that, besides the directorate, special agents are to be appointed to attend to particular matters of business. The authority of such an agent extends, in case of doubt, to all juristic acts which

---

(*z*) Besides the ordinary duties of a statutory agent (164—181), it has certain other special duties. 36, 42, par. 2, 48. In the case of a "registered association", also the duties specified in 59, 67, 71, 72, 76, 78.

(*a*) They are bound to take notice of the limitation of power specified in the articles. Cf. 64, sentence 2.

(*b*) 40.

(*c*) 40.

(*d*) Whether he is a member of the association or not makes no difference.

ordinarily come within the scope of the particular kind of business assigned to him.

31. The association is responsible for any damage which the directorate, a director, or other duly [(e)] appointed agent may cause to a third party by an act giving rise to a claim for compensation, provided that such act was done in the execution of its or his official duties [(f)].

32. The affairs of the association, so far as they are not required to be managed by the directorate or some other representative body of the association, are regulated by resolutions carried at a meeting of the member. It is necessary to the validity of a resolution that the object shall be stated in the notice calling the meeting. A resolution is carried if a majority of the members present vote in favour of it [(g)].

A resolution is also valid without a meeting of the members if all the members declare in writing their consent to the resolution [(h)].

33. For a resolution involving an alteration in the articles a majority of three-fourths of the members present is necessary. For an alteration in the objects for which the association was formed the consent of all the members is necessary; the consent of members not present must he given in writing [(i)].

If the juristic personality of the association depends upon grant, for very alteration in the articles the ratification of the State, or, in case the grant is made by the Federal Council, the ratification of the Federal Council, is necessary [(k)].

34. A member shall not vote [(l)] upon any resolution which relates to the

---

(*e*) The word "duly" is a somewhat free translation of the German expression *verfassungsmässig*, which means literally "in accordance with the articles".

(*f*) This provision enlarges the liability provided for in 831.

(*g*) No resolution if the votes are equal.

(*h*) This provision may be modified by the articles. 40.

(*i*) *Ibid.* In the case of registered association any alteration in the articles must also be registered. 71, 77.

(*k*) Cf. 40.

(*l*) He can, nevertheless, participate in the discussion.

entering into a juristic act between himself and the association, or to the institution or settlement of legal proceedings between himself and the association.

35. Personal rights of one member may not be infringed by resolution at a members' meeting without such member's consent.

36. A members' meeting shall be called in the cases provided for by the articles, and whenever the interest of the association requires it.

37. A members' meeting shall be called if the proportion of the members fixed by the articles, or, in the absence of such a provision, one-tenth of the members demand it in writing, with a statement of the object and reasons [(m)].

If this demand be not complied with, the District Court in whose district the association has its seat may [(n)] authorise the members who have made the demand to call the meeting, and may provide for the chairmanship of the meeting. In the notice calling the meeting reference must be made to such authorisation.

38. Membership is not transferable, and does not pass by inheritance. The exercise of the right of membership may not be delegated to another person [(o)].

39. Members are entitled to withdraw from the association.

It may be provided by the articles that withdrawal is permissible only at the end of a business year, or not until the expiration of a fixed period after notice; such period may amount at most to two years.

40. The provisions of 27, pars. 1, 3, 28, par. 1, and of 32, 33, 38 do not apply where the articles provide otherwise.

41. An association may be dissolved by resolution carried at a members'

(*m*) The directorate cannot question the validity of the reasons for calling the meeting; it has simply to carry out the resolution of the members.

(*n*) But not "must".

(*o*) This does not apply to a "statutory agent" nor to the directorate of a juristic person, because they are not "another person" within the meaning of this provision. Cf. 40.

meeting [p]. For such resolution a majority of three-fourths of the members present is necessary, unless the articles provide otherwise.

42. An association loses juristic personality by the institution of bankruptcy proceedings.

In case of insolvency [q] the directorate shall apply for the institution of bankruptcy proceedings. If the making of the application is delayed, those directors to whom any fault can be imputed causing the delay are responsible to the creditors for any damage arising therefrom; they are liable as joint debtors.

43. Juristic personality may be withdrawn from an association if public interests are endangered by any illegal resolution carried at a members' meeting, or by illegal conduct of the directorate.

Juristic personality may be withdrawn from an association whose object, according to the articles, is not the carrying on of an economic enterprise, if it pursues such an object [r].

Juristic personality may be withdrawn from an association which, according to the articles, has not a political, social-political, or religious object, if it pursues such an object [s].

Juristic personality may be withdrawn from an association whose juristic personality depends upon grant, if it pursues any other object than that specified in the articles.

44. The jurisdiction and the procedure are determined, in the cases provided for by 43, according to the provisions of the State laws applicable to contentious administrative matters. Where there is no contentious administrative

---

(*p*) See 74, par. 2.

(*q*) The fact that the association will be capable of discharging its liabilities after collecting its assets is immaterial. "Insolvency" is, therefore, only a free translation of the word *Überschuldung*, which means literally "overindebtedness".

(*r*) Corollary of 21.

(*s*) Corollary of 61. A further ground for the withdrawal of personality exists in the case of registered associations. See 73.

procedure [t], the provisions of 20, 21 of the Industrial Code [u] apply; the decision is given in the first instance by the superior administrative authority in whose district the association has its seat.

If the juristic personality depends upon grant by the Federal Council, it can be withdrawn (only) by resolution of the Federal Council.

45. On the dissolution of the association or the withdrawal of juristic personality, its property devolves upon the persons [x] designated in the articles.

It may be prescribed in the articles that the persons so entitled shall be designated by resolution carried at a members meeting, or by some other representative body of the association. If the object of the association is not the carrying on of an economic enterprise, a members' meeting may, even without such a provision, assign the property to a public foundation or institution.

If no persons shall have been so designated the property devolves, if the association according to the articles was intended to benefit its members exclusively, upon those who were members at the time of the dissolution or withdrawal of juristic personality, in equal shares; otherwise, upon the Treasury of the State in whose territory the association had its seat [y].

46. If the property of the association devolves upon the Treasury, the provisions relating to inheritances devolving upon the Treasury as statutory heir apply *mutatis mutandis* [z]. The Treasury shall, so far as is possible, use the property in a manner suitable for the carrying out of the objects of the association.

47. If the property of the association does not devolve upon the Treasury, a liquidation must take place [a].

(*t*) *Verwaltungsstreitverfahren.*

(*u*) 20 of the Industrial Code provides in substance that appeal to the next higher authority against the decision is permissible within fourteen days after the decision has been given. 21 specifies the different authorities and the mode of procedure.

(*x*) Whether they are natural or juristic persons makes no difference.

(*y*) See, however, IA, Art. 85.

(*z*) 1922, 1936, 1942, par. 2, 1966, 2011.

(*a*) The articles cannot provide otherwise.

48. The liquidation is effected by the directorate. Other persons may also be appointed liquidators; the provisions applicable to the appointment of the directorate apply also to the appointment of liquidators.

The liquidators have the legal status of the directorate, unless a contrary intention appears from the object of the liquidation.

If there are several liquidators, their resolutions shall be carried unanimously, unless it is otherwise provided.

49. The liquidators shall wind up current business, collect claims, convert the property into money, satisfy the creditors, and distribute the residue among the person entitled to it. The liquidators may also enter upon new transactions for the purpose of winding up uncompleted transactions. The collection of claims and the conversion of the property into money may be dispensed with, in so far as these measures are not necessary for the satisfaction of the creditors, or for the distribution of the residue among the persons entitled to it.

The association is deemed to exist so far as is necessary for carrying out the object of the liquidation until the liquidation is completed.

50. The dissolution of the association or the withdrawal of juristic personality shall be publicly notified by the liquidators. In the notification creditors shall be invited to present their claims. The notification is made in the newspaper selected by the articles for the publication of notices, failing which, in the newspaper selected for the publication of the notices of the District Court in whose district the association had its seat. The notification is deemed to have been effected at the expiration of the second day after the insertion or after the first insertion.

Known creditors shall be invited by special communication to present their claims.

51. The property cannot be distributed to the persons entitled to it before the expiration of one year after the notification of the dissolution of the association or the withdrawal of juristic personality.

52. If a known creditor does not present himself, the amount of his debt shall be lodged [b] for the creditor if the right to make the lodgment exists [c].

If the discharge of a liability is for to the time being impracticable, or if a liability is contested, the property shall be distributed to the persons entitled to it only if security has been given to the creditor [d].

53. Liquidators who fail to perform the duties imposed upon them by 42, par. 2, and 50 to 52, or distribute the property to those entitled to it before the satisfaction of the creditors, are, if any fault can be imputed to them, responsible to the creditor for any damage arising therefrom; they are liable as joint debtors.

54. Associations which have not juristic personality are subject to the provisions relating to partnership. If a member of such an association, acting in the name of the association, enters into a juristic act with a third party, that member is personally liable; if several members so act, they are liable as joint debtors [e].

2. *Registered Associations*.

55. The registration of an association of the kind specified in 21 shall be made in the register of associations in the District Court in whose district the association has its seat [f].

56. Registration should take place only if the number of members amounts to at least seven [g].

57. The articles must state the objects, the name and the seat of the association, and must show that the association is to be registered.

The name should be readily distinguishable from the names of existing associations registered in the same place or in the same commune.

(*b*) 372 *et seq.*

(*c*) 372.

(*d*) 232 *et seq.*

(*e*) See 705 *et seq.*

(*f*) 24.

(*g*) 73.

58. The articles should contain provisions:

(1) concerning the admission and withdrawal of members;

(2) as to whether and what contributions are to be made by the members;

(3) concerning the constitution of the directorate;

(4) concerning the conditions under which meetings of the members shall be called, the form of the notice calling the meetings, and the authentication of resolutions.

59. The directorate shall make an application [(h)] for registration of the association.

To the application shall be annexed:

(1) the articles in original and copy;

(2) a copy of the minutes relating to the appointment of the directorate.

The articles should be signed by at least seven members, and should contain a statement of the date when the articles were adopted.

60. If the application for registration does not satisfy the requirements of 56 to 59, it shall be rejected by the District Court with a statement of the reasons.

An immediate appeal, according to the provisions of the Code of Civil Procedure [(i)], may be lodged against the order for rejection.

61. If the application is allowed, the District Court shall communicate it to the competent administrative authority.

The administrative authority may take objection to the registration [(k)] if the association is illegal or is liable to be suppressed under the public law of associations, or if it pursues a political, social-political, or religious object.

62. If the administrative authority takes objection, the District Court shall communicate the objection to the directorate.

The objection may be contested by the contentious administrative procedure,

---

(*h*) As to the form of the application, see 77, 129.

(*i*) The appeal (*Beschwerde*) must be lodged within the period of two weeks. For further particulars, see 530—540 of the Code of Civil Procedure.

(*k*) This must take place within six weeks after receipt of the communication. 63.

or where such does not exist, by the procedure of *Rekurs*, subject to the conditions specified in 20 and 21 of the Industrial Code (l).

63. Unless the administrative authority informs the District Court that no objection is taken, registration cannot take place until six weeks have elapsed since the communication of the application to the administrative authority and no objection has been taken, or until the objection taken has been definitely rebutted.

64. In the registration the name and the seat of the association, the date on which the articles were adopted, and the names of the directors shall be entered in the register of associations. Provisions which limit the power of the directorate to represent the association, or regulate the carrying of resolutions by the directorate otherwise than as provided for by 28, par. 1, shall also be entered.

65. Upon registration, the name of the association receives the title "registered association" (m).

66. The District Court shall publish the registration in the newspaper selected for the publication of its notices.

The original of the articles shall be marked "registered", and shall be returned. The copy is certified by the District Court and filed with the other documents.

67. Every change in the directorate, as well as a re-appointment of a director, shall be reported by the directorate for registration. A copy of the minutes recording the change or the re-appointment shall be annexed to the report.

The registration of directors appointed by the Court is done by the Court of its own motion.

(*l*) See note (*u*) to 44.

(*m*) The German term for this is *Eingetragener Verein*. The name of the association must have this title; the abbreviated form *E. V.* is, however, permissible.

68. If a juristic act has been entered into by the former directors with a third party, a change in the directorate may be set up against the third party only if it was registered in the register of associations or known to the third party at the time when the juristic act was entered into. If the change has been registered it does not avail against the third party, if he does not know it [(n)] and his ignorance is not due to negligence.

69. The proof that the directorate consists of the persons named in the register is, as against public authorities, furnished by a certificate of the registration by the District Court.

70. The provision of 68 apply also to provisions which limit the scope of the authority of the directorate to represent the association, or which regulate the carrying of resolutions by the directorate otherwise than as provided for by 28, par. 1.

71. Alterations of the articles require to be entered in the register of associations in order to be effective. The alteration shall be reported for registration by the directorate. To the report shall be annexed the resolution containing the alteration, in original and copy.

The provisions of 60 to 64, and of 66, par. 2, apply *mutatis mutandis*.

72. The directorate shall deliver to the District Court, on demand by the latter at any time, a list of the members of the association [(o)].

73. If the number of the members of the association falls below three, the District Court shall withdraw juristic personality from the association upon application by the directorate, and if the application is not made within three months, of its own motion after a hearing of the directorate. The order to withdraw juristic personality shall be communicated to the association. An immediate appeal according to the provisions of the Code of Civil Procedure [(p)]

(*n*) Since everyone has a right to inspect the register of associations, it is presumed that he has knowledge of it, unless he can offer proof to the contrary.

(*o*) Cf. 78.

(*p*) See note (*i*) to 60.

may be lodged against the order.

The association loses juristic personality as soon as the order ceases to be appealable.

74. Both the dissolution of the association and the withdrawal of juristic personality shall be entered in the register of associations. In the case of the institution of bankruptcy proceedings the entry is dispensed with (q).

Where the association is dissolved by resolution carried at a members meeting, or by the expiration of the time fixed for the duration of the association, the directorate shall report the dissolution for registration. In the former case a copy of the resolution for dissolution shall be annexed to the report.

If juristic personality is withdrawn from the association under 43, or if the association is dissolved under the public law of associations, the registration is made upon notification by the competent authority.

75. The institution of bankruptcy proceedings shall be registered by the Court of its own motion. The same rule applies to the cancellation of the order for the institution of proceedings.

76. The names of the liquidators shall be entered in the register of associations. The same rule applies to provisions which regulate the carrying of resolutions by the liquidators otherwise than as provided for by 48, par. 3.

The report for registration shall be made by the directorate, and in case of later alterations, by the liquidators. To the report for registration of the names of the liquidators appointed by resolution carried at a members' meeting a copy of the resolution shall be annexed; to the report for registration of a provision relating to the carrying of resolutions by the liquidators a copy of the minutes containing the provision shall be annexed.

The registration of liquidators appointed by the Court is done by the Court of its own motion.

77. The reports for the register of associations shall be made both by the

---

(q) Because the institution of bankruptcy proceedings necessarily in the loss of juristic personality (42, par. 1), and must be registered by the Court of its own motion. 75.

directors and by the liquidators by means of a publicly certified declaration [r].

78. The District Court may enforce the observance by the directors of the provisions of 67, par. 1, 71, par. 1, 72, 74, par. 2, and 76 by exacting penalties. A single penalty cannot exceed the sum of three hundred marks.

In the same manner the liquidators may be compelled to observe the provisions of 76.

79. Any person is permitted to inspect the register of associations and the documents submitted to the District Court by the association. A copy of the records may be obtained; the copy shall be certified on demand.

II. Foundations.

80. For the creation of a foundation with juristic personality, besides the act of foundation, the ratification of the State in whose territory the foundation is to have its seat is necessary. If the foundation is not to have its seat in any State, the ratification of the Federal Council is necessary. Unless it is otherwise provided, the place where its affairs are managed is deemed to be the seat of the foundation.

81. An act of foundation *inter vivos* is required to be in Writing [s].

Before the ratification is given the founder is entitled to revoke. If application has been made to the competent authority for its ratification, the revocation may be communicated only to the same authority. The heir of the founder is not entitled to revoke, if the founder has filed his application with the competent authority, or where the act of foundation is authenticated by a court or notary, has instructed the court or the notary at the time of or after the authentication to file the application.

82. If the foundation is ratified the founder is bound to transfer to the foundation the property specified in the act of foundation. Rights which can be

---

(*r*) Cf. 129.

(*s*) Cf. 126.

transferred by a mere contract of assignment (t) pass to the foundation upon ratification, unless a contrary intention of the founder appears from the act of foundation.

83. If the act of foundation consists of a disposition *mortis causa* (u), the Probate Court shall obtain the ratification, unless it is applied for by the heir or the executor.

84. If the foundation is not ratified until after the death of the founder, it is deemed, in respect to the dispositions of the founder, to have been already created before his death.

85. The constitution of a foundation is determined, so far as it does not depend upon Imperial or State law, by the act of Foundation.

86. The provisions of 26, 27, par. 3, and 28 to 31, 42 apply *mutatis mutandis* to foundations; the provision of 27, par. 3, and 28, par. 1, however, only in so far as a contrary intention does not appear from the constitution, *e.g.* from the fact that the affairs of the foundation are managed by a public authority. The provisions of 28, par. 2, and 29 do not apply to foundations whose affairs are managed by a public authority.

87. If the fulfilment of the object of the foundation has become impossible, or if it endangers public interests, the competent authority may apply the foundation to a different object or may suppress it.

In changing the object the intention of the founder shall be considered as far as possible; care is especially to be taken that the proceeds of the property of the foundation continue to be applied as far as possible in accordance with the will of the founder for the benefit of those persons whom he intended to benefit. The authority may alter the constitution of the foundation, so far as the change of object demands it.

Before the change of the object and the alteration of the constitution the

---

(*t*) See 398—400, 870, 931, 1153 *et seq.*, 1274.

(*u*) It may be a unilateral act, as, *e.g.*, a will (2231), or a bilateral act, as, *e.g.*, a contract of inheritance (2274).

directorate of the foundation should be heard.

88. On the extinction of the foundation its property devolves upon the persons designated by its constitution. The provisions of 46 to 53 apply *mutatis mutandis*.

III. Juristic Persons under Public Law (x).

89. The provision of 31 applies *mutatis mutandis* to the Treasury as well as to corporations, foundations and institutions under public law.

The same rule applies to the provisions of 42, par. 2, in so far as bankruptcy is permissible in the case of corporations, foundations and institutions under public law.

SECOND SECTION.
THINGS.

90. Things, in the legal sense, are corporeal objects only.

91. Fungible things, in the legal sense, are moveable things which in ordinary dealings are customarily determined by number, measure, or weight.

92. Consumable things, in the legal sense, are moveable things whose ultimate use consists in being consumed or disposed of.

Consumable things include also moveables which constitute a stock-in-trade or other aggregate of things whose ultimate use consists in being disposed of piecemeal.

93. Component parts of a thing which cannot be separated from one another without destroying or essentially changing the one or the other (*i.e.*, essential component parts) may not be the object of separate rights.

94. The essential component parts of land are things which are firmly

(x) The provisions of 80—88 do not apply to juristic persons under public law.

affixed to the soil, *e.g.*, buildings, and the products of the land, so long as they are connected with the soil. Seed upon being sown, a plant upon being planted (*y*), respectively become essential component parts of the land.

The essential component parts of a building are things which are parts of the structure of the building (*z*).

95. Things do not become component parts of land which are affixed to the soil only for a temporary purpose. The same rule applies to a building or other structure which, in the exercise of a right over another person's land, has been affixed to the land by the person who has such right.

Things which are attached to a building only for a temporary purpose do not become component parts of the building.

96. Rights which are connected with the ownership of land (*a*) are deemed to be component parts of the land (*b*).

97. Accessories are moveable (*c*), which, without being component parts of the principal thing, are intended to serve the economic purpose of the principal thing, and stand in a local relation to it suitable for the carrying out of this intention. A thing is not an accessory if it is not regarded in ordinary dealings as an accessory.

The temporary use of a thing to serve the economic purpose of another does not constitute it an accessory (*d*). The temporary separation of an accessory from the principal thing does not terminate it as accessory.

(*y*) It is not necessary that it should have taken root.

(*z*) Since the different stories of a building are its essential component parts, it is impossible for a person to have ownership of a separate story. An exception to this rule is, however, allowed by Art. 182 of the IA.

(*a*) Such rights are: real servitudes (1018), real right of pre-emption (1094, par. 2), perpetual charges on land (1105, par. 2).

(*b*) That is to say a disposition relating to the land will also affect these rights.

(*c*) A piece of land cannot, therefore, be an accessory of another piece of land, although it can be made a "component part" of the latter by an entry in the land register.

(*d*) The legal effect of a thing becoming an accessory is that, in the majority of cases, any disposition affecting the principal thing affects also the accessory.

98. The economic purpose of the principal thing is served:

(1) in the case of a building permanently fitted up for industrial operations, as a mill, a forge, a brewery, a factory, by the machines and other implements intended for the operations;

(2) in the case of a farm, by the tools and cattle intended for the operations of husbandry, the farm products, so far as they are necessary for the continuation of the husbandry up to the time at which a new supply of the like or similar products will presumably be obtained, and the existing stock of manure produced upon the farm [(e)].

99. Fruits of a thing are the products of the thing, and such other yield as is obtained from the thing consistently with the use for which the thing is intended.

Fruits of a right are the proceeds which the right affords consistently with its object, *e.g.* in the case of a right to the acquisition of component parts of the soil, the component parts acquired.

Fruits include also the proceeds which a thing or a right affords by virtue of a legal relation [(f)].

100. Emoluments are the fruits of a thing or a right as well as the advantages which the use of the thing or the right affords.

101. A person who is entitled to receive the fruits of a thing or of a right up to or from a given time, is, unless it is otherwise provided, entitled to:

(1) the products specified in 99, par. 1, and the component parts, even if he is to receive them as fruits of a right, in so far as they have been separated from the thing during the existence of his right;

(2) other fruits [(g)], in so far as they become due during the existence of his right; if, however, the fruits consist in compensation for the relinquishment of the use or of the enjoyment of the fruits, in interest,

---

(*e*) These two instances are given by way of illustration only; they are not intended to be exhaustive.

(*f*) In the language of German text-books these are usually known as "juristic" or "civil" fruits, as, *e. g.*, rent, interest, &c., while those mentioned in the preceding two paragraphs are usually known as "natural" fruits.

(*g*) *I.e.*, "civil" fruits.

dividends, or other periodical income, he is entitled to a part proportionate to the duration of his right.

102. A person who is bound to hand over fruits may demand compensation for the expenses incurred in the production of the fruits, in so far as these were incurred by proper methods of production, and do not exceed the value of the fruits.

103. A person who is bound to bear the charges upon a thing or a right up to or from a given time shall, unless it is otherwise provided (h), bear the periodical charges proportionately to the duration of his obligation; and other charges, in so far as they are payable during the existence of his obligation.

THIRD SECTION.
JURISTIC ACTS.

FIRST TITLE.
Disposing Capacity.

104. A person is incapable of disposing:

(1) who has not completed his seventh year of age;

(2) who is in a condition of morbid disturbance of the mental activity incompatible with a free determination of the will, in so far as the condition is not temporary in its nature;

(3) who has been interdicted on account of insanity (i).

105. The declaration of intention of a person incapable of disposing is void (k).

A declaration is also void which is made in a condition of unconsciousness or temporary disturbance of the mental activity.

(h) By juristic act (*e.g.*, contract, will, &c.) or by law (*e.g.*, 955, 1047).

(i) Those persons interdicted on other grounds are only "limited in disposing capacity". 114, 106.

(k) A declaration of intention made *to* a person incapable of disposing is also void. 131, par. 1.

106. A minor who has completed his seventh year of age is limited in disposing capacity [l] as provided for in 107 to 113.

107. A minor requires, for a declaration of intention whereby he does not merely acquire a legal advantage, the approval [m] of his statutory agent.

108. If the minor enters into a contract without the necessary approval of his statutory agent the contract is void, unless ratified by the agent [n].

If the other party demands the agent to declare whether or not he ratifies, the declaration may be made only to him; a ratification or refusal to ratify declared to the minor before the demand is of no effect. The ratification may be declared only before the expiration of two weeks after receipt of the demand; if it is not given it is deemed to have been refused.

If the minor has become capable of disposing without limitation, his own ratification takes the place of the ratification of the agent.

109. Before ratification of the contract the other party is entitled to revoke it. The revocation may also be declared to the minor.

If the other party was aware of the minority, he may revoke only if the minor has stated, contrary to the truth, that he had the approval of his agent; even in this case he may not revoke if he knew, at the time the contract was entered into, that the approval had not been given.

110. A contract entered into by a minor without the consent of his statutory agent is deemed to be valid *ab initio* if the minor has effected the performance agreed upon with means entrusted to him for this purpose, or for his free disposal, by the agent or, with his consent, by a third party.

111. A unilateral juristic act which the minor enters into without the necessary approval of his statutory agent is void. If the minor enters into such a juristic act with another party with this approval, the juristic act is void if the

---

(*l*) Cf. 131, par. 2. For the capacity to enter into a marriage, see 1303, 1304; to make a will, 2229.

(*m*) *I.e.*, precedent consent. 183.

(*n*) As to the form of the ratification, see 182, par. 2; as to its effects, see 184.

minor does not produce the approval in writing, and the other party without delay rejects the juristic act for this reason. The right to reject is barred if the agent had given the other party information of his approval.

112. If the statutory agent, with the ratification of the Guardianship Court, authorises the minor to carry on business independently, the minor is then capable, without limitation, to do such juristic acts as are within the scope of the business. Juristic acts for which the agent requires the ratification of the Guardianship Court are excepted [(o)].

The authorisation may be revoked by the agent only with the ratification of the Guardianship Court.

113. If the statutory agent authorises the minor to enter into service or employment as a labourer [(p)], the minor is then capable without Limitation to do such juristic acts as relate to the entry into or the cessation of the relation of service or employment of the kind permitted, or to the fulfilment of the obligation arising from such a relation. Contracts for which the agent requires the ratification of the Guardianship Court are excepted [(q)].

The authorisation may be revoked or limited by the agent [(r)].

If the statutory agent is a guardian [(s)] the authorisation may, if refused by him, be supplied by the Guardianship Court on the application of the minor. The Guardianship Court shall give the authorisation if it is in the interest of the ward [(t)].

An authorisation given for a single case is deemed, in case of doubt, to be a general authorisation for entering into other relations of the same kind.

(*o*) Cf. 1643, 1686, 1814 *et seq.*, 1821 *et. seq.*, 1909, 1915.

(*p*) Unlike the case under 112, the ratification of the Guardianship Court is not necessary. A minor who has entered into service or employment as a labourer has less independence than one who carries on business independently of the statutory agent, since the authorisation may be revoked or limited at any time. See par. 2.

(*q*) See note (*o*) to 112.

(*r*) The ratification of the Guardianship Court is not necessary. Otherwise in the case of 112.

(*s*) Or curator. See 1909, 1915.

(*t*) If the service or employment is for a longer period than one year, the guardian must have the ratification of the Guardianship Court in order to give the authorisation. 1822 (7).

114. A person who has been interdicted on account of feeblemindedness, prodigality, or habitual drunkenness, or who has been placed under interim guardianship as provided in 1906, is, in respect to disposing capacity, in the same position as a minor who has completed his seventh year of age.

115. If the order of interdiction is annulled in consequence of an action to set it aside [(u)], the validity of juristic acts entered into by or with the person interdicted may not be called in question on the ground of the order. The annulment has no effect on the validity of the juristic acts entered into by or with the statutory agent.

These provisions apply *mutatis mutandis* if, in the case of interim guardianship, the application for interdiction is recalled or is rejected without any right of appeal, or if the order of interdiction is annulled in consequence of in action to set it aside.

SECOND TITLE.
Declaration of Intention.

116. A declaration of intention is not void by reason of the fact that the declarant has made a secret reservation of not willing the matter declared. The declaration is void if made to a person who is aware of the reservation.

117. If a declaration of intention required to be made to a person is with his connivance made only in pretence [(x)], it is void.

If another juristic act is concealed under a pretended transaction, the provisions applicable to concealed juristic acts apply [(y)].

118. A declaration of intention not seriously intended, which is made in the expectation that it will be understood not to be seriously intended, is void [(z)].

(*u*) This is permissible only within the period of one month. Code of Civil Procedure, 672, 684.

(*x*) This occurs most frequently in those cases where the declarant intends to defraud his creditors.

(*y*) A concealed juristic act, although void for this reason, may, however, be valid on other grounds. 140.

(*z*) A person injured through relying on the declaration may in certain cases claim damages. 122.

119. A person who, when making a declaration of intention, was under a mistake as to its purport, or did not intend to make a declaration of that purport at all, may avoid the declaration if it is to be supposed that he would not have made it with knowledge of the state of affairs and with intelligent appreciation of the case[(a)].

A mistake concerning any characteristics of the person or thing which are regarded in ordinary dealings as essential is also deemed to be a mistake concerning the purport of the declaration.

120. A declaration of intention which has been incorrectly transmitted by the person or institution employed for its transmission may be avoided under the same conditions as a declaration of intention made under mistake.

121. The avoidance must be made, in the cases provided for by 119, 120, without delay (*i.e.*, without culpable [(b)] delay), after the person entitled to avoid has obtained knowledge of the grounds for avoidance. An avoidance as against a person who is not present is deemed to have been effected in due time if the avoidance has been forwarded without delay.

The right of avoidance is barred if thirty years have elapsed since the making of the declaration of intention.

122. If a declaration of intention is void under 118, or avoided under 119, 120, the declarant [(c)] shall, if the declaration was required to be made to another, compensate him or any third party for any damage which the other or the third party has sustained by relying upon the validity of the declaration; not, however, beyond the value of the interest which the other or the third party has in the validity of the declaration.

The duty to make compensation does not arise if the person injured knew of the ground on which the declaration was void or voidable, or would have known of it but for his own negligence (*i.e.*, ought to have known it).

(*a*) The question whether the mistake was one of fact or of law, or whether it was due to negligence or not, is immaterial.

(*b*) For the meaning of this word, see 276.

(*c*) The question whether fault can be imputed to him or not is entirely immaterial.

123. A person who has been induced to make a declaration of intention by fraud or unlawfully by threats may avoid the declaration.

If a third party was guilty of the fraud, a declaration which was required to be made to another may be avoided only if the latter knew or ought to have known of the fraud [(d)]. In so far as another person than the one to whom the declaration was required to be made has acquired a right directly through the declaration, the declaration may be avoided as against him if he knew or ought to have known of the fraud.

124. The avoidance of a declaration of intention voidable under 123 may take place only within the period of one year [(e)].

The period beings to run, in the case of fraud, from the moment at which the person entitled to avoid discovers the fraud; in the case of threats, from the moment at which the coercion ceases. The provisions of 203, par. 2, and of 206, 207, applicable to prescription, apply *mutatis mutandis* to the running of this period.

The right of avoidance is barred if thirty years have elapsed since the making of the declaration of intention.

125. A juristic act which is not in the form prescribed by law is void [(f)]. If it is not in the form prescribed by juristic act, it is void in case of doubt.

126. If writing is prescribed by law the document must be signed by the maker with his own hand by subscription of his name, or by mark certified by a Court or notary.

In the case of a contract the signatures of the parties must be attached to the same document. If several identical copies of the contract are drawn up, it is sufficient if each party signs the copy intended for the other party.

Judicial or notarial authentication may be substituted for writing.

(*d*) The qualification contained in this sentence does not apply to a declaration of intention induced by unlawful threats, which may *always* be avoided as against *all* interested parties.

(*e*) As against the person guilty of fraud or using threats, the period is three years; as against all other persons, one year.

(*f*) A defect in form may generally be cured by confirmation. 141.

127. The provisions of 126 apply also, in case of doubt, to writing prescribed by juristic act. It is sufficient, however, for compliance with the form, unless a contrary intention is to be presumed, if it is by telegraphic transmission and, in the case of a contract, by exchange of letters; if such a form is selected, authentication in accordance with 126 may be subsequently required.

128. If judicial or notarial authentication of a contract is prescribed by law, it is sufficient if first the offer and later the acceptance of the offer be authenticated by a Court or notary [(g)].

129. If it is prescribed by law that a declaration shall be publicly certified, the declaration must be drawn up in writing, and the signature of the declarant be certified by the competent authority [(h)], or a competent official [(h)], or notary [(i)]. If the declaration is subscribed by the maker with his mark, the certification of the mark prescribed in 126, par. 1, is necessary and sufficient.

Judicial or notarial authentication of the declaration may be substitute for the public certification.

130. A declaration of intention required to be made to another, if it is made in his absence, becomes effective at the moment when it reaches him. It does not become effective if a revocation reaches him previously or simultaneously.

The effectiveness of the declaration is not affected by the fact that the declarant die or become incapable of disposing after making it.

These provisions apply even if the declaration of intention is required to be made to a public authority [(k)].

131. If a declaration of intention is made to a person incapable of disposing [(l)], it does not become effective before it reaches his statutory agent.

The same rule applies if the declaration of intention is made to a person

(*g*) Both parties need not be simultaneously present. See 152.

(*h*) See 167, 191 of the Voluntary Jurisdiction Act.

(*i*) A notary is always competent for such matters.

(*k*) *E.g.*, 928, 976, 1945.

(*l*) See 104.

limited in disposing capacity (m). If, however, the declaration merely brings a legal advantage to the person limited in disposing capacity, or if the statutory agent has given his approval, the declaration becomes effective at the moment when it reaches the person limited in disposing capacity.

132. A declaration of intention is also deemed to have become effective if it has been delivered through the instrumentality of an executive officer of a Court. The delivery is made according to the provisions of the Code of Civil Procedure (n).

If the declarant is in ignorance, not due to negligence, of the identity of the person to whom the declaration is required to be made, or if the residence of this person is unknown, the delivery may be effected according to the provision of the Code of Civil Procedure relating to the public service of a citation (o). In the farmer case the District Court is competent to authorise the citation in whose district the declarant has his domicile, or, if he has no domestic domicile, his residence; in the latter case the District Court in whose district the person to whom delivery is required to be made last had his domicile, or, if he had no domestic domicile, last had his residence.

133. In the interpretation of a declaration of intention the true intention is to be sought without regard to the literal meaning of the expression (p).

134. A juristic act which is contrary to a statutory prohibition is void, unless a contrary intention appears from the statute.

135. If the disposition of an object is contrary to a statutory prohibition against alienation which aims only at the protection of particular persons, it is inoperative only as to these persons. A disposition effected by means of compulsory execution or distraint is equivalent to a contractual disposition.

The provisions in favour of those who derive rights from a person without

---

(*m*) See 106, 114.

(*n*) Code of Civil Procedure, 166 *et seq*.

(*o*) Code of Civil Procedure, 203—206.

(*p*) In the case of a contract a further rule of interpretation is laid down in 157.

title apply *mutatis mutandis* [q].

136. A prohibition against alienation which is issued by a Court or by any other competent authority is equivalent to a statutory prohibition against alienation of the kind specified in 135.

137. The right the dispose of an alienable right may not be excluded or limited by juristic act [r]. The validity of an obligation not to dispose of such a right is not affected by this provision [s].

138. A juristic act which is *contra bonos mores* is void [t].

A juristic act is also void whereby a person profiting by the difficulties, indiscretion or inexperience of another, causes to be promised or granted to himself or to a third party for a consideration, pecuniary advantages which exceed the value of the consideration to such an extent that, having regard to the circumstances, the disproportion is obvious [u].

139. If part of a juristic act is void the whole juristic act is void, unless it is to be presumed that it would equally have been entered into if the void part had been omitted.

140. If a void juristic act satisfies the requirements of a different juristic act, the former is valid in right of the latter, if it is to be presumed that its validity would have been intended by the parties on knowing of the invalidity.

(*q*) *I.e.*, the provisions relating to the presumption of the correctness of the land register and the *bonâ fide* acquisition of rights and moveables. See 405, 892, 893, 932—938, 1007, 1032, 1207, 1208, 1227, 1242, 1244.

(*r*) An exception to this rule may be found in 399, which provides that the assignment of a claim may be excluded by agreement with the debtor.

(*s*) That is to say, if two persons agree with each other not to dispose of an alienable right, the agreement is perfectly valid as between themselves. If, however, one of the parties disposes of the right contrary to the agreement, the act is valid to all intents and purposes, although he is liable to the other party for breach of contract.

(*t*) Whether a juristic act is *contra bonos* mores or not is determined by the Court according to the public opinion prevailing at the time.

(*u*) A common instance of this is usury. Cf. IA, Art. 47.

141. If a void juristic act is confirmed by the person who entered into it, the confirmation is deemed to be a renewed undertaking.

If a void contract is confirmed by the parties, they are mutually bound, in case of doubt, to do what they would have been bound to do if the contract had been valid *ab initio*.

142. If a voidable juristic act (x) is avoided it is deemed to have been void *ab initio*.

If a person know or ought to have known of the voidability, he is deemed, if the act is avoided, to have known that the juristic act was void.

143. The avoidance is effected by declaration (y) to the party subject to avoidance.

The party subject to avoidance is, in the case of a contract, the other party; in the case provided for by 128, par. 2, sentence 2, the person who has acquired a right directly through the contract.

In the case of a unilateral juristic act required to be entered into with another person, that other person is the party subject to avoidance. The same rule applies in the case of a juristic act required to be entered into with another person or with a public authority, even if the juristic act has been entered into with the authority.

In the case of a unilateral juristic act of any other kind, the person who has acquired a legal advantage directly founded upon the juristic act is the party subject to avoidance. The avoidance may, however, if the declaration of intention was required to be made to a public authority, be effected by a declaration to the authority; the authority should communicate the avoidance to those persons who have been directly affected by the juristic act.

144. If a voidable juristic act is confirmed by the person entitled to avoid, it ceases to be voidable.

The confirmation need not be in the form prescribed for the juristic act.

(*x*) A voidable juristic act is valid until it is avoided.

(*y*) As a general rule the declaration may be either verbal or in writing. Cf., however, 1341, 1945, 1955, 2282, &c.

THIRD TITLE.
Contract.

145. If a person offers to another the making of a contract he is bound by the offer [z], unless he has excluded this obligation.

146. An offer ceases to be binding if it is declined to the offerer, or if it is not accepted in his favour in due time according to 147 to 149.

147. An offer made to a person who is present may be accepted only there and then. This applies also to an offer made by one person to another on the telephone.

An offer made to a person who is not present may be accepted only before the moment when the offerer may expect to receive an answer under ordinary circumstances.

148. If the offerer has fixed a period of time [a] for acceptance of the offer, the acceptance may take place only within that period.

149. If an acceptance arrives out of time, though it has been transmitted to the offerer in such manner that it would have arrived in due time with ordinary forwarding, and the offerer must have recognised this [b], on receipt of the acceptance he shall without delay notify the acceptor of the delay, unless this has already been done. If he delay so to notify him the acceptance is deemed not to have been out of time.

150. If the acceptance of an offer arrives out of time it is deemed to be a new offer.

An acceptance with amplifications, limitations, or other alterations is deemed to be a refusal coupled with a new offer.

(*z*) He is immediately bound by the offer even before acceptance by the offeree.

(*a*) Cf. 186 *et seq.*

(*b*) *I.e.*, by the exercise of ordinary care. 276.

151. A contract is concluded by the acceptance of an offer, although the acceptance is not communicated to the proposer, if such a communication is not to be expected according to ordinary usage, or if the offerer has waived it. The moment at which the offer ceases to be binding is determined according to the intention of the offerer to be inferred from the offer or the circumstances.

152. If a contract is judicially or notarially authenticated without both parties being simultaneously present, the contract is, unless otherwise provided, concluded upon authentication of the acceptance as provided for in 128. The provision of 151, sentence 2, applies.

153. The conclusion of a contract is not prevented by the fact that the offerer dies or becomes incapable of disposing before acceptance [(c)], unless a contrary intention of the offerer is to be inferred.

154. So long as the parties have not agreed upon all points of a contract upon which, according to the declaration of even one party, agreement is essential, the contract is, in case of doubt, not concluded. An understanding concerning particular points is not binding, even if they have been noted down.

If authentication of the contemplated contract has been agreed upon, in case of doubt the contract is not concluded until the authentication has taken place.

155. If the parties to a contract which they regard as concluded have in fact not agreed upon one point concerning which an agreement should have been arrived at, that which is agreed upon is valid if it is to be inferred that the contract would have been concluded even without a settlement of this point.

156. At an auction a contract is not concluded until the hammer falls. A bid ceases to be binding if a higher bid is made, or the auction is closed before the hammer falls [(d)].

157. Contracts shall be interpreted according to the requirements of good

---

(*c*) This is a corollary of 130, par. 2.

(*d*) In the case of "compulsory auction" the special provisions of 817 of the Code of Civil Procedure and the Compulsory Auction Act apply.

faith, ordinary usage being taken into consideration [(e)].

FOURTH TITLE.
Conditions. Limitation of Time.

158. If a juristic act is entered into subject to a condition precedent, the operative effect dependent upon the condition comes into being on the fulfilment of the condition.

If a juristic act is entered into subject to a condition subsequent the operative effect of the juristic act comes to an end on the fulfilment of the conditions; from and after that moment the previous legal position is restored [(f)].

159. If, according to the scope of the juristic act, the consequences incident to the fulfilment of the condition are to become operative as from an earlier time, then on the fulfilment of the condition the parties are bound to perform reciprocally what they would have been bound to perform, if the consequences had become operative at the earlier time.

160. A person who is entitled subject to a condition precedent may, on the fulfilment of the condition, demand compensation from the other party, if the latter during the time pending the fulfilment has by his fault destroyed or impaired the right dependent upon the condition.

In the case of a juristic act entered into subject to a condition subsequent the person in whose favour the previous legal position is restored has the like claim under the same conditions.

161. If a person has disposed of an object subject to a condition precedent, every further disposition which he makes of the thing pending the fulfilment of the condition is void on the fulfilment of the condition in so far as it would destroy or impair the operative effect dependent upon the condition. Equivalent to such a disposition is a disposition which is effected, pending the

---

(*e*) Further rules of interpretation may be found in 133, 242.

(*f*) The fulfilment of a condition *in fact* may be held to be no fulfilment *in law*, and *vice versâ*. 162.

fulfilment of a condition precedent, by means of compulsory execration or distraint, or by a trustee in bankruptcy.

The same applies, in thecase of a condition subsequent, to the dispositions of a person whose right is extinguished upon the fulfilment of the condition.

The provisions in favour of those who derive rights from aperson without title apply *mutatis mutandis* [(g)].

162. If the fulfilment of a condition is prevented in bad faith by the party to whose disadvantage it would operate, the condition is deemed to have been fulfilled.

If the fulfilment of a condition is brought about in bad faith by the party to whose advantage it would operate, the condition is deemed not to have been fulfilled.

163. If, when a juristic act is entered into, a time has been fixed at which it shall begin to be or cease to be operative, then in the former case the provisions applicable to conditions precedent, in the latter case those applicable to conditions subsequent, contained 158, 160, 161, apply *mutatis mutandis*.

FIFTH TITLE.
Agency. Power of Agency.

164. A declaration of intention which a person makes in the name of a principal within the scope of a delegated authority operates directly both in favour of and as against the principal. It is immaterial whether the declaration is made expressly in the name of the principal, or from the circumstances it appears that the intention was to make it in his name.

If the intention to act in the name of another does not appear manifest, the absence of intention on the part of the agent to act in his own name is not taken into consideration [(h)].

(*g*) See note (*g*) to 135.

(*h*) That is to say, if the other party does not know that the agent acts on behalf of his principal, the agent is himself liable, no matter whether he intends to act for himself or not.

The provisions of par. 1 apply *mutatis mutandis* if a declaration of Intention required to be made to another is made to his agent.

165. The validity of a declaration of intention made by or to an agent is not impaired by the fact that he is limited in disposing capacity [i].

166. In so far as the legal effectiveness of a declaration of intention is vitiated by defective intention [k], or by knowledge or culpable ignorance of certain circumstances, regard is had to the principal, not to the agent.

If, when delegated authority (*i.e.*, power of agency) is conferred by juristic act, the agent has acted according to definite instructions of the principal, the latter may not set up the ignorance of the agent with regard to such circumstances as he himself knew. The same applies to circumstances which the principal ought to have known, so far as the obligation to know is equivalent to actual knowledge.

167. A power of agency is conferred by declaration to the person who is to exercise the power, or to the third party with whom the business delegated is to be transacted.

The declaration need not be in the form prescribed for the juristic act to which the power of agency relates.

168. The power of agency is terminated according to the legal relation upon which its creation is based. The power of agency is also revocable during the subsistence of the legal relation, unless a contrary intention appears from such relation. The provision of 167, par. 1, applies *mutatis mutandis* to the declaration of revocation.

169. In so far as a terminated power of agency of a mandatory or a managing partner is deemed to continue as provided for in 674, 729, it is not valid in favour of a third party who, at the time when a juristic act is entered into, knows or ought to know of the termination of the power.

(*i*) The rule is otherwise in the case of a person incapable of disposing.

(*k*) As a result of mistake, fraud, or unlawful threats. See 116—119, 123.

170. If a power of agency is conferred by declaration to a third party, it remains in force in respect to him until he is notified of its termination by the principal [(l)].

171. If a person has announced by special communication to third party or by public notification that he has given a power of agency to another, then the latter by virtue of the notice becomes an authorised agent, in the former case with reference to the said third party, in the latter case with reference to any third party.

The agency remains in force until the notice is revoked in the same manner as it was given [(m)].

172. It is equivalent to the special communication of a power of agency by the principal, if he has delivered to the agent a written power of agency and the agent produces it to the third party.

The agency remains in force until the written power of agency is returned to the principal or declared invalid [(n)].

173. The provisions of 170, 171, par. 2, and 172, par. 2, do not apply, if the third party knows or ought to know of the termination of the agency at the time when the juristic act is entered into.

174. A unilateral juristic act which an agent enters into with another party is ineffective, if the agent does not produce a written power of agency and the other party without delay rejects the juristic act for this reason. The right to reject is barred if the principal had informed him of the agency.

175. After the termination of the power the agent shall return the written power of agency to the principal; he has no right of lien on it.

176. The principal may declare the power of agency invalid by a public notification; the declaration of invalidity must be published according to the

---

(*l*) See 173.

(*m*) Cf. 173.

(*n*) See Code of Civil Procedure, 204.

provisions of the Code of Civil Procedure (n) applicable to the public service of a citation. The declaration of invalidity takes effect upon the expiration of one month after the last insertion in the public Journal.

Both the District Court in whose district the principal is generally subject to jurisdiction and the District Court which would be competent to entertain an action for the restitution of documents without regard to the value of the object in dispute are equally competent to authorise the publication.

The declaration of invalidity is ineffective if the principal cannot revoke the power of agency.

177. If a person enters into a contract in the name of another without authority, the contract is valid in favour of and as against the principal only if he ratifies.

If the other party demands the principal to declare whether or not he ratifies, the declaration may be made only to him; a ratification or refusal to ratify declared to the agent before the demand is of no effect. The ratification may be declared only before the expiration of two weeks after receipt of the demand; if it is not declared it is deemed to have been refused.

178. Before ratification of the contract the other party is entitled to revoke it, unless he knew of the absence of authority at the time when the contract was entered into. The revocation may also be declared to the agent.

179. A person who has entered into a contract as agent is, if he has not given proof of his authority, bound to the other party at his election (o) either to carry out the contract or to compensate him, if the principal refuses to ratify the contract.

If the agent did not know that he had no authority, he is bound to compensate only for the damage which the other party has sustained by relying upon the authority; not, however, beyond the value of the interest which the other party has in the validity of the contract.

The agent is not liable, if the other party knew or ought to have known of the

(n) See Code of Civil Procedure, 204.

(o) Cf. 263—265.

absence of authority. The agent is also not liable if he was limited in disposing capacity, unless he had acted with the consent of his statutory agent.

180. In the case of a unilateral juristic act agency without authority is not permissible. If, however, the person with whom such a juristic act purported to be entered into has not demurred to the authority claimed by the agent at the time of entering into the juristic act, or if he has agreed that the agent should act without authority, then the provisions relating to contracts apply *mutatis mutandis*. The same rule applies if a unilateral juristic act be entered into with an unauthorised agent with his assent.

181. An agent may not without leave enter into a juristic act in the name of his principal with himself in his own name, or as agent of a third party, unless the juristic act consists exclusively in the fulfilment of an obligation.

SIXTH TITLE.
Approval. Ratification.

182. If the validity of a contract or of a unilateral juristic act which purports to be entered into with another depends upon the consent of a third party, the giving or refusal of consent may be declared as well to the one as to the other party.

The consent need not be in the form prescribed for the juristic act.

If a unilateral juristic act whose validity depends upon the consent of a third party is entered into with the approval of the third party, the provisions of 111, sentences 2, 3, apply *mutatis mutandis*.

183. Precedent consent (*i.e.*, approval) is revocable until the juristic act has been entered into, unless a contrary intention appears from the legal relation by virtue of which the approval is given. The revocation may be declared as well to the one as to the other party.

184. Subsequent consent (*i.e.*, ratification) operates as from the moment when the juristic act was entered into, unless it is otherwise provided.

Dispositions affecting the object of the juristic act which before the ratification have been made by the party ratifying, or which have been effected by means of compulsory execution or distraint or by a trustee in bankruptcy, are not invalidated by the retrospective operation of the ratification.

185. A disposition affecting any object which is made by a person without title, if made with the approval of the person entitled, is valid.

The disposition is effective if the person entitled ratifies it, or if the disposer acquires the object, or if the person entitled becomes his heir and liable for the liabilities of the estate without limitation. In the last two cases, if several incompatible dispositions have been made affecting the object, only the earliest disposition is effective.

FOURTH SECTION.
PERIODS OF TIME. DATES.

186. The rules of interpretation of 187 to 193 apply to the fixing of periods and dates contained in statutes, judicial orders and juristic acts.

187. If a period begins to run from an event or a point of time occurring during the course of a day, then in reckoning the period the day in which the event or the point of time occurs is not counted.

If the beginning of a day is the point of time from which a period begins to run, then this day is counted in reckoning the period. The same rule applies to the day of birth in the reckoning of age.

188. A period described by days ends with the expiration of the last day of the period.

A period described by weeks, by months, or by a period of time covering several months—*i.e.*, year, half-year, quarter—ends, in the case provided for by 187, par. 1, on the expiration of that day of the last week or of the last month which corresponds in name or number to the day in which the event or the point of time occurs; in the case provided for by 187, par. 2, on the expiration of that day of the last week or of the last month which precedes the day which corresponds in name or number to the initial day of the period.

If, in the case of a period described by months, the decisive day for its expiration is wanting in the last month, the period ends with the expiration of the last day of the month.

189. By a half-year a period of six months, by a quarter a period of three months, by a half-month a period of fifteen days is understood.

If a period is fixed at one or several entire months and a half-month the fifteen days shall be counted last.

190. In case of the extension of a period the new period is reckoned from the expiration of the former period.

191. If a period of time is described by months or by years in such a manner that they need not run consecutively, a month is reckoned as thirty days, a year as three hundred and sixty-five days.

192. By the beginning of a month the first, by the middle of a month the fifteenth, by the end of a month the last day of the month is understood.

193. If, on a given day or within a given period, a declaration of intention is required to be made or any act of performance to be done, and if the given day or the last day of the given period falls upon a Sunday or a day officially recognised in the place (*p*) of making or performance as a public holiday, then the next business day takes the place of the Sunday or holiday.

FIFTH SECTION.
PRESCRIPTION.

194. The right to demand an act or forbearance from another (*i.e.*, a claim) is subject to prescription (*q*).

(*p*) Cf. 269.

(*q*) Only "claims" are subject to prescription. Ownership and other rights in things are not subject to prescription, since they do not consist in an act or forbearance.

A claim arising from a relation of family law is not subject to prescription, so far as it has for its object the establishment for the future of the condition proper to the relation [r].

195. The regular period of prescription is thirty years [s].

196. The period of prescription is two years [t] for the following claims [u]:

(1) claims of merchants, manufacturers, artisans and those who practise industrial arts, for delivery of goods, performance of work and care of others' affairs, including disbursements, unless the service is rendered for the carrying on of an industry conducted by the debtor [v];

(2) claims of those whose industry is agriculture or forestry, for delivery of agricultural or forest products, so far as the delivery is for the domestic use of the debtor [x];

(3) claims of carriers by railroad, freighters, boatmen, cabdrivers and messengers, for fare, freight, hire, and fees, including disbursements;

(4) claims of innkeepers and those who make a business of providing food and drink, for supplying lodging and food or for other services rendered to the guest to satisfy their need, including disbursements;

(5) claims of those who sell lottery tickets, for the sale of the tickets, unless the tickets are delivered for further sale [y];

(6) claims of those who make a business of letting moveables under an ordinary Lease, for the rent;

(7) claims of those who, without belonging to the classes specified in (1), make a business of the care of others' affairs or the rendering of

---

(*r*) Such as, for instance, the right to demand restitution of conjugal community. See 1353.

(*s*) Besides 196, 197, there are also the following exceptions to this rule: sale (477), especially sale of cattle (490); ordinary lease (558); contract for work (638); order (786); obligation to bearer (801); unlawful acts (852); usufruct (1057); right of pledge (1226); betrothal (1302); conception through illicit intercourse (1715); gift made in breach of duty (2287); compulsory portion (2332).

(*t*) The period begins to run from the close of the year in which the claim arose. 201.

(*u*) If the claim has been established by judgment, it is barred by prescription in thirty years. 218.

(*v*) In which case the period of prescription is four years, see 196, last paragraph.

(*x*) If the delivery is not for the domestic use of the debtor, the period of prescription is four years. 196, last paragraph.

(*y*) In which case the period of prescription is four years, see 196, last paragraph.

This provision does not apply to the pleas of right of lien, of unperformed contract, of absence of security, or of *beneficium excussionis*, nor to the pleas available to a surety as provided for by 770 and to an heir as provided for by 2014, 2015.

203. Prescription is suspended so long as the obligee is prevented from enforcing his right by the cessation of the administration of justice within the last six months of the period of prescription.

The same rule applies if such prevention is brought about in any other manner by *vis major*.

204. The prescription of claims between spouses is suspended so long as the marriage continues. The same rule applies to claims between parents and children during the minority of the children, and to claims between guardian and ward during the continuance of the guardianship.

205. The period during which prescription is suspended is not reckoned in the period of prescription.

206. If a person incapable of disposing or limited in disposing capacity has no statutory agent, a prescription running against him is not compete before the expiration of six months after the time at which the person becomes capable of disposing without limitation [(c)] or the want of a statutory agent ceases [(d)]. If the period of prescription is shorter than six months, the period fixed for the prescription is substituted for the six months.

These provisions do not apply where a person limited in disposing capacity is capable of suing and being sued [(e)].

207. The prescription of a claim belonging to an estate or running against an estate is not complete before the expiration of six months after the time at which the inheritance is accepted by the heir, or bankruptcy proceedings are instituted against the estate, or from which a claim of an agent or against an

---

(*c*) *E.g.*, when he has attained his majority.

(*d*) *E.g.*, when a guardian has been appointed.

(*e*) In the cases under 112, 113. See 52 of the Code of Civil Procedure.

agent may be enforced. If the period of prescription is shorter than six months, the period fixed for the prescription is substituted for the six months.

208. Prescription is interrupted if the obligor acknowledges the claim towards the obligee by part payment, payment of interest, giving of security, or in any other manner.

209. Prescription is interrupted if the obligee brings an action for satisfaction, or for acknowledgment of the claim, for award of an order for execution, or for issue of a judicial decree for the enforcement of a foreign judgment [(f)].

The following are equivalent to bringing an action:

(1) the service of an order for payment in hortatory process [(g)];

(2) the presentation of the claim in bankruptcy proceedings [(h)];

(3) the pleading of a set-off to the claim in legal process;

(4) the notice of intention to contest the process upon the result of which the claim depends;

(5) the institution of proceedings in execution, and where the compulsory execution is in the hands of the Courts or other public authorities, the presentation of the application for compulsory execution [(k)].

210. If the leave to institute legal proceedings depends upon a prior decision of a public authority, or if the designation of the competent Court is required to be made by a higher Court, the prescription is interrupted by the presentation of a petition to the public authority or the higher Court in the same manner as by bringing action, if the action is brought within three months after the answer to the petition is given. The provisions of 203, 206, 207 apply *mutatis mutandis* to such period.

211. Interruption by bringing action continues until the case is decided [(l)] or otherwise disposed of without any right of appeal.

(*f*) 211, 212.

(*g*) 213.

(*h*) 214.

(*k*) 216.

(*l*) See 219.

If the process is suspended in consequence of an agreement or because it is not prosecuted, the interruption ends with the last step in the process taken by the parties or the Court. The new prescription beginning after the termination of the interruption is interrupted by further prosecution of the process by one of the parties in the same manner as by bringing action.

212. Bringing action is deemed to be no interruption if the action is withdrawn or dismissal by a non-appellable decree not deciding the principal matter.

If the obligee brings action anew within six months, the prescription is deemed to have been interrupted by the bringing of the first action. The provisions of 203, 206, 207 apply *mutatis mutandis* to such period.

213. Service of an order for payment in hortatory process is deemed to be no interruption, if the effects of commencement of action become extinguished [(m)].

214. Interruption by presentation in bankruptcy proceedings continues until the proceedings are ended.

If the presentation is withdrawn, it is deemed to have been no interruption.

If, on the termination of the proceedings, a sum is held back for a claim which is in dispute in consequence of a protest raised at the examination, the interruption continues even after the termination of the proceedings; the end of the interruption is determined according to the provisions of 211.

215. Interruption by pleading set-off in legal process or by notice of intention to contest continues until the process is decided or otherwise disposed of without any right of appeal; the provisions of 211, par. 2, apply.

The interruption is deemed not to have taken place if, within six months after the termination of the process, action be not brought for satisfaction or establishment of the claim. The provisions of 203, 206, 207 apply *mutatis mutandis* to such period.

216. Institution of proceedings in execution is deemed to be no interruption, if the proceedings are discontinued upon the application of the obligee, or on account of the non-fulfilment of the statutory conditions.

(*m*) See Code of Civil Procedure, 697, 701.

Presentation of application for compulsory execution is deemed to be no interruption, if the application is not allowed, or the application is withdrawn before the institution of proceedings in execution, or the proceedings already taken are discontinued as in par. 1.

217. If prescription is interrupted the time elapsed before the interruption is not taken into consideration; a new prescription may not begin before the termination of the interruption.

218. A claim established by a non-appellable judgment is barred by prescription in thirty years, even if it is itself subject to a shorter period of prescription. The same rule applies to a claim arising from an executory compromise or an executory deed, and to a claim becoming executory through settlement in bankruptcy proceedings.

In so far as the settlement relates to periodical payments becoming due only in the future, the shorter period of prescription is sufficient [(n)].

219. A non-appellable decision within the meaning of 211, par. 1, and 218, par. 1, including also a non-appellable judgment issue under reservation [(o)].

220. If a claim is required to be enforced before a Court of arbitration or a special tribunal, before an administrative Court or an administrative authority, the provisions of 209 to 213, 215, 216, 218, 219, apply *mutatis mutandis*.

If the arbitrators are not nominated in the agreement as to arbitration, or if the nomination of an arbitrator is necessary for any other reason, or if the Court of arbitration cannot be invoked until after the fulfilment of some other condition, the prescription is already interrupted by the obligee taking the steps necessary on his part for the settlement of the matter.

221. If a thing with regard to which a claim *ad rem* exists comes by succession in title into the possession of a third party, the time of prescription elapsed during the possession by the predecessor in title is reckoned in favour of the successor in title.

(*n*) *I.e.*, four years. 197.

(*o*) See, *e.g.*, 302, 540, 599 of the Code of Civil Procedure.

222. After the lapse of the period of prescription the obligor is entitled to refuse performance [(p)].

If any act of performance is done in satisfaction of a claim barred by prescription, the value of such performance may not be demanded back, even if the performance has been effected in ignorance of the prescription. The same rule applies to a contractual acknowledgment of liability and to the giving of security by the obligor.

223. The prescription of a claim for which there is a hypotheca or a right of pledge does not prevent the obligee from satisfying himself out of the object in custody.

If a right has been transferred to secure a claim, its re-transfer may not be demanded on the ground of the prescription of the claim.

These provisions do not apply to the case of prescription of claims for arrears of interest or other periodical acts of performance.

224. With the principal claim the claims for accessory acts of performance [(q)] dependent upon it are also barred by prescription, even if the particular prescription applying to the accessory claim is not yet complete.

225. Prescription may neither be excluded nor made more onerous by juristic act [(r)]. Prescription may be facilitated, especially by shortening the period of prescription.

SIXTH SECTION.

EXERCISE OF RIGHTS. SELF-DEFENCE. SELF-HELP.

226. The exercise of a right which can only have the purpose of causing

---

(*p*) The party in whose favour the prescription operates has to plead it, since the Court does not take judicial notice of the prescription of a claim. After the prescription of a claim a natural obligation exists which may have legal effect in certain cases. 222, par. 2, 223, 390, sentence 2.

(*q*) *E.g.*, payment of interest.

(*r*) Cf. 477, par. 1; 638, par. 2.

injury to another is unlawful.

227. An act required for purposes of necessary defence is not unlawful [(s)].

Necessary defence is that defence which is necessary in order to repel an actual unlawful attack [(t)] upon oneself or another.

228. If a person injures or destroys a thing belonging to another in order to avert from himself or from another a danger threatened by it, he does not act unlawfully, if such injury or destruction is necessary to avert the danger, and the damage is not out of proportion to the danger. If the danger was caused by such person's fault he is liable to make compensation.

229. If a person, for the purpose of self-help, destroys or injures a thing, or for the purpose of self-help apprehends an obligor who is suspected of intending flight or overcomes the resistance of the obligee to an act which the latter is bound to permit, he does not act unlawfully if the help of a magistrate is not obtainable in a reasonable time, and there is danger that if he does not act immediately the realisation of the claim will be frustrated or seriously impeded [(u)].

230. Self-help must not be carried further than is necessary to avert the danger.

In case of the seizure of things, unless compulsory execution is effected, leave to distrain shall be applied for.

In case of the apprehension of the obligor, unless he is again set at liberty, leave for the precautionary detention of his person shall be applied for to the District Court in whose district the apprehension took place; the obligor shall be brought before the Court without delay.

If the application to the Court is delayed or rejected, the restitution of the things seized and the liberation of the person apprehended shall take place

---

(*s*) The same provision appears in 53 of the Criminal Code.

(*t*) The attack need not necessarily be against the person; it may be against property or other rights. Blum's *Annalen*, Vol. II., p. 289.

(*u*) The Code permits self-help also in the following special cases: 559—561, 859, 910, 961, 962, 1228.

without delay.

231. If any person does one of the acts specified in 229 under the erroneous assumption that the necessary conditions exist to render his act lawful, he is liable to compensate the other party, even if the error was not due to negligence.

SEVENTH SECTION.
GIVING OF SECURITY.

232. If a person has to give security, he may do so:

(a) by lodging money or negotiable instruments;

(b) by pledge of claims which have been registered in the Imperial debt ledger or the State debt ledger of one of the States;

(c) by pledge of moveables;

(d) by charging hypothecas on land situate within the Empire;

(e) by pledge of claims secured by hypotheca on land situate within the Empire, or by pledge of land charges or annuity charges on land situate within the Empire.

If security cannot be given in this manner it is permissible to furnish a proper surety [(x)].

233. By the lodgment the person entitled acquires a right of pledge over the money or negotiable instruments lodged, and if, according to the provisions of the State law, the title to the money or the negotiable instruments passes to the Treasury or to the institution designated as the lodgment office, a right of pledge on the claim for restitution.

234. Negotiable instruments are suitable to be given as security only if they are payable to bearer, have a market value, and belong to a species in which money belonging to a ward may be invested [(y)]. Instruments to order indorsed

(*x*) 239.

(*y*) 1807.

in blank are equivalent to instruments to bearer.

With the negotiable instruments are to be lodged the interest coupons, annuity coupons, dividend coupons, and renewal coupons.

Security may be given in negotiable instruments only to the extent of three-fourths of their market value.

235. If a person has given security by lodging money or negotiable instruments, he is entitled to exchange the money lodged for suitable negotiable instruments, or the negotiable instruments lodged for other suitable negotiable instruments, or for money.

236. An uncertificated claim against the Empire or against a State may be given as security only to the extent of three-fourths of the market value of the negotiable instruments whose issue the creditor may demand in satisfaction of his claim.

237. A moveable may be given as security only to the extent of two-thirds of its estimated value. Things may be refused as security if deterioration in them is to be apprehended, or if their custody involves special difficulties.

238. A hypothecary claim, a land charge or an annuity charge is suitable to be given as security only if it fulfils the conditions under which, according to the law of the place where the security is required to be given, money belonging to a ward may be invested in hypothecary claims, land charges, or annuity charge.

A claim secured by a cautionary hypotheca [z] is not suitable to be given as security.

239. A proper surety is a person who possesses property proportional [a] to the amount of security to be given and is subject to domestic jurisdiction.

The declaration of suretyship [b] must contain a waiver of the plea of *bene-*

(*z*) See 1184.

(*a*) Cf. 234, par. 3; 236, 237.

(*b*) This must be in writing.

ficium excussionis [c].

240. If the security given become insufficient without any fault on the part of the obligee, it shall be supplemented or new security be given.

(c) 771, 773.

SECOND BOOK.
Law of Obligations [(a)].

FIRST SECTION.
SCOPE OF OBLIGATIONS.

FIRST TITLE.
Obligation of Performance.

241. By virtue of an obligation the creditor is entitled to claim performance from the debtor. The performance may consist in a forbearance.

242. The debtor is bound to effect the performance according to the requirements of good faith, ordinary usage being taken into consideration.

243. A person who owes a thing designated only by species shall deliver a thing of average kind and quality.

If the debtor has done everything required on his part for the delivery of such a thing, his obligation is limited to the thing intended to be delivered.

244. If a money debt expressed in a foreign currency is payable within the Empire, payment may be made in the currency of the Empire, unless payment in the foreign currency is expressly stipulated for.

The commutation is made according to the rate of exchange current in the place of payment [(b)] at the time of payment.

(*a*) The word "obligation" is a free translation of the term *Schuldverhältnis*, which means literally "obligatory relation".

(*b*) See 269, 270.

245. If a money debt is payable in a specific kind of money which is no longer current at the time of payment, the payment shall be made as if the kind of money were not specified.

246. If by law (c) or juristic act a debt is to bear interest, four per cent. per annum (d) shall be paid, unless some other rate is specified (e).

247. If a higher rate of interest than six per cent. per annum is agreed upon, the debtor may, after the expiration of six months, give notice of payment of the principal, six months notice being required. The right of payment on notice may not be excluded or limited by contract. These provisions do not apply to obligations to bearer.

248. An agreement made in advance (f) that interest due shall again bear interest is void.

Savings banks, credit institutions and bankers may agree in advance that interest on deposits not drawn shall be considered as a new interest-bearing deposit. Credit institutions which have been authorised to issue interest-bearing obligations to bearer for the amount of the loans made by them, may cause to be promised to them in advance on such loans payment of interest on arrears of interest.

249. A person who is bound to make compensation shall bring about the condition which would exist if the circumstance making him liable to compensate had not occurred. If compensation is required to be made for injury to a person (g) or damage to a thing, the creditor may demand, instead of restitution in kind, the sum of money necessary to effect such restitution.

(*c*) The principal cases are provided for by 288—290, and 291. Other cases may be found in 256, 347, 452, 641, par. 2, 668, 698, 820, 849, 1133, 1834.

(*d*) In commercial transactions the statutory rate of interest is 5 per cent. (Commercial Code, 352, 353), and in the case of a debt founded on a bill of exchange, 6 per cent.

(*e*) The parties may agree upon any rate of interest, subject, however, to the provision of 138.

(*f*) However, a *subsequent* agreement to the effect that interest *already* due shall accumulate as capital (*i.e.*, shall again bear interest) is valid.

(*g*) In such a case the compensation is usually in the form of a money annuity. 842—847.

250. The creditor may fix a reasonable period for the restitution in kind by the person liable to compensate with a declaration that he will refuse to accept restitution after the expiration of the period. After the expiration of the period the creditor may demand the compensation in money if the restitution is not effected in due time; the claim for restitution is barred.

251. In so far as restitution in kind is impossible or is insufficient to compensate the creditor, the person liable shall compensate him in money.

The person liable may compensate the creditor in money if restitution in kind is possible only through disproportionate outlay.

252. The compensation required to be made includes also lost profits. Profit is deemed to have been lost which could have been expected with probability according to the ordinary course of things or according to the particular circumstances, *e.g.*, according to the preparations and provisions made.

253. For an injury which is not an injury to property compensation in money [(h)] may be demanded only in the cases specified by law [(i)].

254. If any fault of the injured party has contributed in causing the injury, the obligation to compensate the injured party and the extent of the compensation to be made depends upon the circumstances, especially upon how far the injury has been caused chiefly by the one or the other party.

This applies also even if the fault of the injured party consisted only in an omission to call the attention of the debtor to the danger of an unusually serious injury which the debtor neither knew nor ought to have known, or in an omission to avert or mitigate the injury. The provision of 278 applies *mutatis mutandis*.

255. A person who is required to make compensation for the loss of a thing or of a right is bound to make compensation only upon assignment to him of the claims which belong to the person entitled to compensation by virtue of his ownership of the thing or by virtue of his right as against third parties.

(*h*) It is to be noticed that this provision applies only to compensation in money, and not to compensation in the form of restitution in kind. 249.

(*i*) For such cases, see 847, 1300, 1715, par. 1.

256. A person who is bound to reimburse another for outlay shall pay interest from the time of the outlay on the amount expended, or if other objects than money have been used, on the amount to be paid as compensation for their value. If any outlay has been incurred upon an object which is to be delivered to the person bound to make reimbursement, interest shall not be paid for the time during which the person entitled to reimbursement receives the emoluments or the fruits of the object without making compensation.

257. A person who is entitled to demand reimbursement of outlay which he incurs for a specific purpose may, if he has incurred an obligation for such purpose, demand relief from the obligation. If the obligation is not yet due, the person bound to make reimbursement may give him security instead of relieving him.

258. A person who is entitled to remove an attachment from a thing which he is required to deliver to another shall, in case of the removal, put the thing in its former condition at his own expanse. If the other party acquires possession of the thing he is bound to permit the removal of the attachment; he may refuse permission until security is given to him for the damage involved in the removal.

259. A person who is bound to render an account of his management of an affair involving receipts or disbursements [(k)] shall furnish the person entitled to it with an account containing a systematic statement of the receipts or disbursements, and shall, so far as it is customary to give vouchers, submit vouchers.

If there is reason to suspect that the statements contained in the account relating to the receipts have not been made with the necessary amount of care [(l)], he shall, on demand, swear an oath of disclosure to the effect:

> that he, according to the best of his knowledge, has stated the receipts as completely as he was in a position to do.

In matters of trivial importance [(m)] the obligation to swear such oath of disclosure does not exist.

(*k*) *E.g.*, a mandatory, guardian, or executor.

(*l*) The *onus probandi* is upon the person requiring the oath to be sworn.

(*m*) It is for the Court to decide whether the matter is of trivial importance or not.

260. A person who is bound to deliver an aggregate of objects or to give a statement of the contents of such an aggregate shall submit to the person entitled to it an inventory of the contents.

If there is reason to suspect that the inventory has not been drawn up with the necessary amount of care (n), he shall on demand swear an oath of disclosure to the effect:

> that he, according to the best of his knowledge, has stated the contents as completely as he was in a position to do.

The provision of 259, par. 3, applies.

261. The oath of disclosure, unless it is required to be sworn before the Court in which process is pending, shall be sworn before the District Court of the place in which the obligation of giving account or submitting the inventory is required to be fulfilled. If the person who is under such obligation has his domicile or residence within the Empire, the oath of disclosure may be sworn before the District Court of the place of his domicile or residence.

The Court may order a modification of the form of the oath corresponding to the circumstances.

The costs of swearing the oath shall be borne by the person who requires the oath to be sworn.

262. If several acts of performance are due in such a manner that only one of them is required to be done, the right to elect belongs to the debtor in case of doubt.

263. The election is made by declaration to the other party (o).

The performance elected is deemed to be the only one due *ab initio.*

264. If the debtor entitled to elect does not make the election before the levy of compulsory execution, the creditor may, at his election, levy execution on any one of the acts of performance; the debtor may, nevertheless, relieve himself from his obligation, so long as the creditor has not received the elected

---

(*n*) Cf. note (*l*) to 259.

(*o*) The election is irrevocable after it has once been made.

performance wholly or in part, by doing any one of the other acts of performance.

If the creditor entitled to elect is in default [(p)], the debtor may demand the creditor to make an election within a fixed reasonable period of time. After the expiration of the period the right to elect passes to the debtor if the creditor does not make his election in due time.

265. If one of the acts of performance is impossible *ab initio*, or if it subsequently becomes impossible, the obligation is limited to the other acts of performance. This limitation does not arise if the performance becomes impossible in consequence of a circumstance for which the party not entitled to elect responsible.

266. A debtor is not entitled to perform in part [(q)].

267. If a debtor does not have to perform in person, a third party may effect the performance [(r)]. The approval of the debtor is not necessary.

The creditor may decline the performance if the debtor objects to it.

268. If the creditor levies compulsory execution upon an object belonging to the debtor, any person who through the execution incurs danger of losing a right in the object is entitled to satisfy the creditor. The same right belongs to the possessor of a thing if he incurs danger of losing possession through the execution.

The satisfaction may also be made by lodgment or by set-off.

If a third party satisfies the creditor the claim is transfers to him [(s)]. The transfer may not be enforced to the detriment of the creditor.

269. If a place for performance [(t)] is neither fixed nor to be inferred from

---

(*p*) See 293 *et seq.*

(*q*) The rule is otherwise in the case of a bill of exchange. See sect. 38 of the Bills of Exchange Act.

(*r*) The creditor must accept the performance, otherwise he will be in default. 293.

(*s*) *Ipso facto*. Cf. 412.

(*t*) The place of performance is determined: *first*, according to the intention of the parties (cf. 133, 157, 242); *secondly*, according to the special provisions of law which are applicable to the particular case (*e.g.*, 697, 700, 811, 1194, Art. 92 of the Introductory Act); *thirdly*, according to the circumstances, especially according to the nature of the obligation (cf. 133, 157, 242); and *lastly*, according to 269.

the circumstances, *e.g.*, from the nature of the obligation, performance shall be effected in the place where the debtor had his domicile at the time the obligation arose.

If the obligation arose in the conduct of the debtor's industrial operations, and if the debtor's industry is located in another place, such place is substituted for the domicile.

It is not to be inferred from the mere circumstance that the debtor has assumed the expense of transmittal, that the place to which transmittal is required to be made is the place of performance.

270. In case of doubt the debtor shall remit money at his own risk and expense to the creditor at the latter's domicile.

If the claim arose in the conduct of the creditor's industrial operations, and if the creditor's industry is located in another place, such place is substituted for the domicile.

If, in consequence of a change of the creditor's domicile or the location of his industry occurring after the obligation arose, the cost or the risk of remitting is increased, the creditor shall bear the additional cost in the former case and the risk in the latter case.

The provisions relating to the place of performance remain unaffected.

271. If a time for performance (u) is neither fixed nor to be inferred from the circumstances, the creditor may demand the performance forthwith, and the debtor may perform his part forthwith.

If a time is fixed it is to be presumed, in case of doubt, that the creditor may not demand the performance before that time; the debtor, however, may perform earlier (x).

272. If the debtor pays before maturity a debt not bearing interest he is not

---

(*u*) The time of performance is determined: *first*, according to the intention of the parties (133, 157, 242); *secondly*, according to the special provisions of law which are applicable to the particular case (rent, 551; rent, 584; loan for use, 604; loan for consumption, 608, 609; contract for service, 614; contract for work, 640); *thirdly*, according to the circumstances (133, 157, 242); and *lastly*, according to 271.

(*x*) Cf. 299.

entitled to any reduction on account of *interim* interest.

273. If the debtor has a matured claim against the creditor arising from the same legal relation [y] upon which his own obligation is based, he may, unless a contrary intention appears from the obligation, refuse to effect the performance due from him until the performance due to him is effected (*i.e.*, a right of lien).

A person who is bound to hand over an object has the same right, if he has a matured claim on account of outlay incurred on the object, or on account of any injury caused to him by it, unless he has acquired the object by a wilful unlawful act.

The creditor may avert the exercise of the right of lien by giving security. The giving of security by sureties is not permitted.

274. As against suit by the creditor the enforcement of the right of lien has only the effect that the debtor is adjudged to perform on receipt of the performance due to him (*i.e.*, contemporaneous performance).

By virtue of such a judgment the creditor may pursue his claim by means of compulsory execution without effecting the performance due from him if the debtor is in default of acceptance.

275. The debtor is relieved from his obligation to perform if the performance becomes impossible in consequence of a circumstance for which he is not responsible [z] occurring after the creation of the obligation [a].

If the debtor, after the creation of the obligation, becomes unable to perform, it is equivalent to a circumstance rendering the performance impossible [b].

276. A debtor is responsible, unless is otherwise provided, for wilful default

---

(*y*) In commercial transactions the matured claim of the debtor need not arise out of the same legal relation. Both debtor and creditor must, however, be "merchants" as defined by the Commercial Code. See 369—372 of the Commercial Code.

(*z*) Cf. 280, par. 1.

(*a*) If the circumstance occurred before the creation of the obligation, the contract is void. 306.

(*b*) 281 applies to all cases under 275.

and negligence [c]. A person who does not exercise ordinary care acts negligently. The provisions of 827, 828 apply.

A debtor may not be released beforehand from responsibility for wilful default.

277. A person who is answerable only for such care as he is accustomed to exercise in his own affairs [d] is not relieved from responsibility for gross negligence.

278. A debtor is responsible for the fault of his statutory agent, and of persons whom he employs in fulfilling his obligation, to the same extent as for his own fault [e]. The provision of 276, par. 2, does not apply.

279. If the object owed is designated only by species, and so long as delivery of an object of the designated species is possible, the debtor is responsible for his inability to deliver, even though no fault is imputable to him.

280. Where the performance becomes impossible in consequence of a circumstance for which the debtor is responsible, the debtor shall compensate the creditor for any damage arising from the non-performance.

In case of partial impossibility the creditor may, by declining the still possible part of the performance, demand compensation for non-performance of the entire obligation, if he has no interest in the partial performance. The provisions of 346 to 356 applicable to the contractual right of rescission apply *mutatis*

(*c*) This enunciates the general principle, to which there are the following exceptions:

(A) Liability for accident, as in the case where the debtor is in default (287); management of affairs without mandate (678); and innkeepers (701).

(B) Liability for gross negligence, as in the case of a gift (521); loan for use (599); management of affairs without mandate in the special case provided for by 680; finding (968); and creditors default of acceptance (300).

(C) Liability for such care as is exercised by a person in his own affairs. See note (*d*) to 277.

(*d*) Those who are responsible for such degree of care are partners *inter se* (708), spouses *inter se* (1359), gratuitous depositary (690), father and mother in the exercise of the parental power (1664), and limited heirs (2131).

(*e*) He may, however, contract himself out of this responsibility.

mutandis [(f)].

281. If, in consequence of the circumstance which makes the performance impossible, the debtor acquires a substitute or a claim for compensation for the object owed [(g)], the creditor may demand delivery of the substitute received or assignment of the claim for compensation.

If the creditor has a claim for compensation on a count of non-performance, the compensation to be made to him is diminished, if he exercises the right specified in par. 1, by the value of the substitute received or of the claim for compensation.

282. If it is disputed whether the impossibility of performance is the result of a circumstance for which the debtor is responsible, the burden of proof is upon the debtor.

283. If non-appellable judgment has been delivered against the debtor, the creditor may allot him a reasonable period for performance, with a declaration that he refuses to accept the performance after the expiration of the period. After the expiration of the period the creditor may demand compensation for non-performance, if the performance be not effected in due time; the claim for performance is barred. The liability for compensation does not arise if the performance becomes impossible in consequence of a circumstance for which the debtor is not responsible.

If at the expiration of the period the performance is only in part not effected, the creditor has also the right specified in 280, par. 2.

284. If the debtor does not perform after warning given by the creditor after maturity, he is in default through the warning. Bringing an action for the performance and the service of an order for payment in hortatory process are equivalent to warning.

If a time by the calendar is fixed for the performance, the debtor is in default without warning if he does not perform at the fixed time. The same rule

---

(*f*) In the case of mutual contracts the provisions of 325 apply.

(*g*) *E.g.*, in the case of insurance.

applies if a notice is required to precede the performance, and the time if fixed in such manner that it may be reckoned by the calendar from the time of notice.

285. The debtor is not in default so long as the performance is not effected in consequence of a circumstance for which he is not responsible.

286. The debtor shall compensate the creditor for any damage arising from his default [h].

If the creditor has no interest in the performance in consequence of the default, he may, by refusing the performance, demand compensation for non-performance. The provisions of 346 to 356 applicable to the contractual right of rescission apply *mutatis mutandis*.

287. A debtor is responsible for all negligence during his default. He is also responsible for impossibility of performance arising accidentally during the default, unless the injury would have arisen even if he had performed in due time.

288. A money debt bears interest during default at 4 per cent. per annum. If the creditor can demand higher interest on any other legitimate ground [i], this shall continue to be paid. Proof of further damage is admissible.

289. Interest for default shall not be paid upon interest. The right of the creditor to compensation for any damage arising from the default remains unaffected.

290. If the debtor is bound to make compensation for the value of an object which has perished during the default, or which cannot be delivered for a reason which has arisen during the default, the creditor may demand interest on the amount to be paid as compensation, from the time which serves as the basis for the estimate of the value. The same rule applies if the debtor is bound to make compensation for the diminution in value of an object which has deteri-

---

(*h*) As a general rule the creditor cannot rescind the contract on the ground of the default of the debtor. See, however, par. 2.

(*i*) *E.g.*, in commercial transactions the legal rate of interest is 5 per cent., or in case a higher rate of interest has been agreed upon.

orated during the default.

291. A debtor shall pay interest on a money debt from the date of action commenced [(k)], even if he is not in default; if the debt does not become due until after the date [(l)] it bears interest from the date of maturity. The provisions of 288, par. 1, and 289, sentence 1, apply *mutatis mutandis*.

292. If a debtor has to deliver a specific object, the claim of the creditor for compensation for deterioration, destruction, or impossibility of delivery arising from any other cause is, after the date of action commenced, determined according to the provisions [(m)] which apply to the relations between an owner and a possessor after the date of action commenced on a claim of ownership, unless a contrary intention in favour of the creditor appears from the obligation itself or from the default of the debtor.

The same rule applies to the claim of the creditor for delivery of, or compensation for, emoluments and to the claim of the debtor for reimbursement of outlay incurred.

SECOND TITLE.
Default of the Creditor.

293. A creditor is in default if he does hot accept the performance tendered to him [(n)].

294. The performance must be actually tendered to the creditor in the manner in which it is to be effected [(o)].

(*k*) This rule obtains even in the case where the action is brought merely for arrears of interest.

(*l*) Where an action is brought for establishing a right to periodical payments, a declaration as to the right to future payments may be claimed in the action.

(*m*) See 987 *et seq*.

(*n*) No matter whether fault is imputable to him or not.

(*o*) That is to say, in the proper manner (242 *et seq*.), at the proper time (271, 299), and in the proper place (269, 270).

295. A verbal tender by the debtor is sufficient if the creditor has declared to him that he will not accept the performance, or if for effecting the performance an act of the creditor is necessary, *e.g.*, if the creditor has to take away the thing owed. A summons to the creditor to do the necessary act is equivalent to tender of performance.

296. If a time according to the calendar is fixed for the act to be done by the creditor, tender is required only if the creditor does the act in due time. The same rule applies if notice is required to precede the act, and the time for the act is fixed in such manner that it may be reckoned by the calendar from the time of notice.

297. A creditor is not in default if the debtor is not in a position to effect the performance at the time of tender, or, in the case provided for by 296, at the time fixed for the act of the creditor [(p)].

298. If the debtor is bound to perform his part only upon counter-performance by the creditor, the creditor is in default if, though prepared to accept the performance tendered, he does not offer the required counter-performance [(q)].

299. If the time of performance is not fixed, or if the debtor is entitled to perform before the fixed time, the creditor is not in default by reason of the fact that he is temporarily prevented from accepting the tendered performance, unless the debtor has given him notice of his intended performance a reasonable time beforehand.

300. During the default of a creditor his debtor is responsible only for wilful default and gross negligence.

If a thing designated only by species [(r)] is owed, the risk passes to the creditor from the moment at which he is first in default by not accepting the thing tendered.

(*p*) The *onus probandi* lies on the creditor.

(*q*) See 320, 321, 273, 274.

(*r*) Cf. 243.

301. Upon an interest-bearing money debt the debtor does not have to pay interest during the default of the creditor.

302. If a debtor has to hand over the emolument of an object or to make compensation for them, his liability during the default of the creditor is limited to the emoluments which he actually draws [(s)].

303. If the debtor is bound to give up the possession of a piece of land [(t)], he may relinquish its possession after the occurrence of the creditor's default. The creditor must be previously warned of the relinquishment, unless the warning is impracticable.

304. The debtor may, in case of the default of the creditor, demand compensation for the excess of outlay which he has been obliged to incur for the ineffective tender as well as for the custody and preservation of the object owed.

SECOND SECTION.
OBLIGATIONS EX CONTRACTU.

FIRST TITLE.
Creation of an Obligation. Scope of a Contract.

305. For the creation of an obligation by juristic act, and for any alteration of the substance of an obligation, a contract between the parties is necessary, unless it is otherwise provided by law [(u)].

(*s*) He is not, however, responsible for any emoluments which he wilfully or negligently omits to draw.

(*t*) See 928. In the case of moveables which are suitable to be lodged, such as money, negotiable instruments, or other valuables, the debtor may lodge them (372); in the case of moveables of any other kind he may cause them to be sold at public auction and lodge the proceeds (383).

(*u*) A unilateral juristic act is sufficient in the case of a foundation (80, 81), promise of reward (657 *et seq.*), obligations to bearer (793 *et seq.*), and, inferentially, of contracts in favour of a third person (328 *et seq.*).

306. A contract for an impossible performance is void [x].

307. A person who, in concluding a contract for an impossible performance, knew or ought to have known that it was impossible, is bound to make compensation for any damage which the other party has sustained by relying upon the validity of the contract; not, however, beyond the value of the interest which the other party has in the validity of the contract. The duty to make compensation does not arise if the other party knew or ought to have known of the impossibility.

These provisions apply *mutatis mutandis* if the performance is only partially impossible, and the contract is valid in respect of the possible part, or if only one of several acts of performance promised with election [y] between them is impossible.

308. The impossibility of performance does not prevent the validity of the contract if the impossibility can be removed, and the contract is intended to be binding only if the performance becomes possible.

If an impossible performance is promised subject to any other condition precedent [z] or limitation of a definite time, after which it is to become binding, the contract is valid if the impossibility is removed before the fulfilment of the condition or the arrival of the time.

309. If a contract is contrary to a statutory prohibition [a], the provisions of 307, 308, apply *mutatis mutandis.*

310. A contract whereby one party binds himself to convey his future property or a fractional part of his future property or to charge it with a usufruct, is void.

311. A contract whereby one party binds himself to convey his present

---

(*x*) Cf. the maxim: *Ultra posse nemo obligatur.* Mere *inability* to perform on the part of the person bound is insufficient. The impossibility must exist prior to or at the time of the conclusion of the contract, otherwise the provisions of 275, 323, *et seq.* apply. For the case of partial impossibility, see 139.

(*y*) See 262—265.

(*z*) *I.e.*, subject to a condition precedent other than that mentioned in the preceding paragraph.

(*a*) See 134, 135, 138, 139.

property or a fractional part of his present property or to charge it with a usufruct, requires judicial or notarial authentication [(b)].

312. A contract relating to the estate of an existing third person is void. The same rule applies to a contract relating to the compulsory portion or a legacy from the estate of an existing third person.

These provisions do not apply to a contract entered into between future statutory heirs relating to the statutory portion or the compulsory portion of one of them. Such a contract requires judicial or notarial authentication.

313. A contract whereby one party binds himself to transfer ownership of a piece of land [(c)] requires judicial or notarial authentication. A contract concluded without observance of this form becomes valid in its entirety if conveyance by agreement and entry in the land register have taken place.

314. If a person binds himself to alienate or give a charge upon a thing, the obligation extends, in case of doubt, also to the accessories of the thing.

315. If the mode of performance is to be determined by one of the contracting parties, it is to be presumed, in case of doubt, that the determination is to be made in an equitable manner.

The determination is made by declaration to the other party.

If the determination is to be made in an equitable manner, the determination made is binding upon the other party only if it is equitable. If it is inequitable the determination is made by judicial decree; the same rule applies if the determination is delayed.

316. If the extent of the counter-performance promised for an act of performance is not determined the determination, in case of doubt, is to be made by the party who is entitled to demand the counter-performance.

317. If the determination of the performance is left to a third party, it is to

---

(*b*) See 125, 128.

(*c*) Ownership of land cannot be transferred on the mere strength of a contract, entry in the land register is necessary. 873.

be presumed, in case of doubt, that it shall be made in an equitable manner.

If the determination is to be made by several third parties, the agreement of all is necessary in case of doubt; if a sum is to be specified, and if various sums have been specified, the average is to be taken.

318. The determination of the performance left to a third party is made by declaration to one of the contracting parties.

The determination made may be set aside on the ground of mistake, threats, or fraud, at the instance only of the contracting parties; the other party is defendant. The action must be brought without delay after the person entitled to bring it has obtained knowledge of the ground for attack. The right is barred if thirty years have elapsed after the determination has been made.

319. If a third party is to determine the performance in an equitable manner, the determination made is not binding upon the contracting parties if it is evidently inequitable. The determination in this case is made by judicial decree; the same rule applies if the third party cannot or will not make the determination, or if he delays it.

If the third party is to make the determination at his discretion the contract is not binding, if the third party cannot or will not make the determination, or if he delays it.

SECOND TITLE.
Mutual Contract.

320. A person who is bound by a mutual contract may refuse to perform his part until the other party has performed his part, unless the former is bound to perform his part first. If the performance is for the benefit of several persons, the part due to one of them can be refused until the entire counter-performance has been effected. The provision of 273, par. 3, does not apply.

If one party has partially performed his part, counter-performance may not be refused if the refusal under the circumstances, *e.g.*, on account of the relative insignificance of the part not performed, would constitute bad faith.

321. A person who is bound by a mutual contract to perform his part first may, if after the conclusion of the contract a serious change for the worse in the financial circumstances of the other party comes about whereby the claim for the counter-performance is endangered, refuse to perform his part until the other party has performed his part or given security for it.

322. If one party bring an action for the performance due to him under a mutual contract, the enforcement of the right in the other party to refuse performance until the counter-performance has been effected has only the effect that judgment is to be delivered against the latter for contemporaneous performance [(d)].

If the party bringing the action has to perform his part first he may, if the other party is in default of acceptance, bring an action for performance after receipt of the counter-performance.

The provision of 274, par. 2, applies to compulsory execution.

323. If the performance due from one party under a mutual contract becomes impossible in consequence of a circumstance for which neither he nor the other party is responsible, he loses the claim to counter-performance; in case of partial impossibility the counter-performance is diminished in conformity with 472, 473.

If the other party demands delivery under 281 of the substitute received for the object owed, or assignment of the claim for compensation, he remains bound to effect the counter-performance; this is diminished, however, in conformity with 472, 473, in so far as the value of the substitute or of the claim for compensation is less than of the value of the performance due.

If the counter-performance has been effected which according to these provisions was not due, the value of the performance effected may be demanded back under the provisions relating to the return of unjustified benefits [(e)].

324. If the performance due from one party under a mutual contract becomes impossible in consequence of a circumstance for which the other party is

---

(*d*) See 273, 274.

(*e*) See 818—822.

responsible, he retains his claim for counter-performance. He must, however, deduct what he saves in consequence of release from the performance, or what he acquires or maliciously omits to acquire by a different application of his faculties.

The same rule applies if the performance due from one party becomes impossible, in consequence of a circumstance for which he is not responsible, at the time when the other party is in default of acceptance.

325. If the performance due from one party under a mutual contract becomes impossible in consequence of a circumstance for which he is responsible, the other party may demand compensation for non-performance, or rescind the contract. In case of partial impossibility, if he has no interest in the partial performance of the contract [(f)], he is entitled, subject to the conditions specified in 280, par. 2, to demand compensation for non-performance of the entire obligation, or to rescind the entire contract. In lieu of the claim for compensation and of the right of rescission he may avail himself of the rights specified for the case provided for by 323.

The same rule applies in the case provided for by 283, if the performance is not effected before the expiration of the period, or if at that time it is in part not effected.

326. If, in the case of a mutual contract, one party is in default in respect of the performance due from him, the other party may allot him a fixed reasonable period for performing his part with a declaration that he will decline the performance after the expiration of the period. After the expiration of the period he is entitled to demand compensation for non-performance, or to rescind the contract, if the performance has not been effected in due time; the claim for performance is barred. If the performance is in part not effected before the expiration of the period, the provision of 325, par. 1, sentence 2, applies *mutatis mutandis*.

If, in consequence of the default, the performance of the contract is of no use to the other party, such other party has the rights specified in par. 1 without the fixing of a period being necessary.

(*f*) The *onus probandi* lies upon him.

327. The provisions of 346 to 356 applicable to the contractual right of rescission apply *mutatis mutandis* to the right of rescission specified in 325, 326. If the contract is rescinded on account of a circumstance for which the other party is not responsible, such other party is liable only under the provisions relating to the return of unjustified benefits [g].

THIRD TITLE.
Promise of Performance in favour of a Third Party.

328. An act of performance in favour of a third party may by contract be stipulated for in such manner that the third party acquires a direct right to demand the performance.

In the absence of express stipulation it is to be inferred from the circumstances, especially from the object of the contract whether the third party shall acquire the right, whether the right of the third party shall arise forthwith or only under certain conditions, and whether any right shall be reserved to the contracting parties to take away or modify the right of the third party without his consent.

329. If in a contract one party binds himself to satisfy a creditor of the other party without assuming the debt [h], it is not to be presumed, in case of doubt, that the creditor shall acquire a direct right to demand satisfaction from him.

330. If, in a contract for life insurance or an annuity, payment of the insurance or annuity to a third party is stipulated for, it is to be presumed, in case of doubt, that the third party shall acquire a direct right to demand the payment. The same rule applies, if in a gratuitous transfer of property the duty to perform an act in favour of a third party is imposed upon the recipient, or if a person, on taking over the whole of another persons property or goods, promises an act of performance in favour of a third party for the purpose of compounding a

---

(*g*) *I.e.*, 818—822.

(*h*) Cf. 414—419.

liability.

331. If the performance in favour of the third party is to be effected after the death of the person to whom it was promised, in case of doubt the third party acquires the right to the performance upon the death of the promisee.

If the promisee dies before the birth of the third party, the promise to perform in favour of the third party can be revoked or altered only if the right to do so has been reserved.

332. If the promisee has referred to himself the right of substituting another for the third party named in the contract without the consent of the promisor, this may also be done, in case of doubt, by disposition *mortis causa*.

333. If the third party rejects, by declaration to the promisor, the right acquired under the contract, the right is deemed not to have been acquired.

334. Defences arising from the contract are available to the promisor even as against the third party.

335. The promisee may, unless a contrary intention of the contracting parties is to be presumed, demand performance in favour of the third party, even though the right to the performance is in the latter [i].

FOURTH TITLE.
Earnest. Stipulated Penalty.

336. If, on entering into a contract, something is given as earnest, this is deemed to be proof of the conclusion of the contract.

In case of doubt the earnest is not deemed to be a forfeit.

337. The earnest shall, in case of doubt, be credited on the performance due from the giver, or, when this cannot be done, shall be returned on per-

(*i*) There will be two creditors, and the debtor may at his option perform his obligation in favour of the one or the other creditor. 428—430.

formance of the contract.

If the contract is rescinded the earnest shall be returned.

338. If the performance due from the giver becomes impossible in consequence of a circumstance for which he is responsible [(k)], or if the rescinding of the contract is due to his fault, the holder of the earnest is entitled to retain it. If the holder of the earnest demand compensation for non-performance, the earnest shall, in case of doubt, be credited, or, if this cannot be done, shall be returned on payment of the compensation.

339. If the debtor promises the creditor the payment of a sum of money as penalty in case he does not perform his obligation or does not perform it in the proper manner, the penalty is forfeited if he is in default [(l)]. If the performance due consists in a forbearance [(m)], the penalty is forfeited as soon as any act in contravention of the obligation is committed.

340. If the debtor has promised the penalty for the case of his not fulfilling his obligation, the creditor may demand the forfeited penalty in lieu of fulfillment. If the creditor declares to the debtor that he demands the penalty, the claim for fulfilment is barred.

If the creditor has a claim for compensation for non-performance [(n)], he may demand the forfeited penalty as the minimum amount of the damage. Proof of further damage is admissible.

341. If the debtor has promised the penalty for the case of his not fulfilling the obligation in the proper manner, *e.g.*, not at the fixed time, the creditor may demand the forfeited penalty in addition to the fulfilment.

If the creditor has a claim for compensation on account of improper fulfilment, the provisions of 340, par. 2, apply.

If the creditor accepts the fulfilment, he may demand the penalty only if on acceptance he reserves the right to do so.

(*k*) See 276—279, 282.

(*l*) Cf. 284, 285.

(*m*) As to the burden of proof, see 345.

(*n*) See 286 *et seq.*, 325, 326.

342. If another performance than the payment of a sum of money is promised as penalty, the provisions of 339 to 431 apply; the claim for compensation is barred if the creditor demands the penalty.

343. If a forfeited penalty is disproportionately high, it may be reduced to a reasonable amount by judicial decree obtained by the debtor [(o)]. In the determination of reasonableness every legitimate interest of the creditor, not merely his property interest, shall be taken into consideration. After payment of the penalty the claim for reduction is barred.

The same rule applies also, apart from the cases provided for by 339, 342, if a person promises a penalty for the case of his doing or forbearing to do some act.

344. If the law declares the promised performance invalid, an agreement made for a penalty for non-fulfilment of the promise is also invalid, even if the parties knew of the invalidity of the promise.

345. If the debtor contests the forfeiture of the penalty on the ground of having fulfilled his obligation, he shall prove the fulfilment, unless the performance due from him consisted in a forbearance [(p)].

FIFTH TITLE.
Rescission [(q)].

346. If in a contract one party has reserved to himself the right of rescission, and if rescission takes place, the parties are bound to return to each other the consideration received. For services rendered and for allowing the use of a thing the value shall be made good, or, if in the contract a counter-payment in money is stipulated for, this shall be paid.

(*o*) A penalty promised by a "merchant" cannot be reduced, unless he be a retail dealer. 348, 351 of the Commercial Code.

(*p*) In which case the creditor has the *onus probandi*.

(*q*) This title deals with the *contractual* right of rescission. It applies, however, also to the *statutory* right of rescission in cases of mutual contracts (327), sale (467), and contract for work (634, par. 4).

347. The claim to compensation on account of deterioration, destruction or impossibility of delivery arising from any other cause is determined, in case of rescission, and after receipt of the consideration according to provisions which apply to the relation between an owner and a possessor after the date of action commenced on a claim of ownership [r]. The same rule applies to the claim for delivery of, or compensation for emolument, and to the claim for reimbursement of outlay incurred. A sum of money bears interest [s] from the time of its receipt.

348. The obligations of the parties resulting from rescission shall be fulfilled contemporaneously. The provisions of 320, 322 apply *mutatis mutandis*.

349. Rescission is effected by declaration [t] to the other party [u].

350. The right of rescission is not barred by the fact that the object which the party entitled to rescind has received has been accidentally destroyed.

351. The right of rescission is barred if the party entitled is to blame for any essential deterioration, destruction, or impossibility for other reasons of delivering the object received. The destruction of a considerable part is equivalent to the essential deterioration of the object; the fault of another person for which, according to 278, the party entitled is responsible is equivalent to his own fault.

352. The right of rescission is barred if the party entitled has altered the form of the object received by working up or remodelling into a thing of another kind [x].

353. If the party entitled has alienated the object received or a considerable part of it, or has charged it with a right in favour of a third party, the right of rescission is barred if the conditions of 351 or of 352 have arisen in

---

(*r*) See 987, 989, 994 *et seq.*

(*s*) At 4 per cent. 246.

(*t*) The declaration is irrevocable.

(*u*) Cf. 356.

(*x*) Cf. 950 *et seq.*

the case of the party who has acquired the object in consequence of the disposition.

A disposition which is effected by means of compulsory execution or distraint, or by a trustee in bankruptcy, is equivalent to a disposition of the party entitled.

354. If the party entitled is in default [(y)] with the return of the object received or of a considerable part of it, the other party may allot him a fixed reasonable period with a declaration that he refuses to accept after the expiration of the period. The rescission becomes ineffective if the return is not made before the expiration of the period.

355. If a period for the exercise of the right of rescission has not been agreed upon, a reasonable period for its exercise may be allotted to the party entitled to it by the other party. The right of rescission is extinguished if rescission is not declared before the expiration of the period.

356. If in a contract there are several persons on the one or the other side, the right of rescission may be exercised only by all and against all. If the right of rescission is extinguished in respect of one of those persons entitled, it is extinguished also in respect of the others.

357. If one party has reserved the right of rescission for the case of the other party not fulfilling his obligation, the rescission is ineffective if the other party could have relieved himself from the obligation by set-off, and makes a declaration of set-off without delay after the rescission.

358. If one party has reserved the right of rescission for the case of the other party not fulfilling his obligation, and the latter contests the admissibility of the declared rescission on the ground that he has fulfilled it, he shall prove fulfilment unless the performance due from him consists in a forbearance [(z)].

359. If the right of rescission is reserved on payment of a forfeit, the res-

---

(y) Cf. 284, 285.

(z) In which case the person entitled to rescind has the *onus probandi*.

cission is ineffective if the forfeit is not paid before or at the time of the declaration of rescission, and the other party without delay rejects the declaration for this reason. The declaration is, however, effective if the forfeit is paid without delay after the rejection.

360. If a contract is entered into with the proviso that the debtor shall forfeit his rights under the contract if he does not fulfil his obligation, the creditor is entitled to rescind the contract on failure of the debtor so to fulfil it.

361. If it is agreed in a mutual contract that the performance due from one of the parties shall be effected exactly at a fixed time or within a fixed period, it is to be presumed, in case of doubt, that the other party shall be entitled to rescind if the performance is not effected at the fixed time or within the fixed period [(a)].

THIRD SECTION.
EXTINCTION OF OBLIGATIONS.

FIRST TITLE.
Fulfilment.

362. An obligation is extinguished if the performance due be effected in favour of the creditor [(b)].

If the performance is effected in favour of a third party for the purpose of fulfilment, the provisions of 185 apply.

(*a*) This is true even in the case where no fault is imputable to the person bound to effect the performance. The party entitled to the performance may not only rescind the contract, but may also claim, compensation for any damage arising from non-performance; he may, of course, insist upon the fulfilment of the contract, and then claim compensation for any damage arising from the default of the other party as provided for by 286, 325, 326.

(*b*) As to the person effecting the performance, see 267, 268; as to the manner, time and place of performance, see 242 *et seq.*, 269—271.

363. If the creditor has accepted as fulfilment an act of performance done in his favour as fulfilment, the burden of proof is upon him if he will not admit the performance to be valid as fulfilment on the ground that it is other than the performance due, or that it was incomplete.

364. An obligation is extinguished if the creditor accepts in lieu of fulfilment another performance than that agreed upon.

If the debtor, for the purpose of satisfying the creditor, assumes a new obligation towards him, it is not to be presumed, in case of doubt, that he assumes the obligation in lieu of fulfilment.

365. If a thing, a claim against a third party, or any other right is given in lieu of fulfilment, the debtor shall warrant in the same manner as a seller against a defect of title or a defect of quality [c].

366. If a debtor is bound to the creditor to do similar acts of performance by virtue of several obligations, and if the performance effected by him is insufficient for the discharge of all the debts, that debt is discharged which he specifies on effecting the performance.

If the debtor makes no specification, among several debts due that one is first discharged which affords the creditor least security; among several equally secure debts the one most burdensome to the debtor; among several equally burdensome debts the oldest debt; and where several are equally old every debt proportionately.

367. If the debtor has to pay interest and costs besides the principal performance, the value of an act of performance insufficient to discharge the whole debt is applied first to the costs, then to the interest, and lastly to the principal performance.

If the debtor specifies any other application the creditor may refuse acceptance of the performance.

368. On receipt of the performance the creditor shall on demand give a

---

(c) Cf. 434 *et seq.*, 459 *et seq.*

written acknowledgment of receipt (*i.e.*, a receipt) [d]. If the debtor has a legal interest in the making of the receipt in any other form [e] he may require it to be made in such other form.

369. The debtor shall bear and advance the cost of the receipt, unless a contrary intention appears from the legal relation existing between him and the creditor.

If in consequence of a transfer of the claim or by way of inheritance, several creditors take the place of the original creditor, the excess of cost shall be borne by the creditors.

370. The bearer of a receipt is deemed to be authorised to receive the performance, unless circumstances known to the party performing rebuts the presumption of such authorisation.

371. If a certificate of indebtedness has been issued for the claim, the debtor may demand the return of the certificate together with the receipt. If the creditor maintains that he is not in a position to return it, the debtor may demand a publicly certified acknowledgment that the debt is extinguished.

SECOND TITLE.
Lodgment.

372. A debtor may lodge for the benefit of his creditor, money, negotiable instruments and other documents and valuables [f] in a public place designated for that purpose, if the creditor is in default of acceptance. The same rule applies if, for any other reason affecting the creditor personally, or in consequence of uncertainty concerning the identity of the creditor, not due to negligence, the debtor cannot fulfil his obligation or cannot fulfil it with safety.

(*d*) This applies even to small purchases of daily life.

(*e*) *E.g.* under seal.

(*f*) In the case of other kinds of moveables the debtor may cause them to be sold by public auction, and lodge the proceeds (383 *et seq.*); in the case of immoveables, the debtor may relinquish possession. 303.

373. If the debtor is bound to perform only after the counter-performance has been effected by the creditor, he may make the right of the creditor to receive the thing lodged dependent upon counter-performance by the creditor.

374. The lodgment shall be made in the lodgment office of the place where the performance is to be effected; if the debtor makes the lodgment in any other place, he shall compensate the creditor for any damage arising therefrom (g).

The debtor shall without delay notify the creditor of the lodgment; if he fails to do to so he is liable for compensation. The notification may be dispensed with if it is impracticable.

375. If the thing lodged is forwarded to the lodgment office by mail, the lodgment operates as from the time of posting.

376. The debtor has the right to withdraw the thing lodged.

The right of withdrawal is barred:

(1) if the debtor declares to the lodgment office that he waives the right of withdrawal;

(2) if the creditor declares his acceptance to the lodgment office;

(3) if non-appellable judgment between the creditor and the debtor declaring the lodgment legitimate is presented at the lodgment office.

377. The right of withdrawal is not subject to judicial attachment.

If bankruptcy proceedings are instituted against the property of the debtor, the right of withdrawal cannot be exercised even by the debtor during the bankruptcy proceedings.

378. If the right to withdraw the thing lodged is barred, the debtor is released, from his obligation through the lodgment in the same manner as if he had performed, his part in favour of the creditor at the time of the lodgment.

379. If the right to withdraw the thing lodged is not barred, the debtor may refer the creditor to the thing lodged (h).

(*g*) The lodgment itself is, however, valid.

(*h*) So as to prevent compulsory execution from being levied on his property.

As long as the thing is on lodgment the creditor bears the risk, and the debtor is not bound to pay interest or compensation for emoluments not drawn.

If the debtor withdraws the thing lodged, the lodgment is deemed not to have been made.

380. In so far as a declaration of the debtor recognising the creditor's right to receive is necessary or adequate as evidence of such right according to the regulations governing the lodgment office, the creditor may demand from the debtor the delivery of the declaration under the same conditions under which he would have been entitled to demand the performance, if the lodgment had not taken place.

381. The costs of the lodgment shall be borne by the creditor, unless the debtor withdraws the thing lodged.

382. The right of the creditor to the amount lodged is extinguished after the lapse of thirty years since receipt of notice of the lodgment, unless the creditor reports himself at the lodgment office within such period; the debtor is entitled to withdraw even if he has waived the right of withdrawal.

383. If the thing owed is a moveable which is not suitable to be lodged [(i)], and if the creditor is in default, the debtor may cause it to be sold by auction at the place of performance and lodge the proceeds. The same rule applies in the cases provided for by 372 sentence 2, if the destruction of the thing is to be apprehended, or if its custody would involve disproportionate expense.

If a reasonable return is not to be expected from an auction at the place of performance, the thing shall be sold by auction in some other appropriate place.

The auction shall be held publicly by a Court officer appointed for the place of auction, or by some other official authorised to conduct auctions, or by a publicly appointed auctioneer (*i.e.*, public auction). The time and place of the auction, with a general description of the thing, shall be publicly advertised.

(*i*) *I.e.*, if it does not belong to the class of things mentioned in 372.

384. The auction is not permissible until after the creditor has been warned of it. The warning may be dispensed with if the thing is liable to deterioration, and there is danger in delaying the auction.

The debtor shall without delay notify the creditor of the auction; if the debtor fail to do so he is liable for compensation.

The warning and the notice may be dispensed with if they are impracticable.

385. If the thing has an exchange or market price the debtor may effect the sale by private sale at the current price through a broker publicly empowered to conduct such sales, or through a person authorised to conduct public auctions.

386. The costs of the auction or of the sale made under 385 shall be borne by the creditor, unless the debtor withdraws the proceeds lodged.

THIRD TITLE.
Set-off.

387. If two persons mutually owe acts of performance which are of the same kind according to their object, either party may set off his claim against the claim of the other party as soon as he can demand the performance due to him and effect the performance due from him (k).

388. The set-off is made by declaration (l) to the other party. The declaration is ineffective, if made subject to any condition or limitation of time.

389. The set-off has the effect that the claims, in so far as they cover each other (m), are deemed to have been extinguished at the moment at which, being suitable for set-off, they are balanced against each other.

390. A claim against which there is a defence may not be set off. Prescription does not exclude set-off, if the claim barred by prescription was not barred at

---

(k) Exceptions: 391, par. 2, 393, 394.

(l) *I.e.*, set-off does not operate *ipso jure*.

(m) Hence partial set-off is permissible, although partial performance is not allowed. 266.

the time at which it could have been set off against the other claim.

391. Set-off is not excluded by the fact that different places for performance or delivery exist for the claims. The party making the set-off shall, however, compensate for any damage which the other party suffers by reason of the fact that, in consequence of the set-off, he does not receive or cannot effect the performance in the fixed place.

If it is agreed that the performance shall be effected at a fixed time in a fixed place, it is to be presumed, in case of doubt, that the set-off of a claim for which there is another place of performance (*n*) is to be excluded.

392. By the judicial attachment of a claim the set-off of a claim of the debtor against the creditor is excluded only if the debtor has acquired his claim after the attachment, or if his claim has become due only after the attachment and after the maturity of the claim attached.

393. Set-off is not permissible against a claim arising from a wilful unlawful act (*o*).

394. If a claim is not subject to judicial attachment (*p*), it is not subject to set-off. Against sums to be drawn out of sick, aid, or burial funds (*e.g.*, out of journeymen's funds and funds of journeymen's unions), contributions due may, however, be set off.

395. Against a claim of the Empire, of a State, or of a commune, or any other communal union, set-off is permissible only if the performance is due to the same fund out of which the claim of the party making the set-off is to be paid.

396. If either party has several claims suitable for set-off, the party making the set-off may specify the claims which are to be set off against each other. If the set-off is declared without such specification, or if the other party objects

(*n*) Cf. 269—271.

(*o*) Cf. 273, par. 2, 823 *et seq.*

(*p*) 851 of the Code of Civil Procedure provides that, "in the absence of any special provision to the contrary, a claim is subject to judicial attachment only if it is transferable". See further, 377 of the present Code, Art. 81 of the Introductory Act, and 850—852 of the Code of Civil Procedure.

without delay, the provision of 366, par. 2, applies *mutatis mutandis*.

If the party making the set-off owes the other party intend and costs in addition to the principal performance, the provisions of 367 apply *mutatis mutandis*.

FOURTH TITLE.
Release.

397. An obligation is extinguished if the debtor is released from the obligation by contract with the creditor.

The same rule applies if the creditor, by contract with the debtor, acknowledges that the obligation does not exist [(q)].

FOURTH SECTION.
TRANSFER OF CLAIMS.

398. A claim may, by contract with another person, be transferred by the creditor to him (*i.e.*, assignment) [(r)]. On the conclusion of the contract the assignee takes the place of the assignor.

399. A claim is not assignable if the performance cannot be effected in favour of any person other than the original creditor without alteration of its substance, or if assignment is excluded by agreement with the debtor.

400. A claim is not assignable if it is not subject to judicial attachment.

401. With the assigned claim the rights of hypotheca or pledge existing on its account and the rights arising from a suretyship established for it, pass to the assignee.

The assignee may also enforce any right of preference connected with the

---

(*q*) The contract need not be in writing. Cf. 781.

(*r*) The contract of assignment may be either verbal or in writing. Cf., however, 403. The consent of the debtor is not necessary for the assignment, since he is protected by 410.

claim in case of compulsory execution or bankruptcy.

402. The assignor is bound to give to the assignee all information necessary for the enforcement of the claim, and to deliver to him all documents which sever as evidence of the claim, if they are in his possession.

403. The assignor shall on demand execute in favour of the assignee a publicly certified instrument assignment [(s)]. The assignee shall bear and advance the costs.

404. The debtor may set up all defences against the assignee which, at the time of the assignment of the claim, were available against the assignor.

405. If the debtor has executed an instrument for the debt, and if the claim assigned upon production of the instrument, he may not as against the assignee maintain that the incurring or acknowledgment of the obligation was only pretended, or that the assignment was excluded by agreement with the assignor, unless the assignee, at the time of the assignment, knew or ought to have known of the state of affairs.

406. The debtor may also set off against the assignee an existing claim which he has against the assignor, unless he had knowledge of the assignment at the time of the acquisition of the claim, or unless the claim did not become due until after he had acquired such knowledge and after the maturity of the assigned claim [(t)].

407. An act of performance done by the debtor in favour of the assignor after the assignment, or a juristic act entered into between the debtor and the assignor in respect of the claim after the assignment, is valid as against the assignee, unless the debtor knew of the assignment at the time of performance or of entering into the juristic act.

If, in an action between the debtor and the assignor subsequent to the assignment, a non-appellable judgment relating to the claim has been delivered,

---

(*s*) Cf. 129.

(*t*) The *onus probandi* rests upon the assignee.

the judgment is valid as against the assignee, unless the debtor knew of the assignment at the date when the action was first commenced.

408. If an assigned claim be re-assigned by the assignor to a third party, and if the debtor effects the performance in favour of such, third party, or if a juristic act is entered into or an action is commenced between the debtor and such third party, the provisions of 407 apply *mutatis mutandis* in favour of the debtor as against the former assignee.

The same rule applies if the assigned claim is re-assigned to a third party by judicial order, or if the assignor makes acknowledgment to the third party that the assigned claim is transferred to the third party by operation of law [(u)].

409. If the creditor notifies the debtor that he has assigned the claim, the assignment of which he has given notice avails against himself in favour of the debtor, even though it was not made or is invalid. It is equivalent to notice, if the creditor has executed an instrument of assignment to the assignee named in the instrument, and the latter produces it to the debtor.

The notice may be revoked only with the consent of the person who has been named as the assignee.

410. The debtor is bound to perform in favour of the assignee only upon production of an instrument of assignment executed by the assignor. A notice or a warning by the assignee is of no effect, if it is given without production of such an instrument, and the debtor without delay rejects it for this reason.

These provisions do not apply if the assignor has given written notice of the assignment to the debtor.

411. If a person in military service, an official, a clergyman, or a teacher in a public institution of learning assigns the transferable part of his service-pay, pay for engagement pending vacancy, or pension, the pay-office shall be notified of the assignment by presentation of a publicly certified instrument executed by the assignor. Until the notice is given, the office is deemed to have no knowledge of the assignment.

(*u*) Cf. 412.

412. The provisions of 399 to 404, 406 to 410 apply *mutatis mutandis* to the transfer of a claim by operation of law [(x)].

413. The provisions relating to the transfer of claims apply *mutatis mutandis* to the transfer of other rights [(y)], unless the law provides otherwise.

FIFTH SECTION.
ASSUMPTION OF DEBT.

414. A debt may be assumed by a third party by contract with the creditor in such manner that the third party takes the place of the former debtor [(z)].

415. If the assumption of the debt is agreed upon by the third party and the debtor it is invalid, unless ratified by the creditor. Ratification may not take place until the debtor or the third party has informed the creditor of the assumption of the debt. Before ratification the parties may modify or rescind the contract.

If ratification is refused, the assumption of the debt is deemed not to have been effected. If the debtor or the third party demands the creditor to declare whether or not he will ratify within a fixed period of time, ratification may be declared only before the expiration of the period; if it is not declared, it is deemed to have been refused.

So long as the creditor has not ratified the person assuming the debt is, in case of doubt, bound to the debtor to satisfy the creditor in due time. The same rule applies if the creditor refuses to ratify.

416. If the grantee of a piece of land, by contract with the grantor, assumes a debt of the grantor for which there is a hypotheca on the land, the

---

(x) The transfer of a claim takes place by operation of law in the following cases: 268, par. 3; 426, par. 2; 774, par. 1; 1143, par. 1; 1225; 1249, sentence 2; 1438, par. 2; 1519, par. 2; 1549; 1607, par. 2; 1709, par. 2.

(y) *E.g.* copyright.

(z) The former debtor is *ipso facto* discharged from his obligation, even without his knowing it.

creditor may ratify the assumption of the debt only if the grantor communicates it to him. If six months have elapsed since receipt of the communication, ratification is deemed to have been given [a], unless the creditor has refused it to the grantor within such period; the provision of 415, par. 2, sentence 2, does not apply.

The communication may not be made by the grantor until after the grantee has been registered in the land register as owner. It must be made in writing and contain reference to the fact that the person assuming the debt takes the place of the former debtor, unless the creditor declares his refusal within six months.

The grantor shall, on demand by the grantee, communicate to the creditor the assumption of the debt. As soon as the question whether to ratify or not is settled the grantor shall notify the grantee.

417. The person assuming the debt may set up against the creditor all defences arising from the legal relations between the creditor and the former debtor. He may not set off a claim belonging to the former debtor.

The person assuming the debt may not set up any defences against the creditor arising from the legal relations between himself and the former debtor upon which the assumption of the debt is founded.

418. In consequence of the assumption of a debt the liability of sureties and pledges given for the claim are extinguished [b]. If there is a hypotheca for the claim, the consequence is the same as if the creditor had relinquished the hypotheca [c]. These provisions do not apply if the surety or the person to whom the object pledged belongs at the time of the assumption of the debt consents to such assumption.

A right of preference connected with the claim in case of bankruptcy may not be enforced in the bankruptcy proceedings instituted against the property of the person assuming the debt.

(*a*) Unlike the case provided for by 415, silence is deemed to be ratification.

(*b*) The reason being that a surety or pledgor should not be held liable for a new debtor with whom he may not even be acquainted.

(*c*) Cf. 1168, 1175.

419. If a person takes over the whole of another's property under a contract [(d)], the creditors of the latter, without prejudice to the continuance of the liability of the transferor, may, after the conclusion of the contract, enforce their claims existing at that time even as against the transferee.

The liability of the transferee is limited to the value of the property transferred and the claims which he has under the contract. If the transferee sets up any such limitation of liability, the provisions of 1990, 1991, applicable to the liability of an heir apply *mutatis mutandis* [(e)].

The liability of the transferee may not be excluded or limited by agreement between him and the former debtor.

SIXTH SECTION.

PLURALITY OF DEBTORS AND CREDITORS.

420. If several persons owe a divisible performance or if a divisible performance is owed to severe persons, each debtor is, in case of doubt, liable only for an equal share, and each creditor is entitled only to an equal share [(f)].

421. If several persons owe an act of performance in such manner that each is bound to effect the whole performance, though the creditor is entitled to demand the performance only once (*i.e.* joint debtors) [(g)], the creditor may demand the performance at his option from any one of the debtors, in whole or in port. Until the whole performance has been effected all of the debtors

(*d*) Cf. 311, 2371 *et seq.*

(*e*) For the liability of a person taking over the entire business of another for the debts of the business, see 25 *et seq.* of the Commercial Code.

(*f*) The application of this general principle has been so restricted by the many important exceptions provided for by the Code, that in actual practice joint liability in accordance with 421 is almost the universal rule. See note (*g*) to 421.

(*g*) The most important cases of joint liability provided for in the Code are: 427, 769, 840, 1388, 1833, 2058, and many others.

remain bound [(h)].

422. Fulfilment of the obligation by one join debtor operates in favour of the other debtors. The same rule applies to any act of performance in lieu of fulfilment of the obligation, to lodgment and to set-off.

A claim belonging to one of the joint debtors may not be set off by the other debtors.

423. A release agreed upon between the creditor and one joint debtor avails also in favour of the other debtors, if the parties making the agreement intended to terminate the whole obligation.

424. The default of the creditor towards one joint debtor avails also in favour of the other debtors.

425. Facts other than those specified in 422 to 424 avail, unless a contrary intention appears from the nature of the obligation, in favour of and as against only the joint debtor to whom they particularly refer.

This applies, *e.g.*, to the giving of notice, default, imputability of fault, impossibility of performance on the part of one joint debtor, prescription or its interruption or suspension, merger of the claim in the debt, and non-appellable judgment.

426. As between themselves joint debtors are liable in equal shares, unless it is otherwise provided. If from one of the joint debtors the contribution due from him cannot be obtained, the deficiency shall be borne by the other debtors who are bound to make contribution.

If one joint debtor satisfies the creditor and can demand contribution from the other debtors, the claim of the creditor against the other debtors is transferred to him. The transfer may not be enforced to the detriment of the creditor.

427. If in a contract several persons bind themselves in common to effect a divisible performance, they are liable, in case of doubt, as joint debtors.

(*h*) This provision applies only as between the creditor and the joint debtors. As between themselves joint debtors are liable in equal shares. 426.

428. If several persons are entitled to demand an act of performance in such manner that each can demand the whole performance, though the debtor is bound to perform only once (*i.e.* joint creditors), the debtor may at his option perform in favour of any one of the creditors. This applies even if one of the creditors has already brought an action for the performance.

429. Default on the part of one joint creditor avails also against the other creditors.

If claim and debt become merged in one joint creditor, the rights of the other creditors against the debtor are extinguished.

For the rest the provisions of 422, 423, 425 apply *mutatis mutandis*. *E.g.*, if one joint creditor transfers his claim to another person, the rights of the other creditors remain unaffected.

430. Joint creditors are, as between themselves, entitled to equal shares, unless it is otherwise provided.

431. If several persons owe an indivisible performance they are liable as joint debtors.

432. If an indivisible performance is owed to several persons, and if they are not joint creditors, the debtor may only perform in favour of all in common, and each creditor may only demand the performance in favour of all. Each creditor may demand that the debtor lodge the thing owed for the benefit of all the creditors, or if the thing is not suitable to be lodged, that it be consigned to a custodian appointed by the Court.

For the rest a fact which refers only to one creditor does not avail in favour of nor as against the other creditors.

SEVENTH SECTION.
PARTICULAR KINDS OF OBLIGATIONS.

FIRST TITLE.
Sale. Exchange.

I. General Provisions (i).

433. By a contract of sale the seller of a thing is bound to deliver the thing to the purchaser and to transfer ownership of the thing (k). The seller of a right is bound to transfer the right to the purchaser, and if the right involves the possession of a thing (l), to deliver the thing.

The purchaser is bound to pay to the seller the purchase price (m) agreed upon and to take delivery of the thing purchased.

434. The seller is bound to transfer to the purchaser the sold object free from rights enforceable by third parties against the purchaser (n).

435. The seller of a piece of land or of a right over a piece of land is bound to procure at his own expense the cancellation of non-existent rights entered in the land register, if they would in case of their existence injure the right to be transferred to the purchaser.

The same rule applies, in the case of the sale of a ship or of a right in a

(i) Since a contract of sale is in the nature of a mutual contract, the provisions of 320—327 also apply. 373 *et seq.* of the Commercial Code contains special provisions relating to "commercial sale" (*Handelskauf*).

(k) See 448, 854, 929 *et seq.*, and especially 873, 925 relating to the transfer of ownership of land.

(l) Such rights are usufruct (1036) and the special kind of "limited personal servitude" mentioned in 1093.

(m) The purchase price need not be a sum certain in money. See 315—319; also 453, 473.

(n) 434 *et seq.* deal with warranty of *title*, in contradistinction to the warranty of *quality* dealt with in 459 *et seq.*

ship, to the rights entered in the ship register [o].

436. The seller of a piece of land does not warrant the land to be free from public taxes and other public burdens which are not suitable to be entered in the land register.

437. The seller of a claim or any other right warrants the legal existence of the claim or of the right.

The seller of a negotiable instrument warrants that it has not been called in for cancellation.

438. If the seller of a claim warrants the solvency of the debtor, the warranty shall, in case of doubt, refer only to solvency at the date of the assignment.

439. A seller is not responsible for any defect of title, if the purchaser knows [p] of the defect at the time of the sale.

The seller shall extinguish all hypothecas, land charges, annuity charges, and pledges with which the object sold is charged, even though the purchaser knows of their existence [q]. The same rule applies to a caution to secure the claim for charging the sold object with any one of these rights.

440. If the seller does not fulfil the obligations imposed upon him by 433 to 437, 439, the rights of the purchaser are determined according to the provisions of 320 to 327.

If a moveable has been sold and delivered to the purchaser for the purpose of transfer of ownership, the purchaser may not demand compensation for non-performance on account of the right of a third party involving the possession of the thing, unless he has delivered the thing to the third party in consideration of his right, or has returned it to the seller, or unless the thing has been destroyed.

(*o*) Cf. 1259 *et seq.*

(*p*) Notice that the words "or ought to have known" are omitted, *i.e.*, the purchaser must have *actual* (not merely *constructive*) knowledge of the defect. The *onus probandi* rests upon the seller.

(*q*) The purchaser may, however, agree to assume the burden of these rights.

It is equivalent to delivery of the thing to the third party, if the third party become heir to the purchaser, or *vice versâ*, or if the purchaser acquires the right of the third party in any other manner, or buys out the third party.

If the purchaser has a claim for delivery against another person, the assignment of the claim is sufficient in lieu of the return of the thing.

441. The provisions of 440, pars. 2 to 4, apply even if a right in a moveable involving the possession of the thing has been sold (r).

442. If a seller disputes a defect of title asserted by the purchaser, the purchaser shall prove the defect.

443. An agreement whereby the obligation of warranty of title imposed upon the seller by 433 to 437, 439 to 442, is released or limited is void, if the seller fraudulently conceals the defect.

444. The seller is bound to give to the purchaser all necessary information concerning the legal relations affecting the object sold, *e.g.*, in the case of the sale of a piece of land, concerning the boundaries, privileges and burdens; and to deliver to him all documents serving as evidence of the right in so far as they are in his possession. If the contents of such a document relate also to other affairs, the seller is bound to give only a publicly certified extract (s).

445. The provisions of 433 to 444 apply *mutatis mutandis* to other contracts for alienating or giving a charge upon any object for valuable consideration.

446. On the delivery of the thing sold the risk of accidental destruction and accidental deterioration passes to the purchaser. After delivery the emoluments accrue to the purchaser, and he bears the burdens attached to the thing.

If the purchaser of a piece of land is registered in the land register as owner before delivery, these consequences begin with the registration.

(*r*) Cf. note (*l*) to 433.

(*s*) This applies only after the conclusion of the sale.

447. If at the request of the purchaser the seller transmits the thing sold to a place other than the place of performance [(t)], the risk passes to the purchaser as soon as the seller has delivered the thing to the forwarder, freighter, or other person or institution designated to carry out the transmission.

If the purchaser has given special instructions as to the manner of forwarding, and the seller deviates from the instructions without urgent reason, the seller is responsible to the purchaser for any damage arising therefrom.

448. The costs of delivery of the thing sold, *e.g.*, the costs of measuring and weighing, are borne by the seller; the costs of taking delivery of the thing or of forwarding the thing to a place other than the place of performance are borne by the purchaser.

If a right is sold the costs of the creation or transfer of the right are borne by the seller.

449. The purchaser of a piece of land shall bear the costs of conveyance and registration; the purchaser of a right over a piece of land shall bear the costs of the registration in the land register necessary for the creation or transfer of the right, including the costs of the declaration necessary for the registration. In both cases the costs of authentication of the purchase shall also be borne by the purchaser.

450. If the risk has passed to the purchaser before delivery of the thing sold, and the seller incurs any outlay on the thing before delivery, which has become necessary after the passing of the risk, he may demand compensation from the purchaser as if the purchaser had charged him with the care of the thing.

The obligation of the purchaser to compensate for any other outlay is determined according to the provisions relating to management of affairs without mandate.

451. If a right to a thing is sold which involves the possession of the

---

(*t*) Cf. 269.

thing [(u)], the provisions of 446 to 450 apply *mutatis mutandis*.

452. The purchaser is bound to pay interest [(x)] on the purchase price from the date at which the emoluments of the purchased object accrue to him [(y)], unless the purchase price is payable at a fixed time.

453. If the market price is specified as the purchase price, in case of doubt the standard market price at the place and time of performance is deemed to be the price agreed upon [(z)].

454. If the seller has carried out the contract and has fixed a time for payment of the purchase price, he has not the right of rescission specified in 325, par. 2, and 326 [(a)].

455. If the seller of a moveable has reserved ownership until payment of the purchase price, it is to be presumed, in case of doubt, that the transfer of ownership takes place subject to the condition precedent of payment in full of the purchase price, and that the seller is entitled to rescind the contract, if the purchaser is in default with the payment.

456. At a sale under compulsory execution the person charged with making or conducting the sale and the assistants employed by him, including the registrar, are not permitted to purchase the object put up for sale, either for themselves personally or through another, or as representative of another [(b)].

457. The provision of 456 applies also to a sale other than that under compulsory execution, if the authorization to sell has been given by virtue of a provision of law empowering the person giving the authorization to cause the object to be sold on account of another, *e.g.*, in the cases of a sale of a pledged

---

(*u*) Cf. note (*l*) to 433.

(*x*) In the absence of any special agreement, 4 per cent.; in commercial transactions, 5 per cent. See 246.

(*y*) *I.e.*, as a general rule, from the date of delivery. See 446, par. 1.

(*z*) Cf. 269, 271.

(*a*) *I.e.*, there is no *statutory* right of rescission, but there may be a *contractual* right of rescission.

(*b*) If they infringe this provision, they are liable to make compensation as provided for in 823.

object and of a sale permitted by 383, 385; and also to a sale by a trustee in bankruptcy.

458. The validity of a purchase made in contravention of the provisions of 456, 457, and of the transfer of the purchased object depends upon the consent of the persons interested in the sale as debtor, owner, or creditor. If the purchaser demands an interested party to declare whether or not he will ratify, the provision of 177, par. 2 apply *mutatis mutandis*.

If, in consequence of a refusal to ratify a new sale is made, the former purchaser shall be responsible for the costs of the new sale and also for any deficiency.

II. Warranty against Defects of Quality.

459. The seller of a thing warrants the purchaser that, at the time when the risk passes to the purchaser [(c)], it is free from defects which diminish or destroy its value or fitness for its ordinary use or the use presupposed in the contract. An insignificant diminution in value or fitness is not taken into consideration.

The seller also warrants that, at the time the risk passes [(c)], the thing has the promised qualities.

460. A seller is not responsible for a defect of quality in the thing sold if the purchaser knew of the defect at the time of entering into the contract [(d)]. If a defect of the kind specified in 459, par. 1 has remained unknown to the purchaser in consequence of gross negligence, the seller is responsible, unless he has guaranteed that the thing is free from the defect, only if he has fraudulently concealed it.

461. A seller is not responsible for a defect of quality in the thing sold if it is sold by public auction under the law of pledge and designated as a pledge.

(*c*) See 446, 447.

(*d*) The seller has the burden of proof.

462. On account of a defect for which the seller is responsible under the provisions of 459, 460, the purchaser may demand annulment of the sale (*i.e.*, cancellation), or reduction of the purchase price (*i.e.*, reduction) (e).

463. If a promised quality is the thing sold was absent at the time of the purchase (f), the purchaser may demand compensation for non-performance, instead of cancellation or reduction. The same rule applies if the seller has fraudulently concealed a defect.

464. If the purchaser accepts a defective thing although he knows of the defect, he is entitled to the claims specified in 462, 463, only if on acceptance he reserves his rights on account of the defect.

465. Cancellation or reduction is effected if the seller, on demand (g) by the purchaser, declares his consent thereto.

466. If the purchaser asserts against the seller a defect of quality, the seller may offer cancellation and require him to declare within a fixed reasonable period whether he demands cancellation. In such a case cancellation may be demanded only before the expiration of the period (h).

467. The provisions of 346 to 348, 350 to 354, 356, applicable to the contractual right of rescission apply *mutatis mutandis* to cancellation; in the case provided for by 352, however, cancellation is permitted if the defect has not been discovered until the remodelling of the thing. The seller shall also reimburse the purchaser for the expense of the contract.

468. If the seller of a piece of land promises the purchaser certain specified dimensions, he is responsible for the dimensions as for a promised

---

(*e*) The purchaser may elect either the one or the other remedy, unless the law provides otherwise, as in the case of a sale of cattle. 481, 487.

(*f*) Not "at the time when the risk passes", as in the case provided for by 459.

(*g*) Such a demand amounts to a proposal which is binding on the purchaser. 145.

(*h*) After the expiration of the period reduction is the only remedy open to the purchaser, except in the case of the sale of a thing designated by species. 480.

quality [i]. The purchaser may, however, demand cancellation on account of the absence of the promised dimensions only if the deficiency is so considerable that the fulfilment of the contract is of no use to him [k].

469. If of several things sold some only are defective, cancellation may be demanded only in respect of these, even if an aggregate price has been fixed for all the things. If, however, the things were sold as belonging together, either party may demand that the cancellation be extended to all the things, if the defective things cannot be separated from the others without injury to him [l].

470. Cancellation on account of a defect of quality in the principal thing extends also to an accessory. If the accessory thing is defective, cancellation may be demanded only in respect of such accessory.

471. If, in the case of a sale of several things for an aggregate price cancellation is effected only with regard to some of them, the aggregate price shall be reduced in the proportion which at the time of the sale the aggregate value of the things in a condition free from defects would have borne to the value of the things unaffected by the cancellation.

472. In case of reduction the purchase price shall be reduced in the proportion which at the time of the sale the value of the thing in a condition free from defect would have borne to the actual value.

If, in the case of a sale of several things for an aggregate price, reduction is effected only in respect of some of them, then in reducing the price the aggregate value of all the things shall be taken as a basis.

473. If, besides the purchase price fixed in money, other considerations are stipulated for which have non-fungible things as their objects, these considerations, in the cases provided for by 471, 472, shall be estimated in money according to their value at the time of the sale. The reduction of the pur-

---

(*i*) Cf. 459, par. 2, 460, sentence 1, 462, 463.

(*k*) He has the burden of proof.

(*l*) The purchaser has to prove that the things were sold as belonging together, and that the defective things cannot be separate from the others without injury to him.

chaser's counterconsideration is made out of the price fixed in money; if this is less than the amount to be deducted, the seller shall make good to the purchaser the balance.

474. If there are several parties on either side, reduction may be demanded by each and against each.

If reduction (m) demanded by one of the purchasers is effected, cancellation is not permitted.

475. If reduction is made on account of one defect, the right of the purchaser to demand cancellation or reduction on account of another defect is not barred.

476. An agreement whereby the obligation of the seller for warranty against defects of quality is released or limited is void, if the seller fraudulently conceals the defect.

477. The claim for cancellation or reduction and the claim for compensation on account of the absence of a promised quality are barred by prescription, unless the seller has fraudulently concealed the defect (n), in the case of moveables in six months after delivery; in the case of land in one year after the transfer. The period of prescription may be extended by contract (o).

If the purchaser moves for judicial admission of evidence for the purpose of preserving the evidence (p), the prescription is thereby interrupted. The interruption continues until the termination of the proceedings. The provisions of 211, par. 2, and of 212 apply *mutatis mutandis*.

The suspension or interruption of prescription of one of the claims specified in par. 1 results also in the suspension or interruption of prescription of the other claims.

478. If the purchaser has notified the seller of the defect or forwarded notice thereof to him before the claim for cancellation or reduction is barred by

(*m*) Cf. 465.

(*n*) In which case the period of prescription is thirty years, see 195.

(*o*) Exception to 225.

(*p*) Cf. 485 *et seq.*, and 488 of the Code of Civil Procedure.

prescription, he may, even after the lapse of the period of prescription, refuse to pay the purchase price, in so far as he would be entitled to do so by reason of cancellation or reduction. The same rule applies if the purchaser moves for judicial admission of evidence for the purpose of preserving the evidence before the lapse of the period of prescription, or, in an action commenced between him and a subsequent acquirer of the thing on account of the defect, has given notice of the action to the seller.

If the seller has fraudulently concealed the defect, notice or an act which according to par. 1 is equivalent to notice is not necessary.

479. The claim for compensation [q] may be set off after the lapse of the period of prescription only if the purchaser has previously done one of the acts specified in 478 [r]. This limitation does not arise if the seller has fraudulently concealed the defect.

480. The purchaser of a thing designated only by species may demand, instead of cancellation or reduction, that instead of the defective thing one free from defect be delivered to him. The provisions of 464 to 466, 467, sentence 1, and 469, 470, 474 to 479, applicable to cancellation, apply *mutatis mutandis* to this claim.

If, at the time at which the risk passes to the purchaser [s], a promised quality was absent, or if the seller has fraudulently concealed a defect, the purchaser may demand compensation for non-performance instead of cancellation, reduction, or delivery of a thing free from defect.

481. The provisions of 459 to 467, 469 to 480 apply to the sale of horses, asses, mules, hinnies, cattle, sheep and swine only in so far as it is not otherwise provided by 482 to 492 [t].

482. The seller is responsible only for certain defects [u] (*i.e.*, principal

---

(*q*) 463.

(*r*) Exception to 390.

(*s*) Cf. 446, 447.

(*t*) This provision does not apply to animals other than those mentioned in the text.

(*u*) For other defects he is responsible only where he has undertaken to warrant against them. 492.

defects), and then only if they are discovered within specified periods (*i.e.*, periods of warranty) [x].

The principal defects and the periods of warranty are prescribed by an Imperial Ordinance to be issued with the consent of the Federal Council [y]. Its provisions may be extended and modified in the same manner.

483. The period of warranty begins to run from the expiration of the day on which the risk passes to the purchaser [z].

484. If a principal defect is discovered within the period of warranty, it is presumed [a] that the defect was already present at the time when the risk passed to the purchaser.

485. The purchaser loses the rights belonging to him on account of the defect if he does not, at the latest, within two days after the expiration of the period of warranty, or, where the animal has been slaughtered or has perished in any other manner before the expiration of the period, within two days after the death of the animal, notify the seller of the defect or send notice thereof to him, or bring an action against the seller on account of the defect, or give him notice of intention to bring the action, or move for judicial admission of evidence for the purpose of preserving the evidence. The rights are not lost if the seller has fraudulently concealed the defect.

486. The period of warranty may be extended or shortened by contract [b]. The period agreed upon takes the place of the statutory period.

487. The purchaser may demand cancellation only; he may not demand reduction.

(*x*) The effect of the period of warranty is this: if the defect is discovered within the period there is a *primâ facie* presumption that the defect existed at the time of delivery, but the presumption is rebuttable. 484. If the defect is not discovered until after the expiration of the period, it is *conclusively* presumed that the defect did not exist at the time of delivery.

(*y*) See Imperial Ordinance of March 27th, 1899.

(*z*) Cf. 446, 447.

(*a*) The presumption is rebuttable.

(*b*) Which may be either verbal or in writing.

Cancellation may also be demanded in the cases provided for by 351 to 353, *e.g.*, when the animal has been slaughtered; instead of returning the animal the purchaser shall make good its value. The same rule applies to all other cases in which the purchaser is not in a position to return the animal in consequence of a circumstance for which he is responsible [(c)], *e.g.*, a disposal of the animal.

If, before the cancellation is effected, an unessential deterioration of the animal has come about in consequence of a circumstance for which the purchaser is responsible, the purchaser shall make good the diminution in value.

The purchaser has to make compensation for emoluments [(d)] only in so far as he has drawn them [(e)].

488. In case of cancellation the seller shall also compensate the purchaser for the expense of fodder and care; of veterinary examination and treatment; and, in case of necessity, the expense of slaughter and removal of the animal.

489. If an action on the claim for cancellation is commenced, sale by public auction and lodgment of the proceeds shall be ordered by provisional decree [(f)], obtained by either party, as soon as inspection of the animal is no longer necessary.

490. The claim for cancellation and the claim for compensation on account of a principal defect, the absence of which the seller has warranted, are barred by prescription in six weeks after the expiration of the period of warranty. For the rest the provisions of 477 remain unaffected.

A period of six weeks takes the place of the periods specified in 210, 212, 215.

The purchaser may refuse to pay the purchase price even after the prescription of the claim for cancellation. A set-off of the claim for compensation is not

---

(*c*) See 276—278.

(*d*) See 100.

(*e*) He does not have to compensate for emoluments which he has wilfully or negligently omitted to draw. He is liable only for those emoluments which he has *actually* drawn.

(*f*) So as to save the expense of fodder and care. The issue of provisional decrees is regulated by 935 of the Code of Civil Procedure.

subject to the limitation specified in 479 [g].

491. The purchaser of an animal designated only by species may demand, instead of cancellation, that in place of the animal one free from defect be delivered to him. The provisions of 488 to 490 apply *mutatis mutandis* to such claim.

492. If the seller gives a warranty against any defect other than a principal defect, or if he warrants a particular quality in the animal, the provisions of 487 to 491, and, if a period of warranty is agreed upon, the provisions also of 483 to 485 apply *mutatis mutandis*. The prescription specified in 490 begins to run, if a period of warranty is not agreed upon, from the delivery of the animal.

493. The provisions relating to the obligation of the seller in respect of warranty against defects of quality apply *mutatis mutandis* to other contracts which are for alienating or for giving a charge upon a thing for valuable consideration.

III. Particular Kinds of Sale.

1. *Sale according to Sample. Sale on Approval* [h].

494. In a sale according to sample or according to pattern the qualities of the sample or pattern are deemed to have been warranted [i].

495. In a sale on approval or on inspection, the approval of the object bought is at the option of the purchaser. In case of doubt the purchase is made subject to the condition precedent of approval.

The seller is bound to permit the purchaser to examine the object.

496. Approval of an object purchased on approval or on inspection may be

---

(*g*) That is to say, 485 applies.

(*h*) The word "approval" is used here in its ordinary sense, and not in the technical sense which has been assigned to it in this translation. See "approval" in Glossary (Appendix D).

(*i*) The seller is responsible for the qualities of the sample or of the pattern under the rules laid down in 459, par. 2, 460, 463.

declared only within the period agreed upon, and, in the absence of any such period, only before the expiration of a fixed reasonable period allotted by the seller to the purchaser. If the thing was delivered to the purchaser for the purpose of trial or inspection, his silence is deemed to be approval.

2. *Re-purchase* [k].

497. If a seller in a contract of sale, has reserved to himself the right of repurchase [l], the re-purchase is effected by a declaration made by the seller to the purchaser that he exercises his right of re-purchase. The declaration need not be in the form prescribed for the contract of sale.

In case of doubt the price at which the sale has been made is also the price of re-purchase.

498. The original purchaser is bound to deliver to the original seller the purchased object and its accessories.

If, before the exercise of the right of re-purchase, the return of the purchased object has become impossible on account of deterioration, destruction, or for any other reason through some fault of the original purchaser, or if he has essentially altered the object, he is responsible for any damage arising therefrom. If the object has deteriorated without any fault on the part of the original purchaser, or if it is only unessentially altered, the original seller may not demand reduction of the purchase price.

499. If the original purchaser has disposed of the purchased object before the exercise of the right of re-purchase, he is bound to extinguish the rights of third parties thereby created [m]. A disposition which is effected by means of compulsory execution or distraint or by a trustee in bankruptcy is equivalent to a disposition by the original purchase.

(*k*) The right of re-purchase is transferable and transmittable on death. It is available however, only against the original purchaser, and not against a third party, not even against a person who had knowledge of its existence at the time of acquiring the object; to use the Roman legal phraseology, it is a right *in personam* and not a right *in rem*.

(*l*) The right of re-purchase may also be created by subsequent agreement between the parties.

(*m*) Even though no fault is imputable to him.

500. The original purchaser may demand compensation for outlay which he has incurred on the purchased object before the re-purchase in so far as the value of the object is increased by such outlay. He may remove an attachment with which he has provided the thing to be returned (n).

501. If the estimated value which the purchased object has at the time of re-purchase is agreed upon as the price of re-purchase, the original purchaser is not responsible for any deterioration, destruction, or impossibility of returning the object arising from any other cause; and the original seller is not bound to compensate him for outlay incurred (o).

502. If several persons have a right of re-purchase in common, it may be exercised only as a whole. If it is extinguished in respect of one of the persons entitled, or if one of them does not exercise his right, the others are entitled to exercise the right of re-purchase as a whole (p).

503. The right of re-purchase may be exercised, in the case of land, only before the expiration of thirty years, or, in the case of other objects, only before the expiration of three years after the formation of the agreement reserving the right. If a period is fixed for its exercise, this takes the place of the statutory period.

3. *Pre-emption* (q).

504. A person who is entitled to pre-emption in respect of an object may exercise the right of pre-emption as soon as the person bound by it has concluded with a third party a contract of sale (r) relating to the object.

(*n*) Cf. 256—258, 273, 274.

(*o*) The contract may, however, provide otherwise.

(*p*) The rule is different in the case of the right of rescission. 356.

(*q*) The right of pre-emption dealt with under this title exists only as between the contracting parties, and is not available against third parties. It is a *jus in personam*, and is to be distinguished from the real right of pre-emption dealt with in 1094 *et seq.*, which is a *jus in rem*, available against third parties. For a co-heir's *statutory* right of pre-emption, see 2034.

(*r*) A gift or an "exchange" of the object does not justify the exercise of the right of pre-emption.

505. The exercise of the right of pre-emption is effected by a declaration made to the parson bound. The declaration need not be in the form prescribed for the contract of sale.

Upon the exercise of the right of pre-emption the sale is effected between the person entitled and the person bound on the same terms as those which the latter had agreed upon with the third party.

506. An agreement of the person bound with the third party whereby the sale is made subject to the non-exercise of the right of pre-emption, or the right of rescission is reserved to the person bound in case of the exercise of the right of pre-emption, is not binding upon the person entitled to pre-emption.

507. If the third party has bound himself in the contract to execute an accessory consideration which the person entitled is not in a position to execute, the latter shall, instead of executing the accessory consideration, pay its value. If the accessory consideration cannot be estimated in money, the exercise of the right of pre-emption is barred; no regard, however, is paid to the agreement for the accessory consideration, if the contract would have been entered into even though the accessory consideration had not been promised.

508. If the third party has purchased the object to which the right of pre-emption relates together with other objects for an aggregate price, the person entitled to pre-emption shall pay a proportionate part of the aggregate price. The person bound may demand that the pre-emption be extended to all the things which cannot be separated without injury to him.

509. If in the contract a future date has been fixed for payment of the purchase price by the third party, the person entitled to pre-emption may claim the same right of delay only if he gives security for the deferred payment.

If a piece of land is the object of pre-emption, security is not required to be given, in so far as the charging of a hypotheca on the land for the deferred payment has been agreed upon, or a debt for which a hypotheca exists on the land has been assumed as part of the purchase price.

510. The person bound shall without delay communicate to the person entitled to pre-emption the terms of the contract concluded with the third party.

Communication by the third party takes the place of communication by the person bound.

The right of pre-emption may be exercised, in the one of land, only before the expiration of two months, or, in the case of other objects, only before the expiration of one week after receipt of the communication. If a period is fixed for its exercise, this takes the place of the statutory period.

511. In case of doubt the right of pre-emption does not extend to a sale made to a statutory heir in consideration of his future right of inheritance.

512. The right of pre-emption is barred, if the sale is made under compulsory execution or by a trustee in bankruptcy.

513. If the right of pre-emption belongs to several persons in common, it may be exercised only as a whole. If it is extinguished in respect of one of the persons entitled, or if one of them does not exercise his right, the others are entitled to exercise the right of pre-emption as a whole.

514. The right of pre-emption is not transferable and does not pass to the heirs of the person entitled to it, unless it is otherwise provided. If the right is limited to a fixed time, it passes by inheritance in case of doubt.

4. *Exchange* (s).

515. The provisions relating to sale apply *mutatis mutandis* to exchange (t).

(s) The difference between "exchange" and "sale" lies in the fact that in the former case there is no purchase price, but a thing, a right in a thing or any consideration other than money is given in return for the thing exchanged.

(t) That is, each of the contracting parties is a "seller" in respect of the consideration promised by him, and is at the same time a "purchaser" in respect of the consideration promised to him.

SECOND TITLE.
Gift [u].

516. A disposition whereby a person out of his own property confers a benefit on another is a gift, if both parties agree [x] that the disposition is made gratuitously [y].

If the disposition is made without the consent of the other party, the person making it may demand him to declare whether or not he will accept it within a fixed reasonable period. After the expiration of the period the gift is deemed to have been accepted, unless the other party has declined it within the period. If the gift is declined, the return of what has been given may be demanded under the provisions relating to the return of unjustified benefits [z].

517. It is not a gift if a person for the benefit of another abstains from acquiring any property, or relinquishes a right accruing to but not yet finally vested in him, or disclaims an inheritance or a legacy.

518. For the validity of a contract whereby an act of performance is promised gratuitously, judicial or notarial authentication of the promise [a] is necessary. If a promise of debt or an acknowledgment of debt of the kind specified in 780, 781, be made gratuitously, the same rule applies to the promise or the declaration of acknowledgment.

Any defect of form is cured by the performance of the promise.

519. A donor is entitled to refuse fulfilment of a promise made gratuitously

---

(*u*) Under various heads may be found other provisions relating to gift. See Index. See, further, 685, par. 2, 1618, which are of great practical importance in the family life of every day. 86, 87 of the Introductory Act contain special provisions relating to gifts made to juristic persons, members of religious orders and aliens.

(*x*) A gift is therefore a contract for which there must be an offer and an acceptance.

(*y*) A money gift or a gift of moveables, no matter how valuable it may be, need not be made in writing, provided it be executed forthwith. Judicial or notarial authentication is necessary only in the case of a gift of immoveables, or of property (311—313), or in the case of a *promise* of a gift (518).

(*z*) See 818—822.

(*a*) This does not apply, however, to the acceptance of the promise.

in so far as, having regard to his other obligations, he is not in a position to fulfil the promise without endangering his own maintenance suitable to his station in life or the duties to furnish maintenance to others imposed upon him by law.

If the claims of several donees conflict, the claim which first arose takes priority.

520. If a donor promises a subsistence consisting in periodical payments, the obligation is extinguished on his death, unless a contrary intention appears from the promise.

521. A donor is responsible only for wilful default and gross negligence.

522. A donor is not bound to pay interest for default.

523. If a donor fraudulently conceals a defect of title (b), he is bound to compensate the donee for any damage arising therefrom.

If the donor has promised to give an object which he must first acquire, the donee may demand compensation for non-fulfilment on account of a defect of title, if the defect was known to the donor at the time of the acquisition of the object or remained unknown on account of gross negligence. The provisions of 433, par. 1, 434 to 437, 440, pars. 2 to 4, and 441 to 444, applicable to a seller's duty of warranty apply *mutatis mutandis*.

524. If a donor fraudulently conceals a defect (c) of quality in the thing given, he is bound to compensate the donee for any damage arising therefrom.

If the donor has promised to give a thing designated only by species, which he must first acquire, and if the thing given was defective, and the defect was known to the donor at the time of acquiring the thing, or remained unknown on account of gross negligence, the donee may demand the in place of the defective thing one free from defect be furnished to him. If the donor fraudulently concealed the defect, the donee may demand, instead of delivery of a thing free from defect, compensation for non-performance. The provisions applicable to

(b) See 434—437.

(c) The donor is not responsible for a defect unknown to him.

warranty against defects of quality in a thing sold apply *mutatis mutandis* (d) to such claims.

525. A person who makes a gift subject to a burden may demand the execution of the burden, if he on his part has executed the gift (e).

If the execution of the burden is of public interest, after the death of the donor the competent public authority may also demand its execution.

526. In so far as in consequence of a defect of title or of quality in the thing given, the value of the gift does not cover the outlay necessary for the execution of the burden, the donee is entitled to refuse execution until the deficiency caused by the defect is made up. If the donee executes the burden in ignorance of the defect, he may demand from the donor compensation for any outlay incurred in the execution, in so far as such outlay, in consequence of the defect, exceeds the value of the gift.

527. If the execution of the burden remains unperformed the donor may, under the conditions specified for the right of rescission in the case of mutual contracts (f), demand the return of the gift under the provisions relating to the return of unjustified benefits (g) in so far as the gift ought to have been applied to the execution of the burden.

This claim is barred if a third party is entitled to require the execution of the burden.

528. Where the donor, after the execution of the gift, is not in a position to maintain himself in a manner suitable to his station in life, and to fulfil the statutory duty to furnish maintenance imposed upon him in favour of his relatives by blood (h), his wife, or his former wife, he may demand the donee to return

---

(*d*) 480, 491.

(*e*) Whether a third party in whose favour the burden is imposed acquires any direct right against the donee or not is determined according to 328—335.

(*f*) See 325—327.

(*g*) See 818—822.

(*h*) See 1601.

the gift under the provisions relating to the return of unjustified benefits [(i)]. The donee may avoid the return by payment of the sum necessary for such maintenance. The provisions of 760 and the provision of 1613 applicable to the duty of furnishing maintenance to relatives by blood, and, in case of the death of the donor, the provisions also of 1615 apply *mutatis mutandis* to the obligation of the donee.

Among several donees a prior donee is liable only in case a subsequent donees is not bound.

529. The claim to the return of the gift is barred if the donor has brought about his poverty wilfully or by gross negligence, or if at the time of his impoverishment ten years have elapsed since the delivery of the object given.

The same rule applies if the donee, having regard to his other obligations, is not in a position to return the gift without endangering his own maintenance suitable to his station in life, or the fulfilment of the duties to furnish maintenance to others imposed upon him by law.

530. A gift may be revoked if the donee renders himself guilty of gross ingratitude by any serious misconduct towards the donor or a near relation of the donor [(k)].

The right to revoke belongs to the heir of the donor only if the donee has wilfully and unlawfully killed the donor, or prevented him from revoking.

531. Revocation is effected by declaration to the donee.

If the gift is revoked its return may be demanded under the provisions relating to the return of unjustified benefits [(l)].

532. The right to revoke is barred if the donor has forgiven the donee, or if a year has elapsed since the time at which the person entitled to revoke had

---

(*i*) Cf., however, 529, par. 1, and 534.

(*k*) The word "relation" (*Angehöriger*) is not defined by the Code. 52 of the Criminal Code enumerates the following as "*Angehöriger*": relatives by blood or by marriage in the ascending or descending line, adopted parents or children, foster parents or children, husband and wife, brothers and sisters and their spouses or intended spouses.

(*l*) See 818—822.

knowledge of the occurrence of the facts giving him such right. After the death of the donor revocation is no longer permissible.

533. The right to revoke may be waived only after the ingratitude has become known to the person entitled to revoke.

534. Gifts which are made in compliance with a moral duty (m) or the rules of social propriety (n) are not subject to recall or revocation.

THIRD TITLE.
Ordinary Lease. Usufructuary Lease.

I. Ordinary Lease.

535. By a contract of ordinary lease the lessor is bound to give to the lessee the use of the leased thing during the term of the lease. The lessee is bound to pay to the lessor the rent agreed upon.

536. The lessor shall deliver to the lessee the leased thing in a condition fit for the stipulated use, and shall keep it in such condition during the term of the lease (o).

537. If the leased thing is, at the time of delivery to the lessee, affected with a defect which destroys or diminishes its fitness for the stipulated use, or if such a defect arises during the term of the lease, the lessee is released from payment of the rent for the time during which its fitness is destroyed; for the time during which its fitness is diminished he is bound to pay only a part of the rent to be estimated according to 472, 473.

The same rule applies if a promised quality is absent or disappears sub-

---

(m) *E.g.*, a gift made to a poor relative by blood.

(n) *E.g.*, a reward for voluntary service.

(o) This is a corollary of 535. It follows from this that the lessor has to bear the expenses of necessary repairs which are not caused by any fault on the part of the lessee.

sequently. In the letting of a piece of land the promise of specified dimensions is equivalent to the promise of a quality.

538. If a defect of the kind specified in 537 exists at the time of entering into the contract, or if such a defect arises subsequently in consequence of a circumstance for which the lessor is responsible, or if the lessor is in default in respect of the removal of a defect, the lessee may demand compensation for non-fulfilment, instead of enforcing the rights specified in 537.

If the lessor is in default the lessee may himself remove the defect and demand compensation for any necessary outlay.

539. If the lessee knew of the defect of the leased thing at the time of entering into the contract, the rights specified in 537, 538 do not belong to him. If a defect of the kind specified in 537, par. 1, remains unknown to the lessee in consequence of gross negligence, or if he accepts a defective thing although he knows of the defect, he may enforce these rights only under the conditions under which warranty is given to the purchaser of a defective thing as provided in 460, 464.

540. An agreement whereby the obligation of the lessor as to responsibility for defects of title or quality in the leased thing is released or limited, is void if the lessor fraudulently conceals the defect [(p)].

541. If, through the right of a third party, the stipulated use of the leased thing is wholly or in part taken away from the lessee, the provisions of 537, 538, 539, sentence 1, and 540, apply *mutatis mutandis*.

542. If the stipulated use of the leased thing is wholly or in part not given to the lessee in due time, or taken away from him subsequently, the lessee may give notice to terminate the lease without observance of any term of notice. The notice may not be given until after the lessor has allowed a reasonable period of time fixed by the lessee to elapse without affording any remedy. The fixing of such a period is not necessary if the lessee has no interest in the fulfilment of the contract in consequence of the circumstance justifying the notice.

(*p*) The same rule applies in the case of sale. 443, 476.

Notice to terminate the lease may be given on account of an insignificant hindering or withholding of the use only if it is justified by a special interest of the lessee.

If the lessor contests the permissibility of the notice given on the ground that he has given the use of the thing in due time, or has effected the remedy before the expiration of the period, the burden of proof it upon him.

543. The provisions of 539 to 541, and the provisions of 469 to 471 applicable to the cancellation of a sale apply *mutatis mutandis* to the right of giving notice to terminate which the lessee has under 542.

If the rent has been paid in advance for a future time, the lessor shall pay it back in accordance with 347, or, if the notice to terminate is given on account of a circumstance for which he is not responsible, in accordance with the provisions relating to the return of unjustified benefits [q].

544. If a dwelling place or any other place intended for human habitation is in such condition that its use is attended with serious danger to health, the lessee may give notice to terminate the lease without observance of any term of notice even if at the time of entering into the contract he knew of the dangerous condition or waived the rights belonging to him on account of this condition [r].

545. If, during the term of the lease, a defect in the leased thing is discovered, or if precautions become necessary for the protection of the thing against any unforeseen danger, the lessee shall notify the lessor without delay. The same rule applies if a third party claims a right to the thing.

If the lessee fails to give such notice he is bound to make compensation for any damage arising therefrom; where the lessor was not in a position to afford any remedy in consequence of the omission of the notification, the lessee is not entitled to avail himself of the rights specified in 537, nor to give notice to terminate without fixing a period as provided for in 542, par. 1, sentence 3, nor to demand compensation for non-fulfilment.

(*q*) See 812—822.

(*r*) This is an exception to the general principles of an ordinary lease, and is justified only on the ground of public policy. *Salus populi suprema lex.*

546. The lessor shall bear the charges imposed upon the leased thing.

547. The lessor is bound to compensate the lessee for any necessary outlay [s] incurred upon the thing. The lessee of an animal shall, however, bear the cost of provender.

The obligation of the lessor to compensate the lessee for any other outlay [t] is determined according to the provisions relating to management of affairs without mandate [u]. The lessee is entitled to remove an attachment with which he has provided the thing [x].

548. A lessee is not responsible for any alteration or deterioration of the leased thing which is brought about by the stipulated use [y].

549. A lessee is not entitled, without the permission of the lessor, to transfer to a third party the use of the leased thing, *e.g.*, to sublet the thing. If the lessor refuses permission, the lessee may give notice to terminate the lease with observance of the statutory term [z], unless a grave reason exists affecting such third party personally.

If the lessee transfers the use to a third party he is responsible for any fault committed by the third party in the use, even if the lessor has given permission for the transfer.

550. If a lessee uses the thing leased in a way which violates the contract, and if he continues so to use it notwithstanding a remonstrance of the lessor, the latter may apply for an injunction.

551. The rent is payable at the end of the term of lease [a]. If the rent is measured by periods of time, it is payable after the expiration of each of the periods.

(*s*) Cf. 256, 257. The claim is barred by prescription in six months. 558.

(*t*) *I.e.*, any outlay which is not strictly necessary.

(*u*) Cf. 683.

(*x*) Cf. 258.

(*y*) For any other alteration or deterioration he is responsible only if fault is imputable to him.

(*z*) Cf. 565—568.

(*a*) If the lessee is in a bad financial condition, the lessor may insist on his giving security.

The rent for a piece of land [b], unless measured by shorter periods, is payable after the expiration of each quarter of the calendar year on the first business day of the following month [c].

552. A lessee is not released from payment of the rent by the fact that he is hindered in the exercise of his right of use by a cause personal to himself [d]. The lessor must, however, deduct the value of any expenditure [e] saved by him, and of any advantages which he derives from the use being otherwise turned to account. So long as the lessor is not in a position to give the use to the lessee in consequence of transfer of the use to a third party, the lessee is not bound to pay the rent.

553. A lessor may give notice to terminate his lease without observance of any term of notice, if the lessee or any person to whom the lessee has transferred the use of the thing leased, notwithstanding a remonstrance of the lessor, continues to use the thing in a way which violates the contract and seriously impairs the rights of the lessor, *e.g.*, if the lessee leaves to a third party the use which he has transferred to the latter without authority, or seriously endangers the thing by neglecting the care imposed upon him [f].

554. A lessor may give notice to terminate his lease without observance of any term of notice if the lessee is in default in respect of payment of the rent or a part of the rent for two successive instalments [g]. Such notice may not be given if the lessee has satisfied the lessor before it is given.

The notice is ineffective if the lessee could release himself from his debt by set-off, and declares the set-off without delay after the notice [h].

555. If the lessor exercises the right of giving notice which he has under

---

(*b*) Cf. 580.

(*c*) As to the place of payment, see the general provisions of 269, 270.

(*d*) *E.g.*, illness.

(*e*) *E.g.*, expenditure for water, light, &c.

(*f*) Cf. 276, 549, 550.

(*g*) Cf. 551.

(*h*) The parties may, however, exclude the set-off by agreement.

553, 554, he shall, in accordance with 347, pay back the rent paid in advance for a future time.

556. The lessee is bound to return the leased thing after the termination of the lease.

The lessee of a piece of land has no right of lien on account of his claims against the lessor (i).

If the lessee has transferred the use of the thing to a third party, the lessor may, after the termination of the lease, demand the return of the thing even from such third party.

557. If a lessee does not return the leased thing after the termination of the lease, the lessor may demand the rent agreed upon as compensation for the time during which the thing is retained. Proof of further damage is admissible.

558. The claims of a lessor for compensation on account of alteration or deterioration of the leased thing, and the claims of a lessee for compensation for outlay incurred, or for permission to remove an attachment, are barred by prescription in six months.

The prescription of the lessor's claims for compensation begins to run from the time at which he receives the thing back; the prescription of the claims of the lessee begins to run from the termination of the lease.

After the prescription of the claim of the lessor for the return of the thing, his claims for compensation are also barred by prescription.

559. The lessor of a piece of land (k) has, by way of security for his claims arising from the lease, a right of pledge over the things brought upon the premises by the lessee (l). The right of pledge may not be enforced for future claims for compensation, nor for any rent for a later time than the current and following year of the lease. It does not extend to things not subject to judicial

---

(*i*) An exception to 273.

(*k*) Cf. 580.

(*l*) This is a "statutory right of pledge" to which, according to 1257, the provisions of 1204 *et seq.* relating to "pledges constituted by juristic act" apply *mutatis mutandis*.

attachment [m].

560. The lessor's right of pledge is extinguished by the removal of the things from the land, unless the removal takes place without the knowledge or in spite of an objection of the lessor. The lessor may not object to the removal if it takes place in the regular course of business of the lessee, or in accordance with the ordinary affairs of life, or if the things remaining on the premises are evidently sufficient for the security of the lessor.

561. The lessor may, even without application to the Court, prevent the removal of the things subject to his right of pledge in so far as he is entitled to object to the removal, and may also, if the hirer moves out, take possession of the things.

If the things have been removed without the knowledge or in spite of an objection of the lessor, he may demand their delivery for the purpose of replacing them on the land, and may, if the lessee has move out, demand the transfer of possession. The right of pledge is extinguished on the expiration of one month after the lessor had knowledge of the removal of the things, unless he has enforced his claim in court within such period.

562. The lessee may prevent the enforcement of the lessor's right of pledge by giving security; he may release each individual thing from the right of pledge by giving security to the extent of its value.

563. If a thing subject to the lessor's right of pledge is judicially attached by a judgment creditor, then as against such creditor the right of pledge may not be enforced in respect of any rent due for an earlier time than the last year before the judicial attachment.

564. A lease terminates on the expiration of the time for which it was entered upon.

If the term of the lease is not fixed, either party may give notice of its termination as provided for in 565.

(*m*) See 811 of the Code of Civil Procedure.

565. In the case of land notice to terminate the lease may be given only for the end of a quarter of the calendar year; it shall be given, at the latest, on the third business day of the quarter. If the rent is measured by months, notice may be given only for the end of a calendar month; it shall be given, at the latest, on the fifteenth of the month. If the rent is measured by the week, notice may be given only for the end of a calendar week; it shall be given, at the latest, on the first business day of the week.

In the cases of moveables, notice shall be given, at the latest, on the third day before the day on which the lease is to terminate.

If the rent for a piece of land or for a moveable is measured by days, notice may be given on any day for the following day.

The provisions of par. 1, sentence 1, and of par. 2, apply also to all cases in which the lease may be terminated by notice before its expiration with observance of the statutory term (n).

566. A contract relating to the lease of a piece of land which is entered into for a longer term than one year is required to be in writing. If the contract is not in writing it is deemed to have been entered into for an indeterminate time; notice may not, however, be given for an earlier time than the end of the first year (o).

567. If a contract of lease is entered into for a longer term than thirty years, either party may, after thirty years, give notice to terminate the lease with observance of the statutory term. Such notice may not be given if the contract has been entered into for the life of the lessor or of the lessee.

568. If, after the expiration of the term of lease, the use of the thing is continued by the lessee, the lease is deemed to have been extended for an indeterminate time (p), unless the lessor or the lessee declares a contrary intention

---

(*n*) *E.g.*, 549, par. 1, 569, 570, &c. The parties may, of course, stipulate otherwise than as provided in 565.

(*o*) In such a case the contract is not void (contrary to the general rule, see 125, 126), but is deemed to have been entered into for the term of one year (564, par. 2, 565), and may even be renewed for an indeterminate time by implication as provided in 568.

(*p*) At least for one year, in the case of leases of land. 566, sentence 2.

to the other party within a period of two weeks. The period begins to run, as against the lessee, from the time of the continuance of the use; as against the lessor, from the time at which he has knowledge of the continuance.

569. If the lessee dies, both his heir and the lessor are entitled to give notice to terminate the lease with observance of the statutory term [(q)]. The notice may be given only for the first terminal date for which it is permissible [(r)].

570. Person in military service, officials, clergymen, and teachers in public institutions of learning may, in case of their removal to another place and after observance of the statutory term, give notice to terminate the lease [(s)] of the places which they have leased for themselves or their families in the former place of garrison or residence. The notice may be given only for the first terminal date for which it is permissible.

571. If the leased land is alienated to a third party by the lessor after delivery to the lessee, the alienee takes the place of the lessor in the rights and obligations arising from the lease during the existence of his ownership.

If the alienee does not fulfil his obligations, the lessor is liable as a surety who has waived the plea of *beneficium excussionis* [(t)] for any damage for which the alienee is bound to make compensation. If the lessee has knowledge of the transfer of ownership through communication by the lessor, the lessor is released from liability if the lessee does not give notice to terminate the lease for the first terminal date for which notice is permissible.

572. If the lessee of the alienated land has given to the lessor security for the fulfilment of his obligations, the alienee takes by subrogation the rights thereby created. He is bound to return the security only if it is delivered to

---

(*q*) Cf. 565, 566.

(*r*) It is to be noticed that in the case where husband and wife have jointly entered into a contract of ordinary lease with another person, the surviving spouse *as such* (*i.e.* not in his or her capacity of heir), cannot avail himself or herself of the right provided for in this section.

(*s*) Cf. 565, 566.

(*t*) Cf. 771.

him, or if he assumes towards the lessee the obligation of returning it.

573. A disposition which the lessor has made before the transfer of ownership relating to the rent due for the time when the alienee has title, is operative in so far as it relates to the rent for the calendar quarter current at the time of transfer of ownership and the following quarter. A disposition relating to the rent for a future time is valid as against the alienee, if he knew of the disposition at the time of the transfer of ownership.

574. A juristic act entered into between the lessee and the lessor in respect of any claim for rent, *e.g.*, the payment of the rent, is effective against the alienee, in so far as it does not relate to the rent for a later time than the calendar quarter in which the lessee has knowledge of the transfer of ownership and the following quarter. A juristic act entered into after the transfer of ownership is, however, ineffective if the lessee has knowledge of the transfer of ownership at the time of entering into the juristic act.

575. In so far as the payment of the rent to the lessor is effective against the alienee as provided for in 574, the lessee may set off against the alienee's claim for the rent a claim belonging to him against the lessor. The set-off is barred, if the lessee has acquired the counterclaim after having obtained knowledge of the transfer of ownership, or if the counterclaim has not become due until after the knowledge was obtained and after the rent accrued due.

576. If the lessor gives notice to the lessee that he has transferred to a third party the ownership of the leased land, the transfer of which he has given notice avails against himself in favour of the lessee in respect of the claim to rent, even if the transfer has not taken place or if it is invalid [(u)].

The notice may be revoked only with the consent of the person who has been named as the new owner.

577. Where the leased land is made subject by the lessor to the right of a third party after delivery to the lessee, the provisions of 571 to 576 apply

---

(*u*) This rule obtains also in the case where the transfer has been entered in the land register, although no notice thereof has been given to the lessee. Cf. 893.

mutatis mutandis, if the lessee is deprived of the stipulated use by the exercise of the right. If the exercise of the right results only in a limitation of the stipulated use by the lessee, the third party is bound towards the lessee to abstain from exercising such right, in so far as it would interfere with the stipulated use.

578. If, before delivery of the leased land to the lessee, the lessor has alienated the land to a third party, or made it subject to a right by whose exercise the stipulated use is taken away from the lessee or is limited, then the same rule applies as in the cases provided for by 571, par. 1, and 577, if the alienee has assumed towards the lessor the fulfilment of the obligations arising from the lease.

579. If the leased land is again alienated or made subject to rights of third parties by the alienee, the provisions of 571, par. 1, and 572 to 578 apply *mutatis mutandis*. If the new alienee does not fulfil the obligations arising from the lease, the lessor is liable to the lessee as provided for in 571, par. 2.

580. The provisions relating to leases of land apply also to leases of rooms for habitation and other rooms.

II. Usufructuary Lease.

581. By a contract of usufructuary lease the lessor is bound to give to the lessee during the term of the lease the use of the object leased and the enjoyment of its fruits, in so far as they are to be considered as products according to the rules of proper husbandry. The lessee is bound to pay to the lessor the rent agreed upon.

The provisions relating to an ordinary lease apply *mutatis mutandis* to a usufructuary lease, in so far as a contrary intention does not appear from 582 to 597.

582. A lessee of agricultural land shall make all customary repairs at his own expense, *e.g.*, those of the inhabited and industrial buildings, roads, ditches and fences.

583. A lessee of agricultural land may not, without permission of the lessor, undertake any change in the economic purpose of the land affecting the mode of cultivation beyond the term of the lease [(x)].

584. If in the lease of agricultural land the rent is measured by years, it is payable after the expiration of each year of the lease on the first business day of the following year [(y)].

585. The right of pledge of the lessor of agricultural land may be enforced for the entire rent [(z)], und is not subject to the limitation specified in 563. It extends to the fruits of the land and to all things which under 715 (5) of the Code of Civil Procedure [(a)] are not subject to judicial attachment.

586. If a piece of land with its appurtenant stock is leased, the duty to preserve the individual units composing the stock is imposed upon the lessee.

The lessor is bound to replace any units composing the stock which have perished in consequence of a circumstance for which the lessee is not responsible. The lessee shall, however, make good from the offspring the ordinary decrease in the animals included in the stock, in so far as this is in accordance with the rules of proper husbandry.

587. If the lessee of a piece of land takes the appurtenant stock at an appraised value under the obligation to return it on the termination of the lease at the appraised value, the provisions of 588, 589 apply.

588. The lessee bears the risk of accidental destruction or accidental deterioration of the stock. He may dispose of the individual units thereof within the limits of proper husbandry.

The lessee shall preserve the stock in accordance with the rules of proper husbandry, in the condition in which it is delivered to him. Any units supplied by him become the property of the lessor if incorporated in the stock.

(x) The rights of the lessor are protected by 550, 553.

(y) Cf. 551.

(z) The rule is otherwise in the case of an ordinary lease. Cf. 559.

(a) 715 (5) of the old Code of Civil Procedure is 811 (4) of the new Code of Civil Procedure.

589. The lessee shall return to the lessor the stock existing at the time of the termination of the lease.

The lessor may refuse to accept any units included in the stock supplied by the lessee which, according to the rules of proper husbandry, are superfluous for the land or are too valuable; upon his refusal the ownership of the rejected units passes to the lessee.

If the total appraised value of the units received is greater or less than the appraised value of the units to be returned, the difference shall be made good in the former case by the lessee to the lessor; in the latter case, by the lessor to the lessee.

590. The lessee of a piece of land has, by way of security for his claims against the lessor in respect of the leased stock, a right of pledge over the several units composing the stock which have come into his possession. The provision of 562 applies *mutatis mutandis* to the right of pledge.

591. A lessee of agricultural land is bound to return the land after the termination of the lease in the condition produced by proper husbandry continued during the term of the lease until the return of the land. This applies especially to the tillage [b].

592. If a lease of agricultural land ends during the course of a leasing year, the lessor shall make compensation for any outlay which the lessee has incurred upon fruits not yet gathered but, according to the rules of proper husbandry, to be gathered before the end of the leasing year, in so far as such outlay is incurred in the course of proper husbandry and does not exceed the value of these fruits.

593. The lessee of a farm shall, on the termination of the lease, leave behind so much of the existing agricultural products as is necessary for the continuance of the husbandry up to the time when a new supply of the same or similar products will presumably be obtained, without regard to the question whether he received such products on entry upon the lease.

(*b*) Cf. 593.

In so far as the lessee is bound to leave behind agricultural products in greater quantity or of better quality than he received on entry upon the lease, he may demand compensation for the value from the lessor.

The lessee shall leave behind the existing stock of manure produced upon the farm, without being entitled to compensation for its value.

594. If the lessee of a farm take the farm on the basis of an appraisement of its economic condition with the provision that its return on the termination of the lease is likewise to be made on the basis of such an appraisement, the provisions of 589, pars. 2, 3 apply *mutatis mutandis* to the return of the farm.

The same rule applies, if the lessee receives supplies on the basis of an appraisement with such a provision, to the return of the supplies which he is bound to leave behind.

595. If, in the lease of a piece of land or of a right, the term of the lease is not fixed, notice to terminate the lease may be given only for the end of a leasing year; it shall be given, at the latest, on the first business day of the half-year on the expiration of which the lease is to terminate.

These provisions apply, in the case of a lease of a piece of land or of a right, also to the cases in which notice to terminate the lease may be given before its expiration, with observance of the statutory term.

596. The right to give notice specified in 549, par. 1, does not belong to a usufructuary lessee.

The lessor is not entitled to give notice to terminate the lease under 569.

Notice to terminate the lease under 570 may not be given.

597. If the lessee does not return the object leased after the termination of the lease, the lessor may demand as compensation for the time during which the object is detained, the rent agreed upon in the proportion which the emoluments which the lessee during that time has derived or might have derived, bear to the emoluments of the entire year of lease. Proof of further damage is admissible.

FOURTH TITLE.
Loan for Use.

598. By a contract of loan for use the lender of a thing is bound to permit the borrower to use the thing gratuitously.

599. The lender is responsible only for wilful default and gross negligence [c].

600. If the lender fraudulently conceals a defect of title or of quality in the thing lent, he is bound to compensate the borrower for any damage arising therefrom.

601. The borrower shall bear the ordinary expenses of the preservation of the thing lent, *e.g.*, in the case of the loan of an animal, the cost of provender.

The obligation of the lender to make compensation for other expenses is determined according to the provisions relating to management of affairs without mandate [d]. The borrower is entitled to remove an attachment with which he has provided the thing [e].

602. A borrower is not responsible for any alteration or deterioration of the thing lent which is brought about by the stipulated use of the thing.

603. The borrower may not use the thing lent in any other way than that stipulated for. He is not entitled to transfer to a third party the use of the thing without the permission of the lender [f].

604. The borrower is bound to return the thing lent on the expiration of the time fixed for the loan.

If no time is fixed, the thing shall be returned after the borrower has made

---

(*c*) The reason being that the lender of a gratuitous loan is in the same position as a donor in this respect. 521. The borrower is, on the other hand, responsible even for slight negligence.

(*d*) Cf. 677 *et seq.*

(*e*) Cf. 258.

(*f*) Violation of this provision will render the borrower liable even for accidental loss or destruction of the thing lent. 848.

the use of the thing which appears from the object of the loan. The lender may demand the thing back earlier if so much time has elapsed that the borrower might have made this use of it.

If the time of the loan is neither fixed nor to be inferred from the object of the loan, the lender may demand the thing back at any time.

If the borrower transfers the use of the thing to a third party, the lender may also demand it back from the third party after the termination of the loan.

605. The lender may give notice to terminate the loan:

(1) if he has need of the thing lent in consequence of an unforeseen circumstance;

(2) if the borrower makes any use of the thing in breach of the contract, *e. g.*, transfers the use without authority to a third party, or seriously endangers the thing by neglecting the care imposed upon him;

(3) if the borrower dies [(g)].

606. The claim of the lender for compensation on account of alteration or deterioration of the thing lent, and the claim of the borrower for compensation for outlay or for permission to remove an attachment, are barred by prescription in six months. The provisions of 558, pars. 2, 3 apply *mutatis mutandis*.

FIFTH TITLE.
Loan for Consumption.

607. A person who has received money or other fungible things as a loan is bound to return to the lender what he has received in things of the same kind, quality and quantity.

A person who owes money or other fungible things for any other reason may agree with the creditor that the money or the things shall be owed as a loan [(h)].

(*g*) It is to be noticed that the death of the *lender* has no effect on the loan.

(*h*) A deposit may even be held to be a loan for consumption. 700.

608. If interest is stipulated for on a loan (i) it is payable, unless otherwise provided, at the end of each year, and, if the loan is to be repaid before the end of a year, at the time of repayment.

609. If the time for repayment of a loan is not fixed, its maturity depends upon the giving of notice by the creditor or the debtor (j).

The term of notice is three months in the case of loan of more than three hundred marks; one month, in the case of loans of less amount.

If interest is not stipulated for, the debtor is entitled to make repayment even without notice.

610. A person who promises to make a loan may, in case of doubt, revoke the promise if a serious change for the worse in the financial circumstances of the other party comes about whereby the claim for repayment is endangered (k).

SIXTH TITLE.
Contract for Service (l).

611. By a contract for service, the person who promises service is bound

---

(*i*) Interest is not to be implied from the mere loan. In the absence of any stipulation to the contrary the rate is 4 per cent. per annum. 246.

(*j*) This is a deviation from the general rule laid down in 271, par. 1.

(*k*) The change must take place after the promise has been made. If the change took place before or at the time of the promise, he may revoke his promise only on the ground of fraud or unlawful threats.

(*l*) This title contains what is known in English legal terminology as the law of master and servant. Besides the various provisions which come under this title there are many other special laws and statutes which govern special kinds of service, *viz.* :

(A) Imperial Law (cf. Art. 32, IA).—For assistants and apprentices in trade, see the provisions of 59 *et seq.* of the Commercial Code; for seamen, the Seamen's Act of December 27th, 1872; for inland shippers, the Inland Navigation Act of June 15th, 1895; for industrial journeymen, assistants, apprentices, factory labourers, technologists, overseers, the various provisions of the Industrial Code.

(B) State Laws.—The State laws relating to (1) officials, clergymen, and teachers in public institutions of learning, in the absence of special provisions in the Civil Code (cf. Art. 80, IA); (2) labourers in mines (cf. Art. 67, IA); (3) domestic servants (cf. Art. 95, IA).

to perform the service promised, and the other party is bound to pay the remuneration [(m)] agreed upon.

Service of any kind may be the object of the contract for service.

612. Remuneration is deemed to have been tacitly agreed upon if under the circumstances the performance of the service is to be expected only for remuneration.

If the amount of the remuneration is not specified, and if there is a tariff, the tariff rate of remuneration, or, if there is no tariff, the usual remuneration [(n)] is deemed to have been agreed upon.

613. A servant shall, in case of doubt, perform his service in person. The claim for service is in case of doubt not transferable.

614. The remuneration is payable after the performance of the service. If the remuneration is measured by periods of time, it is payable at the end of each of the periods.

615. If the master is in default in respect of the acceptance of the service, the servant may demand the remuneration agreed upon for the service not performed in consequence of the default, without being bound to perform any subsequent service. He must, however, deduct what he has saved in consequence of non-performance of the service, or has acquired or maliciously omitted to acquire by a different application of his service.

616. A servant does not lose his claim to remuneration by the fact that he is prevented from performing the service for a relatively inconsiderable time by a cause personal to himself without his fault [(o)]. He must, however, deduct the amount which accrues to him for the time he is prevented, from a legally compulsory insurance against sickness or accident.

(*m*) This need not consist in money.

(*n*) This is to be determined in an equitable manner by the party who has performed the service. 316.

(*o*) *E.g.*, illness.

617. If, in the case of a continuous service relation [(p)] which claims wholly or for the most part the industrial activity of the servant, he is received into his master's household, then in case of his illness the master shall afford him the necessary care and medical attendance for a period of six weeks; not, however, beyond the termination of the service relation; provided that the illness of the servant has not been brought about wilfully or by gross negligence. The care and medical attendance may be provided by placing the servant in a hospital. The expenses may be set off against the wages due for the time of the illness. If notice to terminate the service relation is given by the master on account of the illness, as provided for in 626, the termination of the service relation caused thereby is not taken into consideration.

The obligation of the master does not arise if provision has been made for care and medical attendance by an insurance or by a public institution for the care of the sick [(q)].

618. A master has so to fit up and maintain rooms, appliances and implements which he has to provide for the performance of the service and so to regulate services which are to be performed under his orders or his direction that the servant is protected against danger to life and health as far as the nature of the service permits.

If the servant is taken into the household, the master shall make such arrangements and regulations with regard to living and sleeping rooms, sustenance, and time for labour and for recreation as are necessary with regard to the health, morality and religion of the servant.

If the master does not fulfil the obligations imposed upon him in regard to the safety and health of the servant, the provisions of 842 to 846 applicable to unlawful acts apply *mutatis mutandis* to his obligation to make compensation [(q)].

619. The obligations imposed upon the master by 617, 618 may not be avoided or limited by contract in anticipation.

(*p*) Whether the service relation is continuous or not is to be determined according to the circumstances of each particular case.

(*q*) Cf. 619.

620. A service relation ends on the expiration of the time (r) for which it has been entered upon (s).

If the duration of the service relation is neither fixed nor to be inferred from the nature or object of the service, either party may give notice to terminate the service relation as provided for in 621 to 623.

621. If the remuneration is measured by the day, notice may be given on any day for the following day.

If the remuneration is measured by the week, notice may be given only for the end of a calendar week; if shall be given, at the latest, on the first business day of the week.

If the remuneration is measured by the month, notice may be given only for the end of a calendar month; it shall be given, at the latest, on the fifteenth of the month.

If the remuneration is measured by quarters of a year or longer periods of time, notice may be given only for the end of a quarter and only with observance of a six weeks' term of notice.

622. The service relation of persons who are engaged with regular employment (t) for the performance of services of a superior kind, and whose industrial activity is claimed wholly or for the most part by the service relation, *e. g.*, of teachers, tutors, private secretaries, companions, may be terminated by notice only for the end of a calendar quarter and only with observance of a six weeks' term of notice, even if the remuneration is measured by shorter periods than quarters.

623. If the remuneration is not measured by periods of time (u), notice to terminate the service relation may be given at any time; in the case, however, of a service relation claiming the industrial activity of the servant wholly or for

---

(r) No matter whether specified or to be inferred from the nature or the object of the service.

(s) The service relation comes also to an end, when the performance of the service becomes impossible. 323 *set seq.*

(t) Those persons who are not engaged with regular employment or whose service is not a continuous one can terminate the service relation at any time. 627.

(u) *E.g.*, where the remuneration is measured by the job.

the most part, a two weeks' term of notice shall be observed.

624. If the service relation is entered upon for the lifetime of a person or for a longer term than five years, notice of its termination may be given by the servant (x) after the lapse of five years. The term of notice is six months.

625. If, after the expiration of the time of service, the service relation is continued by the servant with the knowledge of the other party, it is deemed to have been extended for an indeterminate time (y), unless the other party objects without delay.

626. Notice to terminate the service relation may be given by either party without observance of any term of notice if a grave reason exists (z).

627. If a servant, without standing in a permanent service relation with regular employment, has to perform service of a superior kind such as are customarily entrusted to a person by reason of special confidence, then notice is permissible even without the condition specified in 626 (a).

The servant may give notice only in such manner that the master can provide himself with the service elsewhere, unless a grave reason exists for the improper notice. If he gives improper notice without such reason, he shall compensate the master for any damage arising therefrom.

628. If, after the beginning of the performance of service, notice of its termination is given under 626 or 627, the servant may demand a proportional part of the remuneration for the services already performed. If he gives notice not occasioned by the conduct of the other party in breach of the contract, or if by his own conduct in breach of the contract he gives occasion for notice by the other party, he has no claim for remuneration if his services already performed have no value for the other party in consequence of the notice. If the remu-

---

(x) The master does not have such right. This provision aims at the protection of freedom of labour.

(y) Notice to terminate the service relation may be given under 620, par. 2, to 623.

(z) Whether a "grave reason" exists or not is determined by the Court according to the circumstance of each particular case.

(a) *I.e.*, without any "grave reason".

neration has been paid in advance for a future time, the servant shall return it in accordance with 347, or, if the notice is given in consequence of a circumstance for which he is no responsible, in accordance with the provisions relating to the return of unjustified benefit (b).

If the notice is occasioned by the conduct of the other party in breach of the contract, he is bound to make compensation for any damage arising from the termination of the service relation.

629. After notice of the termination of a continuous service relation, the master shall on demand allow the servant a reasonable time for seeking another employment.

630. On the termination of a continuous service relation the servant may demand from the other party a written testimonial as to the service relation and its duration. The testimonial shall on demand contain a statement as to his efficiency and conduct in service.

SEVENTH TITLE.
Contract for Work.

631. By a contract for work the contractor is bound to produce the work promised (c), and the employer is bound to pay the remuneration agreed upon.

The object of the contract for work may be either the production or alteration of a thing, or any other result (d) to be brought about by labour or performance of service (e).

632. Remuneration is deemed to have been tacitly agreed upon if, under the circumstances, the production of the work is to be expected only for remuneration.

(b) See 818—822.

(c) The contractor is unconditionally liable for the work of his employees. 278.

(d) *E.g.*, carriage of passengers or goods.

(e) If the contractor has to furnish not only labour or service, but also materials for the production of the work, the contract is partly a contract for work, and partly a contract of sale. 651.

If the amount of the remuneration is not specified, and if there is a tariff, the tariff rate of remuneration, or, in the absence of a tariff, the usual remuneration (f) is deemed to have been agreed upon.

633. The contractor is bound so to produce the work that it has the promised qualities and is not affected with defects which destroy or diminish its value or fitness for its ordinary or stipulated use (g).

If the work is not of such quality (h), the employer may demand the removal of the defect. The contract is entitled to refuse such removal if it requires disproportionate outlay.

If the contractor is in default in respect of the removal of the defect, the employer may himself remove the defect and claim compensation for them necessary expense.

634. The employer may allot to the contractor a reasonable period for the removal of the defect of the kind specified in 633 with a declaration that he will not permit the removal of the defect after the expiration of the period. If a defect has already been discovered before the delivery of the work, the employer may fix the period forthwith; the period must be so fixed that it does not expire before the period fixed for delivery. After the expiration of the period the employer may demand the annulment of the contract (*i.e.*, cancellation), or reduction of the remuneration (*i.e.*, reduction), unless the defect has been removed in due time; the claim for removal of the defect is barred.

The fixing of a period is not necessary if the removal of the defect is impossible, or is refused by the contractor, or if the immediate enforcement of the claim for cancellation or reduction is justified by a special interest of the employer.

The right to demand cancellation is barred if the defect diminishes only insignificantly the value or fitness of the work.

The provisions of 465 to 467, 469 to 475 applicable to sale apply *mutatis*

(*f*) This is to be determined by the contractor in an equitable manner. 316.

(*g*) The obligation of the contractor may, however, be enlarged or limited by contract, except in the case provided for by 637.

(*h*) No matter whether due to accident or not.

mutandis to the cancellation and reduction.

635. If the defect in the work is caused by a circumstance for which the contractor is responsible (i) the employer may demand compensation for non-fulfilment, instead of cancellation or reduction.

636. If the work is wholly or in part not produced in due time (k), the provisions of 634, pars. 1 to 3, applicable to cancellation, apply *mutatis mutandis*; the right of the employer to rescind the contract under 827 takes the place of the claim for cancellation. The rights of the employer in the case of the default of the contractor remain unaffected (l).

If the contractor contests the permissibility of the rescission on the ground that he has produced the work in due time, the burden of proof is upon him.

637. An agreement whereby the obligation of the contractor as to responsibility for a defect in the work is released or limited, is void if the contractor fraudulently conceals the defect.

638. The claim of the employer for removal of a defect in the work and his claims for cancellation, reduction, or compensation on account of the defect are barred by prescription, unless the contractor has fraudulently concealed the defect (m), in six months; in the case of work on land, in one year; in the case of work on buildings, in five years. The prescription begins to run from the cessation of the work (n).

The period of prescription may be extended by contract.

639. The provisions of 477, pars. 2, 3, and 478, 479, applicable to the prescription of claims of a purchaser, apply *mutatis mutandis* to the prescription of the claims of the employer specified in 638.

If the contractor, by agreement with the employer, submits an investigation

---

(*i*) Cf. 276, 278.

(*k*) For the time of performance, see 271.

(*l*) See 286, 326, 327.

(*m*) In which case the period of prescription is thirty years.

(*n*) Cf. 640, 644.

into the existence of a defect or of the removal of the defect, the prescription is suspended [o] until the contractor informs the employer of the result of the investigation, or declares to him that the defect is removed, or refuses to effect the removal.

640. The employer is bound to take delivery of the work [p] completed according to contract, unless this is impossible by reason of the nature of the work [q].

It the employer accepts a defective work, although he knows of the defect, the claims specified in 633, 634 belong to him only if at the time of acceptance he reserves his rights on account of the defect.

641. The remuneration is payable at the time of taking delivery of the work. If the work is to be accepted in parts and the remuneration has been specified for the several parts, the remuneration for each part is payable at the time of its acceptance.

Remuneration specified in money bears interest [r] from the time of acceptance of the work, unless a future time is fixed for its payment.

642. If, in the production of the work, an act [s] by the employer is necessary, and if he is in default of acceptance [t] by not performing the act, the contractor may demand reasonable compensation.

The amount of the compensation is determined, on the one hand, by the duration of the default and the amount of the remuneration agreed upon, and on the other hand, according to what the contractor has saved in expenditure on account of the default, or is able to acquire by a different application of his energy.

643. The contractor is entitled, in the case provided for by 642, to allot to

---

(*o*) Cf. 202—207.

(*p*) At the place of the contractor's domicile, or at the place where his industry is located. 269.

(*q*) As, *e.g.*, in the case of carriage of passengers.

(*r*) 4 per cent., in the absence of any stipulation to the contrary. 246.

(*s*) *E.g.*, the furnishing of materials.

(*t*) See 293 *et seq.*

the employer a fixed reasonable period to do the act, with a declaration that he will terminate the contract, if the act is not performed before the expiration of the period. The contract is deemed to be annulled if performance is not effected before the expiration of the period (u).

644. The contractor bears the risk before acceptance of the work (x). If the employer is in default of acceptance (y), the risk passes to him. The contractor is not responsible for accidental destruction or accidental deterioration of the material provided by the employer.

If the contractor forwards the work at the request of the employer to a place other than the place of performance, the provisions of 447 applicable to sale apply *mutatis mutandis*.

645. If the work, before its acceptance by the employer (z) is destroyed, or damaged, or becomes impracticable in consequence of a defect in the material provided by the employer, or in consequence of instructions given by him for its execution, without any contributory circumstance for which the contractor is responsible, the contractor may demand a part of the remuneration proportionate to the labour performed, and compensation for any outlay not included in the remuneration. The same rule applies if the contract is annulled under 643.

A further liability of the employer on account of his fault remains unaffected.

646. If the nature of the work is such that delivery is impossible, the completion of the work takes the place of delivery (a) in the cases provided for by 638, 641, 644 and 645.

647. The contractor has, by way of security for his claims arising from the

---

(*u*) Cf. 645, par. 1, sentence 2.

(*x*) See 640, 646, 323 *et seq*.

(*y*) See 293 *et seq*.

(*z*) See 640, 646.

(*a*) Cf. 640.

contract, a right of pledge [(b)] over the moveables of the employer produced or repaired by him, if they have come into his possession in the course of production or for the purpose of repairing.

648. A contractor who undertakes to construct a building or any part of a building may, by way of security for his claims arising from the contract, require the concession of a cautionary hypotheca [(c)] on the building ground of the employer. If the work is not yet complete, he may require the concession of a cautionary hypotheca by way of security for a part of the remuneration proportionate to the labour performed [(d)], and for any outlay not included in the remuneration.

649. The employer may, at any time before the completion of the work, give notice to terminate the contract. If he gives such notice, the contractor is entitled to claim the remuneration agreed upon; the contractor must, however, deduct what he saves in expenses in consequence of the annulment of the contract, or what he acquires or maliciously omits to acquire by a different application of his energy.

650. If the contract is based upon an estimate of cost without the contractor assuming to guarantee the correctness of the estimate, and it proves that the work is not practicable without largely exceeding the estimate, and if the contractor terminates the contract for this reason, the contractor has only the claim specified in 645, par. 1.

If such exceeding of the estimate is to be expected, the contractor shall give notice to the employer without delay [(e)].

651. If the contractor binds himself to produce the work from material provided by him, he shall deliver the thing produced to the employer and

---

(*b*) This is a statutory right of pledge to which the provisions of 1204 *et seq.* apply. Cf. 1257.

(*c*) Cf. 1184, 1185.

(*d*) Hence the concession of the cautionary hypotheca cannot be demanded until after the performance of the labour.

(*e*) Notice need not be given if the employer has knowledge of such fact.

convey ownership in the thing [f]. The provisions applicable to sale apply to such a contract; if a non-fungible thing is to be produced, the provisions relating to contract for work, with the exception of 647, 648, take the place of 433, 446, par. 1, sentence 1, and of 447, 459, 460, 462 to 464, 477 to 179 [g].

If the contractor binds himself only to provide additions or other accessories, the provisions relating to contract for work apply exclusively.

EIGHTH TITLE.
Brokerage [h].

652. A person who promises a broker's fee for information of the opportunity of making a contract or for the procurement of a contract, is bound to pay the fee only if the contract is concluded in consequence of the information, or in consequence of the procurement by the broker. If the contract is concluded subject to a condition precedent, the broker's fee may not be demanded until the condition is fulfilled.

The broker is entitled to be reimbursed for outlay incurred only if this has been agreed upon. This applies even if a contract is not concluded.

653. A broker's fee is deemed to have been tacitly agreed upon if the business entrusted to the broker is, under the circumstances, only to be expected for remuneration.

If the amount of the remuneration is not specified, and if there is a tariff, the tariff fee, or in the absence of a tariff, the usual fee, is deemed to have been agreed upon.

(*f*) Same rule as in the case of sale. 433, sentence 1.

(*g*) The main difference is: (1) In the case of a sale the purchaser bears the risk from the time of delivery (446), whereas in the case of a contract for work, the employer bears the risk after acceptance of the work (640, 644). (2) In the case where a non-fungible thing is affected with a defect, an employer, unlike a purchaser (462), cannot immediately demand cancellation or reduction, but can, in the first instance, only demand removal of the defect under 463 *et seq*.

(*h*) Besides the provisions under this title, there are many others which govern special kinds of brokerage, *e.g.*, 93—104 of the Commercial Code govern "commercial brokerage", and the provisions of State law relating to agency for domestic servants remain in force. Art. 95, IA.

654. The claim for the broker's fee and for reimbursement of outlay is barred if the broker, contrary to the terms of the contract, has acted also for the other party.

655. If, for information of the opportunity to enter into a contract for service or for the procurement of such a contract, a disproportionately high fee has been agreed upon, it may be reduced to a reasonable amount [(i)] by judicial decree obtained by the debtor. After payment of the fee, the right to claim reduction is barred.

656. No obligation is created by the promise of a fee for information of an opportunity to enter into a marriage, or for the procurement of the conclusion of a marriage. What has been paid on account of the promise may not be demanded back by reason of no obligation having existed.

These provisions apply also to an agreement whereby the other party, for the purpose of fulfilment of the promise, enters into an obligation towards the broker, *e.g.*, an acknowledgment of debt [(k)].

NINTH TITLE.
Promise of Reward.

657. A person who by public notice announces a reward for the performance of an act, *e.g.*, for the production of a result, is bound to pay the reward to any person who has performed the act, even if he did not act with a view to the reward [(l)].

658. The promise of reward may be revoked before the performance of the act. The revocation is effective only if it is made known in the same manner as the promise of reward, or by special communication.

(*i*) Cf. 343.

(*k*) Cf. 781.

(*l*) The promise of the reward must be made in a serious manner and not as a mere jest. See 118. The death of the promisor has no effect on the promise.

The revocability may be waived in the promise of reward; in case of doubt a waiver is presumed from the fact that a period of time has been fixed for the performance of the act.

659. If the act for which the reward has been promised has been performed several times, the reward belongs to the person who has first performed the act.

If the act has been performed by several persons simultaneously, an equal share of the reward belongs to each. If the reward is in its nature indivisible, or if by the terms of the promise only one person is to receive it, it is decided by lot [(m)].

660. If several persons have contributed to the result for which the reward is promised, the promisor shall divide the reward among them equitably with regard to the share of each claimant in the production of the result. The division is not binding if it is evidently inequitable; in such a case it is made by judicial decree.

If the division of the promisor is not recognised as binding by one of the claimants, the promisor is entitled to refuse fulfilment until the claimants have settled the dispute among themselves as to their respective rights; each of them may demand the reward to be lodged for the benefit of all.

The provision of 659, par. 2, sentence 2, applies.

661. A promise of reward which has a prize competition for its object is valid only if a period of time for the competition is fixed in the notice [(n)].

The decision whether any competitor fulfils the conditions of the promise of reward within the period, or which among several competitors deserves the preference, shall be made by the umpire named in the notice of reward, or in the absence of any such, by the promisor of the reward. The decision is binding upon the parties concerned.

In case of equality of merit the provisions of 659, par. 2, apply to the award of the prize.

(*m*) The law does not provide for the manner of drawing lots. This is left to the interested parties to agree between themselves.

(*n*) In which case the promise of reward is irrevocable. 658, par. 2.

The transfer of ownership of the thing produced may be demanded by the promisor of the reward if he has specified in the notice of reward that such transfer shall be made.

TENTH TITLE.
Mandate.

662. By the acceptance of a mandate (o) the mandatary binds himself gratuitously to take charge of an affair (p) for the mandator entrusted to him by the latter (q).

663. A person who is publicly appointed or has publicly offered himself (r) for the charge of certain kinds of affairs is bound, if he does not accept a mandate relating to such affairs, to notify the mandator of his refusal without delay. The same rule applies if a person has offered himself to the mandator for the charge of certain kinds of affairs.

664. In case of doubt the mandatary cannot transfer the execution of the mandate to a third party. If the transfer is permitted, he is responsible only for fault imputable to him in making such transfer. For the fault of an assistant (s) he is responsible under 278.

In case of doubt the claim for execution of the mandate is not transferable.

665. A mandatary is entitled to deviate from the instructions of his mandator (t) if, under the circumstances, he can assume that the mandator would approve of the deviation if he had knowledge of the state of affairs. Before

---

(*o*) As to the time within which a mandate can be accepted, see 147.

(*p*) Any affair, be it a juristic act or not.

(*q*) The mandatary is liable to make compensation if he commits a breach of duty. If the mandate contains also a power of agency, the provisions of 164—166, 177—181, apply.

(*r*) *E.g.*, by advertisement in a newspaper.

(*s*) For his own fault, the mandatary is responsible under 276.

(*t*) In which case the provisions relating to management of affairs without mandate (677 *et seq.*) apply.

making any such deviation the mandatary shall give notice to the mandator and await his decision, unless there is danger in delay.

666. The mandatary is bound to give the mandator all necessary information; on demand to make a statement of the condition of the affair and to render an account [(u)] after the execution of the mandate.

667. A mandatary is bound to hand over to his mandator all that he receives for the execution of the mandate and all that he obtains from the charge of the affair.

668. If the mandatary spends money, for his own benefit, which he has to account to the mandator or to spend for him, he is bound to pay interest [(x)] upon it from the time of spending.

669. The mandator shall on demand make advances to the mandatary for the expenses necessary for the execution of the mandate.

670. If, for the purpose of the execution of the mandate, the mandatary incurs any outlay which he can regard as necessary under the circumstances, the mandator is bound to reimburse him.

671. A mandate may be revoked at any time by the mandator, and terminated by notice at any time by the mandatary.

The mandatary can give notice only in such manner that the mandator can make other arrangements for the charge of the affair, unless a grave reason exists for the improper notice. If he gives improper notice without such reason, he shall compensate the mandator for any damage arising therefrom.

If a grave reason exists the mandatary is entitled to give notice even though he has waived the right to do so.

672. In case of doubt a mandate is not extinguished by the death of the mandator, nor by his becoming incapable of disposing. If the mandate is extinguished, and if there is danger in delay, the mandatary shall continue the

(*u*) Cf. 259—261.

(*x*) At 4 per cent. 246.

charge of the affair entrusted to him until the heir or the statutory agent of the mandator can make other arrangements; the mandate is to such extent deemed to be continuing.

673. In case of doubt a mandate is extinguished by the death of the mandatary. If the mandate is extinguished, the heir of the mandatary shall, without delay, notify the mandatory of the death, and shall, if there is danger in delay, continue to take charge of the affair until the mandator can make other arrangements; the mandate is to such extent deemed to be continuing.

674. If a mandate is extinguished otherwise than by revocation, it is, nevertheless, deemed to be continuing in favour of the mandatary until he knows or ought to know of its extinction.

675. The provisions of 663, 665 to 670, 672 to 674 and, if the person bound has the right to give notice without observance of any term of notice, the provisions also of 671, par. 2, apply *mutatis mutandis* to a contract for service or a contract for work which has for its object the charge of an affair.

676. A person who gives advice or a recommendation to another is not bound to compensate for any damage arising from following the advice or the recommendation, without prejudice to his responsibility resulting from a contract or an unlawful act [y].

ELEVENTH TITLE.
Management of Affairs without Mandate [z].

677. A person who takes charge of an affair for another [a] without having received a mandate from him or being otherwise entitled to do so in respect of him, shall manage the affair in such manner as the interest of the principal requires, having regard to his actual or presumptive wishes.

(*y*) Cf. 823, 824, 826.

(*z*) This is the *negotiorum gestio* of the Roman law.

(*a*) Cf. 686.

678. If the undertaking of the management of the affair is opposed to the actual or presumptive wishes of the principal, and if the agent must have recognised this, he is bound to compensate the principal for any damage arising from his management of the affair, even if no fault is otherwise imputable to him.

679. The fact that the management of the affair is opposed to the wishes of the principal is not taken into consideration if, without the management of the affair, a duty of the principal the fulfilment of which is of public interest or a statutory duty to furnish maintenance to others by the principal would not be fulfilled in due time.

680. If the management of the affair has for its object the averting of an imminent danger which threatens the principal [(b)], the agent is responsible only for wilful default and gross negligence.

681. The agent shall notify to the principal, as soon as practicable, the undertaking of the management of the affair, and await his decision, unless there is danger in delay. For the rest the provisions of 666 to 668 applicable to a mandatary apply *mutatis mutandis* to the obligations of the agent.

682. If the agent is incapable of disposing, or limited in disposing capacity, he is responsible only under the provisions relating to compensation for unlawful acts [(c)], and to the return of unjustified benefits [(d)].

683. If the undertaking of the management of the affair is in accordance with the interest and the actual or presumptive wishes of the principal, the agent may demand reimbursement of his outlay as a mandatary. In the cases provided for by 679 this claim belongs to the agent even if the undertaking of the management of the affair is opposed to the wishes of the principal.

684. If the conditions of 683 do not exist, the principal is bound to return to the agent all that he acquires through the management of the affair under the

---

(*b*) Or a near relative of the principal.

(*c*) Cf. 823 *et seq*.

(*d*) Cf. 812 *et seq*.

provisions relating to the return of unjustified benefits. If the principal ratifies the management of the affair, the claim specified in 683 belongs to the agent.

685. The agent does not have any claim if he had not the intention to demand reimbursement from the principal [(e)].

If parents or grandparents furnish maintenance to their descendants, or *vice versâ*, it is to be presumed, in case of doubt, that there is do intention to demand reimbursement from the recipient.

686. If the agent is under a mistake as to the identity of the principal, the actual principal acquires the rights and obligations arising from the management of the affair.

687. The provisions of 677 to 686 do not apply, if a person takes charge of the affair of another in the belief that it is his own.

If a person treats the affair of another as his own, although knowing that he is not entitled to do so, the principal may enforce the claims based on 677, 678, 681, 682. If he does enforce them, he is liable to the agent as provided for in 684, sentence 1.

TWELFTH TITLE.
Deposit [(f)].

688. By a contract of deposit the depositary is bound to keep in his custody a moveable delivered to him by the depositor.

689. Remuneration for the custody is deemed to have been tacitly agreed upon if under the circumstances the undertaking of the custody is to be expected only for remuneration.

690. If the custody is undertaken gratuitously, the depositary shall be responsible only for such care as he is accustomed to exercise in his own affairs.

(*e*) The *onus probandi* rests upon the principal.

(*f*) Any provision under this title may be modified by agreement between the parties.

691. The depositary is, in case of doubt, not entitled to deposit the deposited thing with a third party. If deposit with a third party is permitted, the depositary is responsible only for his fault in making such deposit. For the fault of an assistant he is responsible as provided for in 278.

692. A depositary is entitled to change the manner of custody agreed upon if, under the circumstances, he may assume that the depositor would approve of the change if he had knowledge of the state of affairs. Before making any such change the depositary shall give notice to the depositor and await his decision, unless there is danger in delay.

693. If a depositary, for the custody of the deposited thing, incurs any outlay which, under the circumstances, he may regard, as necessary, the depositor is bound to reimburse him.

694. The depositor shall compensate the depositary for any damage caused, by the character of the thing deposited, unless at the time of the deposit he neither knew nor ought to have known of the dangerous character of the thing, or unless he gave notice of it to the depositary, or the latter knew it without notice.

695. The depositor may at any time demand the return of the thing deposited, even if a time is fixed for the custody.

696. The depositary may, if a time for the custody is not fixed, require that the thing deposited be taken back at any time [(g)]. If a time is fixed, he may require that it be taken back before the time only if a grave reason exists.

697. The return of the thing deposited shall be made at the place where the thing was to be kept [(h)]; the depositary is not bound to bring the thing to the depositor [(i)].

698. If the depositary spends any deposited money for his own benefit he

(*g*) The depositor must, however, be allowed a reasonable time to remove the thing.

(*h*) The depositor bears the costs and the risk of the return of the thing.

(*i*) The depositary has a right of lien on the thing deposited. 273.

is bound to pay interest [k] upon it from the time of the spending.

699. The depositor shall, at the time of the termination of the custody, pay the remuneration agreed upon. If the remuneration is measured by periods of time it is payable at the end of each of the periods.

If the custody ends before the expiration of the time fixed for it, the depositary may demand a part of the remuneration proportional to his services rendered, unless a contrary intention appears from the agreement as to remuneration.

700. If fungible things are deposited in such manner that the ownership is to pass to the depositary, and he is to be bound to return things of the same kind, quality and quantity, the provisions relating to loan for consumption apply. If the depositor permits the depositary to consume deposited fungible things, the provisions relating to loan for consumption apply as from the time at which the depositary appropriates the things [l]. In both cases, however, the time and place of return is determined, in case of doubt, according to the provisions relating to the contract of deposit.

In the case of deposit of negotiable instruments, an agreement of the kind specified in par. 1 is valid only if it be made in express terms.

THIRTEENTH TITLE.

Delivery of Things to Innkeepers [m].

701. An innkeeper who makes a business of receiving and lodging guests shall compensate a guest received in the course of business for any damage which the latter suffers through the loss or damage of things brought upon his

---

(*k*) At the rate of 4 per cent. 246.

(*l*) This may be tacitly agreed upon. The rule is otherwise in the case of deposit of negotiable instruments. See the following paragraph.

(*m*) Proprietors of restaurants and those who let rooms (whether with or without board) are not innkeepers. Delivery of things to a hotel agent at a railway station has been held, according to the former decisions, to be delivery to the innkeeper.

premises. The duty to make compensation does not arise if the damages is caused by the guest, an attendant of the guest, or a person whom he has received, or if it occurs by reason of the character of the things, or by *vis major* (n).

Things are deemed to have been brought upon the premises which the guest has delivered to the innkeeper or the innkeeper's servants who have been appointed to receive the things or in the circumstances are deemed to have been so appointed, or which he has brought to a place designated to him by them, or in the absence of such designation, to a place provided for such purpose.

A posted notice whereby the innkeeper disclaims liability is of no effect (o).

702. For money, negotiable instruments, and valuables the innkeeper is liable under 701 only to the amount of one thousand marks, unless he receives these objects into his custody with knowledge of their character as valuables, or refuses to undertake the custody (p), or unless the damage is due to the fault of himself or of his servants.

703. The claim which a guest has under 701, 702, is extinguished, unless the guest gives notice to the innkeeper without delay after he has knowledge of the loss or the damage. The claim is not extinguished if the things were delivered to the innkeeper to be kept by him in his custody.

704. The innkeeper has a right of pledge over the things brought upon the premises by the guest by way of security for his claims for lodging and other services afforded to the guest in satisfaction of his needs, including disbursements. The provisions of 559, sentence 3, and 560 to 563 applicable to the right of pledge (q) of an ordinary lessor apply *mutatis mutandis*.

(n) In all these cases the *onus probandi* rests upon the innkeeper.

(o) He may, however, limit or entirely exclude his liability by special agreement with the guest.

(p) He cannot, however, refuse to *receive* these objects. He is then liable only to the amount of one thousand marks.

(q) Generally speaking, the right of pledge is extinguished on the removal of the thing from the premises. The guest can, however, prevent the exercise of the right of pledge by giving security in conformity with 232.

FOURTEENTH TITLE.
Partnership [r].

705. By a contract of partnership [s] the partners bind themselves mutually to promote the attainment of a common object in the manner specified by the contract, *e.g.*, to make the contributions [t] agreed upon.

706. In the absence of a contrary agreement, the partners shall make equal contributions.

If fungible or consumable things are to be contributed, it is to be presumed, in case of doubt, that they become common property of the partners [u]. The same rule applies to non-fungible and non-consumable things if they are to be contributed according to a valuation which is not intended merely for the distribution of profits.

The contribution of a partner may also consist in service to be rendered.

707. A partner is not bound to provide an increase of the contribution agreed upon, nor to make up the capital diminished by losses [x].

708. A partner, in the fulfilment of the duties imposed upon him, is responsible only for such care as he is accustomed to exercise in his own affairs.

709. The management of the affairs of the partnership belongs to all the partners in common; for every affair the consent of all the partners is necessary [y].

If, according to the contract of partnership, the majority of votes is to decide, the majority shall, in case of doubt, be reckoned according to the

---

(*r*) Book II of the Commercial Code contains special provisions relating to "commercial partnerships" (*Handelsgesellschaften*).

(*s*) Apart from the case provided for by 311, a contract of partnership may be either verbal or in writing.

(*t*) The contribution may consist in money, objects, or even services to be rendered.

(*u*) A partner who has contributed such things is liable as a seller for any defect thereof. 445, 493.

(*x*) Cf. 735.

(*y*) This is true even in the case where there is danger in delaying the affair.

number of the partners [z].

710. If, in the contract of partnership, the management of affairs is entrusted to one partner or to several partners, the other partners are excluded from the management of the business [a]. If the management of the business is entrusted to several partners the provisions of 709 apply *mutatis mutandis*.

711. If, according to the contract of partnership, the management of affairs belongs to all or to several partners in such manner that each is entitled to act alone, then each may oppose the undertaking of any affair by another. In case of opposition the affair must be left undone.

712. The authority conferred upon one partner by the contract of partnership to manage the business may be withdrawn from him by a unanimous resolution, or where, according to the contract of partnership the majority of votes decides, by a majority resolution of the other partners if a grave reason exists; such a reason is, *e.g.*, gross breach of duty or incapacity for the proper management of business.

The partner may also on his part resign the management of the business if a grave reason exists; the provisions of 671, pars. 2, 3 applicable to mandate apply *mutatis mutandis*.

713. The rights and obligations of the managing partners are determined according to the provisions of 664 to 670 applicable to mandate, unless a contrary intention appears from the partnership relation.

714. Where the authority to manage the business belongs to one partner according to the contract of partnership he is also authorized, in case of doubt, to represent the other partners in respect of third parties.

715. If, in the contract of partnership, one partner is authorized to represent the other partners in respect of third parties, the representative authority may be withdrawn only in conformity with 712, par. 1; and if it has been

---

(*z*) *I.e.*, not according to their share in contributions. Cf. 745.

(*a*) Cf. 716.

conferred in connection with the authority to manage the business, it may be withdrawn only in connection with such authority.

716. A partner may, even if he is excluded from the management of the business, personally inform himself of the affairs of the partnership; inspect the business books and papers of the partnership; and from them draw up a summary statement of the condition of the partnership property.

An agreement excluding or limiting this right does not prevent its exercise, if there is reason to suspect dishonest management of the business.

717. The claims which the partners have against each other arising from the partnership relation are not transferable. Claims belonging to a partner arising from his management of the business, where their satisfaction can be demanded before liquidation, and claims to a dividend and to what accrues to a partner in case of liquidation are excepted.

718. The contributions of the partners and the objects acquired for the partnership through the management of the business become common property of the partners (*i.e.*, partnership property).

Partnership property includes also what is acquired by virtue of a right forming part of the partnership property, or as compensation for the destruction, damage, or deprivation of an object forming part of such property.

719. A partner may not dispose of his share in the partnership property, or in the several objects belonging thereto; he is not entitled to demand partition [(a)].

A debtor may not set off a claim which he has against a single partner against a claim which belongs to the partnership property.

720. The fact that a claim acquired under 718, par. 1, belongs to the partnership property does not avail against the debtor until he has knowledge of such fact; the provisions of 406 to 408 apply *mutatis mutandis*.

(*a*) He may only give notice of the dissolution of the partnership under 723, and then bring about a liquidation under 730.

721. A partner may not demand a balancing of accounts and the division of profit and loss until after the dissolution of the partnership.

If the partnership is of more than one year's duration, in case of doubt the balancing of accounts and division of profits shall be made at the end of each business year.

722. If the shares of the partners in profit and loss are not specified, each partner has an equal share in the profit and loss, without regard to the kind and amount of his contribution.

If only the share in profit or in loss is specified, in case of doubt the provision applies to profit and loss.

723. If a partnership is not entered into for a fixed time, every partner may at any time give notice of its dissolution [(b)]. If a time is fixed, notice of dissolution may be given before the expiration of the time if a grave reason exists; such a reason exists, *e.g.*, where another partner wilfully or by gross negligence commits a breach of an important duty imposed upon him by the contract of partnership, or where the performance of such a duty becomes impossible. Under the same conditions, if a term of notice of dissolution is fixed notice may be given without observance of such term.

Notice may not be given at an improper time unless a grave reason exists for the improper notice. If a partner gives improper notice without such reason, he shall make compensation to the other partners for any damage arising therefrom.

An agreement whereby the right of giving notice is excluded or limited contrary to these provisions is void.

724. If a partnership is entered into for the lifetime of one of the partners, notice of its dissolution may be given in the same manner as in the case of a partnership entered into for an indeterminate time. The same applies if a partnership is tacitly continued after the expiration of the fixed time.

725. If a creditor of one partner has levied judicial attachment on the

---

(*b*) Cf. 736.

share of the partner in the partnership property, he may give notice of the dissolution of the partnership without observance of any term of notice, unless his title in the debt is only provisionally executory.

So long as the partnership exists the creditor may not enforce the right of the partner arising out of the partnership, with the exception of the claim to a dividend.

726. A partnership is dissolved if the object agreed upon has been attained or its attainment has become impossible.

727. A partnership is dissolved by the death of one of the partners, unless a contrary intention appears from the contract of partnership [(c)].

Where the partnership is dissolved by the death of one of the partners the heir of the deceased partner that without delay give notice of the death to the other partners, and shall, if there is danger in delay, carry on the affairs entrusted to the deceased by the contract of partnership until the other partners in common with him can make other arrangements [(d)]. In the same manner the other partners are bound to temporarily carry on the affairs entrusted to them. The partnership is to such extent deemed to be continuing.

728. A partnership is dissolved by the institution of bankruptcy proceedings against the property of one of the partners [(e)]. The provisions of 727, par. 2, sentence 2 and 3, apply.

729. Where a partnership is dissolved otherwise than by notice of dissolution, the authority to manage the business conferred by the contract of partnership on one partner is, nevertheless, deemed to be continuing in his favour, until he knows or ought to know of the dissolution.

730. After the dissolution of a partnership liquidation takes place among the partners in respect of the partnership property.

For the winding up of current affairs, for the taking up of new affairs

---

(*c*) Cf. 736

(*d*) The heir is liable in the same manner and to the same extent as the deceased partner.

(*e*) Cf. 736.

necessary thereto, and for the preservation and management of the partnership property, the partnership is deemed to be continuing so far as is necessary for carrying out the object of the liquidation (f). The authority to manage the business which one partner has under the contract of partnership is, however, extinguished on the dissolution of the partnership, unless a contrary intention appears from the contract; the management of the business belongs, from and after the dissolution, to all the partners in common.

731. The liquidation takes place, in the absence of a contrary agreement, in accordance with 732 to 735 (g). For the rest the provisions relating to community of ownership apply to the partition.

732. Objects which a partner has made over to the partnership for use shall be given back to him. He may not demand compensation for an object which has been destroyed or damaged by accident.

733. Out of the partnership property shall first be settled the common debts (h), including those debts which, in respect of the creditors, are apportioned between the partners, or for which the other partners are liable as debtors to one partner (i). If a debt is not yet due or is contested, the amount necessary for its settlement shall be reserved.

Out of the partnership property remaining over after the settlement of the debts the contributions shall be returned. For contributions which did not consist in money, their value at the time they were made shall be substituted. For contributions which consisted in services or in the transfer of the use of an object compensation may not be demanded.

For the settlement of the debts and the return of the contributions the partnership property shall be converted into money so far as necessary.

734. After the settlement of the common debts and the return of the contributions the residue, if there is any, accrues to the partners in proportion to their

---

(f) This provision applies not only as between the parties *inter se*, but also as against third parties.

(g) Liquidators may be appointed to carry out the liquidation.

(h) *I.e.*, those obligations incurred in the course of the partnership business.

(i) This relates to the claims of a partner arising from his management of the partnership affairs.

shares in profit [k].

735. If the partnership property is not sufficient for the settlement of the common debts and the return of the contributions, the partners are responsible for the deficiency in the proportion in which they have to bear the losses [k]. If the contribution due from one of the partners cannot be obtained from him, the other partner shall bear the deficiency in the same proportion.

736. Where it is provided in the contract of partnership that if one of the partners gives notice of dissolution or dies, or if bankruptcy proceedings are instituted against his property, the partnership shall continue among the other partners, then in the event of such an occurrence such partner [l] retires from the partnership.

737. Where it is provided in the contract of partnership that if a partner gives notice of dissolution the partnership shall continue among the other partners, a partner may be removed from the partnership in respect of whom a circumstance occurs which, according to 723, par. 1, sentence 2, entitles the other partners to give notice of dissolution. The right of removal belongs to the other partners in common. The removal is effected by a declaration made to the partner to be removed.

738. If a partner retires from the partnership, his share in the partnership property accrues to the other partners. They are bound to return to the retiring partner, in conformity with 732, the objects which he has made over to the partnership for use; to release him from the common debts; and to pay to him what he would have received in liquidation, if the partnership had been dissolved at the time of his retirement. If common debts are not yet due, the other partners may give security to the retiring partner, instead of releasing him.

The value of the partnership property shall be ascertained, so far as necessary, by means of appraisement.

(*k*) Cf. 722.

(*l*) Or his heirs, in the case of his death.

739. If the value of the partnership property is not sufficient to cover the common debts and the contributions, the retiring partner shall be responsible to the other partners for the deficiency in the proportion of his share in losses (m).

740. The partner who has retired shares in the profit and loss which result from the affairs pending at the time of his retirement. The other partners are entitled to wind up these affairs in such manner as appears to them most advantageous.

The partner who has retired may, at the end of each business year, require an account of the affairs (n) wound up in the meantime, payment of the amount due to him, and information concerning the condition of still pending affairs (o).

FIFTEENTH TITLE.
Community of Ownership.

741. If a right belongs to several persons in common, the provisions of 742 to 758 apply (*i.e.*, community by undivided shares), unless it is otherwise provided by law (p).

742. In case of doubt it is to be presumed that equal shares belong to the participants.

743. To each participant a fractional part of the fruits (q) accrues proportional to his share.

Each participant is authorized to use the common object in so far as the joint use of the other participants is not thereby interfered with.

744. The management of the common object belongs to the participants in

(*m*) Cf. 722.

(*n*) Cf. 259.

(*o*) A partner who has retired cannot demand inspection of the business books and papers of the partnership.

(*p*) *E.g.*, partnership, community of goods under the various matrimonial régimes. 1437 *et seq.*

(*q*) Cf. 99 *et seq.*

common.

Each participant is entitled to take any measure necessary for the preservation of the object without the consent of the other participants; he may require that they give their approval in advance for such a measure.

745. By a vote of the majority regulations for management and use corresponding to the character of the common object may be determined upon. The vote of the majority shall be reckoned according to the value of the shares (r).

Each participant may, if the management and use are not regulated by agreement or by a vote of the majority, demand management and use in an equitable manner, having regard to the interests of all the participants.

An essential alteration of the object cannot be voted nor demanded. The right of the individual participant to a fractional part of the emoluments proportional to his share may not be infringed without his consent.

746. If the participants have regulated the management and use of the common object, the regulations made are effective both in favour of and as against all successors in title (s).

747. Each participant may dispose of his share (t). The participants may dispose of the common object only as a whole and only when they are acting in common.

748. Each participant is bound towards the other participants to bear the burdens of the common object and the costs of preservation, management and common use in proportion to his share.

749. Each participant may at any time demand dissolution of the community.

If the right to demand dissolution is excluded by agreement permanently or for a time, the dissolution may, nevertheless, be demanded if a grave reason

---

(r) The rule is different in the case of partnerships. 709, par. 2.

(s) Cf. 1010. A judgment creditor who has levied compulsory execution on the share of a participant is also deemed to be a "successor in title" within the meaning of this provision.

(t) The other participants have no *statutory* right of pre-emption.

exists. Under the same conditions, if a term of notice is fixed dissolution may be demanded without observance of such term.

An agreement whereby the right to demand dissolution is excluded or limited contrary to these provisions is void.

750. If the participants have excluded for a time the right to demand dissolution of the community, in case of doubt the agreement becomes void on the death of one of the participants.

751. If the participants have excluded permanently or for a time the right to demand dissolution of the community, or have fixed a term of notice, the agreement is valid both in favour of and as against all successors in title [(u)]. If a creditor has levied judicial attachment on the share of one participant, he may demand dissolution of the community without regard to the agreement, unless his title in the debt is only provisionally executory.

752. The dissolution of the community is effected by partition in kind, if the common object or objects can be distributed without diminution of value into similar parts proportional to the shares of the participants. The distribution of equal parts among the participants is made by lot [(x)].

753. If partition in kind is impossible, the dissolution of the community is effected by sale of the common object under the provisions relating to sale of pledges [(y)]; in the case of land, by compulsory auction [(z)] and distribution of the proceeds. If alienation to a third party is not permitted [(a)], the object shall be sold by auction among the participants.

If the attempt to sell the object has no result, each participant may demand a second attempt; he shall, however, bear the costs if the second attempt fails.

754. The sale of a common claim is permissible only if it cannot as yet be

---

(*u*) See note (*s*) to 746.

(*x*) Cf. note (*m*) to 659.

(*y*) Cf. 1235 *et seq*.

(*z*) See 180 *et seq*. of the Compulsory Auction Act of March 24th, 1897.

(*a*) *E.g.*, by reason of a testamentary provision.

collected. If collection is possible each participant may demand common collection.

755. If the participants are liable as joint debtors for an obligation which they, in conformity with 748, have to fulfil in proportion to their shares, or which they have incurred far the purpose of fulfilling such an obligation, each participant [(b)] may, on the dissolution of the community, require that the debt be satisfied out of the common object.

The claim may also be enforced against all successors in title [(c)].

Where a sale of the common object is necessary for the satisfaction of a debt, the sale shall be made in the manner provided for by 753.

756. If one participant has a claim against another participant which is based on the community [(d)] he may, on the dissolution of the community, require satisfaction of his claim out of the part of the common object accruing to the debtor. The provisions of pars. 2, 3 apply.

757. If, on the dissolution of the community, a common object is allotted to one of the participants, each of the other participants for his share shall give a warranty against defects of title [(e)] or of quality [(f)] in the same manner as a seller.

758. The claim for dissolution of the community is not subject to prescription [(g)].

(*b*) But not the creditors.

(*c*) See note (*s*) to 746.

(*d*) *E.g.*, the claim for compensation under 748.

(*e*) See 433—444.

(*f*) See 459—493.

(*g*) Other claims arising from the community are subject to prescription.

SIXTEENTH TITLE.
Annuities.

759. A person who is bound to provide an annuity (h) shall, in case of doubt, pay the annuity for the lifetime of the annuitant.

The amount specified for the annuity is, in case of doubt, the yearly amount of the annuity (i).

760. The annuity is payable in advance.

A money annuity is payable in advance by quarterly instalments; as regards any other kind of annuity the period of time for which it shall be paid in advance is determined according to the nature and object of the annuity.

If the annuitant was alive at the beginning of the period for which the annuity is to be paid in advance, the whole amount due for the period accrues to him.

761. For the validity of a contract whereby an annuity is promised the promise is required to be in writing (k), unless some other form is prescribed.

SEVENTEENTH TITLE.
Gaming. Betting.

762. No obligation is created by gaming or betting. What has been given by reason of the gaming or betting may not be demanded back on the ground that no obligation existed (l).

These provisions apply also to an agreement whereby the losing party, for the purpose of satisfying a gaming debt or a bet, incurs an obligation towards the

---

(*h*) This may be created either by contract or by testamentary disposition.

(*i*) The claim for arrears of annuity is barred by prescription in four years. 197.

(*k*) See 126. The acceptance of the promise used not be in writing.

(*l*) The claim for the return of what has been given may, however, be enforced on other grounds, *e.g.*, fraud, threats, &c.

other party, *e.g.*, an acknowledgment of debt [(m)].

763. A lottery contract or a raffle contract is binding if the lottery or the raffle is ratified by the Government. In all other cases the provisions of 762 apply.

764. If a contract purporting to be for the delivery of goods or negotiable instruments is entered into with the intention that the difference between the price agreed upon and the exchange or market price at the time of delivery shall be paid by the losing to the winning party, the contract shall be deemed to be a gaming contract. This applied also if only one of the parties knows or ought to know of this intention.

EIGHTEENTH TITLE.

Suretyship.

765. By a contract of suretyship [(n)], the surety binds himself to the creditor of a third party to be responsible for the fulfilment of the obligation of the third party [(o)].

Suretyship may also be assumed for a future or conditional obligation.

766. A written statement [(p)] of the declaration of suretyship is necessary for the validity of the contract of suretyship. Where the surety fulfils the principal obligation all defects of form are cured.

767. The extent of the principal obligation at any time determines the obligation of the surety. This applies also, *e.g.*, where the principal obligation becomes altered by the fault or default of the principal debtor. The obligation of the surety is not increased by any juristic act entered into by the principal debtor after the assumption of the suretyship.

(*m*) See 781 *et seq.*

(*n*) For cases of what might be termed "statutory suretyship", see 571. par. 2, 1251, par. 2.

(*o*) If the obligation of the third party is void, the contract of suretyship is also void.

(*p*) The acceptance of the declaration of suretyship need not be in writing.

The surety is liable for the costs of notice and suit to be paid by the principal debtor to the creditor.

768. A surety may set up all defences belonging to the principal debtor. If the principal debtor dies the surety may not avail himself of the fact that the heir has only a limited liability for the obligation.

The surely does not lose a defence by reason of the fact that the principal debtor has waived it.

769. If several persons make themselves sureties for the same obligation they are liable as joint debtors, even though they do not assume the suretyship in common.

770. A surety may refuse to satisfy the creditor so long as the principal debtor has the right to avoid the juristic act on which his obligation is based [q].

The surety has the same right, so long as the creditor can satisfy himself by set-off against a matured claim of the principal debtor.

771. A surety may refuse to satisfy the creditor so long as the creditor has not attempted compulsory execution against the principal debtor without result (*i.e.*, a plea of *beneficium excussionis*).

772. If a suretyship exists for a money claim compulsory execution on the moveables of the principal debtor must be attempted at his place of domicile, and if the principal debtor's industry is located in another place, also at such other place; in the absence of a domicile and of an industrial location, at the place of his residence.

If the creditor has a right of pledge or lien on a moveable of the principal debtor, he must also seek satisfaction out of such moveable. If such a right in the thing belongs to the creditor also for another claim, this applies only if both claims are covered by the value of the thing.

773. The plea of *beneficium excussionis* is barred:

(*q*) The surety may not, however, avoid the juristic act himself.

(1) if the surety has waived the plea, *e.g.*, if he has assumed the suretyship in such manner that he is himself a principal debtor [(r)];

(2) if the difficulty of bringing an action against the principal debtor is materially increased in consequence of a change of domicile, industrial location, or place of residence of the principal debtor, occurring after the assumption of the suretyship;

(3) if bankruptcy proceedings have been instituted against the property of the principal debtor;

(4) if it may be presumed that compulsory execution on the property of the principal debtor will not lead to the satisfaction of the creditor.

In the cases provided for by (3) and (4) the plea of *beneficium excussionis* is permissible where the creditor can satisfy himself out of a moveable of the principal debtor over which he has a right of pledge or lien; the provision of 772, par. 2, sentence 2, applies.

774. Where the surety satisfied the creditor the claim of the creditor against the principal debtor is transferred to him. The transfer may not be enforced to the detriment of the creditor. Defences of the principal debtor arising from a legal relation existing between him and the surety remain unaffected.

Co-sureties are liable to each other only according to 426.

775. If the surety has assumed the suretyship by reason of a mandate [(s)] of the principal debtor, or if he has the rights of a mandatary against the principal debtor under the provisions relating to management of affairs without mandate [(t)] on account of the assumption of the suretyship, he can demand from him relief from the suretyship:

(1) if the pecuniary condition of the principal debtor has become materially worse;

(2) if the difficulty of bringing an action against the principal debtor is materially increased in consequence of a change of domicile, industrial location, or place of residence of the principal debtor, occurring after

(*r*) In this case the surety and the principal debtor are liable as joint debtors. 421.

(*s*) Cf. 662 *et seq.*

(*t*) Cf. 677 *et seq.*, especially 683, 684, sentence 2.

the assumption of the suretyship;

(3) if the principal debtor is in default with the fulfilment of his obligation;

(4) if the creditor has obtained an executory judgment for fulfilment against the surety.

If the principal obligation is not yet due the principal debtor may give security to the surety instead of relieving him.

776. If the creditor waives a right of preference connected with his claim, or a hypotheca or a right of pledge by which his claim is secured, or his right against a co-surety, the surety is discharged in so far as he could have obtained compensation by virtue of the waived right as provided for is 774. This applies also if the waived right was not created until after the assumption of the suretyship.

777. If a surety has assumed his suretyship for an existing obligation for a fixed time he is discharged after the expiration of the fixed time, unless the creditor proceeds without delay to the collection of the claim in conformity with 772, continues the process without serious delay, and, after the termination of the process, notifies the surety without delay that he has recourse to him. If the surety has not the plea of *beneficium excussionis* he is discharged after the expiration of the fixed time, unless the creditor gives him notice without delay.

If notice is given in due time the liability of the surety is limited, in the case provided for by par. 1, sentence 1, to the extent of the principal obligation at the time of the termination of the process; in the case provided for by par. 1, sentence 2, to the extent of the principal obligation at the expiration of the fixed time.

778. A person who gives a mandate to another to give credit to a third party in his own name and on his own account is liable to the mandatary as a surety for the obligation of the third party arising from the giving of credit [(u)].

(*u*) Before the credit has been given, the provisions relating to mandate apply; the mandate need not be in writing (cf. 766), and is revocable at any time (671). After the credit has been given, the provisions relating to suretyship apply.

NINETEENTH TITLE.
Compromise (x).

779. A contract whereby the dispute (y) or the uncertainty of the parties concerning a legal relation is ended by way of mutual concession (*i.e.*, a compromise) is not binding if the state of affairs taken as the basis according to the terms of the contract do not correspond with the actual facts, and if the dispute or the uncertainty would not have arisen if the state of affairs had been known.

It is equivalent to uncertainty concerning a legal relation, if the realisation of a claim is uncertain (z).

TWENTIETH TITLE.
Promise of Debt. Acknowledgment of Debt.

780. For the validity of a contract whereby an act of performance is promised in such manner that the promise itself (a) is to create the obligation (*i.e.*, a promise of debt), a written statement (b) of the promise is necessary unless some other form is prescribed.

781. For the validity of a contract whereby the existence of an obligation is acknowledged (*i.e.*, an acknowledgment of debt), a written statement (b) of the declaration of acknowledgment is necessary. If some other form is prescribed for the creation of the obligation whose existence is acknowledged, the contract of acknowledgment shall be made in such other form.

(x) A contract of compromise is subject to the general provisions relating to contracts; it used not, therefore, be made in any particular form. However, where alienation of land, gift or suretyship forms an essential part of a contract of compromise, the respective forms prescribed for such juristic acts must be observed.

(y) The dispute need not be a law-suit.

(z) *E.g.*, owing to the insolvency of the debtor.

(a) That is to say, the obligation rests *solely upon the fact of the promise*, no matter what the ground for the promise might be, as, for instance, a loan or a sale, or a gift, &c.

(b) The acceptance, however, need not be in writing.

782. If a promise of debt or an acknowledgment of debt is issued in consequence of an agreed account [c], or by way of compromise, the written form prescribed in 780, 781 is not necessary.

TWENTY-FIRST TITLE.
Orders to Pay or Deliver.

783. If a person delivers an instrument to a third party in which he directs another to pay or deliver money, negotiable instruments, or other fungible things [d] to the third party, the latter is authorized to procure payment or delivery in his own name from the drawee; the drawee is authorized to pay or deliver to the payee of the order on account of the drawer.

784. If the drawee accepts the order he is bound to make payment or delivery to the payee; he may set up against him only the defences which affect the validity of the acceptance, or result from the tenor of the order or of the acceptance, or which the drawee has directly against the payee.

The acceptance is made by a written note on the order. If the note has been placed on the order before its delivery to the payee, the acceptance becomes effective in his favour only upon delivery.

785. The drawee is bound to make payment or delivery only on delivery of the order.

786. The claim of the payee against the drawee arising from the acceptance is barred by prescription in three years [e].

787. In the case of an order upon a debt the drawee, by his payment or delivery, is released from the debt to the amount thereof.

The drawee is not bound to the drawer to accept the order or to make

---

(*c*) See 350 of the Commercial Code.

(*d*) Cf. 91.

(*e*) The period begins to run from the delivery of the order to the payee. Cf. 198.

payment or delivery to the payee merely because he is a debtor of the drawer.

788. If a drawer issues an order for the purpose of making payment or delivery due from him to the payee, then, even if the drawee accepts the order, the payment or delivery is not made until payment or delivery by the drawee to the payee.

789. If a drawee refuses acceptance before the arrival of the time for payment or delivery, or if he refuses the payment or delivery, the payee shall give notice [(f)] to the drawer without delay. The same applies even if the payee cannot or will not enforce the order.

790. A drawer may revoke his order as against the drawee, so long as the drawee has not accepted the order in favour of the payee, or has not made payment or delivery. This applies even though the drawer by the revocation acts contrary to an obligation imposed upon him in favour of the payee.

791. An order to pay or deliver is not extinguished by the death or occurrence of disposing incapacity of one of the parties.

792. The payee may, by contract with a third party, transfer the order to him, even if it has not yet been accepted. The declaration of transfer is required to be in writing. The delivery of the order to the third party is necessary for such transfer.

The drawer may exclude the transfer. The exclusion is effective against the drawee only if it appears from the order itself, or if it has been communicated by the drawer to the drawee before the latter accepts the order or makes payment or delivery.

If the drawee accepts the order in favour of the transferee, he may not set up any defences from any legal relation existing between himself and the payee. For the rest, the provisions applicable to the assignment of a claim [(g)] apply *mutatis mutandis* to the transfer of the order.

(*f*) Failure to give such notice will render him liable to make compensation.

(*g*) Cf. 398 *et seq.*

TWENTY-SECOND TITLE.
Obligations to Bearer.

793. If a person has issued an instrument in which he promises to perform an act [(h)] in favour of the bearer [(i)] of the instrument (*i.e.*, an obligation to bearer [(k)]), the bearer may require him to effect the promised performance, unless he is not entitled to dispose of the instrument [(l)]. The maker is, however, released from his obligation by performing in favour of a bearer, even though the latter is not entitled to dispose of the instrument.

The validity of the signature may, by a provision contained in the instrument, be made subject to the observance of a particular form. For the signature a subscription made by means of mechanical reproduction is sufficient.

794. The maker is bound by an obligation to bearer even if it has been stolen from him, or lost by him, or has otherwise passed into circulation without his consent.

The validity of an obligation to bearer is not affected by the fact that the instrument is issued after the maker has died or has become incapable of disposing.

795. Obligations to bearer issued within the Empire in which the payment of a certain sum of money is promised may be put in circulation only with the ratification of the Government [(m)].

The ratification is given by the central authority of the State in whose territory the maker has his domicile or his industrial location. The giving of the ratification and the conditions under which it is given shall be published in the *Deutscher Reichsanzeiger* [(n)].

(*h*) The act need not necessarily be the payment of a sum of money or the delivery of a thing.

(*i*) *I.e.*, not to a person named in the instrument. Cf. 808.

(*k*) The most common examples are Government bonds, bank notes, theatre tickets, railway tickets, meal tickets, bathing tickets, and many others. Shares of stock in a joint-stock company are not, however, "obligations to bearer", since they do not contain any promise to perform an act.

(*l*) *E.g.*, if he is a mere depositary, finder, or thief.

(*m*) Cf. IA, Art. 34, IV.

(*n*) *I.e.*, Imperial German Gazette.

An obligation which has passed into circulation without the ratification of the Government is void; the maker shall compensate the bearer for any damage caused by its issue.

These provisions do not apply to obligations which are issued by the Empire or by a State.

796. The maker may set up against the bearer of the obligation only the defences which affect the validity of the issue [o], or appear from the instrument itself, or which the maker has directly against the bearer.

797. The maker is bound to perform only upon delivery of the instrument. Upon delivery he acquires ownership of the instrument, even if the bearer is not entitled to dispose of it.

798. If an obligation to bearer is no longer fit for circulation in consequence of damage or defacement, the bearer may, where its essential contents and its distinctive marks are still recognisable with certainty, require the maker to issue a new obligation to bearer on delivery of the damaged or defaced one. The bearer shall bear and advance the costs.

799. A lost or destroyed obligation to bearer may, unless the contrary is provided for in the instrument, be declared void by means of the procedure by public summons [p]. Interest coupons, annuity coupons, dividend coupons, and non-interest bearing obligations payable at sight are excepted.

The maker is bound to give to the former bearer on demand all information necessary for the public summons or for stoppage of payment, and to issue the necessary certificates. The former bearer shall bear and advance the costs of the certification.

800. If an obligation to bearer has been declared void, the person who has obtained the decree far avoidance may, without prejudice to his right to enforce the claim arising from the instrument, require the maker to issue a new obligation to bearer in place of the one declared void. The person who requires the

---

(*o*) *E.g.*, the defence of the disposing incapacity of the maker.

(*p*) See 946 *et seq.* and 1003 *et seq.* of the Code of Civil Procedure.

issue of the new obligation shall bear and advance the costs.

801. Any claim arising from an obligation to bearer is extinguished on the expiration of thirty years after the arrival of the time fixed for performance, unless the instrument is presented to the maker for redemption before the expiration of the thirty years. If the presentation is made the claim is barred by prescription in two years from the expiration of the term for presentation. The enforcement in court of the claim arising from the instrument is equivalent to presentation.

In the case of interest coupons, annuity coupons, and dividend coupons, the term for presentation is four years. The term begins to run from the expiration of the year in which the time fixed for performance arrives.

The duration and beginning of the term for presentation may be otherwise provided for in the instrument by the maker.

802. The beginning and the running of the term for presentation and also prescription are suspended in favour of the applicant by the stoppage of payment. The suspension begins with the presentation of the application for the stoppage of payment; it ends on the termination of the proceedings by public summons; and, where the stoppage of payment has been ordered before the institution of the proceedings, the suspension also comes to an end if six months have elapsed since the removal of the obstacle preventing the institution of the proceedings and such institution has not previously been applied for. The provisions of 203, 206, 207 apply *mutatis mutandis* to this term.

803. If interest coupons have been issued for an obligation to bearer, the coupons, unless they contain a contrary provision, remain in force even if the principal obligation is extinguished or the obligation to pay interest is extinguished or modified.

If the interest coupons are not returned on the redemption of the principal obligation, the maker is entitled to retain the amount which he is bound to pay for the coupons as provided for in par. 1.

804. If an interest coupon, annuity coupon, or dividend coupon has been lost or destroyed, and the former bearer has given notice of the loss to the maker before the expiration of the term for presentation, the former bearer may demand performance by the maker after the expiration of the term. The claim is barred if the lost coupon has been presented to the maker for redemption, or the claim arising from the coupon has been enforced in court, unless the presentation or the enforcement in court has occurred after the expiration of the term. The claim is barred by prescription in four years.

As regards interest coupons, annuity coupons, or dividend coupons, the claim specified in par. 1 may be excluded [q].

805. New interest coupons or annuity coupons for an obligation to bearer may not be delivered to the bearer of an instrument authorizing receipt of the coupon (*i.e.*, a renewal coupon) if the bearer of the obligation has prohibited the delivery. In such a case the coupons shall be delivered to the bearer of the obligation if he presents it.

806. The conversion of an obligation made payable to bearer into an obligation to a named payee may be effected only by the maker. The maker is not bound so to convert it.

807. If tickets, checks, or similar instruments in which a creditor is not named are issued by the maker under circumstances from which it appears that he intends to be bound to perform in favour of the bearer, the provisions of 793, par. 1, and 794, 796, 797 apply *mutatis mutandis*.

808. If an instrument in which the creditor is named is issued with the provision that the performance promised in the instrument may be effected in favour of any bearer, the debtor is discharged by performing in favour of the bearer of the instrument. The bearer is not entitled to demand performance.

The debtor is bound to perform only upon delivery of the instrument. If the instrument is lost or destroyed, it may be declared void, unless it is otherwise provided, by means of the procedure by public summons. The provisions contained in 802 relating to prescription apply.

(*q*) Cf. IA, Art. 100 (2).

TWENTY-THIRD TITLE.
Production of Things.

809. A person who has a claim against the possessor of a thing in respect of the thing, or wishes to ascertain whether he has such a claim [r], may, if the inspection of the thing is of interest to him for this reason require the possessor to produce the thing for his inspection or to permit his inspection [s].

810. A person who has a legal interest in the examination of a document in the possession of another may demand the possessor to permit him to examine it, if the document is made in his interest, or if in the document a legal relation existing between himself and another is recorded, or if the document contains the negotiations of any juristic act which have been carried on between him and another person, or between one of them and a common intermediary.

811. In the cases provided for by 809, 810 the production shall be made in the place where the thing to be produced is. Either party may require production in some other place if a grave reason exists [t].

The risk and the cost shall be borne by the person asking for the production. The possessor may refuse production until the other party advances to him the costs and gives security against the risk.

TWENTY-FOURTH TITLE.
Unjustified Benefits.

812. A person who, through an act performed [u] by another, or in any other manner, acquires something at the expense of the latter without legal

---

(*r*) An example of this is the case where he believes that another person is in possession of a thing stolen from him.

(*s*) The person asking for inspection has to prove that the conditions exist which give him the right to do so.

(*t*) *E.g.*, illness of the person asking for the production of the thing.

(*u*) Performance may consist in a forbearance. 241.

ground, is bound to return it [x] to him. He is so bound even if a legal ground originally existing disappears subsequently, or a result originally intended to be produced by an act of performance done by virtue of a juristic act is not produced [y].

Recognition of the existence or non-existence of a debt [z], if made under a contract, is also deemed to be an act of performance.

813. The value of an act of performance done for the purpose of fulfilling an obligation may be demanded back even if there was a defence to the claim whereby the enforcement of the claim was permanently barred. The provision of 222, par. 2, remains unaffected.

If an obligation due on a certain date is fulfilled in advance, the claim for return is barred; the discounting of *interim* interest may not be demanded.

814. The value of an act of performance done for the purpose of fulfilling an obligation may not be demanded back if the person performing knew that he was not bound to effect the performance, or if the performance was in compliance with a moral duty, or the rules of social propriety.

815. The claim for return on account of the non-production of the result intended to be produced by an act of performance is barred, if the production of the result was impossible *ab initio*, and the person performing knew this, or if he has prevented the production of the result in bad faith.

816. If a person without title makes a disposition of an object which is binding upon the person having title, he is bound to hand over to the latter what he has obtained by the disposition. If the disposition is made gratuitously, the same obligation is imposed upon the person who acquires a legal advantage directly through the disposition.

If an act of performance is done for the benefit of a person not entitled thereto, which is effective against the person entitled, the former is bound to hand over to the latter the value of such performance.

(*x*) In accordance with 813, 814.

(*y*) A striking instance of this is the revocation of a gift.

(*z*) Cf. 782, 397, par. 2.

817. If the purpose of an act of performance was specified in such manner that its acceptance by the recipient constitutes an infringement of a statutory prohibition or is *contra bonos mores*, the recipient is bound to make restitution. The claim for return is barred if the person performing is *in pari delicto* unless the performance consisted in the incurring of an obligation; what has been given for the performance of such an obligation may not be demanded back.

818. The obligation to return extends to emolument [(a)] derived, and to whatever the recipient acquires either by virtue of a right obtained by him, or as compensation for the destruction, damage or deprivation of the object obtained.

If the return is impossible on account of the nature of the object obtained [(b)], or if the recipient for any other reason [(c)] is not in a position to make the return, he shall make good the value.

The obligation to return or to make good the value is excluded where the recipient is no longer benefited [(d)].

After the date of action commenced the recipient is liable under the general provisions [(e)].

819. If the recipient knows of the absence of legal ground at the time of the receipt, or if he subsequently learns it, he is bound to return from the time of receipt or of acquisition of the knowledge as if an action on the claim for return were commenced at that time [(f)].

If the recipient, by the acceptance of an act of performance, infringes a statutory prohibition or acts *contra bonos mores*, he is bound in the same manner after the receipt of the performance.

820. If a result was intended to be produced by an act of performance,

---

(*a*) Cf. 100.

(*b*) *E.g.*, supply of light, heat, &c.

(*c*) *E.g.*, on account of confusion or specification. 946—951. The *onus probandi* rests upon the recipient.

(*d*) The recipient has the *onus probandi*.

(*e*) Cf. 291, 292, 987—990.

(*f*) Cf. note (*e*) to 818.

and if the production of such a result was, according to the scope of the juristic act, regarded as doubtful, the recipient is, where the result is not produced, bound to return in the same manner as if action were commenced on the claim for return at the time of the receipt (g). The same rule applies if the performance was made on a legal ground whose disappearance was regarded as possible according to the scope of the juristic act, and the legal ground disappears.

The recipient is bound to pay interest (h) only from the time at which he learns that the result hat not been produced, or that the legal ground has disappeared; for the return of emoluments he is not bound in so far as he is no longer benefited at that time.

821. A person who incurs an obligation without legal ground may refuse performance, even if the claim for release from the obligation has been barred by prescription.

822. If the recipient of a benefit transfers such benefit gratuitously to a third party, and if in consequence of this the obligation of the recipient for return of the benefit is excluded, the third party is bound to return the benefit as if he had received it from the creditor without legal ground.

TWENTY-FIFTH TITLE.
Unlawful Acts.

823. A person who, wilfully or negligently (i), unlawfully injures the life (k), body, health, freedom, property or any other right of another is bound to compensate him (l) for any damage arising therefrom.

A person who infringes a statutory provision intended for the protection of

---

(*g*) Cf. note (*e*) to 818.

(*h*) At the rate of 4 per cent. 246.

(*i*) Cf. 276.

(*k*) Injury to life = killing. Other injuries, although endangering the life of the injured party, are deemed to be injuries to "body" and "health".

(*l*) As to the extent of the compensation, see 842—853.

others incurs the same obligation. If, according to the purview of the statute, infringement is possible even without any fault on the part of the wrong-doer, the duty to make compensation arises only if some fault can be imputed to him.

824. A person who maintains or publishes, contrary to the truth, a statement calculated to endanger the credit of another, or to injure his earnings or prosperity in any other manner, shall compensate the other for any damage arising therefrom, even if he does not know of its untruth, provided he ought to know it.

A person who makes a communication the untruth of which is unknown to him, does not thereby render himself liable to make compensation, if he or the receiver of the communication has a legal interest in it.

825. A person who by fraud or threats, or by an abuse of a relation of dependence, induces a woman to permit illicit cohabitation, is bound to compensate her for any damage arising therefrom.

826. A person who wilfully causes damage to another in a manner *contra bonos mores* is bound to compensate the other for the damage (m).

827. A person who causes damage to another in a condition of unconsciousness, or in a condition of morbid disturbance of the mental activity, incompatible with a free determination of the will, is not responsible for the damage (n). If he has brought himself into a temporary condition of this kind by spirituous liquors or similar means (o), he is responsible for any damage which he in this condition unlawfully causes in the same manner as if negligence were imputable to him; the responsibility does not arise if he has been brought into this condition without fault (p).

828. A person who has not completed his seventh year of age is not res-

(m) A juristic act *contra bonos mores* is void. 138.

(n) For exception, see 829. He cannot be held criminally responsible in any case. 51 of the Criminal Code.

(o) *E.g.*, opium, morphine.

(p) The *onus probandi* rests upon the person who avails himself of this excuse.

ponsible for any damage which he causes to another.

A person who has completed his seventh but not his eighteenth year of age is not responsible for any damage which he causes to another, if he at the time of committing the damaging act did not have the understanding necessary for realising his responsibility. The same rule applies to a deaf mute [(q)].

829. A person who, in any one of the cases specified in 823 to 826, is, by virtue of 827, 828 not responsible for any damage caused by him, shall, nevertheless, where compensation cannot be obtained from a third party charged with the duty of supervision [(r)], make compensation for damage in so far as according to the circumstances; *e.g.*, according to the relative positions of the parties [(s)], equity requires compensation [(t)], and he is not deprived of the means which he needs for his own maintenance suitable to his station in life and for the fulfilment of his statutory duties to furnish maintenance to others.

830. If several persons have caused any damage by an act committed in common, each is responsible for the damage [(u)]. The same rule applies if it cannot be discovered which of several participants has actually caused the damage.

Instigators and accomplices are in the same position, as joint-doers.

831. A person who employs another to do any work is bound to compensate for any damage which the other unlawfully causes to a third party in the performance of his work. The duty to compensate does not arise if the employer has exercised ordinary care in the selection of the employee, and, where he has to supply appliances or implements or to superintend the work, has also exercised ordinary care as regards such supply or superintendence or if the damage would have arisen, notwithstanding the exercise of such care [(x)].

(*q*) Responsibility is, however, the rule. The absence of the necessary understanding must be proved by the person asserting it.

(*r*) Cf. 832.

(*s*) *E.g.*, if the child causing the damage belongs to a rich family and the injured party is very poor.

(*t*) The determination of the question is within the discretion of the judge.

(*u*) They are liable as joint debtors. 840.

(*x*) The *onus probandi* rests upon the employer.

The same responsibility attaches to a person who, by contract with the employer, undertakes to take charge of any of the affairs specified in par. 1, sentence 2.

832. A person who is bound by law to exercise supervision over a person [(y)] who needs supervision on account of minority, or on account of his mental or physical condition, is bound to make compensation for any damage which the latter unlawfully causes to a third party. The duty to make compensation does not arise if he fulfils his duty of supervision, or if the damage would have been occasioned notwithstanding the exercise of proper supervision.

The same responsibility attaches to a person who undertakes the supervision by contract [(z)].

833. If a person is killed, or the body or health of a person is injured, or a thing is damaged by an animal [(a)], the person who keeps the animal [(b)] is bound to compensate the injured party for any damage arising therefrom.

834. A person who undertakes to take charge of an animal [(c)] under a contract with the keeper of the animal, is responsible for any damage which the animal causes to a third party in the manner specified in 833. The responsibility does not arise if he has exercised ordinary care in taking charge of the animal, or if the damage would have been occasioned notwithstanding the exercise of such care.

835. If land over which its owner does not have the sporting rights [(d)] is damaged by wild boar, red deer, elk, fallow deer, roe deer, or pheasants [(e)],

---

(*y*) *E.g.*, parents (1627, 1631, 1634), the mother of an illegitimate child (1707), a guardian (1793, 1800, 1897, 1901), the employer of an apprentice (126, 127 of the Industrial Code).

(*z*) *E.g.*, tutor, governor, &c.

(*a*) No matter whether it is a domestic animal or not.

(*b*) Whether he is the owner of the animal or whether any fault is imputable to him or not, is immaterial.

(*c*) *E.g.*, a herdsman.

(*d*) If the owner has the sporting rights, he can protect the land by shooting the animal.

(*e*) As to damage caused by other animals, see IA, Art. 71.

the person who has the sporting rights is bound to compensate the injured party [(f)] for the damage. The duty to make compensation extends to all damage which the animals do to products of the land which have been harvested, though not yet gathered in.

If the exercise of the sporting rights belonging to the owner is withdrawn from him by law, the person who is by law entitled to exercise the sporting rights has to make compensation for the damage. If the owner of a piece of land over which the sporting rights, on account of the situation of the land, can be exercised only in common with the sporting right over anther piece of land, has leased the sporting rights to the owner of such other piece of land under a usufructuary lease, the latter is responsible for the damage.

If for the purpose of a common exercised of the rights of sporting, the landowners of a district have been united by law into an association which is not liable as such, they are responsible for damage in proportion to the size of their landed properties.

836. If, by the fall of a building or other structure attached to a piece of land, or by the detachment of parts of the building or structure, a person is killed, or the body or health of a person is injured, or a thing is damaged, and if the fall or the detachment was caused by defective construction or insufficient maintenance, the possessor of the land is bound to compensate the injured party for any damage arising therefrom. The duty to make compensation does not arise if the possessor has exercised ordinary care for the purpose of averting the danger [(g)].

A former possessor of the land is responsible for the damage, if the fall or the detachment occurs within one year after the termination of his possession, unless during his possession he exercised ordinary care, or unless a subsequent possessor would have been able to avert the danger by the exercise of such care [(h)].

(*f*) Owner, or lessee, or usufructuary, &c., as the case may be.

(*g*) The possessor has the *onus probandi*.

(*h*) The former possessor has the *onus probandi*.

Only a proprietary possessor is a possessor within the meaning of these provisions (i).

837. If a person, in the exercise of a right, possesses a building or other structure on the land of another (k), the responsibility specified in 836 attaches to him instead of to the possessor of the land.

838. A person who undertakes for the possessor the maintenance of a building or a structure attached to land, or who has to maintain the building or the structure by virtue of a right of use belonging to him, is responsible in the same manner as the possessor for any damage caused by its fall or the detachment of its parts.

839. If an official wilfully or negligently commits a breach of official duty incumbent upon him as towards a third party, he shall compensate the third party for any damage arising therefrom (l). If only negligence is imputable to the official, he may be held liable only if the injured party is unable to obtain compensation elsewhere (m).

If an official commits a breach of his official duty in giving judgment in an action, he is not responsible for any damage arising therefrom, unless the breach of duty is punished with a public penalty to be enforced by criminal proceedings (n). This provision does not apply to a breach of duty consisting in the refusal or delay in the exercise of the office.

The duty to make compensation does not arise if the injured party has wilfully or negligently omitted to obviate the injury by making use of a legal

---

(*i*) A Lessee or usufructuary, although entitled to the possession of the thing which is subject to his right, is not deemed to be a possessor within the meaning of 836. Cf., however, 837.

(*k*) *E.g.*, in the case of where a person entitled to a heritable building right (1012—1014) or a usufructuary lessee has erected a building or other structure on the land.

(*l*) Cf. 249 *et seq.*

(*m*) The *onus probandi* rests upon the injured party. For the liability of a judge of a Guardianship Court, see 1674, 1848; for the liability of officials for the unlawful acts of their representatives and deputies, see IA, Art. 78.

(*n*) See 334, 336 of the Criminal Code.

remedy [o].

840. If several persons are jointly responsible for any damage arising from an unlawful act, they are liable, subject to the provision of 835, par. 3, as joint debtors [p].

If a person is liable under 831, 832 to make compensation for the damage caused by another for which such other is also liable, as between themselves only the latter is liable [q], or in the case provided for by 829, only the person who has the duty of supervision.

If a person is liable under 833 to 838 to make compensation for any damage for which a third party is also liable, as between themselves only such third party is liable [q].

841. If an official who, by virtue of his official duty, has to appoint another [r] to conduct an affair for a third party, or has to supervise the conduct of such affair, or by his ratification of juristic acts has to concur in them, is, where he commits any breach of duty, liable jointly with such other person for any damage caused by the latter, then as between themselves only the latter is liable.

842. The obligation to make compensation for any damage on account of an unlawful act committed against the person of another extends to the detriment which the act occasions to his earnings or prosperity [s].

843. If, in consequence of an injury to the body or health of another, the earning capacity of the injured party is destroyed or impaired, or an increase of his necessities arises, compensation shall be made to the injured party by the payment of a money annuity.

(*o*) This section deals with the personal liability of officials. For the liability of the State, a municipality, or any other public corporation for the unlawful acts of its officials, see 89; also IA, Art. 77, and Imperial Land Registration Act, s. 12.

(*p*) *I.e.*, each is liable for the whole damage. 421, 426.

(*q*) *I.e.*, he has to compensate the other co-debtor for what the latter has paid as compensation.

(*r*) *E.g.*, a guardian, a trustee in bankruptcy, &c.

(*s*) The liability is stricter in all cases under 847.

The provisions of 760 apply to the annuity. Whether, in what manner, and to what amount, the person bound to make compensation has to give security is determined according to the circumstances.

Instead of the annuity the injured party may demand a settlement in a lump sum, if a grave reason exists [(t)].

The claim is not barred by the fact that another person has to furnish maintenance to the injured party.

844. In the case of causing death the person bound to make compensation shall make good the funeral expenses to the person on whom the obligation of bearing such expenses lies [(u)].

If the deceased at the time of the injury stood in a relation to a third party by virtue of which he was or might be bound by law to furnish maintenance to such third party, and if in consequence of the death such third party is deprived of the right to claim maintenance, the person bound to make compensation shall compensate the third party by the payment of a money annuity, in so far as the deceased would have been bound to furnish maintenance during the presumable duration of his life; the provisions of 843, pars. 2 to 4, apply *mutatis mutandis*. The obligation to make compensation arises even if at the time of the injury the third party was only *en ventre sa mère*.

845. In the case of causing death, or of causing injury to the body or health of another, or in the case of deprivation of liberty, if the injured party was bound by law to perform service in favour of a third party in his household or industry [(x)], the person bound to make compensation shall compensate the third party for the loss of service by the payment of a money annuity. The provisions of 843, pars. 2 to 4, apply *mutatis mutandis*.

846. If, in the cases provided for by 844, 845, some fault of the injured party has contributed in causing the damage which the third party has sustained,

---

(*t*) *E.g.*, if the person liable dies and his heirs live in a distant place.

(*u*) *I.e.*, the person bound to furnish maintenance to the deceased (1615, 1713) or the heir of the deceased (1968).

(*x*) *I.e.*, a wife (1356), or children (1617); but not domestic servants, as they are bound to perform service, not by law, but by virtue of a contract for service.

the provisions of 254 apply to the claim of the third party.

847. In the case of injury to the body or health of another, or in the case of deprivation of liberty, the injured party may also demand an equitable compensation in money for the damage which is not a pecuniary loss [(y)]. The claim is not transferable, and does not pass to the heirs, unless it has been acknowledged by contract, or an action on it has been commenced.

A like claim belongs to a woman against whom an immoral crime or offence is committed, or who is induced by fraud, or by threats, or by an abuse of a relation of dependence to permit illicit cohabitation.

848. A person who is bound to return a thing of which he has deprived another by an unlawful act is also responsible for the accidental destruction of the thing, or for accidental impossibility of returning it arising from any other cause, or for its accidental deterioration, unless the destruction or the impossibility of returning it, or the deterioration would have come about even if the deprivation had not taken place.

849. If on account of the taking of a thing its value, or, on account of damage to a thing, its diminution in value is to be made good, the injured party may demand interest [(z)] on the amount to be made good from the time which serves as the basis for the estimate of the value.

850. If a person bound to return a thing taken by him incurs any outlay on the thing, he has the rights against the injured party which a possessor has against an owner on account of outlay incurred [(a)].

851. If a person bound to make compensation for any damage on account of the taking or damaging of a moveable compensates the person in whose possession the thing was at the time of the taking or damage, he is discharged by so doing even if a third party was owner of the thing, or had some other right in the thing, unless the right of the third party is known to him or remains unknown

---

(*y*) See the general rule laid down in 253.

(*z*) At the rate of 4 per cent. 246.

(*a*) Cf. 257, 273, par. 1; 994—1003.

in consequence of gross negligence.

852. The claim for compensation for any damage arising from an unlawful act is barred by prescription in three years from the time at which the injured party has knowledge of the injury and of the identity of the person bound to make compensation; in the absence of such knowledge, in thirty years from the commission of the act [(b)].

If the person bound to make compensation has acquired anything by the unlawful act at the expense of the injured party, he is, even after the lapse of the period of prescription, bound to return it under the provisions relating to the return of unjustified benefits [(c)].

853. If a person acquires, by an unlawful act committed by him, a claim against the injured party [(d)], the latter may refuse satisfaction even if the claim for avoidance of the claim is barred by prescription.

(*b*) This is true even in the case where the injury did not become apparent until after this period.

(*c*) Cf. 818 *et seq*.

(*d*) *E.g.*, on the ground of fraud, threats.

THIRD BOOK.
Law of Things.

FIRST SECTION.
POSSESSION.

854. Possession [(a)] of a thing is acquired by the attainment of actual power [(b)] over the thing [(c)].

A real agreement [(d)] between the former possessor and the acquirer is sufficient for the acquisition of possession if the acquirer is in a position to exercise power over the thing.

855. Where a person exercises actual power over a thing for another in the latter's household or business, or in a similar relation by virtue of which he has to follow the directions of the other concerning the thing, then only the latter [(e)] is possessor.

856. Possession is lost by reason of the fact that the possessor relinquishes or otherwise loses actual power over the thing.

Possession is not lost when the exercise of the power is prevented by some

---

(a) The codifiers intentionally refrained from giving any definition of possession, because, as was said in the "Motive", "possession cannot be defined in a satisfactory manner showing how it may be retained and lost". See *Motive zu dem ersten Entwurfe des Bürgerlichen Gesetzbuchs*, 1888, s. 797.

(b) Whether "actual power" has been acquired or not is a question of fact to be determined according to the circumstances of each particular case.

(c) An intention on the part of the acquirer to attain actual power over the thing is not necessary. Hence persons labouring under mental incapacity, as *e.g.*, children under seven years of age and insane persons, can also acquire possession.

(d) See "real agreement" in Glossary (Appendix D).

(e) He has therefore, in case of unlawful interference the right to bring a possessory action, while the person who exercises "actual power" on his behalf has only the right of self-help. See 860.

cause which is temporary in its nature [f].

857. Possession passes to be the heir of the possessor[g].

858. A person who deprives a possessor against his will of his possession, or disturbs him in his possession, acts unlawfully (*i.e.*, unlawful interference), unless the law authorizes the deprivation or disturbance [h].

Possession acquired by unlawful interference is defective [i]. The defect avails against a successor in possession who is the heir of the possessor, or who knew of the defect of his predecessor's possession at the time of acquiring it.

859. A possessor [k] may forcibly resist unlawful interference [l].

If a moveable is taken away from the possessor by unlawful interference, he may retake it by force from the wrongdoer if he be caught in the act or immediately pursued [m].

If a possessor of land is deprived of possession by unlawful interference, he may, immediately [n] upon being dispossessed, recover possession by the expulsion of the wrongdoer [m].

The possessor has the same rights against a person who according to 858, par. 2, is in defective possession [o].

860. A person who exercises actual power on behalf of the possessor under 855 is also authorized to exercise the rights which the latter has under 859.

861. If a possessor is deprived of possession by unlawful interference, he

---

(*f*) Whether it is temporary in its nature or not is to be determined according to the circumstances of each case.

(*g*) That is to say, on the death of the possessor the heir acquires possession of all things belonging to the inheritance, even though he has not acquired actual power over them. Cf. 854.

(*h*) For such cases, see 227—230, 859, pars. 2, 3.

(*i*) For the effects of defective possession, see 861, 862.

(*k*) Cf. 860.

(*l*) This is only an application of the general principle laid down in 229.

(*m*) The right of "self-help" accorded to a possessor is more extensive than that provided for in 229.

(*n*) If this is not immediately done, he has no right of "self-help".

(*o*) If the possessor cannot or will not exercise the right of "self-help", he has the rights specified in 861, 862 and 867.

may demand relinquishment of possession to him from the person who is in defective possession as against him (p).

The claim is barred if the possession of which the possessor has been deprived was defective as against the present possessor or his predecessor in title, and was acquired within a year prior to the deprivation.

862. Where a possessor is disturbed in his possession by unlawful interference, he may require the disturber to move the disturbance. If further disturbance is to be apprehended the possessor may apply for an injunction (q).

The claim is barred if the possessor is in defective possession as against the disturber or his predecessor in title, and the defective possession was acquired within a year prior to the disturbance.

863. As against the claims specified in 861, 862, a right to possession or to disturb the possessor may only be asserted to establish the contention that the deprivation or the disturbance of the possession is not unlawful interference.

864. A claim based upon 861, 862, is extinguished on the expiration of one year after the act of unlawful interference, unless within such period the claim has been enforced by bringing action.

The claim is also extinguished, even though after the act of unlawful interference it is established by a non-appellable judgment that a right over the thing (r) belongs to the wrongdoer by virtue of which he may demand restoration of possession in a manner corresponding to his act of interference.

865. The provisions of 858 to 864 apply also in favour of a person who possesses only a part of a thing, *e.g.*, separate rooms for habitation or other rooms.

866. If several persons possess a thing in common, no possessory action lies as between themselves, in so far as the question relates to the limits of the use belonging to the individuals.

(*p*) The possessor may also claim damages under 823 if fault is imputable to the wrongdoer.

(*q*) He may also claim damages under 823 if fault is imputable to the wrongdoer.

(*r*) *E.g.*, ownership, real servitude, &c.

867. If a thing comes out of the power of its possessor and is afterwards found on a piece of land in the possession of another, the possessor of the land shall permit him to search for and remove it, unless the thing has been taken possession of in the meantime. The possessor of the land may demand compensation for any damage arising from the search and removal. He may, if injury is to be apprehended, refuse his permission until security is given; the refusal is not permitted if there is danger in delay.

868. If a person possesses a thing as usufructuary, pledgee, ordinary or usufructuary lessee, depositary, or in a similar relation by virtue of which he is for a time entitled or bound to possess the thing on behalf of another, then such other person is also possessor (*i.e.*, indirect possession).

869. If unlawful interference is committed against a possessor, the claims specified in 861, 862 belong also to an indirect possessor [(s)]. In case of deprivation of possession the indirect possessor is entitled to demand relinquishment of possession to the former possessor; if the latter cannot or will not re-assume possession, the indirect possessor may demand that possession be relinquished to himself. Under the same conditions he may, in the case provided for by 867, demand permission to search for and remove the thing.

870. Indirect possession may be transferred to another by the assignment to the latter of the claim for the return of the thing.

871. If the indirect possessor stands to a third party in a relation of the kind specified in 868, such third party is also an indirect possessor.

872. A person who possesses a thing as belonging to him is a proprietary possessor [(t)].

(*s*) The indirect possessor is entitled to exercise the right of self-defence and "self-help" only under 227—231, and not under 859.

(*t*) A proprietary possessor has no possessory action. The question whether a person is proprietary possessor or not is of importance in the case of acquisition of ownership (cf. 900, 927, 937 *et seq.*, 955 and 958) and in other minor cases (cf., *e.g.*, 836, par. 3, and 1127).

SECOND SECTION.
GENERAL PROVISIONS RELATING TO RIGHTS OVER LAND.

873. For the transfer (u) of ownership of land, or the creation of any right in another over land, or for the transfer of or the creation of a charge (x) upon such a right, a real agreement between the person entitled and the other party relating to the change of title and registration of the change of title in the land register are necessary, unless the law provides otherwise (y).

Before registration the parties are bound by the agreement only if the declarations have been judicially or notarially authenticated, or have been made or filed in the land registry office, or if the person entitled has delivered to the other party an authorisation for registration conformable with the provisions of the Land Registration Act (z).

874. In the registration of a right over land reference may be made to the authorisation for registration for fuller specification of the extent of the right, unless the law provides otherwise.

875. For the release of a right over land the declaration of the person entitled that he surrenders the right and the cancellation of the right in the land register are necessary (a), unless it is otherwise provided by law (b). The declaration shall be communicated to the land registry office, or to the person

---

(u) *I.e.*, by means of a juristic act *inter vivos*. This provision is not applicable to the transfer of ownership of land by operation of law (as, *e.g.*, succession, compulsory auction, compulsory execution, &c.).

(x) *E.g.*, pledge of a right of usufruct.

(y) For the "assignment" of a hypotheca, a land charge, or an annuity charge, registration in the land register is not necessary. (See 1154, par. 1; 1192, par. 1; and 1199, par. 1.) For further exceptions, see 1159, 1107, 1192, par. 2; and 1200, par. 1.

(z) The authorisation for registration may be given at the land registry office to be then and there recorded, or it may be conferred by a public or publicly certified act. See sect. 29 of the Land Registration Act.

(a) Cf. 873, par. 1.

(b) *E.g.*, 1181. For dispensation from the necessity of cancellation, see 1178, 1107, 1192, par. 2; and 1200, par. 1.

in whose favour is made.

Before cancellation the person entitled is bound by his declaration only if he has communicated it to the land registry office, or has delivered to the person in whose favour it is made an authorisation for cancellation conformable with the provisions of the Land Registration Act [(c)].

876. If a right over land is charged with a right of a third party, the consent of such third party is necessary for the release of the charged right. If the right to be released belongs to the owner for the time being of another piece of land, and if such other piece of land is charged with the right of a third party, the consent of such third party is necessary, unless his right is not affected by the release. The consent shall be declared to the land registry office, or to the person in whose favour it is given; it is irrevocable.

877. The provisions of 873, 874, 876 apply also to alterations in the substance of a right over land.

878. A declaration made under 873, 875, 877 by the person entitled is not invalidated by the fact that the declarant becomes limited in his power of alienation [(d)] after the declaration has become binding on him, and after the application for registration has been filed in the land registry office.

879. The order of priority among several rights to which land is subject is determined, if the rights have been registered in the same division of the land register, by the order of registration. If the rights have been registered in different divisions, the right registered as of earlier date has priority; rights registered as of the same date have equal rank [(e)].

The registration is conclusive for the order of priority, even though the real agreement necessary according to 873 for the acquisition of the right has not been completed until after the registration.

A different arrangement of the order of priority requires registration in the

---

(*c*) The rules are the same as in the case of an authorisation for registration. See note (*z*) to 873.

(*d*) *E.g.*, by the institution of bankruptcy proceedings against him.

(*e*) For exceptions to this rule, see 914, pars. 1, 2; 917, par. 2. In the case of rights which do not require registration, their order of priority is determined by the date of creation.

land register.

880. The order of priority may be subsequently altered.

For an alteration of the order of priority, a real agreement between the person whose right is postponed and the person whose right obtains priority, and registration of the change in the land register are necessary; the provisions of 873, par. 2, and 878 apply. If a hypotheca, a land charge, or an annuity charge is to be postponed, the consent of the owner is also necessary. The consent shall be declared to the land registry office or to one of the parties; it is irrevocable.

If the right which is postponed is subject to a right of a third party, the provisions of 876 apply *mutatis mutandis*.

The rank accorded to the right obtaining priority is not lost by the fact that the right which is postponed is released by juristic act.

Rights which have rank between the one postponed and the one obtaining priority are not affected by the change of rank.

881. In charging land with a right the owner may reserve to himself the authority to have another right, the extent of which is specified, registered with priority to the former right.

The reservation is required to be entered in the land register; the entry must be annexed to the entry of the right that is to be postponed.

If the land is alienated, the reserved authority passes to the acquirer.

If, before registration of the right for which the priority is reserved, the land has been charged with another right without a similar reservation, the priority is without effect in so far as the right registered with the reservation would be impaired in excess of the reservation in consequence of the intervening right.

882. Where land is charged with a right for whose value, according to the provisions applicable to compulsory auction [(f)], the person having the right is to be compensated out of the proceeds of a sale whereby his right is extinguished, the maximum amount of the compensation may be specified. The specification requires registration in the land register.

(*f*) See sect. 92 of the Compulsory Auction Act.

883. A million may be entered in the land register for securing a claim for the concession or release of a right affecting land or affecting a right over land, or for the alteration of the substance or rank of such a right. The registration of a caution is also permissible for securing a future or conditional claim.

A disposition which is made affecting the land or the right after the registration of the caution is ineffective, in so far as it would defeat or impair the claim. This applies even where the disposition is made by means of compulsory execution or distraint, or by a trustee in bankruptcy.

The rank of the right for the concession of which the claim is made is determined by the date of the registration of the caution.

884. Where a claim is secured by a caution the heir of the person bound thereby cannot set up any limitation of his liability [(g)].

885. The registration of a caution is effected by virtue of a provisional decree [(h)], or of an authorisation by the person whose land or right is affected by the caution. It is not necessary for the issue of the provisional decree that *primâ facie* evidence be given that the claim to be secured is likely to be endangered.

In the registration reference may be made to the provisional decree or to the authorisation for registration for fuller specification of the claim to be secured.

886. If the person whose land or right is affected by the caution has a defence whereby the enforcement of the claim secured by the caution is permanently barred, he may require the creditor to cancel the caution.

887. If the creditor whose claim is secured by the caution is unknown, he may be excluded from his right by means of public summons, if the conditions specified in 1170 for the exclusion of a hypotheca-creditor exist. The effect of the caution is extinguished upon the issue of the decree for exclusion.

888. Where the acquisition of a registered right or a right over such a right is ineffective against the person in whose favour the caution is made, the latter

---

(*g*) Cf. 1975 *et seq.*

(*h*) Cf. 935 *et seq.* of the Code of Civil Procedure.

may require the acquirer to give his consent to the registration or cancellation which is necessary for the realisation of the claim secured by the caution.

The same rule applies if the claim is secured by a prohibition against alienation.

889. A right over the land of another is not extinguished by the fact that the owner of the land acquires the right, or the person having the right acquires the ownership of the land [(i)].

890. Several pieces of land may be united into one piece by the fact that the owner causes them to be registered in the land register as one piece.

One piece of land may be made a component part of another piece of land by the fact that the owner causes it to be ascribed to the latter in the land register [(k)].

891. If in the land register a right has been registered in the name of any person, it is presumed that the right belongs to him [(l)].

If a right registered in the land register has been cancelled, it is presumed that the right does not exist [(l)].

892. In favour of a person who acquires a right over land or a right over such a right by juristic act [(m)], the entries of the land register are deemed to be correct [(n)], unless an objection to its correctness is registered [(o)], or the incorrectness is known to the acquirer. If a person entitled to a right registered

---

(*i*) In other words, there is no merger of the right in the ownership. The former lies dormant until it is again separated from the latter.

(*k*) Cf. IA, Art. 119.

(*l*) The presumption is rebuttable.

(*m*) This provision does not apply to acquisition of land otherwise than by juristic act, *e.g.*, by inheritance.

(*n*) An exception to this rule will be found in 1028. If the entry in the land register is in fact incorrect, the true owner can require the registered owner to return to him all property rights acquired by the latter under the provisions relating to the return of unjustified benefits (816, par. 1, sentence 1; par. 2); compensation may also be demanded in certain cases under the provisions relating to unlawful acts. 823 *et seq.*

(*o*) See 899.

in the land register is limited in this power of alienation over it (p) in favour of a particular person, the limitation is effective against the acquirer only if it appears from the land register itself, or is known to the acquirer.

If registration is necessary for the acquisition of the right (q), the question as to the good faith of the acquirer is determined by his state of knowledge at the time of the presentation of the application for registration, or, if the real agreement required by 873 has not been formed until after that time, at the time of the formation of the agreement (r).

893. The provisions of 892 apply *mutatis mutandis*, if a person in whose name a right has been entered in the land register has received the benefits of an act of performance (s) done by virtue of such right, or if a juristic act, not coming within the provisions of 892 and containing a disposition affecting such right (t), has been entered into between him and another person.

894. If the entry in the land register with regard to a right over land, or a right over such a right, or a limitation of the power of alienation of the kind specified in 892, par. 1 is not in accordance with the actual legal situation, the person whose right has not, or has not correctly, been registered, or has been impaired by the registration of a non-existent right over the land or of a limitation of the power of alienation, may require the person whose right is affected by the rectification of the land register to give his consent to such rectification.

895. If the rectification of the land register cannot be made until after the right of the person who is bound by 894 to consent thereto has been registered, he shall, if required to do so, cause his right to be so registered.

896. If the production of a certificate of hypotheca, land charge, or annuity charge is necessary for the rectification of the land register, the person in whose favour the rectification is to be made may require the possessor of the

(p) *E.g.*, by the institution of bankruptcy proceedings.

(q) Cf. note (y) to 873.

(r) If registration is not necessary for the acquisition of a right, the time of acquisition is material.

(s) *E.g.*, payment of interest.

(t) *E.g.*, the giving of notice in the case of a hypotheca.

certificate to produce it at the land registry office.

897. The costs of the rectification of the land register and of the declarations necessary thereto shall be borne by the person who demands the rectification, unless a contrary intention appears from a juristic relation existing between him and the person bound.

898. The claims specified in 894 to 896 are not subject to prescription.

899. In the cases provided for by 894 an objection to the correctness of the land register may be registered.

The registration is made by virtue of a provisional decree [(u)] or of an authorisation by the person whose right is affected by the rectification of the land register. It is not necessary for the issue of the provisional decree that *primâ facie* evidence be given that the right of the objecting party is likely to be endangered.

900. A person who has been registered in the land register as owner of a piece of land without having obtained ownership acquires ownership thereof, if the registration has remained for thirty years and during that time he has proprietary possession of the land [(x)]. The period of thirty years is reckoned in the same manner as the period for the acquisition of a moveable by usucapion [(y)]. The running of the period is suspended so long as an objection to the correctness of the registration has been entered in the land register [(z)].

These provisions apply *mutatis mutandis*, if there has been registered in the land register in the name of any person a right not belonging to him which involves possession of land [(a)], or the exercise of which is protected by the provisions applicable to possession. The rank of such a right is determined by the date of its registration.

901. If a right over the land of another has been improperly cancelled in

---

(*u*) Cf. 935 *et seq.* of the Code of Civil Procedure.

(*x*) Cf. 872.

(*y*) Cf. 937 *et seq.*

(*z*) In accordance with 899.

(*a*) *E.g.*, a right of usufruct.

the land register, it is extinguished if the claim of the person entitled to it against the owner is barred by prescription [b]. The same rule applies if a right over the land of another created by operation of law has not been entered in the land register.

902. Claims arising from registered rights are not subject to prescription. This does not apply to claims for arrears of periodical payments [c] or for compensation [d].

A right on account of which an objection to the correctness of the land register [e] has been entered is equivalent to a registered right.

THIRD SECTION.

OWNERSHIP.

FIRST TITLE.

Scope of Ownership.

903. The owner of a thing may, in so far as the law [f] or the rights of third parties admit, deal with the thing as he pleases and exclude others from any interference with it.

904. The owner of a thing is not entitled to forbid the interference of another with the thing, if the interference is necessary for averting a present danger and the threatened injury is disproportionately great in comparison with the injury caused to the owner by the interference [g]. The owner may require

---

(*b*) See 194 *et seq.*

(*c*) These are barred by prescription in four years. 197.

(*d*) See also 1028, 1090.

(*e*) Cf. 899.

(*f*) For the statutory limitation of the use of a thing, see *e.g.*, 226 and 904 *et seq.*

(*g*) Prohibition by the owner against such interference would constitute an unlawful act which gives rise to a claim for compensation. 823, par. 2.

compensation for the damage caused to him.

905. The right of the owner of a piece of land extends to the space above the surface and to the substance of the earth beneath the surface. The owner may not, however, forbid interference which takes place at such a height or depth that he has no interest in its prevention.

906. The owner of a piece of land may not forbid the discharge of gases, vapours, odours, smoke, soot, heat, noise, vibrations and similar interferences proceeding from another piece of land, in so far as the interference does not, or does not essentially, injure the use of his land, or is caused by a use of the other land which is customary according to the local customs for lands in such situation. Discharge by a special conduit is not permitted.

907. The owner of a piece of land may prevent the construction or erection, on an adjoining piece of land, of structures from which it can be foreseen with certainty that their condition or use will result in an inadmissible interference with his land. If a structure complies with the provisions of the State law which prescribe a specified distance from the boundary or other protective measures, the removal of the structure can be required only if the inadmissible interference actually takes place.

Trees and shrubs [(h)] are not structures within the meaning of these provisions.

908. If a piece of land is threatened with the danger of being injured by the fall of a building or other structure erected on an adjoining piece of land, or by the detachment of parts of the building or structure, the owner may require the person who, according to 836, par. 1, or 837, 838 would be responsible for resulting injury, to take the necessary measures for averting the danger.

909. Land may not be excavated in such manner that the soil of an adjoining piece of land loses its necessary support, unless some other method is provided for adequate support.

910. The owner of a piece of land may cut off and retain roots of a tree or

(*h*) These are regulated by 910.

of a shrub which have penetrated from an adjoining piece of land. The same rule applies to overhanging branches, if the owner has allotted to the possessor of the adjoining piece of land a reasonable period for their removal, and the removal has not been effected within such period.

The owner has not this right if the roots or the branches do not interfere with the use of the land (i).

911. Fruits falling from a tree, or a shrub standing on an adjoining piece of land are deemed to be fruits of such land. This provision does not apply if the adjoining piece of land serves for public use.

912. If the owner of a piece of land, without wilful default or gross negligence (k), has erected a building (l) beyond his boundary, the adjoining owner is bound to submit to the encroachment, unless he has raised an objection before or immediately after the trespass (m).

The adjoining owner shall be compensated by a money rent. The amount of the rent is determined as at the date of the trespass.

913. The rent for the encroachment is payable to the owner for the time being of the adjoining piece of land (n) by the owner for the time being of the other piece of land.

The rent is payable yearly (o) in advance.

914. The right to the rent takes priority to all rights with which the land is charged, even older rights. It is extinguished upon the removal of the encroachment (p).

(*i*) Cf. IA, Arts. 122, 124, 183.

(*k*) The *onus probandi* is upon the owner.

(*l*) The provisions of 912—916 do not apply to structures other than buildings. Cf. *Motive zu dem ersten Entwürfe des Bürgerlichen Gesetzbuchs*, 857—860.

(*m*) The *onus probandi* is upon the adjoining owner.

(*n*) It is immaterial whether he was aware of his right to such rent or not at the time of acquiring the land.

(*o*) To be reckoned from the time of the trespass.

(*p*) The *right* to the rent is not subject to prescription, although the individual claims to arrears of rent are barred by prescription in four years. 197.

The right is not registered in the land register. Registration is necessary for a waiver of the right, and for the determination of the amount of the rent by contract [q].

For the rest those provisions are applicable which apply to a perpetual charge on land existing in favour of the owner for the time being of a piece of land [r].

915. The person entitled to the rent [s] may at any time demand that the person who is bound to pay it shall compensate him, on the transfer of ownership of the encroached part of the land [t], for the value which such part had at the time of the trespass. If he exercises such right, the rights and obligations of both parties are determined according to the provisions relating to sale [u].

The rent shall continue to be paid until the transfer of ownership.

916. If a heritable building right [x] or a servitude [y] over an adjoining piece of land is interfered with by the encroachment, the provisions of 912 to 914 apply *mutatis mutandis* is favour of the person entitled to such building right or servitude.

917. If a piece of land has not the means of connection with a public road necessary for its proper use, the owner may require his adjoining owners to permit him to use their lands for making the necessary connection until the defect is remedied. The direction of the way of necessity and the extent of the right to its use are determined, if necessary, by judicial decree [z].

The adjoining owners over whose lands the way of necessity leads shall be compensated by a money rent. The provisions of 912, par. 2, sentence 2, and

---

(*q*) The amount of the rent fixed by a competent Court in an action brought by one of the interested parties need not be entered in the land register.

(*r*) See 1105 *et seq.*

(*s*) But not the person bound to pay the rent.

(*t*) The ownership of that part of the building which stands upon the encroached land belongs *ab initio* to the person bound to pay the rent. See 95, par. 1.

(*u*) See especially 433—436, 439.

(*x*) See 1012 *et seq.*

(*y*) See 1018 *et seq.*, 1030 *et seq.*, 1090 *et seq.*

(*z*) Cf. IA, Art. 123.

913, 914, 916 apply *mutatis mutandis*.

918. The obligation to permit the way of necessity does not arise, if the former connection of the land with the public road is destroyed by an arbitrary act of the owner [(a)].

If, in consequence of the alienation of a part of the land, the part alienated or the part retained is cut off from the connection with the public road, the owner of that part over which the connection formerly existed must permit the way of necessity. The alienation of one of several pieces of land belonging to the same owner is equivalent to the alienation of a part of the land.

919. The owner of a piece of land may require an adjoining owner to concur in the placing of permanent boundary marks and in the restoration of any boundary mark which may have become misplaced or unrecognizable.

The kind and manner of marking are determined by the laws of the State; if they contain no provisions, local custom determines it.

The costs of marking the boundaries shall be borne by the parties in equal shares, unless a contrary intention appears from some legal relation existing between them.

920. If, in case of confusion of boundaries, the proper boundary cannot be determined, the actual possession is decisive in the delimitation of the boundary. If the actual possession cannot be settled, an equal portion of the land in dispute shall be allotted to each of the piece of land.

Where a determination of the boundary in accordance with these provisions leads to a result that is not in accord with the ascertained circumstance, *e.g.*, with the established size of the piece of land, the boundary is to be drawn so as to be equitable under these circumstances.

921. If two pieces of land are separated from each other by an interval, border, corner, ditch, wall, hedge, fence, or any other device which serves for the advantage of both pieces of land, it is presumed that the owner of the lands are entitled to the common use of such device, unless visible signs indicate that

---

(*a*) *E.g.*, destruction of a bridge.

the device belongs exclusively to one of the two owners.

922. If the two owners are entitled to the common use of one of the devices specified in 921, either may use it for the purpose which results from its character [(b)], in so far as the equal use by the other is not thereby interfered with. The costs of maintenance shall be borne by the two owners in equal shares. So long as one of the two owners has an interest in the continuance of the device, it may not be removed or altered without his consent. For the rest the legal relation between the two owners is determined according to the provisions relating to community of ownership [(c)].

923. If a tree stands upon the boundary, its fruits, and if the tree is felled, the tree itself, belong to the two owners in equal shares.

Each of the two owners may require the removal of the tree. The cost of removal is borne by the two owners in equal shares. If one of the two requires its removal he shall, however, bear the cost alone, if the other waives his right to the tree; in such a case he acquires sole ownership of it when it is cut down. The claim for its removal is barred if the tree serves as a boundary mark, and cannot under the circumstances be replaced by another appropriate boundary mark.

The provisions apply also to a shrub standing on the boundary.

924. The claims arising from 907 to 909, 915, 917, par. 1, 918, par. 2, 919, 920, and 923, par. 2, are not subject to prescription.

SECOND TITLE.
Acquisition and Loss of Ownership of Land.

925. The real agreement of the alienor and the acquirer necessary according to 873 for the transfer of ownership of land (*i.e.*, a conveyance by agreement) must be declared at the land registry office in the presence of both parties

(*b*) But not for any other purpose.

(*c*) See 741—758.

simultaneously [d].

A conveyance by agreement made subject to any condition or limitation of time is of no effect.

926. If the alienor and the acquirer have agreed that the alienation shall extend to the accessories of the land [e], the acquirer acquires ownership of the land and of its accessories existing at the time of the acquisition, in so far as they belong to the alienor. In case of doubt it is to be presumed that the alienation extends to the accessories.

If, by virtue of the alienation, the acquirer acquires possession of accessories which do not belong to the alienor, or which are subject to rights of third parties, the provisions of 932 to 936 apply; the question as to the good faith of the acquirer is determined by his state of knowledge at the time of obtaining possession.

927. The owner of a piece of land may, if for thirty years the land has been in the proprietary possession [f] of another, be excluded from his rights by means of public summons [g]. The time of possession is reckoned in the same manner as the period for acquisition of a moveable by usucapion [h]. If the owner has been registered in the land register the public summons is permissible only if he is dead or has disappeared [i] and within thirty years no registration in the land register which requires the consent of the owner has been made.

The person who has obtained the decree for exclusion acquires ownership by causing himself to be registered in the land register as owner.

If, before the issue of the decree for exclusion a third party has been registered as owner, or in objection to the correctness of the land register has been registered on account of the ownership of a third party, the decree is inoperative as against such third party.

(*d*) Cf. 125, 313; and IA, Art. 143.

(*e*) See 97, 98.

(*f*) Cf. 872.

(*g*) The procedure is regulated by 1003 *et seq.* of the Code of Civil Procedure.

(*h*) See 937, 938.

(*i*) And has been declared dead. See 13—17.

936. If an alienated thing is subject to the right of a third party [(y)], the right is extinguished upon the acquisition of ownership. This applies, however, in the case provided for by 929, sentence 2, only if the acquirer had obtained possession from the alienor [(z)]. If the alienation is made under 930, or if the thing alienated under 931 was not in the indirect possession [(a)] of the alienor, the right of the third party is not extinguished until the acquirer obtains possession of the thing by virtue of the alienation.

The right of the third party is not extinguished, if at the time which is material according to par. 1 the acquirer is in bad faith [(b)] in respect of the right.

If in the case provided for by 931 the right belongs to the third possessor, it is not extinguished even in respect of an acquirer in good faith.

II. Usucapion.

937. A person who has a moveable for ten years [(c)] in his proprietary possession [(d)] acquires ownership thereof (usucapion).

Usucapion is excluded if the acquirer was in bad faith [(e)] at the time of acquiring proprietary possession, or if he subsequently [(f)] learns that the ownership does not belong to him.

(*y*) *E.g.*, a right of pledge or a usufruct.

(*z*) *E.g.*, in the capacity of lessee.

(*a*) Cf. 868.

(*b*) *I.e.*, if the right of the third party is known to him or unknown to him as a result of gross negligence.

(*c*) Without interruption.

(*d*) Cf. 854, 872. The possessor has to prove that he has possessed the thing *as his own*. The mere fact of possession is sufficient; there need not be any *justa causa* for the possession.

(*e*) *I.e.*, if, at the time of the acquisition of proprietary possession, he knew or did not know, as a result of gross negligence, that he did not acquire ownership, or if he acquired the thing by a voidable juristic act which was subsequently avoided, and he knew or ought to have known of its voidability (see 932, par. 2; 142, par. 2) at the time when the juristic act was entered into. The person disputing the usucapion of the thing has to prove the absence of good faith on the part of the possessor.

(*f*) *I.e.*, at any time within the period of ten years.

938. If a person has had a thing in his proprietary possession at the beginning and at the end of a period, it is presumed that his proprietary possession has been continuous in the intermediate time [(g)].

939. Usucapion may not begin and, where it has begun, may not be continued, so long as the prescription of the claim of ownership is suspended [(h)], or the provisions of 206, 207 prevent its completion.

940. Usucapion is interrupted by the loss of proprietary possession [(i)].

It is deemed to be no interruption, if the proprietary possessor has lost his proprietary possession against his will and has recovered it within one year, or by means of action brought within such period [(k)].

941. Usucapion is interrupted, if the claim of ownership [(l)] be enforced in court against the proprietary possessor [(m)], or, in case of indirect possession, against the possessor who derives his right to possession from the proprietary possessor; the interruption operates, however, only in favour of the person who has brought it about. The provisions of 209 to 212, 216, 219, 220, applicable to prescription, apply *mutatis mutandis*.

942. If usucapion is interrupted, the time which has elapsed before the interruption is not taken into consideration; a new usucapion may not begin until after the termination of the interruption.

943. If a thing comes into the proprietary possession of a third party by succession in title [(n)], the time of usucapion which has elapsed during the possession if the predecessor in title is reckoned in favour of such third party.

944. The time of usucapion which has elapsed in favour of a possessor of

---

(*g*) The presumption is rebuttable.

(*h*) See 985, 202—204.

(*i*) See 872, 856.

(*k*) The same rule applies to all cases where possession is recovered by means of unlawful interference.

(*l*) See 985.

(*m*) See 872, 868.

(*n*) No matter whether by way of inheritance or by virtue of a juristic act (sale, gift, &c.).

an inheritance (o) is reckoned in favour of the heir.

945. Upon the acquisition of ownership by usucapion all rights of third parties over the thing created before the acquisition of proprietary possession (p) are extinguished, unless the proprietary possessor, at the time of acquiring proprietary possession, was in bad faith (q) in respect of such rights, or subsequently (r) learns of their existence. The period of usucapion must have elapsed also in respect of the rights of such third parties; the provisions of 939 to 944 apply *mutatis mutandis*.

III. Incorporation. Confusion. Specification.

946. If a moveable be attached to a piece of land in such manner (s) that it becomes an essential component part thereof (t), the ownership of the land extends to such moveable (u).

947. If moveables become attached to each other in such manner (s) that they become essential component parts (t) of a single thing, the former owners become co-owners (x) of such thing; their shares are determined in proportion to the value which such moveables had at the time of incorporation.

If one of the things is to be regarded as the principal thing (y), the owner of the principal thing acquires sole ownership.

948. If moveables become inseparably mixed or confused with each other, the provisions of 947 apply *mutatis mutandis*.

(*o*) See 2018.

(*p*) *I.e.*, before the beginning of the usucapion.

(*q*) He is deemed to be in bad faith, if he knows or does not know, as a result of gross negligence, that the thing is subject to the rights of third parties. The burden of proving bad faith on the part of the proprietary possessor is upon such third parties.

(*r*) *I.e.*, at any time within the period of ten years. Cf. 937.

(*s*) The cause of their becoming so attached to each other is entirely immaterial.

(*t*) Cf. 93—95.

(*u*) For the rights of the owner of such moveable, see 951.

(*x*) Cf. 1008.

(*y*) Cf. 97.

It is equivalent to inseparableness, if the mixed or confused things could be separated only through disproportionate outlay.

949. If the ownership of a thing is extinguished under 946 to 948, all other rights over the thing are also extinguished. If the owner of the thing which is subject to the rights acquires co-ownership, these rights continue to exist over the share which takes the place of the thing. If the owner of the thing which is subject to the rights becomes sole owner, these rights extend to the thing annexed.

950. A person, who by manufacture or transformation of one or several materials (z) produces a new moveable, acquires ownership of the new thing, unless the value of the manufacture or transformation is materially less than the value of the material. Writing, drawing, painting, engraving, or any other similar manipulation of the surface of a thing are equivalent to manufacture.

Upon the acquisition of the ownership of the new thing all rights over the material are extinguished.

951. A person who is deprived of any right under the provisions of 946 to 950 may demand the person in whose favour the alteration of right takes place, to make compensation in money under the provisions relating to the return of unjustified benefits (a). Restoration to the former condition may not be demanded.

The provisions relating to the obligation to make compensation for unlawful acts (b), and the provisions relating to reimbursement of outlay incurred (c) and to the right of removing an attachment (d) remain unaffected. In the cases provided for by 946, 947, the right to remove an attachment under the provisions applicable to a possessor's right of removal against an owner (e) is exercisable, even though the incorporation has not been effected by the possessor of

(z) Belonging to another, wholly or in part.

(a) Cf. 812 *et seq.*

(b) Cf. 823 *et seq.*

(c) Cf. 256, 273, 292, 994 *et seq.*

(d) Cf. 258.

(e) Cf. 997.

the principal thing.

952. The ownership of a certificate of indebtedness issued for a claim belongs to the creditor. The right of any third party in the claim extends to such certificate.

The same rule applies to documents relating to other rights whereby an act of performance may be demanded, *e.g.*, certificates of hypotheca, land charge, and annuity charge.

IV. Acquisition of Products and other Component Parts of a Thing.

953. Products [(f)] and other component parts [(g)] of a thing belong to the owner of the thing even after their separation from the thing, in so far as a contrary intention does not appear from 954 to 957 [(h)].

954. A person who, by virtue of a right over a thing belonging to another [(i)], is entitled to appropriate to himself products or other component parts of the thing, acquires the ownership of them upon their separation from the thing [(j)], subject to the provisions of 955 to 957.

955. A person who is in proprietary possession of a thing [(k)] acquires the ownership of its products and other component parts [(l)] which are deemed to be its fruits, upon their separation from the thing [(j)], subject to the provisions of 956, 957. The acquisition is excluded if the proprietary possessor is not entitled to proprietary possession, or if another person by virtue of a right over the thing is entitled to take its fruits, and the proprietary possessor was in bad

(*f*) Cf. 99.

(*g*) Cf. 93—96.

(*h*) Cf. IA, Art. 181, par. 2.

(*i*) *E.g.*, usufruct.

(*j*) Whether the separation is brought about by his own act, or by the act of a third party, or by natural force, is immaterial.

(*k*) Cf. 872.

(*l*) Cf. 93 *et seq.*, 99 *et seq.*

faith [m] at the time of acquiring proprietary possession, or learns of any defect in his title before the separation.

A person who possesses a thing for the purpose of exercising a right of use over it is in the same position as a proprietary possessor.

The provision of 940, par. 2, applies *mutatis mutandis* to proprietary possession and the possession which is equivalent to it [n].

956. Where the owner permits another to appropriate to himself products or other component parts of the thing, the latter acquires ownership in them, if the possession of the thing is relinquished to him, upon separation [o]; otherwise upon taking possession [p]. If the owner is bound to give such permission [q] he may not revoke it so long as the other remains in possession of the thing relinquished to him.

The same rule applies if the permission is given not by the owner, but by another person to whom products or other component parts of a thing belong after separation.

957. The provisions of 956 apply even if the person who permits appropriation by another is not entitled to do so, unless the other, where possession of the thing is relinquished to him, at the time of such relinquishment, otherwise at the time of taking possession of the products or other component parts, is in bad faith [r], or learns of any defect in his title before separation.

V. Appropriation.

958. A person who takes proprietary possession of an ownerless moveable [s] acquires ownership of such moveable.

(*m*) Cf. 932, par. 2.

(*n*) See the preceding paragraph.

(*o*) See note (*k*) to 954 and 955.

(*p*) Cf. 854.

(*q*) *E.g.*, by the terms of a lease.

(*r*) Cf. 932, par. 2.

(*s*) On the appropriation of ownerless immoveables, see 928.

which he may consider necessary under the circumstances, he may require reimbursement from the person who is entitled to receive it [(d)].

971. The finder may demand a reward from the person entitled to receive the thing. The reward amounts to five per cent. of the value of the thing up to three hundred marks, and one per cent. on value in excess; in the case of animals one per cent. If the thing has a value only for the person entitled to receive it, the reward shall be determined in an equitable manner.

The claim is barred if the finder violates the duty of giving notice [(e)], or conceals the finding upon inquiry being made.

972. The provisions of 1000 to 1002 applicable to the claims of a possessor against an owner on account of outlay incurred apply *mutatis mutandis* to the claims specified in 970, 971.

973. Upon the lapse of one year from the notice of the finding to the police authority the finder acquires ownership of the thing [(f)], unless within such period a person entitled to receive it has become known to the finder, or has notified the police authority of his right. Upon the acquisition of ownership all other rights over the thing are extinguished [(g)].

If the thing is not worth more than three marks, the period of one year begins to run from the date of the finding. The finder does not acquire ownership, if he conceals the finding upon inquiry being made. The notification to the police authority of a right does not prevent the acquisition of ownership.

974. If, before the expiration of the period of one year, persons entitled to receive the thing have become known to the finder, or if they have in due time notified the police of their rights in the case of a thing worth more than three marks, the finder may, under the provisions of 1003, call upon them to make a

---

(*d*) Cf. 256, 273.

(*e*) Cf. 965.

(*f*) A finder acquires ownership even in respect of a thing which has been delivered to the police. See 975 and 976, par. 2.

(*g*) Nevertheless the finder is, within three years after the acquisition of ownership, bound to return whatever benefits he may have received during such period. See 977.

declaration whether or not they will satisfy the claims which he has under 970 to 972. Upon the expiration of the period for the declaration the finder acquires ownership, and all other rights over the thing are extinguished, unless the persons entitled to receive the thing duly declare themselves ready to satisfy the claims.

975. The rights of the finder are not affected by delivery of the thing or of the proceeds of its sale by auction to the police authority. If the police authority causes the thing to be sold by auction, the proceeds take the place of the thing. The police authority may restore the thing or the proceeds to a person entitled to receive it only with the consent of the finder.

976. If the finder waives before the police authority his right to acquire ownership of the thing, his right passes to the communal authority of the place of finding.

If the finder, after delivery of the thing or the proceeds of its sale by auction to the police authority, has acquired ownership under the provisions of 973, 974, the ownership passes to the communal authority of the place of finding, unless the finder demands return of the thing or of the proceeds before the expiration of a fixed period allotted to him by the police authority.

977. If a person is deprived of any right under the provisions of 973, 974, 976, he may, under the provisions relating to the return of unjustified benefits, demand the finder in the cases provided for by 973, 974, or the communal authority in the case provided for by 976, to return whatever (h) the finder or the communal authority has obtained through the change of title. The claim is extinguished upon the expiration of three years after the transfer of ownership to the finder or the communal authority, unless the claim has been enforced in court within such period.

978. A person who finds and takes possession of a thing in the business rooms or vehicles of transport of a public office or commercial agency serving for public transportation, shall deliver the thing without delay to the office or com-

---

(h) This may be the thing itself, or the proceeds realized from a sale of the thing by auction.

mercial agency, or to one of their officials. The provisions of 965 to 977 do not apply.

979. The office of commercial agency may cause the thing delivered to them to be sold by public auction. Public offices and commercial agencies of the Empire, of the States or of the communes may cause the auction to be held by one of their officials.

The proceeds take the place of the thing.

980. The auction is not permissible until after the persons entitled to receive the thing have been summoned by a public advertisement of the finding to give notice of their rights within a fixed period and the period has elapsed; it is not permissible if notice has been given in due time.

The advertisement is not necessary if destruction of the thing is to be apprehended, or its custody would involve disproportionate expense.

981. If three years have elapsed since the expiration of the period fixed in the advertisement, and if no one entitled to receive the thing has given notice of his right, the proceeds of the auction accrue to the Treasury of the Empire in the case of Imperial offices and agencies; to the Treasury of the State in the case of State offices and agencies; to the communal authority in the case of communal offices and agencies; and in the case of commercial agencies conducted by a private person to such person.

If the auction has been held without the public advertisement, the three years' period does not begin to run until after the persons entitled to receive the thing have been summoned by a public advertisement of the finding to give notice of their rights. The same rule applies if money found has been handed over to the proper authority.

The costs shall be deducted from the amount to be handed over.

982. The advertisement prescribed in 980, 981 is made according to the provisions enacted by the Federal Council in the case of Imperial offices and agencies, or by the central authority of a State in all other cases.

983. If a public office is in possession of a thing which it is bound to deliver to a person without the obligation resting upon any contract, and if the person entitled to receive it or his residence is unknown to the office, the provisions of 979 to 982 apply *mutatis mutandis*.

984. If a thing is discovered which has been so long concealed that its owner can no longer be found (*i.e.*, treasure trove), and in consequence of the discovery is taken possession of by the discoverer, the ownership as to one moiety is acquired by the discoverer, and as to the other moiety by the owner of the thing wherein the treasure trove was concealed.

FOURTH TITLE.
Claims Arising from Ownership (i).

985. The owner of a thing may demand its return from any possessor (k).

986. The possessor may refuse to return the thing if he or the indirect possessor (l) from whom he derives his right to possession is entitled to the possession as against the owner. If the indirect possessor is not authorised as against the owner to surrender possession to the possessor, the owner may require the possessor to return the thing to the indirect possessor, if the letter cannot or will not resume possession, to himself.

The possessor of a thing which has been alienated under 931 by assignment of the claim for its return, may set up against the new owner any defences which he has against the assigned claim.

987. A possessor shall return to the owner the emoluments which he draws after action commenced.

If the possessor after action commenced does not draw emoluments which he might draw according to the rules of proper husbandry, he is bound to com-

---

(*i*) The claims dealt with under this title are: (1) claims for the return of a thing (985); (2) claims for the removal of interference with rights of ownership; and (3) claims for searching for and removing a thing situate upon the land of another. 1005.

(*k*) No matter whether he is a direct or indirect possessor.

(*l*) Cf. 868.

pensate the owner in so far as fault [m] is imputable to him.

988. If a possessor who possesses a thing as belonging to him, or for the purpose of exercising over the thing a right of use which does not actually belong to him, has acquired the possession gratuitously, he is bound as against the owner to return the emoluments which he has drawn before action commenced, under the provisions [n] relating to the return of unjustified benefits.

989. The possessor, from the date of action commenced, is responsible to the owner for any damage which arises by reason of the fact that the thing, in consequence of his fault, deteriorates, perishes, or cannot be returned by him for any other reason [o].

990. If the possessor, at the time of acquiring possession, was in bad faith [p], he is liable to the owner under the provisions of 987, 989, as from the time of the acquisition. If the possessor subsequently [q] learns that he is not entitled to possession, he is liable in the same manner as from the time of obtaining the knowledge.

A more extensive liability of the possessor on account of default [r] remains unaffected [s].

991. If a possessor [t] derives his right to possession from an indirect possessor [u], the provisions of 990 apply in respect of emoluments only if the conditions of 990 exist with reference to the indirect possessor also, or if action has been commenced against him.

If the possessor was in good faith at the time of acquiring possession he is, nevertheless, responsible to the owner as from the time of acquiring possession,

---

(*m*) Cf. 276.

(*n*) 812 *et seq.*

(*o*) *E.g.*, alienation of the thing by the possessor.

(*p*) Cf. 932, par. 2.

(*q*) Cf. note (*f*) to 937.

(*r*) Cf. 284—290.

(*s*) A *bonâ fide* possessor is liable only under 987—989; and 991, par. 2.

(*t*) *I.e.*, a *malâ fide* possessor.

(*u*) Cf. 868.

for the damage specified in 989, in so far as he is responsible to the indirect possessor.

992. If a possessor has obtained possession by unlawful interference [(x)] or by a criminal act, he is liable to the owner under the provisions relating to compensation for unlawful acts [(y)].

993. If the conditions specified in 987 to 992 do not exist, the possessor shall, under the provisions relating to the return of unjustified benefits [(z)], return the fruits which he has drawn, in so far as such fruits are not to be regarded as the produce of the thing according to the rules of proper husbandry; for the rest he is neither bound to return emoluments nor to make compensation for them.

For the time for which the emoluments remain with the possessor, the provisions of 101 apply.

994. The possessor may require from the owner reimbursement for the necessary outlay [(a)] incurred upon the thing. He shall not, however, be reimbursed for the ordinary costs of preservation for the time for which the emoluments remain with him.

If, after action commenced or after the creation of the liability specified in 990, the possessor incurs necessary outlay, the duty of the owner to make reimbursement is determined according to the provisions relating to management of affairs without mandate [(b)].

995. Necessary outlay within the meaning of 994 includes also any payments which the possessor has made on account of charges on the thing. For the time for which the emoluments remain with the possessor, he is entitled to be reimbursed only for payments on such extraordinary charges as are deemed to be imposed upon the corpus of the thing.

(*x*) Cf. 858.

(*y*) Cf. 823 *et seq.*, especially 848 and 849.

(*z*) Cf. 812 *et seq.*

(*a*) Cf. 256, 273, 995, 996.

(*b*) See 683, 684.

996. The possessor may require reimbursement for unnecessary outlay only where it is incurred before action commenced, and before the creation of the liability specified in 990, and the value of the thing is increased by such outlay at the time at which the owner recovers the thing.

997. If the possessor has attached to the thing another thing as an essential component part (c) he may separate and retain it. The provisions of 258 apply.

The right to separate the thing is barred if the possessor may not require reimbursement of outlay under 994, par. 1, sentence 2, or if the separation is of no use to him (d), or if he is reimbursed for at least the value which the component part would have for him after the separation.

998. If a piece of agricultural land is to be returned the owner shall make reimbursement for any outlay which the possessor has incurred upon fruits which are not yet gathered, but are, according to the rules of proper husbandry, to be gathered before the end of the agricultural year (e), in so far as such outlay is incurred in accordance with the rules of proper husbandry and does not exceed the value of the fruits (f).

999. A possessor may demand reimbursement of outlay incurred by a farmer possessor whose successor in title he has become, to the same extent as the former possessor could have demanded it, if he had had to return the thing.

The obligation of the owner to make reimbursement of outlay extends also to outlay which had been incurred before he acquired the ownership.

1000. The possessor may refuse to return the thing until his claim for reimbursement of outlay is satisfied. He does not have a right of lien (g) if he has obtained the thing by a wilful unlawful act (h).

(*c*) Cf. 93—95.

(*d*) The *onus probandi* is upon the owner. The "use" need not have a *money* value; a mere *sentimental* value is enough.

(*e*) The period of the "agricultural year" is to be determined in each case according to the kind of fruits.

(*f*) This provision applies even in favour of a *malâ fide* possessor.

(*g*) Cf. 273, 274.

(*h*) Cf. 823 *et seq*.

1001. The possessor may enforce his claim for reimbursement of outlay only if the owner recovers the thing, or ratifies (i) the outlay. Before the time of ratifying the outlay, the owner may relieve himself of the claim by returning the thing recovered. The ratification is deemed to have been given, if the owner accepts the thing offered to him by the possessor with reservation of the claim.

1002. If the possessor returns the thing to the owner, the claim for reimbursement of outlay is extinguished upon the expiration of one month, or in the case of land upon the expiration of six months, after the return of the thing, unless within such period the claim is enforced in court, or the owner ratifies the outlay.

The provisions of 203, 206, 207 applicable to prescription apply *mutatis mutandis* to these periods (k).

1003. The possessor may summon the owner, stating the amount required as reimbursement, to declare within a fixed reasonable period whether or not he ratifies the outlay. After the expiration of the period the possessor is, if ratification is not made in due time, entitled to seek satisfaction out of the thing under the provisions relating to sale of pledges (l), or, in the case of land, under the provisions relating to compulsory execution on immoveable property (m).

If the owner disputes the claim before the expiration of the period, the possessor may satisfy himself out of the thing only if, after a determination by a non-appellable decree of the amount of the outlay, he has summoned the owner to make a declaration within a fixed reasonable period, and the period has expired; the right to seek satisfaction out of the thing is barred, if ratification is given in due time.

1004. If ownership is impaired in any other way than by deprivation or withholding of possession, the owner may require the disturber to remove the injury. If a continuance of the injury is to be apprehended, the owner may

---

(i) Cf. 182 *et seq.*

(k) *I.e.*, the periods of one month and six months specified in the preceding paragraphs.

(l) Cf. 1228 *et seq.*

(m) See Act of March 24th, 1897, relating to compulsory auction and compulsory management.

apply for an injunction.

The claim is barred if the owner is bound to submit to the injury.

1005. If a thing is situated upon land which is in the possession of a person other than the owner of the thing, the latter has against the possessor of the land the claim specified in 867.

1006. It is presumed [(n)] in favour of a possessor of a moveable that he is owner of such moveable. This does not apply, however, as against a former possessor from whom the thing has been stolen, or who has lost it, or has otherwise been deprived of it, unless it is money or an instrument payable to bearer.

It is presumed [(n)] in favour of a former possessor of a moveable that he was owner of such moveable during the time of his possession.

In the case of indirect possession the presumption applies to the indirect possessor [(o)].

1007. A person who has had a moveable in his possession may require the return of the thing from its possessor, if the latter was in bad faith at the time of acquiring possession.

If the thing was stolen from the former possessor, or was lost, or if he was otherwise deprived of it, he may require its return even from a possessor in good faith, unless the latter is owner of the thing, or had been deprived of possession of the thing before the time of possession of the former possessor. This provision does not apply to money nor to instruments payable to bearer.

The claim is barred if the former possessor was in bad faith at the time of acquiring possession, or if he has relinquished possession. For the rest the provisions of 986 to 1003 apply *mutatis mutandis*.

(*n*) The presumption is rebuttable.

(*o*) Cf. 868.

FIFTH TITLE.
Co-ownership.

1008. If the ownership of a thing belongs to several persons by undivided shares [(p)] the provisions of 1009 to 1011 apply.

1009. The thing held in co-ownership may be charged with rights even in favour of one of the co-owners.

The charging of a piece of land held in co-ownership with rights in favour of the owner for the time being of another piece of land, or the charging of another piece of land with rights in favour of the owners for the time being of the land held in co-ownership is not excluded by reason of the fact that the other land belongs to one of the owners of the land held in co-ownership.

1010. If the co-owners of a piece of land have regulated the management and use of the land, or have excluded permanently or temporarily the right to demand partition [(q)] or prescribed a term of notice, the arrangement made is not effective as against a successor in title of one of the co-owners unless it has been entered in the land register as a right with which the share is charged.

The claims specified in 755, 756 may not be enforced against a successor in title of one of the co-owners unless they have been entered in the land register.

1011. Every co-owner may enforce as against third parties any claims arising from ownership in respect of the entire thing; the claim for return of the thing, however, only subject to the conditions specified in 432.

(*p*) The provisions of 742—758 relating to community of ownership apply also to co-ownership by undivided shares, unless a contrary intention appears from 1009—1011. The German conception of co-ownership by undivided shares is that each of the co-owners is *sole* owner, not of the *whole* thing, but of *his share* in the thing. The code contains, however, no provisions as to co-ownership by divided shares.

(*q*) In the absence of any agreement to the contrary, each of the co-owners has a right to demand partition at any time. See 749, par. 1.

FOURTH SECTION.
HERITABLE BUILDING RIGHTS.

1012. A piece of land may be charged with a right (r) in such manner that the person in whose favour the right is created has an alienable and heritable right (s) to have a structure (t) upon or beneath the surface of such land (*i.e.*, a heritable building right).

1013. A heritable building right may be extended to the use of a part of the land not necessary for the structure, if it affords an advantage for the use of the structure (u).

1014. The limitation of a heritable building right to a part of a building, *e.g.*, to one particular story, is not permissible (x).

1015. The real agreement between the owner and the acquirer necessary according to 873 for the creation of a heritable building right must be declared at the land registry office, both parties being simultaneously present.

1016. A heritable building right is not extinguished by the destruction of the structure (y).

1017. The provisions relating to land apply to heritable building rights.

The provisions applicable to acquisition of ownership and to claims arising from ownership (z) apply *mutatis mutandis* to heritable building rights.

(r) The provisions of 873 *et seq.* apply.

(s) The right must be heritable, although it may be created for a definite time.

(t) The "structure" (*Bauwerk*) need not necessarily be a "building" (*Gebäude*).

(u) *E.g.*, garden, court-yard.

(x) Similarly the limitation of a heritable building right to a *fractional* part of a building is not permissible. Cf., however, Arts. 131, 182 of the IA.

(y) That is to say, the person having such right is entitled, though by no means bound to restore the structure.

(z) *I.e.*, 94—98, 303, 313, 416, 435, 436, 446, 477, 559 *et seq.*, 565, 566, 571, 873 *et seq.*, 905 *et seq.*, 925—928, 946, 985 *et seq.*, 1018 *et seq.*, 1031, 1094 *et seq.*, 1105 *et seq.*, 1113 *et seq.*

FIFTH SECTION.
SERVITUDES.

FIRST TITLE.
Real Servitudes.

1018. A piece of land may be charged with a right [(a)] in favour of the owner for the time being of another piece of land in such manner that the latter may use the land in certain ways, or that certain acts may not be done on the land, or that the exercise of a right is excluded which arises from the ownership of the servient tenement in respect of the other land (*i.e.*, a real servitude).

1019. A real servitude may consist only in a right which affords an advantage [(b)] for the use of the dominant tenement. The extent of the servitude cannot be stretched beyond the measure resulting from this.

1020. In the exercise of a real servitude the person entitled to it shall, as far as possible, pay regard to the interest of the owner of the servient tenement. If he maintains any structure upon the servient tenement for the exercise of the servitude, he shall maintain it in an orderly condition so far as the interest of the owner demands.

1021. If the exercise of a real servitude involves the erection of a structure upon the servient tenement, it may be required that the owner of such tenement has to maintain the structure [(c)] so far as the interest of the person entitled demands. If the owner has a right to the common use of the structure, it may be required that the person entitled has to maintain the structure so far as is necessary for the owner's exercise of the right of use.

The provisions relating to perpetual charges on land [(d)] apply *mutatis*

(*a*) 873, par. 1.

(*b*) Mere pleasure (*Annehmlichkeit*) is also an "advantage" within the meaning of this provision.

(*c*) *I.e.*, the owner of the servient tenement may be bound to do a punitive act.

(*d*) See 1105 *et seq.*, especially 1107 and 1108.

mutandis to such duty of maintenance.

1022. Where a real servitude consists in a right to maintain a structure upon a structure of the servient tenement, the owner of the servient tenement shall, unless it is otherwise provided maintain his structure so far as the interest of the person entitled demands. The provision of 1021, par. 2, applies also to such duty of maintenance.

1023. Where the exercise for the time being of a real servitude is limited to a part of the servient tenement [(e)], the owner may require the exercise of the servitude to be transferred to another place equally suitable for the person entitled, if the exercise of it in the former place is especially onerous to him; he shall bear and advance the cost of the transfer. This applies even where the part of the land to which the exercise of the servitude is limited is specified by juristic act.

The right to the transfer may not be excluded or limited by juristic act.

1024. Where a real servitude conflicts with another real servitude or other right of use of the land [(f)] in such manner that the rights cannot or cannot completely be exercised concurrently, and if the rights have equal rank [(g)], either of the entitled parties may require the exercise of the rights to be regulated in an equitable manner, having regard to the interests of all the parties concerned.

1025. Where the dominant tenement is divided the real servitude continues in respect of the several parts; its exercise is, however, in case of doubt permissible only in such manner that it does not become more onerous to the owner of the servient tenement. If the servitude affords an advantage to one only of the parts, it is extinguished [(h)] in respect of the remaining parts.

1026. If the servient tenement is divided, and if the exercise of the real servitude is limited to a specified part of the servient tenement [(i)], the parts

---

(*e*) As, *e.g.*, in the case of a right of way.

(*f*) *E.g.*, a heritable building right, a usufruct, or a limited personal servitude.

(*g*) Cf. 879 *et seq.*

(*h*) *Ipso facto.*

(*i*) If the exercise of the real servitude is not so limited, it continues to exist over the several parts.

which lie outside the limits of its exercise are discharged from the servitude.

1027. If injury is done to a real servitude, the party entitled to the servitude has the rights specified in 1004 [(k)].

1028. Where a structure has been erected upon the servient tenement whereby the real servitude is injured, the claim of the person entitled for the abatement of the injury is subject to prescription [(l)], even if the servitude is registered in the land register [(m)]. Upon the prescription of the claim the servitude is extinguished, so far as the existence of the structure is incompatible with it.

The provisions of 892 do not apply.

1029. If a possessor of a piece of land is disturbed in his exercise of a real servitude entered in the land register in the name of the owner, the provisions applicable to protection of possession [(n)] apply *mutatis mutandis*, provided the servitude has been exercised within one year before the disturbance, even though it be only once.

SECOND TITLE.
Usufruct [(o)].

I. Usufruct of Things.

1030. A thing[(p)] may be charged with a right in such manner that the

---

(*k*) Cf. 1029.

(*l*) The period of prescription is thirty years. 195.

(*m*) An exception to 902.

(*n*) Cf. 858—864.

(*o*) This title deals only with those usufructs which are created by juristic acts. The code does not recognise any *statutory* usufructs except the cases of the "usufruct" by the husband of the wife's property (1363 *et seq.*), and the "usufruct" by the father (or by the mother) of the child's property. 1649 *et seq.*, 1685, 1686. These two cases are, however, subject to the special provisions under their respective heads, and the rules of "usufruct" apply only in cases where it has been expressly so provided. See, *e.g.*, 1378, 1383, 1384, 1652 and 1663.

(*p*) Cf. 90—103. For the creation of a usufruct of a piece of land, registration in the land register is necessary. Cf. 873—902.

person in whose favour the right is created is entitled to draw the emolument of the thing (*i.e.*, a usufruct) [q].

A usufruct may be limited by the explosion of certain classes of emoluments [r].

1031. By virtue of the usufruct of a piece of land the usufructuary acquires the usufruct of its accessories [s] under the provisions of 926 applicable to acquisition of ownership.

1032. For the grant of the usufruct of a moveable it is necessary that the owner deliver the thing to the acquirer and a real agreement be made between the parties that the usufruct shall belong to the latter. The provisions of 929, sentence 2, and 930 to 936 apply *mutatis mutandis*; in the cases provided for by 936 the only effect is that the usufruct takes priority to the right of the third party.

1033. The usufruct of a moveable may be acquired by usucapion [t]. The provisions applicable to acquisition of ownership by usucapion apply *mutatis mutandis* [u].

1034. The usufructuary may have the condition if the thing determined by experts at his own expense. The owner has the same right.

1035. In the case of a usufruct of an aggregate of things the usufructuary and the owner are mutually bound to concur in drawing up an inventory. The inventory shall bear the date when it was drawn up, and shall be subscribed by both parties; either party may require that the subscription be publicly certified.

Either party may also require that the inventory be drawn up by the competent public authority, or a competent official, or notary. The party who requires such drawing up or certification shall bear and advance the costs.

(*q*) A usufruct, being a personal servitude, can be created only in favour of a particular person.

(*r*) A usufruct may be created in respect of a fractional part of a thing.

(*s*) *I.e.*, in addition to the usufruct of its component parts. Cf. 93—96. On the meaning of "accessories", see 97 and 98.

(*t*) On the usucapion of a usufruct of land, see 900.

(*u*) *I.e.*, 937—945.

1036. The usufructuary is entitled to the possession of the thing [x].

In the exercise of the right of use he shall continue the former economic purpose of the thing and shall act according to the rules of proper management.

1037. The usufructuary is not entitled to transform the thing or to alter it essentially.

The usufructuary of a piece of land may erect new structures for the purpose of obtaining stone, gravel, sand, loam, clay, marl, peat, and other component parts of the soil [y] in so far as the economic purpose of the land is not thereby essentially altered.

1038. If a forest is the object of a usufruct, both the owner and the usufructuary may require that the extent of the use and the manner of the economic operations shall be settled by a plan of management. If an important change of circumstances comes about, either party may require a corresponding change of the plan of management. Each party shall bear one-half the expenses.

The same rule applies if a mine or other structure designed for obtaining component parts of the soil is the object of the usufruct.

1039. The usufructuary also acquires ownership of any fruit [z] which he takes contrary to the rules of proper husbandry, or which he takes in excess where this has become necessary in consequence of some special occurrence. He is, however, without prejudice to his responsibility for fault [a], bound to make good to the owner at the termination of the usufruct the value to the fruits, and to give security [b] for the fulfilment of such obligation. Both the owner and the usufructuary may require that the amount to be made good be applied to the restoration of the thing in so far as it is consistent with proper husbandry.

If such application to the restoration of the thing is not required, the duty

---

(x) Cf. 854 *et seq.*, 868, 1065.

(y) All component parts of the soil acquired by the usufructuary belong to him. See 99, par. 2; and 954.

(z) Where the fruits consist in products or other component parts of the thing, ownership is acquired upon their separation from the thing. See 954.

(a) If fault is imputable to him, the provisions of 823 *et seq.* are applicable.

(b) See 232—240.

of making compensation is extinguished in so far as the emoluments accruing to the usufructuary are injured by the irregular or excessive taking of the fruit.

1040. The right of the usufructuary does not extend to the share of the owner in treasure trove [(c)] which is found in the thing.

1041. The usufructuary shall take care of the preservation of the thing in its economic condition. The duty to make repairs and renewals is incumbent upon him only in so far as they are connected with the customary preservation of the thing.

1042. If the thing is destroyed, or damaged, or an extraordinary repair or renewal of the thing or a precaution for the protection of the thing against an unforeseen danger becomes necessary, the usufructuary shall give notice to the owner without delay. The same rule applies if a third party claims any right over the thing.

1043. If the usufructuary of a piece of land himself undertakes an extraordinary repair or renewal which has become necessary [(d)] he may, for this purpose, within the limits of proper management, apply component parts of the land which do not belong to the fruits accruing to him.

1044. If the usufructuary does not himself undertake a repair or renewal of the thing which has become necessary, he shall allow the owner to undertake it and, where land is the object of the usufruct, to apply the component parts of the land specified in 1043.

1045. The usufructuary shall, at his own expense, take out insurance against damage by fire and other accidents to the thing for the term of the usufruct, if such insurance is in accordance with the rules of proper management. The insurance shall be taken out in such manner that the claim against the insurer belongs to the owner.

If the thing has already been insured, the payments to be made on the

---

(*c*) For the meaning of the words "treasure trove", see 984.

(*d*) Since he is not bound to do this, he has a claim for compensation as provided for in 1049.

insurance shall be made by the usufructuary during the term of the usufruct in so far as he would be bound to insure the thing[(e)].

1046. The usufructuary has a usufruct of the claim against the insurer under the provisions [(f)] which apply to usufruct of an outstanding claim which bears interest.

If any damage occurs which is covered by the insurance, both the owner and the usufructuary may require that the insurance money be applied to the restoration of the thing or to the creation of a substitute in so far as this is consistent with proper management. The owner may himself take charge of such application or leave it to the usufructuary.

1047. A usufructuary is bound, during the term of the usufruct, to bear on behalf of the owner all public charges upon the thing, with the exception of the extraordinary charges which are deemed to be imposed upon the corpus of the thing; and all private charges upon the thing existing at the time of the grant of the usufruct, *e.g.*, interest upon hypothecary claims and land charges; and also any payments to be made by reason of an annuity charge [(g)].

1048. If a piece of land with its appurtenant stock is the object of a usufruct, the usufructuary may dispose of the individual units of the stock within the limits of proper management. He shall [(h)] provide for making good any deterioration caused by ordinary use, and also the units of the stock which are consumed according to the rules of proper management; the articles provided by him become, upon incorporation in the stock, the property of the person to whom the stock belongs.

If the usufructuary takes the appurtenant stock at an appraised valuation with the obligation to return it at the termination of the usufruct at an appraised valuation, the provisions of 588, 589 apply *mutatis mutandis*.

(*e*) In this case the owner alone has the right to require the usufructuary to make the payments due on the insurance.

(*f*) See 1076—1079.

(*g*) Similarly this provision applies to payments to be made by reason of a perpetual charge on land. 1105 *et seq*.

(*h*) At his own expense.

1049. If the usufructuary incurs any outlay upon the thing, although he is not bound to do so, the duty of the owner to make compensation is determined according to the provisions relating to management of affairs without mandate [(i)].

The usufructuary is entitled to remove an attachment with which he has provided the thing [(k)].

1050. The usufructuary is not responsible for any alteration or deterioration of the thing which is brought about by the proper exercise of the usufruct [(l)].

1051. If the conduct of the usufructuary causes apprehension of a serious violation of the rights of the owner, the owner may require security to be given [(m)].

1052. If the usufructuary is ordered by a non-appellable decree to give security, the owner may require, instead of security, that the exercise of the usufruct be assigned to a receiver to be appointed by the Court to act on behalf of the usufructuary. The decree appointing a receiver may be issued only if a period for the giving of security has been allotted by the Court to the usufructuary upon the application of the owner, and the period has elapsed; the decree may not be issued if the security is given before the expiration of the period.

The receiver is under the supervision of the Court like a receiver appointed by the Court for the compulsory management of land. The owner may also be appointed receiver.

The management by the receiver shall be terminated if security be subsequently given.

1053. If the usufructuary uses the thing in an unauthorised way, and if he continues so to use the thing in spite of a warning by the owner, the latter may apply for an injunction.

1054. If the usufructuary violates the rights of the owner to a serious

---

(*i*) *I.e.*, 677 *et seq.*

(*k*) Cf. 258.

(*l*) As to what constitutes a "proper exercise of the usufruct", see 1036, par. 2; 1037 and 1041.

(*m*) See 232—240.

extent, and if he continues the injury in spite of a warning by the owner, the latter may demand a decree of management as provided for in 1052.

1055. The usufructuary is bound to return the thing to the owner after the termination of the usufruct.

In the case of a usufruct of agricultural land the provisions of 591, 592 apply *mutatis mutandis*; in the case of a usufruct of a farm the provisions of 591 to 593 apply *mutatis mutandis*.

1056. If the usufructuary has let a piece of land under an ordinary or usufructuary lease which extends beyond the term of the usufruct, after the termination of the usufruct the provisions of 571, 572, 573, sentence 1, and 574 to 576, 579 applicable to the case of alienation apply *mutatis mutandis*.

The owner is entitled to give notice of the termination of the lease, subject to the statutory term of notice [(n)]. If the usufructuary relinquishes the usufruct, the notice is permissible only after the time at which the usufruct would become extinct even if it had not been relinquished.

The lessee is entitled to summon the owner to make a declaration within a fixed reasonable period whether or not he will exercise his right of giving notice. The notice may be given only before the expiration of the period.

1057. The claims of the owner for compensation on account of alterations or deterioration of the thing and the claims of the usufructuary for reimbursement of outlay incurred, or for permission to remove an attachment, are barred by prescription in six months. The provisions of 558, pars. 2 and 3 apply *mutatis mutandis*.

1058. As between the usufructuary and the owner the grantor of the usufruct is deemed to be the owner in favour of the usufructuary, unless the usufructuary knows that the grantor is not owner.

1059. Usufruct is not transferable [(o)]. The exercise of the usufruct may

---

(*n*) See 565 and 595.

(*o*) It cannot therefore be pledged. See 1274, par. 2.

be transferred to another [p].

1060. If a usufruct conflicts with another usufruct or another right of use of the thing in such manner that the rights cannot, or cannot completely, be exercised concurrently, and if the rights have equal rank [q], the provision of 1024 applies.

1061. A usufruct is extinguished upon the death of the usufructuary. If the usufruct belongs to a juristic person, it is extinguished upon the loss of juristic personality.

1062. If the usufruct of a piece of land is terminated by a juristic act, in case of doubt the termination extends also to the usufruct of its accessories.

1063. The usufruct of a moveable is extinguished if the ownership and the usufruct merge in the same person [r].

The usufruct is deemed not to be extinguished in so far as the owner has a legal interest in the continuance of the usufruct.

1064. A declaration made by the usufructuary to the own or grantor that he gives up the usufruct is sufficient to terminate the usufruct of a moveable by juristic act.

1065. If the right of the usufructuary is injured, the provisions applicable to claims arising from ownership [s] apply *mutatis mutandis* to the claims of the usufructuary.

1066. If a usufruct exists in the share of one co-owner [t], the usufructuary exercises the rights which result from the community of the co-owners in respect of the management of the thing and the manner of its use.

The dissolution of the community may be demanded only by the co-owners

---

(*p*) The transferee has, in such a case, only a *jus in personam* against the usufructuary.

(*q*) See 879 *et seq.*

(*r*) This provision is not applicable to a usufruct of land. See 889.

(*s*) See 985—1007, 1011.

(*t*) Cf. 1008.

and the usufructuary jointly.

If the community is dissolved, the usufruct of the objects which take the place of the share enure to the usufructuary.

1067. If fungible things [(u)] are the object of a usufruct, the usufructuary becomes owner of the things; after the termination of the usufruct he shall make good to the grantor the value which the things had at the time of the grant. Both the grantor and the usufructuary may have the value determined by experts at his own expense.

The grantor may require security to be given if the claim for making good the value is endangered.

II. Usufruct of Rights.

1068. The object of a usufruct may also be a right.

The provisions relating to the usufruct of things apply *mutatis mutandis* to the usufruct of rights, unless a contrary intention appears from 1069 to 1084.

1069. The grant of a usufruct of a right is effected according to the provisions applicable to the transfer of rights [(x)].

A usufruct of a right which is not transferable may not be granted.

1070. If a right by virtue of which an act of performance can be demanded [(y)] is the object of a usufruct, the provisions which apply to the legal relation between the acquirer and the person bound in the case of a transfer of the right [(z)] apply *mutatis mutandis* to the legal relation between the usufructuary and the person bound.

If the exercise of the usufruct is transferred to a receiver as provided for in 1052, the transfer is effective as against the person bound only if he has knowledge of the decree issued, or if the decree is communicated to him. The same

---

(*u*) Cf. 92.

(*x*) See 398 *et seq.*; and 873.

(*y*) *E.g.*, an interest-bearing claim, or a perpetual charge on land.

(*z*) See *e.g.*, 404—410.

rule applies to the termination of the management by the receiver.

1071. A right subject to a usufruct may be terminated by juristic act only with the consent of the usufructuary. The consent shall be declared to the person in whose favour it is given; it is irrevocable. The provision of 876, sentence 3, remains unaffected.

The same rule applies to the case of an alteration of the right, so far as the alteration impairs the usufruct.

1072. The usufruct may also be terminated in the manner provided for by 1063, 1064, even if the right subject to the usufruct is not a right over a moveable [a].

1073. The usufructuary of an annuity, a right to recurring acts of performance stipulated for in the transfer of a farm, or a similar right, can demand the several payments which can be demanded by reason of the right [b].

1074. The usufructuary of a claim is entitled to collect the claim, and, if its maturity depends upon notice by the creditor, to give such notice. He shall take care for its proper collection. He is not entitled to make other dispositions of the claim.

1075. Upon payment by the debtor to the usufructuary the creditor acquires the object given in payment, and the usufructuary acquires the usufruct of the object.

If fungible things [c] are given in payment, the usufructuary acquires the ownership of such things; the provisions of 1067 apply *mutatis mutandis*.

1076. If a claim bearing interest is the object of a usufruct, the provisions of 1077 to 1079 apply.

1077. The debtor may pay the principal only to the usufructuary and the creditor in common. Either of them may require that payment be made to them in

---

(*a*) *E.g.*, a hypotheca.

(*b*) Cf. IA, Art. 96.

(*c*) Cf. 92.

common; either may demand lodgment on their joint account, instead of payment.

The usufructuary and the creditor may only give notice in common. Notice by the debtor is effective only if it is communicated to the usufructuary and the creditor.

1078. If the claim is matured, the usufructuary and the creditor are mutually bound to concur in its collection. If maturity depends upon notice, either party may require the other to concur in giving notice, if the collection of the claim is required by the rules of proper management of property on account of danger to its security.

1079. The usufructuary and the creditor are mutually bound to concur in the investment of the collected capital under the provisions [(d)] applicable to the investment of money belonging to a ward, and in the simultaneous grant of a usufruct to the usufructuary. The usufructuary determines the manner of investment.

1080. The provisions relating to the usufruct of a claim apply also to the usufruct of a land charge [(e)], or of an annuity charge [(f)].

1081. If the object of a usufruct is an instrument payable to bearer or an instrument to order endorsed in blank, the possession of the instrument and of its renewal coupons belongs to the usufructuary and the owner jointly. The possession of the interest coupons, annuity coupons, or dividend coupons of the instrument belongs to the usufructuary.

For the grant of the usufruct, the creation of joint possession suffices instead of the delivery of the instrument.

1082. The instrument together with its renewal coupons shall, on demand by the usufructuary or owner, be lodged in a lodgment office, subject to the condition that withdrawal can be required only by the usufructuary and the owner in common. The usufructuary may also require lodgment in the Imperial bank.

(*d*) See 1807, 1808.

(*e*) See 1191 *et seq.*

(*f*) See 1199 *et seq.*

1083. The usufructuary and the owner of the instrument are mutually bound to collect the matured principal; to procure new interest coupons, annuity coupons, or dividend coupons; and to concur in other measures which are required by the rules of proper management of property.

In case of the payment of the instrument the provisions of 1079 apply. Any surplus paid at the time of payment is deemed to be part of the principal.

1084. If an instrument to bearer or an instrument to order indorsed in blank is a fungible thing within the meaning of 92, the provisions of 1067 apply.

III. Usufruct of a Person's Whole Property.

1085. A usufruct of the whole property of a person may be granted only in such manner that the usufructuary acquires the usufruct of the individual object comprised in such property. Where the usufruct is so granted, the provisions of 1086 to 1088 apply.

1086. The creditors of the grantor may, in so far as their claims were created before the grant, demand satisfaction out of the objects subject to the usufruct, without regard to the usufruct. If the usufructuary has acquired ownership of fungible things [(g)], the claim of the grantor for reimbursement for the value takes the place of the things; the usufructuary is bound towards the creditors to make immediate reimbursement.

1087. The grantor may, if any claim created before the grant is due, require the usufructuary to return the objects necessary for the satisfaction of the creditor. The grantor has the right of selection; he may, however, only select the appropriate objects. If the objects returned suffice, the grantor is bound to satisfy the creditor on behalf of the usufructuary.

The usufructuary may fulfil the obligation by delivery of the object owed. Where the object owed is not included in the property which is subject to the usufruct, the usufructuary is entitled, for the purpose of satisfying the creditor, to alienate an object belonging to the property, if satisfaction by the grantor

(*g*) Cf. 92, 1067, 1084.

cannot be expected with certainty. He has to select an appropriate object. Where he is bound to make reimbursement for the value of fungible things he cannot alienate.

1088. The creditors of the grantor, whose claims were already bearing interest at the time of the grant, may also demand interest from the usufructuary during the term of the usufruct. The same rule applies to other periodical payments which, in due course of management, are paid out of the income of the property, provided the claim was created before the grant of the usufruct.

The liability of the usufructuary may not be excluded or limited by agreement between him and the grantor.

The usufructuary is liable to the grantor for the satisfaction of the creditors in respect of any of the claims specified in par. 1. The grantor may require the return of any objects for the purpose of satisfying the creditors only if the usufructuary is in default with the fulfilment of the obligation to make such satisfaction.

1089. The provisions of 1085 to 1088 apply *mutatis mutandis* to the usufruct of an inheritance.

THIRD TITLE.

Limited Personal Servitudes [(h)].

1090. A piece of land [(i)] may be charged with a right [(k)] in such manner

---

(*h*) A "limited personal servitude" and a "real servitude" resemble each other in that both consist of the same rights (cf. 1018 and 1090); they differ, however, from each other in that the former may be granted only to a particular person or persons (cf. 1092), while the latter is granted to any person who is the owner "for the time being" of the land to which it refers. Cf. 1018. A limited personal servitude resembles a usufruct in that both may be granted only to a particular person or persons (see 1059, 1061, 1092); but it differs from the latter in two respect: (1) A usufruct may refer to moveables as well as immoveables (see 1030—1033), while a limited personal servitude refers only to immoveables (see note (*i*) to 1090); and (2) in the absence of any express limitation, the grant of a usufruct includes *all* emoluments derived from the usufructuary object; whereas the grant of a limited personal servitude over a piece of land confers a right to use the land "in certain ways" only. Cf. 1030, 1090.

(*i*) A moveable may not be subjected to a limited personal servitude.

(*k*) Cf. 873, par. 1.

that the person in whose favour the right exists is entitled to use the land in certain ways, or that some other authority belongs to him which can constitute the substance of a real servitude (*i.e.*, a limited personal servitude).

The provisions of 1020 to 1024, 1026 to 1029, 1061 apply *mutatis mutandis*.

1091. The extent of a limited personal servitude is determined, in case of doubt, by the personal necessities of the person entitled to such servitude.

1092. A limited personal servitude is not transferable. The exercise of the servitude can be transferred to another person only if the transfer is authorised.

1093. The right to use a building or a part of a building as a dwelling to the exclusion of the owner may also be granted as a limited personal servitude. The provisions of 1031, 1034, 1036, 1037, par. 1., 1041, 1042, 1044, 1049, 1050, 1057, 1062, applicable to usufruct, apply *mutatis mutandis* to such right.

The person so entitled is authorised to take into the dwelling his family and the persons required for service and attendance suitable to his station in life.

If the right is limited to a part of the building the person entitled to such right may make use of all structures and fittings intended for the common use of the inmates.

SIXTH SECTION.
REAL RIGHT OF PRE-EMPTION (*l*).

1094. A piece of land may be charged with a right in such manner that the person in whose favour the right exists is entitled to pre-emption as against the owner (*m*).

The right of pre-emption may also be created in favour of the owner for the time being of another piece of land.

(*l*) Cf. note (*q*), p. 109.

(*m*) The right must be entered in the land register. 873, par. 1.

1095. An undivided share in a piece of land can be charged with a right of pre-emption only if it consists of the share of a co-owner.

1096. The right of pre-emption may be extended to the accessories (n) which are sold with the land. In case of doubt it is to be presumed that the right of pre-emption is to extend to such accessories.

1097. The right of pre-emption is limited to the case of a sale by the owner to whom the land belongs at the time when such right is granted, or by his heirs. It may, however, be created for several or all cases of sale.

1098. The legal relation between the person entitled and the person bound is determined according to the provisions of 504 to 514. The right of pre-emption can be exercised even in the case of a discretionary sale of the land by a trustee in bankruptcy (o).

As against third parties the right of pre-emption has the effect of a caution (p) for the securing of the claim for the transfer of ownership arising from the exercise of the right.

1099. If the land comes into the ownership of a third party, he may communicate to the person entitled to the right the terms of the contract of sale, in the same manner as the person bound by the right and with the same consequences as those specified in 510, par. 2.

The person bound shall inform the new owner as soon as the right of pre-emption is exercised or barred (q).

1100. If the new owner is the purchaser or a successor in title of the purchaser, he may refuse his consent to the registration as owner of the person entitled, and to the delivery of the land until the purchase price agreed upon between the person bound and the purchaser, in case it has been paid, be repaid to him. If the person entitled obtains registration as owner, the former

---

(*n*) Cf. 97, 98.

(*o*) The rule is otherwise in the case of a personal right of pre-emption. See 512.

(*p*) On the effect of a caution, see 883, par. 2; and 888, par. 1.

(*q*) *Scilicet*, by lapse of time.

owner may, upon delivery of the land, demand from him the repayment of the purchase price already paid.

1101. Where the person entitled has to repay to the purchaser or his successor in title the purchase price as provided for in 1100, he is discharged from the obligation to pay the purchase price due on pre-emption.

1102. If, in consequence of the exercise of the right of pre-emption, the purchaser or his successor in title loses his ownership, the purchaser is, where the purchase price owed by him is not yet paid, discharged from his obligation; he may not demand back the purchase price paid.

1103. A right of pre-emption existing in favour of the owner for the time being of a piece of land may not be separated from the ownership of such land.

A right of pre-emption existing in favour of a particular person may not be annexed to the ownership of a piece of land.

1104. Where the person entitled is unknown, he may be excluded from his right by means of public summons if the conditions exist which are specified in 1170 for the exclusion of a hypotheca creditor. Upon the issue of the decree for exclusion the right of pre-emption is extinguished.

These provisions do not apply to a right of pre-emption which exists in favour of the owner for the time being of a piece of land.

SEVENTH SECTION.
PERPETUAL CHARGES ON LAND.

1105. A piece of land may be charged with a right in such manner that periodical acts of performance are to be done with the means derived from the land [(r)] in favour of the person in whose favour the right exists (*i.e.*, a perpetual

---

(r) "The means derived from the land" (*aus dem Grundstücke*) = the "products" of the land, or the "proceeds" of a sale of the land under compulsory execution. Cf. 1147.

charge [s]).

A perpetual charge may also be granted in favour of the owner for the time being of another piece of land.

1106. An undivided share in a piece of land may be charged with a perpetual charge only where it consists of the share of a co-owner.

1107. The provisions relating to interest payments upon a hypothecary claim [t] apply *mutatis mutandis* to the individual acts of performance.

1108. The owner is also personally liable for the acts of performance becoming due during the time of his ownership, unless it is otherwise provided.

If the land is divided the owners of the several parts are liable as joint debtors [u].

1109. If the land of the person entitled is divided the perpetual charge continues to exist for the benefit of the several parts. If the act of performance is divisible, the shares of the owners are determined in proportion to the size of the parts; if it is not divisible, the provisions of 432 apply. The exercise of the right is, in case of doubt, permissible only in such manner that it does not become more onerous for the owner of the land subject to the perpetual charge.

The person entitled may provide that the right shall be attached to only one of the parts. The provision shall be made at the land registry office, and requires entry in the land register. The provisions of 876, 878 apply *mutatis mutandis*. If the person entitled alienates a part of the land without making such a provision, the right remains attached to the part which he retains.

If the perpetual charge is of advantage to only one of the parts it remains attached to such part alone.

1110. A perpetual charge existing in favour of the owner for the time being of a piece of land may not be separated from the ownership of such land.

(*s*) The charge must be entered in the land register. 873, par. 1. This provision may be modified by State legislation. See IA, Art. 115.

(*t*) See, *e.g.*, 1158, 1159, 1178.

(*u*) Cf. 421—426.

1111. A perpetual charge existing in favour of a particular person may not be attached to the ownership of a piece of land.

If the claim for the individual acts of performance is not transferable [x], the right may not be alienated or charged.

1112. If the person entitled is unknown, the provisions of 1104 apply *mutatis mutandis* to the exclusion of his right.

Eighth Section.
HYPOTHECA. LAND CHARGE. ANNUITY CHARGE.

FIRST TITLE.
Hypotheca.

1113. A piece of land [y] may be charged with a right in such manner that to the person in whose favour the right [z] is created a specified sum of money is to be paid out of the land in satisfaction of a claim belonging to him (*i.e.*, a hypotheca).

A hypotheca may also be granted for a future or a conditional claim.

1114. An undivided share in a piece of land may be charged with a hypotheca only if it consists of the share of a co-owner [a].

1115. In the registration of a hypotheca, the name of the creditor, the amount of the claim, and, if the claim bears interest, the rate of interest, and where other accessory payments are to be made, their amount must be stated in the land register; for the rest reference may be made to the authorization for registration for fuller specification of the claim.

In the case of the registration of a hypotheca for a loan for consumption

(*x*) Cf. 399, 400.

(*y*) Or a heritable building right. See 1017, 1114, 1120, 1132.

(*z*) Cf. 873, par. l.

(*a*) Cf. 1008 *et seq.*

made by a credit institution whose charter has been made public by the competent authority, a reference to the charter is sufficient for the specification of such accessory payments as are to be made according to the charter in addition to the interest.

1116. A certificate of hypotheca is issued for the hypotheca [b].

The issue of the certificate may be excluded. The exclusion may also take place subsequently. A real agreement between the creditor and the owner and registration in the land register are necessary for such exclusion; the provisions of 873, par. 2, and 876, 878 apply *mutatis mutandis*.

The exclusion of the issue of the certificate may be set aside; the setting aside is made in the same manner as the exclusion.

1117. In so far as the issue of a certificate of hypotheca is not excluded, the creditor does not acquire the hypotheca until the certificate is delivered to him by the owner of the land. The provisions of 929, sentence 2, and of 930, 931, apply to the delivery.

For the delivery of the certificate may be substituted an agreement that the creditor shall be entitled to have the certificate delivered to him by the land registry office.

If the creditor is in possession of the certificate, it is presumed that the delivery has been made [c].

1118. By virtue of the hypotheca the land is liable both for the statutory interest on the claim and for the costs of notice and of legal proceedings instituted for the purpose of obtaining satisfaction out of the land.

1119. If the claim does not bear interest, or if the rate of interest is less than five per cent., the hypotheca may be enlarged without the consent of persons having rights of equal or inferior rank, to the extent of making the land liable for interest up to five per cent.

For any alteration of the time and place of payment, the consent of persons

---

(*b*) The rule is otherwise in the case of a cautionary hypotheca. 1185, par. 1.

(*c*) The presumption is rebuttable.

having such rights is likewise not necessary.

1120. The hypotheca extends to all products severed from the land and to other component parts [(d)], in so far as they have not passed upon their severance into the ownership of some person other than the owner or proprietary possessor [(e)] of the land a provided for in 954 to 957; and to all accessories of the land [(f)], with the exception of the accessories which have not passed into the ownership of the owner of the land.

1121. Products and other component parts of the land and its accessories are discharged from the liability, if they are alienated [(g)] and removed from the land before they have been distrained upon in favour of the creditor.

If the alienation takes place before the removal, the acquirer may not, as against the creditor, set up that he was in good faith in respect of the hypotheca. If the acquirer removes the thing from the land, a distraint made before the removal is effective against him only if he is in bad faith in respect of the distraint at the time of the removal [(h)].

1122. If the products or component parts have been severed from the land within the limits of proper husbandry, their liability is extinguished even without alienation, if they are removed from the land before being distrained upon, unless the removal is made for a temporary purpose.

Accessories are discharged from the liability without alienation, if before the distraint the accessory character is destroyed [(i)] within the limits of proper husbandry.

1123. If the land is let under an ordinary or usufructuary lease, the hypo-

---

(*d*) Cf. 93—96.

(*e*) Cf. 872.

(*f*) Cf. 97, 98.

(*g*) Whether the alienation conforms with the rules of "proper husbandry" or not, or whether it takes place by voluntary act or by means of compulsory execution, is immaterial.

(*h*) The acquirer is in bad faith if he knows or does not know, as a result of negligence, that the distraint has been made. Cf. 932, par. 2. The burden of proving bad faith is upon the creditor.

(*i*) An accessory ceases to be such when it is permanently separated from the principal thing, or when it ceases to serve the economic purpose of the principal thing. 97.

theca extends to the claim for the rent.

Where the claim is matured, it is discharged from the liability upon the lapse of one year [(k)] since the date of maturity, unless within such period the distraint has been made in favour of the hypotheca creditor. If the rent is payable in advance, such discharge does not extend to any rent for a later time than the current and following calendar quarter at the time of the distraint.

1124. If the rent is collected before it has been distrained upon in favour of the hypotheca creditor, or if any other disposition has been made of it before the distraint, the disposition is effective as against the hypotheca creditor. If the disposition consists of the transfer of the claim to a third party [(l)], the liability of the claim is extinguished; if a third party acquires a right in the claim, it takes priority in rank to the hypotheca.

The disposition is ineffective as against the hypotheca creditor in so far as it relates to any rent for a later time than the current and following calendar quarter at the time of the distraint.

It is equivalent to the transfer of the claim to a third party, if the land is alienated without the claim.

1125. Where the collection of the rent is invalid as against the hypotheca creditor [(m)], the lessee may not set off against the hypotheca creditor a claim belonging to him against the lessor.

1126. If a right to periodical acts of performance is annexed to the ownership of the land [(n)], the hypotheca extends to the claims for such acts of performance. The provisions of 1123, par. 2, sentence 1, 1124, pars. 1, 3, and 1125, apply *mutatis mutandis*. A disposition, made before the distraint, of a claim to an act of performance which does not become due till three months after the distraint, is ineffective as against the hypotheca creditor.

1127. If objects subject to the hypotheca are insured for the owner or

---

(*k*) On the reckoning of the year, see 187, 188.

(*l*) Cf. 398 *et seq.*

(*m*) See 1124.

(*n*) *E.g.*, by virtue of a perpetual charge. 1105 *et seq.*

proprietary possessor [(o)] of the land, the hypotheca extends to the claim against the insurer.

The liability of the claim against the insurer is extinguished if the insured object is restored, or a substitute for it is provided.

1128. If a building is insured, the insurer may not, as against the hypotheca creditor, pay the insurance money to the insured until he or the insured has given notice to the hypotheca creditor of the occurrence of the damage, and one month has elapsed since receipt of the notice. The hypotheca creditor may, before the expiration of such period, prohibit the insurer from making any payment. The notice may be dispensed with if it is impracticable [(p)]; in such a case the month is reckoned from the date at which the insurance money becomes due.

For the rest the provisions applicable to a pledged claim [(q)] apply; the insurer, however, may not set up that he was unaware of a hypotheca discoverable from the land register.

1129. If an object other than a building is insured, the liability of the claim against the insurer is determined according to the provisions of 1123, par. 2, sentence 1, and 1124, pars. 1 and 3.

1130. If according to the conditions of the Insurance the insurer is bound only to pay the insurance money for the restoration of the insured object [(r)], a payment to the insured which satisfies the conditions is effective as against the hypotheca creditor [(s)].

1131. If a piece of land is ascribed to another piece in the land register as provided for in 890, par. 2, all hypothecas existing on such other piece of land extend to the land ascribed. Rights with which the ascribed land is charged

---

(*o*) Cf. 872.

(*p*) *E.g.*, if the whereabouts of the hypotheca creditor is unknown.

(*q*) See 1279—1290.

(*r*) This provision applies to the insurance of a building as well as of any other object.

(*s*) Whether the insured has used the money for the purpose of restoring the insured object or not, is immaterial.

have priority in rank to such hypothecas.

1132. If a claim is secured by a hypotheca on several pieces of land (*i.e.*, a collective hypotheca), each piece of land is liable for the whole claim [t]. The creditor may seek satisfaction at his discretion out of each of the pieces of land, in whole or in part.

The creditor is entitled to distribute the amount of the claim among the several pieces of land in such manner that each piece is liable only for the amount assigned to it. The provisions of 875, 876, 878 apply *mutatis mutandis* to the distribution.

1133. If, in consequence of deterioration of the land, the security of the hypotheca is endangered [u], the creditor may allot to the owner a fixed reasonable period for the removal of the danger. After the expiration of the period the creditor is entitled to seek satisfaction forthwith [x] out of the land, unless the danger has been removed by the improvement of the land, or by the grant of an additional hypotheca. If the claim does not bear interest and is not yet matured, the creditor is only entitled to a sum which, with addition of the statutory interest [y] from the time of payment till maturity, would equal the amount of the claim.

1134. If the owner or a third party [z] deals with the land in such a manner that deterioration of the land endangering the security of the hypotheca is to be apprehended, the creditor may apply for an injunction.

If the act proceeds from the owner, the Court shall, upon the application of the creditor, order the necessary measures for the prevention of the danger. The same rule applies if the deterioration is to be apprehended by reason of the fact that the owner omits the necessary precautions against any interference on the part of third parties, or against other injuries.

(*t*) Cf. 1172.

(*u*) The question as to whether the deterioration was caused by the owner of the land, or by a third party, or by accident, is entirely immaterial.

(*x*) *I.e.*, even before the hypotheca has become due.

(*y*) At 4 per cent. 246.

(*z*) *E.g.*, an ordinary or usufructuary lessee.

1135. It is equivalent to deterioration of the land within the meaning of 1133, 1134, if accessories to which the hypotheca extends [(a)] have deteriorated or are removed from the land contrary to the rules of proper husbandry.

1136. An agreement is void whereby the owner binds himself to the creditor [(b)] not to alienate the land nor to subject it to further rights.

1137. The owner may avail himself, as against the hypotheca, of all defences which the personal debtor has against the claim, and also of all defences which a surety has under 770 [(c)]. If the personal debtor dies, the owner may not set up for himself that the heir has only a limited liability for the debt.

If the owner is not the personal debtor, he does not lose a defence merely because the latter has waived it.

1138. The provisions of 891 to 899 apply to the hypotheca even in respect of the claim and the defences which the owner has under 1137.

1139. If, in granting a hypotheca for a loan for consumption, the issue of a certificate of hypotheca has been excluded, an application made by the owner [(d)] to the land registry office is sufficient for the registration of an objection to the effect that the loan has not been made, provided such application has been presented before the expiration of one month after the registration of the hypotheca. If the objection is registered within the month the registration has the same effect as if the objection had been registered simultaneously with the hypotheca.

1140. Where the incorrectness of the land register appears from a certificate of hypotheca or a memorandum upon the certificate, the provisions of 892, 893 do not apply. An objection to the correctness of the land register which appears from the certificate or a memorandum upon the certificate is equivalent

---

(*a*) See 1120—1122.

(*b*) He may, however, bind himself to any person other than the creditor. Cf. 137, 903.

(*c*) The defence of prescription is excepted from this rule. See 223, par. 1, and 902.

(*d*) According to 29 of the Land Registration Act, the application must be made in publicly certified form.

to an objection entered in the land register.

1141. If the maturity of the claim depends upon notice, the notice is effective in respect of the hypotheca only if it is communicated by the creditor to the owner, or *vice versâ*. In favour of the creditor, the person who is registered in the land register as owner is deemed to be the owner.

If the owner is not domiciled in the Empire, or if the conditions of 132, par. 2, exist, the District Court in whose district the land is situated shall, upon the application of the creditor, appoint a representative of the owner to whom the creditor's notice can be given.

1142. The owner is entitled to satisfy the creditor, if the claim has become due in respect of him, or if the personal debtor is entitled to make payment.

The satisfaction may also be made by lodgment or by set-off.

1143. If the owner is not the personal debtor, and if he satisfies the creditor, the claim [(e)] is transferred to him. The provisions of 774, par. 1, applicable to a surety, apply *mutatis mutandis*.

If the claim is secured by a collective hypotheca [(f)] the provisions of 1173 apply to such hypotheca.

1144. The owner, on satisfying the creditor, may require the delivery of the certificate of hypotheca and of all other documents which are necessary for the rectification of the land register or for the cancellation of the hypotheca.

1145. If the owner satisfies the creditor in part he may not require the delivery of the certificate of hypotheca [(g)]. The creditor is bound to make a memorandum of the partial satisfaction on the certificate, and to produce the certificate at the land registry office for the purpose of rectification of the land register, or for cancellation, or to produce it to the competent authority or a competent notary, for the purpose of drawing up a part certificate for the owner.

(*e*) Cf. 1153.

(*f*) Cf. 1132.

(*g*) He may, however, require the delivery of "the other documents" described in the preceding section.

The provision of par. 1, sentence 2, applies to interest and other accessory payments only if they become due later than the calendar quarter in which the creditor is satisfied or the following quarter. The provision does not apply to costs for which the land is liable as provided for in 1118.

1146. If the conditions arise with reference to the owner under which a debtor is in default [(h)], interest for default is payable to the creditor out of the land.

1147. The satisfaction of the creditor out of the land and the objects to which the hypotheca extends [(i)], is effected by means of compulsory execution.

1148. In the prosecution of the right arising from the hypotheca, the person who is registered in the land register as owner is deemed to be the owner in favour of the creditor. The right of an unregistered owner to set up the defences which he has against the hypotheca remains unaffected.

1149. The owner may not, so long as the claim has not become due as against him, confer upon the creditor the right to require the transfer of the ownership of the land for the purpose of satisfaction or to alienate the land in any manner other than by compulsory execution.

1150. If the creditor requires satisfaction out of the land, the provisions of 268, 1144, 1145 apply *mutatis mutandis.*

1151. If the claim is divided, the consent of the owner is not necessary for the alteration of the relative rank of the partial hypothecas among themselves [(k)].

1152. If the claim is divided, and if the issue of a certificate of hypotheca is not excluded, a part certificate of hypotheca may be issued [(l)] for each part; the consent of the owner of the land is not necessary. The part certificate takes the place, in respect of the part to which it relates, of the former certificate.

(*h*) Cf. 284, 285, 1141.

(*i*) Cf. 1120—1131.

(*k*) An exception to 880, par. 2, sentences 2 and 3.

(*l*) By the land registry office, a Court or a notary. See 61 of the Land Registration Act.

1153. Upon the transfer of the claim [m] the hypotheca passes to the transferee.

The claim may not be transferred without the hypotheca, and *vice versâ*.

1154. For the assignment [n] of the claim the issue of a written declaration of assignment and delivery of the certificate of hypotheca are necessary; the provisions of 1117 apply. Upon the application of the assignee, the assignor shall cause the declaration of assignment to be publicly certified at his own expense.

For the written declaration of assignment may be substituted the registration of the assignment in the land register.

If the issue of the certificate of hypotheca is excluded [o], the provisions of 873, 878 apply *mutatis mutandis* to the assignment of the claim.

1155. If any right, which a possessor of a certificate of hypotheca has in the capacity of creditor, appears from a series of publicly certified declarations of assignment leading back to a registered creditor, the provisions of 891 to 899 apply in the same manner as if the possessor of the certificate were registered in the land register as creditor. A judicial decree of assignment and a publicly certified acknowledgment of the transfer of the claim by operation of law [p] are equivalent to a publicly certified declaration of assignment.

1156. The provisions of 406 to 408 applicable to the transfer of a claim do not apply to the legal relation between the owner and the transferee in respect of the hypotheca [q]. The transferee must, however, permit a notice given by the owner to the transferor to be valid as against himself, unless at the time of the notice the transfer was known to the owner or was registered in the land register.

(*m*) The transfer may be effected by assignment (cf. 1154), or by operation of law (cf. 412), or by means of compulsory execution.

(*n*) Cf. 398—413.

(*o*) Cf. 1116, par. 2.

(*p*) Cf. 412.

(*q*) 1158 contains an exception to this rule.

1157. A defence which the owner has against the hypotheca by reason of a legal relation existing between him and the transferor [(r)] may also be set up against the transferee. The provisions of 892, 894 to 899, 1140 apply also to such defence.

1158. Where the claim is for interest or other accessory payments, which become due not later than the calendar quarter in which the owner has knowledge of the transfer, or the following quarter, the provisions of 406 to 408 apply to the legal relation between the owner and the transferee [(s)]; the transferee cannot set up the provisions of 892 against the defences which the owner has under 404, 406 to 408, 1157.

1159. Where the claim is for arrears of interest or other accessory payments, the transfer as well as the legal relation between the owner and the transferee are determined by the general provisions applicable to the transfer of claims [(t)]. The same rule applies to the claim for reimbursement of costs for which the land is liable as provided for in 1118.

The provisions of 892 do not apply to the claims specified in par. 1.

1160. The enforcement [(u)] of the hypotheca may be opposed, where the issue of a certificate of hypotheca is not excluded [(x)], if the creditor does not produce the certificate; if the creditor is not registered in the land register, the documents specified in 1155 shall also be produced.

A notice or warning given to the owner is ineffective, if the creditor does not produce the necessary documents as provided for in par. 1, and the owner without delay [(y)] rejects the notice or warning for this reason.

These provisions do not apply to the claims specified in 1159.

(*r*) See 1137, 1138.

(*s*) Cf., however, 1156.

(*t*) Cf. 398 *et seq*. That is to say, the transfer need not be registered in the land register.

(*u*) No matter whether by legal proceedings or otherwise.

(*x*) Cf. 1116, par. 2.

(*y*) *I.e.*, without culpable delay. 121.

1161. If the owner is the personal debtor [(z)], the provisions of 1160 apply also to the enforcement of the claim.

1162. If a certificate of hypotheca is lost or destroyed, it may be declared void by public summons [(a)].

1163. If the claim for which the hypotheca is granted is not created, the hypotheca belongs to the owner. If the claim becomes extinct [(b)], the owner acquires the hypotheca.

A hypotheca for which the issue of a certificate is not excluded belongs to the owner until the delivery of the certificate to the creditor.

1164. If the personal debtor satisfies the creditor, the hypotheca passes to him in so far as he can demand reimbursement from the owner or from a predecessor in title of the owner. If only partial reimbursement is to be made to the debtor, the owner may not enforce the hypotheca, where it has passed to him, to the injury of the hypotheca of the debtor.

It is equivalent to the satisfaction of the creditor if claim and debt merge in the same person [(c)].

1165. If the creditor relinquishes the hypotheca, or if he cancels it under 1183, or if he grants priority to another right [(d)], the personal debtor is discharged from his liability in so far as he would have been able to obtain reimbursement under 1164 out of the hypotheca if the creditor had not done any one of such acts.

1166. If the personal debtor is entitled to require reimbursement from the owner, provided he satisfies the creditor, and if the creditor proceeds to the compulsory auction of the land without giving him notice without delay [(e)], he

---

(*z*) If the owner is not a personal debtor, the enforcement of the claim is governed by the general provisions of the law of obligations. See especially 410.

(*a*) See 1003 *et seq.* of the Code of Civil Procedure.

(*b*) As to the different ways in which a claim may become extinct, see 362 *et seq.*

(*c*) Be he the creditor or the personal debtor.

(*d*) Cf. 880.

(*e*) Cf. 121, par. 1.

may refuse to satisfy the creditor on account of a deficiency from the compulsory auction in so far as he suffers damage in consequence of the omission of the notification. The notification may be omitted if it is impracticable [(f)].

1167. If the personal debtor, where he satisfies the creditor, acquires the hypotheca [(g)], or if he has in case of satisfaction any other legal interest in the rectification of the land register, the rights specified in 1144, 1145, belong to him [(h)].

1168. If the creditor relinquishes the hypotheca the owner [(i)] acquires it.

The relinquishment shall be communicated to the land registry office or to the owner, and requires entry in the land register. The provisions of 875, par, 2, and 876, 878 apply *mutatis mutandis.*

If the creditor relinquishes the hypotheca in respect of a part of the claim, the rights specified in 1145 belong to the owner.

1169. If the owner has a defence whereby the enforcement of the hypotheca is permanently excluded, he may require the creditor to relinquish the hypotheca.

1170. Where the creditor is unknown he may be excluded from his rights by means of public summons, if ten years have elapsed since the last entry in the land register relating to the hypotheca, and the right of the creditor has not been recognised within such period by the owner in a manner appropriate according to 208 for the interruption of prescription. If a date has been fixed for the payment of the claim, the period does not begin to run till the expiration of the day of payment.

Upon the issue of the decree of exclusion the owner acquires the hypotheca. The certificate of hypotheca issued to the creditor becomes void.

(*f*) *E.g.*, where the creditor does not know who is the personal debtor, or does not know his whereabouts.

(*g*) As to when this happens, see 1164.

(*h*) If the personal debtor does not acquire the hypotheca, and if he has no legal interest in the rectification of the land register, he may only demand a receipt from the creditor. 368.

(*i*) No matter whether he is also the personal debtor or not.

1171. An unknown creditor may be excluded from his rights by means of public summons, even if the owner is entitled to satisfy the creditor [(k)] or to give notice, and lodges the amount of the claim for the benefit of the creditor with a waiver of the right of withdrawal [(l)]. The lodgment of interest is necessary only if the rate of interest is entered in the land register; interest for an earlier time than the fourth calendar year prior to the issue of the decree of exclusion is not to be lodged.

Upon the issue of the decree of exclusion the creditor is deemed to be satisfied, in so far as satisfaction has not already been made under the provisions relating to lodgment [(m)]. The certificate of hypotheca issued to the creditor becomes void.

The right of the creditor to the amount lodged is extinguished upon the lapse of thirty years after the issue of the decree of exclusion, unless the creditor reports himself at the lodgment office within such period; the person making the lodgment is entitled to withdraw the amount lodged, even if he has waived the right of withdrawal.

1172. A collective hypotheca [(n)] belongs, in the cases provided for by 1163, to the owners of the charged lands in common.

Each owner may, unless it has been otherwise agreed upon, require that the hypotheca on his land be limited according to 1132, par. 2, to the amount which corresponds to the proportion of the value of his land to the aggregate value of the pieces of land, and be allotted to him with such limitation. The value is reckoned with a deduction of the amounts secured by rights which have priority to the collective hypotheca.

1173. If the owner of one of the pieces of land subject to a collective hypotheca satisfies the creditor, he acquires the hypotheca on his own land; the hypotheca on the other pieces of land is extinguished. It is equivalent to the satisfaction of the creditor by the owner if the creditor's right is transferred to the

(*k*) Cf. 1142, par. 1.

(*l*) Cf. 376, par. 2 (1).

(*m*) See 378.

(*n*) Cf. 1132, par. 1.

owner, or if claim and debt merge in the owner.

If the owner who satisfies the creditor may require reimbursement from the owner of one of the other pieces of land or from a predecessor in title of that owner, the hypotheca on the land of that owner also passes to him to the extent of the claim for reimbursement; it remains with the hypotheca on his own land as a collective hypotheca.

1174. If a personal debtor satisfies a creditor who has a collective hypotheca, or if, in the case of a collective hypotheca, the claim and the debt merge in one person, and if the debtor can require reimbursement only from the owner of one of the pieces of land or from a predecessor in title of the owner, the hypotheca on such piece of land passes to him; the hypotheca on the other lands is extinguished.

If only partial reimbursement is to be made to the debtor, and if for this reason the hypotheca passes to him only in respect of a part of the amount, the owner is bound to deduct such part from the share in the residue of the collective hypotheca which accrues to him as provided for in 1172.

1175. If the creditor relinquishes the collective hypotheca, it accrues to the owners of the charged lands in common (o); the provisions of 1172, par. 2, apply. If the creditor relinquishes the hypotheca on one of the pieces of land, the hypotheca on that piece (p) is extinguished.

The same rule applies if the creditor is excluded from his right as provided for in 1170.

1176. If the conditions of 1163, 1164, 1168, 1172 to 1175 exist only in respect of a part of the hypotheca, the hypotheca accruing to the owner, or one of the owners, or to the personal debtor, by virtue of these provisions, may not be enforced to the injury of the hypotheca remaining with the creditor.

1177. If the hypotheca and the ownership merge in one person (q) while

(*o*) See 1168, par. 1; and 1172, par. 2.

(*p*) An exception to 1168, par. 1.

(*q*) The following are the cases of merger of hypotheca in ownership by operation of law: 1143, 1163, 1168, 1170, par. 2, 1171, par 2, 1172, 1173, 1175.

the claim belongs to a person other than the owner, the hypotheca is then converted into a land charge [(r)]. With respect to the question of interest, the rate of interest, the time of payment, notice, and place of payment, the provisions made in respect of the claim are applicable.

If the claim belongs also to the owner, his rights arising from the hypotheca, so long as the merger is operative, are determined according to the provisions applicable to a land charge belonging to the owner [(s)].

1178. The hypotheca in respect of arrears of interest and other accessory payments, and in respect of costs which are to be paid to the creditor, is extinguished if the hypotheca and the ownership merge in one person. The hypotheca is not extinguished where a right to the claim for such a payment belongs to a third party.

For the relinquishment of the hypotheca in respect of the payments specified in par. 1, a declaration to that affect made by the creditor to the owner is sufficient. So long as a right to the claim for such a payment belongs to a third party, the consent of such third party is necessary. The consent shall be declared to the person in whose favour it is given; it is irrevocable.

1179. Where the owner binds himself to another person to cause the hypotheca to be extinguished if the hypotheca and the ownership merge in one person, a caution [(t)] may be entered in the land register for securing the claim for extinction.

1180. For a claim secured by a hypotheca another claim may be substituted. A real agreement between the creditor and the owner and an entry in the land register are necessary for such substitution; the provisions of 873, par. 2, and 876, 878 apply *mutatis mutandis*.

If the claim which is to take the place of the former claim does not belong to the former hypotheca creditor, his consent is necessary; the consent shall be communicated to the land registry office or to the person in whose favour it is

(*r*) Cf. 1191, 1192.

(*s*) Cf. 1197.

(*t*) Cf. 883 *et seq.*

given. The provisions of 875, par. 2, and 876 apply *mutatis mutandis.*

1181. If the creditor is satisfied out of the land [u], the hypotheca is extinguished [x].

If the satisfaction is effected out of one of the pieces of land charged with a collective hypotheca, the other pieces of land are also discharged.

Satisfaction out of the objects to which the hypotheca extends [y] is equivalent to satisfaction out of the land.

1182. If, in the case of a collective hypotheca, the owner of the land out of which the creditor is satisfied can require reimbursement from the owner of one of the other pieces of land or from a predecessor in title of that owner, the hypotheca on the land of that owner passes to him. The hypotheca may not, however, if the creditor is only partially satisfied, be enforced to the injury of the hypotheca remaining with the creditor and, if the land is charged with a right of equal or subsequent rank, not to the injury of that right.

1183. For the release of a hypotheca by juristic act, the consent of the owner is necessary [z]. The consent shall be communicated to the land registry office or to the creditor; it is irrevocable.

1184. A hypotheca may be granted in such manner that the right of the creditor arising from the hypotheca is determined only according to the claim, and the creditor cannot appeal to any registration for evidence of the claim (*i.e.*, a cautionary hypotheca).

The hypotheca must be designated in the land register as a cautionary hypotheca.

1185. In the case of a cautionary hypotheca the issue of a certificate of hypotheca is excluded.

(*u*) By means of compulsory execution as provided for in 1147.

(*x*) Cancellation in the land register is not necessary.

(*y*) See 1120—1131.

(*z*) If the hypotheca does not belong to the owner himself, a declaration by the hypotheca creditor to the effect that he gives up the hypotheca is also necessary. The release must be registered in the land register. Cf. 875.

The provisions of 1138, 1139, 1141, 1156 do not apply.

1186. A cautionary hypotheca may be converted into an ordinary hypotheca, and *vice versâ* [(a)]. The consent of persons having rights of equal or subsequent rank is not necessary.

1187. In respect of a claim arising from an obligation to bearer, a bill of exchange, or any other instrument that can be transferred by indorsement, only a cautionary hypotheca can be granted. The hypotheca is deemed to be a cautionary hypotheca even if it is not designated as such in the land register [(b)]. The provision of 1154, par. 3, does not apply.

1188. A declaration communicated by the owner to the land registry office that he grants the hypotheca and registration in the land register are sufficient for the grant of a hypotheca [(c)] in respect of a claim arising from an obligation to bearer; the provision of 878 applies.

The exclusion of a creditor from his right, at provided for in 1170, is permissible only if the period for presentation specified in 801 has elapsed. If the obligation is presented or the claim upon the instrument is enforced in Court within the period, the exclusion may not be effected until after the lapse of the period of prescription.

1189. In the case of a hypotheca of the kind specified in 1187 a representative of the creditor for the time being may be appointed with the authority to make certain dispositions affecting the hypotheca, which shall be valid both in favour of and as against every subsequent creditor, and to represent the creditor in the enforcement of the hypotheca. For the appointment of the representative, registration in the land register is necessary.

If the owner is entitled to require the creditor to make a disposition which the representative is authorised to make, he may require the representative to make such a disposition.

(*a*) Both the consent of the creditor and of the owner of the charged land, and registration in the land register, are necessary. 877, 878.

(*b*) An exception to 1184, par. 2.

(*c*) "Hypotheca" here means "cautionary hypotheca". 1187.

1190. A hypotheca may be granted in such manner that only the maximum amount for which the land is to be liable is specified, the determination of the claim being in other respects reserved.

The maximum amount must be entered in the land register.

If the claim been interest, the interest is included in the maximum amount.

The hypotheca is deemed to be a cautionary hypotheca, even if it is not designated as such in the land register.

The claim may be transferred under the general provisions applicable to the transfer of claims (d). If it is transferred under those provisions, the transfer of the hypotheca is excluded (e).

SECOND TITLE.

Land Charge. Annuity Charge.

I. Land Charge.

1191. A piece of land may be charged (f) in such manner that a specified sum of money is to be paid out of the land to the person in whose favour the charge is made (*i.e.*, a land charge).

The charge may also be made in such manner that interest upon the sum of money, as well as other accessory payments, is to be paid out of the land (g).

1192. The provisions relating to hypothecas apply *mutatis mutandis* to land charges, except in so far as a contrary intention appears from the fact that a land charge does not presuppose a claim (h).

(*d*) *I.e.*, 398 *et seq.*

(*e*) If the hypotheca also is to pass to the new creditor, registration in the land register is necessary. Cf. 1185, par. 1; and 1154, par. 3.

(*f*) Cf. 873.

(*g*) In such a case the rate of interest and, if there are other accessory payments, their amount must be entered in the land register. See 1192, 1115.

(*h*) The following provisions are therefore inapplicable: 1137—1139, 1143, 1153, 1161, 1163, par. 1, 1164—1167, 1174, 1177, 1180, 1184—1190.

The provisions relating to interest on a hypothecary claim apply [(i)] to interest on a land charge.

1193. The principal of a land charge does not become due until after notice has been given. Both the owner and the creditor have the right to give notice. The term of notice is six months.

Different provisions are permissible [(k)].

1194. The payment of the principal as well as of interest and other accessory payments shall be made, unless otherwise provided, in the place where the land registry office is situated [(l)].

1195. A land charge may be granted in such a manner that the certificate of land charge is drawn to bearer. The provisions relating to obligations to bearer [(m)] apply *mutatis mutandis* to such a certificate.

1196. A land charge may also be granted to the owner.

For the grant of such a land charge, a declaration communicated by the owner to the land registry office of the effect that the land charge is to be registered in his name in the land register, and the registration are necessary; the provision of 878 applies.

1197. If the owner is the creditor, he may not levy compulsory execution for the purpose of satisfaction.

Interest is due to the owner only if the land is judicially attached upon the application of another person for the purpose of compulsory management, and only for the time of the compulsory management.

1198. A hypotheca may be converted into a land charge, and *vice versâ* [(n)]. The consent of persons having rights of equal or subsequent rank is not necessary.

(*i*) *I.e.*, 1115, 1118, 1119, 1145, par. 2, 1146, 1158, 1159, 1171, 1178.

(*k*) Cf. IA, Art. 117, par. 2.

(*l*) Cf., however, 1177, par. 1, sentence 2.

(*m*) *I.e.*, 793—806.

(*n*) Cf. note (*a*) to 1186.

II. Annuity Charge.

1199. A land charge may be granted in such manner that a specified sum of money is to be paid out of the land at regularly recurring periods (*i.e.*, an annuity charge).

In granting an annuity charge the amount, by payment of which the annuity charge may be redeemed, must be specified. The redemption sum must be stated in the land register.

1200. The provisions applicable to interest on a hypothecary claim [(o)] apply *mutatis mutandis* of the individual payments; and the provision applicable to the principal of a land charge apply *mutatis mutandis* to the redemption sum [(p)].

The payment of the redemption sum to the creditor has the same effect as the payment of the principal of a land charge.

1201. The right of redemption belongs to the owner.

The right to demand redemption cannot be conferred upon the creditor. In the case provided for by 1133, sentence 2, the creditor is entitled to demand the payment of the redemption sum out of the land.

1202. The owner can exercise the right of redemption only after notice has been given. The term of notice is six months, unless it is otherwise provided.

A limitation of the right to give notice is permissible only in so far as the owner can give notice after thirty years, with observance of the six months term.

If the owner has given notice, the creditor may, after the expiration of the term of notice, require the payment of the redemption sum out of the land.

1203. An annuity charge may be converted into an ordinary land charge, and *vice versâ* [(q)]. The consent of persons having rights of equal or subsequent rank is not necessary.

(*o*) See note (*i*) to 1192.

(*p*) See note (*h*) to 1192.

(*q*) See note (*a*) to 1186.

Ninth Section.
PLEDGE OF MOVEABLES AND OF RIGHTS.

FIRST TITLE.
Pledge of Moveables.

1204. A moveable may, for the securing of a claim [(r)], be charged in such manner that the creditor is entitled to seek satisfaction out of the moveable [(s)] (*i.e.*, a pledge).

A pledge may also be granted as a security for a future or a conditional claim.

1205. For the grant of a pledge it is necessary that the owner [(t)] deliver the thing to the creditor and make a real agreement with him to the effect that the pledge shall belong to the creditor. If the creditor is in possession of the thing, a real agreement as to the creation of the pledge is sufficient.

The delivery of a thing which is in the indirect possession [(u)] of the owner may be replaced by the owner transferring the indirect possession to the pledgee and notifying the pledge to the possessor.

1206. Instead of delivery of the thing the creation of joint possession is sufficient, if the thing is in the joint custody of the creditor; where it is in the possession of a third party, its delivery can be made only to the owner and the creditor jointly.

1207. If the thing does not belong to the pledgor, the provisions of 932, 934, 935, applicable to the acquisition of ownership, apply *mutatis mutandis* to the grant of a pledge.

(*r*) This need not be a money claim. Cf. 1113.

(*s*) By a sale of the thing pledged. 1228.

(*t*) Cf. 1207.

(*u*) Cf. 868—870.

1208. If the thing is charged with a right [(x)] of a third party, the pledge takes priority to such right, unless the pledgee, at the time of acquiring the pledge, was in bad faith as against such right[(y)]. The provisions of 932, par. 1, sentence 2, 935, and 936, par. 3, apply *mutatis mutandis*.

1209. The rank of a pledge is determined by the date of its grant, even if it was granted as a security for a future or a conditional claim.

1210. The thing pledged is liable for the claim in the condition in which it is at the time of the assertion of the right of pledge, as, *e.g.*, for interest and stipulated penalties [(z)]. If the personal debtor is not the owner of the thing pledged, the liability is not increased by any juristic act which the debtor enters into after the creation of the pledge.

The thing pledged is liable for the claims of the pledgee for reimbursement of outlay [(a)], for the costs of notice and of legal process to be repaid to the pledgee, and also for the costs of a sale of the thing pledged.

1211. The pledgor may set up as against the pledgee any defences which the personal debtor has against the claim, and also any defences which a surety has under 770. If the personal debtor dies, the pledgor may not avail himself of the fact that the heir has only a limited liability for the debt.

If the pledgor is not the personal debtor, he does not lose a defence through its waiver by the latter.

1212. The pledge extends to products which are severed from the thing pledged.

1213. A pledge may be granted in such manner that the pledgee is entitled to draw the emoluments [(b)] of the thing pledged.

(*x*) *E.g.*, a usufruct.

(*y*) The pledgee is deemed to be in bad faith, if the right of the third party was known to him, or was unknown to him as a result of negligence. Cf. 932, par. 2.

(*z*) Cf. 339 *et seq.*

(*a*) Cf. 1216, 256. The pledgee has a right of lien in respect of his claim for reimbursement of outlay. Cf. 273.

(*b*) Cf. 100.

If a thing which naturally bears fruit is delivered to the pledgee for his sole possession, it is to be presumed, in case of doubt, that the pledgee is entitled to take the fruits.

1214. If the pledgee has the right to draw the emoluments, he is bound to take care to secure the emoluments and to render an account [(c)].

The net proceeds of the emoluments shall be applied towards the satisfaction of the principal claim; but where costs and interest are to be paid, the net proceeds shall first be applied to the payment of the costs and interest.

Different provisions are permissible.

1215. The pledgee is bound to take the pledged thing into his custody as though he were a depositary [(d)].

1216. If the pledgee incurs any outlay upon the thing pledged, the pledgor's duty to make reimbursement is determined according to the provisions relating to management of affairs without mandate [(e)]. The pledgee is entitled to remove an attachment with which he has provided the thing pledged [(f)].

1217. If the pledgee violates the rights of the pledgor to a serious extent, and if he continues to do so in spite of a remonstrance of the pledgor, the pledgor may require that the thing pledged be lodged [(g)] at the expense of the pledgee, or if it is not suitable for lodgment, that it be delivered to a custodian appointed by the Court.

Instead of lodgment or delivery of the pledged thing to a custodian, the pledgor may require the return of the thing pledged on satisfaction made to the creditor. If the claim does not bear interest and is not yet due, the pledgee is only entitled to the sum which, with addition of statutory interest from the time

---

(*c*) Cf. 259.

(*d*) For the duty of the pledgor in respect of his custody of the thing pledged, see 688, 691, 692, 694, 697 and 698. The provision of 690 is not applicable to a pledgee who is responsible for all negligence in respect of his custody of the thing.

(*e*) Cf. 677—687.

(*f*) Cf. 258.

(*g*) Cf. 372 *et seq.*

of payment to maturity, would equal the amount of the claim.

1218. If the destruction of the thing pledged or a serious diminution of its value is to be apprehended, the pledgor may require the return of the thing pledged upon giving security in some other manner [(h)]; the giving of security by sureties is excluded.

The pledgee shall, without delay, notify the pledgor of the threatened destruction, if such notice is practicable.

1219. If the security of the pledgee is endangered by the threatened destruction of the thing pledged, or by an apprehended serious diminution in its value, he may cause the thing pledged to be sold by public auction.

The proceeds take the place of the thing pledged. On demand by the pledgor the proceeds shall be lodged [(i)].

1220. The auction sale of the thing pledged is permissible only after the pledgor has been warned of it; the warning may be dispensed with if the thing pledged is liable to be destroyed and there is danger in delaying the auction. In the case of a diminution in value it is necessary, besides the warning, that the pledgee shall have fixed a reasonable period for the pledgor to give further security, and that the period shall have elapsed.

The pledgee shall without delay notify the pledgor of the auction sale; if he fails to give such notice he is bound to make compensation.

The warning, the fixing of a period, and the notice may be dispensed with if they are impracticable.

1221. If the thing pledged has an exchange or market price, the pledgee may make the sale privately at the current price by a broker publicly empowered to make such sales or by a person authorised to hold public auctions.

1222. If a pledge exists over several things, each is liable for the whole claim.

(*h*) Cf. 232 *et seq.*

(*i*) Cf. 372 *et seq.*

1223. A pledge is bound to return the pledged thing to the pledgor after the extinction of the pledge.

The pledgor (k) may require the return of the thing pledged on satisfaction of the pledgee as soon as the debtor is entitled to make satisfaction.

1224. The satisfaction of the pledgee may also be effected by the pledgor by lodgment or set-off (l).

1225. If the pledgor is not the personal debtor, the claim (m) passes to him in so far as he satisfies the pledgee. The provisions of 774 applicable to a surety apply *mutatis mutandis*.

1226. The claims of the pledgor for compensation on account of alterations or deteriorations of the thing pledged, and also the claims of the pledgee for reimbursement of outlay incurred and for permission to remove an attachment (n), are barred by prescription in six months. The provisions of 558, pars. 2 and 3, apply *mutatis mutandis*.

1227. If any right of the pledgee is violated, the provisions applicable to claims arising from ownership (o) apply *mutatis mutandis* to the claims of the pledgee.

1228. The satisfaction of the pledgee out of the thing pledged is effected by sale.

The pledgee is entitled to sell the thing pledged as soon as the claim is due in whole or in part. If the object owed is not money, the sale is permissible only if the claim has been transmuted into a money claim.

1229. An agreement made before the right to sell has arisen, whereby the ownership of the thing is to pass or is to be transferred to the pledgee if satisfaction is not made, or is not made in due time, is void.

(k) No matter whether he himself or a third party is the personal debtor.

(l) The provisions of 372—396 apply *mutatis mutandis*.

(m) Likewise the right of pledge also passes to him. 1250.

(n) Cf. 1216.

(o) See 985—1007, 1011.

1230. Among several things pledged the pledgee may, unless it is otherwise provided, select which are to be sold. He may put up for sale only so many of the things pledged as are necessary for his satisfaction.

1231. If the pledgee is not in sole possession of the thing pledged [(p)], he may, as soon as the right to sell has arisen [(q)], demand the delivery of the thing pledged for the purpose of sale. In lieu of such delivery, the thing pledged shall, on demand by the pledgor, be delivered to a custodian appointed by the parties jointly; the custodian shall, upon acceptance of the thing, bind himself to keep it ready for sale.

1232. The pledgee is not bound to hand over to a pledgee subsequent to himself in rank the thing pledged for the purpose of sale. If he is not in possession of the thing pledged, and if he does not himself require the sale, he cannot prohibit the sale by a subsequent pledgee.

1233. The sale of the thing pledged shall be effected according to the provisions of 1234 to 1240.

If the pledgee has acquired for his right to sell an executory title against the owner, he may also cause the sale to be effected under the provisions [(r)] applicable to the sale of a judicially attached thing [(s)].

1234. The pledgee shall warn the owner in advance of the sale, and shall at the same time specify the amount in money on account of which the sale is to take place. The warning may not be given until after the tight to sell has arisen; it may be dispensed with if it is impracticable.

The sale cannot be made until the expiration of one month after the warning. If the warning is impracticable, the month is to be reckoned from the time when the right to sell arises.

(*p*) Cf. 1205, par. 2; and 1206.

(*q*) See 1228, par. 2.

(*r*) These are contained in 814—825 of the Code of Civil Procedure.

(*s*) The parties may agree upon some other mode of selling the thing as provided for in 1245 and 1246.

the same person. It is not extinguished so long as the claim secured by the pledge is charged with the right of a third party [(k)].

The pledge is deemed not to have been extinguished where the owner has a legal interest in the continuance of the pledge.

1257. The provisions relating to a pledge constituted by juristic act [(l)] apply *mutatis mutandis* to a pledge created by operation of law [(m)].

1258. If a pledge exists in the share of one co-owner [(n)], the pledgee exercises the rights which result from the community of the co-owners in respect of the management of the thing and the mode of its use.

Before the pledgee's right to sell [(o)] arises, the dissolution of the community can only be required in common by the co-owners and the pledgee. After the right to sell has arisen, the pledgee can require the dissolution of the community without the consent of the co-owner being necessary; he is not bound by any agreement whereby the co-owners have excluded permanently or temporarily the right to require the dissolution of the community or have prescribed a term of notice [(p)].

If the community is dissolved, there is due to the pledgee the pledge in the objects which take the place of the share.

The pledgee's right to sell the share remains unaffected.

1259. The special provisions of 1260 to 1271 apply to a pledge affecting a ship entered in the ship register [(q)].

1260. For the grant of such a pledge a real agreement between the owner of the ship and the creditor that the pledge shall belong to the creditor, and an

---

(k) *E.g.*, a pledge or a usufruct.

(l) *I.e.*, 1204—1256.

(m) Pledges created by operation of law are found in the following sections of this code: 233, 559—563, 581 and 585, 590, 647 and 704.

(n) Cf. 1008 *et seq.*

(o) Cf. 1228, par. 2.

(p) Cf. 1010, par. 1.

(q) Ships which have not or cannot be registered are treated in the same manner as any other moveables.

entry of the pledge in the ship register, are necessary. The provisions of 873, par. 2, and 878 apply *mutatis mutandis*.

In the registration must be stated the name of the creditor, the amount in money of the claim, and, if the claim bears interest, the rate of interest. For the detailed description of the claim, reference may be made to the authorisation for registration.

1261. The relative rank of pledges granted in respect of a registered ship is determined according to the provisions of 879 to 881 and 1151.

1262. So long as a pledge is entered in the ship register it remains operative in the case of alienation or charging of the ship, even if the acquirer is in good faith.

If the pledge is wrongfully cancelled and the ship is alienated, the provisions of 936, par. 1, sentence 1, and par. 2 apply, even if the acquirer obtains the ownership without delivery; the provision of 936, par. 3, does not apply. If a pledge which is subsequent in rank to the pledge wrongfully erased is transferred to a third party, the provision of 1208, sentence 1, applies.

1263. If the entries of the ship register in respect of a pledge are not in accord with the actual legal situation, the rectification of the register may be required according to the provisions of 894, 895, 897, 898 applicable to the rectification of the land register.

If a pledge has been wrongfully cancelled, an objection to the correctness of the ship register may be entered in the manner provided for by 899, par. 2. As long as the objection is entered, the same rule applies as against the acquirer in the case of alienation or charging of the ship as if the pledge were registered.

1264. The liability of the ship is limited to the registered amount of the claim and interest according to the registered rate of interest. The liability for statutory interest and for costs is determined according to the provision of 1118 applicable to hypotheca.

If the claim does not bear interest, or if the rate of interest is lower than five per cent., the pledge may, without the consent of persons having rights of equal or subsequent rank, be enlarged to the extent that the ship is liable for interest up to five per cent.

1265. A pledge affecting a registered ship extends to the accessories of the ship, with the exception of accessories which have not come into the ownership of the owner of the ship.

The provisions of 1121, 1122 applicable to hypotheca apply *mutatis mutandis* to the liability of the accessories.

1266. The provisions of 1205 to 1257 do not apply, in so far as modifications result from the fact that the pledgee does not obtain possession of the ship. In the case provided for by 1254 the right to require termination of the pledge takes the place of the claim for the return of the thing pledged.

1267. The pledgor may, upon satisfaction of the pledgee, require the issue of the documents necessary for the cancellation of the pledge. The personal debtor has the same right, if he has a legal interest in the rectification of the ship register.

1268. The pledgee may seek satisfaction out of the ship and its accessories only by virtue of an executory title according to the provisions applicable to compulsory execution [r].

1269. Where the creditor is unknown he may be excluded from his pledge by means of public summons, if the conditions prescribed in 1170 or in 1171 for the exclusion of a hypotheca creditor exist. Upon the issue of the decree of exclusion the pledge is extinguished. The provision of 1171, par. 3, applies.

1270. To the pledge for a claim arising from an obligation to bearer, from a bill of exchange, or from any other instrument which can be transferred by indorsement, the provisions of 1189, and to the pledge for a claim arising from an obligation to bearer, the provisions of 1188 also apply *mutatis mutandis*.

1271. A pledge affecting a registered ship may be granted in such manner

---

(*r*) Compulsory execution on a registered ship can be effected only by means of compulsory auction. 870, par. 2, of the Code of Civil Procedure. For further particulars, see sects. 162 to 171 of the Compulsory Auction Act.

that only the maximum amount for which the ship is to be liable is specified, the determination of the claim being in other respects reserved. The maximum amount must be entered in the ship register.

If the claim bears interest, the interest is included in the maximum amount.

1272. The provisions of 1260 to 1271 apply also to pledge of a share in a ship.

SECOND TITLE.
Pledge of Rights.

1273. A right can also be the object of pledge.

The provisions relating to pledge of moveables apply *mutatis mutandis* to pledge of rights in so far as a contrary intention does not appear from 1274 to 1296. The provisions of 1208 and 1213, par. 2, are not applicable.

1274. The grant of a pledge of a right is effected according to the provisions applicable to the transfer of rights [(s)]. If for the transfer of the right the delivery of a thing is necessary [(t)], the provisions of 1205, 1206 apply.

So long as a right is not transferable, a pledge of the right may not be granted.

1275. If a right by virtue of which an act of performance can be demanded is the object of a pledge, then to the legal relation between the pledgee and the person bound thereto, the provisions which, in the case of transfer of the right, apply to the legal relation between the acquirer and the person bound thereto [(u)], and in the case of an order of the Court issued according to 1217, par. 1, the provision of 1070, par. 2, applies *mutatis mutandis*.

1276. A pledged right may be terminated by juristic act only with the

---

(*s*) Cf. 398 *et seq.* and 873.

(*t*) An instance of this may be found in 1154, par. 1.

(*u*) See especially 401—410.

consent of the pledgee. The consent shall be declared to the person in whose favour it is given; it is irrevocable. The provision of 876, sentence 3, remains unaffected.

The same rule applies in the case of a modification of the right so far as it impairs the pledge.

1277. The pledgee may seek satisfaction out of the right only by virtue of an executory title according to the provisions applicable to compulsory execution [(x)], unless it is otherwise provided. The provisions of 1229 and 1245, par. 2, remain unaffected.

1278. If a right, for the pledging of which the delivery of a thing is necessary, is the object of a pledge, the provisions of 1253 apply *mutatis mutandis* to the termination of the pledge by the return of the thing.

1279. The special provisions of 1280 to 1290 apply to the pledge of a claim.

1280. The pledging of a claim which can be transferred by a mere contract of assignment is effective only if the creditor notifies the debtor of it.

1281. The debtor may only perform his part in favour of the pledgee and the creditor in common [(y)]. Each of them may require that performance be effected in favour of them in common; either may require, in lieu of performance, that the thing owed be ledged [(z)] on their joint account, or, if it is not suitable for lodgment, that it be delivered to a custodian appointed by the Court.

1282. If the conditions specified in 1228, par. 2, have arisen, the pledgee is entitled to collect the claim, and the debtor can perform his part only in favour of him. The right to collect a money claim belongs to the pledgee

---

(x) See 704 *et seq.* of the Code of Civil Procedure. The pledgee cannot seek satisfaction by a "private" extra-judicial sale, as is the case with the pledge of moveables. Cf. 1228.

(y) This provision presupposes that the conditions specified in 1228, par. 2, have not yet arisen. After the fulfilment of the conditions, the debtor is entitled to perform his part only in favour of the pledgee. See 1282, par. 1, sentence 1.

(z) See 372 *et seq.*

only in so far as is necessary for his satisfaction. Where he is entitled to collect the claim, he may also require that the money claim be assigned to him in lieu of payment.

The pledgee is not entitled to make any other disposition affecting the claim; the right to seek satisfaction out of the claim under 1277 remains unaffected.

1283. If the maturity of the pledged claim depends upon notice, the creditor may give notice without the consent of the pledgee, unless the latter is entitled to draw the emoluments of the claim [(a)].

Notice by the debtor is effective only if it is communicated both to the pledgee and to the creditor.

If the conditions specified in 1228, par. 2, have arisen, the pledgee is also entitled to give notice; a communication addressed to the pledgee is deemed to be a notice by the debtor.

1284. The provisions of 1281 to 1283 do not apply where the pledgee and the creditor agree otherwise.

1285. Where payment is to be made to the pledgee and the creditor in common [(b)], both are mutually bound to concur in its collection, if the claim is due.

Where the pledgee is entitled to collect the claim without the concurrence of the creditor [(c)], he shall take care for the proper collection. He shall, without delay, notify the creditor of the collection, unless the notification is impracticable.

1286. If the maturity of the pledged claim depends upon notice, and if the right to give notice does not belong to the pledgee [(d)], he can require notice from the creditor, where the collection of the claim is required by the rules of proper management of property on account of its security becoming endangered.

(*a*) *E.g.*, interest.

(*b*) Cf. 1281.

(*c*) Cf. 1282, 1294.

(*d*) Cf. 1283, par. 3.

Under the same conditions the creditor may require the pledgee to give his consent to the notice, where the consent is necessary (e).

1287. If the debtor makes payment in conformity with 1281, 1282, upon payment the creditor acquires the object given in payment, and the pledgee acquires a pledge over the object. If the payment consists in the transfer of the ownership of a piece of land, the pledgee acquires a cautionary hypotheca (f).

1288. If a money claim is collected in conformity with 1281, the pledge and the creditor are mutually bound to concur, provided it is practicable without injury to the interest of the pledge, in investing the sum collected according to the provisions applicable to the investment of money belonging to a ward (g), and simultaneously a pledge over the sum is granted to the pledge. The creditor determines the manner of investment.

If the collection is made in conformity with 1282, the claim of the pledgee, where the sum collected is due to him for his satisfaction, is deemed to be satisfied by the creditor.

1289. A pledge over a claim extends to the interest on the claim. The provisions of 1123, par. 2, and of 1124, 1125, apply *mutatis mutandis*; a notification by the pledgee to the debtor that he exercises his right of collection takes the place of the distraint.

1290. Where a claim is subject to several pledges, only that pledgee whose pledge has priority to the other pledges is entitled to collect the claim.

1291. The provisions relating to the pledge of a claim apply also to the pledge of a land charge or of an annuity charge.

1292. For the pledging of a bill of exchange or other instrument which can be transferred by indorsement, a real agreement between the creditor and the pledgee and delivery of the indorsed instrument are sufficient.

(*e*) Cf. 1283, par. 1.

(*f*) Registration in the land register is not necessary.

(*g*) See 1807 and 1808.

1293. The provisions relating to the pledge of moveables apply to the pledge of an instrument payable to bearer [h].

1294. If a bill of exchange, or any other instrument which can be transferred by indorsement, or an instrument payable to bearer, is the object of a pledge, the pledgee is, even though the conditions specified in 1228, par. 2, have not yet arisen, entitled to collect the claim, and where notice is necessary, to give notice, and the debtor may only make payment to him.

1295. If a pledged instrument which can be transferred by indorsement has an exchange or market price, the creditor is, after the fulfilment of the conditions specified in 1228, par. 2, entitled to cause the instrument to be sold as provided for in 1221.

1296. The pledge of a negotiable instrument extends to the interest coupons, annuity coupons, or dividend coupons belonging thereto, provided they have been delivered to the pledgee. The pledgor may, unless it is otherwise provided, require the return of the coupons, provided they become due before the fulfilment of the conditions specified in 1228, par. 2.

(*h*) *I.e.*, 1204—1258.

FOURTH BOOK.
Family Law.

FIRST SECTION.
CIVIL MARRIAGE.

FIRST TITLE.
Betrothal.

1297. No action can be brought upon a betrothal for the fulfilment of the promise to marry [(a)].

A promise to pay a penalty in case of non-fulfilment of the promise is void [(b)].

1298. If a betrothed person withdraws from the betrothal, he (or she) shall compensate the other party to the betrothal, the latter's parents, and any third parties who have acted *in loco parentis* for any damage caused by their having incurred outlay or obligations in expectation of the marriage. He shall also compensate the other party to the betrothal for any damage which the latter suffers through having, in expectation of the marriage, taken other measures affecting his (or her) property or employment.

The damage shall be made good only in so far as the incurring of outlay or obligations and the other measures were reasonable under the circumstances.

The duty to make compensation does not arise if a grave reason for the

(a) Betrothal, therefore, creates only a *moral* obligation to fulfil the promise of marriage.

(b) As to the claims of a go-between, see 656.

withdrawal exists [c].

1299. If a betrothed person causes the withdrawal of the other party to the betrothal by any fault which constitutes a grave reason for the withdrawal, the former is bound to make compensation in accordance with 1298, pars. 1 and 2.

1300. If a betrothed woman of unblemished character has permitted the other party to the betrothal to cohabit with her, and if the conditions specified in 1298 or 1299 exist, she may also claim an equitable compensation in money [d] on account of the injury, which is not an injury to property [e].

The claim is not transferable and does not pass to her heirs, unless it has been acknowledged by contract or action has been commenced to recover it.

1301. If the marriage is not concluded, either party to the betrothal may demand from the other the return of what he (or she) has given to the other as a gift or as a token of the betrothal in accordance with the provisions relating to the return of unjustified benefits [f]. In case of doubt it is to be presumed that the claim for return is barred if the betrothal is dissolved by the death of one of the parties to the betrothal.

1302. The claims specified in 1298 to 1301 are barred by prescription in two years after the dissolution of the betrothal [g].

SECOND TITLE.
Conclusion of Marriage.

1303. A man may not marry before attaining majority; a woman may not

---

(*c*) The burden of proof is upon the defendant. Whether a "grave reason" exists or not is determined by the Court, according to the circumstances of each particular case.

(*d*) Cf. 825, 847.

(*e*) *I.e.*, loss of virginity.

(*f*) See 812 *et seq.*, especially 815, 818.

(*g*) On the invalidity of a testamentary disposition in favour of a betrothed person after the dissolution of the betrothal, see 2077.

marry before the completion of her sixteenth year of age [h].

Dispensation from this provision [i] may be granted to a woman.

1304. A person who is limited in disposing capacity [k] requires, for concluding a marriage, the approval of his statutory agent.

If the statutory agent is a guardian, and if the approval is refused by him, it may be supplied by the Guardianship Court upon the application of the ward. The Guardianship Court shall give its approval if the conclusion of the marriage is in the interest of the ward.

1305. A legitimate child requires, before the completion of his twenty-first year of age, the approval of the father for concluding a marriage; an illegitimate child requires, before the same age, the approval of the mother [l]. The mother takes the place of the father if he is dead, or if the rights arising from paternity do not belong to him as provided for in 1701. A child declared legitimate [m] does not require the approval of the mother, even if the father is dead.

It is equivalent to the death of the father or of the mother if they are permanently not in a position to make a declaration, or if their place of residence is permanently unknown.

1306. In respect of an adopted child [n], the right to give the approval for concluding a marriage belongs to the person who has adopted the child, instead of to the natural parents. If a married couple have jointly adopted the child, or if one spouse has adopted the child of the other spouse, the provisions of 1305, par. 1, sentences 1, 2, and par. 2, apply.

(*h*) A marriage celebrated in violation of this provision is not void (1323), but is only voidable (1331).

(*i*) Cf. 1322.

(*k*) See 106, 114.

(*l*) A marriage celebrated without the parental approval is neither void nor voidable. See 1323, 1330. However, if a daughter violates this provision she would lose her claim to any "outfit" (1621), and her parents would retain their right of usufruct of her property. 1661, 1684, 1364.

(*m*) Cf. 1723 *et seq.*

(*n*) Cf. 1741 *et seq.*

The natural parents do not recover the right to give approval even if the legal relation created by the adoption is terminated.

1307. The parental approval may not be given through an agent. If the father or the mother is limited in disposing capacity, the consent of the statutory agent is not necessary.

1308. If the parental approval is refused to a child who is of full age [(o)], it may be supplied by the Guardianship Court upon the application of the child. The Guardianship Court shall give the approval if it is refused without any grave reason.

Before giving the decision, the Guardianship Court should hear the child's relatives by blood or marriage, if it can be done without serious delay and without disproportionate expense. The provision of 1847, par. 2, applies to the reimbursement of expenditure.

1309. No person can conclude a second marriage before his first marriage has been dissolved [(p)] or declared void [(q)]. If a married couple wish to repeat the marriage ceremony [(r)], a previous declaration of nullity is not necessary.

If an action for nullity or for restitution [(s)] is brought against a judicial decree whereby the first marriage was dissolved or declared void, the parties cannot conclude a second marriage before the determination of the suit, unless the action has not been instituted until after the expiration of the prescribed period of five years [(t)].

1310. A marriage cannot be concluded between relatives by blood in the direct line, nor between brothers and sisters of full blood or half-blood, nor

(*o*) A child of full age requires the parental approval only in the rare case where he is not yet twenty-one years old (1305), but has been declared of full age. 3.

(*p*) By the death of one of the parties or by divorce.

(*q*) Cf. 1323 *et seq.*, especially 1326.

(*r*) Because of some doubt as to the validity of the first ceremony.

(*s*) See respectively 579 and 580 of the Code of Civil Procedure.

(*t*) See 586 of the Code of Civil Procedure.

between relatives by marriage in the direct line [(u)].

A marriage cannot be concluded between persons one of whom has had sexual intercourse with parents, grandparents, or descendants of the other.

Relationship by blood, within the meaning of these provisions, exists also between an illegitimate child and his descendants on the one side, and the father and his relatives by blood on the other side [(x)].

1311. A person who has adopted another shall not conclude a marriage with the latter or the latter's descendants so long as the legal relation created by the adoption exists [(y)].

1312. A marriage cannot be concluded between a spouse divorced for adultery and the person with whom the divorced spouse has committed adultery, if the adultery is specified in the judicial decree of divorce as the ground for the divorce [(z)].

Dispensation from this provision [(a)] may be granted.

1313. A woman cannot conclude a second marriage until ten months after the dissolution [(b)] or annulment of her first marriage, unless in the meantime she has given birth to a child [(c)].

Dispensation from this provision [(d)] may be granted.

1314. A person who has a legitimate child who is a minor or who is under his guardianship cannot conclude a marriage until the Guardianship Court has issued to him a certificate that he has fulfilled the obligations specified in 1669,

---

(*u*) On the meaning of "relatives by blood" and "relatives by marriage", see 1589 and 1590 respectively. A marriage concluded in violation of this provision is void. 1327.

(*x*) This provision is necessary because an illegitimate child and his natural father are not deemed to be related by blood. 1589, par. 2.

(*y*) A marriage concluded in contravention of this provision is by no means void. The effect of such a marriage is the termination of the adoption. See 1771.

(*z*) Such a marriage would be void. 1328.

(*a*) Cf. 1322.

(*b*) By the death of the husband or by divorce.

(*c*) The child is legitimate. Exceptions, see 1591 *et seq.*

(*d*) Cf. 1322.

or that they are not imposed upon him.

If, in the case of a continued community of goods, a participating descendant is a minor or is under guardianship, the surviving spouse cannot conclude a marriage until the Guardianship Court has issued to him (or her) a certificate that he (or she) has fulfilled the obligations specified in 1493, par. 2, or that they are not imposed upon him (or her).

1315. Persons in military service and State officials who, according to the State laws, require special permission for concluding a marriage, cannot conclude a marriage without the prescribed permission.

Aliens who, according to the State laws, require permission or a certificate for concluding a marriage, cannot conclude a marriage without such permission or certificate [(e)].

1316. A public summons should precede the celebration of a marriage. The summons ceases to be effective if the marriage is not concluded within six months after the execution of the summons.

The public summons may be dispensed with if the dangerous illness of one of the parties to the betrothal does not permit postponement of the conclusion of the marriage.

Dispensation from the public summons may be granted [(f)].

1317. The marriage is concluded by the parties to the betrothal, personally and simultaneously present, declaring before a registrar their intention to enter into wedlock with each other. The registrar must be ready to receive the declarations [(g)].

The declarations cannot be made subject to any condition or limitation of time.

1318. The registrar should, at the celebration of the marriage, in the presence of two witnesses, direct the question to the parties severally and in

---

(*e*) See also IA, Arts. 13—17.

(*f*) Cf. 1322, pars. 2, 3.

(*g*) Each party bears one-half of the expenses of the marriage ceremonies, in conformity with 420. For the case where one of the parties to the betrothal is an alien, see Arts. 13 and 17 of the IA.

succession whether it is their intention to enter into wedlock with each other and, after the parties have answered the question affirmatively, should pronounce that by virtue of this law they are now legally united married persons.

Persons who have been declared deprived of civil rights should not be called as witnesses during the time for which the deprivation of civil rights is effective, nor should minors. Persons who are related by blood or by marriage with one of the parties to the betrothal, or with the registrar, or with each other, may be called as witnesses.

The registrar should record the celebration of the marriage in the marriage register.

1319. A person is deemed to be a registrar within the meaning of 1317 who, without being a registrar, publicly exercises the office of a registrar, unless the parties to the betrothal know of the absence of official authority at the celebration of the marriage.

1320. The marriage should be concluded before the competent registrar.

The registrar is competent in whose district one of the parties to the betrothal has his (or her) domicile or customary residence.

If neither of the parties has his (or her) domicile or customary residence within the Empire, and, furthermore, if only one of them is a German, the competent registrar is determined by the highest supervising authority of the State of which the German is a subject, and if he is not a subject of any State, by the Imperial Chancellor.

Among several competent registrars the parties have the right to select.

1321. By virtue of a written authorisation by the competent registrar, the marriage may also be celebrated before the registrar of another district.

1322. The right to grant a dispensation permitted by 1303, 1313, belongs to the State of which the woman is a subject; the right to grant a dispensation permitted by 1312 belongs to the State of which the divorced spouse is a subject. In the case of Germans who are not subjects of any State the right to grant such dispensation belongs to the Imperial Chancellor.

The right to grant a dispensation permitted by 1316 belongs to the State in which the marriage is to be celebrated.

The government of the State shall make provisions relating to the issue of the grant belonging to the State.

THIRD TITLE.
Void and Voidable Marriages.

1323. A marriage is void only in the cases provided for by 1324 to 1328.

1324. A marriage is void if in the conclusion of the marriage the form prescribed in 1317 has not been observed.

If the marriage has been entered in the marriage register, and if the parties have lived together as man and wife for ten years after the conclusion of the marriage, or where one of them has previously died, until the death of that one, at the least, however, three years, the marriage is deemed to be valid *ab initio*. This provision does not apply if, at the expiration of the ten years or at the death of one of the parties, action for nullity is brought.

1325. A marriage is void if, at the time of the celebration of the marriage, one of the parties was incapable of disposing, or was in a condition of unconsciousness or temporary disturbance of mental activity.

The marriage is deemed to be valid *ab initio* if the party confirms it after the cessation of the disposing capacity, the unconsciousness or the disturbance of mental activity, before it has been declared void or dissolved [(h)]. The confirmation need not be in the form prescribed for the celebration of the marriage.

1326. A marriage is void if, at the time of the celebration of the marriage, one of the parties was living in lawful wedlock with a third party [(i)].

1327. A marriage is void if it has been concluded between relatives by blood or by marriage contrary to the prohibition of 1310, par. 1.

(*h*) No matter whether by the death of one of the parties or by divorce.

(*i*) Cf. 1309.

1328. A marriage is void if it was prohibited by 1312 on account of adultery.

If subsequent dispensation from the provision of 1312 is granted, the marriage is deemed to be valid *ab initio*.

1329. The nullity of a marriage void under 1325 to 1328, so long as the marriage has not been declared void or dissolved, may be established only by means of an action for nullity. The same rule applies to a marriage void under 1324, if it has been entered in the marriage register.

1330. A marriage may be avoided only in the cases provided for by 1331 to 1335 and 1350 (k).

1331. A marriage may be avoided by a spouse who, at the time of the conclusion of the marriage, or, in the case provided for by 1325, at the time of confirmation, was limited in disposing capacity, if the conclusion of the marriage or the confirmation was effected without the approval of the statutory agent.

1332. A marriage may be avoided by a spouse who, at the conclusion of the marriage, did not know that the affair was the conclusion of a marriage, or who knew this, but did not intend to make a declaration of intention to enter into wedlock (l).

1333. A marriage may be avoided by a spouse who, at the conclusion of the marriage, was under a mistake as to the identity of the other spouse or as to such personal characteristics (m) of the other spouse as would have deterred him from concluding the marriage with knowledge of the state of affairs and with intelligent appreciation of the nature of marriage.

1334. A marriage may be avoided by a spouse who has been induced to conclude the marriage by fraud concerning such circumstance as would have deterred him from concluding the marriage with knowledge of the state of affairs

---

(*k*) A voidable marriage is valid to all intents und purposes until it has been avoided by one of the parties.

(*l*) The question whether this was due to negligence or not is entirely immaterial. 119.

(*m*) Other characteristics may be taken into consideration only in the case provided for by 1334.

and with intelligent appreciation of the nature of marriage. If the other spouse was not guilty of the fraud, the marriage is voidable only if the latter knew of the fraud at the conclusion of the marriage.

A marriage may not be avoided on the ground of fraud concerning pecuniary circumstances (n).

1335. A marriage may be avoided by a spouse who has been illegally induced by threats to conclude the marriage (o).

1336. The avoidance of a marriage may not be effected through an agent. If a spouse entitled to avoid a marriage is limited in disposing capacity, he (or she) does not require the consent of his (or her) statutory agent.

On behalf of a spouse who is capable of disposing, his (or her) statutory agent may avoid the marriage, subject to the ratification of the Guardianship Court. In the cases provided for by 1331, so long as the spouse entitled to avoid the marriage is limited in disposing capacity, only his (or her) statutory agent may avoid the marriage.

1337. The right to avoid the marriage is barred in the cases provided for by 1331, if the statutory agent ratifies the marriage, or if the spouse entitled to avoid the marriage confirms it after he (or she) has become capable of disposing without limitation. If the statutory agent is a guardian, the ratification, if refused by him, may be supplied by the Guardianship Court upon the application of the spouse; the Guardianship Court shall give the ratification if the maintenance of the marriage is in the interest of the spouse.

In the cases provided for by 1332 to 1335, the right of avoidance is barred if the spouse entitled to avoidance confirms the marriage after the discovery of the mistake or of the fraud, or after the cessation of the coercion.

The provisions of 1336, par. 1, apply also to the confirmation.

(*n*) The majority opinion of the *Reichstags-Kommission* was that a marriage should not be degraded into a mere "business affair" (*Handelsgeschäft*), and so this paragraph has been added, while the words "or such personal circumstances", after the words "personal characteristics", have been struck out from 1333.

(*o*) Cf. 1346, 1347.

1338. The right of avoidance is barred after the dissolution of the marriage, unless the dissolution has been brought about by the death of the spouse not entitled to avoidance [(p)].

1339. The avoidance may be effected only within six months.

The period beings to run, in the cases provided for by 1331, from the time at which the conclusion or confirmation of the marriage is known to the statutory agent, or the spouse acquires unlimited disposing capacity; in the cases provided for by 1332 to 1334, from the time at which the spouse discovers the mistake or fraud; in the case provided for by 1335, from the time at which the coercion ceases.

The provisions of 203, 206, applicable to prescription, apply *mutatis mutandis* to this period.

1340. If the statutory agent of a spouse who is incapable of disposing has not avoided the marriage in due time, the spouse personally may, after the cessation of the disposing incapacity, avoid the marriage in the same manner as if he (or she) had not had any statutory agent.

1341. The avoidance is effected, so long as the marriage has not been dissolved, by bringing an action for avoidance.

If the action is withdrawn, the avoidance shall be deemed not to have taken place. The same rule applies if the avoided marriage, before it has been declared void or dissolved, is ratified or confirmed in the manner provided for by 1337.

1342. If the marriage has been dissolved by the death of the spouse not entitled to avoidance, the avoidance is effected by declaration to the Probate Court; the declaration shall be made in publicly certified form.

The Probate Court should communicate the declaration both to the person who, if the marriage were valid, and to the person who, if the marriage were void, would be the heir of the deceased spouse. The Probate Court shall

---

(p) The spouse entitled to avoidance may therefore avoid the marriage, even after the death of the other spouse. 1342.

permit any person to inspect the declaration, provided he can offer *primâ facie* proof that he has a legal interest therein.

1343. If a voidable marriage is avoided, it shall be deemed to have been void *ab initio*. The provision of 142, par. 2, applies.

The nullity of avoidable marriage which has been avoided by means of an action may not be collaterally set up, so long as the marriage has not been declared void or dissolved.

1344. As against a third party no defence can be derived from the nullity of the marriage to a juristic act entered into between him and one of the spouses, or to a non-appellable judgment entered between them, unless at the time when the juristic act was entered into, or at the time when action was commenced, the marriage was declared void or the nullity was known to the third party.

The nullity can be set up without this limitation, if it is based upon a defect in form and the marriage has not been entered in the marriage register.

1345. If the nullity of the marriage was known to one of the spouses at the time of concluding the marriage, the other spouse, unless the nullity was also known to that one, may [(q)], after the declaration of nullity or after the dissolution of the marriage, demand that their relation in respect of property rights, especially in respect of the duty to furnish maintenance, be dealt with as if the marriage had been dissolved at the time of the declaration of nullity or of the dissolution, and the spouse to whom the nullity was known had been declared to be the exclusively guilty party [(r)].

This provision does not apply if the nullity is based upon a defect in form and the marriage has not been entered in the marriage register.

1346. If a marriage voidable on the ground of threats [(s)] is declared void, the right specified in 1345, par. 1, belongs to the spouse entitled to avoidance.

(*q*) Cf. 1347.

(*r*) Cf. 1574, 1578 *et seq*.

(*s*) Cf. 1335.

If a marriage voidable on the ground of mistake [t] is declared void, the right belongs to the spouse who is not entitled to avoidance, unless he (or she) knew or ought to have known of the mistake at the conclusion of the marriage.

1347. If the spouse to whom the right specified in 1845, par. 1, belongs declares to the other spouse that he (or she) exercises the right, he (or she) can no longer assert the consequences of the nullity of the marriage; if he (or she) declares to the other spouse that he (or she) accepts these consequences, the right specified in 1345, par. 1, is extinguished.

The other spouse may demand that the spouse thus entitled declare within a fixed reasonable period, whether or not he (or she) will exercise the right. In such a case the right may be exercised only before the expiration of the period.

FOURTH TITLE.
Re-marriage in case of Declaration of Death.

1348. If one spouse, after the other spouse has been declared dead [u], concludes a new marriage, the new marriage is not void merely because the spouse declared dead is still alive, unless both spouses at the conclusion of the marriage knew that he (or she) was living at the time of the declaration of death.

Upon the conclusion of the new marriage the former marriage is dissolved. It remains dissolved even if the declaration of death is revoked in consequence of an action to set it aside.

1349. If action has been brought to set aside the judicial decree whereby one of the spouses has been declared dead, the other spouse cannot conclude a new marriage before the termination of the process, unless the action to set aside has not been brought until ten years after promulgation of the judicial decree.

(*t*) Cf. 1332, 1333.

(*u*) Cf. 13 *et seq.*

1350. Either spouse of the new marriage [(x)] may, if the spouse declared dead is still alive, avoid the new marriage, unless at the time of concluding the marriage he (or she) had knowledge of the latter being alive. The avoidance may be effected only within six months from the time at which the spouse learned that the spouse declared dead was still alive.

The right of avoidance is barred if the spouse entitled to avoidance confirms the marriage after having obtained knowledge that the spouse declared dead is still alive, or if the new marriage has been dissolved by the death of one of the spouses.

1351. If the marriage is avoided under 1350 by the spouse of the former marriage [(y)], that spouse shall furnish maintenance to the other spouse [(z)], under the provisions of 1578 to 1582 applicable to divorce, unless the other spouse knew at the conclusion of the marriage that the spouse declared dead was living at the time of the declaration of death.

1352. If the former marriage is dissolved under 1348, par. 2, the obligation of the wife to make to the husband a contribution towards the expense of maintenance of their children is determined according to the provisions of 1585 applicable to divorce.

FIFTH TITLE.
Effects of Marriage in General.

1353. The spouses are mutually bound to live in conjugal community [(a)].

If the demand of one of the spouses for restitution of the conjugal community appears to be an abuse of his (or her) right, the other spouse is not bound to conform to the demand. The same rule applies if the other spouse is entitled

(*x*) But not the spouse who has been erroneously declared dead.

(*y*) *I.e.*, by the spouse who was married to the person declared dead.

(*z*) *Scilicet*, of the new marriage.

(*a*) The claim to the restitution of the conjugal community is not subject to prescription. See 194, par. 2.

to petition for divorce [(b)].

1354. The right to decide in all matters affecting the common conjugal life belongs to the husband; he determines especially the place of abode and the dwelling [(c)].

The wife is not bound to conform to the decision of the husband if the decision appears, to be an abuse of his right.

1355. The wife takes the surname of the husband.

1356. The wife is, subject to the provisions of 1354, entitled and bound to conduct the joint household.

The wife is bound to work in the household and in the business of the husband, where such activity is customary according to the circumstances in which the couple live.

1357. The wife is entitled, within the sphere of her domestic activity, to manage the husband's affairs for him and to represent him. Juristic acts which she enters into within such sphere of activity are deemed to be entered into in the husband's name, if it does not appear otherwise from the circumstances.

The husband may limit or exclude the right of the wife. If the limitation or exclusion appears to be an abuse of the husband's right, it may be annulled by the Guardianship Court upon the application of the wife. As against third parties the limitation or exclusion is effective only in accordance with 1435.

1358. If the wife has bound herself to a third party for an act of performance to be done by her in person, the husband may give notice, without any term of notice, of the termination of the legal relation, if he has been authorised to do so by the Guardianship Court upon his own application. The Guardianship Court shall give the authorisation if it appears that the activity of the wife is injurious to the conjugal interests.

(*b*) Cf. 1565—1571.

(*c*) A contract, whether made before or after the marriage, whereby the man binds himself not to move his residence or the wife is exempted from following the husband, is null and void as being *contra bonos mores*.

The right to give notice is barred if the husband has consented to the obligation, or if upon the application of the wife the consent has been supplied by the Guardianship Court. The Guardianship Court may give the consent if the husband is prevented from making a declaration by illness or absence and there is danger in delay, or if the refusal of consent appears to be an abuse of his right. So long as the common domestic life is broken off, the right to give notice does not belong to the husband.

Neither the consent nor the notice may be given through an agent of the husband; if the husband is limited in disposing capacity, he does require the consent of his statutory agent.

1359. The spouses are answerable to each other, in the fulfilment of the obligations arising from the marriage relation, only for such care as they are accustomed to exercise in their own affairs.

1360. The husband shall furnish maintenance to the wife in accordance with his station in life, his means and his earning capacity [(d)].

The wife shall furnish to the husband, if he is not in a position to maintain himself, the maintenance appropriate to his station in life in accordance with her means and her earning capacity.

The maintenance shall be furnished in the manner suitable to the conjugal community [(e)]. The provisions of 1605, 1613 to 1615, applicable to the duty of furnishing maintenance to relatives by blood, apply *mutatis mutandis*.

1361. If the spouses are living apart, and as long as one of them may and dues refuse the restitution of conjugal life [(f)], the maintenance shall be furnished by a money annuity; the provisions of 760 apply to the annuity. The husband shall also deliver to the wife out of the common household for her use all things necessary for the conduct of a separate household, unless such things are indispensable to him or belong to the property subject to the wife's disposition.

(*d*) This is true even where the wife has the means to maintain herself. She has, however, in such a case to contribute towards the expenses of joint household. 1371.

(*e*) That is to say, the maintenance is to be furnished, not by the payment of money, but by providing her (or him) with board, lodging, &c.

(*f*) Cf. 1353, par. 2.

The husband's duty of furnishing maintenance is extinguished or is limited to the payment of a contribution, if its extinction or limitation is equitable, having regard to the necessities, means and earning capacity of the spouses.

1362. It is presumed in favour of the creditors of the husband that all moveables which are in the possession of one of the spouses or of both spouses belong to the husband [(g)]. This applies also to instruments to bearer and to instruments to order indorsed in blank.

In regard to things intended exclusively for the personal use of the wife, *e.g.*, clothing, ornaments, and working implements, the presumption obtains, as between the spouses *inter se* and as between the spouses and their creditors, that the things belong to the wife.

SIXTH TITLE.
Matrimonial Régimes.

I. Statutory Régime.

1. *General Provisions.*

1363. By the conclusion of a marriage the property to the wife becomes subject to the management and usufruct [(h)] by the husband (contributed property) [(i)].

Contributed property includes also the property which the wife acquires during the marriage.

1364. The rights of management and usufruct by the husband do not come

---

(*g*) The presumption is rebuttable. It is also to be noticed that the presumption does not obtain as between the spouses.

(*h*) On the extent of the rights of "management and usufruct", see 1375 *et seq.*

(*i*) All the property of the wife is presumed to be contributed property until the contrary is shown. *Motive zu dem ersten Entwurfe des Bürgerlichen Gesetzbuchs*, 1283. The *ownership* of the contributed property remains vested in the wife.

into being [(k)] if he concludes a marriage with a woman limited in disposing capacity without the approval of her statutory agent.

1365. The management and usufruct by the husband does not extend to the separate property [(l)] of the wife.

1366. Things intended exclusively for the personal use of the wife, *e.g.*, clothing, ornaments, and working implements, are separate property [(m)].

1367. Separate property includes also that which the wife acquires by her labour [(n)] or by the conduct of a separate business [(o)].

1368. Separate property includes also that which is declared to be separate property by the marriage contract.

1369. Separate property includes also that which the wife acquires by succession or legacy, or as a compulsory portion (acquisition *mortis causa*), or which is transferred to her gratuitously by a third party *inter vivos*, provided the testator in his testamentary disposition, or the third party at the time of the transfer, has specified that the acquisition shall be separate property [(p)].

1370. Separate property includes also that which the wife acquires by virtue of a right forming part of the separate property, or as compensation for the destruction, damage, or deprivation of an object forming part of such property,

---

(*k*) In which case separation of goods takes place. 1426.

(*l*) The wife has absolute power to deal with her separate property as though she were, a *feme sole*. 1371.

(*m*) Such things are presumed to belong to the wife, even as against the creditors of the husband. 1362.

(*n*) *I.e.*, by her labour *on her own account*. If she works as an assistant of her husband, then what she acquires is not only not her property, but is the exclusive property of her husband. 1356, par. 2.

(*o*) The question whether she can conduct a separate business or not depends upon whether her duties towards her husband and children would be thereby interfered with or not. In the event of a divergence of opinion between husband and wife, the husband decides as provided in 1354. The presumption, however, is that the wife can conduct a separate business without interfering with her duties as wife and mother.

(*p*) Without such specification the acquisition would belong to the wife's contributed property. 1363, par. 2.

or by a juristic act affecting such property.

1371. The provisions applicable to the property of the wife under the régime of separation of goods [q] apply *mutatis mutandis* to the separate property; the wife is required, however, to contribute towards the expense of the joint household only in so far as the husband has not already received a reasonable contribution through his usufruct of the contributed property.

1372. Either spouse may require the other to concur in determining the condition of the contributed property by the drawing up of an inventory. The provisions of 1035, applicable to usufruct, apply to the drawing up of the inventory.

Either spouse may, at his (or her) own expense, cause the condition of things forming part of the contributed property to be determined by experts.

2. *Rights of Management and Usufruct*.

1373. The husband is entitled to take possession of all things forming part of the contributed property.

1374. The husband shall manage the contributed property in a proper manner. He shall give to the wife, on demand, any information relating to his management.

1375. The husband's right of management does not include any authority to hind the wife by juristic acts, or to dispose of the contributed property without her consent.

1376. Without the consent of the wife the husband may:

(1) dispose of money and other fungible things belonging to the wife;

(2) set-off claims of the wife against those claims against the wife which are enforceable against the contributed property;

(3) discharge liabilities of the wife for the delivery of an object forming part of the contributed property, by the delivery of such object.

(q) *I.e.*, 1427 *et seq.*

1377. The husband should not make any disposition to which he is entitled under 1376 without the consent of the wife, unless the disposition is made in the ordinary course of management of the contributed property [(r)].

The husband shall invest for the benefit of the wife any money forming part of the contributed property according to the provisions applicable to the investment of money belonging to a ward [(s)], unless the money is necessary to meet expenses.

The husband is permitted to alienate or consume other consumable things for his own benefit. If he exercises this right, he shall make good the value of such things after the termination of his rights of management and usufruct; the value shall be made good even before that time, in so far as this is required for the proper management of the contributed property.

1378. If a piece of land with its appurtenant stock forms part of the contributed property, the rights and the duties of the husband in respect of the appurtenant stock are determined according to the provisions of 1048, par. 1, applicable to usufruct.

1379. If a juristic act, for which the husband requires the consent of his wife, is necessary for the proper management of the contributed property, such consent may, if she refuses it without sufficient reason, be supplied by the Guardianship Court [(t)] upon the application of the husband.

The same rule applies if the wife is prevented by illness or absence from making a declaration, and there is danger in delay.

1380. The husband may, in his own name, enforce in Court any right forming part of the contributed property. If he is entitled to dispose of such right without the consent of his wife [(u)], the judgment is operative both in favour of and against her.

(*r*) This provision applies only *as between the spouses*. For the rights of the wife in case of its infringement, see 1391 to 1394.

(*s*) *I.e.*, 1807, 1808.

(*t*) *I.e.*, the Guardianship Court of the place where the husband is domiciled. 45 of the Voluntary Jurisdiction Act.

(*u*) 1376.

1381. If the husband acquires moveables by means of the contributed property, ownership passes to the wife upon such acquisition, unless the husband does not intend to acquire such moveables on account of the contributed property. This applies especially to instruments to bearer and instruments to order indorsed in blank.

The provisions of par. 1 apply *mutatis mutandis* where the husband acquires, by means of the contributed property, any right to things of the kind specified, or any other right which can be transferred by a mere contract of assignment.

1382. Household articles which the husband furnishes in place of those which have been contributed by the wife, but no longer exist or have become worthless, become contributed property [(x)].

1383. The husband acquires the emoluments of the contributed property in the same manner and to the same extent as a usufructuary.

1384. The husband shall bear, besides the expense incurred in the acquisition of the emoluments, the expenses of maintaining objects forming part of the contributed property in accordance with the provisions applicable to usufruct.

1385. During the existence of his rights of management and usufruct the husband is bound to bear on behalf of the wife:

(1) all public charges imposed upon her, except those charges imposed upon her separate property, and those extraordinary charges which are deemed to be imposed upon the capital of the contributed property;

(2) all charges created under private law [(y)] and imposed upon objects forming part of the contributed property;

(3) all premiums required to be paid for the insurance of objects forming part of the contributed property.

(x) This provision is applicable even to the case where the articles have been furnished by the husband *with his own money*.

(y) *E.g.*, hypothecas, land charges, annuity charges, servitudes, &c.

1386. During the existence of his rights of management and usufruct the husband is bound, on behalf of the wife, to bear the interests on those liabilities of the wife which may be required to be discharged out of the contributed property. The same rule applies to periodical payments of any other kind, including those payments owing by the wife by reason of her statutory duty to furnish maintenance to others, in so far as such payments are to be made out of the income of the contributed property in the ordinary course of management.

The husband does not incur this obligation if the liabilities or the payments are, as between the spouses, borne by the wife's separate property [(z)].

1387. The husband is bound to bear on behalf of the wife:

(1) the costs of any action by which he enforces a right forming part of the contributed property and of any action brought by the wife, unless they are to be borne by the separate property [(a)];

(2) the costs of the defence of the wife in any criminal proceedings instituted against her, in so far as payment of the costs is required by the circumstances, or is made with the consent of the husband, without prejudice to the duty of the wife to make compensation in the event of her being sentenced.

1388. In so far as, according to 1385 to 1387, the husband is bound on behalf of his wife to discharge her liabilities, both he and his wife are liable as joint debtors.

1389. The husband shall bear the expenses of the joint household [(b)].

In so far as the net income of the contributed property is necessary for the maintenance of the husband and of the wife and the descendants of the marriage, she may require him to spend the net income for such maintenance without regard to his other obligations.

1390. Where the husband, in the course of his management of the contributed property, incurs any outlay which he may consider necessary under the

---

(z) See 1415 *et seq.*

(a) 1415, 1416.

(b) The wife is, however, liable to make contribution in certain cases. 1371.

circumstances, he may demand compensation from the wife, unless such outlay is to be borne by the husband himself [(c)].

1391. If it is to be apprehended, owing to the conduct of the husband, that the rights of the wife will be infringed in a manner seriously endangering the contributed property, she may require her husband to give security [(d)].

The same rule applies where the claims of the wife to compensation for the value of consumable things [(e)] arising from the husband's rights of management and usufruct are seriously endangered.

1392. If the conditions exist under which the husband is bound to give security, the wife may also require the husband to lodge with a lodgment office or with the Imperial Bank all instruments to bearer forming part of the contributed property, together with their renewal coupons, subject to the condition that their withdrawal may be demanded by the husband only with the consent of the wife. The lodgment of instruments to bearer which are consumable things within the meaning of 92, and of interest coupons, annuity coupons, or dividend coupons, may not be demanded instruments to order indorsed in blank are equivalent to instruments to bearer.

Without the consent of the wife the husband may not make any disposition affecting the lodged instruments, even though he would otherwise be entitled to do so under 1376.

1393. The husband may, instead of lodging the instruments to bearer, as provided for by 1392, transfer them to the name of the wife, or, if they have been issued by the Empire or by a State, cause them to be converted into uncertificated claims against the Empire or the State.

1394. The wife may not enforce any claims which she has against the husband by reason of his rights of management and usufruct until after the termination of such rights, unless the conditions exist under which she may require her husband to give security as provided for in 1391. The claim specified in

---

(c) 1384 *et seq.*

(d) She may, if she chooses, bring an action to establish separation of goods. 1418 (1), 1426.

(e) *Scilicet*, which the husband may have alienated or consumed as provided for by 1377, par 3.

1389, par. 2, is not subject to this limitation.

1395. The wife requires the approval of the husband for making any disposition affecting the contributed property [(f)].

1396. If the wife disposes of any contributed property by contract with a third party without the approval of her husband, the contract is void unless ratified by the husband.

If the other party demands the husband to declare whether or not he will ratify, the declaration may be made only to him; a ratification or refusal to ratify declared to the wife before the demand is of no effect. The ratification may be declared only before the expiration of two weeks after receipt of the demand; if it is not declared, it is deemed to have been refused.

If the husband refuses to ratify the contract, it does not become valid by reason of the fact that his rights of management and usufruct come to an end.

1397. Before ratification of the contract the other party is entitled to revoke. The revocation may also be declared to the wife.

If the other party knew that the woman was a married woman, he may revoke only if the wife has stated, contrary to the truth, that her husband has given his approval; even in this case the other party may not revoke if the absence of approval was known to him at the time when the contract was entered into.

1398. A unilateral juristic act whereby the wife disposes of any contributed property without the approval of her husband is void [(g)].

1399. The consent of the husband is not necessary for juristic acts whereby the wife binds herself to do an act of performance.

If the husband consents to such a juristic act, it is valid as against him in respect of the contributed property. If he does not consent, the juristic act is operative as against him in accordance with the provisions relating to the return of unjustified benefits [(h)], in so far as the contributed property is benefited by

---

(*f*) Exception: 1401, 1402.

(*g*) See 1401, 1403, 1404.

(*h*) 818—822.

the juristic act.

1400. If the wife brings an action without the consent of the husband, the judgment is inoperative as against him in respect of the contributed property.

The wife may not bring an action to enforce any right forming part of the contributed property except with the consent of the husband.

1401. The consent of the husband is not necessary in the cases provided for by 1395 to 1398, 1399, par. 2, and 1400, if the husband is prevented by illness or absence from making a declaration, and there is danger in delay.

1402. If a juristic act for which the wife requires her husband's consent is necessary for the proper care of her personal affairs, such consent may, if he refuses it without sufficient reason, be supplied by the Guardianship Court upon the application of the wife (*i*).

1403. A unilateral juristic act affecting the contributed property shall be entered into with the husband.

A unilateral juristic act affecting any liability of the wife shall be entered into with the wife; the juristic act must, however, also be entered into with the husband, if it is to be effective against him in respect of the contributed property.

1404. The limitations imposed upon the wife by 1395 to 1403 avail against a third party, even if he did not know that the woman was a married woman.

1405. If the husband gives his approval to the conduct of a separate business by the wife, his consent is not necessary for such juristic acts and legal proceedings as come within the scope of the business. Unilateral juristic acts in respect of such business shall be entered into with the wife.

It is equivalent to the approval of the business by the husband if the wife conducts the business with the knowledge of and without any objection by the husband.

An objection or revocation of approval is effective as against third parties

---

(*i*) Cf. note (*t*) to 1379.

only subject to the conditions specified in 1435.

1406. The wife does not require the consent of the husband:

(1) for accepting or disclaiming an inheritance or a legacy, or for renouncing her compulsory portion, or for filing an inventory of an inheritance devolved on her;

(2) for declining an offer to make a contract or a gift;

(3) for entering into a juristic act with the husband.

1407. The wife does not require the consent of her husband:

(1) for continuing an action commenced before the date of the marriage;

(2) for enforcing in Court any right forming part of the contributed property against the husband;

(3) for enforcing in Court any right forming part of the contributed property against a third party, if the husband has disposed of the right without the necessary consent of his wife;

(4) for enforcing in Court a right of objection against compulsory execution.

1408. No right which the husband has in the contributed property by virtue of his rights of management and usufruct is transferable [k].

1409. If the husband is under guardianship, the guardian shall represent him in the rights and the duties which arise from the rights of management and usufruct of the contributed property. This applies even if the wife is the guardian of her husband [l].

3. *Liability for Debts*.

1410. Creditors of the husband may not demand satisfaction out of the contributed property [m].

(*k*) This applies to the right *as such*, and not to things which are acquired *by virtue of* the right (as, *e. g.*, emoluments of the contributed property).

(*l*) Where the husband has been interdicted his wife can be appointed to act as his guardian. 1900.

(*m*) This provision may even be inferred from 1375, 1383.

1411. Creditors of the wife may demand satisfaction out of the contributed property without regard to the husband's rights of management and usufruct, except in so far as a contrary intention appears from 1412 to 1414 [(n)]. They are not subject, in enforcing the claims of the wife, to the limitation specified in 1394.

If the husband has alienated or consumed consumable things under 1377, par. 3, he is bound to make immediate compensation for the benefit of the creditors.

1412. The contributed property is not liable for any liability of the wife arising from a juristic act entered into after the date of marriage, unless the husband has given his consent to the juristic act [(o)], or the juristic act is valid as against him even without his consent [(p)].

The contributed property is liable for the costs of any action to which the wife is a party, even if the judgment is inoperative as against him in respect of the contributed property.

1413. The contributed property is not liable for any liability of the wife arising from the acquisition of an inheritance or of a legacy, if she acquires the inheritance or the legacy as her separate property [(q)] after the date of the marriage.

1414. The contributed property is not liable for any liability of the wife arising after the date of the marriage in consequence of a right forming part of her separate property, or in consequence of her possession of a thing forming part thereof, unless such right or thing exists in connection with a separate business carried on by the wife with the approval of her husband.

1415. As between the spouses the following are borne by the separate property:

(1) the liabilities of the wife arising from any unlawful act committed by

---

(*n*) In actual practice this exception is more important than the general rule.

(*o*) Cf. 1395, 1399, 1405.

(*p*) Cf. 1399, par. 2; 1401, 1402, 1406, 1407.

(*q*) Cf. 1369.

her during the marriage, or arising from any criminal proceedings instituted against her on account of such an act;

(2) the liabilities of the wife arising from any legal relation affecting her separate property, even if they have arisen before the date of the marriage or before the time at which the property became separate property;

(3) the costs of any action to which the wife is a party relating to any of the liabilities specified in (1) and (2).

1416. As between the spouses the costs of any action between them are borne by the separate property, unless the husband is bound to bear them.

The same rule applies to the costs of any action between the wife and a third party, unless the judgment is operative as against the husband in respect of the contributed property. If, however, the action relates to a personal affair of the wife, or to a liability, not coming within the provisions of 1415, (1) and (2), for which the contributed property is liable, then this provision does not apply, provided the costs are necessary under the circumstances.

1417. If any liability imposed upon the separate property by 1415, 1416 is discharged out of the contributed property, the wife shall make compensation to the contributed property out of the separate property to the extent of the latter.

If any liability of the wife which, as between the spouses, is not imposed upon the separate property is discharged out of such property, the husband shall make compensation to the separate property out of the contributed property to the extent of the latter.

4. *Termination of the Rights of Management and Usufruct.*

1418. The wife may bring an action to terminate the rights of management and usufruct:

(1) if the conditions exist under which she may require her husband to give security as provided for in 1391;

(2) if the husband has committed a breach of his duty to furnish maintenance to the wife and to the descendants of the marriage, and a serious danger to the future maintenance is to be apprehended. It is deemed

to be a breach of the duty to furnish maintenance, where the wife and the descendants of the marriage do not receive at least the maintenance which they would have received, if the rights of management and usufruct of the contributed property had been properly exercised;

(3) if the husband has been interdicted [(r)];

(4) if the husband has a curator appointed to take charge of his property affairs as provided for in 1910;

(5) if a curator *absentis* has been appointed for the husband and there is no expectation that the curatorship will come speedily to an end [(s)].

The termination of the rights of management and usufruct takes place as soon as the decree ceases to be appealable.

1419. The rights of management and usufruct come to an end, as soon as an order for the institution of bankruptcy proceedings against the property of the husband ceases to be appealable.

1420. The rights of management and usufruct come to an end, where the husband is declared dead, at the date which is deemed to be the date of his death.

1421. After the termination of the rights of management and usufruct the husband shall return the contributed property to the wife, and shall render to her an account of his management [(t)]. The provision of 592 applies *mutatis mutandis* to the return of agricultural land; the provisions of 592, 593 apply *mutatis mutandis* to the return of a farm.

1422. If the rights of management and usufruct are terminated by judicial decree under 1418, the husband is bound to return the contributed property in such manner as if action on the claim for its return were commenced at the time when action was brought for the termination of the rights of management and usufruct.

(*r*) In which case he is represented by his guardian. 1409.

(*s*) As to the termination of the curatorship, see 1425.

(*t*) The manner of rendering accounts is provided for in 259, 260.

1423. If the husband has let a piece of land forming part of the contributed property under an ordinary or usufructuary lease, and if the term of the lease is still running at the time of the termination of the rights of management and usufruct, the provisions of 1056 apply *mutatis mutandis.*

1424. The husband is, even after the termination of his rights of management and usufruct, entitled to continue the management until he knows or ought to know of the termination. A third party may not take advantage of this right, if he knows or ought to know of the termination of the rights of management and usufruct at the time of entering into a juristic act.

If the rights of management and usufruct come to an end in consequence of the death of the wife, the husband shall take charge of those affairs subject to his right of management which cannot be delayed without risk until her heir can make other arrangements.

1425. If the interdiction or curatorship on account of which the rights of management and usufruct come to an end is itself revoked, or if the order of interdiction is successfully attacked, the husband may bring an action for restitution of his rights. The same rule applies where the husband declared dead is still alive.

The restitution of the rights of the husband takes place as soon as the decree ceases to be appealable. The provision of 1422 applies *mutatis mutandis.*

In case of restitution, that becomes separate property which would have remained or would have become separate property if the rights of the husband had not been terminated.

5. *Separation of Goods.*

1426. If the husband's rights of management and usufruct do not come into being as provided for in 1364, or if they come to an end as provided for in 1418 to 1420, separation of goods takes place [(u)].

The provisions of 1427 to 1431 apply to the separation of goods.

(*u*) Separation of goods arises also in the case where a general community of goods is dissolved. 1468—1470.

1427. The husband shall bear the expenses of the joint household.

For defraying the expenses of the joint household the wife shall make a reasonable contribution (x) to her husband out of the income of her property, and the earnings of her work, or of any separate business carried on by her. The husband may claim contribution in respect of past expenses only in so far as such contribution was in arrear after demand made by the husband. This claim of the husband is not transferable.

1428. If a serious danger to the maintenance which the husband has to furnish to his wife and the descendants of the marriage is to be apprehended, the wife may retain such part of her contribution towards the expenses of the joint household as is necessary for such maintenance (y).

The same rule applies if the husband has been interdicted or if he has a curator appointed to take charge of his property affairs, as provided for in 1910, or if a curator *absentis* has been appointed for him.

1429. If the wife incurs any outlay out of her property for the purpose of defraying the expenses of the joint household, or if she entrusts anything out of her property to her husband for such purpose, it is presumed, in case of doubt, that she does not intend to require compensation.

1430. If the wife entrusts the whole or a part of her property to the management of her husband, he may, at his discretion, use any income which he draws during his management unless the income is necessary for defraying the expenses incurred in the ordinary course of management and for discharging such liabilities of the wife as would, in the ordinary course of management, be discharged out of the income of her property. The wife may provide otherwise.

1431. Separation of goods is effective as against third parties only subject to the conditions specified in 1435 (z).

(x) The question of reasonableness is determined according to the social position of the married couple.

(y) Under the statutory régime she would in such a case be entitled to bring an action to terminate her husband's rights of management and usufruct. 1418 (2).

(z) It matters not whether the separation of goods arises by operation of law or otherwise.

The same rule applies, in the case provided for by 1425, to the restitution of the rights of management and usufruct, if their termination has been entered in the marriage property register.

II. Contractual Régime.

1. *General Provisions*.

1432. Both spouses may regulate their property relations by contract (*i.e.*, a marriage contract), and may also terminate or modify the matrimonial régime even after the date of the marriage.

1433. A matrimonial régime may not be established by reference to a law no longer in force, nor to a foreign law [(a)].

If the husband has his domicile in a foreign country at the time of the marriage, or, where the contract is entered into after the date of the marriage, at the time when the contract was entered into, then reference to any law relating to matrimonial régimes in force at the place of his domicile is permissible.

1434. A marriage contract must be entered into before a court or a notary in the presence of both parties simultaneously [(b)].

1435. If the husband's rights of management and usufruct are excluded or modified by the marriage contract, defences arising from such exclusion or modification to a juristic act entered into between a third party and one of the spouses, or to a non-appellable judgment delivered between them, may be set up against the third party only if, at the time when the juristic act was entered into, or at the time when action was commenced in court, the exclusion or modification was entered in the marriage property register of the competent District Court, or was known to the third party.

The same rule applies if any regulation of the marriage property relations

(*a*) *I.e.*, a matrimonial régime may not be established by *mere* reference to such a law, although its provisions may be embodied in the marriage contract.

(*b*) Either party may, however, be represented by an agent.

entered in the marriage property register is revoked or modified by a marriage contract.

1436. If, by a marriage contract, the husband's rights of management and usufruct are excluded, or a general community of goods, or a community of income and profits, or a community of moveables is dissolved, separation of goods takes place, unless a contrary intention appears from the contract.

2. *General Community of Goods.*

1437. A marriage contract whereby a general community of goods is agreed upon or dissolved may not be entered into through a statutory agent [(c)].

If one of the contracting parties is limited in disposing capacity, he requires the consent of his statutory agent. If the statutory agent is a guardian, ratification by the Guardianship Court is necessary.

1438. Under the general community of goods the property of the husband and the property of the wife become the common property of both spouses (*i.e.*, common property). Common property includes also any property which he or she acquires during the subsistence of the community of goods.

Individual objects become common property without the necessity of transfer by juristic act.

If a right which has been, or may be, entered in the land register becomes common property, either spouse may require the other to concur in rectifying the land register [(d)].

1439. Objects which may not be transferred by juristic act are excluded from the common property. The provisions applicable to the contributed property under the régime of community of income and profits, with the exception of 1524, apply *mutatis mutandis* to such objects.

1440. All separate property is excluded from the common property.

Separate property is that which has been declared to be separate property of

---

(*c*) This does not apply to mere *alterations* in respect of the community of goods.

(*d*) As to such rectification, see 894—896.

one of the spouses in the marriage contract, or which is acquired by one of the spouses under 1369 or 1370 [(e)].

1441. The provisions applicable to the property of the wife under the régime of separation of goods apply *mutatis mutandis* to the separate property of the wife; the wife shall, however, make a contribution towards the expenses of the joint household only in so far as the income accruing to the common property is not sufficient to cover such expenses [(f)].

1442. Neither spouse may dispose of his (or her) share in the common property or in the individual objects belonging thereto; he (or she) is not entitled to demand partition.

A debtor may set off a claim enforceable against the common property only against a claim forming part of the common property.

1443. The common property is subject to the management of the husband. The husband is also entitled to take possession of all things forming part of the common property or to dispose of such property, or to bring actions relating to such property in his own name.

By the husband's acts of management the wife is personally bound neither to third parties nor to her husband.

1444. The husband requires the approval of his wife for a juristic act whereby he binds himself to dispose of the common property as a whole, or to make any disposition affecting such property whereby such an obligation incurred without the consent of the wife is to be fulfilled.

1445. The husband requires the approval of his wife for disposing of any land forming part of the common property, or for incurring an obligation to make such a disposition [(g)].

1446. The husband requires the approval of his wife for making a gift out

---

(*e*) Under this community both spouses may have separate property.

(*f*) There is a similar provision under the statutory régime. 1371.

(*g*) This provision applies only to land itself, and not to any *right* over land (as, *e.g.*, hypothecas, servitudes, &c.) which the husband may dispose of without his wife's consent.

of the common property, or for making any disposition affecting the common property whereby the promise of such a gift given without the consent of the wife is to be fulfilled [(h)]. The same rule applies to the promise of a gift not affecting the common property.

Gifts made in compliance with a moral duty or the rules of social propriety are excepted [(i)].

1447. If a juristic act of the kind specified in 1444, 1445 is necessary for the proper management of the common property, the consent of the wife may, if refused by her without sufficient reason, be supplied by the Guardianship Court upon the application of the husband [(k)].

The same rule applies if the wife is prevented by illness or absence from making a declaration, and there is danger in delay.

1448. If the husband enters into a juristic act of the kind specified in 1444 to 1446 without the approval of the wife, the provisions of 1396, pars. 1, 3, and 1397, 1398, applicable to a disposition made by the wife in respect of the contributed property, apply *mutatis mutandis.*

If in the case of a contract the other party demands the husband [(l)] to procure ratification by the wife, the declaration whether or not she ratifies may be made only to such other party; a ratification or refusal to ratify declared to the husband before the demand is of no effect. The ratification may be declared only before the expiration of two weeks after receipt of the demand; if it is not declared, it is deemed to have been refused.

If the ratification of the wife is supplied by the Guardianship Court, the order of the Court, where a demand has been made under par. 2, is effective only if the husband communicates it to the other party; the provisions of par. 2, sentence 2, apply *mutatis mutandis.*

1449. If the husband disposes of any right forming part of the common

---

(*h*) An "advancement" made to a son or daughter is not deemed to be a gift. 1620.

(*i*) See 534.

(*k*) If the juristic act is in the nature of a gift, the consent of the wife may not be supplied by the Guardianship Court. See 1446.

(*l*) The other party has no right to require the wife to give her ratification.

property without the necessary consent of his wife, she may enforce such right in Court against third parties without the concurrence of the husband (m).

1450. If the husband is prevented by illness or absence from entering into a juristic act relating to the common property, or to bring an action relating to such property, the wife may enter into the juristic act or bring the action in her own name or in the name of her husband, if there is danger in delay (n).

1451. If for the proper charge of the personal affairs of the wife a juristic act which she may not legally enter into in respect of the common property without the consent of her husband is necessary, such consent may, if refused by him without sufficient reason, be supplied by the Guardianship Court upon the application of the wife (o).

1452. The provisions of 1405 apply *mutatis mutandis* to the conduct of a separate business by the wife.

1453. Only the wife is entitled to accept or disclaim an inheritance or a legacy devolved on her; the consent of her husband is not necessary. The same rule applies to the renunciation of her compulsory portion and to the refusal of an offer of a contract or of a gift made to her.

The wife does not require the consent of her husband for filing an inventory relating to an inheritance devolved on her.

1454. The wife does not require the consent of her husband for continuing an action commenced before the time of the commencement of the community of goods.

1455. If the common property is benefited by a juristic act entered into by the husband or the wife without the necessary consent of the other spouse, the return of the benefits out of the common property may be demanded under the provisions relating to the return of unjustified benefits.

(*m*) This is an exception to 1443.

(*n*) All rights and duties arising from acts done by the wife by virtue of this section pass to the common property.

(*o*) Similar to 1402, under the statutory régime.

1456. The husband is not responsible to the wife for his management of the common property [(p)]. He shall, however, make compensation to the common property for any diminution thereof, if he has brought about such diminution with the intention of injuring the wife or by any juristic act which he enters into without the necessary consent of the wife.

1457. If the husband is under guardianship, the guardian shall represent him in the rights and the duties which arise from the management of the common property [(q)]. The same applies even if the wife is the guardian of her husband.

1458. The expenses of the joint household are borne by the common property.

1459. Creditors of the husband and, unless a contrary intention appears from 1460 to 1462, also creditors of the wife, may demand satisfaction out of the common property (liabilities of the common property).

The husband is also personally liable as a joint debtor for the liabilities of the wife which are the liabilities of the common property. His liability is extinguished on the dissolution of the community of goods, if as between the spouses the liabilities are not borne by the common property.

1460. The common property is not liable for any liability of the wife which arises from a juristic act entered into after the commencement of the community of goods, unless the husband gives his consent to the juristic act, or the juristic act is effective in respect of the common property even without his consent.

The common property is liable for the costs of any action to which die wife is a party even if the judgment is inoperative as against the common property.

1461. The common property is not liable for the liabilities of the wife arising in consequence of the acquisition of an inheritance or of a legacy, if the wife acquires the inheritance or the legacy as separate property after the com-

---

(*p*) This is an exception to 1359.

(*q*) Where the husband has been interdicted on the ground of prodigality, his wife may bring an action to dissolve the community of goods as provided for in 1468.

mencement of the community of goods [r].

1462. The common property is not liable for any liability of the wife arising after the commencement of the community of goods in consequence of a right forming part of her separate property, or in consequence of the possession of a thing forming part thereof, unless the right or the thing exists in connection with a separate business carried on by the wife with the approval of her husband [s].

1463. As between the spouses the following liabilities of the common property are borne by that spouse with reference to whom they arise:

(1) the liabilities arising from any unlawful act committed by him (or her) after the commencement of the community of goods, or from any criminal proceedings instituted against him (or her) on account of such an act;

(2) the liabilities arising from any legal relation affecting his (or her) separate property, even if they have arisen before the commencement of the community of goods, or before the time at which the property became separate property;

(3) the costs of any action relating to any of the liabilities specified in (1) and (2).

1464. As between the spouses the costs of any action between them are borne by the wife, unless the husband has to bear them.

The same rule applies to the costs of any action between the wife and a third party, unless the judgment is operative as against the common property. If, however, the action affects a personal affair of the wife, or a liability of the common property incurred by the wife and not provided for by 1463 (1) and (2), this provision does not apply, if the costs are necessary under the circumstances.

1465. As between the spouses an advancement promised or furnished to a child of the marriage out of the common property is borne by the husband, in so

(*r*) Corollary of 1453.

(*s*) Cf. 1414, 1452.

far as it exceeds a reasonable amount of the common property.

If the husband promises or furnishes an advancement out of the common property to a child who is not born of the marriage, such advancement is, as between the spouses, borne by the father or the mother of the child, as the case may be; it is borne by the mother, however, only in so far as she consents to it, or the advancement does not exceed a reasonable amount to the common property (t).

1466. If the husband uses the common property for the benefit of his separate property, he shall make good to the common property the value of what has been expended.

If the husband uses his separate property for the benefit of the common property he may demand reimbursement out of the common property (u).

1467. Whatever a spouse owes to the common property or whatever the wife owes to the separate property of the husband, shall not be returned until after the dissolution of the community of goods; if, however, the separate property of the wife is sufficient for the payment of any debt owed by her, she shall pay the debt even before that time.

If the husband has a claim against the common property, he may not assert the claim until after the dissolution of the community of goods.

1468. The wife may bring an action for dissolution of the community of goods (x):

(1) if the husband has entered into a juristic act of the kind specified in 1444 to 1446 without the consent of the wife, and for the future a serious danger to the interest of his wife is to be apprehended;

(2) if the husband has diminished the common property with the intention of injuring his wife;

(t) Cf. 2054. An "outfit" furnished to a daughter is in all cases to be paid out of the common property.

(u) This applies even to the expenses of the joint household.

(x) A general community of goods may, as a general rule, be dissolved in the following ways: (1) By the dissolution of the marriage; (2) by a special marriage contract; and (3) by action brought under 1468, 1469.

(3) if the husband has committed a breach of his duty to furnish maintenance to the wife and to the descendants of the marriage, and a serious danger to future maintenance is to be apprehended;

(4) if the husband has been interdicted on account of prodigality, or if he seriously endangers the common property through prodigality;

(5) if the common property, in consequence of liabilities incurred by the husband, is burdened with debts to such an extent that a later acquisition of the wife will be seriously endangered.

1469. The husband may bring an action for the dissolution of the community of goods, if the common property, in consequence of liabilities incurred by the wife which, as between the spouses, are not borne by the common property [(y)], is burdened with debts to such an extent that a later acquisition of the husband will be seriously endangered.

1470. In the cases provided for by 1468, 1469, the dissolution of the community of goods takes place as soon as the decree ceases to be appealable. For the future separation of goods takes place.

The dissolution of the community of goods is effective as against third parties only subject to the conditions specified in 1435.

1471. After the dissolution of the community of goods a liquidation in respect of the common property takes place [(z)].

Before the liquidation the provisions of 1442 apply to the common property.

1472. Before the liquidation the right of management of the common property belongs to both spouses in common. The provisions of 1424 apply *mutatis mutandis*.

Either spouse is bound to concur with the other in any measures which are necessary for the proper management of the common property; either spouse may, without the concurrence of the other, take all necessary measures for the preservation of the common property.

(*y*) Cf. 1463—1465.

(*z*) Either spouse may bring an action for liquidation.

1473. That becomes common property which is acquired by virtue of any right forming part of the common property, or as compensation for the destruction, damage or deprivation of any object forming part of such property, or by any juristic act affecting such property.

The fact that a claim acquired by juristic act belongs to the common property is not available against a debtor until he has knowledge of such fact; the provisions of 406 to 408 apply *mutatis mutandis*.

1474. The liquidation is effected in the manner provided for by 1475 to 1481, unless an agreement to the contrary is agreed upon.

1475. The liabilities of the common property shall first be discharged out of the common property. If a liability of the common property is not yet due or if it is in dispute, whatever is necessary for the discharge of such liability shall be retained.

If, as between the spouses, a liability of the common property is borne by only one of the spouses [(a)], such spouse may not demand the discharge of the liability out of the common property.

The common property shall, so far as necessary, be converted into money for the discharge of the liabilities of the common property.

1476. After the discharge of the liabilities of the common property the residue accrues to the spouses in equal shares.

Each of the spouses must deduct from his (or her) share whatever he or she is bound to reimburse to the common property. In so far as the reimbursement is not made by such deduction, he (or she) remains liable if the other spouse [(b)].

1477. The distribution of the residue is made according to the provisions applicable to community of ownership [(c)].

Either spouse may, on making compensation for their value, appropriate

(*a*) See 1464, 1465.

(*b*) The other spouse may claim reimbursement from the separate property of the spouse liable to make reimbursement.

(*c*) 752—757.

the things intended exclusively for his (or her) personal use, *i.e.*, clothing, ornaments, and working implements, and those objects which he (or she) has contributed to the community of goods, or which he (or she) has acquired during the subsistence of the community of goods by succession or legacy, or in consideration of his (or her) future right of inheritance, or by gift, or as an advancement [(d)].

1478. If the spouses have been divorced or judicially separated, and if one of them has been declared to be the exclusively guilty party, the other may demand that to each of the spouses the value of what he (or she) has contributed to the community of goods be returned; if the value of the common property is not sufficient for such return, each spouse shall bear one half of the deficiency.

That is deemed to have been contributed which would have become contributed property if a community of income and profits had been created [(e)]. The value of what has been contributed is determined as at the time of the contribution.

The right specified in par. 1 belongs also to a spouse whose marriage has been dissolved on account of his (or her) insanity [(f)].

1479. If the community of goods is dissolved by judicial decree under 1468 or 1469, the spouse who has applied for the decree may demand that liquidation shall be made in such manner as if action on the claim for liquidation had been commenced at the time of bringing the action for dissolution of the community of goods.

1480. If any liability of the common property is discharged before partition of the common property, each of the spouses is personally liable as a joint debtor to the creditor, even though he (or she) is not so liable at the time of the partition. His (or her) liability is limited to the objects allotted to him (or her); the provisions of 1990, 1991, applicable to the liability of an heir, apply

---

(*d*) This provision applies only as between the spouses.

(*e*) See 1520—1524.

(*f*) 1569.

mutatis mutandis.

1481. If, at the time of the liquidation, the discharge of a liability of the common property which, as between the spouses, is borne by the common property or by the husband is omitted, the husband shall give a guarantee that the wife will not be pursued by the creditor [(g)]. The wife has the same obligation towards the husband, if the discharge of a liability of the common property is omitted which is borne by the wife as between the spouses.

1482. If the marriage is dissolved by the death of one of the spouses, and if no descendant of the marriage [(h)] is living, the share of the deceased spouse in the common property belongs to his (or her) estate. The succession to the spouse takes place according to the general provisions.

1483. If any descendants of the marriage are living at the time of the death of one of the spouses, the community of goods is continued between the surviving spouse and the descendant of the marriage who would be entitled to inherit in the case of statutory succession. The share of the deceased spouse in the common property does not belong to his (or her) estate in this case; for the rest the succession to the spouse takes place according to the general provisions [(i)].

If there are other descendants besides the descendants of the marriage, their rights to inherit and their shares in the estate are determined in such manner as if the continued community of goods had not been created.

1484. The surviving spouse may refuse the continuance of the community of goods [(k)].

The provisions of 1943 to 1947, 1950, 1952, 1954 to 1957, 1959, applicable to the disclaimer of an inheritance, apply *mutatis mutandis* to such refusal. If the surviving spouse is under parental power or under guardianship, the ratification

---

(*g*) She may not, however, require the husband to give security.

(*h*) An illegitimate child which is subsequently "declared to be legitimate" is deemed to be a descendant of the marriage. 1736.

(*i*) *I.e.*, as regards those objects which have been excluded from the common property, the provisions of 1439, 1440 are applicable.

(*k*) A waiver of this right by contract is inoperative. 1518.

of the Guardianship Court is necessary for such refusal.

If the spouse refuses the continuance of the community of goods, the same rule applies as in the case provided for by 1482.

1485. The common property of the continued community of goods consists of the matrimonial common property [(l)], in so far as it does not accrue to a non-participating descendant as provided for in 1483, par. 2, and of the property which the surviving spouse acquires either out of the estate of the deceased spouse or after the commencement of the continued community of goods.

The property which any descendant of the marriage has at the time of the commencement of the continued community of goods, or which he subsequently acquires, does not belong to the common property.

The provisions of 1438, pars. 2, 3, applicable to the matrimonial community of goods, apply *mutatis mutandis* to the common property [(m)].

1486. Separate property of the surviving spouse is that which he (or she) has had heretofore as separate property, or which he (or she) acquires under 1369 or 1370 [(n)].

If objects which cannot be transferred by juristic act belong to the property of the surviving spouse, the provisions applicable to the contributed property of the husband under the régime of the community of income and profits, with the exception of 1524, apply *mutatis mutandis* to such objects.

1487. The rights and liabilities of the surviving spouse and of the participating descendants in respect of the common property of the continued community of goods are determined according to the provision of 1442 to 1449, 1455 to 1457, 1466, applicable to the matrimonial community of goods; the surviving spouse has the legal status of the husband, and the participating descendants have the legal status of the wife.

Whatever the surviving spouse owes to the common property, or whatever he (or she) may claim out of the common property, shall not be returned until

---

(*l*) *I.e.*, the common property under the original community.

(*m*) The continued community of goods is not registered in the marriage property register.

(*n*) The participating descendants do not have separate property.

after the dissolution of the continued community of goods.

1488. The liabilities of the common property of the continued community of goods are the liabilities of the surviving spouse and those liabilities of the deceased spouse which were the liabilities of the common property of the matrimonial community of goods.

1489. The surviving spouse is personally liable for the liabilities of the common property of the continued community of goods.

In so far as the surviving spouse incurs such personal liability only in consequence of the commencement of the continued community of goods, the provisions applicable to the liability of an heir for the liabilities of an estate apply *mutatis mutandis*; the common property in the condition in which it was at the time of the commencement of the continued community of goods takes the place of the estate [(o)].

No personal liability on the part of the participating descendants for the liabilities of the deceased [(p)] or surviving spouse is created by the continued community of goods.

1490. If any participating descendant dies, his share in the common property does not belong to his estate. If he dies leaving descendants who would have become participating descendants if he had not survived the deceased spouse, such descendants take his place. If he dies without leaving any such descendants, his share accrues to the other participating descendants, and where no such other participating descendants survive, to the surviving spouse.

1491. A participating descendant may renounce the share in the common property. The renunciation is effected by declaration to the Court having jurisdiction over the estate of the deceased spouse; the declaration shall be made in

---

(*o*) *I.e.*, the surviving spouse has either of the following remedies to limit his liability: (1) By applying for the appointment of an official administrator to manage the common property (1981—1988); (2) by the institution of bankruptcy proceedings. 214—234 of the Bankruptcy Act.

(*p*) Such a liability may, however, arise in consequence of *succession* to the estate of the deceased spouse.

publicly certified form [q]. The Probate Court should communicate the declaration to the surviving spouse and to the other participating descendants.

The renunciation may be effected by contract with the surviving spouse and the other participating descendants. Such a contract requires judicial or notarial authentication.

If the descendant is under parental power or under guardianship, the ratification of the Guardianship Court is necessary for the renunciation.

The renunciation has the same effects as if the person renunciating had died at the time of the renunciation without leaving any descendants [r].

1492. The surviving spouse may at any time dissolve the continued community of goods. The dissolution is effected by declaration to the Court having jurisdiction over the estate of the deceased spouse; the declaration shall be made in publicly certified form. The Probate Court should communicate the declaration to the participating descendants, and, where the surviving spouse is the statutory agent of any of such descendants, to the Guardianship Court.

The dissolution may be effected by contract between the surviving spouse and the participating descendants. Such a contract requires judicial or notarial authentication.

If the surviving spouse is under parental power or under guardianship, the ratification of the Guardianship Court is necessary for the dissolution.

1493. The continued community of property is dissolved on the re-marriage of the surviving spouse.

Where a participating descendant is a minor or is placed under guardianship, the surviving spouse shall notify the Guardianship Court of his intention to re-marry, file an inventory of the common property, dissolve the community of goods, and bring about a liquidation [s]. The Guardianship Court may permit the dissolution of the community of goods to be postponed until the conclusion to the marriage, and also the liquidation to be postponed until some future date.

(*q*) See 129.

(*r*) The renunciation is binding upon all the descendants of the renunciating party.

(*s*) If the surviving spouse has not done all these things he (or she) cannot enter into a marriage. 1314, par. 2.

1494. The continued community of goods is dissolved on the death of the surviving spouse.

If the surviving spouse is declared dead, the continued community of goods is dissolved at the date which is deemed to be the date of his (or her) death.

1495. Any participating descendant may bring an action against the surviving spouse for the dissolution of the continued community of goods:

(1) if the surviving spouse has entered into a juristic act of the kind specified in 1444 to 1446 without the consent of the descendant, and for the future a serious danger to the interests of the descendant is to be apprehended;

(2) if the surviving spouse has diminished the common property with the intention of injuring the descendant;

(3) if the surviving spouse has committed a breach of duty to furnish maintenance to the descendant, and a serious danger as to the future maintenance is to be apprehended;

(4) if the surviving spouse has been interdicted on account of prodigality, or if he seriously endangers the common property through prodigality;

(5) if the surviving spouse has forfeited his parental power over the descendant, or, if he had had such power, would have forfeited it.

1496. The dissolution of the continued community of goods begins, in the cases provided for by 1495, as soon as the judicial decree ceases to be appealable. The dissolution is effective in respect of all descendants even if the decree is issued in an action brought by only one of them.

1497. After the dissolution of the continued community of goods a liquidation in respect of the common property takes place [(t)].

Before the liquidation, the legal relations between the persons entitled to a share in the common property are determined according to 1442, 1472, 1473.

1498. The provisions of 1475, 1476, 1477, par. 1, and 1479 to 1481 apply to the liquidation; the surviving spouse takes the place of the husband; the

(t) *Ipso facto.*

participating descendants take the place of the wife. The obligation specified in 1476, par. 2, sentence 2, is imposed only upon the surviving spouse.

1499. In the liquidation the following are borne by the surviving spouse:

(1) the liabilities of the common property imposed upon him (or her) at the commencement of the continued community of goods, in so far as the matrimonial common property was not liable for them, or in so far as they were borne by him (or her) as between the spouses [(u)];

(2) the liabilities of the common property which have arisen after the commencement of the continued community of goods, and which as between the spouses would have been borne by him (or her) if they had been incurred by him (or her) during the subsistence of the matrimonial community of goods [(x)];

(3) any advancement which he (or she) has promised or furnished to a participating descendant out of proportion to the common property, or which he (or she) has promised or furnished to a non-participating descendant [(y)].

1500. The participating descendants must at the time of the liquidation deduct from their shares the liabilities of the deceased spouse which were borne by such spouse as between the spouses [(z)], in so far as the surviving spouse could not obtain satisfaction from the heir of the deceased spouse.

In the same manner the participating descendants shall deduct from their shares whatever the deceased spouse was bound to return to the common property.

1501. If a sum of money has been paid out of the common property to any participating descendant in consideration of a renunciation of his share, such sum of money shall be reckoned as part of the common property at the time of liquidation, and deducted from the moiety accruing to the descendants.

The surviving spouse may make a different agreement with the other par-

(*u*) See 1488, 1460—1462.

(*x*) 1463, 1464.

(*y*) 1465, 1624.

(*z*) 1463—1465.

ticipating descendants even before the dissolution of the continued community of goods. Such an agreement requires judicial or notarial authentication; it is binding even on those descendants who did not take part in the continued community of goods until after the agreement has been made.

1502. The surviving spouse is entitled to appropriate the common property or any individual objects belonging thereto on payment of its or their value. This right does not pass to his (or her) heirs.

If the continued community of goods is dissolved by judicial decree under 1495, the surviving spouse does not have the right specified in par. 1. In such a case the participating descendants may, on payment of the value, appropriate any objects which the deceased spouse would be entitled [(a)] to appropriate under 1477, par. 2. The right may be exercised by them only in common.

1503. The participating descendants share the moiety of the common property accruing to them in the proportion in which they would have been entitled to inherit as heirs of the deceased spouse in case of statutory succession, if he (or she) had not died until the time of the dissolution of the continued community of property.

Whatever has been received in advance shall be brought into hotchpot under the provisions applicable to hotchpot between descendants, unless this has already been done at the time of the partition of the estate of the deceased spouse.

If any descendant has received a sum of money paid out of the common property in consideration of a renunciation of his share, such sum of money shall be borne by those descendants who profit by the renunciation.

1504. In so far as the participating descendants are liable to the creditors of the common property as provided for in 1480, they are, as between themselves, liable in proportion to their shares in the common property. Such liability is limited to the objects allotted to them; the provisions of 1990, 1991, applicable to the liability of an heir, apply *mutatis mutandis*.

(*a*) Cf. 1515.

1505. The provisions relating to the right to demand the completion of a compulsory portion apply *mutatis mutandis* in favour of a participating descendant; the dissolution of the continued community of goods takes the place of the accrual of the inheritance; the share in the common property accruing to the descendant at the time of the dissolution is deemed to be his statutory portion; and the moiety of the value of such a share is deemed to be his compulsory portion.

1506. If any participating descendant is unworthy to inherit, he is also unworthy to receive his share in the common property. The provisions relating to unworthiness to inherit apply *mutatis mutandis* [(b)].

1507. The Probate Court shall issue to the surviving spouse, upon his (or her) application, a certificate relating to the continuance of the community of goods. The provisions relating to a certificate of inheritance apply *mutatis mutandis* [(c)].

1508. The spouses may exclude the continuance of the community of goods by a marriage contract.

The provisions of 1437 apply to a marriage contract whereby the continuance of the community of goods is excluded, or whereby such exclusion is revoked.

1509. Either spouse may, in providing for the case where the marriage is dissolved by his (or her) death, exclude the continuance of the community of goods by testamentary disposition, if he (or she) is entitled to deprive the other spouse of the compulsory portion [(d)], or to bring an action for the dissolution of the community of goods. The provisions relating to the deprivation of a compulsory portion apply *mutatis mutandis* to such exclusion [(e)].

1510. If the continuance of the community of goods is excluded, the same

(*b*) 2339 *et seq.*

(*c*) 2353 *et seq.*

(*d*) He may do so whenever he is entitled to petition for divorce. 2335.

(*e*) 2336, 2337.

rule applies as in the case provided for by 1482.

1511. Either spouse may, in providing for the case where the marriage is dissolved by his (or her) death, exclude by testamentary disposition any descendant of the marriage from participating in the continued community of goods [(f)].

The excluded descendant may, without prejudice to his right of inheritance, demand payment, out of the common property of the continued community of goods, of the amount which would have accrued to him as a compulsory portion of the common property of the matrimonial community of goods, if the continued community of goods had not been created. The provisions applicable to the claim to a compulsory portion apply *mutatis mutandis*.

The amount paid to the excluded descendant is, in accordance with 1500, chargeable against all the participating descendants at the time of liquidation. As between the participating descendants themselves such amount is borne by those descendants who profit by the exclusion.

1512. Either spouse may, in providing for the case where the continued community of goods is created on his (or her) death, reduce, by testamentary disposition, to one half the share in the common property accruing to a participating descendant after the dissolution of the continued community of goods [(g)].

1513. Either spouse may, in providing for the case where the continued community of goods is created on his (or her) death, deprive a participating descendant, by testamentary disposition, of the share in the common property accruing to such descendant after the dissolution of the continued community of goods, if he (or she) is entitled to deprive the descendant of his compulsory portion. The provisions of 2336, pars. 2 to 4, apply *mutatis mutandis*.

If the spouse is entitled under 2338 to limit the descendant's right to a compulsory portion, he (or she) may subject the descendant's share in the common

---

(*f*) The consent of the other spouse is necessary. 1516.

(*g*) The part of which the participating descendant has been deprived accrues to the other participating descendants.

property to a similar limitation.

1514. Either spouse may, by testamentary disposition, transfer even to a third party [(h)], the amount of which he (or she) has deprived any descendant under 1512 or 1513, par. 1.

1515. Either spouse may, in providing for the case where the continued community of goods is created on his (or her) death, direct in his (or her) testamentary disposition that a participating descendant shall have the right, at the time of partition, to appropriate the common property or any individual objects belonging thereto on payment of its or their value.

If a farm forms part of the common property, it may be directed that the farm be assessed at the value of its produce [(i)], or at a price not less than the value of the produce. The provisions of 2049, applicable to the order of succession, apply.

The right to appropriate the farm at the value or price specified in par. 2 may also be created by the surviving spouse.

1516. For the validity of the dispositions of either spouse specified in 1511 to 1515, the consent of the other spouse is necessary.

The consent may not be given through an agent [(k)]. If the spouse is limited in disposing capacity, the consent of his (or her) statutory agent is not necessary. The declaration of consent requires judicial or notarial authentication. The consent is irrevocable.

The spouses may also make the dispositions specified in 1511 to 1515 in a joint will.

1517. For the validity of a contract whereby a descendant of the marriage, in the event of the marriage being dissolved by the death of one of the spouses, renounces or revokes the renunciation of his share in the common property of the continued community of goods in favour of such spouse, the consent of the other spouse is necessary. The provisions of 1516, par. 2, sentences 3 and 4, apply

---

(*h*) The provisions of 2147 *et seq.* relating to legacies apply to the transfer.

(*i*) See IA, Art. 137.

(*k*) A spouse under disposing incapacity cannot, therefore, give such consent.

to such consent.

The provisions applicable to the renunciation of an inheritance apply *mutatis mutandis*.

1518. Neither spouse may, by testamentary disposition or by contract, make any provision which is incompatible with the provisions of 1483 to 1517.

3. *Community of Income and Profits*.

1519. That which the husband or the wife acquires during the subsistence of the community of income and profits becomes the common property of both spouses (*i.e.*, common property) [(l)].

The provisions of 1438, pars. 2, 3, and 1442 to 1453, 1455 to 1457, applicable to the general community of goods, apply to the common property.

1520. Contributed property of a spouse includes that which belongs to him (or her) at the commencement of the community of income and profits.

1521. Contributed property of a spouse includes also that which he (or she) acquires *mortis causa*, or in consideration of a future right of inheritance, or as a gift [(m)], or as an advancement. An acquisition which may be considered under the circumstances as income is excepted.

1522. Contributed property of a spouse includes also objects which cannot be transferred by juristic act, and rights which are extinguished on his (or her) death [(n)] or the acquisition of which depends on the death of one of the spouses [(o)].

1523. Contributed property of a spouse includes also that which has been declared to be contributed property in the marriage contract.

1524. Contributed property of a spouse includes also that which he (or

---

(*l*) Exceptions: 1521, 1522, 1524.

(*m*) No matter whether made by the other spouse or by a third party.

(*n*) *E.g.*, a life annuity. 759.

(*o*) *E.g.*, rights under a life insurance policy.

she) acquires by virtue of a right forming part of his (or her) contributed property, or as compensation for the destruction, deterioration, or deprivation of an object forming part of such property, or by a juristic act relating to such property. An acquisition made in connection with the conduct of a business is excepted.

The fact that a claim acquired by juristic act belongs to the contributed property is not available against a debtor until he has knowledge of such fact; the provisions of 406 to 408 apply *mutatis mutandis*.

1525. The contributed property shall be managed on account of the common property in such manner that the emoluments which would accrue to the husband under the provisions applicable to the régime of management and usufruct shall belong to the common property.

For the rest, the provisions of 1373 to 1383, 1390 to 1417, apply *mutatis mutandis* to the contributed property of the wife.

1526. Separate property of the wife includes that which has been declared to be separate property in the marriage contract, or is acquired by the wife under 1369 or 1370.

The husband does not have separate property.

The same rules which apply to the separate property under the régime of general community of goods apply to the separate property of the wife.

1527. It is presumed that the property existing at any time is common property [(p)].

1528. Either spouse may require the other to concur in determining the condition of his (or her) own contributed property and that of the other spouse by drawing up an inventory. The provisions of 1035, applicable to usufruct, apply to the drawing up of the inventory.

Either spouse may cause the condition of the things belonging to the contributed property to be determined by experts at his (or her) own expense.

1529. The expenses of the joint household are borne by the common pro-

---

(*p*) The presumption is rebuttable; it obtains, however, even as between the spouses *inter se*.

perty.

The common property also bears the charges upon the contributed property of both spouses; the extent of such charges is determined according to the provisions of 1384 to 1387 applicable to the contributed property of the wife under the régime of management and usufruct.

1530. The common property is liable for the liabilities of the husband and for such liabilities of the wife as are specified in 1531 to 1534 (*i.e.*, liabilities of the common property) [(q)].

The husband is also personally liable as a joint debtor for the liabilities of the wife which are not the liabilities of the common property [(r)]. His liability is extinguished on the dissolution of the community of income and profits, if the liabilities, as between the spouses, are not borne by the common property.

1531. The common property is liable for the liabilities of the wife which belong to the class of charges upon the contributed property specified in 1529, par. 2.

1532. The common property is liable for any liability of the wife arising out of a juristic act entered into after the commencement of the community of income and profits, and for the costs of any action brought by the wife after the commencement of the community of income and profits, provided the entering into the juristic act or the bringing of the action takes place with the consent of the husband, or is effective in respect of the common property even without his consent [(s)].

1533. The common property is liable for any liability of the wife arising after the commencement of the community of income and profits in consequence of a right belonging to her, or in consequence of the possession of a thing belonging to her, provided the right or the thing exists in connection with a separate

---

(*q*) In other words, the common property is liable not only for *all* the liabilities of the husband, but also for all the liabilities of the wife, with the exception of those liabilities incurred by her before the commencement of the community.

(*r*) Cf. 1459.

(*s*) Cf. 1460.

business carried on by her with the approval of the husband [t].

1534. The common property is liable for the liabilities of the wife imposed upon her by reason of her statutory duty to furnish maintenance to others [u].

1535. As between the spouses the following liabilities of the common property are borne by that spouse with reference to whom they arise:

(1) the liabilities arising from any legal relation relating to his (or her) contributed property, or to his (or her) separate property, even if they have arisen before the commencement of the community of income and profits, or before the time at which the property became contributed property or separate property [x];

(2) the costs of any action, to which the spouse is a party, relating to any of the liabilities specified in (1) [y].

1536. As between the spouses the following are borne by the husband:

(1) the liabilities of the husband which have arisen before the commencement of the community of income and profits;

(2) the liabilities of the husband towards the wife arising from his management of her contributed property, unless the common property is benefited at the time of the dissolution of the community of income and profits [z];

(3) the liabilities of the husband arising from any unlawful act committed by him after the commencement of the community of income and profits, or from any criminal proceedings instituted against him on account of such an unlawful act [a];

(4) the costs of any action, to which the husband is a party, relating to any of the liabilities specified in (1) to (3).

(*t*) It is immaterial whether such business forms part of her contributed property or separate property.

(*u*) Cf. 1386, sentence 2.

(*x*) Cf. 1463 (2).

(*y*) Cf. 1463 (3).

(*z*) The husband has to prove that the common property is so benefited.

(*a*) Cf. 1463 (1).

1537. The provisions of 1535 and 1536 (1) and (4), do not apply in so far as the liabilities are to be borne by the common property as provided for in 1529, par. 2.

The same rule applies to the provisions of 1535 in so far as the liabilities arise in the course of a business conducted on account of the common property, or in consequence of a right or of the possession of a thing connected with such a business.

1538. If the husband promises or furnishes an advancement to a child, the provision of 1465 apply [(b)].

1539. In so far as at the time of the dissolution of the community of income and profits the contributed property of a spouse is benefited at the expense of the common property, or *vice versâ*, compensation must be made to the other property out of the property thus benefited. Further claims [(c)] based on special reasons remain unaffected.

1540. If consumable things which belonged to the contributed property of a spouse no longer exist, it is presumed in favour of such spouse that they have been consumed for the benefit of the common property, and that the latter is benefited to the extent of their value [(d)].

1541. Whatever a spouse owes to the common property or the wife owes to the contributed property of the husband shall not be returned until after the dissolution of the community of income and profits; if, however, both the contributed property and the separate property of the wife are sufficient for the payment of any debt due from her, she shall pay such debt even before that time.

If the husband has a claim against the common property he may not assert the claim until after the dissolution of the community of income and profits [(e)].

1542. The wife may, subject to the conditions specified in 1418 (1),

---

(*b*) See 1624.

(*c*) *E.g.*, claims arising from management of business without mandate. 677 *et seq.*

(*d*) The presumption is rebuttable. Cf. also 1527.

(*e*) Cf. 1467.

(3) to (5), and 1468, and the husband may, subject to the conditions specified in 1469, bring an action for the dissolution of the community of income and profits.

The dissolution becomes effective as soon as the judicial decree ceases to be appealable.

1543. The community of income and profits is dissolved as soon as an order for the institution of bankruptcy proceedings against the property of the husband ceases to be appealable [f].

1544. The community of income and profits is dissolved, where one of the spouses is declared dead, at the date which is deemed to be the date of his (or her) death.

1545. If the community of income and profits is dissolved under 1542 to 1544, the régime of separation of goods takes place for the future.

The dissolution of the community is effective as against third parties subject only to the conditions specified in 1435.

1546. After the dissolution of the community of income and profits a liquidation in respect of the common property takes place. Before the liquidation the legal relations between the spouses are determined according to 1442, 1472, 1473.

In the absence of any agreement [g] to the contrary the liquidation is effected according to the provisions of 1475 to 1477, 1479 to 1481 applicable to the general community of goods.

The provisions of 1421 to 1424 applicable to the régime of management and usufruct apply to the contributed property of the wife.

1547. If the community of income and profits is dissolved by the institution of bankruptcy proceedings against the property of the husband, the wife may [h] bring an action for the re-establishment of the community. Where the community

---

(*f*) Cf. 1419.

(*g*) For the form of such an agreement, see 1432—1436.

(*h*) Even before the termination of the bankruptcy proceedings.

is dissolved in consequence of a declaration of death, the spouse who has been declared dead has the same right, if he is still alive.

If the community is dissolved under 1418 (3) to (5), the husband may, subject to the conditions specified in 1425, par. 1, bring an action for the re-establishment of the community.

1548. The re-establishment of the community of income and profits in the cases provided for by 1547 takes place as soon as the judicial decree ceases to be appealable. The provision of 1422 applies *mutatis mutandis*.

If the dissolution has been entered in the marriage property register, the re-establishment is effective as against third parties subject only to the conditions specified in 1435.

In case of such re-establishment, that which would have remained or would have become separate property if the community had not been dissolved becomes the separate property of the wife[(i)].

4. *Community of Moveables*.

1549. Unless a contrary intention appears from 1550 to 1557, the provisions applicable to the general community of goods apply to the community of moveables and of income and profits (*i.e.*, community of moveables)[(k)].

1550. The contributed property of a spouse is excluded from the common property.

The provisions applicable to the contributed property under the régime of community of income and profits apply to such contributed property[(l)].

1551. Contributed property of a spouse includes immoveables which he (or she) had at the commencement of the community of moveables, or which he (or she) acquires during the subsistence of the community by succession or as a legacy, or in consideration of a future right of inheritance, or as a gift, or as an

---

(*i*) Cf. 1425, 1431.

(*k*) A community of moveables possesses all the characteristics of a community of income and profits, and the two régimes exactly coincide with each other if neither spouse possesses *immoveables*.

(*l*) See 1520—1525, 1535 *et seq*.

advancement.

Immoveables, within the meaning of this provision, include land together with its accessories; rights over land, with the exception of hypothecas, land charges and annuity charges; and claims which have for their object the transfer of ownership of land, or the creation or transfer of one of the rights specified herein, or the discharge of a piece of land from such a right.

1552. Contributed property of a spouse includes also objects which cannot be transferred by juristic act.

1553. Contributed property of a spouse includes also:

(1) that which has been declared to be contributed property in the marriage contract;

(2) that which he (or she) acquires under 1369, provided that it has been specified that the acquisition shall be contributed property.

1554. Contributed property of a spouse includes also that which he (or she) acquires in the manner specified in 1524. That which is acquired as a substitute for objects which are contributed property merely because they cannot be transferred by juristic act [(m)], is excepted.

1555. The husband does not have separate property.

1556. If, during the subsistence of the community of moveables, one of the spouses acquires, by succession or as a legacy, or in consideration of a future right of inheritance, or as a gift, or as an advancement, objects which become partly common property and partly contributed property, the liabilities incurred in consequence of such acquisition are, as between the spouses, borne proportionately by the common property and the spouse who has made the acquisition.

1557. Continued community of goods takes place only if it has been agreed upon in a marriage contract.

(*m*) Cf. 1439. See further 1524, par. 1, sentence 2, which is also applicable to this case.

III. Marriage Property Register (n).

1558. Entries in the marriage property register shall be made in the District Court in whose district the husband has his domicile.

By an order of the Administration of Justice of one of the States a District Court may be charged with the duty of keeping a register for several districts.

1559. If after an entry has been made the husband removes his domicile to another district, the entry must be repeated in the register of such other district. The former entry is deemed to have been renewed if the husband removes his domicile back to the former district.

1560. An entry in the register should be made only on application and only according to the terms of the application. The application shall be made in publicly certified form.

1561. In the cases provided for by 1357, par. 2, and 1405, par. 3 the entry is made on the application of the husband.

In all other cases application on the part of both spouses is necessary; either spouse is bound to concur with the other spouse in making the application.

Application by one of the spouses is sufficient:

(1) for the registration of a marriage contract, or of any modification, ordered by judicial decree, of the property relations of the spouses, provided the marriage contract or a copy of the decree certified to be non-appealable accompanies the application;

(2) for the repetition of an entry in the register of another district, if the application is accompanied by a publicly certified copy of the former entry issued after the abandonment of the former domicile.

1562. The District Court shall publish the entry in the newspaper selected for the publication of its notices.

If any notification of the régime has been registered, the publication shall

---

(*n*) The marriage property register (*Güterrechtsregister*) is entirely separate and distinct from the marriage register (*Heiratsregister*) mentioned in 1318 *et seq.*

be limited to a designation of the régime and, if the régime is regulated otherwise than as provided by law, to a general designation of such notification.

1563. Any person is permitted to inspect the register [(o)]. A copy of the records may be obtained; the copy shall be certified on demand.

SEVENTH TITLE.
Divorce.

1564. A marriage may be dissolved on any one of the grounds [(p)] specified in 1565 to 1569. The dissolution is effected by judicial decree. The dissolution takes place as soon as the decree ceases to be appealable.

1565. Either spouse may petition for divorce if the other spouse has been guilty of adultery [(q)] or of any act punishable under 171, 175 of the Criminal Code.

The right of the spouse to petition for divorce is barred if he (or she) consents to or is an accomplice in the adultery or the criminal act.

1566. Either spouse may petition for divorce if the other spouse makes an attempt against his (or her) life.

1567. Either spouse may petition for divorce if the other spouse has wilfully deserted him (or her).

Wilful desertion exists only:

(1) if either spouse, after having been ordered by a non-appealable decree to restitute the conjugal community, has intentionally disobeyed such

---

(*o*) No matter whether he has a legal interest in making such inspection or not.

(*p*) The grounds entitling a spouse to obtain a divorce or a judicial separation are divided into "absolute" and "qualified" grounds. Where the ground is absolute the relief prayed for must be granted, whereas in the case of a qualified ground the matter is left to the discretion of the Court. The absolute grounds are those specified in 1565, par. 1, 1566, 1567, par. 1; the qualified grounds are specified in 1568, 1569.

(*q*) An attempt to commit adultery constitutes at most a "qualified ground". Cf. 1568.

decree for a year against the will of the other spouse;

(2) if either spouse has been absent intentionally from the conjugal home for a year against the will of the other spouse, and the conditions for public citation [r] have occurred as against him (or her) for the period of one year.

In the case provided for by par. 2 (2), the divorce may not be granted if the conditions for public citation have ceased to exist at the termination of the *viva voce* proceedings upon which the decree is to be issued.

1568. Either spouse may petition for divorce if the other spouse has, by any grave breach of marital duty, or by dishonest or immoral conduct, disturbed the conjugal relations to such an extent that the petitioner cannot be expected to continue the marriage. Gross ill-treatment is also deemed to be a grave breach of duty.

1569. Either spouse may petition for divorce if the other spouse has become insane for three years continuously during the marriage, and the insanity has reached such a stage that the intellectual community between the spouses hat ceased, and there is no hope of its re-establishment.

1570. The right to a divorce is extinguished by condonation in the cases provided for by 1565 to 1568.

1571. In the cases provided for by 1565 to 1568 the petition for divorce must be filed within six months from the time at which the petitioner had knowledge of the ground for divorce. The petition is disallowed if ten years have elapsed since the occurrence of the ground for divorce [s].

The period does not run so long as the conjugal community of the spouses remains dissolved. If the spouse entitled to petition for divorce is required by the other spouse either to restitute the conjugal community or to make the petition, the period begins to run from the receipt of the request.

Citation to appear on the day fixed for condonation is equivalent to the

---

(r) Code of Civil Procedure, 203 of the Revised Edition.

(s) See 606 *et seq.* of the Code of Civil Procedure.

making of the petition. The citation ceases to be operative if the spouse entitled to petition for divorce has not appeared on the day fixed for condonation, or if three months have elapsed since the termination of the process for condonation and the petition has not been made within such period.

The provisions of 203, 206, applicable to prescription, apply *mutatis mutandis*, to the running of the periods of six and three months.

1572. A ground for divorce, even if the period specified in 1571 for its assertion has elapsed, may still be asserted in the course of the proceedings in so far as the period had not elapsed at the time of the making of the petition.

1573. Facts upon which a petition for divorce may no longer be based can be set up in support of a petition for divorce based upon other facts.

1574. If a marriage is dissolved on any one of the grounds specified in 1565 to 1568, the decree shall declare the respondent to be the guilty party of the divorce.

If the respondent has made a cross-petition, and if it is also recognised to be well founded, both spouses shall be declared to be guilty parties.

Upon the application of the respondent, and even without the making of a cross-petition, the petitioner shall also be declared to be a guilty party, if facts exist whereby the respondent could petition for divorce, or, if his (or her) right to petition for divorce has been barred by condonation or lapse of time, was entitled to petition for divorce at the time of the occurrence of the ground for divorce asserted by the petitioner.

1575. A spouse entitled to petition for divorce may petition for judicial separation in lieu of divorce. If the other spouse applies for divorce, and if the petition is well founded, the divorce shall be granted.

The provisions of 1573, 1574 apply to the petition for judicial separation.

1576. If judicial separation has been granted, either spouse may apply for divorce by virtue of the decree for separation, unless the conjugal community has been re-established after the issue of such decree.

The provisions of 1570 to 1574 do not apply; if the marriage is dissolved, the spouse declared to be the guilty party shall also be declared to be the guilty party by the decree for divorce.

1577. A divorced wife retains the surname of her former husband.

A divorced wife may resume her maiden name. If she had been married before the conclusion of the dissolved marriage, she may also resume the name which she had at the time of the conclusion of the dissolved marriage, unless she has been declared to be the exclusively guilty party. The resumption of the name is made by declaration to the competent public authority; the declaration shall be made in publicly certified form.

If the divorced wife has been declared to be the exclusively guilty party, her former husband may prohibit her from using his name. The prohibition is made by declaration to the competent public authority; the declaration shall be made in publicly certified form. The public authority should communicate the declaration to the divorced wife. After she has lost the name of her husband she resumes her maiden name.

1578. A husband declared to be the exclusively guilty party shall furnish maintenance to his divorced wife suitable to her station in life in so far as she cannot furnish such maintenance out of the income of her property and the earnings of her labour, if, under the circumstances under which the spouses have been living, it is usual for the wife to earn money by her labour.

A wife declared to be the exclusively guilty party shall furnish maintenance to her divorced husband suitable to his station in life, in so far as he is not in a position to maintain himself [(t)].

1579. In so far as the spouse declared to be the exclusively guilty party is not in a position, having regard to his (or her) other obligations, to furnish maintenance to the other spouse without endangering his (or her) own maintenance suitable to his (or her) station in life, he (or she) is entitled to retain two-thirds or, where this is insufficient for the necessaries of life, such part of the income available for providing maintenance as is necessary for such purpose. If he (or she) has to furnish maintenance to a minor unmarried child or to his

(t) If both parties have been declared to be guilty parties, neither has a right to claim maintenance from the other.

(or her) new spouse in consequence of his (or her) re-marriage, his (or her) obligation in respect of the divorced spouse is limited to an amount which is equitable, having regard to the necessities, the pecuniary circumstances, and the earning capacities of the parties concerned.

Under the conditions of par. 1 the husband is entirely discharged from his duty to furnish maintenance to his divorced wife, if she can provide for such maintenance out of the capital of her property.

1580. The maintenance shall be furnished by payment of a money annuity subject to the conditions specified in 760. Whether, in what manner, and to what amount the person liable to furnish maintenance has to give security is determined according to the circumstances.

Instead of the annuity, the person entitled may demand settlement in a lump sum, if a grave reason exists.

For the rest, the provisions of 1607, 1610, 1611, par. 1, 1613, and, in the case of the death of the person entitled, the provisions also of 1615, applicable to the duty to furnish maintenance by relatives by blood, apply *mutatis mutandis*.

1581. The duty to furnish maintenance is extinguished on the re-marriage of the person entitled.

In case of the re-marriage of the person liable, the provisions of 1604 apply *mutatis mutandis*.

1582. The duty to furnish maintenance is extinguished on the death of the person liable.

The liability of the heir of the deceased is not subject to the limitations of 1579. The person entitled must, however, allow a reduction of the annuity to one-half of the income which the person liable received out of his property at the time of his death. Income accruing from a right which is extinguishable on the arrival of a certain time or the occurrence of a certain event is not taken into consideration after the time has arrived or the event occurred.

If there are several persons entitled to maintenance, the heir may proportionately reduce their annuities so that they shall together be equal to one-half of the income.

1583. If a marriage has been dissolved on account of the insanity of one of the spouses, the other spouse shall furnish maintenance to him (or her) in the same manner as a spouse declared to be the exclusively guilty party [(u)].

1584. If either spouse has been declared to be the exclusively guilty party, the other spouse may revoke any gifts which he (or she) has made to the guilty spouse during the betrothal or marriage. The provisions of 531 apply.

The right to revoke is barred if one year has elapsed after the decree for divorce has ceased to be appealable, or if the donor or donee has died.

1585. If the husband has to furnish maintenance to a child of the marriage, the wife is bound to furnish a reasonable contribution towards such maintenance out of the income of her property and the earnings of her labour, or of any separate business carried on by her, unless such maintenance may be provided by her husband's right of usufruct of the child's property. The claim of the husband is not transferable.

If the right to take care of the child's person belongs to the wife, and if a serious danger to the maintenance of the child is to be apprehended, she may retain the contribution to be used by her for providing the maintenance of the child.

1586. If judicial separation is granted under 1575, the effects incident to divorce come into being; the conclusion of a new marriage is, however, excluded. The provisions relating to void and voidable marriages apply as if the decree had not been issued [(x)].

1587. If conjugal community is re-established after judicial separation, the effects incident to judicial separation cease to operate, and separation of goods takes place.

(*u*) Cf. 1578, 1579.

(*x*) In other words, a voidable marriage may be avoided even after judicial separation. 1323 *et seq.*

EIGHTH TITLE.
Religious Obligations.

1588. The religious obligations in respect of a marriage are not affected by the provisions of this section.

SECOND SECTION.
RELATIONSHIP.

FIRST TITLE.
General Provisions.

1589. Persons of whom one is descended from the other are relatives by blood in the direct line. Persons who are not related by blood in the direct line, but are descended from one and the same third person, are related by blood in the collateral line. The degree of relationship by blood is determined by the number of intermediate births.

An illegitimate child and his father are not deemed to be related by blood.

1590. Relatives by blood of a spouse are related to the other spouse by marriage. The line and the degree of relationship by marriage are determined by the line and degree of the intermediate relationship by blood.

Relationship by marriage continues even if the marriage whereby it was created has been dissolved.

SECOND TITLE.
Legitimate Descent.

1591. A child born after the conclusion of a marriage is legitimate, if the wife conceived the child before or during the marriage, and the husband cohabited with the wife within the period of possible conception. The child is not legitimate if it is evidently impossible under the circumstance that the wife has conceived the child by the husband.

It is presumed that the husband has cohabited with the wife within the period of possible conception [(y)]. In so far as the period of possible conception falls within a period of time prior to the marriage, the presumption obtains only if the husband has died without having repudiated the legitimacy of the child.

1592. The period of possible conception is the period between the one hundred and eighty-first day and the three hundred and second day, both inclusive, before the day of the birth of the child.

If it is established that the child has been conceived within a period which is remoter than three hundred and two days before the day of birth, such period is, in favour of the legitimacy of the child, deemed to be the period of possible conception.

1593. The illegitimacy of a child born during the marriage or within three hundred and two days after the dissolution of the marriage, may not be set up unless the husband has repudiated the legitimacy, or has died without having lost the right of repudiation [(z)].

1594. The repudiation of legitimacy may be effected only within the period of one year.

The period begins to run from the time at which the husband learns of the birth of the child.

The provisions of 203, 206, applicable to prescription, apply *mutatis mutandis* to the running of the period.

1595. The repudiation of legitimacy may not be effected through an agent. If the husband is limited in disposing capacity, he does not require the consent of his statutory agent.

A statutory agent may repudiate the legitimacy on behalf of the husband

---

(*y*) The presumption is rebuttable.

(*z*) The right of repudiation may be lost by acknowledgment of the paternity of the child (1598), and by lapse of time. 1594.

incapable of disposing only with the ratification of the Guardianship Court. If the statutory agent has not repudiated the legitimacy in due time, the husband may, after the disappearance of his disposing incapacity, himself repudiate the legitimacy in the same manner as though he had not any statutory agent.

1596. The repudiation of legitimacy is effected during the lifetime of the child by bringing an action for repudiation [(a)]. The action shall be brought against the child.

If the action is withdrawn, the repudiation is deemed not to have been effected. The same rule applies if the husband acknowledges the child as his own before the termination of the process.

Before the termination of the process the illegitimacy of the child may not be set up collaterally.

1597. After the death of the child the repudiation of legitimacy is effected by declaration to the Probate Court; the declaration shall be made in publicly certified form.

The Probate Court should communicate the declaration both to the person who, if the child were legitimate, and to the person who, if the child were illegitimate, would be the heir of the child. The Probate Court shall permit any person to inspect the declaration, provided he can offer *primâ facie* proof that he has a legal interest therein.

1598. The right to repudiate legitimacy is barred if the husband acknowledges [(b)] the child as his own after birth.

The acknowledgment may not be made subject to any condition or limitation of time.

The provisions of 1595, par. 1, apply to such acknowledgment. The acknowledgment may also be made by a disposition *mortis causa*.

1599. If an acknowledgment of legitimacy is voidable, the provisions of 1595 to 1597 and, where the voidability is based on fraud or threats, besides

---

(*a*) See 640 of the Code of Civil Procedure.

(*b*) The acknowledgment may be either express or implied.

the provisions of 203, par. 2, and 206, the provisions also of 203, par. 1, apply *mutatis mutandis*.

1600. If a woman who has re-married after the dissolution of a previous marriage gives birth to a child who, according to 1591 to 1599, would be a legitimate child both of the first and of the second husband, the child is, where it is born within two hundred and seventy days after the dissolution of the first marriage, deemed to be the child of the first husband, and where it is born after that period, the child of the second husband.

THIRD TITLE.
Duty to Furnish Maintenance.

1601. Persons related by blood in the direct line are bound to furnish maintenance to one another [c].

1602. A person is entitled to maintenance only if he is not in a position to maintain himself [d].

An unmarried minor child may, even if he has property, claim maintenance from his parents in so far as the income of his property and the earnings of his work are not sufficient for his maintenance.

1603. A person is not bound to furnish maintenance if, having regard to his other obligations, he is not in a position to furnish maintenance to others without endangering his own maintenance suitable to his station in life.

Where the parents are in such a condition, they are bound, as towards their unmarried minor children, to use all available means to maintain themselves and their children at the same time. This obligation does not arise if there is any relative by blood who is bound to furnish maintenance; the obligation does not

---

(*c*) The duty to furnish maintenance does not exist as between relatives by blood in the collateral line, even as between brothers and sisters.

(*d*) The fact that a person has brought himself to such a condition through his own fault, does not affect his *right* to claim maintenance; it affects only the *amount* of maintenance to which he is entitled.

arise in respect of a child whose maintenance may be furnished out of the capital of his property.

1604. In so far as a wife's duty to furnish maintenance to her relatives by blood depends upon the question whether she is in a position to furnish such maintenance, the husband's rights of management and usufruct of the contributed property are not taken into consideration.

If a general community of goods, a community of income and profits, or a community of moveables exists, the husband's or the wife's duty to furnish maintenance to relatives by blood is determined just as though the common property belonged exclusively to that spouse who is bound to furnish maintenance. If the relatives by blood of both spouses are necessitous, the maintenance shall be furnished out of the common property just as though the necessitous relatives stood in the same relationship with both spouses upon which the duty of the spouse bound to furnish maintenance is based.

1605. In so far as a minor child's duty to furnish maintenance to his relatives by blood depends upon the question whether he is in a position to furnish such maintenance, the parental right of usufruct of the child's property is not taken into consideration.

1606. Descendants are liable to furnish maintenance before relatives by blood in the ascending line are liable. The descendants' duty to furnish maintenance is determined according to the statutory order of succession [(e)] and in proportion to their respective shares in the inheritance.

Among relatives by blood in the ascending line those of nearer degree are liable before those of remoter degree; relatives of the same degree are liable in equal shares. The father is, however, liable before the mother; if the mother has a right of usufruct of her child's property [(f)] she is liable before the father is liable.

1607. In so far as a relative by blood is, by virtue of 1603, not bound to

---

(*e*) 1924 *et seq.*

(*f*) 1684 *et seq.*

furnish maintenance, that relative by blood who is liable next after him shall furnish maintenance.

The same rule applies where legal proceedings in a German court against a relative by blood have become impossible or materially more difficult. The claim against such relative passes to the relative by blood who has furnished maintenance.

The transfer may not be enforced to the detriment of the person entitled to maintenance.

1608. The spouse of a necessitous person is liable before the latter's relatives by blood are liable. However, in so far as such spouse, having regard to his (or her) other obligation, is not in a position to furnish maintenance without endangering his (or her) own maintenance suitable to his (or her) station in life, the relatives by blood are liable before the spouse is liable. The provisions of 1607, par. 2, apply *mutatis mutandis*.

The same rule applies to a judicially separated or divorced spouse who is bound to furnish maintenance [g], and to a spouse who is bound by 1351 to furnish maintenance.

1609. If there are several necessitous persons, and if the person liable to furnish maintenance is not in a position to furnish maintenance to all such persons, as between themselves the descendants take precedence to relatives by blood in the ascending line; as between such descendants those who would be entitled to be heirs in case of statutory succession, take precedence to the other descendants; as between relatives by blood in the ascending line, those of nearer degree take precedence to those of remoter degree.

A spouse takes the same rank as unmarried minor children; he (or she) takes precedence to all other children and all other relatives by blood. A judicially separated or divorced spouse [h] and a spouse entitled to maintenance under 1351 take precedence to children of full age, married children, and other relatives by blood.

(*g*) 1578 *et seq.*

(*h*) Cf. 1578, 1579.

1610. The amount of the maintenance to be furnished is determined according to the station in life of the necessitous person (*i.e.*, maintenance suitable to station in life).

Such maintenance includes all the necessaries of life, and where the necessitous person needs education, it includes also the costs of education and of preparation for a profession.

1611. A person who has become necessitous by his own moral fault may demand only the bare necessaries of life.

A descendant's, parent's, or a spouse's claim to maintenance is subject to the same limitation, if they render themselves guilty of any misconduct whereby the person liable to furnish maintenance is entitled to deprive them of their compulsory portions [(i)]; grandparents' claims to maintenance and those of ancestors of remoter degree are subject to the same limitation, if with reference to them the conditions exist under which their children are entitled to deprive them of their compulsory portions.

A necessitous person may not, on account of the limitation of his claim by these provisions, have recourse to any other person liable to furnish maintenance.

1612. Maintenance shall be furnished by payment of a money annuity. The person bound may demand that he be permitted to furnish maintenance in some other manner, if this is justified by special reasons [(k)].

If parents have to furnish maintenance to an unmarried child, they may determine the manner and the period of time for which the maintenance is to be furnished in advance. For special reasons, and upon the application of the child, the Guardianship Court may modify such determination.

For the rest the provisions of 760 apply.

1613. In respect of past maintenance the person entitled may demand payment or compensation for non-payment only as from the time at which the

---

(*i*) 2333 *et seq.*

(*k*) Such reasons may affect either the person bound or the person entitled.

person bound was in default [l] or an action on the claim for maintenance was commenced.

1614. Future maintenance may not be renounced.

By a payment in advance the person bound is, where the person entitled becomes necessitous again, released only in respect of the period specified in 760, par. 2, or, where he has fixed the period himself, only in respect of a period which is reasonable under the circumstances [m].

1615. The claim for maintenance is extinguished on the death of the person entitled or of the person bound, in so far as the claim is not for payment or compensation on account of non-payment in respect of past maintenance, nor for such payments to be made in advance as become due [n] at the time of the death of the person entitled or of the person bound.

In the case of the death of the person entitled, the person bound shall pay the funeral expenses [o] unless they are payable by the heir of the deceased.

FOURTH TITLE.
Legal Status of Legitimate Children.

I. Legal Relations between Parents and Children in general.

1616. A child takes the surname of his father [p].

1617. A child is, so long as he is a member of the parental household,

---

(*l*) 284, 285, 279.

(*m*) On the compounding of a person's liability to furnish maintenance to an illegitimate child, see 1714.

(*n*) Cf. 760, par. 3.

(*o*) Cf. 1968.

(*p*) As to a person's right to his own name, see 12. An illegitimate child takes the surname of its mother. 1706.

and is educated or maintained by his parents, bound to perform services [(q)] in their household and business in a manner corresponding to his capacity and his station in life [(r)].

1618. If a child of full age who is a member of the parental household incurs any outlay out of his property for defraying the household expenses, or if he entrusts anything out of his property to the parents for such a purpose, it is presumed, in case of doubt, that he has no intention to demand compensation [(s)].

1619. If a child of full age who is a member of the parental household entrusts the whole or a part of his property to his father's management, the father may, at his discretion, use any income which he draws during his management unless such income is necessary for defraying the expense of proper management and for the fulfilment of the obligations of the child which, in the course of proper management, are to be discharged out of the income of such property. The child may provide otherwise.

The mother has the same right if the child entrust his property to her management.

1620. The father is bound to furnish to a daughter on her marriage a reasonable outfit for the establishment of a home in so far as, having regard to his other obligations, he is in a position to do so without endangering his own maintenance suitable to his station in life, and the daughter has not property sufficient for procuring such outfit. The same obligation is imposed upon the mother if the father is not in a position to furnish such outfit, or if he is dead.

The provisions of 1604 and 1607, par. 2, apply *mutatis mutandis*.

1621. The father and the mother may refuse to furnish the outfit if the daughter marries without the necessary parental approval [(t)].

(*q*) Without any claim to remuneration.

(*r*) It makes no difference whether the child is a minor or a person of full age.

(*s*) The presumption does not apply to outlay incurred in the course of the parent's business. A similar presumption obtains in favour of the child in respect of maintenance furnished to him by his ancestors. 685, par. 2.

(*t*) 1305.

The same rule applies where the daughter renders herself guilty of any misconduct which entitles the person bound to furnish the outfit to deprive her of her compulsory portion [(u)].

1622. A daughter may not demand an outfit where she has received an outfit from her father or mother for a former marriage.

1623. The claim for an outfit is not transferable. It is barred by prescription in one year after the conclusion of the marriage.

1624. Whatever has been given to a child [(x)] by the father or by the mother in consideration of the child's marriage, or for establishing an independent position in life, or for founding or preserving a home or a position in life (*i.e.*, an advancement), is, even where no obligation to do so exists, deemed to be a gift only in so far as the advancement exceeds a reasonable amount under the circumstances, *e.g.*, the pecuniary circumstances of the father or mother.

The obligation of the person furnishing the advancement in respect of warranty of title or quality is, even though the advancement is not deemed to be a gift, determined according to the provisions applicable to a donor's duty of warranty [(y)].

1625. If a father furnishes an advancement to a child whose property is subject to his management in his capacity of father or guardian, it is to be presumed, in case of doubt, that he has furnished the advancement out of such property. This provision applies *mutatis mutandis* to the mother.

II. Parental Power.

1626. A child is under parental power so long as he is a minor.

(*u*) 2333.

(*x*) No matter whether a son or daughter, a minor or a person of full age.

(*y*) *I.e.*, 521, 523, 524.

1. *Parental Power of the Father.*

1627. A father has, by virtue of his parental power, the right and the duty to take care of his child's person and property.

1628. The right and the duty to take care of the child's person and property does not extend to those affairs of the child for which a curator has been appointed [(z)].

1629. If the curator has the care of the child's person or property, the Guardianship Court decides in case of disagreement between the father and the curator as to any act relating both to the person and to the property of the child.

1630. The care of the child's person and property includes the right to represent him.

The father does not have the right to represent the child in so far as a guardian does not have the right to represent his ward as provided for in 1795. The Guardianship Court may under 1796 deprive the father of his right to represent the child.

1631. The care of the child's person includes the right and the duty to educate him [(a)]; to exercise supervision over him [(b)]; and to determine his place of residence.

The father may, by virtue of his right to educate the child, enforce reasonable discipline upon him. The Guardianship Court shall assist the father on his application by enforcing appropriate discipline.

1632. The care of the child's person includes the right to demand restitution of the custody of the child from any person who unlawfully detains him from the father.

1633. If a daughter has been married, the care of her person is limited to

---

(*z*) See 1909.

(*a*) On the religious education of the child, see IA, Art. 134.

(*b*) Hence the father is liable for the unlawful act of his child. 832.

the right to represent her in the affairs affecting her person.

1634. Besides the father, the mother has, during the subsistence of the marriage, the right and the duty to take care of the child's person; she is not entitled to represent the child, except as provided by 1685, par. 1. In case of disagreement between the parents the opinion of the father prevails.

1635. If the marriage has been dissolved on any one of the grounds specified in 1565 to 1568, and so long as the divorced spouses are still alive [(c)], the care of the child's person [(d)] belongs, where one of the spouses has been declared to be the exclusively guilty party, to the other spouse; where both spouses have been declared to be guilty, the mother has the care of sons under six years of age and of daughters, while the father has the care of sons over six years of age. The Guardianship Court may make a different provision, if such provision is required by special reason in the interests of the child; the Guardianship Court may revoke any such provision, if it is no longer necessary.

The right of the father to represent his children remains unaffected [(e)].

1636. The spouse who does not have the care of the child's person, as provided for by 1635, retains the right to have access to the child. The Guardianship Court may regulate such access in greater details.

1637. If the marriage is dissolved under 1348, par. 2, the same rule applies in respect of the care of the child's person as if the marriage had been dissolved and both spouses had been declared guilty.

1638. The right and the duty to take care of the child's property (*i.e.*, the management of the property) does not extend to the property which the child acquires *mortis causa*, or which is transferred to him gratuitously by a third party *inter vivos*, provided the testator in his testamentary disposition or the third party at the time of the transfer, has specified that the acquisition shall be exempt

---

(*c*) After the death of either spouse the other spouse acquires the parental power, even though he or she be the guilty party.

(*d*) The right to take care of the child's property remains vested in the father.

(*e*) The Guardianship Court may, however, deprive him of such right. 1630, par. 2.

from the fathers right of management.

Whatever the child acquires by virtue of any right forming part of such property, or as compensation for the destruction, damage or deprivation of any object forming part of such property, or by any juristic act relating to such property, is also exempt from the father's right of management [(f)].

1639. Whatever the child acquires *mortis causa*, or whatever is transferred to him gratuitously by a third party *inter vivos*, shall be managed by the father according to the directions of the testator or of the third party, if such directions have been given by the testator in his testamentary disposition, or by the third party at the time of transfer. If the father does not act according to the directions, the Guardianship Court may take the necessary measures to have them carried out.

The father may deviate from the directions in so far as a guardian would be permitted to do so under 1803, pars. 2 and 3.

1640. The father shall draw up an inventory of the child's property subject to his management, which exists at the time of the death of the mother or which accrues to the child subsequently, and shall file the inventory with the Guardianship Court after he has given a guarantee as to its accuracy and completeness [(g)]. In the case of household articles, a statement of their aggregate value is sufficient.

If the inventory filed is insufficient, the Guardianship Court may order another inventory to be drawn up by a competent public authority, a competent official, or a notary. Such order may not be made in respect of the property accruing to the child in consequence of the death of the mother, if the mother has prohibited it in her testamentary disposition.

1641. The father may not make gifts on behalf of the child. Gifts which are made in compliance with a moral duty or the rules of social propriety are excepted.

(*f*) A curator will be appointed to take care of the child's property which is not subject to the father's right of management (1909), but the father retains his right of usufruct of such property (1656), unless he has been expressly deprived of such right. 1651, par. 1 (2).

(*g*) Failure to comply with this provision may work a forfeiture of the right of management. 1670.

1642. The father shall, subject to the provision of 1653, invest the child's money subject to his management [(h)] in the manner provided for by 1807, 1808, applicable to the investment of money belonging to a ward, unless such money is necessary to meet expenses.

The Guardianship Court may for special reasons permit the father to invest such money in some other manner.

1643. For entering into juristic acts on behalf of the child the father requires the ratification of the Guardianship Court in all cases in which a guardian [(i)] would require such ratification as provided for by 1821, par. 1 (1) to (3), par. 2, and 1822 (1), (3), (5), (8) to (11).

The same rule applies to the disclaimer of an inheritance or of a legacy and to the renunciation of a compulsory portion. If the devolution upon the child takes place only in consequence of disclaimer by the father, such ratification is necessary only if the father would be entitled concurrently with the child.

The provisions of 1825, 1828 to 1831 apply *mutatis mutandis*.

1644. If the ratification of the Guardianship Court is necessary for the alienation of certain objects, the father may not without such ratification entrust such objects to the child for the fulfilment of any contract entered into by the latter, nor for his free disposal.

1645. Without the ratification of the Guardianship Court the father should not start a new business in the name of the child.

1646. If the father acquires moveables [(k)] with the means of the child, ownership passes to the child upon acquisition, unless the father does not intend to acquire on account of the child. This applies also to instruments to bearer

---

(*h*) The father does not have the right of management in respect of (1) the child's property for which a curator has been appointed under 1909; and (2) any property acquired by the child in the course of a separate business carried on by him under 112, 113.

(*i*) The father, unlike a guardian, is not bound to render an account, nor to draw up an inventory. Exceptions: 1640, 1667.

(*k*) He may not acquire immoveables except with the ratification of the Guardianship Court. 1643, par. 3, and 1829.

and to instruments to order indorsed in blank.

The provisions of par. 1 apply *mutatis mutandis*, if the father with the means of the child acquires any right over things of the kind specified, or any other right which can be transferred by a mere contract of assignment.

1647. The father's management of the property is terminated as soon as an order for the institution of bankruptcy proceedings against the property of the father ceases to be appealable (*l*).

After the revocation of the proceedings the Guardianship Court may re-transfer the management to the father.

1648. If the father incurs any outlay for the care of the child's person or property, and if he is justified in doing so under the circumstances, he may demand compensation from the child, unless such outlay is to be borne by himself (*m*).

1649. The father has, by virtue of his parental power, a right of usufruct of the child's property.

1650. Things intended exclusively for the personal use of the child, *e.g.*, clothing, ornaments, and working implements, are exempt from the right of usufruct (*i.e.*, privileged property).

1651. Privileged property includes:

(1) that which the child acquires by his labour (*n*) or by the conduct of a separate business permitted to him by 112;

(2) that which the child acquires *mortis causa* (*o*), or which is transferred to him gratuitously by a third party *inter vivos*, provided the testator in his testamentary disposition, or the third party at the time of the transfer has specified that the property shall be exempt from the right

---

(*l*) In such a case the curator appointed by the Guardianship Court stands in the shoes of the father. 1909.

(*m*) Cf. 1654, 1660.

(*n*) *I.e.*, in so far as the labour is performed on his own account, and not in connection with the father's household or business. 1617.

(*o*) Cf. 1638.

of usufruct.

The provisions of 1638, par. 2, apply *mutatis mutandis*.

1652. The father acquires the emoluments of the property subject to his right of usufruct in the same manner and to the same extent as a usufructuary.

1653. The father can alienate or consume, for his own benefit, consumable things (p) which are subject to his right of usufruct; in the case of money, however, the ratification of the Guardianship Court is necessary. If the father exercises such a right, he shall make compensation for the value of such things after die termination of his right of usufruct; the compensation shall be made before that time, if the proper management of the property demands it.

1654. The father shall bear the charges upon the property subject in his right of usufruct. His liability is determined according to the provisions of 1384 to 1386, 1388, applicable to the régime of management and usufruct. Such charges include also the costs of any action brought on behalf of the child, in so far as they are not to be borne by his privileged property; and the costs of the defence of the child in any criminal proceeding instituted against him, without prejudice to the child's duty to make compensation in the event of his being sentenced.

1655. If a business forming part of the property subject to the right of usufruct is carried on by the father in the name of the child, only the yearly net profits of such business accrue to the father. If there is loss in any year, the profits of subsequent years remain with the child until the loss has been made up.

1656. If the father does not have the right to manage the property subject to his right of usufruct, he also may not exercise the right of usufruct; he may, however, demand delivery of all emoluments, unless their use is necessary for the proper management of the property and for the payment of the charges incident to his right of usufruct.

If the parental power of the father is suspended, or if the father is deprived

---

(p) As to non-consumable things, see 1642, 1643.

of the care of the child's person and property by the Guardianship Court, the expenses of the maintenance of the child may be defrayed out of the emoluments in so far as such expenses are to be borne by the father [q].

1657. If the father is not allowed to exercise the right of usufruct, he shall forthwith discharge any liability imposed upon him in favour of the child even if the liability in consequence of the right of usufruct would not have to be discharged until after the termination of the right of usufruct. This provision does not apply to the case where the parental power is suspended.

1658. The right which the father has by virtue of his usufruct of the proper of the child is not transferable.

The same rule applies to claims which the father has under 1655, 1656, so long as they are not due.

1659. The creditors of the child may demand satisfaction out of the property of the child without regard to the parental right of usufruct.

If the father has alienated or consumed consumable things under 1653, he is bound to make immediate compensation for the benefit of the creditors.

1660. The provisions of 1415, 1416, par. 1, and 1417, applicable to the régime of management and usufruct, apply *mutatis mutandis* as between the father and the child in respect of the liabilities of the latter.

1661. The right of usufruct is extinguished on the marriage of the child [r]. The father retains, however, his right of usufruct if the marriage is entered into without the necessary parental consent [s].

1662. The father may renounce his right of usufruct. The renunciation is effected by declaration to the Guardianship Court; the declaration shall be made in publicly certified form.

1663. If the father has, by virtue of his right of usufruct, let a piece of

---

(*q*) Cf. 1601, 1654.

(*r*) "Child" here means "daughter", since a son may not marry before majority.

(*s*) 1304, 1308.

land, forming part of the child's property, under an ordinary or usufructuary lease, and if the term of the lease is still running at the time of the termination of his right of usufruct, the provisions of 1056 apply *mutatis mutandis*.

If a piece of agricultural land forms part of the property subject to his right of usufruct, the provision of 592 applies *mutatis mutandis*; if a farm forms part of such property, the provisions of 592, 593 apply *mutatis mutandis*.

1664. The father shall, in the exercise of his parental power, be responsible to the child only for such care as he is accustomed to exercise in his own affairs.

1665. If the father is prevented [(t)] from exercising the parental power, the Guardianship Court shall, unless his parental power is exercised by the mother as provided for in 1685, take the necessary measures in the interest of the child [(u)].

1666. If the moral or physical welfare of the child is endangered by the fact that the father abuses his right to take care of the child's person, or neglects the child, or is guilty of any dishonest or immoral conduct, the Guardianship Court shall take the necessary measures to avert the danger. The Guardianship Court may, *e.g.*, order the child, for the purpose of his education, to be sent to a suitable family or an institution for education, or a reformatory [(v)].

If the father has disregarded the child's right to maintenance, and if a serious danger to the future maintenance is to be apprehended, both the management of the property and the right of usufruct may be withdrawn from the father.

1667. If the property of the child is endangered by the fact that the father fails to perform the duties connected with the management of property or the right of usufruct [(x)], or by the fact that he is insolvent, the Guardianship Court shall take the necessary measures to avert the danger.

(*t*) Whether by legal hindrance or by other circumstance makes no difference.

(*u*) *E.g.*, the appointment of a curator. 1909.

(*v*) IA, Arts. 34, 135.

(*x*) 1639 *et seq.*

The Guardianship Court may, *e.g.*, order the father to file an inventory of the property and to render an account of his management. The father shall give a guarantee as to the accuracy and completeness of the inventory. If the inventory filed is insufficient, the provision of 1640, par. 2, sentence 1, applies. The Guardianship Court may also, where the child's property includes negotiable instruments, valuables or uncertificated claims against the Empire or one of the States, impose upon the father the same obligation as are imposed upon guardian by 1814 to 1816, 1818; the provisions of 1819, 1820 apply *mutatis mutandis*.

The expenses of the measures taken shall be borne by the father.

1668. If the measures permitted by 1667, par. 2, are not sufficient, the Guardianship Court may require the father to give security for the property subject to his management [(y)]. The kind and the amount of the security to be given is determined by the Guardianship Court at its discretion.

1669. If the father intends to re-marry, he shall notify the Guardianship Court of his intention to do so; present at his own expense an inventory of the property subject to his management; and bring about a liquidation [(z)] if a community between him and the child exists in respect of such property. The Guardianship Court may permit the liquidation to be postponed until after the conclusion of the marriage.

1670. If the father does not comply with the orders made under 1667, 1668, or if he fails to perform the obligation imposed upon him by 1640, 1669, the Guardianship Court may withdraw from him the management of the property [(a)]. Other measures may not be taken to compel him to give security.

1671. During the subsistence of the parental power the Guardianship Court may at any time modify the orders made by it: *e.g.*, it may order any increase, or diminution, or the termination of the security given.

(*y*) He may not, however, be compelled to give security, although he may be deprived of his right of management as provided in 1670.

(*z*) The procedure is regulated by 86—90 of the Voluntary Jurisdiction Act.

(*a*) He retains, however, the right of usufruct. 1656.

1672. In the giving or termination of the security the concurrence of the child is substituted by an order of the Guardianship Court.

The costs of the giving or termination of the security shall be borne by the father.

1673. The Guardianship Court should, before giving any decision whereby the right to take care of the child's person or property, or the right or usufruct is withdrawn from the father or is limited, hear the father, unless it is impracticable to do so.

Before giving the decision the child's relatives by blood, *e.g.*, the mother, or his relatives by marriage, should also be heard, if this can be done without serious delay and without disproportionate expense. The provision of 1847, par. 2, applies to the compensation for disbursements.

1674. If a judge of a Guardianship Court wilfully or negligently fails to perform the duties imposed upon him, he is responsible to the child as provided for in 839, pars. 1 and 3.

1675. The Communal Orphan Council shall notify the Guardianship Court of any case which comes to its knowledge and which requires the interference of the Guardianship Court [(b)].

1676. The parental power of the father is suspended if he is incapable of disposing.

The same rule applies if the father is limited in disposing capacity, or if he has a curator appointed under 1910, par. 1, to take care of his person and property. The right to take care of the person of the child belongs both to the father and to the statutory agent [(c)] of the child; the father is not entitled to represent the child. In case of disagreement between the father and the statutory agent, the opinion of the statutory agent prevails.

1677. The parental power of the father is suspended if it is established by

---

(*b*) See 1665—1667.

(*c*) *I.e.*, the mother if her marriage with the father still subsists (1685), or the guardian in other cases. 1773.

the Guardianship Court that the father is *de facto* prevented from exercising his parental power for a considerable time.

The suspension is terminated if it is established by the Guardianship Court that the ground for suspension no longer exists.

1678. So long as the parental power of the father is suspended the father is not entitled to exercise it; he retains, however, his right of usufruct of the child's property, subject to the provision of 1685, par. 2.

1679. The parental power of the father is terminated, where he is declared dead, at the date which is deemed to be the date of his death.

If the father is still alive he recovers the parental power by declaring to the Guardianship Court his intention to do so.

1680. The father forfeits the parental power if he is sentenced to penal servitude, or to imprisonment for not less than six months, in consequence of a crime or delict wilfully committed against the child. If at the same time another criminal act has been committed, and a cumulative penalty has been imposed, only the penalty for the crime or delict committed against the child is taken into consideration.

The forfeiture of the parental power is effected as soon as the judicial decree ceases to be appealable [(d)].

1681. If the parental power of the father is terminated or is suspended, or if his management of the property comes to an end on any other ground, the father shall return the property to the child, and shall render an account of his management.

1682. The father is entitled, even after the termination of his parental power, to continue to manage the affairs connected with the care of the child's person and property, until he knows or ought to know of such termination. A third party may not take advantage of this right, if he knows or ought to know of the termination of the parental power at the time of entering into a juristic act.

(*d*) Where the father has forfeited his parental power it does not pass to the mother so long as her marriage with the father still subsists. In this case a guardian would be appointed. Cf. 1684.

These provisions apply *mutatis mutandis*, if the parental power of the father is suspended, or his management of property comes to an end on any other ground.

1683. If the parental power is terminated in consequence of the death of the child, the father shall manage the affairs which cannot be delayed without danger until the heir of the child is able to make other arrangement [(e)].

2. *Parental Power of the Mother.*

1684. The parental power belongs to the mother:

(1) if the father has died, or has been declared dead;

(2) if the father has forfeited the parental power and the marriage has been dissolved [(f)].

In the case of declaration of death the parental power of the mother begins at the date which is deemed to be the date of death.

1685. If the father is *de facto* prevented from exercising the parental power, or if his parental power is suspended, the mother during the subsistence of the marriage exercises the parental power, with the exception of the right of usufruct.

If the marriage has been dissolved, the Guardianship Court shall transfer the exercise of the parental power to the mother upon her application, where the parental power of the father is suspended and there is no expectation that the ground for the suspension will disappear. In this case the mother acquires also the right of usufruct of the child's property.

1686. The provisions applicable to the parental power of the father apply *mutatis mutandis* to the parental power of the mother, except so far as a contrary intention appears from 1687 to 1697.

1687. The Guardianship Court shall appoint a supplementary guardian for the mother:

(1) if the father has directed the appointment as provided in 1777;

(*e*) Exception to 1681.

(*f*) See note (*d*) to 1680.

(2) if the mother applies for the appointment;

(3) if for special reasons, *e.g.*, because of the extent or difficulty of the management of the property, or if in the cases provided for by 1666, 1667, the Guardianship Court deems such appointment to be necessary in the interest of the child.

1688. The supplementary guardian may be appointed for all kinds of affairs, for certain kinds of affairs, or for special affairs.

The extent of his authority is fixed by the act of appointment. If the extent is not so fixed all affairs are within his authority.

If the father has directed the appointment, the Guardianship Court shall, in making the appointment, follow the directions given by him under 1777 relating to the supplementary guardian's authority.

1689. The supplementary guardian shall, within the scope of his authority, assist and supervise the mother in her exercise of the parental power: he shall without delay notify the Guardianship Court of any case which requires its interference [(g)].

1690. The ratification of the supplementary guardian within the scope of his authority is necessary for every juristic act for which a guardian requires the ratification of the Guardianship Court [(h)] or of the supervising guardian [(i)]. Juristic acts which the mother may not enter into without the ratification of the Guardianship Court are excepted. The provisions of 1828 to 1831 apply *mutatis mutandis*.

The ratification of the supplementary guardian may be supplied by the ratification of the Guardianship Court.

Before giving any decision relating to such ratification the Guardianship Court should, in all cases where the juristic act is within the scope of the supplementary guardian's authority, hear the supplementary guardian, if there is such one, and it is practicable to do so.

(*g*) Such a case is where she is *de facto* prevented from exercising the parental power (1665), or where the moral or physical welfare of the child (1666) or his property (1667) is endangered.

(*h*) See 1821—1823.

(*i*) 1810, 1812 and 1813.

1691. In so far as the investment of money forming part of the child's property is within the scope of the supplementary guardian's authority, the provisions of 1809, 1810, applicable to the investment of money belonging to a ward, apply *mutatis mutandis*.

1692. If the mother is required to file an inventory of the property, the supplementary guardian shall be called to assist her in drawing up the inventory; he shall also give a guarantee as to the accuracy and completeness of the inventory. If the inventory is insufficient, the provisions of 1640, par. 2, apply *mutatis mutandis*, unless the conditions specified in 1667 exist.

1693. The Guardianship Court may, upon the application of the mother, transfer to the supplementary guardian the whole or a part of the management of the property; if this is done, he has the rights and the duties of a curator.

1694. With regard to the order of precedence in which a person is called upon to act as supplementary guardian, his appointment and supervision, his liability and claims, the compensation promised to him, and the termination of his functions, the same provisions apply as in the case of a supervising guardian [k].

The functions of the supplementary guardian are terminated even if the parental power of the mother is suspended [l].

1695. The Guardianship Court may at any time revoke, in the cases provided for by 1687 (2) and (3), the appointment of the supplementary guardian, or in the case provided for by 1693, the transfer of the management of property to the supplementary guardian.

If the appointment of the supplementary guardian is made under 1687 (2), it should be revoked only with the consent of the mother. The same rule applies to the transfer of the management of property to the supplementary guardian.

1696. If the parental power of the mother is suspended on account of her minority, she has the right and the duty to take care of the child's person; she is

(*k*) Cf. 1792, par. 4, 1833—1836.

(*l*) In such a case a guardian will be appointed. 1773, 1698.

not entitled to represent the child. So long as the mother has the care of the child, the guardian of the child has the legal status of a supplementary guardian.

1697. The mother loses the parental power if she re-marries [(m)]. She retains, however, the right and the duty to take care of the child's person, subject to the limitations specified in 1698.

1698. If a guardian is appointed for the child because the parental power of the father is suspended or forfeited, or because the father is deprived of the right to represent the child, or if a curator has been appointed in the place of the father for the education of the child, the right to take care of the child's person belongs to the mother, together with the guardian or with the curator in the same manner as with the father in the case provided for by 1634.

FIFTH TITLE.

Legal Status of Children Born of Void Marriages.

1699. A child born of a void marriage who, if the marriage were valid, would have been legitimate, is deemed to be legitimate in so far as both spouses did not know at the time of the marriage that the marriage was void.

This provision does not apply if the marriage was void owing to some defect in form, and the marriage has not been entered in the marriage register [(n)].

1700. The legal relations between the parents and a child who is deemed to be legitimate as provided for in 1699 are, except in so far as a contrary intention appears from 1701, 1702, determined according to the provisions which apply to a child born of a dissolved marriage in the case where both spouses have been declared to be guilty parties.

1701. If the father knew at the time of the marriage that the marriage was void, he does not have the rights arising from paternity. The parental power

---

(*m*) A father does not lose his parental power by his re-marriage. 1669.

(*n*) If this marriage has been entered in the marriage register the defect in form is cured. 1324, par. 2.

belongs to the mother [o].

1702. If the mother knew at the time of the marriage that the marriage was void, she has, in respect of the child, only those rights which, in the case of divorce, belong to a wife who has been declared to be the exclusively guilty party.

If the father dies, or if his parental power is terminated on any other ground, the mother has only the right and the duty to take care of the child's person; she is not entitled to represent the child. So long as the mother has the care of the child the guardian of the child has the legal status of a supplementary guardian.

The provisions of par. 2 apply, even if the parental power of the father is suspended on account of his disposing incapacity, or by virtue of 1677 [p].

1703. If the child is not deemed to be legitimate because both spouses knew at the time of the marriage that the marriage was void, he may, however, as a legitimate child, demand maintenance from the father [q] so long as the latter is alive. The father does not have the right specified in 1612, par. 2.

1704. If the marriage is voidable and is avoided on the ground of threats, the spouse entitled to avoid it is in the same position as a spouse who did not know at the time of the marriage that the marriage was void.

SIXTH TITLE.
Legal Status of Illegitimate Children.

1705. An illegitimate child has the legal status of a legitimate child in respect of his mother [r] and her relatives by blood.

1706. An illegitimate child takes the surname of his mother.

(*o*) He may not even be appointed guardian. 1899, par. 3.

(*p*) The mother may not be appointed guardian in this case. 1899, par. 3.

(*q*) As to the amount of the maintenance, see 1602.

(*r*) But not in respect of his father. 1589, par. 2.

If the mother takes any other name in consequence of her marriage, the child takes the surname which the mother had before the marriage. The putative father may, with the child's and mother's approval, give his name to the child by declaration made to the competent public authority; the declaration of the putative father and the child's and mother's declaration of approval shall be made in publicly certified form.

1707. The mother does not have the parental power over an illegitimate child [(s)]. She has the right and the duty to take care of the child's person; she is not entitled to represent the child. So long as the mother has the care of the child the guardian of the child has the legal status of a supplementary guardian.

1708. The father of an illegitimate child is bound to furnish to the child, until the completion of his sixteenth year of age, maintenance suitable to the mother's station in life. Maintenance includes all the necessaries of life and the expenses of education and of preparation for a profession.

If the child, at the time of the completion of his sixteenth year of age, is not in a position to maintain himself in consequence of physical or mental infirmities, the father shall furnish maintenance to him even after that time [(t)]; the provision of 1603, par. 1, applies.

1709. The father is liable to furnish maintenance before the child's mother and maternal relatives by blood are liable.

In so far as the mother or any maternal relative by blood who is liable furnishes maintenance to the child, the claim of the child against the father passes to the mother or to such relative. The transfer may not be enforced to the detriment of the child.

1710. The maintenance shall he furnished by payment of a money annuity.

The annuity is payable in advance by quarterly instalments. The father is

---

(*s*) She may, however, be appointed guardian. 1778, par. 3.

(*t*) The father is not liable to furnish maintenance to such child if the latter's incapacity to maintain himself arises after the completion of his sixteenth year of age.

not released by any payment in advance for a future time [u].

If the child was living at the beginning of a quarter, the whole amount due for that quarter accrues to him.

1711. Past maintenance may also be demanded.

1712. The claim to maintenance is not extinguished on the death of the father; it belongs to the child even if the father died before the birth of the child.

The heir of the father is entitled to compound the liability of the deceased by payment of the amount which would accrue to the child as a compulsory portion if he were legitimate. If there are several illegitimate children, the amount is reckoned just as if they were all legitimate.

1713. The claim to maintenance is extinguished on the death of the child in so far as it is not directed to the payment or compensation for non-payment in respect of past maintenance, or to such payments to be made in advance which became due at the time of the death of the child [x].

The father shall bear the funeral expenses, unless they are payable by the heir of the child.

1714. An agreement between the father and the child [y] relating to future maintenance or the amount to be paid for compounding the liability to furnish maintenance requires the ratification of the Guardianship Court.

A gratuitous renunciation of future maintenance is void.

1715. The father is bound to pay to the mother the expenses of her confinement and the expenses for maintenance for the first six weeks after her confinement, and also any other expenses which are necessary in consequence of her conception or confinement. The mother may require the usual amount of expenses to be paid to her, without regard to the actual expenses incurred.

Such claim belongs to the mother even if the father died before the birth of the child, or if the child was stillborn.

(*u*) Such payment may be made only with the ratification of the Guardianship Court. 1714.

(*x*) Cf. 1710, par. 3.

(*y*) The child is represented by his guardian.

The claim is barred by prescription in four years. The prescription begins to run from the expiration of six weeks after the birth of the child.

1716. Even before the birth of the child it may be ordered by provisions decree obtained by the mother that the father shall, immediately after the birth of the child, pay to the mother or to the guardian the amount for the maintenance to be furnished to the child for the first three months, and shall lodge the necessary sum a reasonable time before the birth of the child. In the same manner it may be ordered upon the application of the mother that payment of the usual amount of expense to be paid under 1715, par. 1, and the lodgment of the necessary sum shall take place.

For the issue of such a provisional decree it is not necessary that there be *primâ facie* proof that the claim is likely to be endangered.

1717. A person who has cohabited with the mother within the period of possible conception is deemed to be the father of the illegitimate child within the meaning of 1708 to 1716, unless another person has also cohabited with her within the same period. A habitation is not, however, taken into consideration, if it is evidently impossible under the circumstances that the mother has conceived the child in consequence of such cohabitation.

The period of possible conception is the period between the one hundred and eighty-first day and the three hundred and second day, both inclusive, before the day of the birth of the child.

1718. A person who, after the birth of the child, acknowledges his paternity by public act, may not avail himself of the fact that another person has cohabited with the mother within the period of possible conception.

SEVENTH TITLE.
Legitimation of Illegitimate Children.

I. Legitimation by Subsequent Marriage.

1719. An illegitimate child acquires, by reason of the fact that the father marries the mother, the legal status of a legitimate child from and after the celebration of the marriage.

1720. The husband of the mother is deemed to be the father of the child, if he has cohabited with her within the period of possible conception specified in 1717, par. 2, unless it is evidently impossible under the circumstances that the mother has conceived the child in consequence of such cohabitation.

If after the birth of the child the husband acknowledges his paternity by public act, it is presumed that he has cohabited with the mother within the period of possible conception.

1721. If the marriage of the parents is void, the provisions of 1699 to 1704 apply *mutatis mutandis.*

1722. The celebration of the marriage between the parents has, in respect of the descendants of the illegitimate child, the effects of legitimation, even if the child was born before the marriage.

II. Declaration of Legitimation (z).

1723. An illegitimate child may, upon the application of the father, be declared legitimate by order of the public authority.

The right to issue a declaration of legitimation belongs to the State of which the father is a subject; if the father is a German who is not a subject of any State, the right belongs to the Imperial Chancellor.

The Government of the State may make provisions as to the issue of such declarations as it has the right to make (a).

1724. A declaration of legitimation may not be made subject to any condition or limitation of time.

1725. The application must contain a declaration by the father that he

(z) This is derived from the *legitimatio per rescriptum principis* of the Roman Law.

(a) The matter is entirely within the discretion of the State Government. Cf. 1734.

acknowledges the child as his own.

1726. For the declaration of legitimation the approval of the child and, if the child has not completed his twenty-first year of age, the approval of the mother are necessary. If the father is married, he requires also the approval of his wife.

The approval shall be given to the father or to the public authority with which the application is to be filed; the approval is irrevocable.

The approval of the mother is not necessary if she is permanently not in a position to make a declaration, or if her place of residence is permanently unknown. The same rule applies to the approval of the father's wife.

1727. If the approval of the mother is refused, it may be supplied by the Guardianship Court on the application of the child, if failure to make the declaration of legitimation would cause disproportionate injury to the child.

1728. The application for the declaration of legitimation and the approval of the persons specified in 1726 may not be made through an agent.

If the child is incapable of disposing, or if he has not completed his fourteenth year of age, his statutory agent may give the approval, subject to the ratification of the Guardianship Court.

1729. If the father is limited in disposing capacity, he requires both the consent of his statutory agent and the ratification of the Guardianship Court for making the application.

If the child is limited in disposing capacity, the same rule applies to the giving of his approval.

If the mother of the child or the wife of the father is limited in disposing capacity, the consent of her statutory agent is not necessary for the giving of her approval.

1730. The application and the declaration of approval of the persons specified in 1726 require judicial or notarial authentication [(b)].

(*b*) The application and the declaration may be authenticated separately. 128.

1731. If the application or the approval of any one of the persons specified in 1726 is voidable [(c)], the provisions of 1728, 1729, apply to the avoidance and confirmation of such voidable declaration.

1732. The declaration of legitimation may not be issued if at the time of the conception of the child a marriage between the parents would be forbidden by 1310, par. 1, on account of relationship by blood or by marriage.

1733. The declaration of legitimation may not be issued after the death of the child.

After the death of the father the declaration of legitimation may be issued only if the father has filed his application with the competent public authority, or at the time or after the authentication of the application by a Court or notary, has instructed the Court or the notary to file such application [(d)].

A declaration of legitimation made after the death of the father has the same effect as though it were made before his death.

1734. A declaration of legitimation may be refused even if there is no legal impediment to it.

1735. It has no effect on the validity of the declaration of legitimation if the applicant is not the father of the child, of if it has been erroneously assumed that the mother of the child or the wife of the father is permanently not in a position to make a declaration or that her place of residence is permanently unknown.

1736. By the declaration of legitimation the child acquires the legal status of a legitimate child.

1737. The effects of a declaration of legitimation extend to the descendants of the child; they do not extend to the father's relatives by blood. The wife of the father is not related to the child by marriage, nor is the spouse of the child

---

(c) *E.g.*, on the ground of mistake, fraud, or unlawful threats. 119 *et seq.*

(d) The application may not be made in a testamentary disposition. See *Protokolle der II. Reichskommission.*

so related to the father [e].

The rights and the duties arising from the relationship by blood between the child and his relatives remain unaffected, unless it is otherwise prescribed by law.

1738. On the declaration of legitimation the mother loses the right and the duty to take care of the child's person. If she has to furnish maintenance to the child such right and duty revive, if the parental power of the father is terminated, or if it is suspended on account of the disposing incapacity of the father or by virtue of 1677.

1739. The father is bound to furnish maintenance to the child and the child's descendants before the mother and maternal relatives by blood are so bound [f].

1740. If the father intends to marry while he has still the parental power over the child, the provisions of 1669 to 1671 apply.

EIGHTH TITLE.
Adoption.

1741. A person [g] who has no legitimate descendants may adopt another [h] by contract with the latter. Such a contract requires the confirmation of the competent Court.

1742. Adoption may not be made subject to any condition or limitation of time.

1743. The fact that there is an adopted child does not prevent the adoption

---

(*e*) The effects of legitimation by declaration are therefore not so extensive as those of legitimation by subsequent marriage, in which case the child is deemed to be legitimate *to all intents and purposes*. 1719. Legitimation by declaration is generally resorted to in all cases in which marriage between the parents has become impossible (*e.g.*, on account of the death or insanity of either parent, &c.).

(*f*) For particulars, see 1602 *et seq.*

(*g*) Man or woman, married or unmarried.

(*h*) Whether a minor or a person of full age makes no difference.

of another child.

1744. The adoptor must have completed his fiftieth year of age, and must be at least eighteen years older than the adopted child.

1745. Dispensation from the requirements of 1744 may be granted; dispensation from the requirement as to the completion of the fiftieth year of age may, however, be granted only if the adoptor is a person of full age [(i)].

The power to grant such dispensation belongs to the State of which the adoptor is a subject; if the adoptor is a German who is not a subject of any State, the power to grant such dispensation belongs to the Imperial Chancellor.

The Government of the State shall make provisions relating to the issue of the grant belonging to the State.

1746. If a person is married, he (or she) may adopt or be adopted only with the approval of his (or her) spouse.

The approval is not necessary if the spouse is permanently not in a position to make a declaration, or if his (or her) place of residence is permanently unknown [(k)].

1747. A legitimate child before the completion of his twenty-first year of age may be adopted only with the approval of his parents [(l)]; an illegitimate child before the same age may be adopted only with the approval of his mother [(m)]. The provision of 1746, par. 2, applies *mutatis mutandis*.

1748. The approval of the persons specified in 1746, 1747 shall be communicated to the adopter or the adopted child, or to the Court competent for the confirmation of the contract of adoption; the approval is irrevocable.

The approval may not be given through an agent. If the person approving is limited in disposing capacity, he does not require the consent of his statutory

---

(*i*) *I.e.*, is twenty-one years old, or has been declared of full age. 2 *et seq.*

(*k*) Cf. 1756.

(*l*) The approval of one of the parents is not sufficient.

(*m*) Where the child is under guardianship, ratification by the Guardianship Court is also necessary. 1751, par. 2.

agent.

The declaration of approval requires judicial or notarial authentication.

1749. A person may be adopted as a joint child by a married couple.

An adopted person, so long as the legal relation created by the adoption exists, may be further adopted only by the spouse of the adoptor [(n)].

1750. The contract of adoption may not be entered into through an agent. If the adopted child has not completed his fourteenth year of age, his statutory agent may enter into the contract subject to the ratification of the Guardianship Court.

The contract of adoption must be entered into before a Court or notary in the presence of both parties simultaneously.

1751. If the adoptor is limited in disposing capacity, he requires, for entering into such a contract, both the consent of his statutory agent and the ratification of the Guardianship Court.

The same rule applies to the adopted child if he is limited in disposing capacity.

1752. If a guardian intends to adopt his ward, the Guardianship Court should not give its ratification so long as the guardian is serving his term of office. If any person intends to adopt his former ward, the Guardianship Court should not give its ratification before he has rendered an account of his management and has given proof of the existence of the property of the ward.

The same rule applies if a curator appointed to take charge of the ward's property intends to adopt his ward or his former ward.

1753. The confirmation of a contract of adoption may not be effected after the death of the adopted child.

After the death of the adoptor confirmation is permissible only if the adoptor or the child has filed an application for confirmation with the competent Court, or, at the time or after the authentication of the contract by a Court or notary, has instructed the Court or the notary to file such application.

(*n*) The same rule applies to termination of adoption. 1768.

Confirmation effected after the death of the adoptor has the same effect as though it were effected before his death.

1754. The adoption becomes effective on confirmation. The contracting parties are bound even before confirmation.

Confirmation may be refused only if some legal requirement of adoption has not been complied with. If the confirmation is definitely refused, the contract ceases to be binding.

1755. If the contract of adoption or the approval of any one of the persons specified in 1746, 1747 is voidable [(o)], the provisions of 1748, par. 2, 1750, par. 1, and 1751 apply to the avoidance and confirmation of such voidable juristic act.

1756. It has no effect on the validity of the adoption, if at the time of the confirmation of the contract of adoption it was erroneously assumed that one of the persons specified in 1746, 1747 was permanently not in a position to make a declaration or that his place of residence was permanently unknown.

1757. By the adoption the child acquires the legal status of a legitimate child of the adoptor [(p)].

If a child is adopted by a married couple jointly, or if one spouse adopts the child of the other spouse, the child acquires the legal status of a joint legitimate child of both spouses.

1758. The child takes the surname of the adoptor. If the child is adopted by a woman who takes another name in consequence of her marriage, the child takes the surname which the woman had before her marriage. In the cases provided for by 1757, par. 2, the child takes the surname of the man.

The child can add his former surname to the new name, unless it is otherwise provided by the contract of adoption.

1759. By the adoption the adoptor does not acquire any right of inheri-

---

(*o*) On the ground of mistake, fraud, or unlawful threats. 119 *et seq.*

(*p*) Even in respect of succession. Cf. 1759.

tance.

1760. The adoptor shall, at his own expense, draw up an inventory of the property of the child in so far as it is subject to his right of management by virtue of the parental power, and shall file the inventory with the Guardianship Court; he shall give a guarantee as to the accuracy and completeness of the inventory. If the filed inventory is insufficient, the provisions of 1640, par. 2, sentence 1, applies.

If the adoptor fails to perform the duty imposed upon him by par. 1, the Guardianship Court may withdraw from him the management of the property. The withdrawal may be revoked at any time.

1761. If the adoptor intends to marry while he has still the parental power over the child, the provisions of 1669 to 1671 apply.

1762. The effects of adoption extend to the descendants of the adopted child. Such effects extend to a descendant living at the time of the conclusion of the contract and any after-born descendants only if the contract was also entered into with the already living descendant.

1763. The effects of adoption do not extend to the adoptor's relatives by blood. The spouse of the adoptor is not related to the child by marriage, nor is the spouse of the child so related to the adoptor.

1764. The rights and the duties arising from the relationship between the child and his relatives by blood are not affected by the adoption, unless it is otherwise provided by law.

1765. After the adoption the natural parents lose the parental power over the child, and if the adopted child is illegitimate, his mother loses the right and the duty to take care of the child's person.

If the father or the mother has to furnish maintenance to the child, the right and the duty to take care of the child's person revive, if the parental power of the adoptor is terminated, or if it is suspended on account of the disposing incapacity of the adoptor, or by virtue of 1677. The right to represent the child does not revive.

1766. The adoptor is liable to furnish maintenance to the child and to the descendants of the child to whom the effects of adoption extend, before the natural parents are liable.

In the case provided for by 1611, par. 2, the adoptor is in the same position as the child's natural relatives by blood in the ascending line.

1767. The adoptor's right of usufruct of the property of the child and the child's right of inheritance in respect of the adoptor may be excluded by the contract of adoption.

For the rest, the effects of adoption may not be modified by the contract of adoption.

1768. The legal relations created by adoption may be terminated. Such termination may not be made subject to any condition or limitation of time.

Such termination is effected by contract between the adoptor of the one part and the adopted child and the descendants of the child to whom the effects of the adoption extend of the other part.

If a married couple have adopted a child jointly, or if one spouse has adopted a child of the other spouse, the concurrence of both spouses is necessary for such termination.

1769. After the death of the child the other interested parties may by contract terminate the legal relations subsisting between them. After the death of one of the spouses the same rule applies in the cases provided for by 1757, par. 2.

1770. The provisions of 1741, sentence 2 and 1750, 1751, 1753 to 1755, applicable to adoption, apply also to such termination.

1771. If persons who are bound together by the tie of adoption intermarry contrary to the provision of 1311 [q], the legal relations created between them by the adoption are terminated on the celebration of the marriage.

If the marriage is void, and if one of the spouses has the parental power

---

(*q*) *I.e.*, before the termination of adoption.

over the other spouse, such power is forfeited on the celebration of the marriage. The forfeiture does not take place if the marriage is void owing to some defect in form [(r)] and the marriage has not been entered in the marriage register.

1772. After the termination of adoption the child and the descendants of the child who are affected by the termination lose the right to use the surname of the adoptor. This provision does not apply in the cases provided for by 1757, par. 2, if the termination takes place after the death of one of the spouses.

THIRD SECTION.
GUARDIANSHIP.

FIRST TITLE.
Guardianship over Minors.

I. Establishment of Guardianship.

1773. A guardian is appointed for a minor, if he is not under parental power, or if the parents are not entitled to represent the child in the affairs affecting his person or property.

A guardian is appointed for a minor even if the family status of the latter cannot be ascertained [(s)].

1774. The Guardianship Court shall establish the guardianship of its own motion [(t)].

(*r*) Cf. 1324.

(*s*) *E.g.*, a foundling.

(*t*) The Guardianship Court of the district where the ward is domiciled is the competent Court. Voluntary Jurisdiction Act, ss. 35 *et seq.*

1775. The Guardianship Court should appoint only one guardian for the ward or wards, if several brothers and sisters are to be placed under guardianship, unless there are special reasons for the appointment of more than one guardian.

1776. The following persons shall (u) be called upon to act as guardian in the order in which they are named:

(1) the person (x) nominated as guardian by the father of the ward (y);

(2) the person (x) nominated as guardian by the legitimate mother of the ward (y);

(3) the paternal grandfather of the ward;

(4) the maternal grandfather of the ward.

Neither grandfather is called upon to act, if the ward has been adopted by a person other than the spouse of his father or mother. The same rule applies if the person from whom the ward is descended has been adopted by a person other than the spouse of his father or mother and the effects of adoption extend to the ward.

1777. The father may nominate a guardian only if he has the parental power over the child at the time of his death; he does not have such right if he is not entitled to represent the child in the affairs affecting the child's person or property (z). The same rule applies to the mother (a).

The father may nominate a guardian for a child born after his death only if he would have been entitled to do so if the child had been born before his death.

The nomination of a guardian is made by testamentary disposition (b).

1778. A person who has been called upon to act as guardian under 1776

(u) *I.e.*, such persons have a *legal* right to be appointed as guardians.

(x) Whether male or female makes no difference.

(y) The nomination may not be entrusted to a third party.

(z) Cf. *e.g.*, 1666.

(a) The mother of an illegitimate child may therefore nominate a guardian so long as she has the parental power.

(b) *I.e.*, by a will (2229 *et seq.*) or by a contract of inheritance. 2299.

can be passed over without his consent only if he may not or should not be appointed guardian as provided for in 1780 to 1784 or if he is prevented from accepting, or delays in accepting, the guardianship, or if his appointment would endanger the interest of the ward.

If the person called upon to act is only temporarily hindered from accepting the office, the Guardianship Court shall, after the cessation of the hindrance and upon his application, appoint him as guardian in the place of the guardian originally appointed.

A husband can be appointed as guardian of his wife in preference to the persons called upon to act under 1776; a mother can be appointed as guardian of an illegitimate child in preference to the grandfather.

A co-guardian cannot be appointed to act concurrently with the person called upon to act except with the latter's consent.

1779. If the guardianship cannot be conferred upon a person called upon to act under 1776, the Guardianship Court shall select a guardian after hearing the Communal Orphan Council [(c)].

The Guardianship Court should select a person competent to act as guardian by reason of his personal relations and pecuniary circumstances and any other circumstances. In making the selection the religious faith of the ward shall be taken into consideration. The child's relatives by blood and by marriage shall have the preference.

1780. A person who is incapable of disposing or has been interdicted on account of feeble-mindedness, prodigality, or habitual drunkenness, may not [(d)] be appointed as guardian.

1781. The following persons should not [(e)] be appointed as guardians:

(1) a minor, or any person who has been placed under *interim* guardianship,

---

(*c*) The hearing is within the discretion of the Guardianship Court; it may appoint a guardian even without any such hearing.

(*d*) This provision is mandatory, and any infringement thereof will render the appointment null and void.

(*e*) This provision is only directory, and infringement thereof will not affect the validity of the appointment.

as provided for in 1906;

(2) any person for whom a curator has been appointed under 1910 to take care of the affairs affecting his property;

(3) a bankrupt during the time of his bankruptcy;

(4) a person who has been declared deprived of civil rights, unless a contrary intention appears from the provisions of the Criminal Code [(f)].

1782. A person should not [(e)] be appointed as guardian if he has been excluded from the guardianship by direction of the father or of the legitimate mother [(g)] of the ward. The mother may not exclude a person who has been nominated as guardian by the father.

The provisions of 1777 apply to such exclusion.

1783. A woman who is married to a person other than the father of the ward [(h)] should [(i)] be appointed as guardian only with the consent of her husband.

1784. An official or a clergyman who requires special permission to accept a guardianship according to the State law, should not[(i)] be appointed as guardian without the prescribed permission.

1785. Every male German shall accept the office of guardianship for which he is selected by the Guardianship Court, unless his appointment to the office is prevented by any one of the grounds specified in 1780 to 1784.

1786. The acceptance of the office of guardianship may be refused by the following persons:

(1) a woman[(j)];

(2) a person who has completed his sixtieth year of age;

(*f*) 34 (6) of the Criminal Code provides that such appointment is permissible if the person deprived of civil rights is the ward's relative by blood in the ascending line, and the supreme public authority over guardianships or the family council has ratified the appointment.

(*g*) The expressions "legitimate mother" and "illegitimate mother" of a ward are adopted for the sake of brevity, although they are never so used in English law.

(*h*) "Ward" here means a ward who is born in lawful wedlock.

(*i*) See note (*e*), preceding page.

(*j*) *I.e.*, any woman, whether married or unmarried, whether a widow or a divorced wife.

(3) a person who has more than four legitimate minor children (k); a child adopted by another person is not counted (l);

(4) a person who is prevented by illness or infirmities from conducting the guardianship properly;

(5) a person who, on account of the distance of his place of domicile from the office of the Guardianship Court, cannot act as guardian without special inconvenience (m);

(6) a person who is required by 1844 to give security;

(7) a person who should be appointed to act as guardian jointly with another person;

(8) a person who has already more than one guardianship or curatorship; a guardianship or curatorship over several brothers and sisters is deemed to be a single guardianship only; two supervising guardianships are equivalent to one guardianship.

The right to refuse is barred if it is not asserted in the Guardianship Court before the appointment (n).

1787. A person who refuses to accept a guardianship without lawful excuse is, if any fault is imputable to him, responsible for any damage which the ward has sustained in consequence of the delay of the appointment of a guardian.

If the Guardianship Court declares the refusal to be without lawful excuse, the person refusing shall, on demand by the Guardianship Court, temporarily accept the guardianship, without prejudice to the legal remedies available to him.

1788. The Guardianship Court may compel the person selected as guardian to accept the office of guardianship by exacting penalties.

No single penalty can exceed the sum of three hundred marks. Successive penalties may be imposed only at an interval of at least a week. No more than three penalties can be imposed.

(*k*) Predeceased children are not taken into consideration.

(*l*) This does not apply, however, to the adoptor.

(*m*) Distance from the *ward*'s domicile is no ground for refusal.

(*n*) If the ground for refusal arises subsequent to the appointment, he may apply for discharge from his office. 1889.

1789. A guardian is appointed by the Guardianship Court before which he assumes the obligation to act as guardian faithfully and conscientiously. The assumption of the obligation should be effected by clasp of hand in lieu of oath.

1790. The appointment of a guardian may be made terminable on the occurrence or non-occurrence of a certain event.

1791. The guardian receives a certificate of appointment.

The certificate should contain the name and the date of the birth of the ward, the names of the guardian, supervising guardian, and co-guardians, and in the case of distribution of functions between several guardians, the manner of the distribution. If a family council has been established, this shall also be stated.

1792. Besides the guardian a supervising guardian may be appointed.

A supervising guardian should be appointed if the guardianship involves the management of property, unless the management is unimportant, or the guardianship is to be conducted by several guardians jointly.

If the guardianship is not conducted by several guardians jointly, the one guardian may be appointed as supervising guardian in respect of the other.

The provisions applicable to the order of precedence in which persons are called upon to act and to the appointment of guardians apply to the order of precedence in which persons are called upon to act as supervising guardians and to the appointment of supervising guardians [(o)].

II. Conduct of Guardianship.

1793. A guardian has the right and the duty to take care of his ward's person and property, and also to represent him.

1794. The right and the duty of the guardian to take care of the ward's person and property do not extend to the affairs of the latter for which a curator has

(o) On the duties of a supervising guardian, see 1799.

been appointed [(p)].

1795. The guardian may not represent the ward:

(1) in any juristic act between his spouse or one of his relatives by blood in the direct line of the one part, and the ward of the other part, unless the juristic act consists exclusively in the fulfilment of an obligation;

(2) in any juristic act which has for its object the transfer or charging of a claim of the ward against the guardian secured by a right of pledge, hypotheca, or suretyship, or the termination or diminution of such security, or the creation of an obligation on the ward for such transfer, charge, termination, or diminution;

(3) in any action between the persons specified in (1), and in any action relating to any matter of the kind specified in (2).

The provision of 181 remains unaffected.

1796. The Guardianship Court may withdraw from the guardian the right to represent the ward in certain affairs or certain kinds of affairs.

The withdrawal should take place only if the interest of the ward is in serious conflict with the interest of the guardian, or of a third party represented by the latter, or of one of the persons specified in 1795 (1).

1797. If there are several guardians they conduct the guardianship jointly. In case of disagreement between them the Guardianship Court decides, unless it was otherwise provided at the time of appointment.

The Guardianship Court may distribute the functions of the guardianship among several guardians by entrusting to each of them authority with a definite limit. Within the limit of authority entrusted to him each guardian conducts the guardianship independently of the others.

Directions which the father or the mother has given under 1777 relating to the decision in cases of disagreement between the guardians nominated by them and to the distribution of functions between such guardians, shall be followed by the Guardianship Court, unless to follow them would endanger the interest of the

---

(*p*) Cf. 1909.

ward.

1798. If the right to take care of the ward's person and property belongs to different guardians, the Guardianship Court decides in case of disagreement as to any act affecting both the person and the property of the ward.

1799. The supervising guardian shall take care that the guardian conducts the guardianship in accordance with his duties. He shall, without delay, notify the Guardianship Court of any breach of duty on the part of the guardian and of any other case which requires the intervention of the Guardianship Court, *e. g.*, the death of the guardian, or the occurrence of any other circumstance in consequence of which the guardian vacates his office, or the dismissal of the guardian is necessary.

The guardian shall, on demand, give to the supervising guardian any information concerning his conduct of the guardianship, and to permit him to inspect all documents relating to the guardianship.

1800. The right and the duty of the guardian to take care of the ward's person are determined according to the provisions of 1631 to 1633, applicable to the parental power.

1801. The right to take care of the religious education [q] of the ward may be withdrawn from the guardian by the Guardianship Court, if the guardian does not belong to the faith in which the ward is to be brought up [r].

1802. The guardian shall draw up an inventory of the property existing at the time of the establishment of the guardianship, or accruing to the ward subsequently, and shall file it with the Guardianship Court after having given a guarantee as to its accuracy and completeness [s]. If there is a supervising guardian, he shall request the supervising guardian to take part in drawing up the inventory; the supervising guardian shall also give a guarantee as to the accuracy and completeness of the inventory.

(*q*) See IA, Art. 134.

(*r*) Cf. 1779, par. 2, sentence 2.

(*s*) The guarantee need not be given under oath.

In drawing up the inventory the guardian may call in the assistance of an official, a notary, or any other expert.

If the filed inventory is insufficient, the Guardianship Court may order another inventory to be drawn up by a competent public authority, or a competent official, or a notary.

1803. Whatever the ward acquires *mortis causa* [(t)], or whatever is transferred to him gratuitously by a third party *inter vivos*, shall be managed by the guardian according to the direction of the testator or of the third party, if, such directions have been given by the testator in a testamentary disposition, or by the third party at the time of the transfer.

With the ratification of the Guardianship Court the guardian can deviate from the directions, if to follow them would endanger the interest of the ward.

For any deviation from the directions which a third party has given at the time of making the transfer *inter vivos*, his consent, if he be still alive, is necessary and sufficient. The consent of such third party may be supplied by the Guardianship Court, if he be permanently not in a position to make a declaration, or if his place of residence be permanently unknown.

1804. A guardian may not make any gifts on behalf of his ward [(u)]. Gifts which are made in compliance with a moral duty or the rules of social propriety are excepted.

1805. A guardian cannot use the property of his ward for his own benefit.

1806. The guardian shall invest all money forming part of the ward's property, unless such money is necessary to meet expenses.

1807. The investment of the ward's money prescribed in 1806 should be made only:

(1) in claims secured by a security hypotheca on land situate within the Empire, or in security land charges or annuity charges on land situate within the Empire;

(*t*) As to the meaning of the expression "acquisition *mortis causa*", see 1369.

(*u*) Not even with the ratification of the Guardianship Court.

(2) in certificated claims against the Empire or a State, and in claims which have been registered in the Imperial debt ledger or in the State debt ledger of one of the States [(x)];
(3) in certificated claims whose interest has been guaranteed by the Empire or a State;
(4) in negotiable instruments, *e.g.*, certificate of pledge, or in certificated claims of any kind against a domestic communal corporation or a credit institution of such a corporation, in so far as such negotiable instruments or claims have been declared by the Federal Council to be proper for the investment of money belonging to a ward;
(5) in a public savings-bank located within the Empire, provided that it has been declared by the competent authority of the State in which it has its seat to be proper for the investment of money belonging to a ward.

In regard to land situate within the territory of a State, the State law may lay down general rules according to which the security of a hypotheca, a land charge, or an annuity charge is to be determined.

1808. If under the circumstances investment cannot be made in the manner specified by 1807, the money shall be invested in the Imperial Bank, a State bank, or any other bank located within the Empire which has been declared by State law to be proper for this purpose, or in a lodgment office [(y)].

1809. A guardian should invest his ward's money in the manner specified by 1807, par. 1 (5), or by 1808, only subject to the condition that the ratification of the supervising guardian or of the Guardianship Court is necessary for the withdrawal of the money.

1810. The guardian should make the investments prescribed by 1806 to 1808 only with the ratification of the supervising guardian; the ratification of the supervising guardian may be supplied by the ratification of the Guardianship Court. If there is no supervising guardian, the investments should be made

---

(x) See Imperial Act of 31st May, 1891; and IA, Art. 97.

(y) See IA, Art. 144.

only with the ratification of the Guardianship Court, unless the guardianship is conducted by several guardians jointly.

1811. The Guardianship Court may for special reasons permit the guardian to invest in any manner other than that prescribed by 1807, 1808.

1812. The guardian may dispose of a claim or of any other right by virtue of which the ward may demand an act of performance, or of a negotiable instrument belonging to the ward only with the ratification of the supervising guardian, unless the ratification of the Guardianship Court is necessary, as provided by 1819 to 1822. The same rule applies to the incurring of an obligation to make such a disposition.

The ratification of the supervising guardian may be supplied by the ratification of the Guardianship Court.

If there is no supervising guardian, the ratification of the Guardianship Court takes the place of the ratification of the supervising guardian [(z)], unless the guardianship is conducted by several guardians jointly.

1813. A guardian does not require the ratification of the supervising guardian for the acceptance of an act of performance due:

(1) if the object of the performance does not consist in money or negotiable instruments [(a)];

(2) if the claim does not exceed the sum of three hundred marks;

(3) if money invested by the guardian is repaid;

(4) if the claim forms part of the emoluments of the ward's property [(b)];

(5) if the claim is for the reimbursement of costs of giving notice, or of legal proceedings, or for any other accessory acts of performance [(c)].

The dispensation allowed by par. 1 (2) and (3), does not extend to the withdrawal of money for whose investment some other provision has been made. The dispensation allowed by par. 1 (3) does not apply to the withdrawal of

---

(z) *I.e.*, if the supervising guardian is prevented from giving his ratification, or if he refuses it without sufficient reason.

(a) *E.g.*, the receipt of anything ordered by the ward.

(b) *E.g.*, interest, rent, &c. even although they exceed the sum of 300 marks.

(c) *E.g.*, forfeiture of a stipulated penalty in the case of a contract.

money which has been invested under 1807, par. 1 (1) to (4).

1814. The guardian shall lodge at a lodgment office or the Imperial Bank instruments to bearer forming part of the ward's property together with their renewal coupons, subject to the condition that the return of the instruments may be demanded only with the ratification of the Guardianship Court. The lodgment of instruments to bearer which are consumable things within the meaning of 92 (d), and of interest coupons, annuity coupons, or dividend coupons, is not necessary. Instruments to order endorsed in blank are equivalent to instruments to bearer.

1815. The guardian may, instead of lodging the instrument to bearer as provided by 1814, cause them to be transferred to the name of the ward subject to the condition that he may dispose of them only with the ratification of the Guardianship Court (e). If the instruments have been issued by the Empire or by a State, he may, subject to the same condition, cause them to be converted into uncertificated claims against the Empire or against the State.

If instruments to bearer which may be converted into uncertificated claims against the Empire or against a State are required to be lodged, the Guardianship Court may order them to be converted into uncertificated claims (f) as provided for in par. 1.

1816. If uncertificated claims against the Empire or a State form part of the ward's property at the time of the establishment of the guardianship, or if the ward subsequently acquires such claims, the guardian shall cause to be entered in the debt ledger the provision that he may dispose of such claims only with the ratification of the Guardianship Court.

1817. The Guardianship Court may for special reasons release the guardian from the obligations imposed upon him by 1814, 1816.

1818. The Guardianship Court may for special reasons order the guardian

---

(d) *E.g.*, bank notes.

(e) That is to say, during the continuance of the guardianship.

(f) 1807 (2).

to lodge, in the manner specified by 1814, those negotiable instruments forming part of the ward's property which he is not bound by 1814 to lodge and the ward's valuables; on the application of the guardian the lodgment of interest coupons, annuity coupons and dividend coupons may be ordered even without any special reason.

1819. So long as the negotiable instruments or valuables lodged under 1814 or 1818 have not been withdrawn, the guardian requires the ratification of the Guardianship Court for making any disposition affecting them, or, if certificates of hypotheca, land charge, or annuity charge have been lodged, for making any disposition affecting the hypothecary claim, land charge or annuity charge. The same rule applies to the incurring of an obligation to make such a disposition.

1820. If instruments to bearer have been transferred to the name of the ward or converted into uncertificated claims under 1815, the guardian also requires the ratification of the Guardianship Court for incurring any obligation to dispose of the principal claims arising from such transfer or conversion.

The same rule applies if, in the case of an uncertificated claim of the ward, the provision specified in 1816 has been registered.

1821. A guardian requires the ratification of the Guardianship Court:

(1) for disposing of land or of any right over land [(g)];

(2) for disposing of a claim which has for its object the transfer of ownership of land, or the creation or transfer of a right over land, or the discharge of a piece of land from such a right;

(3) for incurring an obligation to do any one of the acts of disposition specified in (1) and (2);

(4) for any contract which has for its object the gratuitous acquisition of land or of a right over land.

Hypothecas, land charges and annuity charges are not rights over land within the meaning of these provisions.

(*g*) Rights over land are: usufructs, servitudes, perpetual charges on land, heritable building rights, and real rights of pre-emption.

1822. A guardian requires the ratification of the Guardianship Court:

(1) for any juristic act whereby the ward is bound to dispose of his property as a whole, or of an inheritance devolved upon him, or of his future statutory portion of an inheritance, or of his future compulsory portion; and for making any disposition of the ward's share in an inheritance;

(2) for disclaiming an inheritance or a legacy, for renouncing a compulsory portion, and for any contract relating to the partition of an inheritance;

(3) for any contract which has for its object the acquisition or alienation of a business for a valuable consideration, and for a contract of partnership entered into for the purpose of carrying on a business [(h)];

(4) for any contract of usufructuary lease relating to a farm [(i)] or to any industrial operation;

(5) for any contract of ordinary or usufructuary lease or any other contract whereby the ward is bound to make periodical payments, if the contract is to continue for a longer period than one year after the ward shall have completed his twenty-first year of age;

(6) for any contract of apprenticeship entered into for a longer term than one year [(k)];

(7) for any contract which has for its object the entering into service or employment as a labourer, if the ward is to be bound to do acts of performance personally for a longer period than one year [(l)];

(8) for accepting money on the ward's credit;

(9) for issuing an obligation to bearer, or for incurring an obligation arising from a bill of exchange or from any other instrument which may be transferred by indorsement [(m)];

(10) for the assumption of an obligation of another person, *e.g.*, the assumption of a suretyship;

(*h*) The ratification of the Guardianship Court is not necessary for the *continuance* of a business which has already been started.

(*i*) It makes no difference whether the ward is to be lessor or lessee.

(*k*) Cf. 1827; and the Industrial Code, ss. 126—128.

(*l*) Cf. 1827; and 611 *et seq.*; also Commercial Code, s. 59.

(*m*) Commercial Code, s. 363.

(11) for the issue of a power of procuration [(n)];

(12) for a compromise or a contract of arbitration, unless the object in dispute or the question for compromise or arbitration may be assessed in money and the value does not exceed the sum of three hundred marks;

(13) for any juristic act whereby a security for a claim of the ward is terminated or diminished, or whereby an obligation to do so is created.

1823. Without the ratification of the Guardianship Court the guardian should not start any new business in the name of the ward, nor discontinue an existing business of the ward.

1824. In regard to objects which can be alienated only with the ratification of the supervising guardian or of the Guardianship Court, the guardian may not without such ratification entrust such objects to the ward for the fulfilment of any contract concluded by the latter or for the latter's free disposal.

1825. The Guardianship Court may confer a general authorisation on the guardian to enter into juristic acts for which the ratification of the supervising guardian is necessary as provided for in 1812, and the juristic acts specified in 1822, (8) to (10).

The authorisation should be given only if it is necessary for carrying out the object of the management of property, *e.g.*, for the conduct of a business.

1826. Before giving any decision as to the ratification necessary for any act of the guardian, the Guardianship Court should hear the supervising guardian, if there is such and if it is practicable to do so.

1827. The Guardianship Court should hear the ward before giving any decision as to the ratification of a contract of apprenticeship or of any contract relating to the entering into service or employment as a labourer, and, if the ward has completed his fourteenth year of age, as to his renunciation of German nationality.

If the ward has completed his eighteenth year of age, the Guardianship

---

(*n*) *Ibid.* s. 48.

Court should, as far as possible, hear him before giving any decision as to the ratification of one of the juristic acts specified in 1821 and 1822 (3), and before giving any decision as to the ratification of the starting or discontinuing of a business.

1828. The Guardianship Court may declare its ratification of a juristic act only to the guardian [(o)].

1829. If a guardian enters into a contract without the necessary ratification of the Guardianship Court, the contract is invalid unless it is subsequently ratified by the Guardianship Court. The ratification or refusal to ratify is not valid as against the other party until it has been communicated to him by the guardian.

If the other party requires the guardian to inform him whether ratification has been given, the information as to the ratification may be given only before the expiration of two weeks after receipt of the request; if the ratification is not so communicated, it is deemed to have been refused.

If the ward has become of age, his own ratification takes the place of the ratification of the Guardianship Court.

1830. If the guardian has stated to the other party, contrary to the truth, that the Guardianship Court has given its ratification, the other party is entitled to revoke before communication of the subsequent ratification of the Guardianship Court [(p)], unless the absence of ratification was known to him at the time of entering into the contract [(q)].

1831. A unilateral juristic act entered into by a guardian without the necessary ratification of the Guardianship Court, is invalid. If the guardian enters into such a juristic act with another party with such ratification, the juristic act is invalid, if the guardian does not produce the ratification in writing, and the other party without delay rejects the juristic act for this reason.

(*o*) The ratification need not be in writing.

(*p*) The burden of proof is upon the other party.

(*q*) The burden of proof is upon the guardian.

1832. In so far as a guardian requires the ratification of the supervising guardian for a juristic act [(r)], the provisions of 1828 to 1831 apply *mutatis mutandis*.

1833. A guardian is liable to his ward for any damage arising from any breach of duty, if fault can be imputed to him. The same rule applies to a supervising guardian.

If several persons are jointly responsible for the damage, they are liable as joint debtors [(s)]. If, besides the guardian, the supervising guardian or a co-guardian is responsible for the damage caused by the guardian only on the ground of a breach of the duty of supervision, then as between such persons only the guardian is liable.

1834. If a guardian spends his ward's money for his own benefit, he shall pay interest [(t)] from the time of spending.

1835. If a guardian incurs any outlay for the purpose of conducting the guardianship, he may require his ward to advance money or to make compensation under the provisions of 669, 670, applicable to mandate. A supervising guardian has the same right.

Outlay includes also such services of the guardian or of the supervising guardian as are connected with his industry or profession.

1836. Guardianship is undertaken gratuitously. The Guardianship Court may, however, permit the guardian, and, for special reasons, also the supervising guardian, to claim a reasonable remuneration. Such permission should be given only if the value of the ward's property and the extent and importance of the guardianship business justifies it. The remuneration may at any time be increased, or reduced, or withdrawn for the future.

Before permitting, increasing or reducing, or withdrawing the remuneration the guardian and, if there is a supervising guardian or if such a guardian is to be appointed, the latter also should be heard.

(*r*) Cf. 1812.

(*s*) Cf. 421 *et seq*.

(*t*) At 4 per cent. 246.

III. Precautionary Measures and Supervision by the Guardianship Court.

1837. The Guardianship Court shall exercise supervision over all acts done by a guardian and supervising guardian, and shall interfere by appropriate orders and prohibitions against breaches of duty.

The Guardianship Court may compel the guardian and the supervising guardian to obey its orders by exacting penalties. No single penalty can exceed the sum of three hundred marks.

1838. The Guardianship Court may order the ward, for the purpose of his education, to be removed into a suitable family, or an institution of learning, or a reformatory. If the father or the mother has the care of the ward's person, such an order may be made only under the conditions specified in 1666.

1839. The guardian and supervising guardian shall, on demand at any time, give information to the Guardianship Court as to the conduct of the guardianship and as to the ward's personal affairs.

1840. The guardian shall render an account of his management of the property to the Guardianship Court.

Accounts shall be rendered once a year. The year for which accounts shall be rendered is fixed by the Guardianship Court.

If the management of property is of trivial importance, the Guardianship Court may, after the accounts for the first year have been rendered, order that accounts be rendered at longer intervals not exceeding three years.

1841. The accounts should contain a systematic statement of the receipts and disbursements; should give information as to any increase or diminution of the property; and should, so far as vouchers are customarily given, be furnished with vouchers.

If a business is carried on with commercial account-books, a balance drawn from such account-books is sufficient as an account. The Guardianship Court may, however, demand production of the books and vouchers.

1842. If there is a supervising guardian, or if a supervising guardian is to be appointed, the guardian shall submit to him the accounts together with information as to the condition of the property. The supervising guardian shall make such remarks on the accounts as he deems fit to make after examination of them.

1843. The Guardianship Court shall examine the accounts by calculation and verification, and shall, as far as may be necessary, order them to be corrected or supplemented.

Claims which are in dispute between the guardian and the ward may be enforced in Court even before the termination of the guardianship [(u)].

1844. The Guardianship Court may for special reasons compel the guardian to give security for the property subject to his management [(x)]. The Guardianship Court determines at its discretion the kind and the amount of the security to be given. So long as the office of the guardian continues, the Guardianship Court may at any time order an increase, decrease, or termination of the security.

In the giving, increasing, or decreasing, or terminating of the security, for the concurrence of the ward is substituted the order of the Guardianship Court.

The costs of the giving of security and of its increase or decrease, or termination, are borne by the ward.

1845. If the ward's father or legitimate mother who has been appointed guardian intends to marry, the obligations specified in 1669 are imposed upon him or her.

1846. If a guardian has not yet been appointed, or if an appointed guardian is prevented from performing his duties, the Guardianship Court shall take the necessary measures in the interest of the ward.

1847. Before giving any decision as to any such measures, and upon application by the guardian or supervising guardian, the Guardianship Court should hear the ward's relatives by blood or by marriage, if this can be done without

---

(*u*) A curator may be appointed (1909) to represent the ward for this purpose.

(*x*) In such a case the guardian may refuse to accept the office at the very outset (1786 (6)), or may apply for discharge from office, if it has already been accepted. 1889.

serious delay and without disproportionate expense. In important affairs the hearing should be given even without such application; important affairs are, *e.g.*, declaration of majority, substitution of the necessary approval for entering into a marriage in the case provided for by 1304, substitution of the ratification in the case provided for by 1337 renunciation of German nationality, and declaration of death.

Relatives by blood or by marriage may demand from the ward reimbursement of outlay incurred; the amount of outlay is determined by the Guardianship Court.

1848. If a judge of a Guardianship Court wilfully or negligently commits a breach of the duties imposed upon him, he is responsible to the ward under 839, pars. 1 and 3.

IV. Functions of the Communal Orphan Council (y).

1849. The Communal Orphan Council shall propose (z) to the Guardianship Court the names of the persons who, in each particular case, are competent to act as guardians, supervising guardians, or members of a family council.

1850. The Communal Orphan Council shall, in assisting the Guardianship Court, see that the guardians of the wards residing within its district take care of their wards' person, *e.g.*, their education and their physical welfare, in accordance with duty. The Communal Orphan Council shall notify the Guardianship Court of any default or breach of duty on the part of a guardian which comes to its notice, and shall on demand give information as to the personal welfare and conduct of a ward.

If the Communal Orphan Council has knowledge of any danger to a ward's property, it shall notify this to the Guardianship Court.

1851. The Guardianship Court shall communicate to the Communal Orphan

---

(*y*) The organization of Communal Orphan Councils is regulated by the Introductory Act (*Ausführungsgesetz*) of each particular State.

(*z*) The proposal is not, however, binding upon the Guardianship Court.

Council the establishment of guardianship over a ward residing within the latter's district, stating the names of the guardian and supervising guardian, and any change of guardians or supervising guardians.

If the residence of a ward is removed to the district of another Communal Orphan Council, the guardian shall notify such removal to the Communal Orphan Council of the former place of residence, and the latter shall notify such removal to the Communal Orphan Council of the new place of residence.

V. Exempted Guardianship.

1852. If a father [(a)] has nominated a guardian, he may exclude the appointment of a supervising guardian.

The father may direct that the guardian nominated by him shall be exempt from the limitations specified in 1809, 1810 in respect of the investment of money, and that he shall not require the ratification of the supervising guardian or of the Guardianship Court for the juristic acts specified in 1812. Such directions are deemed to have been given, if the father has excluded the appointment of a supervising guardian.

1853. The father may release a guardian nominated by him from the obligation to lodge instruments to bearer and instruments to order [(b)], or the obligation to cause the provision specified in 1816 to be entered in the Imperial debt ledger or a State debt ledger.

1854. The father may release a guardian nominated by him from the obligation to render accounts during his term of office.

In such a case the guardian shall, at the end of every two years, present to the Guardianship Court a general statement as to the condition of the property subject to his management. The Guardianship Court may order that such general statement be presented at longer intervals not exceeding five years.

If there is a supervising guardian, or if such a guardian is to be appointed,

---

(*a*) Or a mother. 1855.

(*b*) 1814.

the guardian shall present to him such general statement, together with information as to the condition of the property. The supervising guardian shall make such remarks on the general Statement as he deems fit to make after examination.

1855. If a legitimate mother nominates a guardian, she may give the same directions as the father may under 1852 to 1854.

1856. The provisions of 1777 apply to the directions permitted by 1852 to 1855.

1857. The directions given by the father or mother may be set aside by the Guardianship Court if the observance of them would endanger the interest of the ward.

VI. Family Council.

1858. A family council should be established by the Guardianship Court, if the father or the legitimate mother of the ward has directed its establishment.

The father or the mother may make the establishment of the family council dependent upon the occurrence or non-occurrence of a certain event.

The establishment of a family council is dispensed with, if the necessary number of competent persons is not obtainable.

1859. A family council should be established by the Guardianship Court, if any relative by blood or marriage of the ward, or the guardian, or the supervising guardian applies for its establishment, and the Guardianship Court deems it proper in the interest of the ward.

The establishment of a family council is dispensed with, if the father or the legitimate mother of the ward has prohibited it [c].

1860. A family council consists of the judge of the Guardianship Court as president, and no less than two nor more than six members.

1861. A person is called upon to act as a member of the family council if

(c) By will or contract of inheritance. 1868.

he has been nominated as such by the father or the legitimate mother of the ward [(c)]. The provision of 1773, pars. 1 and 2, apply *mutatis mutandis*.

1862. In so far as no person is called upon to act under 1861, or the person called upon to act refuses to accept the office [(d)], the Guardianship Court shall select members necessary to form a quorum of the family council. Before making the selection the Communal Orphan Council and, as provided for in 1847, the ward's relatives by blood, or marriage should be heard.

The family council has the right to determine any greater number of members [(e)], and the mode of their selection.

1863. If, besides the president, there is only the number of members necessary to form a quorum of the family council, one or two supplementary members shall be appointed.

The family council selects the supplementary members, and determines the order of precedence in which they shall come into the family council in the case of a member being unable or failing to act.

If the father or the legitimate mother has nominated supplementary members and has determined the order of precedence in which they are called upon to act, such directions shall be followed.

1864. If the family council does not have a quorum in consequence of the temporary inability of a member to act, and if there is no supplementary member, a supplementary member shall be appointed during the time of such inability. The president has the right to select such supplementary member.

1865. A person who is incapable of disposing or has been interdicted on account of feeble-mindedness, prodigality, or habitual drunkenness, may not be appointed as a member of a family council.

1866. The following persons should not be appointed as members of a family council:

(*c*) By will or contract of inheritance. 1868.

(*d*) 1869.

(*e*) But not more than six. 1860.

(1) the guardian of the ward [f];
(2) a person who should not be appointed as guardian as provided for in 1781 or 1782;
(3) a person who has been excluded from membership by direction of the father or of the legitimate mother of the ward.

1867. A person who is related to the ward neither by blood nor by marriage should not be appointed as member of the family council, unless he has been nominated by the ward's father or legitimate mother, or has been selected by the family council, or has been selected by the president under 1864.

1868. The provisions of 1777 apply to the directions permitted to the father or the mother by 1858, 1859, 1861, 1863, 1866.

Directions given by the father take priority to those given by the mother.

1869. No person is bound to accept membership of a family council.

1870. The members of a family council are appointed by the president, before whom they assume the obligation to exercise their office faithfully and conscientiously. The assumption of the obligation should be effected by clasp of hand in lieu of oath.

1871. The appointment of a member of a family council may be made terminable on the occurrence or non-occurrence of a certain event.

1872. A family council has the rights and the duties of the Guardianship Court. The duty to conduct its affairs is imposed upon the president.

Members of a family council may exercise their functions only in person. They are responsible in the same manner as a judge of a Guardianship Court [g].

1873. Meetings of the family council shall be called by the president. A meeting shall be called if two members or the guardian or the supervising guar-

---

(*f*) The supervising guardian is, however, eligible to membership.

(*g*) Cf. 1848.

dian applies for it, or if the interest of the ward demands it. The members may be notified of the meeting either verbally or in writing.

1874. The presence of the president and of at least two members is necessary to form a quorum of the family council.

Resolutions of the family council are carried according to the majority of votes of those persons present. If the votes are equal the vote of the president decides.

If in any affair the interest of the ward is in serious conflict with the interest of a member, such member is excluded from voting. Any question as to such exclusion is decided by the president.

1875. A member of a family council who does not comply with the notice of meeting without sufficient excuse, or fails to give notice in due time of his inability to be present, or refuses to vote, shall be ordered by the president to make compensation for any damage arising therefrom.

The president may impose upon such member a fine of not more than one hundred marks.

If a sufficient excuse is subsequently found to exist, the measures taken shall be revoked.

1876. If immediate intervention is necessary the president shall take all necessary measures; call a meeting of the family council; notify it of the measures taken; and ask for a resolution as to any further measures which may be necessary.

1877. Members of a family council may demand from the ward reimbursement of outlay incurred; the amount of the outlay is fixed by the president.

1878. A member of a family council vacates his office on the same grounds as those on which a guardian vacates his office as provided for in 1885, 1886, 1889.

A member may, against his will, be discharged from office only by the Court next higher in rank to the Guardianship Court.

1879. The Guardianship Court shall dissolve a family council if the number of its members necessary to form a quorum is absent, and there are no competent persons to make up the deficiency.

1880. The father of a ward may, subject to the conditions specified in 1777, direct the family council established by him to be dissolved on the occurrence or non-occurrence of a future event. The ward's legitimate mother has the same right over a family council established by her.

If such a case occurs the Guardianship Court shall dissolve the family council.

1881. The Guardianship Court shall notify the dissolution of the family council to the persons who are members at that time, the guardian and the supervising guardian.

The guardian and supervising guardian receive new certificates of appointment. The original certificates shall be returned to the Guardianship Court.

VII. Termination of Guardianship.

1882. A guardianship comes to an end on the disappearance of the conditions specified in 1773 for its establishment [(h)].

1883. If a ward is legitimated by subsequent marriage, the guardianship does not come to an end until the paternity of the putative father is established by a non-appellable decree issued between him and the ward, or until the Guardianship Court orders the termination of the guardianship.

The Guardianship Court shall order the termination of the guardianship if it deems the conditions for legitimation to be in existence. So long as the putative father is living the termination should be ordered only if he has acknowledged his paternity, or is permanently prevented from making a declaration, or his place of residence is permanently unknown.

1884. If the ward has disappeared the guardianship does not come to an end until its termination by the Guardianship Court. The Guardianship Court shall terminate the guardianship if it has information of the death of the ward.

Where the ward is declared to be dead the guardianship comes to an end on

---

(*h*) A guardianship also comes to an end on the attainment of majority by the ward.

the issue of the decree for declaration of death.

1885. A guardian vacates his office on his being interdicted.

Where the guardian is declared dead, his office is vacated on the issue of the decree for declaration of death.

1886. The Guardianship Court shall dismiss the guardian from his office where his continuation in office, especially his conduct in breach of duty [(i)], would endanger the interest of the ward [(k)], or where one of the grounds specified in 1781 arises with reference to the guardian.

1887. Where a woman has been appointed guardian the Guardianship Court may dismiss her from office if she marries.

Where a married woman has been appointed guardian the Guardianship Court shall dismiss her from office if her husband refuses to give his consent, or revokes his consent to the acceptance or continuance in office. This provision does not apply where the husband is the father of the ward [(l)].

1888. Where an official or a clergyman has been appointed guardian, the Guardianship Court shall dismiss him from office if the permission, which is necessary according to the State law for accepting the office or for continuance in the office which has been accepted before he becomes an official or clergyman, is refused or revoked, or if the refusal which is permissible by the State law in respect of the continuance in office is given [(m)].

1889. The Guardianship Court shall dismiss a guardian on his own application if a grave reason exists; such a reason is, *e.g.*, the occurrence of a circumstance which, under 1786, par. 1, (2) to (7), would entitle him to refuse acceptance of the office.

1890. A guardian shall, on the termination of his office, hand over to his

---

(*i*) Immoral conduct also constitutes a ground for dismissal.

(*k*) The Guardianship Court may, in the first instance, prevent breaches of duty by orders and prohibitions. 1837.

(*l*) In such a case the guardianship could have been established only if the father had not the parental power.

(*m*) 1784.

ward the property managed by him, and shall give an account of his management [n]. In so far as he has rendered an account to the Guardianship Court, a reference to such account is sufficient.

1891. If there is a supervising guardian, the guardian shall submit the accounts to him. The supervising guardian shall make such remarks on the accounts as he deems fit to make after examination.

The supervising guardian shall on demand give information as to the conduct of the supervising guardianship and, so far as he is in a position to do so, shall also give information as to the property managed by the guardian.

1892. The guardian shall, after having submitted the accounts to the supervising guardian, present them to the Guardianship Court.

The Guardianship Court shall examine the accounts by calculation and verification and shall not accept the accounts except with the concurrence of the supervising guardian and after discussion with the interested parties. In so far as the accounts have been acknowledged to be correct, the Guardianship Court shall authenticate such acknowledgment.

1893. In case of termination of guardianship or the vacation of the office of guardianship, the provision of 1682, 1683, apply *mutatis mutandis*.

The guardian shall return his certificate of appointment to the Guardianship Court on vacating his office.

1894. The heir of a deceased guardian shall without delay notify the Guardianship Court of the death.

The guardian shall without delay notify the Guardianship Court of the death of the supervising guardian or of co-guardian.

1895. The provisions of 1885 to 1889, 1893, 1894, apply *mutatis mutandis* to the supervising guardian.

(*n*) 259—261.

SECOND TITLE.
Guardianship over Persons of Full Age.

1896. If a person of full age has been interdicted, a guardian is appointed for him (o).

1897. Except in so far as a contrary intention appears from 1898 to 1908, the provisions applicable to guardianship over a minor apply to guardianship over a person of full age.

1898. The father and the mother of the ward are not entitled to nominate any guardian, nor to exclude any person from the guardianship (p).

1899. The father or, next after him, the legitimate mother (q) of the ward is called upon to act as guardian in preference to the grandfathers (r).

Neither parent is called upon to act as guardian if the ward has been adopted by a person other than the spouse of his father or mother.

If the ward is born of a void marriage, in the case provided for by 1701, the father is not called upon to act; in the case provided for by 1702 the mother is not called upon to act.

1900. A wife may be appointed guardian of her husband even without his consent.

The spouse of a ward can be appointed guardian in preference to the parents and the grandfathers (r); the legitimate mother can, in the case provided for by 1702, be appointed guardian in preference to the grandfathers.

An illegitimate mother can be appointed guardian in preference to the grandfather.

1901. The guardian shall take care of the ward's person only in so far as it

---

(*o*) After the interdiction has been applied for, and before a guardian has been appointed, an interim guardianship may be established. 1906 *et seq.*

(*p*) The reason being that the ward is no longer under his or her parental power.

(*q*) As to an illegitimate mother, see 1778, par. 3.

(*r*) Cf. 1776.

is necessary for the carrying out of the object of the guardianship.

If a married woman is under guardianship, the limitation specified in 1633 does not arise.

1902. The guardianship may promise or furnish an advancement out of the property of the ward only with the ratification of the Guardianship Court.

For a contract of ordinary or usufructuary lease, and for any other contract whereby the ward is bound to do periodical acts of performance, the Guardian requires the ratification of the Guardianship Court where the contract is entered into for a longer term than four years. The provision of 1822 (4) remains unaffected.

1903. If the father of the ward is appointed guardian, the appointment of a supervising guardian is dispensed with. The father has the right to claim the dispensations which may be granted under 1852 to 1854. The Guardianship Court may set aside the dispensations if they endanger the interest of the ward.

These provisions do not apply where the father would not be entitled to manage the ward's property if the latter were a minor [s].

1904. If the legitimate mother of the ward has been appointed guardian, the same rule applies to her as to the father in the case provided for by 1903. The mother, however, shall be appointed supervising guardian if she applies for such appointment, or if the conditions exist under which a supplementary guardian would have to be appointed for her as provided for in 1687 (3). If a supervising guardian is appointed, the mother does not have the right to claim the dispensations specified in 1852.

1905. A family council may be established only in the manner specified by 1859, par. 1.

Neither the father nor the mother of the ward is entitled to give any directions as to the establishment and termination of a family council or as to its membership.

1906. A person of full age, whose interdiction has been applied for, may

---

(s) *I.e.*, in the cases provided for by 1647, 1666, 1670, 1676, 1677, 1680.

be placed under *interim* guardianship if the Guardianship Court deems it necessary for averting any serious danger to the person or property of such person.

1907. The provisions relating to the order of precedence in which persons are called to act as guardian do not apply to *interim* guardianship.

1908. *Interim* guardianship comes to an end as soon as the application for interdiction has been withdrawn or rejected without any right of appeal.

If the interdiction takes place, the *interim* guardianship comes to an end if a guardian is appointed by virtue of such interdiction.

The *interim* guardianship shall be terminated by the Guardianship Court if the ward no longer requires the protection of the *interim* guardianship.

THIRD TITLE.
Curatorship.

1909. A curator is appointed for a person under parental power or guardianship, to take charge of the affairs of which the parent or guardian is prevented [(t)] from taking charge. A curator is appointed, *e.g.*, for the management of any property which such person acquires *mortis causa*, or which has been transferred to him gratuitously by a third party *inter vivos*, provided that the testator in his testamentary disposition, or the third party at the time of the transfer, has specified that the acquisition shall be exempt from the father's or guardian's management.

If the necessity for a curatorship arises, the parent or guardian shall notify the Guardianship Court without delay.

A curatorship shall also be established even if the conditions for the establishment of a guardianship exist, provided that a guardian has not yet been appointed.

1910. A curator may be appointed for a person of full age who is not under guardianship, to take charge of his person and property, if he is unable to take

(*t*) No matter whether by law or by circumstances.

care of his own affairs in consequence of physical infirmities, *e.g.*, because he is deaf, blind, or dumb.

If a person of full age who is not under guardianship is unable, in consequence of mental or physical infirmities, to take charge of certain of his affairs or certain kinds of affairs, *e.g.*, his property affairs, a curator may be appointed for him to take charge of such affairs.

The curatorship can be established only with the approval of the infirm person [(u)], unless an understanding with him is impossible.

1911. A curator *absentis* may be appointed for a person of full age who is absent and whose place of residence is unknown, to take charge of his property affairs so far as is necessary. Such a curator shall also be appointed for him, even though the absent person has given a mandate or a power of agency for taking charge of his property, if circumstances have arisen which cause the revocation of the mandate or of the power of agency.

The same rule applies to an absent person whose place of residence is known, but who is prevented from returning to take charge of his property affairs.

1912. A curator is appointed for a child *en ventre sa mère* to protect its future rights so far as such rights require protection. The right to protect such rights belongs, however, to the father or mother if the child would have been under his or her parental power had it been already born.

1913. If it is unknown or uncertain who is the interested party in an affair, a curator may be appointed for the interested party to take charge of the affair so far as such care is necessary. For example, a curator may be appointed for a reversionary heir who is not yet born or whose identity cannot be ascertained until after the occurrence of a future event, for the time until the occurrence of reversionary succession[(v)].

1914. Where a fund has been collected for a temporary purpose by public subscription, a curator may be appointed for the purpose of the management and

---

(*u*) The curatorship shall be terminated on his application.

(*v*) See 2100 *et seq.*, especially 2101 and 2139.

use of the fund, if the persons appointed for such purpose have died or ceased to act.

1915. Unless it is otherwise provided by law, the provisions applicable to guardianship apply *mutatis mutandis* to curatorship.

The appointment of a supervising guardian is not necessary.

1916. The provisions relating to the order of precedence in which persons are called upon to act as guardian do not apply to a curatorship to be established under 1909.

1917. If the establishment of a curatorship under 1909, par. 1, sentence 2, is necessary, the person shall be called upon to act as curator who has been nominated as such by the testator in his testamentary disposition, or by the third party at the time of transfer; the provisions of 1778 apply *mutatis mutandis*.

The testator may by testamentary disposition, or the third party may at the time of transfer, grant to the person nominated as curator the dispensations specified in 1852 to 1854. The Guardianship Court may set aside the dispensations granted if they endanger the interest of the person under curatorship.

For making any deviation from the directions of the third party his consent is, so long as he is still living, necessary and sufficient. The consent of the third party may be supplied by the Guardianship Court, if he is permanently not in a position to make a declaration, or if his place of residence is permanently unknown.

1918. The curatorship over a person under parental power or guardianship comes to an end on the termination of the parental power or guardianship.

The curatorship over a child *en ventre sa mère* comes to an end on the birth of the child.

The curatorship for taking charge of a particular affair comes to an end on the completion of the affair.

1919. Curatorship shall be terminated by the Guardianship Court if the ground for its establishment has ceased to exist.

1920. A curatorship established under 1910 shall be terminated by the

Guardianship Court if the person under curatorship applies for the termination.

1921. The curatorship over a person who is absent shall be terminated by the Guardianship Court if the person absent is no longer prevented from taking charge of his property affairs.

If the person absent dies, the curatorship does not come to an end until it is terminated by the Guardianship Court. The Guardianship Court shall terminate it if it has information of the death of the person absent.

If the person absent is declared to be dead, the curatorship comes to an end on the issue of the decree for declaration of death.

FIFTH BOOK.
Law of Inheritance.

FIRST SECTION.
ORDER OF SUCCESSION.

1922. On the death of a person (accrual of the inheritance), his property (the inheritance) passes [(a)] as a whole to one or several other persons (heirs).

The provisions relating to an inheritance apply to the share of a co-heir (share in the inheritance).

1923. Only a person who was living at the time of the accrual of the inheritance may become an heir [(b)].

A person *en ventre sa mère* at the time of the accrual of the inheritance is deemed to have been born before that time.

1924. Statutory heirs of the first class are the descendants of the deceased.

A descendant living at the time of the accrual of the inheritance excludes from succession all descendants related by blood to the deceased through him.

If a descendant has died before the time of the accrual of the inheritance, the descendants related by blood to the deceased through him take his place (succession *per stirpes*).

Children inherit in equal shares.

(*a*) *Ipso jure*. The inheritance may, however, be disclaimed within six weeks. 1942 *et seq*.

(*b*) This provision applies only to a statutory heir, and not to a person (especially a juristic person) appointed by will (2101, 2106, par. 2), nor to a contract of inheritance. 2279.

1925. Statutory heirs of the second class are the parents of the deceased and their descendants.

If the parents are living at the time of the accrual of the inheritance, they alone inherit in equal shares.

If the father or the mother has died before the time of the accrual of the inheritance, the descendants of the deceased parent take his or her place in accordance with the provisions applicable to the succession of heirs of the first class. If there are no descendants, the surviving parent alone inherits.

1926. Statutory heirs of the third class are the grandparents [(c)] of the deceased and their descendants.

If the grandparents are living at the time of the accrual of the inheritance, they alone inherit in equal shares.

If, among the paternal or maternal grandparents, the grandfather or grandmother has died before the time of the accrual of the inheritance, the descendants of the deceased grandfather or grandmother take his or her place. If there are no such descendants, the share of the deceased grandparent on the paternal or maternal side goes to the other share of the grandparents on the other side; and if the latter are not living, to their descendants.

If the paternal or maternal grandparents have died before the time of the accrual of the inheritance, and if there are no descendants of the deceased grandparents on the paternal or maternal side, the grandparents on the other side or their descendants inherit alone.

In so far as descendants take the place of their parents or of their ancestors, the provisions applicable to the succession of heirs of the first class [(d)] apply.

1927. If a person belongs to the first, second or third class of different *stirpes*, he receives the share devolving upon him in respect of each *stirpes*. Each share is deemed to be a separate share in the inheritance [(e)].

(*c*) *I.e.*, four altogether, two on the paternal and two on the maternal side.

(*d*) 1924, pars. 2 to 4.

(*e*) *I.e.*, a share in respect of one *stirps* may be disclaimed without affecting any share in respect of another *stirps*. 1951, par. 1.

1928. Statutory heirs of the fourth class are the great grandparents of the deceased and their descendants.

If the great grandparents are living at the time of the accrual of the inheritance, they alone inherit; if there are several great grandparents, they inherit is equal shares without distinction whether they belong to the same or to different lines.

If the great grandparents have died before the time of the accrual of the inheritance, that one of their descendants inherits who is related by blood to the deceased nearest in degree; several persons of the same degree inherit in equal shares.

1929. Statutory heirs of the fifth class and the subsequent classes are the remoter ascendants of the deceased and their descendants.

The provisions of 1928, pars. 2, 3, apply *mutatis mutandis*.

1930. A relative by blood is not entitled to inherit so long as there is a relative by blood of a preceding class.

1931. The surviving spouse of the deceased, in the capacity of statutory heir, is, concurrently with relatives by blood of the first class, entitled to one-fourth of the inheritance, or, concurrently with relatives by blood of the second class or with grandparents, to one-half of the inheritance. If there are both grandparents and descendants of the grandparents, the spouse takes also the share in the other half which would devolve upon such descendants as provided for in 1926.

If there are neither relatives by blood of the first or second class nor grandparents, the surviving spouse takes the whole inheritance.

1932. If the surviving spouse is statutory heir concurrently with relatives by blood of the second class or with grandparents, such spouse, in addition to his or her share in the inheritance, takes, by way of preferential benefit, all objects connected with the joint household in so far as they are not accessories of land, and all wedding presents.

The provisions applicable to legacies apply to such preferential benefit.

1933. The surviving spouse's right of inheritance and the right to the preferential benefit are barred if the deceased at the time of his death was entitled to petition for divorce by reason of the fault of the spouse (f) and filed a petition for divorce or judicial separation (g).

1934. If the surviving spouse is a relative by blood entitled to the inheritance, he (or she) inherits at the same time as a relative by blood. The share which devolves on him (or her) by reason of relationship by blood is deemed to be a separate share in the inheritance.

1935. If the share of a statutory heir is, in consequence of his failure to inherit, added to the share of another statutory heir, the former share is deemed to be a separate share in the inheritance both in respect of the legacies and testamentary burdens with which the former or the latter heir is charged, and in respect of the hotchpot liability (h).

1936. If neither a relative by blood nor the spouse of the deceased is living at the time of the accrual of the inheritance, the Treasury of the State of which the deceased was a subject at the time of his death becomes statutory heir (i). If the deceased was a subject of several States, the Treasuries of these States are entitled to inherit as statutory heirs in equal shares (k).

If the deceased was a German who was not a subject of any State, the Imperial Treasury becomes statutory heir.

1937. The deceased may name his heir by a unilateral disposition *mortis causa* (a will or testamentary disposition).

1938. The deceased may by will exclude a relative by blood or his (or her) spouse from the statutory succession even without appointing an heir.

1939. The deceased may by will confer any pecuniary benefit on another

---

(*f*) This provision does not apply where the divorce was based on insanity.

(*g*) In such a case a legacy made by will or contract of inheritance is also inoperative. 2077, 2279.

(*h*) 2050, 2051.

(*i*) Cf. IA, Art. 138.

(*k*) An inheritance devolved upon the Treasury cannot be disclaimed. 1942, par. 2.

person without appointing him heir (*i.e.*, a legacy) [(l)].

1940. The deceased may by will bind his heir or a legatee to perform some act without conferring on any person a right to demand performance (*i.e.*, a testamentary burden) [(m)].

1941. The deceased may by contract appoint an heir and create legacies and testamentary burdens (*i.e.*, a contract of inheritance) [(n)].

Both the other contracting party and a third party may be appointed as heir (contractual heir) or legatee.

SECOND SECTION.
LEGAL STATUS OF AN HEIR.

FIRST TITLE.
Acceptance and Disclaimer of an Inheritance. Supervision of the Probate Court.

1942. An inheritance passes [(o)] to the heir entitled to inherit, subject to his right of disclaiming it (devolution of the inheritance).

The Treasury may not disclaim an inheritance devolving upon it as statutory heir.

1943. The heir may not disclaim the inheritance after he has accepted it [(p)], or after the period fixed for the disclaimer has elapsed; at the expiration of the period the inheritance is deemed to have been accepted.

1944. The disclaimer may be effected only within six weeks [(q)].

(*l*) See 2147 *et seq.* A universal legacy (*i.e.*, a legacy of the whole estate) is deemed to be a reversionary succession and not a legacy. 2100 *et seq.*

(*m*) For further particulars, see 2192 *et seq.*

(*n*) See 2274 *et seq.*

(*o*) *Ipso jure.*

(*p*) Either expressly or impliedly.

(*q*) The disclaimer is voidable, but not revocable. 1954 *et seq.*

The period begins to run from the time at which the heir has knowledge of the devolution and of the ground of his being entitled to inherit (r). If the heir is entitled under a disposition *mortis causa*, the period does not begun to run until the publication of the disposition (s). The provisions of 203, 206, applicable to prescription, apply *mutatis mutandis* to the running of the period (t).

The period is six months if the deceased was last domiciled in a foreign country, or if the heir resides in a foreign country (u) at the beginning of the period.

1945. The disclaimer is effected by declaration to the Probate Court (x); the declaration shall be made in publicly certified form.

An authorised agent requires a publicly authenticated power of agency. The power of agency must either accompany the declaration or be annexed to it within the period of disclaimer.

1946. An heir may accept or disclaim an inheritance as soon as accrual of the inheritance has taken place (y).

1947. The acceptance or disclaimer may not be made subject to any condition or limitation of time.

1948. A person who is entitled to inherit under a disposition *mortis causa* may, if he would be entitled to inherit as statutory heir even without the disposition, disclaim the inheritance in the capacity of appointed heir, and accept it in the capacity of statutory heir.

A person who is entitled to inherit both under a will and under a contract of inheritance may accept the inheritance devolved upon him by virtue of his

---

(r) *I.e.*, whether by statutory succession or under a will or a contract of inheritance.

(s) On the publication of a will, see 2260; of a contract of inheritance, see 2300.

(t) In the case of persons of imperfect disposing capacity (114), the period begins to run from the moment at which the statutory agent has such knowledge.

(u) A German colony or protectorate is deemed to be a foreign country within the meaning of this provision.

(x) *I.e.*, the Probate Court of the place where the deceased was last domiciled. Sect. 73 of the Voluntary Jurisdiction Act.

(y) He may do so even before the will has been published.

testamentary right and disclaim the inheritance devolved upon him by virtue of his contractual right, and *vice versâ* (z).

1949. An acceptance is deemed not to have been effected if the heir was under a mistake as to the ground upon which his right to inherit is based (a).

A disclaimer extends, in case of doubt, to all grounds upon which the right to inherit is based (b) and which are known to the heir at the time of making the declaration of disclaimer.

1950. Acceptance or disclaimer may not be limited to a part of an inheritance. Acceptance or disclaimer of a part of an inheritance is of no effect.

1951. A person who is entitled to inherit several shares in an inheritance (c) may, if his right to inherit is based upon different grounds, accept any of such shares and disclaim the others.

If the right to inherit is based on the same ground, the acceptance or disclaimer of one share affects also the other shares even if they devolve upon him after the date of acceptance or disclaimer. The right to inherit is deemed to be based upon the same ground where such right is created by several wills, or by several contracts of inheritance concluded between the same persons.

If a deceased appoints an heir for several shares in his inheritance, he may permit him by disposition *mortis causa* to accept any of such shares and disclaim the other.

1952. The right of an heir to disclaim an inheritance passes by inheritance.

If the heir dies before the expiration of the period of disclaimer, the period does not expire before the expiration of the period of disclaimer fixed for the inheritance of the deceased heir.

(*z*) His obligations in respect of legatees (2161) and testamentary burdens (2192) are not, however, affected by such acceptance or disclaimer.

(*a*) The fact that the mistake was due to negligence is immaterial for this purpose, although he may be liable to make compensation to a third party for any damage which such third party has suffered through relying upon the validity of the acceptance. 122.

(*b*) See note (*r*) to 1944.

(*c*) For instance, by virtue of several degrees of relationship by blood (1927), or by virtue of relationship by blood and by virtue of relationship by marriage. 1934.

If there are several heirs of the deceased heir, each may disclaim the part of the inheritance devolved upon the deceased heir proportional to his share in the inheritance devolved upon them.

1953. If an inheritance is disclaimed, its devolution on the person disclaiming is deemed not to have taken place.

The inheritance devolves on the person who would have been entitled to inherit if the person disclaiming had died before the time of the accrual of the inheritance; the devolution is deemed to have taken place at the time of the accrual of the inheritance.

The Probate Court should communicate the disclaimer to the person upon whom the inheritance has devolved in consequence of the disclaimer [(d)]. The Probate Court shall permit any person to inspect the declaration of disclaimer, provided he can offer *primâ facie* proof that he has a legal interest therein.

1954. Where an acceptance or disclaimer is voidable, the avoidance may be effected only within six weeks [(e)].

Where the acceptance or disclaimer is voidable on the ground of threats, the period begins to run from the time at which the coercion ceases; in all other cases, from the time at which the person entitled to avoid has knowledge of the ground for avoidance. The provisions of 203, 206, 207, applicable to prescription, apply *mutatis mutandis* to the running of the period.

The period is six months where the deceased was last domiciled in a foreign country [(f)], or where the heir resided in a foreign country at the beginning of the period.

The right of avoidance is barred if thirty years have elapsed since the acceptance or disclaimer.

1955. The avoidance of the acceptance or of the disclaimer is effected by

---

(*d*) The object of this provision is to enable the period of disclaimer specified in 1944 to run against the other heirs. If they are unknown, the Probate Court shall take the necessary measures for the protection of the estate as provided for by 1960.

(*e*) For the effects of avoidance, see 142.

(*f*) Cf. note (*u*) to 1944.

declaration to the Probate Court [g]. The provisions of 1945 apply to such declaration.

1956. The omission to disclaim within the period of disclaimer may be avoided in the same manner as an acceptance.

1957. The avoidance of an acceptance is deemed to be a disclaimer, and the avoidance of a disclaimer is deemed to be an acceptance.

The Probate Court should communicate the avoidance of a disclaimer to the person on whom the inheritance devolved in consequence of the disclaimer. The provision of 1953, par. 3, sentence 2, applies.

1958. Before acceptance [h] of an inheritance a claim running against the estate may not be enforced in Court against the heirs.

1959. If an heir takes charge of the affairs of an inheritance before disclaiming, he has the rights and the duties of a manager of affairs without mandate as against the person who ultimately becomes heir.

If the heir disposes of any object forming part of the estate before disclaiming, the validity of the disposition is not affected by a disclaimer, provided the disposition could not be delayed without injury to the estate.

A juristic act which must be entered into with the heir as such remains, if it is entered into with the person disclaiming before the disclaimer, effective even after the disclaimer.

1960. Before acceptance of the inheritance the Probate Court shall, so far as is necessary, take all precautionary measures for the preservation of the estate. The same rule applies if the heir is unknown, or if it is uncertain whether he has accepted the inheritance or not.

The Probate Court may, *e.g.*, order the affixing of seals [i], the lodgment of money, negotiable instruments and valuables, and the drawing up of an inven-

---

(*g*) An exception to 143.

(*h*) See 1943, 1946 *et seq.*, and 1959.

(*i*) A testamentary disposition prohibiting the drawing up of an inventory of the estate or the affixing of seals is invalid.

tory of the estate; and it may appoint a curator for the person who will become heir (a curator of the estate).

The provision of 1958 does not apply to a curator of an estate.

1961. The Probate Court shall, in the cases provided for by 1960, par. 1, appoint a curator of the estate, if such appointment is applied for by a person entitled to a claim against the estate for the purpose of enforcing his claim in Court.

1962. In respect of the curatorship of an estate the Probate Court takes the place of the Guardianship Court.

1963. If, at the time of the accrual of an inheritance, the birth of an heir is expected, and if the expectant mother is not in a position to maintain herself, she may, until the time of delivery, claim maintenance suitable to her station in life out of the estate, or out of the child's share, if other persons have also become entitled to inherit. In determining such share it is presumed that only one child will be born.

1964. If an heir has not been found within a period which is reasonable under the circumstances, the Probate Court shall decide as the fact that there is no heir other than the Treasury [(k)].

The decision establishes the presumption that the Treasury is statutory heir [(l)].

1965. The decision shall be preceded by a public citation for notification by any person claiming any right of inheritance; the manner of advertising the public citation and the duration of the period for notification are determined by the provisions applicable to the procedure by public summons. The public citation may be dispensed with if its expense is disproportionate to the value of the estate.

A right of inheritance is not taken into consideration if, within three months after the expiration of the period for notification, it has not been proved to the

---

(*k*) Cf. 1936.

(*l*) The presumption is rebuttable under 292 of the Code of Civil Procedure.

Probate Court that the right of inheritance exists, or that such right has been enforced in Court by action against the Treasury. If a public citation has not been issued the three months' period begins to run from the time when citation has been issued by the Court to prove that such right is in existence or that such action has been brought.

1966. No right may be enforced, in Court by or against the Treasury in the capacity of statutory heir until after it has been decided by the Probate Court that no other heir than the Treasury is in existence.

SECOND TITLE.
Liability of an Heir for the Liabilities of the Estate.

I. Liabilities of the Estate.

1967. An heir is liable for the liabilities of the estate.

The liabilities of the estate include not only the debts incurred by the deceased, but also the obligations imposed upon the heir as such, *e.g.*, the obligations arising from any rights to compulsory portions, legacies and testamentary burdens.

1968. The heir bears the funeral expenses of the deceased suitable to the latter's station in life [(m)].

1969. The heir is bound, as towards all the members of the deceased's family who, at the time of the death of the deceased, belonged to the latter's household and were maintained by the latter, to furnish maintenance to them for the first thirty days after the accrual of the inheritance to the same extent as the deceased himself; and to permit them to use the house and all household articles. The testator may give a different direction in his testamentary disposition.

The provisions relating to legacies apply *mutatis mutandis*.

(*m*) If the heir does not defray such expenses, they are borne by the persons who were bound to furnish maintenance to the deceased. 1601 *et seq.*, especially 1608.

II. Public Summons of the Creditors of an Estate.

1970. The creditors of an estate may be required by public summons to present their claims.

1971. Pledgees and creditors who stand on an equal footing with pledgees in bankruptcy proceedings, or who, in the case of compulsory execution on immoveables, have a right to claim satisfaction out of such immoveables, are not affected by the public summons so far as satisfaction out of the objects subject to their rights is concerned. The same rule applies to creditors whose claims have been secured by a caution, or who in bankruptcy proceedings have a right of privilege in respect of any object subject to their right.

1972. Rights to compulsory portions, legacies and testamentary burdens are, subject to the provision of 2060 (1), not affected by the public summons.

1973. An heir may refuse to satisfy a creditor of the estate who is excluded by the public summons in so far as the estate is exhausted through satisfaction of the creditors who are not so excluded. The heir shall, however, satisfy the excluded creditor before performing his obligations arising from rights to compulsory portions, legacies and testamentary burdens, unless the creditor has not enforced his claim in Court until after the performance of such obligations.

The heir shall, under the provisions relating to the return of unjustified benefits, hand over any surplus of the estate for the purpose of satisfying the creditor in compulsory execution proceedings. The heir may refuse to hand over any existing objects belonging to the estate by payment of their value. A non-appellable decree directing the heir to satisfy an excluded creditor has, as against another creditor, the same effect as satisfaction itself [(n)].

1974. A creditor of the estate who asserts his claim against the heir after five years since the accrual of the inheritance stands on an equal footing with an excluded creditor, unless his claim has become known to the heir before the expiration of the five years, or has been notified in the proceedings by public

---

(*n*) Cf. 995 of the Code of Civil Procedure, and sect. 219 of the Bankruptcy Act.

summons. In the case of the inheritance of a person who has been declared dead, the period of five years does not begin to run until the issue of the decree for declaration of death.

The obligation imposed upon the heir by 1973, par. 1, sentence 2, arises, as between the obligations arising from rights to compulsory portions, legacies, and testamentary burdens, only in so far as the creditor would have priority in rank in case of bankruptcy proceedings against the estate (o).

In so far as a creditor is not affected by the public summons, as provided in 1971, the provisions of par. 1 do not apply to him.

III. Limitation of the Liability of an Heir.

1975. The liability of an heir for the liabilities of an estate is limited to the estate, if a curatorship over the estate has been established for the satisfaction of the creditors of the estate (*i.e.*, administration of the estate), or if bankruptcy proceedings have been instituted against the estate (p).

1976. If the administration of the estate has been ordered, or bankruptcy proceedings against the estate have been instituted, the legal relations, extinguished in consequence of the accrual of the inheritance by the merger of a right in an obligation or of a right in a charge, are deemed not to have been extinguished (q).

1977. If, before the administration of the estate has been ordered or before bankruptcy proceedings have been instituted against the estate, a creditor of the estate has set off his claim against a claim of the heir not forming part of the estate, without the latter's consent, then after the date of the order for administration or the institution of the bankruptcy proceedings the set-off is deemed not to have been effected.

The same rule applies if a creditor who is not a creditor of the estate has set

(*o*) See Bankruptcy Act, s. 226, par. 3.

(*p*) For exceptions, see 1994, par. 1, sentence 2; 2005, par. 1; 2013.

(*q*) Under sect. 225 of the Bankruptcy Act the heir may assert any claims which he has against the deceased.

off a claim which he has against the heir against a claim forming part of the estate.

1978. If administration of the estate has been ordered, or bankruptcy proceedings against the estate have been instituted, the heir is responsible to the creditors of the estate for the administration of the estate prior to the date of the order or bankruptcy proceedings just as if he had administered the estate on their behalf as a mandatory after the acceptance of the inheritance. The provisions relating to management of affairs without mandate apply *mutatis mutandis* to the affairs of the inheritance managed by the heir before its acceptance.

The claims which the creditors of the estate have under par. 1 are deemed to be part of the estate.

Any outlay incurred by the heir shall be reimbursed to him out of the estate in so far as he could claim reimbursement under the provisions relating to mandate or relating to management of affairs without mandate.

1979. The discharge of a liability of the estate by the heir is deemed, as against the creditors of the estate, to have been made on account of the estate if under the circumstance the heir might presume that the estate was sufficient for discharging all the liabilities of the estate.

1980. If the heir does not apply for the institution of bankruptcy proceedings against the estate without delay [r] after having had knowledge of the insolvency of the estate, he is responsible to the creditors for any damage arising therefrom. In determining the question of insolvency of the estate the obligations arising from legacies and testamentary burdens are not taken into consideration.

Ignorance due to negligence is equivalent to actual knowledge of insolvency. It is deemed to be negligence if, *e.g.*, the heir does not apply for a public summons of the creditors of the estate [s], although he has reason to believe in the existence of unknown liabilities of the estate; such public summons is not

---

(*r*) *I.e.*, without culpable delay. 121.

(*s*) See 1970 *et seq.*

necessary if the cost of the proceedings is disproportionate to the value of the estate [t].

1981. The administration of the estate shall be ordered by the Probate Court if the heir applies for such order.

Upon the application of a creditor of the estate the administration of the estate shall be ordered if there is reason to believe that satisfaction of the creditors of the estate out of the estate will be endangered by the conduct or pecuniary circumstances of the heir. The application may not be made after two years have elapsed since the acceptance of the inheritance [u].

The provisions of 1785 do not apply.

1982. The order for the administration of the estate may be refused if the assets are insufficient for the payment of costs.

1983. The Probate Court shall publish the order for the administration of the estate in the newspaper selected for the publication of its notices.

1984. Upon the issue of the order for the administration of the estate the heir loses his right to administer the estate and his right to dispose of it. The provisions of sects. 6 and 7 of the Bankruptcy Act apply *mutatis mutandis* [x]. A claim against the estate may be enforced in Court only against the administrator of the estate.

Compulsory execution or distraint on the estate in favour of a creditor who is not a creditor of the estate is not permitted [y].

1985. The administrator of the estate shall administer the estate, and shall discharge the liabilities of the estate out of the estate.

(*t*) See Bankruptcy Act, s. 228, par. 2.

(*u*) The heir may not be appointed administrator of the estate.

(*x*) These two sections of the Bankruptcy Act are now numbered 7 and 8 in the Revised Edition. Sect. 7 provides that juristic acts entered into by the heir after the issue of the decree for administration are invalid as against the creditors of the inheritance. Sect. 8 provides that any payment made to the heir by virtue of an obligation to be performed in favour of the estate is not valid as against creditors of the estate unless the assets of the estate are actually increased by such payment.

(*y*) See 784 of the Code of Civil Procedure.

The administrator is responsible even to the creditors of the estate for his administration of the estate. The provision of 1978, par. 2, and 1979, 1980, apply *mutatis mutandis* [(z)].

1986. The administrator cannot surrender the estate to the heir until the known liabilities of the estate have been discharged.

If the discharge of a liability is impracticable for the time being, or if it is contested, the surrender of the estate can be made only if security has been given to the creditor. Security need not be given for a conditional claim where the possibility of the fulfilment of the condition is so remote that the claim has no present money value.

1987. The administrator may claim a reasonable remuneration for acts done in the discharge of his office.

1988. The administration of the estate comes to an end on the institution of bankruptcy proceedings against the estate.

The administration of the estate may be terminated if it is apparent that the assets are insufficient for the payment of costs.

1989. If the bankruptcy proceedings against the estate have been terminated by the distribution of the estate or by the payment of a composition, the provisions of 1973 apply *mutatis mutandis* to the liability of the heir.

1990. Where an order for the administration of the estate or institution of bankruptcy proceedings may be refused by reason of the insufficiency of the assets for the payment of costs, or where the administration of the estate is terminated or the bankruptcy proceedings are discontinued [(a)] for such reason, the heir may refuse to satisfy a creditor of the estate in so far as the estate is insufficient for his satisfaction. In such a case the heir is bound to hand over the estate for the purpose of satisfying the creditor in compulsory execution proceedings.

This right of the heir is not barred by the fact that the creditor, after the

---

(*z*) An inventory period (1994) may not be fixed as against the administrator. 2012.

(*a*) On the "discontinuance" (*Einstellung*) of bankruptcy proceedings, see Bankruptcy Act, s. 204.

accrual of the inheritance, has acquired a right of pledge or a hypotheca by means of compulsory execution or distraint, or has acquired a caution by means of a provisional disposition [b].

1991. If the heir exercises the rights which he has under 1990, the provisions of 1978, 1979 apply to his liability and to the re-imbursement of outlay incurred.

The legal relations extinguished in consequence of the accrual of the inheritance by the merger of a right in an obligation or of a right in a charge are, as between the heir and the creditors, deemed not to have been extinguished [c].

A non-appellable decree directing the heir to satisfy a creditor has, as against another creditor, the same effect as satisfaction itself.

The heir shall perform all obligations arising from rights to compulsory portions, legacies and testamentary burdens just as if they had been presented for performance in the case of bankruptcy proceedings.

1992. If the insolvency of the estate is due to legacies and testamentary burdens, the heir is, even though the conditions specified in 1990 have not occurred, entitled to perform such obligations in accordance with the provisions of 1990, 1991. He may refuse to hand over any existing objects belonging to the estate by payment of their value [d].

IV. The Filing of an Inventory. Unlimited Liability of an Heir.

1993. An heir is entitled to file an inventory of the estate (*i.e.*, inventory) with the Probate Court (*i.e.*, the filing of an inventory).

1994. The Probate Court shall, upon the application of a creditor of the estate, fix a period for the heir to file the inventory (*i.e.*, inventory period). After the expiration of the period the heir is liable without limitation for the liabilities of the estate unless an inventory has been filed within such period.

(*b*) See 883, 884.

(*c*) See note (*q*) to 1976.

(*d*) This provision is similar to that contained in 1973, par. 2.

The applicant shall offer *primâ facie* proof of his claim. The validity of the fixing of the period is not affected by the fact that the claim proves to be non-existent.

1995. The inventory period should not be less than one month nor more than three months. It begins to run from the time of the service of the order fixing the period.

If the period has been fixed before acceptance of the inheritance, it does not begin to run until acceptance of the inheritance.

The Probate Court may, upon the application of the heir, extend the period at its discretion.

1996. If the heir has been prevented by *vis major* from filing the inventory in due time, or from applying for extension of the inventory period, which he is justified in doing under the circumstances, the Probate Court shall, upon his application, fix a new inventory period. The same rule applies if the heir, without any fault on his part, has no knowledge of the service of the order fixing the inventory period.

The application must be filed within two weeks after the removal of the preventing cause, and at the latest before the expiration of one year after the lapse of the period originally fixed [(e)].

Before giving any decision the Probate Court should, if possible, hear the creditor of the estate upon whose application the original period has been fixed.

1997. The provisions of 203, par. 1, and 206, applicable to prescription, apply *mutatis mutandis* to the running of the inventory period and of the period of two weeks specified in 1996, par. 2.

1998. If the heir dies before the expiration of the inventory period or the period of two weeks specified in 1996, par. 2, the period does not expire before the lapse of the period fixed for disclaimer of the inheritance by the heir.

1999. If the heir is under parental power or guardianship, the Probate Court should communicate the fixing of the inventory period to the Guardianship

(*e*) See 234 of the Code of Civil Procedure.

Court.

2000. The fixing of an inventory period is ineffective where administration of the estate has been ordered or bankruptcy proceedings against the estate have been instituted. During the continuance of the administration or of the bankruptcy proceedings an inventory period may not be fixed. If the bankruptcy proceedings have been terminated by the distribution of the estate or by the payment of a composition, the filing of an inventory is not required for terminating the unlimited liability.

2001. The objects belonging to the estate existing at the time of the accrual of the inheritance and the liabilities of the estate (*f*) should be fully stated in the inventory.

The inventory should contain a description of the objects belonging to the estate, where such description is necessary for determining their value, and also a statement of their value.

2002. The heir must call in the assistance of a competent public authority, or a competent official, or a notary for making the inventory (*g*).

2003. The Probate Court shall, upon the application of the heir, either make the inventory itself or instruct a competent public authority, a competent official, or a notary to make it. Presentation of the application is deemed to be the observance of the inventory period.

The heir is bound to give any information necessary for making the inventory.

The inventory shall be filed with the Probate Court by such public authority, official, or notary.

2004. If the Probate Court has already in its possession an inventory which complies with the requirements of 2002, 2003, it is sufficient if the heir declares to the Probate Court before the expiration of the inventory period that

---

(*f*) Including all liabilities which have been incurred after the accrual of the inheritance, *e.g.*, the funeral expenses of the deceased.

(*g*) The cost of the inventory is borne by the estate. Bankruptcy Act, s. 224 (4).

such inventory shall be valid as though it had been filed by him.

2005. If the heir has intentionally caused any serious omission in the statement of the objects belonging to the estate contained in the inventory, or if he causes any non-existent liability of the estate to be included in the inventory with the intention of injuring the creditors of the estate, he is liable without limitation for the liabilities of the estate. The same rule applies if he refuses or intentionally delays in a serious manner to give the information in the case provided for by 2003.

If the statement of the objects belonging to the estate is incomplete under circumstances other than those specified in par. 1, a new inventory period [(h)] may be fixed for the heir to complete the inventory.

2006. The heir shall, on demand by a creditor of the estate swear an oath of disclosure [(i)] in the Probate Court to the effect:

> that he, according to the best of his knowledge, has stated the objects belonging to the estate as completely as he was in a position to do.

The heir may complete the inventory before swearing such oath.

If the heir refuses to swear such oath, he is liable without limitation to the creditor who has made the application. The same rule applies if he does not appear on the day fixed for appearance nor on the day fixed upon the application of the creditor, unless there is a sufficient excuse for non-appearance on the fixed day.

A repetition of such oath may be required by the same or another creditor only if there is reason to suspect that other assets of the estate have become known to the heir after the swearing of the oath.

2007. If an heir is entitled to several shares in the inheritance [(k)], his liability for the liabilities of the estate in respect of each of the shares is determined just as if the shares belonged to different heirs. In cases of the right of

---

(*h*) This provisions of 1994—2000 are applicable to such period.

(*i*) As to its procedure, see sect. 79 of the Voluntary Jurisdiction Act.

(*k*) 1951.

accrual [l] and in those provided for by 1935 this applies only where the shares are unequally charged.

2008. If a married woman becomes heiress, and if the inheritance forms part of her contributed property or common property, the fixing of an inventory period is effective only if it is made to affect her husband also. So long as the period has not expired as against the husband, it does not expire as against the wife. The filing of an inventory by the husband is also available in favour of the wife.

If the inheritance forms part of the common property, these provisions apply even after the dissolution of the community of goods.

2009. If the inventory has been filed in due time, it is presumed, as between the heir and the creditors of the estate, that at the time of the accrual of the inheritance there were no other assets of the estate than those stated in the inventory [m].

2010. The Probate Court shall permit any person to inspect the inventory, provided that he can offer *primâ facie* proof that he has a legal interest therein.

2011. An inventory period may not be fixed as against the Treasury as statutory heir. The Treasury is bound to give to the Probate Court any information relating to the condition of the estate.

2012. An inventory period may not be fixed as against a curator of an estate appointed under 1960, 1961. A curator of an estate is bound as towards the creditors of the estate to give any information relating to the condition of the estate. The curator of the estate may not waive the limitation of the liability of the heir.

These provisions apply also to an administrator of an estate.

2013. If an heir is liable without limitation for the liability of an estate, the provisions of 1973 to 1975, 1977 to 1980, 1989 to 1992 do not apply; the

---

(*l*) 2094, 2095.

(*m*) The presumption is rebuttable.

heir is not entitled to apply for an order for the administration of the estate (n). The heir may, however, avail himself of any limitation of his liability arising under 1973 or 1974, if the case provided for by 1994, par. 1, sentence 2, or 2005, par. 1, arises subsequently.

The provisions of 1977 to 1980 and the right of an heir to apply for an order for the administration of the estate are not barred by the fact that he is liable without limitation to some creditors of the estate.

V. Dilatory Pleas.

2014. An heir is entitled to refuse the discharge of a liability of the estate before the expiration of three months after the acceptance of the inheritance, but not after the date of the filing of an inventory (o).

2015. If the heir has presented his application for the issue of a public summons to the creditors of the estate within one year after the acceptance of the inheritance, and if the application is allowed, the heir is entitled to refuse the discharge of a liability of the estate until the termination of the proceedings of the public summons.

It is equivalent to termination of the proceeding of the public summons if the heir does not appear on the day fixed by the public summons, and does not within two weeks apply for the fixing of another day, or if he does not appear on such other day.

If the decree of exclusion is issued, or the application for the issue of such decree is rejected, the proceedings are not deemed to have been terminated before the expiration of a period of two weeks since the publication of the decree, nor before the decision of any appeal taken within the prescribed period.

2016. The provisions of 2014, 2015 do not apply where the heir is liable without limitation.

The same rule applies, in so far as a creditor is not affected by a public

(n) Cf. 1975.

(o) A claim based upon 1969 is not deemed to be a "liability of the estate" within the meaning of this provision.

summons to the creditors of the estate as provided in 1971, with the result that any right acquired after the accrual of the inheritance by means of compulsory execution or distraint, and any caution acquired by means of a provisional decree after that time are not taken into consideration [(p)].

2017. If a curator of an estate has been appointed to administer the estate after the acceptance of the inheritance, the periods specified in 2014 and 2015, par. 1, begin to run from the time of such appointment [(q)].

THIRD TITLE.
Petitio Hereditatis.

2018. The heir may require any person to return to him whatever [(r)] the latter has acquired out of the inheritance by virtue of an alleged right of inheritance to which he in fact is not entitled (a possessor of the inheritance).

2019. Whatever the possessor of the inheritance acquires through a juristic act by means of the inheritance is also deemed to be acquired out of the inheritance.

The fact that a claim acquired in this manner forms part of the inheritance is not available against the debtor until he has knowledge of such fact; the provisions of 406 to 408 apply *mutatis mutandis*.

2020. The possessor of the inheritance shall surrender to the heir all the emoluments drawn by him; the obligation to make such surrender extends also to fruits the ownership of which he has acquired.

2021. In so far as the possessor of the inheritance is not in a position to make such surrender, his obligation is determined according to the provisions relating to the return of unjustified benefits.

(*p*) Cf. 1990, par. 2.

(*q*) The curator may also set up any plea which is available to an heir as provided for by 2014, 2015.

(*r*) *I.e.*, whether it be *res corporales* or *res incorporales* makes no difference.

2022. The possessor of the inheritance is bound to surrender the things forming part of the inheritance only upon reimbursement of all outlay incurred upon them, in so far as such outlay is not covered by setting off the benefits to be returned under 2021. The provisions of 1000 to 1003, applicable to claims arising from ownership, apply *mutatis mutandis*.

Outlay includes also any expenses incurred by the possessor of the inheritance for the payment of charges upon the inheritance or for the purpose of the discharge of any liabilities of the estate.

In so far as the heir, in respect of the outlay which has been incurred not upon individual objects, *e.g.*, the outlay specified in par. 2, has to make reimbursement thereof to a greater extent under the general provisions than under these provisions, the claim of the possessor of the inheritance under the general provisions remains unaffected.

2023. If the possessor of the inheritance has to surrender things forming part of the inheritance, the claim of the heir for compensation for the damage or destruction of the things or the impossibility of returning them arising from any other cause is, after the date of action commenced, determined according to the provisions which apply to the legal relations between an owner and a possessor after the date of action commence on a claim of ownership [(s)].

The same rule applies to the claim of the heir for the surrender of or compensation for emoluments, and to the claims of the possessor of the inheritance for reimbursement of outlay incurred [(t)].

2024. If the possessor of the inheritance was in bad faith at the time of possession of the inheritance, he is liable just as if action on the claim of the heir were commenced at such time. If the possessor of the inheritance subsequently learns that he is not an heir, he is liable in the same manner after he has acquired such knowledge. Any further liability on account of default [(u)] remains unaffected.

(*s*) See 989 *et seq.*

(*t*) A *malâ fide* possessor may only claim reimbursement of necessary outlay incurred by him under the provisions relating to management of affairs without mandate. 677 *et seq.*

(*u*) See 284, 285.

2025. If the possessor of the inheritance has acquired an object belonging to the inheritance by a criminal act, or has acquired a thing forming part of the inheritance by unlawful interference, he is liable under the provisions relating to compensation for unlawful acts. A *bonâ fide* possessor of the inheritance is, however, liable for unlawful interference under those provisions only if the heir had already attained actual possession of the thing [(x)].

2026. So long as the *petitio hereditatis* is not barred by prescription, the possessor of the inheritance may not, as against the heir, avail himself of the usucapion of a thing which he has in his possession as part of the inheritance.

2027. The possessor of the inheritance is bound to give to the heir any information respecting the condition of the inheritance and the place where the objects belonging to the inheritance may be found.

The same obligation is imposed upon any person who, without being a possessor of the inheritance, takes possession of a thing out of the estate before the heir has attained actual possession of such thing.

2028. Any person who was a member of the deceased's household at the time of the accrual of the inheritance, is bound to give to the heir, on demand, any information as to which of the affairs of the inheritance he has managed, and the place, if known to him, where the objects belonging to the inheritance may be found.

If there is reason to suspect that the information has not been given with the necessary care, the person bound shall, on demand by the heir, swear an oath of disclosure to the effect:

> that he, according to the best of his knowledge, has made the statement as completely as he was in a position to do.

The provisions of 259, par. 3, and 261 apply.

2029. The liability of a possessor of an inheritance [(y)] is, even as against the claims which the heir has in respect of the individual objects belonging to

---

(*x*) An exception to 857.

(*y*) Whether *bonâ fide* or *malâ fide* makes no difference.

the inheritance, determined according to the provisions relating to claims arising from ownership.

2030. Any person who acquires an inheritance by contract with a possessor of the inheritance is, as against the heir, in the same position as a possessor of the inheritance.

2031. If a person declared to be dead survives the date which is deemed to be the date of his death, he may demand the return of his property under the provisions applicable to *petitio hereditatis*. So long as the person declared dead is still living, the prescription of his claim is not complete until the lapse of one year after the time at which he has knowledge of the declaration of death.

The same rule applies, where the death of a person has been erroneously assumed without a declaration of death [z].

FOURTH TITLE.
Plurality of Heirs.

I. Legal Relations between the Heirs "Inter se".

2032. If the deceased leaves several heirs, the estate becomes the common property of the heirs.

Before partition the provisions of 2033 to 2041 apply.

2033. Each co-heir may dispose of his share in the estate. A contract whereby a co-heir disposes of his share requires judicial or notarial authentication.

A co-heir may not dispose of his share in the individual objects belonging to the estate.

2034. If a co-heir sells his share to a third party, the other co-heirs are entitled to pre-emption [a].

(z) *E.g.*, where a dead body has been erroneously identified.

(a) The right of pre-emption belongs to the other heirs *jointly*. On the exercise of this right, see 504 *et seq*.

The period for the exercise of the right of pre-emption is three months. The right of pre-emption passes by inheritance.

2035. If the share sold has been transferred to the purchaser, the co-heirs may, as against the purchaser, exercise the right of pre-emption which they have as against the seller under 2034. The right of pre-emption as against the seller is extinguished on the transfer of the share.

The seller shall without delay notify the co-heirs of the transfer [(b)].

2036. Upon the transfer of the share to the co-heirs the purchaser is discharged from his liability for the liabilities of the estate. His liability continues, however, to exist in so far as he is responsible to the creditors of the estate under 1978 to 1980; the provisions of 1990, 1991, apply *mutatis mutandis.*

2037. If the purchaser transfers the share to a third party, the provision of 2033, 2035, 2036, apply *mutatis mutandis.*

2038. The right to administer the estate belongs to the heirs in common. Each co-heir is bound as towards the others to concur in all measures which are necessary for the proper administration of the estate; each co-heir may take any measures necessary for the preservation of the estate even without the concurrence of the others.

The provisions of 743, 745, 746, 748, apply. No distribution of fruits is made until partition of the estate. If partition is excluded for a longer period than one year [(c)], each co-heir may demand distribution of net profits at the end of each year.

2039. If a claim forms part of the estate, the person bound may perform his obligation only in favour of all the heirs jointly, and each co-heir may demand performance only in favour of all the heirs. Each co-heir may require the person bound to lodge, for the benefit of all the heirs, the thing to be delivered, or, where the thing is not suitable to be lodged, to deliver it to a custodian appointed by the Court.

(*b*) 510, par. 1, is applicable.

(*c*) Cf. 2044.

2040. The heirs may dispose of an object belonging to the estate only in common.

A debtor may not set off a claim which he has against a single co-heir against a claim forming part of the estate.

2041. Whatever is acquired by virtue of a right forming part of the estate, or as compensation for the destruction, damage, or deprivation of an object belonging to the estate, or by a juristic act relating to the estate, forms part of the estate. The provision of 2019, par. 2, applies to any claim acquired by such a juristic act.

2042. Each co-heir may demand partition at any time except in so far as a contrary intention appears from 2043 to 2045.

The provisions of 749, pars. 2, 3, and 750 to 758 apply.

2043. In so far as the shares in the inheritance are not yet determined on account of the expected birth of a co-heir [(d)], partition is excluded until the uncertainty is removed.

The same rule applies in so far as the shares in the inheritance are not yet determined because a decision on a declaration of legitimation, or on the confirmation of adoption, or on the ratification of a foundation established by the deceased, is still pending.

2044. The deceased may by testamentary disposition exclude partition in respect of the estate or the individual objects belonging to the estate, or make it dependent upon the observance of a period after notice. The provisions of 749, pars. 2, 3, 750, 751, and 1010, par. 1, apply *mutatis mutandis*.

The disposition is ineffective if thirty years have elapsed since the accrual of the inheritance. The deceased may, however, direct that the disposition is to be effective until the occurrence of a certain event with reference to one of the co-heirs, or, where he has created any reversionary succession or legacy, until the occurrence of reversionary succession or the devolution of the legacy. If the co-heir with reference to whom the event is to occur is a juristic person, a

---

(*d*) Cf. 1963.

period of thirty years is to be observed.

2045. Each co-heir may demand that partition be suspended until the termination of the proceedings by public summons permitted by 1970, or until the expiration of the period for presentation specified in 2061. If public summons has not yet been applied for, or if public citation under 2061 has not yet been issued, the suspension may be demanded only if the application has been made or the citation has been issued without delay.

2046. The liabilities of the estate shall be first discharged out of the estate. If a liability of the estate is not yet due or is contested, whatever is necessary for the discharge of the liability shall be retained [(e)].

If a liability of the estate is borne by only some of the co-heirs, such liability may be discharged only out of what accrues to them at the time of partition.

The estate shall, as far as necessary, be converted into money for the discharge of its liabilities.

2047. After the discharge of the liabilities of the estate the residue accrues to the heirs in proportion to their shares in the inheritance.

Documents relating to the personal affairs of the deceased, or to his family, or to the whole estate, remain the joint property of the co-heirs [(f)].

2048. The deceased may give directions as to partition in a testamentary disposition. He may, *e.g.*, direct that partition shall be effected by a third party in an equitable manner. Any decision given by such third party by virtue of the direction is not binding upon the heirs, if it is evidently inequitable; in such a case the decision is given by judicial decree.

2049. If the deceased has directed that one of the co-heirs shall have the right to appropriate any farm forming part of the estate, it is to be presumed, in case of doubt, that the farm shall be assessed at the value of its products [(g)].

(*e*) This provision applies only as between the co-heirs *inter se*. As between the co-heirs and the creditors of the estate the provisions of 2058 *et seq.* apply.

(*f*) The provisions of 745 are applicable to this case.

(*g*) See IA, Art. 137.

The value of the products is determined by the permanent net profits which may be derived from the farm consistently with its former economic purpose, in accordance with the rules of proper husbandry.

2050. Descendants who succeed to the inheritance as statutory heirs are mutually bound, at the time of partition (h), to bring into hotchpot whatever they have received from the deceased by way of advancement during the letter's lifetime, unless the deceased has direct of otherwise at the time of making the advancement.

Additional payments made for the purpose of being used as income, and expenses incurred in the preparation for a profession shall be brought into hotchpot in so far as they exceed a reasonable amount of the property of the deceased.

Other gifts made *inter vivos* shall be brought into hotchpot if the deceased has so directed at the date of making the gifts.

2051. If any descendant, who would have been subject to the hotchpot liability in the capacity of heir, fails to inherit before or after the accrual of the inheritance, the descendant who takes his place is bound to bring into hotchpot the gifts which he has received.

If the deceased has appointed a substitutional heir for a descendant who fails to inherit, it is to be presumed, in case of doubt, that such substitutional heir shall receive no more than such descendant would receive, having regard to his hotchpot liability.

2052. If the deceased has appointed his descendants as heirs for the shares which they would receive as statutory heirs, or if he has fixed their shares in the inheritance in such a manner that they stand, as between themselves, in the same relation as in the case of statutory succession, it is to be presumed, in case of doubt, that such descendants shall be subject to hotchpot liability as provided in 2050, 2051.

2053. If a descendant of remoter degree has received a gift from the deceased

(*h*) The hotchpot liability lapses after the partition is complete.

before failure to inherit on the part of a descendant of nearer degree who excludes such remoter descendant from statutory succession, or if a descendant who takes the place of another descendant as substitutional heir has received any gift from the deceased, such gift shall not be brought into hotchpot, unless the deceased has otherwise directed at the time of making the gift.

The same rule applies where a descendant, before acquiring the legal status of a descendant, has received a gift from the deceased.

2054. A gift made out of the common property under the *régime* of general community of goods, or community of income and profits, or community of moveables, is deemed to have been made by both spouses in equal shares. If, however, a gift is made to a descendant who is descended from one only of the spouses, or if one of the spouses has to make compensation to the common property on account of a gift, such gift is deemed to have been made by such spouse alone.

These provisions apply *mutatis mutandis* to a gift made out of the common property under the *régime* of continued community of goods.

2055. At the time of partition each co-heir shall deduct, from his share in the inheritance, the value of any gift which he is bound to bring into hotchpot. The value of all the gifts which are liable to be brought into hotchpot shall be added to the estate, in so far as the estate accrues to the co-heirs who are subject to the hotchpot liability.

The value is determined as at the date of the gifts.

2056. If a co-heir, through any gift made to him, has received more than he would receive at the time of partition, he is not bound to surrender the amount in excess. In such a case the estate is distributed among the other heirs, no regard being paid to the value of such co-heir's gift and his share in the inheritance.

2057. Each co-heir is bound on demand to give to the other co-heirs all information as to any gifts which he is bound to bring into hotchpot, as provided for in 2050 to 2053. The provisions of 260, 261, relating to the obligation to swear an oath of disclosure, apply *mutatis mutandis*.

II. Legal Relations between the Heirs and the Creditors of the Estate.

2058. The heirs are liable as joint debtors for the common liabilities of the estate.

2059. Before distribution of the estate each co-heir may refuse to discharge the liabilities of the estate out of any property which he has in addition to his share in the estate [(i)]. If he is liable without limitation for a liability of the estate, he does not have this right in respect of his share in the liability proportional to his share in the inheritance.

The right of the creditors of the estate to demand satisfaction from all the co-heirs out of the undistributed estate remains unaffected.

2060. After the distribution of the estate each co-heir is liable for his share in a liability of the estate in proportion of his share in the inheritance:

(1) if the creditor has been excluded by public summons [(k)]; the Procedure by public summons extends also to the creditors specified in 1972, and to the creditors to whom the co-heir is liable without limitation [(l)];

(2) if the creditor enforces his claim after five years since the time specified in 1974, par. 1, unless the claim has become known to the co-heir before the expiration of the five years, or has been presented in the proceedings by public summons; this provision does not apply in so far as the creditor is not affected by the public summons as provided for in 1971;

(3) if bankruptcy proceedings have been instituted against the estate, and have been terminated by the distribution of the estate or by the payment of a composition [(m)].

2061. Each co-heir may issue a public citation to the creditors of the estate

---

(*i*) *I.e.*, out of his private property.

(*k*) See 1973, 2015.

(*l*) 2006, 2013.

(*m*) 1975, 1989.

to present their claims to him or to the Probate Court within six months [n]. Where such citation has been issued, each co-heir is, after the distribution of the estate, liable only for his share in the claim proportional to his share in the inheritance, unless presentation is made before the expiration of the prescribed period, or the claim has become known to him at the time of the distribution.

The public citation shall be published in the *Deutscher Reichsanzeiger* [o], and in the newspaper selected for the publication of the notices of the Probate Court. The prescribed period begins to run from the date of the last insertion. The costs are borne by the heir who issues the citation.

2062. An order for the administration of the estate may be applied for only by the heirs jointly [p]; it may not be issued after the estate has been distributed.

2063. The filing of an inventory by one co-heir avails also in favour of the other co-heirs, unless their liability for the liabilities of the estate is unlimited.

A co-heir may, as against the other co-heirs, avail himself of his limitation of liability even if he is liable without limitation as against the other creditors of the estate [q].

THIRD SECTION.
WILLS.

FIRST TITLE.
General Provisions.

2064. A person may make a will only in person.

2065. The testator may not make a testamentary disposition in such a manner

---

(*n*) Unlike the case provided for by 1970 *et seq.*, the public citation is not issued by the Court but by the co-heir himself.

(*o*) *I.e.*, German Imperial Gazette.

(*p*) 1981.

(*q*) As between themselves *inter se*, co-heirs have always the privilege of limited liability.

that another person has to determine whether it is or is not to be operative.

The testator may not leave to another person the designation of the person who is to receive a testamentary gift nor the selection of the object to be given to a testamentary beneficiary.

2066. If a testator has made a testamentary gift to his statutory heirs without any further direction, the persons who would be his statutory heirs at the time of the accrual of the inheritance are entitled to the gift in proportion to their statutory portions. If the gift is made subject to a condition precedent, or is made to be operative from a given day, and if the condition has not been fulfilled or the day has not arrived until after the accrual of the inheritance, the persons who would have been statutory heirs if the testator had died at the time of the fulfilment of the condition or the arrival of the day are deemed, in case of doubt, to be entitled to the gift.

2067. If a testator has made a testamentary gift to his relatives by blood, or to his nearest relatives by blood without any further direction, the relatives by blood who would be his statutory heirs at the time of the accrual of the inheritance are, in case of doubt, deemed to be entitled to the gift in proportion to their statutory portions. The provision of 2066, sentence 2, applies.

2068. If a testator has made a testamentary gift to his children without any further direction, and if a child has died leaving descendants before the making of the will, it is to be presumed, in case of doubt, that the descendants are entitled to the gift in so far as they would take the place of such child in the case of statutory succession.

2069. If a testator has made a testamentary gift to one of his descendants, and if the latter fails to receive the gift after the making of the will, it is to be presumed, in case of doubt, that the latter's descendants are entitled to the gift in so far as they would take the latter's place in the case of statutory succession.

2070. If a testator has made a testamentary gift to the descendants of a third party without any further direction, it is to be presumed, in case of doubt, that the descendants are not entitled to the gift who were not yet conceived at the time of the accrual of the inheritance, or, where the gift has been made subject to a condition precedent or has been made to become operative from a given day, and the condition has not been fulfilled or the given day has not arrived until after the accrual of the inheritance, then at the time of the fulfilment of the condition or the arrival of the day.

2071. If a testator has made a testamentary gift to a certain class of persons or to certain persons without any further direction, who stand in service relation or business relation with him, it is to be presumed, in case of doubt, that the persons who belonged to the specified class or who stood in the specified relation at the time of the accrual of the inheritance are entitled to the gift.

2072. If a testator has made a testamentary gift to the poor without any further direction, it is to be presumed, in case of doubt, that the public poor relief fund of the commune in whose district he was last domiciled is entitled to take the gift subject to the testamentary burden to distribute it among the poor.

2073. If a testator has designated the testamentary beneficiary in such a manner that the designation applies to several persons, and if it cannot be ascertained which of them is to receive the testamentary gift, they are deemed to be entitled to the gift in equal shares.

2074. If a testator has made a testamentary gift subject to a condition precedent, it is to be presumed, in case of doubt, that the gift is to be operative only if the beneficiary survives the fulfilment of the condition [(r)].

2075. If a testator has made a testamentary gift subject to the condition that the beneficiary shall forbear from or continue to do some act during a period of uncertain length, and if the forbearance or the act depends entirely on the free will of the beneficiary, it is to be presumed, in case of doubt, that the gift is made subject to the condition subsequent that the beneficiary does or forbears from doing the act.

2076. If a testamentary gift is made subject to a condition which is

---

(*r*) If the condition has been fulfilled before the death of the testator, the legatee must have also survived the testator.

intended for the benefit of a third party, the condition is, in case of doubt, deemed to have been fulfilled, if the third party refuses the concurrence necessary for the fulfilment of the condition.

2077. A testamentary disposition whereby a testator has made a testamentary gift to his spouse, is inoperative, if the marriage is void, or if it has been dissolved before the death of the testator. It is equivalent to the dissolution or the marriage, if the testator was entitled, at the time of his death, to petition for divorce by reason of the fault of the other spouse, and had filed a petition for divorce or judicial separation.

A testamentary disposition whereby a testator has made a testamentary gift to his betrothed, is inoperative if the betrothal has ceased before the death of the testator.

The disposition is not ineffective if it is to be presumed that the testator would have made it even though such a case had occurred.

2078. A testamentary disposition may be avoided in so far as the testator was under a mistake as to the purport of his declaration, or did not intend to make a declaration of that purport at all, and in so far as it is to be presumed that he would not have made the declaration if he had known of the state of affairs.

The same rule applies in so far as the testator has been influenced to make the disposition by the erroneous assumption or expectation of the occurrence or non-occurrence of a circumstance, or unlawfully by threats.

The provisions of 122 do not apply.

2079. A testamentary disposition may be avoided if the testator has passed over a compulsory beneficiary [(s)] living at the time of the accrual of the inheritance, whose existence was not known to him at the time of the making of the disposition, or who has been born or has become compulsory beneficiary after the making of the disposition [(t)]. The right of avoidance is barred in so far as it is to be presumed that the testator would have made the disposition even if he

---

(*s*) 2303.

(*t*) Such a person may be the wife married to, or a child legitimated or adopted by the testator after the making of the disposition.

had known of the state of affairs.

2080. The person is entitled to avoid the disposition who would directly benefit by the revocation of the testamentary disposition.

If, in the cases provided for by 2078, the mistake relates only to a particular person, and if such person is entitled to avoid or would have been entitled to avoid if he had been living at the time of the accrual of the inheritance, no other person is entitled to avoid the disposition.

In the case provided for by 2079, the right of avoidance belongs only to the compulsory beneficiary.

2081. The avoidance of a testamentary disposition whereby an heir is appointed, or a statutory heir is excluded from succession, or an executor is nominated, or a disposition of such kind is revoked, is made by declaration to the Probate Court.

The Probate Court should communicate the declaration of avoidance to the person who benefits directly by the avoided disposition. The Probate Court shall permit any person to inspect the declaration, provided that he can offer *primâ facie* proof that he has a legal interest therein.

The provision of par. 1 applies also to the avoidance of a testamentary disposition whereby a right is not created in favour of another person, *e.g.*, the avoidance of a testamentary burden.

2082. The avoidance may be made only within the period of one year.

The period begins to run from the time at which the person entitled to avoid has knowledge of the ground for avoidance.

The provisions of 203, 206, 207, applicable to prescription, apply *mutatis mutandis* to the running of the period.

The right of avoidance is barred if thirty years have elapsed since the accrual of the inheritance.

2083. If a testamentary disposition whereby the obligation to perform an act is created [(*u*)], is voidable, the person under such obligation may refuse

(*u*) Such act may be either the giving of a legacy or the execution of a testamentary burden.

performance even if the right of avoidance is barred by 2082.

2084. If the purport of a testamentary disposition admits of several interpretations, in case of doubt the interpretation according to which the disposition is to be operative shall be preferred.

2085. The invalidity of one of several dispositions contained in a will does not result in the invalidity of the other dispositions, unless it is to be presumed that the testator would not have made such other dispositions if the first invalid disposition had been omitted.

2086. If the right to make a supplementary disposition is reserved in a testamentary disposition, and if the supplementary disposition has not been made, the disposition is valid, unless it is to be presumed that its validity was intended to be made dependent upon the supplementary disposition.

SECOND TITLE.
Appointment of Heirs.

2087. If a testator has bequeathed his property or an aliquot part of his property to a beneficiary, the disposition is deemed to be the appointment of an heir even if the beneficiary has not been named as an heir.

If particular objects only have been given to the beneficiary, it is not to be presumed, in case of doubt, that he is to be an heir, even if he has been named as an heir.

2088. If a testator has appointed only one heir, and if the appointment is limited to an aliquot part of the inheritance, statutory succession takes place in respect of the other parts.

The same rule applies, if the testator has appointed several heirs with a limitation of each to an aliquot part, and the parts do not exhaust the whole inheritance.

2089. If it was the intention of the testator that the appointed heirs shall become sole heirs, and if each of them has been appointed for an aliquot part of the inheritance and their aliquot parts do not exhaust the whole inheritance, each part shall be increased proportionally.

2090. If each of the appointed heirs has been appointed for an aliquot part of the inheritance, and if the parts exceed the whole inheritance, each part shall be diminished proportionally.

2091. If several heirs have been appointed without their respective shares in the inheritance being specified, they are appointed for equal shares, unless a contrary intention appears from 2066 to 2069.

2092. If, of several heirs, some have been appointed for several aliquot parts while the others have been appointed without any aliquot parts, the latter shall receive the remaining part of the inheritance.

If the specified aliquot parts exhaust the whole inheritance, each part shall be proportionately reduced in such manner that each of the heirs appointed without any aliquot parts shall receive a part equal to the smallest aliquot part expressly given by the will.

2093. If, of several heirs, some have been instituted for one and the same aliquot part of the inheritance (*i.e.*, a joint share in the inheritance), the provisions of 2089 to 2092 apply *mutatis mutandis* to such joint share in the inheritance.

2094. If several heirs have been appointed in such manner that statutory succession is excluded, and if one of the heirs fails to inherit before or after the accrual of the inheritance, his share accrues to the other heirs in proportion to their respective shares in the inheritance. If some of the heirs have been appointed for a joint share, such accrual takes place among them in the first instance.

If a part only of the inheritance is disposed of by the appointment of several heirs, and if statutory succession takes place in respect of the other part, such accrual takes place among the appointed heirs only in so far as they have been appointed for a joint share.

The testator may exclude the right of accrual.

2095. The share in an inheritance devolving upon an heir by virtue of the right of accrual is deemed to be a separate share in respect of all legacies and testamentary burdens with which such heir or the heir failing to inherit is charged, and also in respect of the hotchpot liability.

2096. A testator may provide for the case where an heir fails to inherit before or after the accrual of the inheritance by appointing another person as heir (*i.e.*, a substitutional heir).

2097. If any person has been appointed substitutional heir for the case where the heir entitled to inherit in the first instance cannot become an heir, or for the case where he will not be an heir, it is to be presumed, in case of doubt, that he has been appointed for both cases.

2098. If several heirs have been appointed as mutual substitutional heirs, or if in respect of one of them the others have been appointed substitutional heirs, it is to be presumed, in case of doubt, that they have been instituted substitutional heirs in proportion to their shares in the inheritance.

If several heirs have been appointed mutual substitutional heirs, the heirs who have been appointed for a joint share take precedence, in case of doubt, to the others in their capacity of substitutional heir for such joint share.

2099. The right of a substitutional heir takes priority to the right of accrual.

THIRD TITLE.
Appointment of Reversionary Heirs.

2100. A testator may appoint an heir in such manner that the latter does not become an heir until after another person has previously become an heir (*i.e.*, a reversionary heir) (x).

2101. If a person has been appointed heir who was not conceived at the

(x) The distinction between a reversionary heir and a substitutional heir (2096) lies in the fact that the former becomes an heir only if another person has previously become an heir; while the latter does not become an heir if another person has previously become an heir.

time of the accrual of the inheritance, it is to be presumed, in case of doubt, that he has been appointed reversionary heir. If it was not the intention of the testator that the appointed person should be reversionary heir, the appointment is of no effect.

The same rule applies to the appointment as heir of a juristic person who has not come into being until after the accrual of the inheritance; the provision of 84 remains unaffected.

2102. The appointment of a person as reversionary heir results, in case of doubt, also in the appointment of such person as substitutional heir.

If it is doubtful whether a person has been appointed substitutional heir or reversionary heir, he is deemed to have been appointed substitutional heir.

2103. If the deceased has directed the heir to surrender the inheritance to another person on the arrival of a certain time or the occurrence of a certain event, it is to be presumed that such other person has been appointed reversionary heir.

2104. If the deceased has directed that the heir shall be heir only until the arrival of a certain time or the occurrence of a certain event without specifying who is to receive the inheritance ultimately, it is to be presumed that the persons have been appointed reversionary heirs who would have become the statutory heirs of the deceased if he had died at the arrival of the time or on the occurrence of the event. The Treasury is not a statutory heir within the meaning of this provision.

2105. If the deceased has directed that the appointed heir shall not receive the inheritance until the arrival of a certain time or the occurrence of a certain event without specifying who is to be heir in the meantime, then the statutory heirs of the deceased become limited heirs.

The same rule applies where the identity of the heir is to be determined by an event occurring after the accrual of the inheritance, or where a person, not conceived at the time of the accrual of the inheritance, or a juristic person not having come into being at that time, has been appointed heir, but is deemed to have been appointed only as reversionary heir under 2101.

2106. If the deceased has appointed a reversionary heir without specifying any time or event, after which the reversionary succession is to take place, the inheritance devolves upon the reversionary heir on the death of the limited heir.

If the appointment as heir of a person not yet conceived is deemed to be the appointment of a reversionary heir under 2101, par. 1, the inheritance devolves upon such reversionary heir at his birth. In the case provided for by 2101, par. 2, the devolution takes place on the coming into being of the juristic person.

2107. If the deceased has named a reversionary heir to act as such on the death of a descendant who, at the time of the making of a testamentary disposition, had no descendant, or had a descendant unknown to the deceased at that time, it is to be presumed that the reversionary heir has been appointed only for the case where the deceased's descendant dies without issue.

2108. The provisions of 1923 apply *mutatis mutandis* to reversionary succession.

If the appointed reversionary heir dies before an occasion arises for reversionary succession, but after the accrual of the inheritance, his right passes to his heirs, unless a contrary intention of the testator is to be inferred. If the reversionary heir has been appointed subject to a condition precedent, the provision of 2074 applies.

2109. The appointment of a reversionary heir becomes inoperative after the lapse of thirty years since the accrual of the inheritance, unless an occasion for reversionary succession has arisen within such period. Even after the lapse of such period the appointment remains operative:

(1) if the reversionary succession has been directed for the case where a certain event occurs with reference to the limited heir or to the reversionary heir, and the person with reference to whom the event is to occur was living at the time of the accrual of the inheritance;

(2) if, in providing for the case where a brother or sister has been born to the limited or reversionary heir, such brother or sister has been named as reversionary heir.

If the limited or reversionary heir with reference to whom the even is to occur, is a juristic person, a period of thirty years shall be observed.

2110. The right of a reversionary heir extends, in case of doubt, to the share in the inheritance which devolves upon the limited heir in consequence of failure to inherit on the part of a co-heir [y].

The right of a reversionary heir does not extend, in case of doubt, to any preferential legacy [z] made to a limited heir.

2111. The inheritance includes that which the limited heir acquires by virtue of a right forming part of the inheritance, or as compensation for the destruction, damage, or deprivation of an object belonging to the inheritance, or by a juristic act entered into a account of the inheritance, unless the acquisition accrues to the limited heir by way of emoluments. The fact that a claim acquired by a juristic act belongs to the inheritance is not available as against the debtor until he has knowledge of such fact; the provisions of 406 to 408 apply *mutatis mutandis*.

The inheritance includes also that which the limited heir has incorporated with the appurtenant stock of a piece of land forming part of the inheritance.

2112. A limited heir may dispose of any objects forming part of the inheritance, unless a contrary intention appears from the provisions of 2113 to 2115 [a].

2113. A disposition made by a limited heir affecting a piece of land forming part of the inheritance or affecting a right over land forming part of the inheritance is, where reversionary succession takes place, inoperative in so far as it would frustrate or impair the right of the reversionary heir.

The same rule applies to a disposition affecting an object belonging to the inheritance which is made gratuitously or for the purpose of fulfilling a promise of a gift made by the limited heir. Gifts which are made in compliance with a moral duty or the rules of social propriety, are excepted.

The provisions in favour of those who derive rights from a person without

(*y*) See 1935, 2094.

(*z*) Cf. 2150.

(*a*) Cf. 2129.

title apply *mutatis mutandis* [(b)].

2114. If a hypothecary claim, a land charge or an annuity charge forms part of the inheritance, the right to give notice [(c)] and the right to collect belong to the limited heir. The limited heir may, however, only demand that the capital be paid to him after production of the approval of the reversionary heir, or that it be lodged on the joint account of himself and the reversionary heir. The provisions of 2113 apply to any other dispositions affecting hypothecary claims, land charges and annuity charges.

2115. A disposition affecting an object belonging to the inheritance made by means of compulsory execution or distraint, or by a trustee in bankruptcy is, where reversionary succession takes place, ineffective in so far as it would frustrate or impair the right of the reversionary heir. The disposition is effective without such limitation if the claim of a creditor of the estate is enforced in Court, or an existing right over an object belonging to the inheritance which is enforceable against the reversionary heir in case of reversionary succession, is enforced in Court.

2116. A limited heir shall, on demand by a reversionary heir, lodge at a lodgment office or in the Imperial Bank all instruments to bearer forming part of the inheritance, together with their renewal coupons, subject to the condition that their withdrawal may be demanded only with the consent of the reversionary heir. The lodgment of instruments to bearer which are fungible things [(d)] within the meaning of 92, and of interest coupons, annuity coupons, or dividend coupons, may not be demanded. Instruments to order indorsed in blank are equivalent to instruments to bearer.

The limited heir may dispose of the lodged instruments only with the consent of the reversionary heir [(e)].

2117. The limited heir may, instead of lodging the instruments to bearer

(*b*) See note (*q*) to 135.

(*c*) See, *e.g.*, 1141, 1160, &c.

(*d*) *E.g.*, bank notes.

(*e*) The reversionary heir is bound to give his approval in certain cases. 2120.

as provided for in 2116, cause them to be transferred to his own name subject to the condition that he may dispose of them only with the consent of the reversionary heir. If the instruments have been issued by the Empire or by a State he may, subject to the same condition, cause them to be converted into uncertificated claims against the Empire or the State.

2118. If uncertificated claims against the Empire or a State form part of the inheritance, the limited heir is, on demand by the reversionary heir, bound to cause to be entered in the Imperial or State debt ledger the provision that he may dispose of the claims only with the consent of the reversionary heir.

2119. Money which, according to the rules of proper management, has to be permanently invested, can be invested by the limited heir only in accordance with the provisions applicable to investment of money belonging to a ward [(f)].

2120. If a disposition which the limited heir may not legally make as against the reversionary heir, is necessary for the proper management of the estate, *e.g.*, for the discharge of the liabilities of the estate, the reversionary heir is bound as towards the limited heir to give his approval to the disposition. The approval shall on demand be given in publicly certified form. The cost of certification is borne by the limited heir.

2121. The limited heir shall give to the reversionary heir on demand an inventory of the objects belonging to the inheritance. The inventory shall be marked with the date on which it is made, and shall be signed by the limited heir; the limited heir shall on demand cause his signature to be publicly certified.

The reversionary heir may demand that he be called to take part in the making of the inventory.

The limited heir is entitled, and, on demand by the reversionary heir, is bound to cause the inventory to be made by the competent public authority, a competent official, or a notary.

The costs of making the inventory and of its certification are borne by the

---

(*f*) See 1807, 1808.

inheritance.

2122. The limited heir may cause the condition of the things forming part of the inheritance to be determined by experts at his own expense. The reversionary heir has the same right.

2123. If a forest form part of the inheritance, both the limited heir and the reversionary heir may require that the extent and the manner of its use be settled by a plan of management. If an important change of circumstances comes about, either party may require corresponding change of the plan of management. The expenses are borne by the inheritance.

The same rule applies, if a mine or other structure designed for obtaining component parts of the soil forms part of the inheritance.

2124. The limited heir is bound as towards the reversionary heir to bear the customary expenses of maintaining the objects belonging to the inheritance.

Other expenses which the limited heir may regard as necessary under the circumstances for maintaining the objects belonging to the inheritance may be defrayed out of the inheritance. If he defrays such expenses out of his own property, the reversionary heir is, where reversionary succession takes place, bound to make reimbursement.

2125. If the limited heir incurs expenses on the inheritance which are not provided for by 2124, the reversionary heir is, where reversionary succession takes place, bound to make reimbursement under the provisions relating to management of affairs without mandate.

The limited heir is entitled to remove an attachment with which he has provided a thing forming part of the inheritance [(g)].

2126. The limited heir is not, as against the reversionary heir, bound to bear extraordinary charges which are deemed to be imposed upon the capital of the objects belonging to the inheritance. The provisions of 2124, par. 2, apply to such charges.

(*g*) Cf. 258.

2127. The reversionary heir is entitled to require the limited heir to give all information concerning the condition of the inheritance [(h)], if there is reason to suspect that the limited heir seriously violates the rights of the reversionary heir by his management.

2128. If it is to be apprehended from the conduct or financial difficulties of the limited heir that the rights of the reversionary heir will be seriously violated, the reversionary heir may require security to be given.

The provisions of 1052, applicable to a usufructuary's obligation to give security, apply *mutatis mutandis*.

2129. If the limited heir is deprived of his right of management under 1052, he loses his right to dispose of any objects belonging to the inheritance.

The provisions in favour of those who derive rights from a person without title apply *mutatis mutandis* [(i)]. The deprivation of the right of management is not effective as against a debtor in respect of claims forming part of the inheritance until he has knowledge of the order of deprivation, or until such order is communicated to him. The same rule applies to the revocation of such deprivation.

2130. After reversionary succession has taken place, the limited heir is bound to surrender to the reversionary heir the inheritance in the condition in which it would have been if it had been properly managed continuously until the time of its surrender. The provision of 592 applies *mutatis mutandis* to the surrender of agricultural land; the provisions of 592, 593, apply *mutatis mutandis* to the surrender of a farm.

The limited heir shall render an account on demand [(k)].

2131. The limited heir shall be responsible to the reversionary heir in respect of his management only for the same care as he is accustomed to exercise in his own affairs.

(*h*) The duty of giving information includes also the duty to swear an oath of disclosure. 260.

(*i*) See note (*q*) to 135.

(*k*) 259.

2132. The limited heir shall not be responsible for any alteration or deterioration of the things belonging to the inheritance which is brought about by proper use.

2133. If the limited heir takes any fruits contrary to the rules of proper husbandry, or if he takes any fruits in excess where this has become necessary in consequence of some special occurrence, the value of such fruits accrues to him only in so far as the emoluments accruing to him are diminished by the improper or excessive taking, and the value of such fruits is not to be used for the restoration of the thing according to the rules of proper husbandry.

2134. If the limited heir has used an object belonging to the inheritance for his own benefit, he is, after reversionary succession has taken place, bound to make good its value to the reversionary heir. Any further liability on account of fault remains unaffected.

2135. If the limited heir has let, under an ordinary or usufructuary lease, a piece of land forming part of the inheritance, and if the term of the lease is still running at the time of reversionary succession, the provisions of 1056 apply *mutatis mutandis*.

2136. The deceased may release the limited heir from the limitations and obligations specified in 2113, par. 1, and 2114, 2116 to 2119, 2123, 2127 to 2131, 2133, 2134.

2137. If the deceased has appointed the reversionary heir for the residue of the inheritance remaining at the time of reversionary succession, a release from all the limitations and obligations specified in 2136 is deemed to have been granted.

In case of doubt the same rule is deemed to be applicable where the deceased has directed that the limited heir shall be entitled to have free disposal of the inheritance.

2138. In the cases provided for by 2137 the limited heir's duty to make surrender is limited to the existing objects belonging to the inheritance which still remain with him. He may not demand compensation for expenses incurred on the objects which he is not bound to surrender in consequence of such limitation of his duty.

If the limited heir has disposed of an object belonging to the inheritance contrary to the provision of 2113, par. 2, or if he has diminished the inheritance with the intention of injuring the reversionary heir, he is bound to make compensation to the reversionary heir.

2139. Upon the occurrence of an occasion for reversionary succession the limited heir ceases to be an heir, and the inheritance devolves upon the reversionary heir.

2140. Even after the occurrence of an occasion for reversionary succession the limited heir is entitled to dispose of the objects belonging to the inheritance to the same extent as before the reversionary succession, until he knows or ought to know of such occurrence. A third party may not take advantage of this right if he knows or ought to know of it at the time when a juristic act is entered into.

2141. If the birth of a reversionary heir is to be expected at the time of the occurrence of an occasion for reversionary succession, the provisions of 1963 apply *mutatis mutandis* to the expectant mother's claim to maintenance.

2142. A reversionary heir is entitled to disclaim the inheritance as soon as accrual of the inheritance has taken place [(l)].

If the reversionary heir disclaims the inheritance, it remains with the limited heir, unless the deceased has directed otherwise.

2143. If reversionary succession takes place, the legal relations extinguished in consequence of the accrual of the inheritance by merger of a right in a liability or of a right in a charge, are deemed not to have been extinguished.

2144. The provisions relating to an heir's limitation of liability for the liabilities of an estate apply also to a reversionary heir; the residue of the inheritance accruing to the reversionary heir, including the claims which he has against the limited heir as such, takes the place of the estate.

(*l*) *I.e.*, he need not wait till the occurrence of an occasion for reversionary succession.

An inventory filed by the limited heir is also available in favour of the reversionary heir.

The reversionary heir may, as against the limited heir, avail himself of his limitation of liability even if he be liable without limitation to the other creditors of the estate.

2145. The limited heir is, even after the occurrence of an occasion for reversionary succession, liable for the liabilities of the estate in so far as the reversionary heir is not liable. The limited heir's liability continues to exist also in respect of the liabilities of the estate which are borne by the limited heir as between himself and the reversionary heir.

After the occurrence of an occasion for reversionary succession, the limited heir may, unless his liability is unlimited, refuse to discharge the liabilities of the estate in so far as that which accrues to him from the inheritance is not sufficient to discharge them. The provisions of 1990, 1991, apply *mutatis mutandis*.

2146. The limited heir is bound as towards the creditors of the estate to notify without delay to the Probate Court the occurrence of the reversionary succession. Notice by the reversionary heir is a substitute for notice by the limited heir.

The Probate Court shall permit any person to inspect the notice, provided that he can offer *primâ facie* proof that he has a legal interest therein.

FOURTH TITLE.
Legacies.

2147. An heir or a legatee may be charged with a legacy. Unless the testator has otherwise provided, the heir is deemed to have been charged.

2148. If several heirs or several legatees are charged with the same legacy, in case of doubt the heirs are charged in proportion to their shares in the inheritance, and the legatees are charged in proportion to the value of their legacies.

2149. If the testator has provided that an object belonging to the inheritance shall not devolve on the appointed heir, the object is deemed to have been bequeathed to the statutory heirs. The Treasury is not a statutory heir within the meaning of this provision.

2150. A legacy given to an heir (a preferential legacy) is deemed to be a legacy even if the heir himself is charged therewith.

2151. A testator may give a legacy to several persons in such manner that the person charged or a third party has to decide which of the several persons [(m)] shall receive the legacy.

The decision of the person charged is made by declaration to the person who is to receive the legacy; the decision of the third party is made by declaration to the person charged.

If the person charged or the third party cannot give the decision, the legatees become joint-creditors. The same rule applies, if the Probate Court [(n)], upon the application of one of the interested parties, has fixed a period for the person charged or the third party to make the declaration, and the period has expired, unless the declaration has been made within such period. The beneficiary who receives the legacy is, in case of doubt, not liable to make partition.

2152. If a testator has given a legacy to several persons in such manner that only one of them is to receive the legacy, it is to be presumed that the person charged shall decide which of them is to receive the legacy.

2153. A testator may give a legacy to several persons in such manner that the person charged or a third party has to decide the share in the bequeathed object which each is to receive. The decision is made in the manner provided for by 2151, par. 2.

If the person charged or the third party cannot give the decision, legatees are entitled to equal shares. The provision of 2151, par. 3, sentence 2, applies *mutatis mutandis*.

(*m*) Such persons must be designated either by name or by a general description; otherwise the legacy is deemed to be a "testamentary burden" only. 2194.

(*n*) *I.e.*, the Probate Court of the place where the testator was last domiciled.

2154. A testator may give a legacy in such manner that the legatee is to receive one of several objects. In such a case if the right to select the object has been given to a third party, it is exercised by declaration to the person charged.

If the third party cannot make the selection, the right of selection passes to the person charge. The provision of 2151, par. 3, sentence 2, applies *mutatis mutandis*.

2155. If the testator has designated the bequeathed thing only by species, a thing suitable to the legatee's station in life shall be given [(o)].

If the right to designate the thing is given to the legatee or to a third party, the provisions contained in 2154, applicable to the right of selection given to a third party, apply.

If the designation made by the legatee or by the third party is evidently not suitable to the legatee's station in life, the person charged has so to carry out the legacy as though the testator had made no provision concerning the designation of the thing.

2156. If a testator has determined the purpose for which a legacy is intended, he may give to the person charged with such legacy or to a third party the right to determine an equitable mode in which the legacy is to be carried out. The provisions of 315 to 319 apply *mutatis mutandis* to such a legacy.

2157. If the same object has been bequeathed to several persons, the provisions of 2089 to 2093 apply *mutatis mutandis*.

2158. If the same object has been bequeathed to several persons, and if one of them fails to receive his share before or after the accrual of the inheritance, such share accrues to the other legatees in proportion to their shares. This applies also even though the testator has determined the shares of the legatees. If some of the legatees are entitled to one and the same share, the right of accrual arises among such legatees first.

(*o*) The person charged with the legacy is responsible, as a seller, for defects of quality or title in the thing given. 2182, 2183.

The testator may exclude the right of accrual.

2159. Any share devolving on a legatee by virtue of the right of accrual is, in respect of the legacies and testamentary burdens with which such legatee or the legatee failing to receive the share is charged, deemed to be a separate legacy.

2160. A legacy is inoperative if the legatee was not living at the time of the accrual of the inheritance.

2161. Unless a contrary intention of the testator is to be inferred, a legacy remains operative even where the person charged does not become heir or legatee. In such a case the person is deemed to be charged who benefits directly through the failure to carry out the legacy on the part of the person originally charged.

2162. If a legacy has been given subject to a condition precedent, or has been made to be operative from a given day, it becomes inoperative after the expiration of thirty years since the accrual of the inheritance, unless the condition has been fulfilled or the given day has arrived within such period.

If the legatee was not conceived at the time of the accrual of the inheritance, or if his identity is determined only by an event occurring after the accrual of the inheritance, the legacy becomes inoperative upon the expiration of thirty years since the accrual of the inheritance, unless within such period the legatee has been conceived or the event has occurred whereby his identity is determined.

2163. In the cases provided for by 2162, a legacy remains operative even after the expiration of thirty years:

(1) if it has been made for the case where a certain event occurs with reference to the person charged or the legatee, and such person or legatee was living at the time of the accrual of the inheritance;

(2) if, in providing for the case where a brother or sister is born to him, an heir, or a reversionary heir, or a legatee is charged with the legacy in favour of such brother or sister.

If the person charged or the legatee with reference to whom the event is to occur is a juristic person, the period of thirty years is effective.

2164. A legacy of a thing extends, in case of doubt, to its accessories existing at the time of the accrual of the inheritance [(p)].

If the testator, on account of damage done to the thing after the making of the legacy, has a claim for compensation for the diminution of its value, the legacy extends, in case of doubt, to such claim.

2165. If an object forming part of the inheritance has been bequeathed, the legatee may not, in case of doubt, demand the discharge of rights with which the object is charged. If the claim to such discharge belongs to the testator, the legacy extends, in case of doubt, to such claim.

If a hypotheca, land charge, or annuity charge belonging to the testator himself exists over a piece of bequeathed land, it is to be inferred from the circumstances whether the hypotheca, land charge, or annuity charge is to be deemed to have been bequeathed with the land.

2166. If a piece of bequeathed land forming part of the inheritance is charged with a hypotheca for a debt of the testator, or for a debt which the testator is bound to pay on behalf of the debtor, the legatee is, in case of doubt, bound as towards the heir to satisfy the creditor in due time, in so far as the debt is covered by the value of the piece of land. The value is determined as at the time at which ownership passes to the legatee; the value is calculated by deducting the value of all charges which take priority in rank to the hypotheca.

If a third party is bound as towards the testator to pay the debt, such obligation of the legatee exists only in so far as the heir may not require the third party to pay the debt.

These provisions do not apply to a hypotheca of the kind specified in 1190.

2167. If, besides the bequeathed land, other pieces of land forming part of the inheritance have been charged with the hypotheca [(q)], the obligation of the legatee specified in 2166 is, in case of doubt, limited to a part of the debt

---

(p) The person charged with the legacy shall likewise surrender all fruits taken by him. 2184.

(q) Such a hypotheca is called a "collective hypotheca". 1132.

which bears to the whole debt the same proportion which the value of the bequeathed land bears to the whole value of all the pieces of land. The value is calculated in the manner provided for by 2166, par. 1, sentence 2.

2168. If a collective land charge or a collective annuity charge exists over several pieces of land forming part of the inheritance, and if one of such pieces of land has been bequeathed, the legatee is, in case of doubt, bound as towards the heir to satisfy the creditor for a part of the land charge or annuity charge which bears to the whole charge the same proportion which the value of the bequeathed land bears to the value of all the pieces of land. The value is calculated in the manner provided for by 2166, par. 1, sentence 2.

If, besides the bequeathed piece of land, another piece of land not forming part of the inheritance has been charged with a collective land charge or collective annuity charge, and if, at the time of the accrual of the inheritance, the testator was bound as towards the owner of the other piece of land or a predecessor in title of such owner to satisfy the creditor, the provisions of 2166, par. 1, and 2167 apply *mutatis mutandis*.

2169. A legacy of a specific object is inoperative in so far as the object does not form part of the inheritance at the time of the accrual of the inheritance, unless the object was intended to be bequeathed to the legatee even in the case where it does not form part of the inheritance.

If the testator had possession only of the bequeathed object, the possession is, in case of doubt, deemed to have been bequeathed, unless it affords no legal advantage to the legatee.

If the testator had a claim for the delivery of the bequeathed object, or a claim for compensation for its value where it had been destroyed or taken away from the testator after the making of the legacy, such claim is, in case of doubt, deemed to have been bequeathed.

An object which the testator is bound to alienate to another person is not deemed to be a part of the inheritance within the meaning of par. 1.

2170. If a legacy of an object not forming part of the inheritance at the time of the accrual of the inheritance is operative under 2169, par. 1, the person charged with the legacy shall procure the object for the legatee.

If the person charged is not in a position to procure the object, he shall pay its value. If the object can only be procured through disproportional outlay, the person charged may release himself by payment of its value.

2171. If a legacy has for its object an act of performance which is impossible, or is prohibited by law at the time of the accrual of the inheritance, the legacy is inoperative [(r)]. The provisions of 308 apply *mutatis mutandis*.

2172. The delivery of a bequeathed thing is also deemed to be impossible where the thing is incorporated or confused or mixed with a thing belonging to another person in such manner that the ownership of such other thing extends to the bequeathed thing, as provided for in 946 to 948, or in such manner that co-ownership has been created; or where the bequeathed thing has been manufactured or transformed in such manner that the person who has created the new thing has become owner thereof, as provided for in 950.

Where the incorporation, confusion or mixing has been made by a person other than the testator [(s)], and where the testator has thereby acquired co-ownership, such co-ownership is, in case of doubt, deemed to have been bequeathed; where the testator has a right to remove the incorporated thing [(t)], such right is, in case of doubt, deemed to have been bequeathed. In the case of manufacture or transformation by a person other than the testator, the provision of 2169, par. 3, is applicable.

2173. Where a testator has bequeathed a claim belonging to him which is satisfied before the accrual of the inheritance, and where the object delivered in satisfaction of the claim is still existing as part of the inheritance, it is to be presumed, in case of doubt, that such object has been bequeathed to the legatee. Where the claim was for the payment of a sum of money, the sum of money received by the testator is, in case of doubt, deemed to have been bequeathed, even though the inheritance does not comprise cash to that amount.

(*r*) Where the impossibility arises after the date of accrual, the person charged with the legacy is discharged, unless the impossibility is due to his own fault.

(*s*) If the testator himself has made the incorporation, confusion or mixing, the legacy is deemed to have been revoked.

(*t*) 258.

2174. A legacy creates a right in favour of the legatee to claim delivery of the bequeathed object from the person charged with the legacy.

2175. Where a testator has bequeathed a claim which he has against the heir, or where he has bequeathed a right with which a thing or a right belonging to the heir is charged, the legal relations extinguished in consequence of the accrual of the inheritance by the merger of the right in the liability or of the right in the charge are deemed not to have been extinguished in respect of the legacy.

2176. The claim of a legatee (u) comes into being (devolution of a legacy) on the accrual of the inheritance, subject to his right to disclaim the legacy.

2177. If the legacy has been given subject to a condition precedent, or has been made to be operative from a given day, and where the condition is fulfilled or the day has arrived after the accrual of the inheritance, the devolution of the legacy takes place on the fulfilment of the condition or the arrival of the day.

2178. If the legatee was not conceived at the time of the accrual of the inheritance, or if his identity is to be determined by an event occurring after the accrual of the inheritance, in the former case the devolution of the legacy takes place at the date of birth; in the latter case, on the occurrence of the event.

2179. For the time between the accrual of the inheritance and the devolution of the legacy in the cases provided for by 2177, 2178, the provision applicable to a case where an act of performance is promised subject to a condition precedent apply (x).

2180. If a legatee has accepted a legacy he may do longer disclaim it.

The acceptance or disclaimer of a legacy is made by declaration to the person charged with the legacy (y). The declaration may not be made until the accrual of the inheritance; the declaration is ineffective if made subject to any

---

(u) See 2174.

(x) *I.e.*, 160—162.

(y) Unlike the case of an inheritance there is no prescribed period for the acceptance or disclaimer of a legacy.

condition or limitation of time.

The provisions of 1950, 1952, pars. 1, 3, and 1953, pars. 1, 2, applicable to the acceptance or disclaimer of an inheritance, apply *mutatis mutandis*.

2181. If the time for carrying out a legacy is to be fixed by the person charged therewith at his discretion, in case of doubt the legacy becomes due on the death of such person.

2182. If a thing designated only by species has been bequeathed, the person charged with the legacy has the same obligations as a seller as provided for in 433, par. 1, 434 to 437, 440, pars. 2 to 4, and 441 to 444.

Where a specific object not forming part of the inheritance has been bequeathed [(z)], the same rule applies in case of doubt, subject, however, to the limitation of liability based on 2170.

If a piece of land is the object of a legacy, the person charged therewith does not, in case of doubt, warrant the land free from real servitudes, limited personal servitudes and perpetual charges.

2183. If a thing designated only by species has been bequeathed, and if the thing delivered is defective, the legatee may demand that in the place of the defective thing one free from defects be delivered to him. If the person charged with the legacy has fraudulently concealed a defect, the legatee may demand compensation for non-performance instead of delivery of a thing free from defect. The provisions applicable to warranty against defects of quality in a thing sold apply *mutatis mutandis* to such claims [(a)].

2184. If a specific object forming part of the inheritance has been bequeathed, the person charged with the legacy shall surrender also to the legatee the fruits taken after the devolution of the legacy, whatever he has acquired by virtue of any bequeathed right. The person charged is not bound to make compensation for emoluments which are not deemed to be fruits.

2185. If a specific thing forming part of the inheritance has been bequeathed,

---

(*z*) Cf. 2165.

(*a*) 459 *et seq*.

the person charged with the legacy may, under the provisions which apply to the relations between a possessor and an owner [(b)], demand compensation for outlay incurred on the bequeathed thing after the date of the accrual of the inheritance, and for any payments made by him after such date for the charges upon the thing.

2186. If a legatee is charged with a legacy or testamentary burden, he is not bound to execute the legacy or testamentary burden until he is entitled to claim execution of the legacy given to him [(c)].

2187. A legatee who has been charged with a legacy or testamentary burden may refuse to execute the legacy or testamentary burden even after acceptance of the legacy bequeathed to him in so far as that which he has received from such legacy is not sufficient for the purpose of execution.

If another person takes the place of the charged legatee as provided for in 2161, such person is liable to no greater extent than the legatee himself.

The provisions of 1992, applicable to the liability of an heir, apply *mutatis mutandis*.

2188. If performance due to a legatee is reduced by reason of the heir's limitation of liability [(d)], or by virtue of a claim to compulsory portion, or in accordance with 2187, the legatee may, unless a contrary intention of the testator is to be inferred, proportionately reduce the charges imposed upon him.

2189. In providing for the case where any legacies or testamentary burdens imposed upon the heir or a legatee are reduced by reason of the heir's limitation of liability, or by virtue of a claim to compulsory portion, or in accordance with 2187, 2188, the testator may direct by testamentary disposition that any one of such legacies or testamentary burdens shall have priority in rank to the other legacies or testamentary burdens with which the heir or legatee is charged.

2190. Where a testator has bequeathed an object to a substitutional legatee

---

(*b*) 994 *et seq.*

(*c*) See 2176, 2178.

(*d*) See 1975 *et seq.*

in the event of the original legatee failing to receive the legacy, the provisions of 2097 to 2099, applicable to the appointment of a substitutional heir, apply *mutatis mutandis*.

2191. Where a testator has bequeathed an already bequeathed object to a third party on the arrival of a certain time or the occurrence of a certain event after the devolution of the legacy, the original legatee is deemed to have been charged with such legacy.

The provisions of 2102, 2106, par. 1, 2107, and 2110, par. 1, applicable to the appointment of a reversionary heir, apply *mutatis mutandis* to such a legacy.

FIFTH TITLE.
Testamentary Burdens.

2192. The provisions of 2065, 2147, 2148, 2154 to 2156, 2161, 2171, 2181, applicable to a testamentary gift, apply *mutatis mutandis* to a testamentary burden [(e)].

2193. A testator may, in creating a testamentary burden the purpose of which he has specified, give to the person charged therewith or to a third party the right to determine the person in favour of whom the burden is to be executed.

Where the right to make the determination belongs to the person charged, and where he has been ordered by a non-appellable decree to execute the burden, the person who has obtained such decree may fix reasonable period for him to execute the burden; after the expiration of such period the plaintiff is entitled to make the determination unless execution is effected in due time.

Where the right to make the determination belongs to a third party it is exercised by declaration to the person charged. If the third party cannot make any such determination, the right passes to the person charged. The provision

(e) The special provisions of 2186—2189 apply to testamentary burdens given to a legatee.

of 2151, par. 3, sentence 2, applies *mutatis mutandis*; the person charged and all other persons who are entitled to demand execution of the burden are deemed to be interested parties within the meaning of that provision.

2194. The execution of a testamentary burden may be demanded by the heir, a co-heir, or any other person who would be affected directly by the failure to execute the burden on the part of the person charged therewith. If execution of the testamentary burden is of public interest, the competent public authority may demand its execution.

2195. The invalidity of a testamentary burden does not result in the invalidity of the legacy subject to the burden, unless it is to be presumed that the testator would not have given the legacy without the burden.

2196. If execution of a testamentary burden becomes impossible in consequence of a circumstance for which the person charged therewith is responsible [(f)], the person who would be affected directly by the failure to execute the burden on the part of the person charged therewith may, under the provisions relating to the return of unjustified benefits, demand surrender of any testamentary gift in so far as such gift would have to be applied to the execution of the burden [(g)].

The same rule applies where a person charged with a testamentary burden has been ordered by a non-appellable decree to execute the burden which may not be executed by a third party, and the available legal remedies have been resorted to against such person without success.

SIXTH TITLE.

Executors.

2197. A testator may by will appoint one or more executors.

The testator may appoint a substitutional executor to act in the event of the

(*f*) 276.

(*g*) *I.e.*, the person charged with the burden is not bound to surrender the whole gift.

original appointee failing or ceasing to be an executor before or after acceptance of the office.

2198. The testator may give to a third party the right to determine who is to accept the office of executor. The right is exercised by declaration to the Probate Court [h]; the declaration shall be given in publicly certified form [i].

The right of the third party is extinguished on the expiration of a period fixed for him by the Probate Court upon the application of one of the interested parties.

2199. The testator may authorise the executor to appoint one or more co-executors.

The testator may authorise the executor to appoint a successor to himself.

The appointment is made in the manner provided for by 2198, par. 1, sentence 2.

2200. If the testator has in his will requested the Probate Court to appoint an executor, the Probate Court may make the appointment.

The Probate Court should, before making any such appointment, hear the interested parties, if this can be done without serious delay and without disproportionate expense.

2201. The appointment of an executor is invalid if, at the time at which he is to enter upon the duties of the office, he is incapable of disposing, or is limited in his disposing capacity, or a curator has been appointed for him to take charge of his property affairs as provided for in 1910.

2202. The functions of an executor begin at the time at which the appointee accepts the office.

The acceptance or refusal of the office is effected by declaration to the Probate court. The declaration may not be made until after the accrual of the inheritance; the declaration is ineffective if it is made subject to any condition or limitation of time.

The Probate Court may, upon the application of one of the interested

---

(*h*) *I.e.*, the Probate Court of the place where the testator was last domiciled.

(*i*) Any interested party is entitled to inspect the declaration.

parties, fix for the appointee a period of time within which to make a declaration whether or not he accepts the office. After the expiration of the period the office is deemed to have been refused, unless acceptance has been declared within such period.

2203. The executor shall carry out the testamentary dispositions of the testator.

2204. The executor shall, if there are several heirs, bring about a partition among them in accordance with 2042 to 2056.

The executor shall, before carrying out the partition, hear the heirs on the scheme of partition.

2205. The executor shall administer the estate. He is entitled to take possession of the estate and to dispose of any objects belonging thereto. He is entitled to make gratuitous dispositions only in so far as they are made in compliance with a moral duty or the rules of social propriety.

2206. An executor is entitled to incur obligations on account of the estate in so far as this is necessary for its proper administration. Where he is entitled to dispose of any object belonging to the estate, he may also incur, on account of the estate, an obligation for the disposal of such an object.

The heir is bound to give his approval to the incurring of any such obligation, subject, however, to his right of setting up his limitation of liability for the liabilities of the estate.

2207. The testator may direct that the executor shall have unlimited right to incur obligations on account of the estate. Even in such a case the executor is entitled to make a promise of a gift only subject to the conditions specified in 2205, sentence 3.

2208. An executor has not any of the rights specified in 2203 to 2206 in so far as it may be presumed that the testator intended that he should not have them. If only particular objects belonging to the estate are subject to the administration of the executor, he has the powers specified in 2205, sentence 2, only in respect of such objects.

If the executor is not bound to carry out the dispositions of the testator himself, he can require the heir to carry them out, unless a contrary intention of the testator is to be inferred.

2209. The testator may give to his executor the right to administer the estate without imposing upon him any other duties than those connected with the administration [(k)]; he may also direct that the executor shall continue the administration after the performance of any other duties imposed upon him. In case of doubt it is to be presumed that the authorisation specified in 2207 has been given to such an executor.

2210. Any direction given under 2209 is ineffective if thirty years have elapsed since the accrual of the inheritance. The testator may, however, direct that the administration shall continue until the death of the heir or of the executor, or until the occurrence of any other event affecting either of them. The provision of 2163, par. 2, applies *mutatis mutandis*.

2211. The heir may not dispose of any object belonging to the estate subject to the administration of the executor.

The provisions in favour of those who derive rights from a person without title apply *mutatis mutandis* [(l)].

2212. A right subject to the administration of the executor may be enforced in Court only by the executor.

2213. A claim against the estate may be enforced in Court both against the heir and against the executor. If the right to administer the estate does not belong to the executor, the claim may be enforced only against the heir. A claim to compulsory portion may be enforced only against the heir, even if the right of administering the estate belongs to the executor.

The provision of 1958 does not apply to an executor.

A creditor of the estate who enforces his claim against the heir may also enforce his claim against the executor to the extent that the latter has to suffer

(*k*) *E.g.*, the duty as to partition. 2204.

(*l*) See note (*q*) to 135.

compulsory execution on the objects belonging to the estate subject to his administration.

2214. Creditors of the heir who are not creditors of the estate may not have recourse to objects belonging to the estate subject to the administration of the executor.

2215. The executor shall, after acceptance to the office, give to the heir without delay a list of the objects of the estate subject to his administration, and of any liabilities of the estate which are known to him, and shall render any other assistance which is necessary for the making of an inventory (*n*).

The list shall bear the date when it was made, and shall be signed by the executor; the executor shall on demand cause his signature to be publicly certified.

The heir may demand that he be called to take part in making the list.

The executor is entitled and, on demand by the heir, is bound to have such a list made by the competent public authority, or by a competent official, or by a notary.

The costs of making the list and of its certification are borne by the estate.

2216. The executor is bound to administer the estate in a proper manner.

Any direction which the testator has given in his testamentary disposition for the administration of the estate shall be followed by the executors. They may, however, upon the application of the executor or of any other interested party, be set aside by the Probate Court, if to follow them would seriously endanger the estate. The Court should, as far as possible, hear the interested parties before giving any decision.

2217. The executor shall on demand transfer to the heir for the latter's free disposal any objects belonging to the estate of which he has evidently no need for the performance of his duties. His right of administration over such objects is extinguished as soon as they have been transferred to the heir.

(*n*) The reason being that the list may not satisfy all the requirements of an "inventory". 2001, par. 2, 2002, 2003.

The executor may not refuse to transfer such objects on the ground of any liabilities of the estate not arising from a legacy or testamentary burden, nor on the ground of any legacies or testamentary burdens made subject to a condition or limitation of time, if the heir gives security for the discharge of the liabilities or for the execution of the legacies or testamentary charges.

2218. The provisions of 664, 666 to 668, 670, 673, sentence 2, and 674, applicable to mandate, apply *mutatis mutandis* to the legal relations between the executor and the heir.

Where the administration is of more than one year's duration the heir may require an account to be rendered every year [(o)].

2219. Where an executor commits a breach of the duties imposed upon him, he is, if fault is imputable to him, responsible to the heir and, in so far as a legacy is to be carried out, also to the legatee for any damage arising therefrom.

If there are several executors to whom fault is imputable, they are liable as joint debtors.

2220. The testator may not release the executor from the duties imposed upon him by 2215, 2216, 2218, 2219.

2221. An executor may claim reasonable remuneration for the discharge of his duties, unless the testator has provided otherwise.

2222. A testator may also appoint an executor to exercise the rights and perform the duties of a reversionary heir until the occurrence of reversionary succession.

2223. A testator may also appoint an executor to supervise the execution of any legacies or testamentary burdens with which a legatee is charged.

2224. Where several executors have been appointed, they shall discharge their duties jointly; in case of disagreement the Probate Court decides. If any

---

(*o*) He may also be required to swear an oath of disclosure. 259.

of them ceases to act the others shall continue alone to discharge the duties. The testator may provide otherwise.

Each executor is entitled, even without the consent of the other executors, to take any measures which are necessary for the preservation of any object belonging to the estate which is subject to their joint administration.

2225. The office of an executor is vacated if he dies, or if circumstances arise which would render the appointment invalid as provided for in 2201.

2226. An executor may at any time give notice of his intention to retire from office [(p)]. Such notice is effected by declaration to the Probate Court. The provision of 671, pars. 2, 3, apply *mutatis mutandis*.

2227. The Probate Court may, upon the application of an interested party, dismiss an executor from office if a grave reason exists; such a reason is, *e.g.*, gross breach of duty or incapacity to manage the affairs properly.

The executor should, if possible, be heard before being dismissed.

2228. The Probate Court shall permit any person to inspect the declarations made under 2198, par. 1, sentence 2, 2199, par. 3, 2202, par. 2, 2226, sentence 2, provided he can offer *primâ facie* proof that he has a legal interest therein.

SEVENTH TITLE.

The Making and Revocation of a Will.

2229. A person who is limited in disposing capacity does not require the consent of his statutory agent for making a will.

A minor may not make a will until he has completed his sixteenth year of age [(q)].

A person who is interdicted on account of feeble-mindedness, prodigality or

---

(*p*) He need not give any reason for doing so.

(*q*) Cf. 2238, par. 2, 2247.

habitual drunkenness, may not make a will. Such incapacity begins immediately on the presentation of the application, by virtue of which the interdiction takes place.

2230. Where an interdicted person has made a will before the decree for interdiction is made absolute, the interdiction does not invalidate the will if the interdicted person dies before the decree is made absolute.

The same rule applies if the interdicted person makes a will after the presentation of an application for revocation of the interdiction, and the interdiction is revoked according to the terms of the application.

2231. A will may generally be made in the following manner:

(1) before a judge or notary;

(2) by a declaration of the testator, written and signed with his own hand [r], stating the place where and the date at which it is made.

2232. The provisions of 2233 to 2246 apply to the making of a will before a judge or notary [s].

2233. In superintending the making of a will, the judge must be attended by a registrar or by two witnesses [t]; the notary must be attended by another notary or by two witnesses.

2234. The following persons may not take part as a judge, notary, registrar or witness in superintending the making of a will:

(1) the spouse of the testator, even though the marriage no longer subsists;

(2) any person who is related to the testator by blood or marriage in the direct line or within the second degree in the collateral line.

2235. A person who will be a beneficiary under the will or who stands in the relation of the kind specified in 2234 with the beneficiary, may not take part in superintending the making of the will as a judge, notary, registrar or witness.

(*r*) A type-written declaration is insufficient for such a purpose.

(*s*) Cf. IA, Art. 151.

(*t*) Cf. IA, Art. 149.

Participation on the part of any such person has only the effect that the testamentary gift to the beneficiary is void.

2236. A person who stands in the relation of the kind specified in 2234 with the judge or notary may not take part in superintending the making of the will as a registrar, assisting notary or witness.

2237. The following persons should not take part as a witness in superintending the making of a will:

(1) a minor;

(2) a person declared to have been deprived of civil rights for the time for which the deprivation has been ordered [(u)];

(3) a person who, under the provisions of the criminal code, is incapable of being called as a witness under oath [(x)];

(4) a person who is in the service of the judge or notary as a domestic servant or employee [(y)].

2238. The will shall be made in the following manner: The testator either makes an oral declaration of his last will to the judge or notary, or delivers to him a written statement accompanied by an oral declaration that the written statement contains his last will. The written statement may be delivered open or sealed. It may be written by the testator himself or by any other person.

A minor or a person who cannot read may make a will only by oral declaration.

2239. All persons taking part in superintending the making of a will must be present during the whole proceedings.

2240. A protocol relating to the making of the will must be drawn up in the German language.

2241. The protocol must contain:

(*u*) See Criminal Code, ss. 32, 34, 36.

(*x*) *Ibid.* s. 161.

(*y*) A servant or employee of the testator is, however, not disqualified as a witness.

(1) the name of the place and the date of the proceedings;

(2) the names of the testator and of all persons taking part in the proceedings;

(3) the declarations of the testator required by 2238, and, where a written statement is delivered, the fact that the written statement has been delivered.

2242. The protocol must be read out to and ratified by the testator, and signed by him with his own hand. In the protocol the fact that this has been done must be recorded. The protocol should on demand be laid before the testator for his perusal.

If the testator declares that he cannot write (z), a record of such declaration in the protocol is substituted for his signature.

The protocol must be signed by all the persons taking part in the proceedings.

2243. A person who is believed by the judge or the notary to be dumb or otherwise prevented from speaking may make his will only by the delivery of a written statement. He must, during the proceedings, write with his own hand in the protocol or on a separate piece of paper, which must be annexed to the protocol as an appendix thereto, the declaration that the written statement contains his last will (a).

Both the fact that the declaration is holograph and the fact that the judge or notary believes that the testator is prevented from speaking, must be recorded in the protocol. The protocol need not be expressly ratified by the testator.

2244. If the testator declares that he does not understand the German language, a sworn interpreter must be called to take part in the making of the will. The provisions of 2234 to 2237, applicable to a witness, apply *mutatis mutandis* to the interpreter.

The protocol must be translated into the language in which the testator makes his declaration. The translation must be made or certified and read out by the interpreter; the translation must be annexed to the protocol as an appen-

---

(z) Cf. 2238, par. 2.

(a) The code does not provide for the case of a dumb person who can neither read nor write.

dix thereto.

The protocol must contain the declaration of the testator that he does not understand the German language, the name of the interpreter, and the fact that the interpreter has made or certified and read the translation. The interpreter must sign the protocol.

2245. If all the persons taking part in the proceedings affirm that they understand the language in which the testator makes his declaration, the assistance of an interpreter is not necessary.

If the assistance of an interpreter is not required, the protocol must be drawn up in the foreign language, and must contain the declaration of the testator that he does not understand the German language, and the affirmation of the persons taking part in the proceedings that they understand the foreign language. A German translation should be annexed as an appendix.

2246. The protocol which is drawn up relating to the making of the will should, together with its appendices, and, where the will is made by delivery of a written statement, together with such statement, be sealed by the judge or notary with the official seal in the presence of the testator and all other persons taking part in the proceedings; it should be provided with an indorsement signed by the judge or notary describing the will in a precise manner, and should be taken into official custody.

A certificate as to the official custody of the will should be issued to the testator.

2247. A minor or a person who cannot read (b) may not make a will in the manner provided for by 2231 (2).

2248. A will made in the manner provided for by 2231 (2) shall be taken into official custody on demand by the testator. The provision of 2246, par. 2, applies.

2249. Where a testator apprehends that he will die before he is able to make a will before a judge or notary, he may make his will before the chief officer of

(b) Cf. 2238, par. 2.

the commune in which he resides, or, where he resides in the district of a communal union (*Verband*) or rural district (*Gutsbezirk*) which has the legal status of a commune under State law, before the chief officer of such communal union or rural district. The chief officer must be attended by two witnesses. The provisions of 2234 to 2246 apply; the chief officer takes the place of the judge or notary.

The fact that the testator apprehends that he will not be able to make a will before a judge or notary must be stated in the protocol. The validity of the will is not affected by the fact that the apprehension was groundless [(c)].

2250. If a person resides in a place which, in consequence of an epidemic or any other extraordinary circumstances, is isolated from the outer world in such a manner that it is impossible or very difficult to make a will before a judge or notary, he may make a will either in the manner provided for by 2249, par. 1, or by oral declaration before three witnesses.

If oral declaration before three witnesses is selected, a protocol concerning the making of the will must be drawn up [(d)]. The provisions of 2234, 2235, 2237 (1) to (3) apply to such witnesses; the provisions of 2240 to 2242, 2245 apply to such protocol. A will may not be made in this manner with the assistance of an interpreter.

2251. If a person is on board a German vessel which does not belong to the Imperial navy, and which is outside a German port in the course of a sea voyage, he may make a will by oral declaration before three witnesses as provided for in 2250 [(e)].

2252. A will made in the manner provided for by 2249, 2250, or 2251 is deemed not to have been made if three months have elapsed since the making of the will and the testator is still living.

The beginning and running of the period of three months are suspended, so long as the testator is not in a position to make a will before a judge or notary.

(*c*) Cf. 2252.

(*d*) Either by the testator himself or by one of the witnesses.

(*e*) See IA, Art. 44.

If, in the case provided for by 2251, the testator starts upon another sea voyage before the expiration of the period, the period is so far interrupted that after the termination of the new voyage the full period begins to run *de novo*.

If the testator is declared dead after the expiration of the period, the will retains its validity if the period had not yet elapsed at the time when the testator was last reported to be still alive.

2253. A will or any particular dispositions contained therein may be revoked by the testator at any time.

Interdiction of the testator on account of feeble-mindedness, prodigality, or habitual drunkenness does not prevent the revocation of a will made before the interdiction.

2254. The revocation is effected by a new will.

2255. A will may also be revoked by reason of the fact that the testator, with the intention of revoking it, destroys the testamentary document or makes alterations in it whereby the intention to revoke a written declaration of intention is customarily expressed.

If the testator has destroyed or altered the testamentary document in this manner, it is presumed that he intended to revoke his will.

2256. A will made before a judge or notary, or in the manner provided for by 2249, is deemed to have been revoked if the document taken into official custody has been returned to the testator.

The testator may demand the return of his will at any time. The return may be made only to the testator in person.

The provision of par. 2 applies also to a will taken into custody under 2248; the return of such a will does not affect the validity of the will.

2257. If the revocation by will of a testamentary disposition is itself revoked [(f)], the disposition is valid as though it had not been revoked.

2258. A will is revoked by the making of a second will in so far as the

---

(*f*) Revocation of a revocation of a will must also be made by will.

latter is inconsistent with the former.

If the second will is revoked, the first will becomes operative to the same extent as if it had not been revoked.

2259. Any person who is in possession of a will which has not been taken into official custody is bound to deliver it without delay to the Probate Court after he has knowledge of the death of the testator.

If a will is in the custody of a public authority other than a Court, or if it is taken into official custody by a notary, it shall be delivered to the Probate Court after the death of the testator. The Probate Court shall demand its delivery if it has knowledge of the existence of the will.

2260. The Probate Court (g) shall, as soon as it has knowledge of the death of the testator, fix a day for the opening of his will, if it is in its official custody. The statutory heirs of the testator and all other interested parties should, if possible, be summoned to be present on that day.

On the fixed day the will shall be opened, read out to the interested parties, and on demand submitted to them for perusal. Where the will is submitted for perusal, the formality of reading aloud the will can be dispensed with.

A protocol concerning the opening of the will shall be drawn up. If the will was sealed, the protocol shall state whether the seal was broken or not before it was opened.

2261. If a Court other than the Probate Court has the will in its official custody, the duty of opening the will is imposed upon such Court. The will, together with a certified copy of the protocol drawn up concerning the opening of the will, shall be sent to the Probate Court; a certified copy of the will shall be retained.

2262. The Probate Court shall notify to any interested parties who were not present at the opening of the will, any part thereof in which they are interested.

2263. Any direction given by the testator forbidding the opening of his will immediately after his death is void.

(g) *I.e.*, the Probate Court of the place where the testator was last domiciled.

2264. Any person is entitled to inspect the will after it has been opened, and to demand a copy or any part thereof, provided that he can offer *primâ facie* proof that he has a legal interest therein; the copy shall be certified on demand.

EIGHTH TITLE.
Joint Will.

2265. A joint will may be made only by a married couple.

2266. A joint will may be made in the manner provided for by 2249, even if the conditions of 2249 exist with reference to only one of the spouses.

2267. It is sufficient for making a joint will in the manner provided for by 2232. If one of the spouses makes a will in the manner prescribed therein, and the other spouse makes a declaration that the will shall be deemed also to be his or her will. The declaration must be written and signed by his (or her) own hand, stating the place where and date at which it is made.

2268. A joint will is invalid in its entirety in the cases provided for by 2077.

If the marriage is dissolved before the death of one of the spouse, or if the conditions of 2077, par. 1, sentence 2, exist, the dispositions remain operative in so far as it may be presumed that they would have been made even if the testator had known of such circumstances.

2269. Where the spouses have directed in a joint will whereby each appoints the other heir, that after the death of the surviving spouse the estate of both shall devolve on a third party, it is to be presumed, in case of doubt, that the third party has been appointed heir of the surviving spouse for the whole estate.

Where the spouses have created a legacy by such a joint will which is to be carried out after the death of the surviving spouse, it is to be presumed, in case of doubt, that the legacy is not to devolve upon the legatee until after the death of the surviving spouse.

2270. Where the spouses have made dispositions in a joint will from which it may be presumed that the disposition of the one would not have been made if the disposition of the other had been omitted, then, if one of the dispositions is void or is revoked, the other also is rendered void.

Such a relation of interdependence of the dispositions is, in case of doubt, to be presumed, if the spouses have mutually made testamentary gifts to each other; or if a testamentary gift has been made by either spouse to the other and a disposition, operative in the event of the latter surviving the former, has been made in favour of any person who is related by blood or who is on intimate terms with the former.

The provision of par. 1 does not apply to any dispositions other than those relating to the appointment of an heir, legacies, or testamentary burdens (h).

2271. The revocation of a disposition which stands in the relation of the kind specified in 2270 with a disposition of the other spouse shall be effected during the lifetime of both spouses in the manner provided for by 2296, applicable to rescission from a contract of inheritance. Neither spouse may, during the lifetime of the other, unilaterally make any new disposition *mortis causa* revoking his (or her) original disposition.

The right of revocation is extinguished on the death of the other spouse; the surviving spouse may, however, revoke his (or her) disposition, if he (or she) disclaims the testamentary gift given to him (or her). Even after acceptance of the testamentary gift the surviving spouse is entitled to revoke under 2294 and 2336.

If a testamentary gift has been given to any descendant, entitled to compulsory portion, of both spouses or of one of the spouses, the provision of 2289, par. 2, applies *mutatis mutandis*.

2272. A joint will may be withdrawn from official custody only by both spouses in the manner provided for by 2256.

2273. In the opening of a joint will the dispositions of the surviving spouse shall not, in so far as they can be separated from the others, is read out, nor shall they be brought to the knowledge of the interested parties in any other

(h) *E.g.*, nomination of a guardian.

manner. A certified copy of the dispositions of the deceased spouse shall be made. The will shall be re-sealed and re-taken into official custody (i).

FOURTH SECTION.
CONTRACT OF INHERITANCE.

2274. A testator can conclude a contract of inheritance only in person (k).

2275. No person may enter into a contract of inheritance in the capacity of testator, unless he be capable of disposing without limitation.

A spouse may, in the capacity of testator, enter into a contract of inheritance with his (or her) spouse, even though he (or she) be limited in disposing capacity. In such a case he (or she) requires the consent of his (or her) statutory agent; if the statutory agent is a guardian, ratification by the Guardianship Court is also necessary (l).

The provisions of par. 2 apply also to betrothed persons.

2276. A contract of inheritance may be entered into only before a judge or notary in the presence of both parties simultaneously. The provisions of 2233 to 2245 apply; any provisions contained therein which are applicable to a testator apply also to each of the contracting parties.

For a contract of inheritance between spouses or between betrothed persons which is recorded in the same document as a contract of marriage, the form prescribed for the contract of marriage is sufficient (m).

2277. A document recording a contract of inheritance should be sealed in the manner provided for by 2246, and indorsed and taken into official custody, unless the parties demand otherwise. The parties are deemed, in case of doubt,

---

(i) *Scilicet*, if the will has been placed in official custody.

(k) A contract of inheritance may be entered into not only between spouses or persons betrothed to each other, but also between any persons who are capable of making a valid contract.

(l) Ratification by the Guardianship Court is not necessary if the spouse is under parental power.

(m) See 1434. The formal requirements provided for in 2233—2245 are therefore dispensed with.

to have demanded otherwise if the contract of inheritance is recorded in the same document in which some other contract (n) is recorded.

A certificate relating to the custody of the contract of inheritance taken into official custody should be issued to each of the contracting parties.

2278. Each of the parties to a contract of inheritance may make contractual dispositions *mortis causa*.

Dispositions other than those relating to the institution of an heir, legacies, and testamentary burdens may not be made (o).

2279. The provisions applicable to testamentary gifts and testamentary burdens apply *mutatis mutandis* to contractual testamentary gifts and contractual testamentary burdens.

The provisions of 2077 apply to a contract of inheritance between spouses or betrothed persons even though a third party is a beneficiary under the contract.

2280. Where spouses have provided in a contract of inheritance whereby they are mutually appointed heirs, that the estate of both shall devolve upon a third party after the death of the surviving spouse, or have directed that a legacy shall be carried out after the death if the surviving spouse, the provision of 2269 applies *mutatis mutandis*.

2281. A contract of inheritance may be avoided by the testator under 2078, 2079; for avoidance under 2079 it is necessary that the compulsory beneficiary be living at the time of avoidance (p).

Where a disposition made in favour of a third party is avoided by the testator after the death of the other contracting party, the avoidance shall be declared to the Probate Court. The Probate Court should communicate the declaration to the third party.

(n) *E.g.*, a contract of marriage.

(o) *Unilateral* depositions relating to other matters than those mentioned in the text, as, *e.g.*, the appointment of an executor, may, however, be made. Cf. 2299.

(p) The avoidance must be effected against the other contracting party during the latter's lifetime. 143.

2282. The avoidance may not be made by an agent of the testator. If the testator is limited in disposing capacity, he does not require the consent of his statutory agent for making the avoidance.

Where a testator is incapable of disposing, his statutory agent may, with the ratification of the Guardianship Court, avoid a contract of inheritance on behalf of such testator.

A declaration of avoidance requires judicial or notarial authentication.

2283. Avoidance may be effected by a testator only within the period of one year.

The period begins to run, in the case of avoidance on the ground of threats, from the time at which the coercion ceases; in all other cases, from the time at which the testator has knowledge of the ground for avoidance. The provisions of 203, 206, applicable to prescription, apply *mutatis mutandis* to the running of the period.

If, in the case provided for by 2282, par. 2, the statutory agent has not avoided the contract of inheritance in due time, the testator himself may, after the cessation of his disposing incapacity avoid his contract of inheritance in the same manner as though he had not had a statutory agent.

2284. Confirmation of a voidable contract of inheritance may be made only by the testator in person [(q)]. If the testator is limited in disposing capacity, the right to confirm the contract is barred.

2285. The persons specified in 2080 may no longer avoid a contract of inheritance under 2078, 2079, if the testator's right of avoidance is extinguished [(r)] at the time of the accrual of the inheritance.

2286. The right of the testator to dispose of his property by juristic act *inter vivos* is not limited by a contract of inheritance.

2287. If the testator has made a gift with the intention of injuring his contractual heir, the contractual heir may, after the inheritance has devolved upon

(*q*) The confirmation is not subject to any formal requirements.

(*r*) By confirmation of the contract or by lapse of time.

him, require the donee to return the gift under the provisions relating to the return of unjustified benefits.

The claim is barred by prescription in three years after the devolution of the inheritance.

2288. If the testator has destroyed, removed, or damaged the object of a legacy made under a contract of inheritance, with the intention of injuring the legatee, the value of the object takes the place of the object in so far as the heir is thereby rendered incapable of carrying out the legacy [(s)].

If the testator has alienated or given a charge upon the object with the intention of injuring the legatee, the heir is bound to procure the object or to extinguish the charge for the legatee; the provisions of 2170, par. 2, apply *mutatis mutandis* to such obligation. If the alienation or charge is made by way of gift, the legatee has, in so far as he may not demand compensation from the heir, the claim specified in 2287 against the donee.

2289. A prior testamentary disposition made by the testator is revoked by a contract of inheritance in so far as it would impair the right of a beneficiary under the contract. A subsequent disposition *mortis causa* is, subject to the provision of 2297, inoperative to the same extent.

Where the beneficiary is a descendant of the testator entitled to a compulsory portion, the testator may, by a subsequent testamentary disposition, give any of the directions permitted to him by 2238.

2290. A contract of inheritance or any individual contractual disposition may be revoked by contract between the parties to the contract of inheritance. Revocation may not be effected after the death of either party.

The testator may enter into the contract to revoke only in person [(t)]. If he is limited in disposing capacity, he does not require the consent of his statutory agent [(u)].

If the other party is under guardianship, ratification by the Guardianship

(*s*) This provision presupposes that the legacy has not been revoked by the testator.

(*t*) A person incapable of disposing may not enter into such a contract.

(*u*) Cf. 2282.

Court is necessary. The same rule applies if he is under parental power, unless the contract is entered into between spouses or betrothed persons [x].

The contract is required to be in the form prescribed in 2276 for the contract of inheritance.

2291. A contractual disposition whereby a legacy or a testamentary burden is created, may by revoked by a will made by the testator. The consent of the other contracting party is necessary for the validity of the revocation; the provisions of 2290, par. 3, apply.

A declaration of consent requires judicial or notarial authentication; the consent is irrevocable.

2292. A contract of inheritance concluded between spouses may also be revoked by a join will of the spouses [y]; the provisions of 2290, par. 3, apply.

2293. A testator may rescind his contract of inheritance, if he has reserved the right to do so in the contract [z].

2294. A testator may rescind a contractual disposition, if the beneficiary has been guilty of any misconduct which entitles the testator to deprive him of his compulsory portion, or, where the beneficiary does not belong to the class of persons entitled to compulsory portions, would entitle the testator to deprive him of his compulsory portion if he were a descendant of the testator [a].

2295. A testator may rescind a contractual disposition if it is made in consideration of a duty, imposed upon the beneficiary by a juristic act, to make periodical payments to the testator during the latter's lifetime, *e.g.*, payments to be made in respect of a claim for maintenance, and the duty is extinguished before the death of the testator.

2296. The rescission may not be made through an agent. If the testator is limited in disposing capacity, he does not require the consent of his statutory agent.

(*x*) Cf. 2275.

(*y*) Cf. 2265 *et seq.*

(*z*) The other party does not have such right.

(*a*) Such right need not be expressly reserved by the testator in his contract of inheritance.

The rescission is effected by declaration to the other contracting party. The declaration requires judicial or notarial authentication.

2297. In so far as the testator is entitled to rescind, he may, after the death of the other contracting party, revoke the contractual disposition by a will. In the cases provided for by 2294, the provisions of 2336, pars. 2 to 4, apply *mutatis mutandis*.

2298. If both parties have made contractual dispositions in a contract of inheritance, the nullity of any one of these dispositions renders the entire contract invalid [(b)].

If the right of rescission has been reserved in such a contract, the whole contract is revoked by rescission on the part of one of the contracting parties [(c)]. The right of rescission is extinguished on the death of the other contracting party. The surviving party may, however, revoke his disposition by will if he disclaims the gift conferred upon him by the contract [(d)].

The provisions of par. 1 and par. 2, sentences 1 and 2, do not apply if a contrary intention of the contracting parties is to be inferred.

2299. Either of the contracting parties may unilaterally make any disposition in the contract of inheritance which may be made by will [(e)].

To such a disposition the same applies as if it had been made by will [(f)]. The disposition may also be revoked by any contract whereby a contractual disposition may be revoked [(g)].

Where the contract of inheritance is revoked by the exercise of the right of rescission or by contract, the disposition is thereby invalidated, unless a contrary intention of the testator is to be inferred.

(*b*) Cf. 139.

(*c*) When the rescission refers only to a particular disposition contained in the contract, it is presumed that the contract remains binding in respect of the other dispositions.

(*d*) Cf. 2271, par. 2.

(*e*) *E.g.*, nomination of a guardian.

(*f*) The party making the disposition may revoke it at any time.

(*g*) 2290.

2300. The provisions 2259 to 2263, 2273, applicable to the opening of a will, apply *mutatis mutandis* to a contract of inheritance; the provisions of 2273, sentence 2 and 3, however, only in so far as the contract of inheritance is in official custody.

2301. The provisions relating to dispositions *mortis causa* apply to a promise of a gift made subject to the condition that the donee shall survive the donor. The same rule applies to a promise of debt or acknowledgment of debt of the kind specified in 780, 781, made by way of gift subject to the same condition.

If the donor executes the gift by delivery of the object given, the provisions relating to gifts *inter vivos* apply.

2302. A contract whereby a person binds himself to make or not to make, to revoke or not to revoke a disposition *mortis causa*, is void.

FIFTH SECTION.
COMPULSORY PORTION.

2303. If a descendant of a testator is excluded from succession by disposition *mortis causa*, he may demand his compulsory portion from the heir. The compulsory portion is equal to one-half of the statutory portion (h).

The same right belongs to the parents and spouse of the testator, if they have been excluded from succession by a disposition *mortis causa* (i).

2304. The giving of a compulsory portion is, in case of doubt, not deemed to be an appointment of heir.

2305. If a share in the inheritance has been left to a compulsory beneficiary which is less than one-half of his statutory portion, the compulsory beneficiary may claim the deficiency from his co-heirs as his compulsory portion.

(*h*) A compulsory portion may be renounced by the person entitled thereto. 2346 *et seq.*

(*i*) It is to be noticed that a brother or sister of the testator is not entitled to any compulsory portion.

2306. If a compulsory beneficiary entitled to inherit as heir has been limited by the appointment of a reversionary heir, or of an executor, or by a direction for the partition of the estate, or if he has been charged with a legacy or testamentary burden, the limitation or charge is deemed not to have been created if the share in the inheritance left to him does not exceed one-half of his statutory portions. Where his share in the inheritance is greater than one-half of his statutory portion, he may claim his compulsory portion if he disclaims his share in the inheritance [k]; the period for disclaimer does not begin to run until the compulsory beneficiary has knowledge of the limitation or charge.

It is equivalent to a limitation by the appointment of an heir, if the compulsory beneficiary has been appointed reversionary heir.

2307. Where a legacy has been given to a compulsory beneficiary, he may claim his compulsory portion if he disclaims the legacy. If he does not disclaim the legacy, he has a right to a compulsory portion only in so far as the value of the former is less than the value of the latter; in calculating the value of the legacy any limitations and charges of the kind specified in 2306 are not taken into consideration.

The heir who is charged with the legacy may fix a reasonable period for the compulsory beneficiary to declare whether or not he will accept the legacy [l]. Upon the expiration of the period the legacy is deemed to have been disclaimed unless acceptance has been declared within such period.

2308. Where a compulsory beneficiary who, as heir or legatee, has been limited or charged in the manner specified in 2306, has disclaimed the inheritance or legacy, he may avoid the disclaimer if the limitation or charge has disappeared by the time of the disclaimer and such disappearance was unknown to him.

(*k*) A compulsory beneficiary has a right to his compulsory portion free from all charges. Where his share in the inheritance which is subject to a limitation or charge is greater than his compulsory portion, he may either claim his compulsory portion free from all charges, or accept his share in the inheritance subject to the limitation or charge.

(*l*) If he claims the compulsory portion, he is presumed to have disclaimed the legacy.

The provisions, applicable to the avoidance of a disclaimer of an inheritance [(m)], apply *mutatis mutandis* to the avoidance of a disclaimer of a legacy. The avoidance is effected by declaration to the person charged with the legacy.

2309. Descendants of remoter degree and the parents of the testator are not entitled to compulsory portions in so far as a descendant of nearer degree, who would exclude them from statutory succession, is entitled to compulsory portion, or accepts any testamentary gift left to him.

2310. In determining the value of a share in the inheritance which is taken as a basis for calculating the value of a compulsory portion, the persons who have been excluded from succession by testamentary disposition, or have disclaimed the inheritance, or have been declared unworthy to inherit [(n)], are also counted [(o)]. A person who has been excluded from statutory succession by renunciation of the inheritance is not counted.

2311. The condition and value of the estate at the time of the accrual of the inheritance are taken as a basis for calculating the value of a compulsory portion. In calculating the value of the compulsory portion due to the testator's parents, any preferential benefit [(p)] due to the surviving spouse of the testator is not taken into consideration.

The value shall, so far as is necessary, be ascertained by appraisement. A valuation made by the testator is not conclusive.

2312. If the testator has directed, or if it is to be presumed, as provided for in 2049, that one of the heirs shall have the right to appropriate a farm forming part of the estate at the value of its products [(q)], and if such right is exercised, the value of the products is also conclusive for calculating the value of a compulsory portion. Where the testator has fixed some other price of appro-

(*m*) *I.e.*, 1954 *et seq.*

(*n*) Cf. 2339 *et seq.*

(*o*) Heirs who died before the testator's death are not counted.

(*p*) 1932.

(*q*) 2049; and IA, Art. 137.

priation, such price is conclusive if it is not less than the value of the products nor more than the value of appraisement.

If the testator leaves only one heir, he may direct that the value of the products or any other price fixed in the manner provided for by par. 1, sentence 2, shall be taken as a basis for calculating the value of a compulsory portion.

These provisions apply only where the heir who acquires the farm belongs to the class of persons specified in 2303 who are entitled to compulsory portions.

2313. In determining the value of the estate, rights and liabilities which are subject to a condition precedent are not taken into consideration. Rights and liabilities which are subject to a condition subsequent are taken into consideration as if they were unconditional. Where the condition is fulfilled, a reduction corresponding to the new legal situation shall be made.

The same rule applies to uncertain or insecure rights and doubtful liabilities, just as if they were rights and liabilities subject to a condition precedent. The heir is bound as towards the compulsory beneficiary to determine the condition of uncertain rights, and to enforce insecure rights in so far as this is required by the rules of proper management of property.

2314. If a compulsory beneficiary is not an heir (r), the heir shall give to him on demand all information concerning the condition of the estate (s). The compulsory beneficiary demand that he be called to take part in making an inventory of the objects belonging to the estate which is to be presented to him, as provided for in 260, and that the value of the objects belonging to the estate be communicated to him. He may also demand that the inventory be made by the competent public authority, or by a competent official, or by a notary.

The cost is borne by the estate.

2315. A compulsory beneficiary shall deduct from his compulsory portion any benefit which has been conferred on him by the testator by a juristic act *inter vivos*, with the direction that such benefit shall be deducted from his com-

---

(*r*) This happens whenever the compulsory beneficiary has been expressly excluded from succession, or has disclaimed any share in the inheritance as provided for in 2306.

(*s*) The compulsory beneficiary does not have any such right as against an executor.

pulsory portion [(t)].

The value of such benefit is added to the estate in calculating the value of the compulsory portion. The value of such benefit is determined as at the time at which the benefit was conferred.

Where the compulsory beneficiary is a descendant of the testator, the provision of 2051, par. 1, applies *mutatis mutandis.*

2316. Where there are several descendants among whom a gift made by the testator would be subject to hotchpot liability in case of statutory succession, the value of the compulsory portion of each of the descendants is determined by the statutory portion which would accrue to him at the time of partition, regard being had to the hotchpot liability. A descendant who has been excluded from statutory succession by renunciation of the inheritance is not taken into consideration in calculating the value.

Where the compulsory beneficiary is an heir, and where the value of the compulsory portion, calculated in the manner provided for by par. 1, is greater than the value of the share in the inheritance given to him, he may demand from the co-heirs the excess in value as his compulsory portion, even if the share given to him is equal to or greater than one-half of his statutory portion.

The testator may not, to the detriment of a compulsory beneficiary, exclude any benefits of the kind specified in 2050, par. 1, from being taken into consideration.

Where any benefit to be taken into consideration, as provided for in par. 1, is to be deducted at the same time from the compulsory portion as provided for in 2315, such reduction takes place only in respect of one-half of the value of such benefit.

2317. The claim for a compulsory portion comes into being on the accrual of the inheritance [(u)].

The claim passes by inheritance and is transferable.

(*t*) Such direction may be either express or implied. As the testator was under obligation to furnish an "advancement" to his child, he could not have directed the advancement to be deducted from the child's compulsory portion. 1624.

(*u*) See 1922.

2318. An heir may reduce a legacy with which he is charged, in so far as the liability in respect of compulsory portions is borne by him and the legatee proportionately. The same rule applies to a testamentary burden.

As against a legatee who is also a compulsory beneficiary, such reduction of his legacy is not permissible to the extent of depriving him of his own compulsory portion.

Where the heir is himself a compulsory beneficiary, he may, on account of his liability in respect of compulsory portions, reduce any legacy or testamentary burden to the extent that he is not deprived of his own compulsory portion.

2319. Where one of several heirs is a compulsory beneficiary, he may, after partition of the estate, refuse to satisfy another compulsory beneficiary to the extent that he is not deprived of his own compulsory portion. The other heirs are liable for any deficiency due to such other compulsory beneficiary.

2320. A person who becomes an heir in the place of a compulsory beneficiary shall, as between himself and the other co-heirs, bear the burden in respect of the compulsory portion, and shall, where the compulsory beneficiary has accepted a legacy given to him, bear the burden of such legacy to the extent of the benefits received.

In case of doubt the same rule applies to a person to whom the testator has, by a disposition *mortis causa*, given the compulsory beneficiary's share in the inheritance.

2321. Where a compulsory beneficiary has disclaimed a legacy given to him, then as between the heirs and the legatees the person who benefits by the disclaimer shall bear the burden in respect of the compulsory portion to the extent of the benefit received [(x)].

2322. If an inheritance or a legacy disclaimed by one of the compulsory beneficiaries, has been charged with a legacy or testamentary burden, the person who benefits by such disclaimer [(y)] may reduce [(z)] the legacy or testa-

---

(x) Cf. 2307.

(y) And who consequently bears the burden to the legacy or testamentary burden. 2320, 2321.

(z) Cf. 2188, 2318.

mentary burden to the extent that he is not deprived of the amount sufficient for the payment of the compulsory portion.

2323. An heir may not refuse to execute a legacy or testamentary burden under 2318, par. 1, in so far as he has not to bear the burden in respect of compulsory portions as provided for in 2320 to 2322.

2324. A testator may, by disposition *mortis causa*, impose, as between the heirs themselves, the burden in respect of compulsory portions, upon one or more of them, and may give any directions varying the provisions of 2318, par. 1, and 2320 to 2323.

2325. Where a testator has made a gift to a third party [(a)], a compulsory beneficiary may claim, by way of augmentation of his compulsory portion [(b)], the amount whereby the compulsory portion would be increased if the object given were added to the estate.

A consumable thing is estimated at the value which it had at the date of the gift. An object other than a consumable thing is estimated at the value which it had at the time of the accrual of the inheritance; if its value at that time is greater than its value at the date of the gift, only the latter is taken into consideration.

The gift is not taken into consideration if, at the time of the accrual of the inheritance, ten years have elapsed since delivery of the object given; if the gift was made by the testator to his surviving spouse, the period does not begin to run until the dissolution of the marriage.

2326. The compulsory beneficiary may claim an augmentation of his compulsory portion even if one-half of his statutory portion has already been given to him. If more than one-half of his statutory portion has been given to him, such claim is barred to the extent of the excess in value which he has received.

2327. Where the compulsory beneficiary has himself received a gift from

---

(*a*) That is, to a person who is not a compulsory beneficiary. For a gift made to a compulsory beneficiary, see 2327.

(*b*) *Ergänzung des Pflichtteils.*

the testator, the value of the gift shall be added to the estate in the same manner as if it were made to a third party (c), and shall at the same time be deducted from the compulsory beneficiary's augmentation of his compulsory portion. The value of a gift to be deducted in the manner provided for by 2315, shall be deducted from the total value of the compulsory portion and of any augmentation of such portion.

Where the compulsory beneficiary is a descendant of the testator, the provision of 2051, par. 1, applies *mutatis mutandis* (d).

2328. If an heir is himself a compulsory beneficiary, he may refuse augmentation of another compulsory beneficiary's portion to the extent that he is not deprived of his own compulsory portion, including what would accrue to him by way of augmentation of his own compulsory portion.

2329. In so far as an heir is not liable for augmentation of a compulsory portion, the compulsory beneficiary may, under the provisions relating to the return of unjustified benefits (e), require any donee of the testator to return the gift for the purpose of making up the deficiency. If the compulsory beneficiary is sole heir, he has the same right.

The donee may refuse to return the gift by payment of its value.

Among several donees a prior donee is liable only in so far as a subsequent donee is not liable.

2330. The provisions of 2325 to 2329 do not apply to gifts which are made in compliance with a moral duty or the rules of social propriety (f).

2331. A gift made out of any common property under the régime of general community of goods, community of income and profits, or community of moveables, is deemed to have been made by both spouses in equal shares. If, however, the gift was made to a person who is a descendant of one only of the spouses, or of whom one only of the spouses is a descendant, or if one of the

---

(*c*) "Third party" here means "a person who is not a compulsory beneficiary".

(*d*) The period of ten years specified in 2325, par. 3, does not apply to this case.

(*e*) See 818—822.

(*f*) See notes (*m*) and (*n*) to 534.

spouses has to make compensation to the common property for the value of the gift, it is deemed to have been made by such spouse alone.

These provisions apply *mutatis mutandis* to a gift made out of any common property under the régime of continued community of goods [(g)].

2332. The claim to compulsory portion is barred by prescription in three years from the time at which the compulsory beneficiary has knowledge of the accrual of the inheritance and of any disposition whereby his compulsory portion is injured; in the absence of such knowledge, in thirty years from the accrual of the inheritance.

Any claim which a compulsory beneficiary has against a donee under 2329 is barred by prescription in three years from the accrual of the inheritance.

The prescription is not suspended by the fact that such claims may not be enforced until after a disclaimer of the inheritance or legacy [(h)].

2333. A testator may deprive a descendant of his compulsory portion:

(1) if the descendant makes an attempt against the life of the testator, or of his spouse, or of any of his descendants;

(2) if the descendant has been guilty of wilful corporal ill-treatment of the testator or his spouse; in the case of ill-treatment of his spouse, however, only where the descendant is also descended from such spouse;

(3) if the descendant has been guilty of any crime, or any serious wilful offence against the testator or his spouse;

(4) if the descendant maliciously commits a breach of his statutory duty to furnish maintenance to the testator;

(5) if the descendant leads a dishonourable or immoral life contrary to the testator's wishes.

2334. A testator may deprive his father of his compulsory portion, if the latter has been guilty of any of the offences specified in 2333 (1), (3), (4). The testator has the same right against his mother if she has been guilty of any

(*g*) Cf. 1483.

(*h*) See 2306 *et seq.*

such offence.

2335. A testator may deprive his (or her) spouse of his (or her) compulsory portion if the spouse is guilty of an offence by virtue of which the testator is entitled to petition for divorce as provided for in 1565 to 1568.

The right of deprivation is not extinguished by the lapse of the period specified in 1571 for the assertion of the ground for divorce.

2336. The deprivation of a compulsory portion is effected by testamentary disposition.

The ground for deprivation must exist at the time of making the disposition and must be stated therein.

The burden of proving the existence of such ground is upon the person who sets up the deprivation.

In the case provided for by 2333 (5) deprivation is ineffective if the descendant has permanently ceased to lead a dishonourable or immoral life.

2337. The right of deprivation of a compulsory portion is extinguished by condonation. A disposition whereby a testator has directed any such deprivation is invalidated by condonation [(i)].

2338. Where a descendant has, by prodigality or insolvency, endangered his future acquisition to a serious extent, the testator may limit such descendant's right to compulsory portion by directing that after the latter's death his statutory heirs shall receive, as reversionary heirs or as reversionary legatees, the share which has been given to him, or the compulsory portion accruing to him, in proportion to their statutory portions. The testator may also direct that his share or compulsory portion shall be subject to the management of an executor during the lifetime of the descendant; in such a case the descendant has a claim to the net profits of his share or compulsory portion [(k)].

The provisions of 2336, pars. 1 to 3, apply *mutatis mutandis* to such directions. Any such directions are inoperative if at the time of the accrual of the

---

(*i*) The condonation may be either express or implied.

(*k*) Such a limitation of a descendant's right to compulsory portion is known under German legal terminology as *Enterbung in guter Absicht* (*Exheredatio bona mente*).

inheritance the descendant permanently reforms himself in respect of prodigality, or the insolvency constituting the ground for such directions no longer exists.

SIXTH SECTION.
UNWORTHINESS TO INHERIT.

2339. A person is unworthy to inherit:

(1) who has wilfully and unlawfully killed or attempted to kill the testator, or has brought him to a condition in consequence of which the testator became incapable, down to the date of his death, of making or revoking a disposition *mortis causa*;

(2) who has wilfully and unlawfully prevented the testator from making or revoking a disposition *mortis causa*;

(3) who has, by fraud or unlawful threats, induced the testator to make or revoke a disposition *mortis causa*;

(4) who has, in respect of a disposition *mortis causa* made by the testator, been guilty of any act punishable under the provisions of 267 to 274 of the Criminal Code [(*l*)].

In the cases provided for by par. 1 (3), (4), the unworthiness to inherit does not arise if, before the accrual of the inheritance, the disposition which the testator has been induced to make or in respect of which the criminal act has been committed, has become inoperative, or the disposition which he has been induced to revoke, would have become inoperative even if it had not been revoked.

2340. Unworthiness to inherit is set up by an avoidance of the acquisition of the inheritance.

The avoidance is not permissible until after the devolution of the inheritance. As against a reversionary heir the avoidance may be effected as soon as the inheritance has devolved upon the limited heir.

(*l*) These provisions deal with falsification of documents.

The avoidance may be effected only within the period specified in 2082.

2341. Any person is entitled to avoid who benefits by the failure to inherit on the part of the person who is unworthy to inherit, even if he does not benefit thereby until the failure to inherit on the part of another person also.

2342. The avoidance is effected by bringing an action for avoidance. The action shall be brought for the purpose of having the heir declared unworthy to inherit.

The effect of such avoidance does not come into being until the decree ceases to be appealable.

2343. The right of avoidance is barred if the testator has condoned the person unworthy to inherit.

2344. Where an heir has been declared unworthy to inherit, the devolution of the inheritance upon him is deemed not to have taken place.

The inheritance devolves upon the person who would have been entitled to inherit if the person unworthy to inherit had died at the time of the accrual of the inheritance; the devolution is deemed to have taken place at the time of the accrual of the inheritance.

2345. Where a legatee has been guilty of any one of the offences specified in 2339, par. 1, his claim arising from the legacy is voidable. The provisions of 2082, 2083, 2339, par. 2, and 2341, 2343, apply.

The same rule applies to a claim for compulsory portion, if the compulsory beneficiary has been guilty of any one of such offences (*m*).

(*m*) In all cases under 2345, the avoidance is not effected by an action for avoidance (cf. 2342), but by a declaration of avoidance made to the Probate Court.

SEVENTH SECTION.
RENUNCIATION OF INHERITANCE (n).

2346. Relatives by blood and the spouse of a person may renounce their statutory (o) rights of inheritance in respect of such person's inheritance by contract with him (p). The party renouncing is excluded from statutory succession as though he had died before the accrual of the inheritance; he has no right to any compulsory portion.

The renunciation may be limited to the right to compulsory portion.

2347. Where the party renouncing is under guardianship, ratification by the Guardianship Court is necessary for the renunciation; where he is under parental power, the same rule applies unless the contract is entered into between spouses or betrothed persons.

The person to whose inheritance the renunciation refers may enter into the contract only in person; if he is limited in disposing capacity, he does not require the consent of his statutory agent (q). If the person to whose inheritance the renunciation refers, is incapable of disposing, the contract may be entered into through his statutory agent; ratification by the Guardianship Court is necessary to the same extent as is provided for in par. 1.

2348. A contract of renunciation requires judicial or notarial authentication.

2349. If a descendant or a relative by blood in the collateral line of the person to whose inheritance the renunciation refers renounces his statutory right of inheritance, the effect of the renunciation extends to his descendants, unless

---

(n) A renunciation of an inheritance (*Erbverzicht*) must not be confounded with a disclaimer of an inheritance (*Ausschlagung der Erbschaft*) dealt with in 1942—1966. An inheritance can be "renounced" only during the lifetime of the person to whose estate the renunciation refers, and only by a contract with him, whereas the right of disclaiming an inheritance does not come into existence until the devolution of the inheritance (1942), and can be exercised only within a prescribed period (1944) by declaration to the Probate Court. 1945.

(o) Or testamentary. 2352.

(p) Or with his statutory heirs. 312, par. 2.

(q) Cf. 2290.

it is otherwise provided.

2350. If any person renounces his statutory right of inheritance in favour of another, it is to be presumed, in case of doubt, that the renunciation is intended to be operative only in the event of such other person becoming an heir.

If a descendant of the person to whose inheritance the renunciation refers, renounces his statutory right of inheritance, it is to be presumed, in case of doubt, that the renunciation is to be operative only in favour of the other descendants and the spouse of such person.

2351. The provisions of 2348, and, in respect of the person to whose inheritance the renunciation refers, the provisions also of 2347, par. 2, apply to a contract whereby a renunciation of the inheritance is revoked.

2352. A person who has been appointed heir or has been made a legatee under a will, may renounce the testamentary gift by contract with the testator. The same rule applies to a gift made to a third party by a marriage contract [(r)]. The provisions of 2347, 2348, apply.

EIGHTH SECTION.
CERTIFICATE OF INHERITANCE.

2353. The Probate Court shall issue to the heir on demand a certificate relating to his right of inheritance, and, where he is entitled only to a share in the inheritance, relating to the value of his share (*i.e.*, a certificate of inheritance).

2354. A person who, as a statutory heir, applies for the issue of a certificate of inheritance, shall state:

(1) the date of the testator's death;

(2) the relationship upon which his right of inheritance is based;

(*r*) The fact whether or not such third party is an heir or a legatee is entirely immaterial. He, and not the other contracting party, has the right to renounce.

(3) whether any persons, and, if so, who exist or existed, by whom he would be excluded from succession, or by whom his share in the inheritance would be diminished;

(4) whether any, and if so what, dispositions *mortis causa* of the testator exist;

(5) whether any action relating to his right of inheritance is pending.

If a person fails to inherit who would exclude the applicant from succession, or in whose favour his share in the inheritance would he diminished, the applicant shall state the manner in which such person fails to inherit.

2355. A person who applies for the issue of a certificate of inheritance by virtue of a disposition *mortis causa* shall specify the disposition upon which his right of inheritance is based; shall state whether any and what other dispositions *mortis causa* of the testator exist; and shall make a statement as to the matters prescribed in 2354, par. 1 (1) (5), and par. 2.

2356. The applicant shall prove by public act [(s)] the accuracy of the statements made in accordance with 2354, par. 1 (1) (2), and par. 2; and shall, in the case provided for by 2355, produce the document in which his right of inheritance is recorded. Where the document cannot be procured or can be procured only at disproportionate expense, the production of other evidence is sufficient.

In regard to the other statements required to be made by 2354, 2355, the applicant shall, before a Court or notary, give a guarantee, instead of swearing an oath, to the effect that he is not aware of any circumstance which is inconsistent with the statements made. The Probate Court may dispense with the guarantee if it deems such a step unnecessary.

These provisions do not apply in so far as the facts are known to the Probate Court.

2357. Where there are several heirs, a joint certificate of inheritance shall be issued upon application. The application may be made by any one of the heirs.

(*s*) See Code of Civil Procedure, s. 380.

In the application the names of the heirs and their shares in the inheritance shall be stated.

Where the application is not made by all the heirs, it shall contain a statement to the effect that the other heirs have accepted the inheritance (t). The provisions of 2356 apply also to any statements made by the applicant relating to the other heirs.

The guarantee in lieu of oath shall be given by all the heirs, unless the Probate Court holds the guarantee by one or more of them to be sufficient (u).

2358. The Probate Court shall, of its own motion and after having considered the evidence offered by the applicant, make any verification which is necessary for establishing the facts of the case, and shall admit any proper evidence which has been offered.

The Probate Court may issue a public citation to all other persons to notify it of their rights of inheritance; the manner of publication and the period for notification are determined by the provisions relating to public summons (x).

2359. The certificate of inheritance may be issued only if the Probate Court holds that the facts necessary to support the application have been established.

2360. If an action relating to the right of inheritance is pending, the opponent of the applicant should be heard before the issue of the certificate of inheritance.

Where a disposition upon which the right of inheritance is based is not recorded in any public act submitted to the Probate Court, then before the issue of a certificate of inheritance the person who would be heir if the disposition were invalid should be heard on the question of its validity.

It is not necessary that he should be heard if it is impracticable.

(*t*) The reason being that a certificate of inheritance may not be issued before the acceptance of the inheritance. Application for the issue of such a certificate is, however, *primâ facie* proof of acceptance of the inheritance.

(*u*) Where a co-heir has obtained a certificate of inheritance, the other co-heirs are released from the obligation of giving the guarantee.

(*x*) See 948 *et seq.* of the Code of Civil Procedure.

2361. If it appears that any certificate of inheritance which has been issued is inaccurate, the Probate Court shall order it to be returned. The certificate of inheritance becomes void upon being returned.

Where the certificate of inheritance cannot be returned forthwith, the Probate Court shall order it to be cancelled [y]. The order shall be published in accordance with the provisions of the Code of Civil Procedure applicable to the public service of a citation [z]. The cancellation becomes operative upon the expiration of one month after the last publication of the order in the public journal.

The Probate Court may, of its own motion, verify the accuracy of any certificate of inheritance issued by it.

2362. The true heir may require any person who is in possession of an inaccurate certificate of inheritance to return it to the Probate Court.

Any person to whom an inaccurate certificate of inheritance has been issued shall give to the true heir all information relating to the condition of the inheritance and the place where the objects belonging to the inheritance may be found [a].

2363. A certificate of inheritance issued to a limited heir shall state the fact that reversionary succession has been directed; the conditions under which it will take place; and the name of the person who will become the reversionary heir [b]. Where the testator has appointed the reversionary heir for the residue of the inheritance remaining at the time of the occurrence of reversionary succession, or where he has directed that the limited heir shall be entitled to have free disposition of the inheritance, this shall also be stated.

The reversionary heir has the right specified in 2362, par. 1.

2364. Where the testator has appointed an executor, the appointment shall be stated in the certificate of inheritance.

(*y*) No appeal (*Beschwerde*) lies against such an order. See Voluntary Jurisdiction Act, s. 84.

(*z*) See Code of Civil Procedure, 204.

(*a*) Such person may, in certain cases, be required to swear an oath of disclosure as provided for in 260, 261.

(*b*) See 2100 *et seq.*

The executor has the right specified in 2362, par. 1.

2365. It is presumed that the person who is named as heir in the certificate of inheritance has the right of inheritance stated in the certificate, and that he is not limited by any directions other than those stated therein.

2366. If any person acquires, by a juristic act entered into with the person named in the certificate of inheritance as heir, any object belonging to the inheritance or any right over such object or a release from a right forming part of the inheritance, the contents of the certificate are deemed to be accurate in his favour to the extent of the presumption created by 2365, unless he knows [(c)] of the inaccuracy, or knows that the Probate Court has demanded the certificate to be returned on account of its inaccuracy.

2367. The provisions of 2366 apply *mutatis mutandis*, where any act of performance has been done in favour of the person named as heir in the certificate of inheritance, by reason of a right forming part of the inheritance, or where a juristic act, containing a disposition affecting such a right and not coming within the provision of 2366, has been entered into between him and another relating to such a right.

2368. The Probate Court shall issue to an executor on demand a certificate of his appointment. Where the executor is limited in his administration of the estate, or where the testator has directed that the executor shall have an unlimited right of incurring obligations on account of the estate, this shall be stated in the certificate.

Where the appointment is not recorded in any of the public acts produced to the Probate Court, then before the issue of the certificate the heir should, if possible, be heard on the question of the validity of the appointment.

The provisions relating to a certificate of inheritance apply *mutatis mutandis* to such a certificate; the certificate becomes inoperative upon vacation of office by the executor.

(c) But not "or ought to have known"; in other words, *constructive* knowledge is insufficient for this purpose.

2369. Where objects situate within the Empire form part of an inheritance in respect of which no German Probate Court is competent to issue a certificate of inheritance, the issue of a certificate of inheritance relating to such objects may be required.

An object in respect of which a book or register is kept by a German public authority for the registration of any person entitled thereto, is deemed to be situate within the Empire. A claim is deemed to be within the Empire if a German Court is competent to entertain an action thereon.

2370. If a person declared to be dead was living at or died before the date which is deemed to be the date of his death, the person who would be heir by virtue of the declaration of death is, even without the issue of a certificate of inheritance, deemed to be heir in favour of a third party in respect of the juristic acts specified in 2366, 2367, unless the third party is aware of the incorrectness of the declaration of death, or knows that the declaration of death has been revoked in consequence of an action to set it aside.

Where a certificate of inheritance has been issued, the person declared to be dead has, if he is still living, the rights specified in 2362. A person whose death has been erroneously presumed without a declaration of death has the same rights [(d)].

NINTH SECTION.

PURCHASE OF AN INHERITANCE [(e)].

2371. A contract, whereby an heir sells the inheritance which has devolved on him, requires judicial or notarial authentication [(f)].

(*d*) *E.g.*, where a dead body has been erroneously identified.

(*e*) A purchaser of an inheritance does not acquire any *right* of inheritance in the strict sense of the term, but only *all the individual objects* belonging to the inheritance. The general provisions relating to sale (433 *et seq.*), in so far as they are not is inconsistent with the provisions under the present title, apply *mutatis mutandis* to the purchase of an inheritance.

(*f*) Where a co-heir sells his share in the inheritance, the other co-heirs have the right of pre-emption. 2034. A sale of an inheritance to a third party before its devolution is void. 312.

2372. Any benefits which result from the lapse of a legacy or testamentary burden, or from the hotchpot liability (g) of a co-heir, accrue to the purchaser.

2373. Any share in the inheritance which devolve on the seller after the conclusion of the sale by virtue of reversionary succession, or in consequence of the failure to inherit on the part of a co-heir (h), and any preferential legacy (i) given to the seller are, in case of doubt, not deemed to have been included in the sale. The same rule applies to any documents or pictures of the deceased's family.

2374. The seller is bound to deliver to the purchaser the objects belonging to the inheritance existing at the time of the sale, including what he has acquired before the sale by virtue of any right forming part of the inheritance, or as compensation for the destruction, deterioration or deprivation of an object belonging to the inheritance, or by a juristic act which related to the inheritance.

2375. If the seller has consumed, gratuitously alienated or given a charge upon any object belonging to the inheritance before the sale, he is bound to compensate the purchaser for the value of the object consumed or alienated, or for any diminution in value in consequence of the charge. The duty to make compensation does not arise if the purchaser knew at the time of the purchase that the object had been consumed or disposed of gratuitously.

For the rest, the purchaser may not claim compensation for any deterioration, destruction, or impossibility (k), arising from any other reason, of delivery of an object belonging to the inheritance.

2376. The obligation of the seller to give a warranty against defects of title (l) is limited to a warranty that the right of inheritance belongs to him; that it is not limited by the right of any reversionary heir or by the appointment of an executor; that his right of inheritance is not subject to any legacy, testamentary

---

(*g*) See 2050 *et seq.*

(*h*) As to the right of accrual (*jus accrescendi*), see 2094.

(*i*) See 2150.

(*k*) See 275, par. 2.

(*l*) Cf. 434.

burden, compulsory portion, hotchpot liability, nor to any direction as to partition (m); and that unlimited liability (n) to all or some of the creditors of the estate has not been incurred.

The seller is not responsible for defects of quality in a thing forming part of the inheritance.

2377. The legal relations extinguished in consequence of the accrual of the inheritance by merger of a right in a liability or of a right in a charge are, as between the purchaser and the seller, deemed not to have been extinguished. Such a legal relation shall be restored, if necessary.

2378. The purchaser is bound as towards the seller to discharge the liabilities of the estate, unless the seller warrants that they do not exist as provided for in 2376.

If the seller has discharged a liability of the estate before the sale, he may demand re-imbursement from the purchaser.

2379. Emoluments becoming due for the period prior to the sale remain vested in the seller. He bears the charges payable during such period, including any interests on the liabilities of the estate. However, all charges payable out of the inheritance (o) and all extraordinary charges which are deemed to have been imposed on the capital of the objects belonging to the inheritance are borne by the purchaser.

2380. The purchaser assumes, after the conclusion of the purchase, the risk of accidental loss or accidental deterioration of the objects belonging to the inheritance. From and after that date all emoluments accrue to him, and he bears all charges.

2381. The purchaser shall re-imburse the seller for the necessary outlay which the latter has incurred on the inheritance before the sale.

In respect of any other outlay incurred before the sale, the purchaser shall

(*m*) Cf. 2048.

(*n*) See 1967, 1975 *et seq*.

(*o*) See 103.

make re-imbursement in so far as the value of the inheritance is increased by such outlay at the time of the sale.

2382. The purchaser is, after the conclusion of the purchase, liable to the creditors of the estate, without prejudice to the continuance of the seller's liability (p). The same rule applies also to any liabilities for the discharge of which the purchaser is not liable to the seller as provided for in 2378, 2379.

The liability of the purchaser to the creditors may not be excluded or limited by agreement between the purchaser and the seller.

2383. The provisions relating to the limitation of an heir's liability apply to the liability of the purchaser (q). The purchaser is liable without limitation, in so far as the seller at the time of the sale was liable without limitation. If the liability of the purchaser is limited to the inheritance, his claims arising from the purchase are deemed to be part of the inheritance.

The filing of an inventory (r) by the seller or purchaser avails also in favour of the other party, unless the latter is liable without limitation.

2384. The seller is bound as towards the creditors of the estate to notify without delay to the Probate Court (s) the sale of the inheritance and the name of the purchaser. Notification by the purchaser takes the place of notification by the seller.

The Probate Court shall permit any person to inspect the notification, provided he can offer *primâ facie* proof that he has a legal interest therein.

2385. The provisions relating to the purchase of an inheritance apply *mutatis mutandis* to the purchase of an inheritance acquired by the seller by contract, and to any other contracts which are for the alienation of an inheritance which has devolved on the alienor or which has been acquired by him in some other manner.

In the case of a gift the donor is not bound to make compensation for any

---

(*p*) That is, both contracting parties are liable to the creditors of the estate.

(*q*) See 1975 *et seq*.

(*r*) See 1993.

(*s*) That is, the Probate Court of the place where the testator was last domiciled.

objects belonging to the inheritance which have been consumed or alienated gratuitously before the date of the gift, nor for any charge upon such objects created gratuitously before such date. The obligation specified in 2376 in respect of warranty against defects of title is not imposed on the donor; if the donor has fraudulently concealed a defect, he is bound to compensate the donee for any damage arising therefrom.

In testimony whereof We have signed with Our own hand and have affixed the Imperial Seal.

Given in the New Palace, the 18th day of August, 1896.

[L. S.] WILHELM.

PRINCE OF HOHENLOHE.

APPENDIX A.

INTRODUCTORY ACT TO THE CIVIL CODE.
(August 18th, 1896.)

WE, **WILLIAM**, by the Grace of God, German Emperor, King of Prussia, &c., decree in the name of the Empire, with the consent of the Federal Council and the Imperial Parliament, as follows:

FIRST SECTION.
GENERAL PROVISIONS [a].

ART. 1. The Civil Code shall come into force on the 1st day of January, 1900; at the same time the following laws shall also come into force: The Act relating to Alterations in the Act for the Organization of the Judiciary, the Code of Civil Procedure and the Bankruptcy Act; the Act relating to Compulsory Auction and Compulsory Management; the Land Registration Act; and the Voluntary Jurisdiction Act [b].

ART. 2. Every legal rule (*Rechtsnorm*) is law (*Gesetz*) within the meaning of the Civil Code and of the present Act [c].

(*a*) These "general provisions" (Arts. 1—31) deal mainly with the subject of "Conflict of Laws" or "Private International Law", to use the favourite expression of Continental jurists.

(*b*) The Compulsory Auction and Compulsory Management Act and the Land Registration Act were passed on March 24, 1897; all the other Acts mentioned in the text were passed on May 17, 1898. The Revised Commercial Code of May 10, 1897, also came into force on the same day as the Civil Code.

(*c*) A Government Ordinance, or a provision contained in a treaty with a foreign power, or a rule of customary law of the Empire (but not of the individual States), is deemed to be a "legal rule" within the meaning of this provision.

ART. 3. If, in the Civil Code or in the present Act, the right to legislate has been reserved to the States, or if it has been provided therein that certain provisions of the State laws remain unaffected or may be enacted, then the existing provisions of the State laws remain in force, and new provisions may be enacted by State laws.

ART. 4. If, in the Imperial or State laws, reference is made to provisions which are repealed by the Civil Code or by the present Act, the corresponding provisions of the Civil Code or of the present Act shall take their place.

ART. 5. The Imperial territory of Alsace-Lorraine is deemed to be a State within the meaning of the Civil Code and of the present Act.

ART. 6. In civil actions in which a claim is enforced by action or counter-action under the Civil Code, the procedure and the decision of the last instance, within the meaning of sect. 8 of the Introductory Act to the Act of the Organization of the Judiciary, is assigned to the Imperial Court.

ART. 7. The disposing capacity of a person is determined by the law of the country of which he is a subject.

If an alien who is of full age or who has the legal status of a person of full age becomes a subject of the Empire, he retains the legal status person of full age, even though he be not of full age under German law [(d)].

If an alien enters into a juristic act within the Empire for which he is incapable or is limited in capacity, he is deemed to be capable of entering into the juristic act in so far as he would be capable under German law. This provision does not apply to juristic acts under the family law and the law of inheritance, nor to juristic acts whereby a piece of land situated in a foreign country is disposed of.

ART. 8. An alien may be interdicted within the Empire under German law, provided he has his domicile or, where he has no domicile, his residence within the Empire.

(*d*) Cf. Code of Civil Procedure, 55, and Bill of Exchange Act, s. 84.

ART. 9. A person who has disappeared may within the Empire be declared dead under German law, provided he was a German at the time of his disappearance.

If, at the time of his disappearance, he was a subject of a foreign country, he may be legally declared dead within the Empire under German law in respect of the legal relations which are determined by German law, and also in respect of his property situated within the Empire; the provisions of 2369, par. 2, of the Civil Code apply *mutatis mutandis*.

If an alien who has disappeared was domiciled within the Empire, and if his wife who has remained or has returned within the Empire is a German, or was a German until her marriage with the person who has disappeared, such person may, upon the application of the wife, be declared dead within the Empire under German law without the limitation specified in par. 2.

ART. 10. An association belonging to a foreign country and having juristic personality under the laws of that country is, if it could acquire juristic personality within the Empire only under the provisions of 21, 22 of the Civil Code, deemed to have juristic personality if its juristic personality has been recognised by a resolution of the Federal Council. The provisions relating to partnership and the provision of 54, sentence 2, of the Civil Code apply to foreign associations of the kind specified which have not been so recognised.

ART. 11. The form of a juristic act is determined by the laws which govern the legal relation forming the object of the juristic act. However, compliance with the laws of the place where the juristic act is entered into is sufficient.

The provision of par. 1, sentence 2, does not apply to a juristic act whereby a right to a thing is created or whereby such a right is disposed of [(e)].

ART. 12. By reason of an unlawful act committed in a foreign country, no greater claims can be enforced against a German than those constituted by German law [(f)].

ART. 13. The conclusion of a marriage, even if only one of the parties is a

---

(e) Such a juristic act is governed by the *lex rei sitae* (Art. 28).

(f) This provision does not apply in favour of aliens.

German, is determined in respect of each of the parties by the laws of the country of which he (or she) is a subject [(g)]. The same rule applies to an alien who concludes a marriage within the Empire [(h)].

In respect of the wife of an alien declared dead under Article 9, par. 3, the conclusion of a new marriage is determined by German law.

The form of a marriage which is concluded within the Empire is determined exclusively by German law.

ART. 14. The personal legal relations of German spouses *inter se* are determined by German law, even if the spouses have their domicile in a foreign country.

The German law applies even though the husband has lost the German nationality, provided the wife has retained her German nationality.

ART. 15. The matrimonial régime is determined by the German law if the husband was a German at the time of the conclusion of the marriage.

If the husband acquires German nationality after the conclusion of the marriage, or if foreign spouses have their domicile within the Empire, the laws of the country of which the husband was a subject at the time of the conclusion of the marriage govern the matrimonial régime; the spouses may, however, enter into a marriage contract, even though it would not be permissible under the laws of that country.

ART. 16. If alien spouses, or spouses who acquire the German nationality after the conclusion of the marriage, have their domicile within the Empire, the provisions of 1435 of the Civil Code apply *mutatis mutandis*; the foreign statutory régime is equivalent to a contractual régime.

The provisions of 1357, 1362, 1405 of the Civil Code apply, in so far as they are more favourable to third parties than the foreign laws.

ART. 17. Divorce is governed by the laws of the country of which the husband is a subject at the time when the petition is filed.

(*g*) In other words, the marriage must be valid under the laws to which both parties are subject.

(*h*) This is true even in a case where both parties are aliens.

A fact which occurred while the husband was a subject of another country may be set up as a ground for divorce only if the fact is also a ground for divorce or judicial separation under the laws of that country.

If at the time when the petition is filed the husband has lost his German nationality, while the wife is a German, German law applies.

A divorce or judicial separation may not be granted within the Empire by virtue of a foreign law, unless a divorce would be permitted both by the foreign law and by German law.

ART. 18. The legitimate descent of a child is determined by German law if the husband of the mother is a German at the time of the birth of the child, or, where he has died before the birth of the child, was a German at the time of his death (*i*).

ART. 19. The legal relations between the parents and a legitimate child are determined by German law if the father, or, if the father has died, the mother, possesses German nationality. The same rule applies if the German nationality of the father or of the mother is lost, provided the child retains German nationality (*j*).

ART. 20. The legal relations between an illegitimate child and the mother are determined by German law, if she is a German. The same rule applies if she has lost her German nationality while the child has retained its German nationality.

ART. 21. The father's duty to furnish maintenance to an illegitimate child, and his duty to reimburse the mother for the expenses of pregnancy, confinement and maintenance is determined by the law of the country of which the mother is a subject at the time of the birth of the child; no greater claims, however, can be enforced than what have been constituted by German law.

ART. 22. The legitimation of an illegitimate child and the adoption of a child is determined by German law if the father at the time of the legitimation,

---

(*i*) This provision is applicable even to the case where the child has subsequently lost his German nationality.

(*j*) Cf. Art. 28.

or the adoptor at the time of the adoption, possesses German nationality.

If the father or the adoptor is a subject of a foreign country, while the child possesses German nationality, the legitimation or adoption is ineffective if the necessary approval, under German law, of the child or of a third party with whom the child stands in a family relation, has not been given.

ART. 23. A guardianship or a curatorship may be established within the Empire, even over an alien, in so far as the government of the country of which he is a subject does not assume to take care of him, provided the alien requires guardianship or curatorship under the laws of that country, or has been interdicted within the Empire.

The German Guardianship Court may take provisional measures so long as no guardianship or curatorship has been established.

ART. 24. Succession to the estate of a German, even if he had his domicile in a foreign country, is determined by German law.

If a German had, at the time of his death, his domicile in a foreign country, his heirs may, in respect of their liability for the liabilities of the estate, invoke the laws in force at the place of the domicile of the deceased.

If an alien who has made or revoked a disposition *mortis causa* acquires the German nationality, the validity of the making or of the revocation is determined by the law of the country of which he was a subject at the time of making or revoking the disposition; he retains also his capacity to make a disposition *mortis causa*, even if he has not attained the age required by German law. The provision of Article 11, par. 1, sentence 2, remains unaffected.

ART. 25. Succession to the estate of an alien who, at the time of his death, had his domicile within the Empire, is determined by the law of the country of which he was a subject at the time of his death. A German may, nevertheless, enforce claims arising from his right of inheritance, even if they are constituted only by German law, unless, according to the law of the country of which the deceased was a subject, succession to the estate of a German who had his domicile in that country is determined exclusively by German law.

ART. 26. If, out of an estate which has accrued in a foreign country, property situated within the Empire is transferred to the heirs or legatees entitled to it according to the law in force in that country, through the instrumentality of German authorities, a third person may not object to the transfer on the ground that he has a claim to the property as heir or legatee.

ART. 27. If German law is declared to be applicable by the law of a foreign country whose law is declared to be applicable by Article 7, par. 1, Article 13, par. 1, Article 15, par. 2, Article 17, par. 1, and Article 25, then German law applies.

ART. 28. The provisions of Articles 15, 19, 24, par. 1, 25 and 27, do not apply to objects which are not within the territory of the country whose laws are applicable according to these provisions, and which, according to the laws of the country within whose territory they are, are subject to special provisions.

ART. 29. If a person is a subject of no country, his legal relations, so far as the laws of the country of which a person is a subject have been declared to be applicable, are determined according to the laws of the country of which the person was last a subject, and if he has not previously been a subject of any country, according to the laws of the country in which he has or had, at the time which is material, his domicile, and, in the absence of a domicile, his residence.

ART. 30. The application of a foreign law is not permitted if the application would be *contra bonos mores*, or contrary to the object of a German law.

ART. 31. It may be provided by order of the Imperial Chancellor, with the consent of the Federal Council, that a right of reprisal may be exercised against a foreign country, its subject and their legitimate successors (k).

SECOND SECTION.
RELATION OF THE CIVIL CODE TO THE IMPERIAL LAWS.

ART. 32. The provisions of the Imperial Laws (l) remain in force. Nevertheless, they are repealed in so far as the repeal results from the Civil Code and the

(*k*) Cf. Code of Civil Procedure, 110 (1).

(*l*) Including all treaties concluded between the Empire and foreign powers.

present Act [m].

ART. 33. In so far as relatives by blood or by marriage of a person incur legal consequences through him in the manner provided for by the Act for the Organisation of the Judiciary, the Code of Civil Procedure, the Code of Criminal Procedure, the Bankruptcy Act and the Act of July 21, 1879 (*Reichs-Gesetzbl.*, p. 277), relating to the Avoidance of Juristic Acts of a Debtor apart from Bankruptcy Proceedings, the provisions of the Civil Code relating to relationship by blood or by marriage apply.

ART. 34. [This article contains a few amendments to the Criminal Code.]

ART. 35. [This article contains a few amendments to the Code of Criminal Procedure.]

ART. 36. [This article contains a few amendments to the Industrial Code.]

ART. 37. Sect. 2 of the Act of November 1, 1867, relating to the Freedom of Removal (*Freizügigkeit*) (*Bundes-Gesetzbl.*, p. 55), is amended as follows:

A person who claims any rights arising from German nationality shall, on demand, furnish proof of his German nationality, and, where he is under parental power or guardianship, furnish proof of the ratification of his statutory agent.

A married woman requires the ratification of her husband.

ART. 38. The Act of November 8, 1867, relating to the Organisation of the Consulate of the Confederation and the Rights and Duties of Consuls of the Confederation (*Bundes-Gesetzbl.*, p. 137) is thus supplemented:

I. Sect. 16 contains the following as par. 2:

In respect of the making of a disposition *mortis causa* the right of acting as a notary, specified in par. 1, belongs to a trading consular officer (*Wahlkonsul*) [n] only when such right has been specially conferred on him by the Imperial Chancellor.

(*m*) The repeal may be made in express terms or by implication.

(*n*) See Oppenheim's International Law, 1905, Vol. I. s. 420, and foot-note.

II. The following provision is added as 17a:

The provisions of the Civil Code, and not the provisions of 17, apply to the making of a disposition *mortis causa*.

ART. 39. The Act of November 14, 1867, relating to Stipulated Interest (*Bundes-Gesetzbl.*, p. 159) is repealed.

ART. 40. The Act of May 4, 1870, relating to the Conclusion of Marriage and the Authentication of the Civil Status of Subjects of the Confederation in a Foreign Country (*Bundes-Gesetzbl.*, p. 599), is amended as follows:

I. In 3, par. 1, sentence 1, 9, 11, par. 2, and 12, par. 1, sentence 2, for the word "must" is substituted the word "should".

II. The following provisions take the place of 7, 8:

Sect. 7.

[Re-enacts 1317 of the Civil Code.]

Sect. 7a.

[Re-enacts 1318 of the Civil Code.]

Sect. 8.

[Re-enacts 1319 of the Civil Code.]

Sect. 8a.

A marriage concluded before an official authorized to celebrate marriages (1), or before an official having the legal status of such an official, is not void on account of a defect in form unless the form prescribed in 7 has not been observed at the time of the celebration.

[The second paragraph re-enacts 1324 of the Civil Code.]

ART. 41. The Act of June 1, 1870, relating to Acquisition and Loss of the Nationality of the Confederation and of the States (*Bundes-Gesetzbl.*, p. 355) is amended as follows:

I. The following provisions take the place of 11:

The grant of State nationality extends, unless an exception thereto is made, at the same time to the wife and to minor children, in respect of whom the grantee or naturalized person is the statutory agent by virtue of the parental power. Daughters who are or have been married are excepted.

II. The following provisions are added as 14a:

The release (*Entlastung*) from State nationality of a person who is under parental power or guardianship may be applied for by his statutory agent only with the ratification of the Guardianship Court.

The ratification of the Guardianship Court is not necessary if the father or the mother applies for the release for himself or herself, and at the same time for the child by virtue of the parental power. If the scope of authority of a supplementary guardian appointed for the mother extends to the care of the child's person, the mother in such a case requires the ratification of the supplementary guardian for the application for the release of the child from State nationality.

III. The following provisions take the place of 19:

The release of a person from nationality extends, unless an exception thereto is made, at the same time to his wife and to children in respect of whom such person is the statutory agent by virtue of the parental power.

This provision does not apply to daughters who are or have been married, nor to children who are under the parental power of the mother, if she requires for making an application for the release of the children from nationality, the ratification of the supplementary guardian as provided for in 14a, par. 2, sentence 2.

IV. The following provisions take the place of 21, par. 2:

The loss of State nationality under these provisions extends at the same time to the wife and to children in respect of whom the releasee is the statutory agent by virtue of the parental power, provided the wife or the children are with him. Daughters who are or have been married are excepted.

ART. 42. The Act of June 7, 1871, relating to the Obligation to make Compensation for causing Death or Bodily Injuries in the Working of Railways, Mines, &c. (*Reichs-Gesetzbl.*, p. 207), is amended as follows:

I. The following provisions take the place of 3:

Sect. 3.

In the case of causing death compensation (1 and 2) shall be made by the reimbursement of the expenses of an attempted cure, and any pecuniary loss which the deceased has sustained by reason of the fact that during his illness his earning capacity was destroyed or impaired, or an increase of his necessities occurred. The person liable to make compensation shall also make good the funeral expenses to the person upon whom the duty of defraying such expenses is imposed.

If at the time of the injury the deceased stood in a relation to a third party by virtue of which he was or might be bound by law to furnish maintenance to such third party, and if such third party is deprived of his right to maintenance in consequence of the death, the person liable to make compensation shall make compensation to such third party in so far as the deceased would be liable to furnish such maintenance during the presumable period of his life. The duty to make such compensation arises even if the third party was only *en ventre sa mère* at the time of the injury.

Sect. 3a.

In the case of bodily injury compensation (1 and 2) shall be made by reimbursement of the expenses of an attempted cure, and all pecuniary loss which the injured person has suffered by reason of the fact that in consequence of the injury his earning capacity has been destroyed or impaired, or an increase of his necessities has arisen, permanently or temporarily.

II. In 5 for the words "of the provisions contained in 1 to 3" are substituted the words:

"of the provisions contained in 1 to 3a".

III. The following provisions take the place of 7, 8, 9:

Sect. 7.

The compensation for the destruction or diminution of the earning capacity and the increase of the necessities of the injured person, and the compensation to be made to a third party as provided for in 3, par. 2, shall, of the future, be made by payment of a money annuity.

The provisions of 843, pars. 2 to 4, of the Civil Code, and 648 (6) of the Code of Civil Procedure, apply *mutatis mutandis*. The same rule applies, in respect of the money annuity to be paid to the injured person, to the provision of 749, par. 3, and, in respect of the money annuity to be paid to the third party, to the provision of 749, par. 1 (2), of the Code of Civil Procedure.

If, at the time when judgment was delivered against the person bound to pay a money annuity, security has not been ordered to be given, the person entitled may, nevertheless, require security to be given if the pecuniary condition of the person bound has become materially worse; under the same conditions, the person entitled may require an increase of the security fixed in the judgment.

Sect. 8.

Claims for compensation (1 to 3a) are barred by prescription in two years after the time of the accident. As against the person to whom the person killed had to furnish maintenance (3, par. 2), the prescription begins to run from the death. For the rest, the provisions of the Civil Code relating to prescription apply.

Sect. 9.

The statutory provisions remain unaffected, according to which, apart from the cases provided for by the present Act, a contractor who undertakes to build a structure of the kind specified in 1 and 2, or any other person who is, *e.g.*, responsible on account of his own fault, is liable for any damage arising from causing death or bodily injury to a human being in the construction of the structure.

ART. 43. Sect. 6, par. 2, of the Act of March 31, 1873 (*Reichs-Gesetzbl.*, p. 61), relating to the Legal Relations of Imperial Officials, is repealed.

ART. 44. The provisions of 44 of the Imperial Military Act of May 2, 1874 (*Reichs-Gesetzbl.*, p. 45), apply *mutatis mutandis* to persons who are members of the crew of a ship in the service of the Imperial Navy so long as the ship is outside of a domestic port, or so long as such persons are in the custody of an enemy as prisoners of war or hostages; and other persons taken on board of such a ship, so long as they are on board, and so long as the ship is outside of a domestic port. The period upon whose expiration a testamentary disposition ceases to be operative begins from the time at which the ship returns to a domestic port, or the person who has made the disposition is no longer on board the ship, or ceases to be a prisoner of war or hostage in the custody of the enemy. Other vessels of the Imperial Navy are in the same position as ships.

ART. 45. Sect. 45, par. 2, sentence 2, of the Imperial Military Act of May 2, 1874 (*Reichs-Gesetzbl.*, p. 45), is repealed.

ART. 46. The Act of February 6, 1875, relating to the Authentication of Civil Status and the Conclusion of Marriage (*Reiehs-Gesetzbl.*, p. 23), is amended as follows:

I. Sects. 28 to 40, 42, 43, 51 to 53 are repealed.

II. The following provisions take the place of 41, 44, 50, 55:

Sect. 41.

The celebration of a marriage is governed by the provisions of the Civil Code.

Sect. 44.

For the issue of an order for the public summons to be issued before the celebration of a marriage any registrar is competent, before whom the marriage may be celebrated, as provided for in 1320 of the Civil Code.

Sect. 50.

The registrar should not celebrate a marriage without public summons, unless a certificate by a medical officer is produced to him to the effect that the dangerous illness of one of the parties does not permit postponement of the celebration of the marriage.

Sect. 55.

If a marriage has been declared void, or if the non-existence of a marriage has been established in an action which has for its object the determination whether or not a marriage exists between the parties, or if a marriage has been dissolved before the death of one of the spouses, or if a judicial separation has been granted under 1575 of the Civil Code, this shall be recorded in the margin of the entry relating to the celebration of the marriage.

If the conjugal community is restored after a judicial separation, this shall on demand be recorded in the margin.

III. Sect. 67 contains the following as par. 2:

It is not deemed to be a criminal act where a clergyman or any person in religious service proceeds to the religious celebration of a marriage in a case where the dangerous illness of one of the parties does not permit postponement of the marriage.

IV. In 69 for the words "in this Act" are substituted the words:

"in this Act and in the Civil Code".

V. In 75, par. 1, for the words "according to the provisions of this Act" are substituted the words:

"according to the provisions of the Civil Code".

ART. 47. Sect. 3 of the Usury Act of May 24, 1880 (*Reichs-Gesetzbl.*, p. 109), as contained in Article II. of the Act of June 19, 1893, supplementary to the provisions relating to usury (*Reichs-Gesetzbl.*, p. 197), is repealed.

ART. 48. Sect. 16, par. 2, of the Act of April 20, 1881, relating to The Care of Widows and Orphans of Imperial Officers of the Civil Service (*Reichs-Gesetzbl.*, p. 85), is repealed.

ART. 49. Sect. 18, par. 2, of the Act of June 17, 1887, relating to the Care of Widows and Orphans of Persons serving in the Imperial Army and the Imperial Navy (*Reichs-Gesetzbl.*, p. 237), is repealed.

ART. 50. Sect. 9 of the Act of May 31, 1891, relating to the Imperial debt ledger (*Reichs-Gesetzbl.*, p. 321), is amended as follows:

A married woman is permitted to make an application without the consent of the husband.

A married woman requires the consent of her husband, if a provision in the letter's favour has been registered. Such a provision shall be registered if the married woman or the husband with her consent applies for its registration. The married woman is bound to give her consent to the husband if under the matrimonial *régime* existing between them she may not dispose of the uncertificated claim without the consent of the husband.

ART. 51. Sect. 8, par. 2, of the Act of June 13, 1895, relating to the Care of Widows and Orphans of Persons serving in the Imperial Army and the Imperial Navy of and above the rank of sergeant-major (*Reichs- Gesetzbl.*, p. 261), is repealed.

ART. 52. If, under an Imperial Act, compensation is to be paid to the owner of a thing on account of the deprivation, damage, or use of the thing, or on account of the limitation of his right of ownership in the interests of the public, and if a right in the thing belongs to a third party, for which special compensation is not paid, such third party has, in so far as his right is violated, the rights to the claim for compensation which he would have in respect of the proceeds of an auction if his right had been extinguished by compulsory auction.

ART. 53. If compensation is to be paid to the owner of a piece of land in a case provided for by Article 52, the provisions of 1128 of the Civil Code apply *mutatis mutandis* to the claim for compensation. If the person entitled takes objection, within the period specified in 1128, to the payment of the compensation to the owner, the owner and any other person entitled thereto may apply for the institution of proceedings for partition under the provisions applicable to distribution of proceeds in the case of compulsory auction. In such a case payment shall be made to the Court having jurisdiction over the proceedings for partition.

If the right of the third party is a perpetual charge on land, a hypotheca, a land charge, or an annuity charge, the liability of the claim for compensation is extinguished, if the damaged object has been restored, or a substitute has been provided for the moveable of which its owner has been deprived. If compensation is to be paid on account of the use of the land, or on account of the deprivation or damage of fruits and accessories, the provisions of 1123, par. 2, sentence 1, and 1124, pars. 1, 3, of the Civil Code apply *mutatis mutandis*.

ART. 54. The provision of 36, par. 4, of the Act of December 21, 1871, relating to Limitation of the Right of Ownership of Land in Fortified Places (*Reichs- Gesetzbl.*, p. 459), is not affected by the provisions of Articles 52 and 53. If proceedings for partition take place according to the provisions of Articles 52 and 53, the compensation shall, at the request of the Court having jurisdiction over the proceedings, be paid to such Court, in so far as payment is still outstanding at the time of the presentation of the request.

The provision of 37 of the same Act is amended as follows:

If a piece of land is charged with a right which is impaired by any limitation of the right of ownership, the person entitled may, before the lapse of one month after the owner has communicated to him the limitation of the right of ownership, apply for the institution of proceedings for partition.

THIRD SECTION.

RELATION OF THE CIVIL CODE TO STATE LAW.

ART. 55. The provisions of the private laws of the States are repealed unless it is otherwise provided for in the Civil Code and in the present Act.

ART. 56. The provisions of the treaties which a State has concluded with a foreign country before the date when the Civil Code comes into force remain unaffected.

ART. 57. In respect of the sovereigns of the States, members of their families, and members of the Princely House of Hohenzollern, the provisions of the Civil Code apply only in so far as the special provisions of the constitution of the House or of the State laws contain no provisions to the contrary.

The same rule applies in respect of members of the former Royal House of Hanover, the former Princely House of the Electorate of Hesse, and the former Princely House of the Duchy of Nassau.

ART. 58. In respect of the family relations and the properties of the Houses which were formerly members of the Empire, and have been mediatized since 1806, or which have obtained the legal status of such Houses in respect of their family relations and properties by resolution of the former German Confederation or by State law before the date when the Civil Code comes into force, the provisions of the State laws and, subject to the conditions provided for in the State laws, the provisions of the constitutions of the Houses remain unaffected.

The same rule applies in favour of the former Imperial nobility and of the families of the feudal nobility which, before the date when the Civil Code comes into force, have acquired under State law the legal status of the former Imperial nobility.

ART. 59. The provisions of State laws relating to family fideicommissa (*Familienfideikommisse*) and fiefs, including allodial fiefs, and the provisions relating to family settlements (*Stammgüter*) remain unaffected.

ART. 60. The provisions of State laws remain unaffected which permit the granting of a hypotheca, Land charge, or annuity charge on a piece of land, which can be charged only to a limited extent according to the provisions of Articles 57 to 59, in such a manner that the creditor may seek satisfaction out of the land exclusively by means of compulsory management by a receiver.

ART. 61. If the alienation or charging of a piece of land is not permitted, or is permitted only to a limited extent by the provisions of Articles 57 to 59, then in respect of an acquisition in violation of such provisions, the provisions of the Civil Code apply *mutatis mutandis* in favour of those who derive rights from a person without title.

ART. 62. The provisions of State laws relating to property subject to a rent charge (*Rentengüter*) remain unaffected.

ART. 63. The provisions of State laws relating to the heritable right of emphyteusis (*Erbpachtrecht*), including the right of small peasant proprietors (*Büdnerrecht*) and the right of small tenant farmers (*Häuslerrecht*), remain unaffected in those States in which such rights exist. The provisions of 1017 of the Civil Code apply *mutatis mutandis* to such rights.

ART. 64. The provisions of State laws relating to the right of a single heir (*Anerbenrecht*) in respect of agricultural and forest lands, together with their appurtenances, remain unaffected.

The State laws may not limit the right of a testator to make a disposition *mortis causa* affecting land subject to the right of such heir.

ART. 65. The provisions of State laws relating to rights to the use of water

(*Wasserrecht*), including right water-mills (*Mühlenrecht*) and the rights of inland navigation (*Flössereirecht*), the provisions relating to the promotion of irrigation and drainage of lands, and the provisions relating to accretion, islands formed by natural forces, and dry river beds, remain unaffected.

ART. 66. The provisions of State laws relating to the right of constructing a dike or to sewage works remain unaffected.

ART. 67. The provisions of State laws which belong to the mining law remain unaffected.

If, according to the provisions of State law, compensation is to be paid on account of damage to a piece of land caused by the working of a mine, the provisions of Articles 52, 53 apply, unless the State laws provide otherwise.

ART. 68. The provisions of State laws remain unaffected which permit the charging of a piece of land with a well-defined heritable and alienable right to obtain ores which are not subject to the provisions of the mining law. The provisions of 874, 875, 876, 1015, 1017 of the Civil Code apply *mutatis mutandis*.

ART. 69. The provisions of State laws relating to sporting and fishing remain unaffected, subject to the provision of 958, par. 2, of the Civil Code, and the provisions of the Civil Code relating to compensation for damage caused by game.

ART. 70. The provisions of State laws containing general principles by which damage caused by game is to be determined, and the provisions of State laws under which the claim to compensation for damage caused by game must be enforced in the competent Court within a fixed period, remain unaffected.

ART. 71. The provisions of State laws remain unaffected, according to which:

(1) the obligation to make compensation for damage caused by game arises even in a case where the damage is caused by animals which are suitable for sport, but are not those species specified in 835 of the Civil Code;

(2) the owner or the possessor of an enclosure is responsible for damage

caused by an animal suitable for sport running outside the enclosure;

(3) the owner of a piece of land is, where the sporting rights over another piece of land may be exercised only in common with the sporting rights over his own land, liable for damage caused by game on the other piece of land even if he has declined an offer of the sporting usufructuary lease made to him;

(4) the damage caused by game to gardens, orchards, vineyards, tree-nurseries and isolated trees, is not to be made good even if the preventive measures which are sufficient for preventing the damage under ordinary circumstances have been omitted;

(5) the obligation to make good the damage is regulated otherwise than in the case provided for by 835, par. 3, of the Civil Code;

(6) a communal authority, in the place of the owners of separate pieces of land united together as a single district for sporting purposes, is liable to make good any damage caused by game, and is entitled to have recourse against such owners; or the lessee under a sporting usufructuary lease, in the place of the owners or of the owners' union, or of the municipality, or jointly with them, is bound to make good the damage;

(7) a person bound to make compensation for any damage caused by game may require re-imbursement for the amount paid by him as compensation from the person who is entitled to exercise the sporting rights in another district.

ART. 72. If a right of use, unlimited in respect of time, exists over a piece of land, the provisions of 835 of the Civil Code relating to the obligation to make compensation for any damage caused by game apply, the person entitled to such right of use taking the place of the owner.

ART. 73. The provisions of State laws relating to Royal prerogatives remain unaffected.

ART. 74. The provisions of State laws relating to rights of restraint (*Zwangsrechte*), rights of ban (*Bannrechte*), and real rights to the conduct of an industry (*Realgewerbeberechtigungen*) remain unaffected.

ART. 75. The provisions of State laws relating to insurance remain unaffected unless special provisions have been enacted in the Civil Code.

ART. 76. The provisions of State laws relating to copyrights remain unaffected.

ART. 77. The provisions of State laws remain unaffected which relate to the liability of a State, or of the communes and other communal unions (provincial, circuit, and district unions), for any damage caused by their officials in the exercise of the public authority entrusted to them; similarly the provisions of the State laws remain unaffected which exclude the right of an injured party to require compensation from the officer for such an injury, in so far as the State or the communal union is liable.

ART. 78. The provisions of State laws remain unaffected, according to which officers are liable for the deputies and assistants employed by them to a greater extent than as provided for in the Civil Code.

ART. 79. The provisions of State laws remain unaffected, according to which experts appointed for the official estimation of the value of lands are liable for any damage caused by a breach of official duty to a greater extent than as provided for in the Civil Code.

ART. 80. Unless a special provision has been enacted in the Civil Code, the provisions of State laws remain unaffected which relate to pecuniary claims and obligations of officials, clergymen, and teachers in public institutions of learning, arising from their official or service relation, including claims of their heirs.

The provisions of State laws relating to prebendal rights (*Pfründenrecht*) remain unaffected.

ART. 81. The provisions of State laws which limit the transferability of claims of the persons specified in Article 80, par. 1, in respect of salaries, pay for engagement pending vacancy, pensions, widows' and orphans' pensions; and also the provisions of State laws which permit set-off against such claims otherwise than as provided for in 394 of the Civil Code, remain unaffected [(a)].

ART. 82. The provisions of State laws relating to the constitution of associations whose juristic capacity depends upon State grant remain unaffected.

ART. 83. The provisions of State laws relating to forestry associations remain unaffected.

ART. 84. The provisions of State laws under which a religious association or an ecclesiastical association may acquire juristic capacity only by means of legislation remain unaffected.

ART. 85. The provisions of State laws under which the property of a dissolved association devolves, in the case provided for by 45, par. 3, of the Civil Code, upon a corporation, foundation, or institution under public law instead of the Treasury, remain unaffected [(b)].

ART. 86. The provisions of State laws which limit the acquisition of rights by juristic persons, or make the acquisition subject to ratification by the State, in so far as the provisions relate to objects of more than five thousand marks in value, remain unaffected. If the ratification necessary under the State laws for an acquisition *mortis causa* is given, it is deemed to have been given before the accrual of the inheritance [(c)]; if the ratification is refused, the juristic person in respect of the devolution is deemed to be non-existent; the provision of 2043 of the Civil Code applies *mutatis mutandis*.

ART. 87. The provisions of State laws which make the validity of gifts to members of religious orders or similar congregations subject to State ratification remain unaffected.

The provisions of State laws according to which members of religious orders or similar congregations may acquire *mortis causa* only with State ratification remain unaffected. The provisions of Article 86, sentence 2, apply *mutatis mutandis*.

(*a*) See Code of Civil Procedure. 850.

(*b*) Similar to Arts. 129, 138.

(*c*) Cf. Civil Code, 84.

Members of such religious orders or similar congregations who are not bound to take any vows for life or for an indeterminate time are not subject to the provisions specified in pars. 1 and 2.

ART. 88. The provisions of State laws which make acquisition of lands by aliens subject to State ratification remain unaffected.

ART. 89. The provisions of State laws which permit extrajudicial attachment of things for the protection of land and its products, including the provisions relating to the payment of pledge money and compensation money, remain unaffected.

ART. 90. The provisions of State laws relating to the legal relations which arise out of the giving of security under public law on account of the discharge of an office or on account of the conduct of an industry remain unaffected.

ART. 91. The provisions of State laws under which the Treasury, a corporation, foundation, or institution under public law, or a foundation subject to the management of a public authority is, for the purpose of securing certain of its claims, entitled to require the registration of a hypotheca on land of the debtor; and the provisions of State laws under which the registration of the hypotheca is to take place at the request of a certain public authority, remain unaffected. The hypotheca may be registered only as a cautionary hypotheca; it comes into being upon registration.

ART. 92. The provisions of State laws which provide that payments out of public funds shall be received at the pay-office remain unaffected.

ART. 93. The provisions of State laws relating to the periods upon the expiration of which places leased under ordinary leases are to be vacated at the expiration of the leases remain unaffected.

ART. 94. The provisions of State laws relating to the conduct of business by pawnbrokers and pawnbroking institutions remain unaffected.

The provisions of State laws remain unaffected under which public pawnbroking institutions have the right to refuse to return any pledged thing to its owner until payment of the loan for which the thing was pledged.

ART. 95. The provisions of State laws relating to domestic servants (*Gesinderecht*) remain unaffected. The same rule applies also to the provisions relating to the duty to make compensation on the part of any person who induces a domestic servant to desert his master illegally, or accepts him into his service with knowledge of a still existing service relation, or issues an incorrect service testimonial.

The provisions of 104 to 115, 131, 278, 617 to 619, 624, 831, 840 (par. 2), and 1358 of the Civil Code apply; the provisions of 617, however, only in so far as State law does not give any greater claims to domestic servants than as provided for by the Civil Code.

A master has no right to inflict corporal punishment upon a domestic servant.

ART. 96. The provisions of State laws remain unaffected which relate to a contract of life annuity (*Leibgeding*), life pension (*Leibzucht*), old man's part (*Altenteil*) [(d)], or periodical acts of performance in consideration of the transfer of a farm (*Auszug*) [(e)]; provided the contract is entered into in respect of the transfer of land, and provided the provisions of State law regulate the obligation arising from such a contract only in the absence of any special agreement to the contrary.

ART. 97. The provisions of State laws remain unaffected which regulate the registration of creditors of a State in the State debt ledger, and the legal relations arising from the registration, *e.g.*, the transfer of and the giving of a charge upon an uncertificated claim.

In so far as a married woman is entitled under those provisions to make an application independently of her husband, such right is barred if a provision has been registered in the debt ledger in favour of the husband. Such a provision shall be registered if the wife or the husband with her consent has applied for the

(*d*) For a short account of the "old man's part", see Dr. Schuster's "The Principles of German Civil Law", p. 400.

(*e*) *Ibid*. p. 400.

registration. The wife is bound as towards the husband to give the consent if, under the matrimonial *régime* existing between them, she may not dispose of the uncertificated claim in question except with the consent of the husband.

ART. 98. The provisions of State laws relating to the repayment or conversion of interest bearing State debts for which instruments to bearer have been issued or which have been registered in the State debt ledger remain unaffected.

ART. 99. The provisions of State laws relating to public savings-banks remain unaffected, subject, however, to the provisions of 808 of the Civil Code and the provisions of the Civil Code relating to the investment of money belonging to a ward.

ART. 100. The provisions of State laws remain unaffected which enact that, in the case of obligations to bearer issued by a State, or one of its corporations, foundations, or institutions created under public law:

(1) the validity of a signature shall be subject to the observance of a special form, even if such form has not been provided for in the instrument;

(2) the claim specified in 804, par. 1, of the Civil Code shall be barred, even if such bar has not been provided for in the interest coupon or annuity coupon.

ART. 101. The provisions of State laws remain unaffected which bind a State, or one of its corporations, foundations, or institutions created under public law, in a manner other than that provided for by 806, sentence 2, of the Civil Code, to transfer the obligations to bearer issued by it, to the name of a specific person entitled thereto; similarly the provisions of State laws which regulate the legal relations arising from the transfer of such an obligation, including the declaration of cancellation, remain unaffected.

ART. 102. The provisions of State laws relating to declaration of cancellation and stoppage of payment in respect of the instruments specified in 807 of the Civil Code remain unaffected.

The provisions of State laws remain unaffected which prescribe any procedure other than the procedure by public summons for the declaration of cancellation of the instruments specified in 808 of the Civil Code.

ART. 103. The provisions of State laws remain unaffected under which a State, a union, or an institution which is bound by public law to furnish maintenance to a person may demand reimbursement of the outlay incurred in respect of such maintenance from the person to whom it has furnished the maintenance, or from any other persons who were bound by the provision of the Civil Code to furnish the maintenance.

ART. 104. The provisions of State laws relating to the claim for reimbursement in respect of public contributions which have been improperly raised, or in respect of costs of any legal proceedings, remain unaffected.

ART. 105. The provisions of State laws remain unaffected according to which an undertaker of a railway enterprise, or of any other enterprise involving danger to the public, is responsible for any damage arising from such enterprise to a greater extent than according to the provisions of the Civil Code.

ART. 106. The provisions of State laws remain unaffected which, in permitting a piece of land serving public use to be used in connection with a structure or a business, hold the owner of the structure or business responsible for any damage caused to the public use of the land by such structure or business.

ART. 107. The provisions of State laws relating to the duty of making compensation for damage caused by the infringement of a penal statute intended for the protection of land remain unaffected.

ART. 108. The provisions of State laws relating to the duty of making compensation for damage caused by a mob, riot, or insurrection remain unaffected.

ART. 109. The provisions of State laws relating to the removal, damage, or use of a thing in the interests of the public, or to the limitation of rights of ownership and the deprivation or limitation of other rights in the interests of the public, remain unaffected. Unless law provides otherwise the provisions of Articles 52, 53 apply to the compensation required by State law to be made on account of any one of these acts.

ART. 110. The provisions of State laws remain unaffected which, in providing for the case where buildings destroyed are restored in a different situation, regulate the respective rights over the different pieces of land concerned.

ART. 111. The provisions of State laws which, in the interest of the public, limit the rights of ownership [(f)] in respect of *de facto* acts of disposition [(g)] remain unaffected [(h)].

ART. 112. The following provisions of State laws remain unaffected: those relating to the consolidation of lands dedicated to railways of large or small gauge, and of any other properties (*i.e.*, consolidated railway, *Bahneinheit*); those relating to the alienation of or the giving of a charge upon such a consolidated railway or its component parts, particularly the giving of a charge in respect of the issue of part obligations to bearer (*Teilschuldverschreibungen auf den Inhaber*), and relating to the legal relations arising in connection therewith; and those relating to liquidation for the purpose of satisfying the creditors who have a preferential right to claim satisfaction out of the component parts of the consolidated railway.

ART. 113. The provisions of State laws remain unaffected which relate to the consolidation of pieces of land, partition of community, the regulating of roads, the regulating of the relations between a lord of a manor and his tenant, and the cancellation, conversion or limitation of servitudes and perpetual charges. This applies also to the provisions which regulate any affairs which are common to the parties concerned and which result from any one of the above-mentioned matters, or which relate to the acquisition of ownership, or the creation, alteration, or extinction of any other rights over land, and to the rectification of the land register.

(*f*) Whether in respect of a moveable or of an immoveable makes no difference.

(*g*) A limitation of a right of ownership is said to relate to a *de facto* act of Disposition (*tatsächliche Verfügung*), when it affects the *manner* in which such right may be exercised, as, *e.g.*, an ordinance prohibiting the erection of a building beyond a certain height; while a limitation affecting the *right of ownership itself*, and not merely the *manner* in which such right may be exercised, is said to be a limitation in respect of a *de jure* act of disposition (*rechtliche Verfügung*). Examples of the latter case may be found in Arts. 115, 116, 117, 119 and 124.

(*h*) Cf. 903.

ART. 114. The provisions of State laws remain unaffected according to which redemption rents and other perpetual charges belonging to the State or to a public institution in consequence of any regulation of the relations between a lord of a manor and his tenants, or in consequence of the redemption of servitudes and perpetual charges, or in consequence of its right of lord paramount, do not require registration for their creation and validity as against the public faith of the land register.

ART. 115. The provisions of State laws which prohibit or limit the charging of a piece of land with certain real servitudes, or limited personal servitudes, or perpetual charges, remain unaffected; and the provisions of State laws which specify the nature and the extent of such rights also remain unaffected.

ART. 116. The provisions of State laws specified in Articles 113 to 115 do not apply to any money annuity required to be paid as provided for in 912, 916, 917 of the Civil Code, nor to the duties of furnishing maintenance specified in 1021, 1022 of the Civil Code.

ART. 117. The provisions of State laws which prohibit the charging of a piece of land beyond a certain value remain unaffected.

The provisions of State laws remain unaffected which prohibit the charging of a piece of land with a hypotheca or land charge not terminable by giving notice, or which, in the case of hypothecary claims and land charges, limit temporarily, or, in the case of annuity charges, permit for a period shorter than that specified in 1202, par. 2, of the Civil Code, the exclusion of the right of giving notice of termination by the owner.

ART. 118. The provisions of State laws remain unaffected which confer priority in rank to other charges over a piece of land, on a money annuity, hypotheca, land charge, or annuity charge belonging to the State or to a public institution on account of a loan for the improvement of the charged land.

The provisions of 892, 893 of the Civil Code apply in favour of a third party.

ART. 119. The provisions of State laws remain unaffected which:

(1) limit the right of alienation in respect of land;

(2) prohibit or limit the partition of a piece of land, or the alienation of one or more of several pieces of land which have hitherto been cultivated together;

(3) prohibit or limit the consolidation of several pieces of land permitted by 890, par. 1, of the Civil Code, or the ascribing of a piece of land to another piece of land permitted by 890, par. 2, of the Civil Code.

ART. 120. The provisions of State laws remain unaffected according to which, in the case of alienation of a part of a piece of land, the part alienated is free from any charges upon the land if it is established by the competent authority that such legal change is not injurious to the interested parties.

Under the same conditions the provisions of State laws remain in force, according to which:

(1) in the case of the partition of a piece of land charged with a perpetual charge, the perpetual charge is divided among the several parts of the piece of land;

(2) in the case of the extinction of a right which the owner for the time being of a piece of land has over another piece of land, the consent of the person is not necessary in whose favour the land of the person entitled is charged;

(3) in the cases provided for by 1128 of the Civil Code and Article 52 of the present Act, the claim to compensation belonging to the owner becomes free from rights of a third party to the claim.

ART. 121. The provisions of State laws remain unaffected according to which, in the case of the partition of a piece of land charged with a perpetual charge in favour of the State or a public institution, only a part of the piece of land remains charged with the perpetual charge and in favour of the owner for the time being of such part, the remaining parts are charged with perpetual charges of the same kind in consideration thereof.

ART. 122. The provisions of State laws remain unaffected which regulate the rights of an owner of a piece of land in respect of fruit trees standing on the boundary or on an adjoining piece of land otherwise than as provided for by 910 and 923, par. 2, of the Civil Code.

ART. 123. The provisions of State laws which confer the right to a way of necessity for the purpose of connecting a piece of land with a waterway or with a railway, remain unaffected.

ART. 124. The provisions of State laws remain unaffected which subject the ownership of a piece of land in favour of its adjoining owners to restrictions other than those specified in the Civil Code. This applies also to the provisions under which structures, trees and shrubs may be respectively erected or planted only at a specified distance from the boundary.

ART. 125. The provisions of State laws which extend the provision of 26 of the Industrial Code to railways, steamships and similar undertakings remain unaffected.

ART. 126. By State legislation rights of ownership of a piece of land belonging to the State may be transferred to a communal union, and the rights of ownership of a piece of land belonging to a communal union may be transferred to another communal union or to the State.

ART. 127. The provisions of State laws relating to the transfer of ownership of a piece of land which has not been registered in the land register, and which, according to the provisions of the Land Registration Act, is not required to be registered after the transfer, remain unaffected.

ART. 128. The provisions of State laws relating to the creation or extinction of a servitude over a piece of land which has not been registered in the land register, and which is not required to be registered according to the provisions of the Land Registration Act, remain unaffected.

ART. 129. The provisions of State laws which confer the right of appropriation in respect of a piece of land abandoned under 928 of the Civil Code to a specific person other than the Treasury remain unaffected.

ART. 130. The provisions of State laws relating to the right of appropriation in respect of pigeons belonging to another and found in a state of liberty remain unaffected.

ART. 131. The provisions of State laws remain unaffected, which, in the case where each of the co-owners of a piece of land upon which a building has been erected, has the exclusive use of a part of such building, regulate their relations in respect of the community of ownership, or exclude the application of 749 to 751 of the Civil Code, or deprive a trustee in bankruptcy of the right to require dissolution of the community in the event of bankruptcy proceedings being instituted against the property of one of the co-owners.

ART. 132. The provisions of State laws relating to taxes for the erection of churches and schools remain unaffected.

ART. 133. The provisions of State laws relating to the right to have a seat in a building dedicated to public religious service or to occupy a place in a public cemetery remain unaffected.

ART. 134. The provisions of State laws relating to the religious education of children remain unaffected.

ART. 135. The provisions of State laws relating to the compulsory education of minors remain unaffected. The compulsory education is, subject to the provisions of 55, 56 of the Criminal Code, permissible only if it is ordered by the Guardianship Court. Such order may, apart from the cases provided for by 1666, 1838 of the Civil Code, be made only if the compulsory education is necessary for protecting a minor from moral perdition.

State law may confer upon an administrative authority the right to decide whether the minor whose compulsory education has been ordered is to be removed to a family, or an educational institution or a reformatory if the minor is to be brought up at public expense.

ART. 136. The provisions of State laws remain unaffected under which:

(1) the directorate of an educational or charitable institution subject to State management or supervision, or any other public official has all or any of the rights and duties of a guardian in respect of the minors who are educated or taken care of either by the institution or by a family or institution selected by the directorate or official under its or his supervision; and the directorate of the institution or the official

retains, subject to the power of the Guardianship Court to appoint another guardian, such rights and duties even after the termination of the education or care of the minors and until their attainment of majority;

(2) in the case of illegitimate minor children the provisions of (1) apply also even if such minors are being educated or taken care of in their mother's household under the supervision of the directorate or official;

(3) the directorate of an educational or charitable institution subject to State management, or an employee of the institution designated by it, or any other public official may be appointed guardian over the minors specified in (1) and (2) in preference to the persons who would be called upon to act as guardian as provided for by 1776 of the Civil Code;

(4) in the case of the appointment of a guardian made under the provisions of (1) to (3) a supervising guardian is not to be appointed, while the guardian has the exemptions permitted by 1852 of the Civil Code.

ART. 137. The provisions of State laws remain unaffected which lay down the general principles whereby the value of the proceeds of a farm is to be determined in the cases provided for by 1515, pars. 2 and 3, and 2049, 2312 of the Civil Code.

ART. 138. The provisions of State laws under which a corporation, foundation, or institution under public law becomes statutory heir in the place of the Treasury, in the case provided for by 1936 of the Civil Code, remain unaffected.

ART. 139. The provisions of State laws remain unaffected under which the Treasury or any other juristic person acquires a right of inheritance, a claim to a compulsory portion, or a right to specific things in respect of the estate of a person taken care of or supported by the Treasury or the juristic person.

ART. 140. The provisions of State laws remain unaffected under which the Probate Court may or should, of its own motion, and under conditions other than those specified in 1960, par. 1, of the Civil Code, order an inventory of an estate to be drawn up, and, before the inventory has been drawn up, take all necessary precautionary measures, as, *e.g.*, the affixing of seals.

ART. 141. State law may provide that only the Courts or only the notaries are competent for the authentication of juristic acts which, according to the provisions of the Civil Code, require judicial or notarial authentication.

ART. 142. The provisions of State laws remain unaffected which enact that, in respect of land situated within the territory of the State, not only the Courts and notaries, but also any other public authorities or officials, are competent for the authentication of the contract specified in 313 of the Civil Code, and for the authentication of the declarations which are required by 873, par. 2, of the Civil Code, in order to make the contract binding upon the parties concerned.

ART. 143. The provisions of State laws remain unaffected, which enact that, in the cases provided for by 925, 1015 of the Civil Code, a real agreement of the parties in respect of land situated within the territory of the State, may be declared not only to the land register office, but also to the Court, a notary, or any other public authority or official.

The provisions of State laws remain unaffected, which enact that the presence of both parties simultaneously is not necessary for the conveyance of a piece of land, if it has been sold by auction by a Court or notary, provided the conveyance is unaffected on the day of the auction.

ART. 144. The provisions of State laws, relating to the *jurisdictio rei* and *jurisdictio loci* (*sachlich und örtlich Zuständigkeit*) of lodgment offices, remain unaffected. State law may provide that the investment of money belonging to a ward as provided for in 1808 of the Civil Code, shall not be made at the lodgment-offices of the State.

ART. 145. State law may contain minor regulations as to lodgment; it may, *e. g.*, regulate the manner of proof of any right to receive the things lodged, and may prescribe that the ownership of any moneys or negotiable instruments lodged shall pass to the Treasury or the institution designated as the lodgment-office, subject to the obligation to make restitution; that a sale of the things lodged may be ordered by the Treasury or the institution of its own motion; and that the claim to restitution shall, in favour of the Treasury or of the institution, be extinguished upon the expiration of a fixed period of time, or subject to some other conditions. In the cases provided for by 382, 1171, par. 3, and 1269, sentence 3, of the Civil Code, the person making the lodgment must be permitted to withdraw the sum of money lodged, at least during the year after the date at which the right of the creditor to the sum of money lodged is extinguished.

The lodgment may not be made subject to any judicial order.

ART. 146. Where it is provided by State law that lodgment-offices shall also accept things other than money, negotiable instruments, or any other instruments or valuables, the provisions of 372 to 382 of the Civil Code apply to the obligation in respect of the delivery of such things.

ART. 147. The provisions of State laws remain unaffected, under which public authorities other than Courts are competent to exercise the functions of a Guardianship Court or Probate Court.

Where the functions of a Probate Court have been conferred by State law upon a public authority other than a court, the district Court in whose district such public authority has its office, is competent to administer the oath of disclosure prescribed in 2006 of the Civil Code.

ART. 148. State law may exclude the jurisdiction of a Probate Court in respect of the making of an inventory.

ART. 149. The provisions of State laws remain unaffected under which a judge may, in officiating at the making of a disposition *mortis causa*, be assisted by a person specially appointed to authenticate documents in the place of a registrar or of two witnesses.

The provisions of 2234 to 2236 of the Civil Code apply to such person.

ART. 150. The provisions of State laws remain unaffected according to which, in the case provided for by 2249 of the Civil Code, an officially appointed person is competent in the place of or concurrently with the chief officer.

ART. 151. The general provisions of State laws relating to the making of judicial or notarial documents remain unaffected by the provisions of 2234 to 2245, 2276 of the Civil Code and Article 149 of the present Act. An infringement of any such provisions is, subject to the provisions relating to the consequences of defects in respect of the *jurisdictio rei*, without effect upon the validity of a disposition *mortis causa*.

ART. 152. The provisions of State laws remain unaffected which determine the conditions, in respect of legal proceedings which are not to be settled according to the provisions of the Code of Civil Procedure, under which the effects incident to the bringing of an action or the commencement of an action under the provisions of Civil Code, come into being. In the absence of any such provisions the provisions of the Code of Civil Procedure apply *mutatis mutandis*.

FOURTH SECTION.
TEMPORARY PROVISIONS.

ART. 153. A person who, at the date when the Civil Code comes into force, has not completed his twenty-first year of age, but has been declared of full age, or has otherwise acquired the legal status of a person of full age, is, from and after that date, in the same position as a person of full age.

ART. 154. A person who has been emancipated or liberated from power under the French law or the law of Baden is, from and after the date when the Civil Code comes into force, in the same position as a person of full age if he has at that date completed his eighteenth year of age; if not, then he is in the same position as a minor.

ART. 155. A person who, at the date when the Civil Code comes into force, has been interdicted on account of insanity is, from and after that date, in the same position as a person who has been interdicted on account of insanity under the provisions of the Civil Code.

ART. 156. A person who, at the date when the Civil Code comes into force, has been interdicted on account of prodigality is, from and after that date, in the same position as a person who has been interdicted on account of prodigality under the provisions of the Civil Code.

The same rule applies to a person over whom and on account of whose prodigality a supplementary guardian has been appointed under the French law or the law of Baden.

ART. 157. The provisions of the French Law and of the law of Baden relating to an elective domicile remain in force in respect of the legal relations which are governed by such law, in so far as the domicile has been elected prior to the date when the Civil Code comes into force.

ART. 158. The effects of a declaration of death made prior to the date when the Civil Code comes into force are determined by the former law, unless a contrary intention appears from Articles 159 and 160.

ART. 159. The spouse of a person declared dead prior to the date when the Civil Code comes into force may enter into a new marriage after the date when the Civil Code comes into force, even if the remarriage would not be permitted by the former law. The provisions of 1348 to 1352 of the Civil Code apply *mutatis mutandis*.

ART. 160. In so far as in consequence of a declaration of death under the provisions of the Civil Code the parental power over a person who has disappeared, a guardianship or curatorship, or the functions of a guardian, supervising guardian, curator, supplementary guardian, or member of a family council come to an end, such provisions apply, from and after the date when the Civil Code comes into force, even to a declaration of death made prior to such date.

ART. 161. A legal process which is pending at the date when the Civil Code comes into force, and which has for its object a declaration of death, a declaration of disappearance, or the provisional putting of a presumptive heir into possession, or the use of the property of a person who has disappeared, shall be settled by the former law.

If, prior to the date when the Civil Code comes into force, a declaration that a person has disappeared, or the provisional putting of a presumptive heir into possession, or the use of the property of a person who has disappeared, takes place, the former law determines also the declaration of death or the definitive putting of a presumptive heir into possession.

The effects of a decision given under pars. 1 and 2 are also determined by the former law. In the case of the declaration of death the provisions of Articles 159, 160 apply.

Art. 162. In so far as the definitive putting of a presumptive heir into possession or the use of the property of a person who has disappeared, effected under the former law, or permitted by Article 161, par. 2, is without effect on the legal relations to which the effects of a declaration of death under the Civil Code extend, then a declaration of death under the provisions of the Civil Code is permissible after the date when the Civil Code comes into force; the effects are limited to such legal relations.

Art. 163. Unless a contrary intention from Articles 164 to 166, the provisions of 25 to 53, 85 to 89 of the Civil Code apply from and after the date when the Civil Code comes into force to juristic persons existing at that date.

Art. 164. The provisions of State laws remain in force, which relate to communes (*Realgemeinden*) and such similar unions, existing at the date when the Civil Code comes into force, whose members as such are entitled to the use of agricultural and forest lands, mills, breweries, and similar structures. It makes no difference whether the communes or other unions are juristic persons or not, and whether the right of the members is attached to the possession of land or not.

Art. 165. The provisions of the Bavarian laws of April 29, 1869, relating to the status of associations and business and agricultural partnerships formed under private law remain in force in respect of associations and registered partnerships which exist by virtue of such laws at the date when the Civil Code comes into force.

Art. 166. The provisions of the Saxon law of June 15, 1868, relating to juristic persons, remain in force in respect of associations of persons which, at the date when the Civil Code comes into force, have acquired juristic personality by registration in a partnership register.

Art. 167. The provisions of State laws which relate to the credit institutions of the peasantry or of the nobility existing at the date when the Civil Code comes into force, remain in force.

ART. 168. A limitation of the right of disposal existing at the date when the Civil Code comes into force, remains effective, subject, however, to the provisions of the Civil Code in favour of those who derive rights from a person without title.

ART. 169. The provisions of the Civil Code relating to prescription apply to claims which have arisen, but are not yet barred by prescription before the date when the Civil Code comes into force. The beginning, suspension and interruption of prescription are determined, however, for the time prior to the date when the Civil Code comes into force, according to the former law.

If the period of prescription is shorter under the Civil Code than under the former law, the shorter period is reckoned from the date when the Civil Code comes into force. If, however, the longer period fixed by the former law expires sooner than the shorter period fixed by the Civil Code, the prescription is complete upon the expiration of the longer period.

ART. 170. An obligation which has arisen before the date when the Civil Code comes into force is determined by the former law.

ART. 171. A contract of ordinary or usufructuary lease, or a contract for service, existing at the date when the Civil Code comes into force, is, unless after that date notice to terminate the contract is given on the first day for which such notice may be given under the former law, determined, after such day, by the provisions of the Civil Code.

ART. 172. If a thing which, at the date when the Civil Code comes into force, has been leased under an ordinary or usufructuary lease is, after that date, alienated or charged with a right, the lessee has, as against the acquirer of the thing or of the right, the rights specified in the Civil Code. Any further rights which the lessee has under the former law remain unaffected, subject, however, to the provision of Article 171.

ART. 173. From and after the date when the Civil Code comes into force its provisions apply to a community by undivided shares existing at that date.

ART. 174. From and after the date when the Civil Code comes into force the provisions of 798 to 800, 802, 804, and 806, sentence 1, of the Civil Code apply to obligations to bearer issued prior to that date. In the case of obligations which are payable at sight and do not bear interest, and in the case of interest coupons, annuity coupons, and dividend coupons the former law remains, however, in force in respect of declaration of cancellation and stoppage of payment.

The prescription of the claims arising from obligations to bearer issued prior to the date when the Civil Code comes into force is determined by the former law, subject, however, to the provision of 802 of the Civil Code.

ART. 175. Interest coupons, annuity coupons, and dividend coupons issued after the date when the Civil Code comes into force in respect of an instrument to bearer issued prior to that date are determined by the laws which apply to coupons of the same kind issued after that date.

ART. 176. After the date when the Civil Code comes into force an obligation to bearer may no longer be taken out of circulation. The putting out of circulation of an obligation to bearer prior to that date loses its effect when the Civil Code comes into force.

ART. 177. After the date when the Civil Code comes into force, the provisions of 808, par. 2, sentences 2, 3, of the Civil Code, and Article 102, par. 2, of the present Act apply to instruments issued before that date and belonging to the kind specified in 808 of the Civil Code, in so far as the debtor is bound to effect performance only upon delivery of the instrument.

ART. 178. Any legal process pending at the date when the Civil Code comes into force, and having for its object the cancellation of an obligation to bearer or of an instrument of the kind specified in 808 of the Civil Code, or the stoppage of payment of such an instrument, shall he settled according to the former law. The effects of the process and of the judgment are also determined by the former law.

ART. 179. Where a claim arising from an obligation has acquired validity as against third parties by entry in a public register as provided for by the former law, such claim retains its validity even after the date when the Civil Code comes into force.

ART. 180. The provisions of the Civil Code apply, subject to Article 191, and after the date when the Civil Code comes into force, to possession existing at that date.

ART. 181. The provisions of the Civil Code apply, from and after the date when the Civil Code comes into force, to ownership existing at that date.

If, at the date when the Civil Code comes into force, ownership of a thing belongs to several persons not by undivided shares, or if separate ownership of the products of a piece of land, *e.g.*, trees, has been created at that date, such rights continue to exist.

ART. 182. Ownership of a particular story of a building, existing at the date when the Civil Code comes into force, continues to exist. The legal relations between the interested parties *inter se* are governed by the former law.

ART. 183. In favour of a piece of land which has become a forest at the date when the Civil Code comes into force, and until the next renovating season of the forest, the provisions of State laws remain in force which regulate the rights of the owner of an adjoining piece of land in respect of trees and bushes standing on the boundary or on the forest otherwise than as provided for in 910 and 923, pars. 2 and 3, of the Civil Code.

ART. 184. Rights with which a thing or a right is charged at the date when the Civil Code comes into force remain to the same extent and with the same rank as under the former law, except in so far as a contrary intention appears from Articles 192 to 195. After the date when the Civil Code comes into force, however, the provisions of 1017 apply to a heritable building right; the provisions of 1020 to 1028 of the Civil Code apply to a real servitude.

ART. 185. If, at the date when the Civil Code comes into force, the usucapion of ownership or usufruct of a moveable is not yet complete, the provisions of Article 169 apply *mutatis mutandis* to such usucapion.

ART. 186. The procedure according to which land registers are to be kept, and the time at which a land register is deemed to have been kept for a district are determined in each State by an ordinance of the Government of the State.

Where a land register for a district is deemed to have been kept, the register is also deemed to have been kept for those lands which are situate within such district and for which no section has been provided in the land register, unless such lands have been excepted by special ordinance.

ART. 187. A real servitude, existing at the time at which the land register is deemed to have been kept, is not required to be registered in order to retain its effect as against the public faith of the land register. Registration shall, however, take place, if it is demanded by the person entitled to the servitude or by the owner of the servient tenement; the cost shall be borne and advanced by the person who demands the registration.

It may be provided by State law that all existing real servitudes or certain kinds thereof must, at the time or subsequent to the time when a land register is kept, be registered in the land register in order to retain their effect as against the public faith of the land register. The provision may be limited to certain land registration districts.

ART. 188. It may be provided by an ordinance of the State Government that Statutory rights of pledge, existing at the time at which a land register is deemed to have been kept, are not required to be registered in order to retain their effect as against the public faith of the land register, for a period not exceeding ten years reckoned from the date when the Civil Code comes into force.

It may be provided by an ordinance to the State Government that rights under ordinary or usufructuary leases, which are existing in the nature of rights over land at the time specified in par. 1, are not required to be registered in order to retain their effect as against the public faith of the land register.

ART. 189. The acquisition and loss of ownership, and the creation transfer, charge and extinction of any other right over land or of a right over such a right are, even after the date when the Civil Code comes into force, governed by the former law until the time at which a land register is deemed to have been kept. The same rule applies to any change affecting the substance or rank of such rights. A right not permitted by the provisions of the Civil Code may no longer be created after the date when the Civil Code comes into force.

If at the late at which the land register is deemed to have been kept a possessor has been registered in a land register as the person entitled, the provisions of Article 169 apply *mutatis mutandis* to a usucapion which was not yet complete at such date, but which is permitted by 900 of the Civil Code.

The cancellation of a right with which a piece of land, or a right over land, is charged at the time at which the land register is deemed to have been kept is, even after such time, governed by the former law until the right is entered in the land register.

ART. 190. The right of appropriation which the Treasury has under 928, par. 2, of the Civil Code extends to all lands which are ownerless at the time at which the land register is deemed to have been kept. The provision of Article 129 applies *mutatis mutandis*.

ART. 191. The former law relating to the possessory protection of a real servitude or of a limited personal servitude applies even after the date when the Civil Code comes into force until the land register is deemed to have been kept in respect of the servient tenement.

After the time at which the land register is deemed to have been kept the provisions of the Civil Code applicable to protection of possession apply *mutatis mutandis* to the protection of the exercise of a real servitude involving the maintenance of a permanent structure, so long as real servitudes of such kind are not required to be registered in order to retain their effect as against the public faith of the land register as provided in Article 128 or Article 187. The same rule applies to real servitudes of any other kind to the extent that possessory protection is afforded only if the servitude has been exercised at least once in each of the three years prior to its infringement.

ART. 192. A right of pledge over a piece of land existing at the time at which the land register is deemed to have been kept is, after that time, deemed to be a hypotheca for which the issue of a certificate of hypotheca is excluded. If the amount of the claim for which the right of pledge exists is not specified, the right of pledge is deemed to be a cautionary hypotheca.

If the right of pledge is limited in such manner that the creditor may seek satisfaction out of the land only by means of compulsory management, such limitation continues to exist.

ART. 193. It may be provided by State law that a right of pledge which is not deemed to be a cautionary hypotheca under Article 192 shall be deemed to be a cautionary hypotheca or a hypotheca for which a certificate of hypotheca may be issued; and that an instrument issued for such right of pledge shall be deemed to be a certificate of hypotheca.

ART. 194. It may be provided by State law that a creditor, whose right of pledge exists at the time specified in Article 192, is entitled to demand cancellation of a right of pledge prior or equal in rank, where the right and ownership merges in the same person, in the same manner as though a caution had been entered in the land register for securing the right to such cancellation.

ART. 195. A land charge existing at the time at which the land register is deemed to have been kept is, after that time, deemed to be a land charge within the meaning of the Civil Code, and an instrument issued for the land charge is deemed to be a certificate of land charge. The provision of Article 192, par. 2, applies *mutatis mutandis*.

It may be provided by State law that a land charge, existing at the time specified in par. 1, shall be deemed to be a hypotheca for which a certificate of hypotheca may be issued, or to be a cautionary hypotheca; and that an instrument issued in respect of the land charge shall be deemed to be a certificate of hypotheca.

ART. 196. It may be provided by State law that the provisions of the Civil Code relating to land shall apply to a heritable and transferable right of use of a piece of land, and that the provisions of the Civil Code, applicable to the acquisition of ownership of land, shall apply to the acquisition of such a right.

ART. 197. The provisions of State law remain in force which, in respect of a piece of land of which a right of use, not coming under Article 63, exists in favour of a tenant at the date when the Civil Code comes into force, permit a new right of a similar nature to be created after the extinction of the old right of use, and which compel the lord of the manor to create such new right.

ART. 198. The validity of a marriage celebrated before the date when the Civil Code comes into force is determined according to the former law.

A marriage void or invalid under the former law is deemed to have been valid *ab initio* if the spouses are still living together as married people at the date when the Civil Code comes into force, and the ground upon which the nullity or invalidity is based would not, under the provisions of the Civil Code, result in or would have lost the effect of the nullity or avoidability of a marriage. The period fixed for avoidance by the Civil Code does not begin to run until the date when the Civil Code comes into force.

A declaration of invalidity of a marriage made under the former law is equivalent to a declaration of nullity under the Civil Code.

ART. 199. The personal legal relations of spouses *inter se*, *e.g.*, the mutual duty to furnish maintenance, are, even in respect of marriages existing at the date when the Civil Code comes into force, determined according to the provisions of the Civil Code.

ART. 200. The former law remains in force in respect of the matrimonial *régime* of a marriage existing at the date when the Civil Code comes into force. This applies also to the provisions relating to the effects of the *régime* in respect of rights of inheritance and to the provisions of the French law and the law of Baden relating to the procedure regulating separation of goods (*Vermögensabsonderungen*) between spouses.

A regulation of a matrimonial *régime* permitted by the provisions of the Civil Code may be made by a marriage contract even if such contract would not be permitted by the former law.

In so far as a wife is limited in disposing capacity in consequence of the matrimonial *régime* or of the marriage as provided by the former law relating to the former matrimonial *régime*, such limitation remains operative so long as the former *régime* exists.

ART. 201. After the date when the Civil Code comes into force a divorce or a judicial separation takes place under the provisions of the Civil Code.

If, before the date when the Civil Code comes into force, a spouse has been guilty of any offence of the kind specified in 1565 to 1568 of the Civil

Code, a petition for divorce or judicial separation may be granted only if the offence was a ground for divorce or judicial separation under the former law.

ART. 202. The effects of a permanent or temporary separation *a mensa et toro*, granted before the date when the Civil Code comes into force, are governed by the former law. This applies also to the provisions under which a separation, continuing to exist up to the time of the death of one of the spouses, is equivalent to the dissolution of the marriage in all or some respects.

ART. 203. The legal relations between parents and a legitimate child born before the date when the Civil Code comes into force are determined by the provisions of the Civil Code after it has come into force. This applies also in respect of the property which the child has acquired prior to that date.

ART. 204. If, at the date when the Civil Code comes into force, the father or the mother is limited by an order of the competent public authority in his or her right to take care of the child's person or property, such limitation remains operative. The Guardianship Court may set the order aside under 1671 of the Civil Code.

If the father or the mother is deprived of the right of usufruct of the child's property by an order of the competent public authority, the Guardianship Court shall upon application set the order aside unless the deprivation of the usufruct is justified by 1666, par. 2, of the Civil Code.

ART. 205. If, before the date when the Civil Code comes into force, the father has under the former law excluded the mother from the guardianship over the child, or has directed the appointment of a supplementary guardian for the mother, such direction of the father is, after the date when the Civil Code comes into force, deemed to be an order for the appointment of a supplementary guardian for the mother within the meaning of the Civil Code.

ART. 206. Where under the former law a divorce has been granted, or a marriage has been dissolved in consequence of a declaration of death of one of the spouses, or a separation *a mensa et toro* has been granted, the right and the duty of the parents to take care of the person of the children of the marriage are determined according to the former law; the provisions of 1635, par 1, sentence

2, par. 2, and 1636 of the Civil Code, however, apply.

ART. 207. The question as to how far children of a void or invalid marriage, celebrated before the date when the Civil Code comes into force, are deemed to be legitimate children, and the question as to how far the father and the mother have the duties and the rights of parents of legitimate children are determined according to the former law.

ART. 208. The legal status of an illegitimate child born before the date when the Civil Code comes into force is, after such date, determined according to the provisions of the Civil Code; the question of paternity, the right of the child to use the father's surname, and the father's duty to furnish maintenance are, however, determined according to the former law.

The question as to how far a child conceived out of lawful wedlock before the date when the Civil Code comes into force acquires, for special reasons, *e.g.*, conception after betrothal, the legal status of a legitimate child, and the question as to how far the father and mother of such a child have the duties and the rights of parents of legitimate children, are determined according to the former law.

The provisions of par. 1 apply also to a child acknowledged by a person as his child under the French law or the law of Baden.

ART. 209. The question as to how far a child legitimated or adopted before the date when the Civil Code comes into force has the legal status of a legitimate child, and the question as to how far the father and mother have the duties and the rights of parents of legitimate children are determined according to the former law.

ART. 210. After the date when the Civil Code comes into force the provisions of the Civil Code apply to guardianship or curatorship existing at that date. If the guardianship has been established on account of the bodily infirmities of the ward, it is deemed to be a curatorship established under 1910, par. 1, of the Civil Code. If the guardianship has been established on account of the feeble-mindedness of the ward without any interdiction having taken place, it is deemed to be a curatorship created over the affairs affecting the property of such ward as provided for in 1910, par. 2, of the Civil Code.

The guardians and curators originally appointed remain in office. The same rule applies to a family council and its members in the territories subject to the Prussian Guardianship Act of July 5, 1875. A supervising guardian shall be dismissed from office if such a guardian could not have been appointed under the provisions of the Civil Code.

ART. 211. The appointment of a supplementary guardian appointed over a feeble-minded person under the French law or the law of Baden ceases to be operative upon the expiration of six months after the date when the Civil Code comes into force.

ART. 212. The provisions of State law whereby certain negotiable instruments have been declared suitable for the investment of money belonging to a ward remain in force.

ART. 213. The legal relations arising under the law of inheritance in respect of the estate of a person who has died before the date when the Civil Code comes into force are determined according to the former law. The same applies also to the provisions relating to the procedure of liquidation in matters of inheritance.

ART. 214. Where a disposition *mortis causa* has been made or revoked before the date when the Civil Code comes into force, such making or revocation is governed by the former law even if the testator dies after the date when the Civil Code comes into force.

The same rule applies to the obligation of the testator in making a contract of inheritance or a joint will, in so far as the contract of inheritance or the will has been made before the date when the Civil Code comes into force.

ART. 215. A person who, before the date when the Civil Code comes into force, has acquired the capacity to make and has actually made a disposition *mortis causa*, retains such capacity even if he has not yet attained the age required by the Civil Code.

The provisions of 2230 of the Civil Code apply to a will which has been made before the date when the Civil Code comes into force by a person who dies after that date.

ART. 216. The provisions of State laws under which members of certain families of the nobility are not limited by the right to compulsory portion in regulating succession to their estates, remain in force in respect of those families to which such right to compulsory portion belongs at the date when the Civil Code comes into force.

ART. 217. Where a contract for the renunciation of an inheritance has been made before the date when the Civil Code comes into force, the making and the effects of such a contract are determined according to the former law.

The same rule applies to a contract entered into before the date when the Civil Code comes into force, whereby a contract for the renunciation of an inheritance has been revoked.

ART. 218. In so far as the former State laws remain applicable under the provisions of this section, such laws may be modified by State legislation even after the date when the Civil Code comes into force.

In testimony whereof, We have signed the present Act with Our own hand, and have affixed the Imperial Seal.

Given in the New Palace, the 18th day of August, 1896.

[L. S.] WILHELM.

PRINCE OF HOHENLOHE.

APPENDIX B.

BIBLIOGRAPHY.

[The following is a select list of the more important works on German Civil Law and Cognate Topics.]

I. Bibliographical Works.

Maas: Bibliographie des bürgerlichen Rechts, 1888—1898; Nachträge, 1899—1904.

—Bibliographie d. amtl. Materialien z. BGB, 1897.

—Jurisprudent Germaniae, 1905, Berlin, 1906; Published yearly.

Mühlbrecht: Wegweiser durch die neuere Literatur der Staats- und Rechtswissenschaft, 2 Bde, 1893—1901.

—Bibliographie des BGB, I—III, 1898—1901.

[Short bibliographical notes may also be found in the larger German text-books.]

II. Codes and Statutes referred to in the Text or Footnotes.

Code of Civil Procedure (Civilprozessordnung) of June 30, 1877; Revised edition, May 20, 1898.

Commercial Code (Handelsgesetzbuch) of May 10, 1897.

Criminal Code (Strafgesetzbuch) of May 15, 1871.

Industrial Code (Gewerbeordnung) of July 26, 1900.

Billsof Exchange Act, July 5, 1869 (Allgemeine deutsche Wechselordnung).

Bankruptcy Act, February 10, 1877 (May 20, 1898) (Konkursordnung).

Compulsory Auction and Compulsory Management Act, March 24, 1897 (Gesetz über die Zwangsversteigerung und Zwangsverwaltung).

Imperial Ordinance (Kaiserliche Verordnung) of March 27, 1899.

Introductory Act to the Civil Code, August 18, 1896 (Einführungsgesetz zum BGB).

Land Registration Act, March 24, 1897 (May 20, 1898) (Grundbuchordnung).

Voluntary Jurisdiction Act, May 17, 1898 (May 20, 1898) (Gesetz über die Angelegenheiten der freiwilligen Gerichtsbarkeit).

III. General Works.

Deutsches Reichs-Gesetzbuch für Industrie, Handel und Gewerbe einschliesslich Handwerk und Landwirtschaft. Vollständige Sammlung aller einschlägigen Reichsgesetze, Verordnungen, Ausführungsbestimmungen usw. mit Erläuterungen, Formular buch und Sachregister. Bearbeitet und herausgegeben von der Redaction des Reichs-Gesetzbuches für Industrie, Handel und Gewebe, 2 Bde., 39. Aufl., 1905.

Birkmeyer: Encyklopädie der Rechtswissenschaft, 3. Aufl., 1904.

Holtzendorff: Encyklopädie der Rechtswissenschaft in systematischer Bearbeitung, Herausgegeben von Dr. Josef Kohler; Sechste, der Neubearbeitung erste Aufl., 2 Bde., 1904.

Stephan: Handbuch des gesamten Rechts, 1903.

IV. Sources of the Civil Code.

The following are the principal sources (cf. Meulenaere's Code civil allemand et loi d'introduction, p. 1) from which the various provisions of the Civil Code are derived:

Foreign Laws:

(1) Roman Law.

(2) Code Napoléon (1807).

(3) Das österreichische allgemeine bürgerliche Gesetzbuch (1811).

(4) The Swiss Federal Code of Obligations (1883).

German Laws:

(1) Das preussische Landrecht (1794).

(2) The various draft Codes of Dresden (1886), Bavaria (1860 and 1864), and Hesse (1841—1853).

(3) Sächsisches bürgerliches Gesetzbuch (1863).

V. WORKS RELATING TO THE CIVIL CODE.

(a) **Official Publications:**

Bericht der Reichstags-Kommission über den Entwurf eines BGB, und Einführungsgesetz einer Zusammenstellung der Kommissionsbeschlüsse, Berlin, 1896.

Denkschrift zum Entwurfe eines BGB, 1896.

Entwurf eines BGB, Erste Lesung, 1888, Zweite Lesung, 1895.

Motive zu dem ersten Entwurfe des BGB, 1888.

Motive zu dem Entwurfe zweiter Lesung, 1894.

Protokolle der Kommission für die zweite Lesung des Entwurfes des BGB. Im Auftrage des Reichsjustizamtes bearbeitet von Achilles, Gebhard und Spann, 6 Bde. u. Reg.-Bd., 1897—1899.

(b) **Advanced works on the Civil Code:**

Cosack: Lehrbuch des deutschen bürgerlichen Rechts, 4. Aufl., 2 Bde., 1903—1904.

Crome: System des Deutschen bürgerlichen Rechts, I—III, 1900—1905.

Dernburg: Das bürgerliche Recht des deutschen Reichs und Preussens, I. Bd., 3. Aufl., 1906; II. Bd., 3. Aufl., 1906; III. Bd., 3. Aufl., 1904; IV. Bd., 2. Aufl., 1903; V. Bd., 2. Aufl., 1905. Ergänz.-Bde., 1903—1906.

Endemann: Lehrbuch des bürgerlichen Rechts, I. Bd., 9. Aufl., 1903; II. Bd., 8—9. Aufl., 1905; III. Bd., 7. Aufl., 1900.

Enneccerus u. Lehmann: Das bürgerliche Recht, 2 Bde., 2. Aufl., 1901.

Goldmann u. Lilienthal: Das BGB, systematisch dargestellt, 2. Aufl. I. Bd., 1903; II. Bd., 1905.

Kohler: Lehrbuch des bürgerlichen Rechts, I—II, 1904—1906.

Matthias: Lehrbuch des bürgerlichen Rechts, 2 Bde., 3. Aufl., 1900.

(c) **Elementary Works on the Civil Code:**

Engelmann: Das bürgerliche Recht Deutschlands, 4. Aufl., 1906.

Grünewald u. Freudenthal: Grundriss zur Einführung in das BGB, 1898.

Heilfron: Lehrbuch des bürgerlichen Rechts, 4 Bde., 1900—1905.

Krückmann: Institutionen des BGB, 3. Aufl., 1901.

Müller u. Meikel: Das bürgerliche Recht des deutschen Reichs, 2. Aufl., 2 Bde., 1904.

Siméon: Recht und Rechtsgang im deutschen Reich, 2 Bde., 3. u. 4. Aufl., 1906.

Zitelmann: Das Recht des BGB, I, 1900.

(d) **Commentaries:**

Hölder u. a.: 3 Bde., 1900—1904.

hlenbeck: Das BGB, erläutert, 2. Aufl., 1—3. Bd., 1903—1904.

Planck u. a.: BGB, erläutert, 6 Bde., 3. Aufl., 1903—1906.

Rehbein: Das BGB, mit Erläuterungen, I—II, 1899—1903.

Scherer: 6 Bde. u. 4 Erg.-Bde., 1897—1904.

Staudinger u. a.: 2. Aufl., 7 Bde., 1903—1906.

(e) **Annotated Editions:**

Achilles, André u. a.: 4. Aufl., 1903.

Brandis, W. u. F.: 5. Aufl., 1903.

Fischer u. Henle: 7. Aufl., 1906.

Landé: 3 Bde., 1900.

Neumann: 3 Bde., 4. Aufl., 1905.

Rosenthal: 7. Aufl., 1906.

(f) **Translations**:

French.

Bufnoir, Challamel, Drioux, Gény, Hamel, Lévy-Ullmann et Saleilles: Code civil allemand, Paris, 1904. (Prepared with Government assistance.) Not yet complete.

Gruber, Jules: Code civil pour l'empire d'allemand avec la loi d'introduction; Texte allemand avec traduction française; Deuxième édition, Strasbourg, 1900.

Meulenaere: Code civil allemand et loi d'introduction traduits et annotés, Paris, 1897.

Raoul de la Grasserie: Code civil allemand et loi d'introduction, suivis de la loi sur les livres fonciers et de celle sur la vente et l'admi-nistration forcées, traduits et annotés, avec introduction; Deuxième édition, Paris, 1901.

Italian.

Eusebio: Codice civile dell' imperio germanico promulgato il 18 Agosto 1896 seguito dalla legge introduttiva; Traduzione Italiana, Torino, 1897.

Spanish.

A. García Moreno: Texto y comentario al Código civil del Imperio alemán, promulgado el 18 de Agosto de 1896, con la exposicíon de motivos, ley de introducción y disposiciones transitorias; traduccíon directa del alemán, revisada, anotada y comentada pot la redacción de la Revista de los Tribunales y de legislación universal, Madrid, 1897.

(g) **Comparative Study of the Civil Code**:

Barre: BGB, und Code civil, Vergleichende Darstellung, 2. Aufl., Berlin, 1897.

—Code civil allemand et Code civil français comparés entre eux, 2. éd, Trad. par Hartmann, Berlin, 1899.

Förtsch: Vergleichende Darstellung des Code civil und des BGB, Berlin, 1899, 2. Aufl.

Schuster, E. J. : The Principles of German Civil Law, Oxford, 1907.

Wierex: Het ontwerp van het burgerlijk wetboek voor het Duitsche Rijk vergeleken met het Nederlandsch burglerlijk wetboek. 's Gravenhage, 1895.

(h) Lexicons and Miscellaneous Works:

Bernhardi: Handwörterbuch zum BGB, 3. Aufl., 1902.

Christiani: Bürgerliches Rechtslexikon, 2. Aufl., 1901.

Cohn: Das neue bürgerliche Recht in Sprüchen, 4 Teile, 1899—1900.

Dispeker: Alphab. geordneter Führer durch das BGB, 1901.

Ehmcke: Wörterbuch des BGB, Neue Ausg., 3 Bde., 1904.

Gradenwìtz: Wortverzeichnis zum BGB, 1902.

Haidlen: Das BGB, mit den Motiven und sonstigen gesetzgeberischen Vorarbeìten, 5 Bde., 1897.

Kaden: Handlexikon des BGB, 1899.

APPENDIX C.

LIST OF GERMAN TECHNICAL TERMS EXPRESSLY DEFINED BY THE CODE.

Abtretung = assignment (398).
Anfall der Erbschaft = devolution of the inheritance (1942).
Anfall des Vermächtnisses = devolution of the legacy (2176).
Anspruch = claim (194).
Auflage = testamentary burden (1940).
Auflassung = conveyance by agreement (925).
Ausstattung = advancement (1624).
Beschränkte persönliche Dienstbarkeit = limited personal servitude (1090).
Ehevertrag = marriage contract (1432).
Eigenbesitzer = proprietary possessor (872).
Eingebrachtes Gut = contributed property (1363).
Einrede der Vorausklage = plea of *beneficium excussionis* (771).
Einwilligung = approval (183).
Erbbaurecht = heritable building right (1012).
Erben = heirs (1922).
Erbfall = accrual of the inheritance (1922).
Erbfolge nach Stämmen = succession *per stirpes* (1924).
Erbschaft = inheritance (1922).
Erbschaftsbesitzer = possessor of the inheritance (2018).
Erbschein = certificate of inheritance (2353).
Erbteil = share in an inheritance (1922).
Erbvertrag = contract of inheritance (1941).

Erfüllung Zug um Zug = contemporaneous performance (274).

Erneuerungsschein = renewal coupon (805).

Ersatzerbe = substitutional heir (2096).

Ersitzung = usucapion (937).

Erwerb von Todeswegen = acquisition *mortis causa* (1369).

Fahrlässigkeit = negligence (276).

Fahrnisgemeinschaft = community of moveables (1549).

Freies Vermögen = privileged property (1650).

Früchte eines Rechtes = fruits of a right (99).

Früchte einer Sache = fruits of a thing (99).

Gemeinschaft nach Bruchteilen = community by undivided shares (741).

Gemeinschaftlicher Erbteil = joint share in an inheritance (2093).

Genehmigung = ratification (184).

Gesammtgläubiger = joint creditors (428).

Gesammthypothek = collective hypotheca (1132).

Gesammtgut = common property (1438, 1519).

Gesammtgutsverbindlichkeiten = liabilities of the common property (1459, 1530).

Gesammtschuldner = joint debtors (421).

Gesellschaftsvermögen = partnership property (718).

Gewährfristen = periods of warranty (482).

Grunddienstbarkeit = real servitude (1018).

Grundschuld = land charge (1191).

Guter Glaube = good faith (932).

Hauptmängel = principal defects (482).

Hypothek = hypotheca (1113).

Inventar = inventory (1993).

Inventarfrist = inventory period (1994).

Inventarerrichtung = filing of the inventory (1993).

Kennen musste = ought to have known (122).

Letzwillige Verfügung = testamentary disposition (1937).

Minderung = reduction (462, 643).

Mittelbarer Bisitz = indirect possession (868).

Nacherbe = reversionary heir (2100).

Nachlasspfleger = curator of an estate (1960).
Nachlassverwaltung = administration of an estate (1975).
Niessbrauch = usufruct (1030).
Notwekr = necessary defence (227).
Nutzungen = emoluments (100).
Öffentliche Versteigerung = public auction (383).
Pfandrecht = [right of] pledge (1204).
Quittung = receipt (368).
Reallast = perpetual charge [on land] (1105).
Rentenschuld = annuity charge (1199).
Sachen = things (90).
Schatz = treasure trove (984).
Schenkung = gift (516).
Schuldanerkenntnis = Acknowledgment of debt (781).
Schuldverschreibung auf den Inhaber = obligation to bearer (793).
Schuldversprechen = promise of debt (780).
Sicherungshypothek = cautionary hypotheca (1184).
Standesmässiger Unterhalt = maintenance suitable to station in life (1610).
Testament = will (1937).
*Unverz*üglich = without delay (121).
Verbrauchbare Sachen = consumable things (92).
Verbotene Eigenmacht = unlawful interference (858).
Vergleich = compromise (779).
Vermächtnis = legacy (1939).
Vermögensverwaltung = management of property (1638).
Vertragserbe = contractual heir (1941).
Vertretbare Sachen = fungible things (91).
Vollmacht = power of agency (166).
Vorausvermächtnis = preferential legacy (2150).
Wandelung = cancellation (462, 634).
Wesentliche Bestandteile = essential component parts (93).
Zubehör = accessories (97).
Zurückbehaltungsrecht = [right of] lien (273).

APPENDIX D.

GLOSSARY OF TECHNICAL TERMS.

A.

Accessories = *Zubehör*. Defined by 97. See further Schuster, p. 56.

Accrual of an Inheritance = *Erbfall*. Defined by 1922.

Acknowledgment of Debt = *Schuldanerkenntnis*. Defined by 781. See also "Debt".

Acquisition *mortis causa* = *Erwerb von Todeswegen*. Defined by 1369.

Administration of an Estate = *Nachlassverwaltung*. Defined by 1975.

Advancement = *Ausstattung*. Defined by 1624.

Agricultural Land = *Wirtschaftliches Grundstück*. See "Farm".

Annuity = *Leibrente*. In ordinary English the word "annuity" is applied to periodical payments of money. In this translation the word is used in a somewhat broader sense, and refers to any periodical acts of performance. See "Performance".

Annuity Charge = *Rentenschuld*. Defined by 1199.

Approval = *Einwilligung*. Defined by 183. Cf. "Consent".

Appurtenant Stock = *Inventar*. This is a collective term which is used to denote live stock, farming implements, furniture, and all other things connected with farming purposes.

Assignment = *Abtretung*. Defined by 398.

Authorization = *Ermächtigung*. See "Consent".

B.

Beneficium Excussionis [Plea of] = *Einrede der Vorausklage.* Defined by 771.

C.

Cancellation = *Wandelung.* Defined by 462 and 634.

Cautionary Hypotheca = *Sicherunghypothek.* Defined by 1184. The fundamental distinction between a cautionary hypotheca and an ordinary hypotheca lies in the fact that the presumption of the correctness of the land register does not apply to the former (see 891), while it does apply to the latter (see 1138). It follows that in the case of a cautionary hypotheca the debtor may avail himself of all defences connected with the debt (especially those arising subsequent to registration in the land register) not only as against the creditor, but also as against a subsequent (even *bonâ fide*) acquirer of the hypotheca. Cautionary hypothecas are made use of especially where the parties do not intend the hypotheca to be circulated in the market, but merely intend that the hypotheca shall serve as a security for the performance of an obligation.

Certificate of Inheritance = *Erbschein.* Defined by 2353.

Children = *Kinder.* "Children" refers only to sons and daughters, while "descendants" includes also grand-children, great grand-children, &c.

Claim = *Anspruch.* Defined by 194.

Collective Hypotheca = *Gesammthypothek.* Defined by 1132.

Commencement of Action = *Rechtshängigkeit.* An action is deemed to commence at the date of the service of citation, or, where a supplementary claim is brought forward at any hearing of the action, at the date of such hearing. See Code of Civil Procedure, sects. 253, 263, 281.

Common Property = *Gesammtgut.* Defined by 1438 and 1519.

Community by Undivided Shares = *Gemeinschaft nach Bruchteilen.* Defined by 741.

Community of Moveables = *Fahrnisgemeinschaft*. Defined by 1549. A "community of moveables" lies midway between a "general community of goods" and a "community of income and profits". It extends to all contributed moveables (*Fahrnis*) existing at the date of the marriage, as well as to all income and profits derived during the subsistence of the marriage, as provided for in 1551.

Compromise = *Vergleich*. Defined by 779.

Compulsory Beneficiary = *Pflichtteilsberechtigter*. A compulsory beneficiary is a person who is entitled to a compulsory portion (*q. v.*). Schuster uses the expression "compulsory heir", which is misleading, as a "compulsory beneficiary" need not necessarily be—and is usually not—an "heir" in the strict sense of the term. Cf. 2304.

Compulsory Portion = *Pflichtteil*. A compulsory portion is that portion of an inheritance of which a statutory heir cannot be deprived without some lawful reason. Cf. the *portio legitima* in Roman law, the *réserve* in French law, and the legitim in Scotch law.

Consent = *Zustimmung*. The Code uses the word "consent" in a general sense, denoting both "approval" (see 183) and "ratification" (see 184). "Approval" must be distinguished from "authorization" (*Ermächtigung*), which means the *conferring* of a right to enter into a juristic act, whereas "approval" is only a condition precedent to the *exercise* of such a right.

Consumable Things = *Verbrauchbare Sachen*. Defined by 92.

Contemporaneous Performance = *Erfüllung Zug um Zug*. Defined by 274.

Contra bonos mores = *Gegen die guten Sitten*. "*Contra bonos mores*" must not be taken to be synonymous with the word "immoral". "The expression", says Schuster (p. 91), "like the English expression 'acts against public policy', is applied to such classes of acts as could not be enforced by the Courts without giving offence to public feeling (*quae facta laedunt pietatem, existimationem, verecundiam nostram et, ut generaliter dixerim, contra bonos mores fiunt*)". Dig. 28, 7, 15, Papinian.

Contractual Heir = *Vertragserbe*. Defined by 1941.

Contract of Inheritance = *Erbvertrag*. Defined by 1941.

Contributed Property = *Eingebrachtes Gut*. Defined by 1363.

Conveyance by Agreement = *Auflassung*. Defined by 925.

Creditor = *Gläubiger*. The word "creditor" is here used in a much broader sense than it usually has under English law. It means a person to whom any act of performance (*q. v.*) is due. Cf. "Debt".

Creditors of an Estate = *Nachlassgläubiger*. Under German law, legatees, compulsory beneficiaries, and persons who are entitled to enforce testamentary burdens are also deemed to be "creditors of an estate". Cf. 1967.

Curator of an Estate = *Nachlasspfleger*. Defined by 1960.

D.

Debt = *Schuld*. The word "debt" is used in the translation in a much wider sense than it has in ordinary English. A "debt" (in the sense in which it is here used) may be roughly defined to be an act of performance (*q. v.*) which is due from one person (*i.e.*, the debtor) to another person (*i.e.*, the creditor).

Debtor = *Schuldner*. See "Debt".

Declaration of Death = *Todeserklärung*. A person who has disappeared or has been missing, and who has not been heard of for a considerable time, is known in German law as a *Verschollener*. Such a person may, subject to certain conditions, be declared dead by an order of the competent court obtained on the application of an interested party. Such a judicial order is known as a "declaration of death". For particulars, see Code of Civil Procedure, sects. 946—971; Schuster, pp. 26—28.

Declaration of Intention = *Willenserklärung*. A declaration of intention is the active or passive manifestation of the human will intended to create a juristic act (*q. v.*); as *e.g.*, the delivery of a thing, deliberate acquiescence, &c. See Schuster, p. 73.

Delivery [of a thing]. See "Performance".

Descendants = *Abkömmlinge*. See "Children".

Devolution of an Inheritance = *Anfall der Erbschaft*. Defined by 1942.

Devolution of a Legacy = *Anfall des Vermächtnisses*. Defined by 2176.

Disclaimer of an Inheritance = *Ausschlagung der Erbschaft*. See p. 520, footnote (*n*).

Disposing Capacity = *Geschäftsfähigkeit*. Disposing capacity is the capacity to enter into a juristic act which may be either unilateral or bilateral, as the case may be (see "Juristic Act"). The expression has therefore a much broader meaning than the more familiar English expression "contractual capacity".

Disposition [or Disposal] = *Verfügung*. A disposal of an object (*q. v.*) does not necessarily mean the alienation (*Veräusserung*) or re-linquishment (*Verzicht*) of the object. The charging of the object with a right in favour of another (*Belastung*) is also deemed to be a disposal of the object.

Disposition *mortis causa* = *Verfügung von Todes wegen*. This is a general expression which may refer to a will or to a contract of inheritance, as the case may be.

Doubt. The phrase "in case of doubt" (*im Zweifel*), which occurs very frequently in the Civil Code, means that the provision in question is a mere rule of interpretation (*Auslegungsregel*), and applies only in the absence of any evidence to the contrary.

E.

Effect [of no]. See "Void".

Emoluments = *Nutzungen*. Defined by 100.

Essential Component Parts = *Wesentliche Bestandteile*. Defined by 93.

Estate = *Nachlass*. See "Inheritance". For the sake of brevity the word "estate" is used in this work to mean the estate of a deceased person.

F.

Farm = *Landgut*. The Code draws a distinction between a piece of "agricultural land" (*wirtschaftliche Grundstück*) and a "farm" (see, *e. g.*, 98, 582 *et seq.*, 591 *et seq.*, 1822 (4), 2049, 2312). A farm is a piece of land which is fully provided with all structures and implements which are necessary for farming purposes. Mere size does not necessarily constitute it a farm. Several pieces of land which are cultivated together constitute but a single farm. On the other hand, a parcel of land, no matter whether situated in the city or in the country, which is under cultivation but which is not fully provided with all the necessary farming structures and implements, is not called a farm, but a piece of agricultural land (as, *e.g.*, a field in which a person plants potatoes for his domestic use, or a meadow in which a person pastures his cattle).

Filing of an Inventory = *Inventarerrichtung*. Defined by 1993.

Forfeiture of Parental Power. See "Suspension of Parental Power".

Foundation = *Stiftung*. Under German law, not only an association of persons but a foundation—*i.e.*, a fund or a collection of things—devoted to the furtherance of a particular purpose, be it charitable or otherwise, may also be clothed with juristic personality. A person who wishes to devote a fund for the erection of a museum, for instance, may, according to German law, accomplish his object in any one of three ways: (1) he may transfer the fund to an existing juristic person (*e.g.*, a municipality), and charge it with the duty of using the fund for the specified purpose; or (2) he may form an association with juristic personality for the purpose of administering the fund; or (3) he may create a juristic person out of the fund itself.

Fungible Things = *Vertretbare Sachen*. Defined by 91.

G.

Gift = *Schenkung*. Defined by 516.

Good Faith = *Guter Glaube*. Defined by 932.

Guardian = *Vormund*. Where several persons act jointly as guardian, they are called co-guardians (*Mitvormünder*). A supervising guardian (*Gegenvormund*) is a person who is appointed to supervise the acts of the guardian. A supplementary guardian (*Beistand*) is a person appointed to assist and supervise a mother in her exercise of the parental power.

H.

Heirs = *Erben*. Defined by 1922.

Heritable Building Right = *Erbbaurecht*. Defined by 1012.

Hortatory Process = *Mahnverfahren*. Regulated by sects. 688—703 of the Code of Civil Procedure.

Hypotheca = *Hypothek*. Defined by 1113.

I.

Indirect Possession = *Mittelbarer Besitz*. Defined by 868.

Ineffective. See "Void".

Inheritance = *Erbschaft*. Defined by 1922. An inheritance is the estate of a deceased person viewed as a whole (*Universitas juris*). For the distinction between a "renunciation of an inheritance" and a "disclaimer of an inheritance", see p. 520, footnote (*n*).

Inoperative. See "Void".

Interdiction = *Entmündigung*. The word "interdiction", which is borrowed from the French legal vocabulary, means the judicial reduction of a person of full age to the status of a minor.

Interruption of Prescription. See "Suspension of Prescription".

Invalid. See "Void".

Inventory = *Inventar*. Defined by 1993.

Inventory Period = *Inventarfrist*. Defined by 1994.

J.

Joint Share in an Inheritance = *Gemeinschaftlicher Erbteil.* Defined by 2093.

Joint Creditors = *Gesammtgläubiger.* Defined by 428.

Joint Debtors = *Gesammtschuldner.* Defined by 421.

Judicial Attachment = *Pfändung.* See Code of Civil Procedure, sects. 803 *et seq.*

Juristic Act = *Rechtsgeschäft.* A juristic act may be provisionally defined to be an act constituted by a declaration of intention (*q. v.*) and intended to create, transfer, or extinguish a right. A juristic act may be either unilateral (as, *e.g.*, a will) or bilateral (as, *e.g.*, a contract). The phrase "juristic act" is borrowed from the French rendering (*acte juridique*). The term "act-in-the-law", which is adopted by Schuster, is perhaps the best English expression for the German word, but it is unfortunately too cumbersome.

L.

Land Charge = *Grundschuld.* Defined by 1191.

Lease. German law distinguishes two kinds of leases; viz., Ordinary Leases (*Miete*) and Usufructuary Leases (*Pacht*). An ordinary lease differs from a usufructuary lease in two respects: (1) the subject-matter of an ordinary lease is always a "thing" (*i.e.*, a *res corporalis*, see 90), whereas that of a usufructuary lease may be a *res corporalis* or a *res incorporalis* (*e.g.*, a right of usufruct or a right to a patent may be leased under a usufructuary lease); (2) an ordinary lease confers only the right to the use of the thing leased, whereas a usufructuary lease confers not only the right to use the object leased, but also the right to take its fruits. Cf. 535 and 581. The expressions "lessor", "lessee", "rent", and "the term of the lease", are, for the sake of brevity, used in connection with both kinds of leases. The context will show whether they refer to the one or the other. An ordinary lease differs from a loan for use (*Leihe*) in that the former is for a remuneration while the latter is gratuitous. Cf. 535 and 598.

Legacy = *Vermächtnis*. Defined by 1939. See also "Testamentary Burden".

Liabilities of the Common Property = *Gesammtgutsverbindlichkeiten*. Defined by 1459 and 1530.

Lien [Right of] = *Zurückbehaltungsrecht*. Defined by 273. The term "lien" is used in this work in a somewhat wider meaning than in English law. A German lien confers on the person entitled to it not only the right to retain a thing belonging to the debtor, but also the right to refuse the performance of any act which is due to the debtor until the debtor performs his own obligation. See Schuster, p. 176.

Limited Personal Servitude = *Beschränkte persönliche Dienstbarkeit*. Defined by 1090.

Loan for Use = *Leihe*. For the distinction between a loan for use and an ordinary lease, see "Lease".

Lodgment = *Hinterlegung*. Lodgment may be provisionally defined to be the official deposit of certain classes of things (generally money, negotiable instruments and other documents and valuables: see 372 and IA 146) in a public lodgment-office established under State law (Cf. IA 144).

M.

Maintenance suitable to Station in Life = *Standesmässiger Unterhalt*. Defined by 1610.

Management of Property = *Vermögensverwaltung*. Defined by 1638.

Marriage Contract = *Ehevertrag*. Defined by 1432.

Matrimonial Régime = *Eheliches Güterrecht*. This expression is used to denote the effects of a marriage on the property of each of the spouses at the date of the marriage, or acquired subsequent to that date.

Must = *müssen*. See "Should".

N.

Necessary Defence = *Notwehr*. Defined by 227.

Negligence = *Fahrlässigkeit*. Defined by 276.

O.

Object = *Gegenstand*. The word "thing" (*Sache*) means *res corporalis* only (see 90), while the word "object" refers both to *res corporalis* and to *res incorporalis*.

Obligation to Bearer = *Schuldverschreibung auf den Inhaber*. Defined by 793.

Ought to have known = *kennen musste*. Defined by 122.

P.

Participating Descendants = *Anteilsberechtigte Abkömmlinge*. Participating descendants are the descendants who participate in a "continued community of goods".

Partnership Property = *Gesellschaftsvermögen*. Defined by 718.

Payment. See "Performance".

Performance = *Leistung*. "Performance" may be provisionally defined to be an act or forbearance which is due from one person to another. The word "Leistung" has such a variety of meanings that it is impossible to render it always by the word "performance". Sometimes it is translated by the word "delivery" (when speaking of a thing), and sometimes by the word "payment".

Periods of Warranty = *Gewährfristen*. Defined by 482.

Perpetual Charge [on Land] = *Reallast*. Defined by 1105.

Pledge [Right of] = *Pfandrecht*. Defined by 1204.

Power of Agency = *Vollmacht*. Defined by 166. Under German law a power of agency may be conferred either in express words or by implication. Hence the expression must not be taken to be synonymous with the more familiar English expression "power of attorney" which implies the presence of a formal document. See Schuster, p. 106.

Possessor of an Inheritance = *Erbschaftsbesitzer*. Defined by 2018.

Preferential Legacy = *Vorausvermächtnis*. Defined by 2150.

Principal Defects = *Hauptmängel*. Defined by 482.

Privileged Property = *Freies Vermögen*. Defined by 1650.

Promise of Debt = *Schuldversprechen*. Defined by 780.

Proprietary Possessor = *Eigenbesitzer*. Defined by 872.

Provisional Decree = *Einstweilige Verfügung*. The issue of "provisional decrees" is regulated by sects. 935 *et seq*. of the Code of Civil Procedure.

Public Auction = *Öffentliche Versteigerung*. Defined by 383.

"Public Faith of the Land Register" = *Der öffentliche Glaube des Grundbuchs*. This expression refers to the presumption of the correctness of the land register as provided for in 892.

Public Summons [Procedure by] = *Aufgebotsverfahren*. This procedure is regulated by sects. 946—1024 of the Code of Civil Procedure.

R.

Ratification = *Genehmigung*. Defined by 184. Cf. "Consent".

Real Agreement = *Einigung*. An agreement which *propria vigore* creates, transfers or extinguishes a real right is called a real agreement. See further Schuster, p. 342.

Real Servitude = *Grunddienstbarkeit*. Defined by 1018.

Receipt = *Quittung*. Defined by 368.

Reduction = *Minderung*. Defined by 462 and 634.

Régime. See " Matrimonial Régime".

Renewal Coupon = *Erneuerungsschein*. Defined by 805.

Renunciation of an Inheritance = *Erbverzicht*. For the distinction between a "renunciation of an inheritance" and a "disclaimer of an inheritance", see p. 520, footnote (*n*).

Reversionary Heir = *Nacherbe*. Defined by 2100. For the distinction between a "reversionary" heir and a "substitutional" heir, see footnote (*x*) to 2100.

S.

Self-help = *Selbsthilfe*. Self-help is the protection or assertion of one's rights without the assistance of the Courts.

Service [Contract for]. See "Work".

Share in an Inheritance = *Erbteil*. Defined by 1922.

Should = *Sollen*. German rules of interpretation draw a sharp distinction between the word "should" and the word "must" (*müssen*). The French official translation of the Civil Code is the only translation which brings out this distinction clearly. A provision containing the word "should" is merely directory, and non-compliance therewith does not invalidate the proceeding, although the person infringing the provision may, in certain cases, be liable to pay a penalty or to pay damages. On the other hand a provision containing the word "must" (or "cannot") is mandatory, and non-observance thereof renders the transaction absolutely null and void for all intents and purposes. Cf., *e.g.*, 1780 and 1781; 56, 57 and 58.

State = *Bundesstaat*. The word "State" refers to one of the States of the German Confederation. The Imperial territory Alsace-Lorraine is also deemed to be a "State" within the meaning of the Civil Code and of the Introductory Act. See IA 5.

Statutory Agent = *Gesetzlicher Vertreter*. A statutory agent is a person who is by law entitled and bound of act on behalf of another person under disposing incapacity, or in concurrence with another person of limited disposing capacity. See Index, "Statutory Agent".

Statutory Portion = *Gesetzlicher Erbteil*. The share of an inheritance to which a statutory heir is entitled in the absence of any testamentary or contractual disposition is called his "statutory portion".

Substitutional Heir = *Ersatzerbe*. Defined by 2096. For the distinction between a "substitutional" heir and a "reversionary" heir, see footnote (*x*) to 2100.

Succession *per stirpes* = *Erbfolge nach Stämmen*. Defined by 1924.

Supervising Guardian. See "Guardian".

Supplementary Guardian. See "Guardian".

Suspension of Parental Power. When a father's parental power is "suspended" (*ruht*), he does not thereby lose his usufruct over his child's property; where his parental power is forfeited (*verwirkt*), he loses *ipso facto* his right of usufruct.

Suspension of Prescription. "Suspension" (*Hemmung*) of prescription must be distinguished from "interruption" (*Unterbrechung*) of prescription. Where a prescription is suspended, the time which has run prior to the date of suspension is counted; where a prescription is interrupted, the time which has run before the date of interruption is not counted. Cf. 205 and 217.

T.

Testamentary Burden = *Auflage*. Defined by 1940. A testamentary burden differs from a legacy in that the person for whose benefit the burden is imposed on the heir or legatee has no direct right to claim the benefit; whereas a legatee has a direct right to claim the legacy bequeathed to him.

Testamentary Disposition = *Letztwillige Verfügung*. Defined by 1937.

Testamentary Gift = *Letztwillige Zuwendung*. This is a general expression denoting either a share in an inheritance given to an "heir" or a "legacy".

Things = *Sachen*. Defined by 90.

Treasure Trove = *Schatz*. Defined by 984.

Treasury = *Fiskus*. The word "Treasury" is an approximate translation of the word "Fiskus", which is the State viewed from the standpoint of private law. It is capable of having rights and of being subject to duties, and may therefore be sued even without its consent.

U.

Uncertificated Claim = *Buchforderung*. An uncertificated claim is one in respect of which a certificate cannot be issued.

Unlawful Interference = *Verbotene Eigenmacht*. Defined by 858.

Usucapion = *Ersitzung*. Defined by 937.

Usufruct = *Niessbrauch*. Defined by 1030.

V.

Void = *Nichtig*. A defective juristic act may be:

(A) "void". A juristic act which is void is considered as absolutely non-existent in the eye of the law; it is void *ab initio* for all intents and purposes. Any interested party is entitled to set up the fact that an act is void. The word "void" is, however, used in a somewhat different sense in connection with marriage. A void marriage is not void *per se*, but is deemed to be valid until it is declared void by a non-appealable decree obtained in an action brought especially in that behalf. Such an action is known as an action for nullity (*Nichtigkeitsklage*);

(B) "voidable" (*anfechtbar*). A voidable juristic act is and remains valid until it is avoided by a declaration made by the party entitled to avoid it. After a voidable act has been avoided, it is deemed to be void *ab initio* (cf. 142), and the rules relating to void juristic acts apply. The word "voidable" is used in a different sense with reference to marriage. A voidable marriage is and remains valid until it is avoided by a nonappealable decree obtained in an action for avoidance (*Anfechtungsklage*);

(C) "inoperative", "invalid", "ineffective", "of no effect" (*unwirksam*). The expression "*unwirksam*" is used in the Code in different senses. Sometimes it means "void" (see, *e. g.*, 111); sometimes it means that the juristic act is void not for all intents and purposes, but only in certain respects or as against certain persons (see, *e.g.*, 135, 161); sometimes it means that the juristic act has *not yet* fulfilled, but *may subsequently fulfil, one or more of the requirements necessary to its validity* (*see*, *e.g.*, 108, 174, 185).

W.

Will = *Testament*. Defined by 1937.

Without Delay = *Unverzüglich*. Defined by 121.

Work [Contract for] = *Werkvertrag*. A contract for Service (*Dienstvertrag*) is a contract for the *performance* of service, while a contract for work is for the production of a *result* to be brought about by the performance of service (as, *e.g.*, repair of a thing). Cf. the Roman distinction between *locatio operarum* and *locatio operis*.

INDEX.

IA=Introductory Act (Appendix A).

BOOK REVIEW. [1]

A CHINESE COMMENTARY ON THE GERMAN CIVIL CODE. [2]

ERNEST J. SCHUSTER, LL. D.

THE fact that the first English translation of the *German Civil Code* should have been produced by a citizen of the Celestial Empire proves that the East and West have, after all, come much nearer to each other than is generally supposed. The translator is obviously a man of exceptional ability and industry, and he must be congratulated on the completion of a task which, even for one who is not handicapped by the difficulty of translating from an acquired into an acquired language, would have been sufficiently arduous. As a general rule, the translation is not only correct, but as intelligible as a literal reproduction of the highly technical forms of expression of the *German Civil Code* can possibly be. It would have been miraculous if mistakes had been avoided entirely, but the non-accomplishment of such a miracle does not diminish our admiration for the translator's talents. It may however be useful to point out some deficiencies which, in our opinion, would have been avoidable, and which somewhat detract from the usefulness of the work.

The expressions by which German technical terms are rendered are to a

[1] From *Journal of the Society of Comparative Legislation*, Vol. 8, Part 2 (1907), pp. 247–250.

[2] Chung Hui Wang, *The German Civil Code*, translated and annotated with a historical introduction and appendices, London: Stevens and Sons, Limited, 1907, pp. xxv and 631.

large extent—perhaps to a larger extent than the courteous and complimentary acknowledgment in the preface implies—taken from the present writer's work on *German Civil Law*. Without claiming any special merit in respect of the choice of these expressions, he may be allowed to express his approval of this course, on the ground that it is obviously desirable that English authors who write on continental law should, as much as possible, establish a uniform terminology. I cannot, therefore, help regretting that Dr. Wang, having once made such an extensive surrender of originality, should not have entirely refrained from the difficult task of coining new expressions, more particularly as some of the terms invented by him are eminently calculated to mislead English readers. As the elucidation of each particular instance of this fact requires an undue sacrifice of space, one example must suffice. The terms *Vorbehaltsgut* and *Eingebrachtes Gut* are respectively rendered by " separate property " and " contributed property". This necessarily creates the entirely mistaken impression that the *Eingebrachtes Gut* is not the separate property of the spouse to which it belongs, and that in the case of spouses living under any régime of community of goods, the "contributed property" forms part of the common fund. The provision of s. 1555, which refers to spouses living under the régime of community of movables, and which Dr. Wang translates: "the husband does not have separate property", will be taken by any uninformed reader to mean that under the régime in question the whole of the husband's property must necessarily belong to the common fund, which reading is, of course, entirely opposed to the true meaning of the section. The fact that Dr. Wang, very naturally, does not always know whether a particular word has a technical meaning in German law is another source of error. If, for instance, he had known that the word *Niederlassung* has a well-defined technical meaning, he would not have said, as he does in his translation of s. 7, that "a person who *habitually resides* in a place establishes his domicile in that place", and would not thereby have created an entirely mistaken impression as to the meaning of "domicile" in German law.

The footnotes form the least satisfactory part of the book. If the use of a Code is not to be a pitfall, it is absolutely necessary to mention in their appropriate places the separate enactments by which the rules contained in the Code are supplemented or modified. This is done with respect to some of the provisions of the Codes, but in the majority of cases these supplemental references are either omitted entirely or given in an incomplete or inadequate manner. Thus, for instance, a reader is led to believe by s. 765 that no guarantee is valid unless evidenced by a document signed by the surety, whilst in reality (owing to the effect of Commercial Code s. 350, to which the translator fails to call attention) no writing is required for any *commercial* guarantees. The note to s. 12 states that the provision contained in that section for the protection of names applies to the names of "juristic persons" as well as to the names of natural persons, but it omits to call attention to the elaborate rules as to the firm-names of single traders and commercial partnerships and companies contained in Commercial Code ss. 17, 18. In the note to s. 22, which deals with associations established to carry out "economic enterprises", and which explains that the term "economic enterprises" includes "commercial enterprises", as well as others which are not of a commercial nature, the translator fails to point out that the section does not at all apply to associations established for commercial purposes, as these are entirely governed by the rules relating to them contained in the Commercial Code or in other Statutes. The notes to the sections dealing with "powers of agency" fail to notice the extremely wide power of agency which German law attributes to a "procuration holder" by virtue of s. 49 of the Commercial Code. The translator does not call attention to the fact that the provision against compound interest contained in s. 248 is subject to a most important exception provided for by s. 355 of the Commercial Code.

These, and numerous other omissions of the same kind, cannot be excused on the ground of want of space, as many of the notes contained in the book might well have been dispensed with, being either superfluous or unintelligible or inaccurate. Statements, for instance, like that contained in the note to s. 793 (which mentions "theatre tickets, meal tickets, and bathing tickets" among "the most common examples" of obligations to bearer), or like that contained in the note to s. 872 (which tells the reader that "a proprietary possessor has no possessory action"), ought not to appear in the work of an author so learned and talented as Dr. Wang.

The idea of having a glossary of English technical terms (*i.e.* of English terms used as equivalents of German technical terms) is a happy one, but the explanation of the terms is not always satisfactory, and the glossary is very incomplete, as it omits the equivalents of many technical expressions of German law which quite specially call for explanation. Thus, the equivalents of *Verzug*, *Verschulden*, *Vorsatz*, *beschränkte Geschäftsfähigkeit*, *Bereicherung*, *Schuldübernahme*, and many other similar highly technical terms, are not contained in the glossary, whilst some of the English expressions used for them by the translator are particularly liable to be misunderstood (*e. g.* the expression "default", by which the word *Verzug* is generally translated, but which in s. 425 is also used as the equivalent of *Verschulden*, and the expression "fault", which in other places is intended to reproduce the last-mentioned term).

The publishers deserve recognition for the excellence of the printing and the magnificence of the outward appearance of the book. It is to be hoped that they will be rewarded by an extensive sale, and that in a new edition the book will be made as useful and trustworthy as it can easily be made by judicious correction.

编校絮语

（一）

我国法律界通称的《德国民法典》，1896年7月1日由德意志帝国议会（Reichstag）通过，1896年8月18日经皇帝签署，1896年8月24日公布于《帝国法律公报》（Reichsgesetzblatt），自1900年1月1日起施行。

1907年，王宠惠先生的《德国民法典》英译本，由英国伦敦斯蒂文森有限责任公司出版，是《德国民法典》的第一个英文译本。时年王宠惠先生二十六岁。

（二）

《德国民法典》公布后，在世界范围获得了广泛的赞誉。就此，王宠惠先生在《德国民法典》英译本翻译前言（Preface）中例举了英国当时两位重要法学家的评价。一是弗雷德里克·威廉·梅特兰（Frederic William Maitland）在其所译《中世纪政治理论》的译者导言（Introduction）中，盛赞《德国民法典》是“有史以来最精心制定的国家法律”〔1〕。二是亚历山大·皮尔斯·希金斯（Alexander Pearce Higgins）在其文章《德国民法典的制定》中对《德国民法典》的高度推崇，称《德国民法典》是“所有将要制定成文法典的国家效法的样本”〔2〕。而

---

〔1〕 语见 *Political Theories of the Middle Age*, Translator's Introduction, p. xvii。按：《中世纪政治理论》1900年由Cambridge University Press出版，系梅特兰译自德国著名法学家奥托·祁克（Otto Gierke, 1841-1921）所著《德意志合作社法》（Das deutsche Genossenschaftsrecht）第三卷第十一章（第502—644页），德文标题为Die publicistischen Lehren des Mittelalters。王宠惠先生在《德国民法典》英译本翻译前言（Preface）中的文字表达，容易使人将梅特兰误解为该书作者。

〔2〕 语见 Alexander Pearce Higgins, “The Making of the German Civil Code”, in: *Journal of the Society of Comparative Legislation*, Vol. 6, 1905, pp. 95-105。

在王宠惠先生本人看来,《德国民法典》是德国最有学识的法学者们历时二十二年精心研究成果的结晶,整部法典结构科学,条文表述精细严谨,是一部不朽的法典文献,即使在英语的文化世界中,也享有相当崇高的地位,具有学术研究上和法律实务上的价值。因此应当为《德国民法典》出版英译本。然而,迄至王宠惠先生着手英译《德国民法典》时,却没有英译本。〔1〕这或许是王宠惠先生英译《德国民法典》的最主要动因。

(三)

王宠惠先生出生于1881年。1895年考入北洋大学堂法科,1899年毕业,因学习成绩优异,于翌年取得"钦字第一号考凭"〔2〕。1901年东渡日本。1902年受官派,自日本赴美留学,先在加利福尼亚州立大学就读,不久转入耶鲁大学法学院。1903年取得法学硕士学位〔3〕,成绩列法学院第一名,获 Magna Cum Laude 荣誉〔4〕,"受卒业证书时","代表全校四千余人致答词"〔5〕。1905年取得民法学博士学位(D. C. L., Doctor of Civil Law)〔6〕,获 Summa Cum Laude 荣誉〔7〕,博士论文的题目为"住所:比较法上的研究"(Domicil: A Study in Comparative Law)。随后前往

---

〔1〕 Chung Hui Wang, *The German Civil Code*, translated and annotated with a historical introduction and appendices, London: Stevens and Sons, Limited, 1907, Preface, pp. v-vi.

〔2〕 所称"考凭",即学位文凭,王宠惠先生因此被认为是中国第一张大学文凭的获得者。

〔3〕 关于王宠惠先生1903年在耶鲁大学法学院毕业时取得的法学硕士学位,国内学者有写LL. M. 者,有写M. L. 者。前者为拉丁语 Legum Magister 的缩写,后者为英语 Master of Laws 的缩写,依陆谷孙主编《英汉大词典》(上海译文出版社1993年版)说明,二者等同(同义)。

〔4〕 见 Bulletin of Yale University, Law School Catalogue, 1903-1904, at 50; 引自王伟:《中国近代留洋法学博士考(1905-1950)》,上海人民出版社2011年版,第63页。按:Magna Cum Laude,拉丁语,意为"学业成绩优等"。

〔5〕 梁启超:《新大陆游记》,见《梁启超全集》(第二册),北京出版社1999年版,第1149页。

〔6〕 关于王宠惠先生博士学位的类别,见王宠惠先生在其《德国民法典》英译本所署;关于王宠惠先生取得博士学位的时间,见王宠惠先生博士论文首页所载(王宠惠博士论文的中文翻译,参见张仁善编:《王宠惠法学文集》,法律出版社2008年版,第117—146页)。另据王伟在《中国近代留洋法学博士考(1905-1950)》第63页的记述,王宠惠先生取得博士学位的具体时间为1905年6月28日。

〔7〕 见 Bulletin of Yale University, Law School Catalogue, 1905-1906, at 76; 引自王伟:《中国近代留洋法学博士考(1905-1950)》,上海人民出版社2011年版,第63页。按:Summa Cum Laude,拉丁语,意为"学业成绩最优异"。

欧洲，在英国伦敦和德国柏林从事法学研究，至1911年9月回国。

王宠惠先生旅欧期间，来回于英国伦敦和德国柏林；在伦敦取得英国律师资格[1]，在德国被选为柏林比较法学会会员，1907年《德国民法典》英译本在英国伦敦出版。

关于王宠惠先生英译《德国民法典》，国内学者一般认为是王宠惠先生到欧洲之后在半年左右的时间内完成的。例如，张生教授在文章中说：[2]

> 1907年，在德国柏林比较法学会研修期间，王宠惠即开始对德国民法典产生了浓厚的兴趣。

并说：

> 至1907年8月1日，在短短的半年多的时间里，王宠惠完成了英文本《德国民法典》的翻译，……

祝曙光教授说：[3]

> 王宠惠获得耶鲁大学法学博士学位后，继续在欧洲求学，考取了英国的律师资格，并被选为“柏林比较法学会”会员，是会员中唯一的亚洲人。在“柏林比较法学会”的讨论中，王宠惠萌生了英译《德国民法》的念头。

刘宝东博士也说：[4]

> 此时[5]，他做了一件令西方法学界震惊的事——以令人惊讶的工作效率和隽永畅达的文笔，用了半年左右的时间，将晦涩难懂的《德国民法典》翻译成英文，并于1907年由英国伦敦著名的斯蒂芬

---

〔1〕 在所接触到的关于王宠惠的资料中，一般都只说王宠惠先生在伦敦取得英国律师资格，唯刘昕杰博士在文章《王宠惠评传》（刊于《政治法学研究》2014年第1卷）中说王宠惠先生是在伦敦中殿律师学院（Middle Temple，亦译中殿律师协会）取得的英国律师资格。

〔2〕 张生：“王宠惠与中国法律近代化——一个知识社会学的分析”，载《比较法研究》2009年第3期。

〔3〕 祝曙光：《法官外交家王宠惠》，福建教育出版社2015年版，第31页。

〔4〕 刘宝东：《出山未比在山清：王宠惠》，团结出版社2010年版，第47页。除上述外，台北《传记文学》第44卷第1期所刊吴相湘《王宠惠是蜚声国际法学家》一文亦说，王宠惠先生到欧洲后“抽暇将1900年德国民法译为英文，1907年刊行”；亦见胡文俊编：《王宠惠与中华民国》，广东人民出版社2006年版，第48页。

〔5〕 指王宠惠先生到欧洲之后。

斯书店出版。

但国外有学者却有不同的看法。1975 年和 1994 年出版的《德国民法典》英译本在“译者说明和致谢”中都有如下文字：

> It is proof of this academic and comparative legal interest that two English translations of the BGB were made and published within ten years of its entry into force. The first, and perhaps the better, of these translations was done by Dr. Chung Hui Wang, who subsequently became the Chinese justice on the Permanent Court of International justice, and was published in London (although drafted at Yale Law School) in 1907. Wang's achievement is all the more remarkable in view of his non-English-speaking origins.[1]

依上述引文括号内的文字，译者显然认为王宠惠先生事实上在耶鲁大学法学院期间就已开始翻译《德国民法典》。

以上两种说法，目前似乎均无有力的材料以资证实。不过，我们还是认为后者应更为可信。

首先，《德国民法典》被称为法学家之作品，概念严谨抽象，条文表达精密，各种法律术语在整个法典中始终保持相同含义，各条款间相互指示适用繁复，内容艰涩难懂，即便德国法院，对《德国民法典》都至少经历二十年才能熟练适用，[2]再者，整部法典及其施行法二者条文总量不少，因此，要在短期内高品质地翻译成任何一种其他语言，相信都是十分困难的。

其次，国内学者认为王宠惠先生到了欧洲以后才开始翻译《德国民法典》，可能主要是基于：①王宠惠先生的《德国民法典》英译本出版于王宠惠先生到欧洲之后的 1907 年；②段彩华所著《民国第一位法学家王宠惠传》对王宠惠先生翻译《德国民法典》的生动描写。

考虑到国内一般读者目前还不容易读到这部传记作品，也为读者对

---

〔1〕 Ian S. Forrester, Simon L. Goren, Hans-Michael Ilgen (translators), *The German Civil Code*, Fred B. Rothman & Company, 1975, Transltors' Comments and Acknowledgments, p. xxi; Simon L. Goren (translators), *The German Civil Code*, Fred B. Rothman & Company, 1994, Transltors' Comments and Acknowledgments, p. xxiii.

〔2〕 参见［德］罗伯特·霍恩、海因·科茨、汉斯·G. 莱塞：《德国民商法导论》，楚建译，谢怀栻校，中国大百科全书出版社 1996 年版，第 70 页。

王宠惠先生英译《德国民法典》拥有美好的想象，容节录原文于此：[1]

> 一九〇七年，他二十六岁，对《德国民法》有着浓厚的兴趣，不但精研了它，背诵了它，并且着手把它译成英文本。
>
> 当时《德国民法》……被世界各国所推崇，认为是法律学上的新纪元。在“柏林比较法学会”里，也被各种国籍的会员们，认为是学术上的瑰宝。
>
> 在学会的讨论中，他提出那本书的价值和优点，为大家所折服。当他提到要翻译成英文时，别人反倒觉得好笑了。
>
> “王先生，”德国的史普林说：“这本《德国法》，早有英国的法学权威约翰森扬言要翻译。”
>
> “是呀，”英国的乔埃士也说：“美国的法学专家鲁韦，已经在两年前就着手翻译了，只是还没有译完而已。”
>
> “你，一个中国人，不会比英国人译得更好的。”别的人向他提供意见。
>
> “更不会比美国人译得标准。”另外的会员说。
>
> 可是，王宠惠对这件事有决心和兴趣，看成是一种责任，不管别人怎样说，他打开那本书，伏在桌案上，开始翻译了。思潮澎湃，志气昂扬，工作一开始便无法停止，黄昏当早晨，晚上当下午，每天除了正常的读书做事外，别的时间都用在翻译那本书上。
>
> 一气呵成，他的英译《德国民法》脱稿了。让情绪冷静几天，再用阅读者的心情，仔细评赏一遍，自己深具信心，很快坐船到伦敦去，想法子接洽书店或出版社把它印出来。

然而，值得说明的是，以上文字只能以“小说家言”视之，而不能作为信史。作者在“后记”中明确说：为王宠惠先生写传记，遇到的困难之一是，“王先生是一位从事立法、司法、行政和外交工作的人，生活非常严肃，一举一动都可以做世人的模范。为他写传记，要让人尊敬他信服他，比较容易，而想让读者觉得他的生平在严肃中也有趣味的一面，爱不忍释的看下去，是很费斟酌的事”。为此，其在写作上，采用的是“小说的表现形式，除了让事件前后连贯，脉络相通外，描写尽可能求其

〔1〕 段彩华：《民国第一位法学家王宠惠传》，近代中国出版社1982年印行，第101—103页。特别感谢华东政法大学法律学院陈颐教授数年前惠赠该书影印件。笔者于此抄录书中文字，容有机会当面向著者表示感谢。

活泼、轻松、完整。每一件经历、事迹，形成一个单元，自成一个小段落。让读者在欣赏时，觉得是读小说和资治通鉴一类的故事”。[1]

再次，在王宠惠先生法学博士论文《住所：比较法上的研究》所列参考书目中，关于德语部分有以下四项：[2]

1. *Bürgerliches Gesetzbuch für das Deutsche Reich*. (《德意志帝国民法典》)

2. *Motive zu dem Entwurfe eines Bürgerlichen Gesetzbuches für das Deutsche Reich*, Berlin und Leizig, 1888. (《民法典草案立法理由书》，柏林和莱比锡，1888年出版)[3]

3. Christian Friedrich Mühlenbruch: *Lehrbuch des Pandecten-Rechts*, Halle, 1844, 3 vols. (克里斯蒂安·弗里德里希·米伦布鲁赫：《学说汇纂教科书》，哈勒，1844年出版，三卷)[4]

4. Friedrich Carl von Savigny: *System des heutigen Römischen Rechts*, Berlin, 1848, 8 vols. (弗里德里希·卡尔·冯·萨维尼：《当代罗马法体系》，柏林，1848年出版，八卷)[5]

从博士论文的参考文献可以看到，王宠惠先生已完全具备英译《德国民法典》的德语能力（英语能力固不待论），加之王宠惠先生对“目前美国只有耶鲁大学法学院固定开设德国民法课程”的观察，以及关于“英语国家自然不会想到要将《德国民法典》译成英文本”的认识，[6]我们有理由相信，以王宠惠先生的智慧、卓识（对《德国民法典》价值的认识）和远见，在撰写博士论文期间应该就已经有英译《德国民法典》的想法，甚至至少已着手英译《德国民法典》的准备工作。[7]我们甚至

---

〔1〕 参见段彩华：《民国第一位法学家王宠惠传》，近代中国出版社1982年印行，第291—292页。

〔2〕 参见张仁善编：《王宠惠法学文集》，法律出版社2008年版，第119—121页。

〔3〕 所称《民法典草案理由书》系第一委员会就其民法典草案所提交的立法说明，共五卷，分总则、债法、物法、亲属法和继承法各一卷，于1888年出版。

〔4〕 米伦布鲁赫所著《学说汇纂教科书》共三卷，第一卷出版于1835年，第二卷出版于1836年，第三卷出版于1837年。

〔5〕 萨维尼所著《当代罗马法体系》共八卷，第一卷至第三卷出版于1840年，第四卷和第五卷出版于1841年，第六卷出版于1847年，第七卷出版于1848年，第八卷出版于1849年。

〔6〕 Chung Hui Wang, *The German Civil Code*, translated and annotated with a historical introduction and appendices, London: Stevens and Sons, Limited, 1907, Preface, p. v, and note *a*.

〔7〕 前文提到1975年和1994年《德国民法典》英译本的译者认为王宠惠先生在耶鲁大学法学院期间已将《德国民法典》草译成英文（drafted at Yale Law School）。

猜想，王宠惠先生之所以在取得耶鲁大学法学博士学位后，去到欧洲的英国和德国继续从事法学研究，其中一个重要的原因可能就是为了最终完成《德国民法典》的翻译工作，并寻找机会在英国出版《德国民法典》英译本。〔1〕

最后，附带说一句，倘若前述传记关于王宠惠先生在柏林比较法学会讨论会中提出要将《德国民法典》翻译成英文的描述是真实的，那么，以王宠惠先生的稳重，即便不是翻译工作已近完成，也不会只是“着手翻译”或才开始有将《德国民法典》译成英文的想法，就在那样场合做那样的表示。

（四）

关于王宠惠先生英译《德国民法典》，还有一个饶有趣味的问题：倘若旧金山当年不发生地震，沃尔特·鲁韦（Walter Loewy）的工作室和图书室没有毁于地震或随后的火灾，王宠惠是否仍然能成为《德国民法典》的第一个英译者。

沃尔特·鲁韦的《德国民法典》英译本于1909年出版后，有书评说，鲁韦1906年开始英译《德国民法典》，因发生“旧金山大火”〔2〕，其图书室被毁，翻译工作不得不中断，《德国民法典》英译本的出版因此

---

〔1〕 至少到王宠惠先生在耶鲁大学研习法律学的那个年代，比较法研究在整个美国都并不很受重视。而在欧洲，王宠惠先生至少看到：在德国有柏林国际比较法学和国民经济学联合会（Die Internationale Vereinigung für vergleichende Rechtswissenschaft und Volkswirtschaftslehre zu Berlin），在英国则有比较立法学会（The Society of Comparative Legislation）。而且，对于英国，王宠惠先生应该至少还会看到以下一些事实：①英国学界重视德国的法学和立法。前已述及，德国著名法学家奥托·祁克著作的一些内容被译成英文在英国出版，Alexander Pearce Higgins 发表专文介绍《德国民法典》的制定（The Making of the German Civil Code）。除此以外，《比较立法学会杂志》等刊物常有关于德国法律的文章或报道。②英国一些著名学者对《德国民法典》赞誉有加，且都颇推崇（见前文）。③当时英国从事德国法研究的专家，欧内斯特·约瑟夫·舒斯特（Ernest Joseph Schuster），对德国私法有相当程度的研究。舒斯特在1896年，即《德国民法典》颁布的那一年，先后在英国伦敦的内殿律师协会（The Inner Temple）和林肯律师协会（Lincoln's Inn）发表演讲，介绍《德国民法典》的制定情况和立法成就（两次演讲的内容分别刊于 *The Law Quarterly Review*, Vol. 12, 1896, pp. 17-35 和 *Journal of the Society of Comparative Legislation*, Vol. 1, 1896-1897, pp. 191-211，文章标题均为 The German Civil Code）。

〔2〕 1906年4月18日旧金山发生7.8级强烈地震并引发大火，给旧金山整座城市造成毁灭性的影响，旧金山市当时的有力人士为增强城市的未来发展，着意减少地震在灾害方面的角色而称之为“旧金山大火”。

被推迟，结果，王宠惠先生的英译本先于鲁韦的英译本出版。[1]言下之意，倘若鲁韦的图书室没有被地震所毁，《德国民法典》的第一个英译者应当是鲁韦，而不是王宠惠先生。

就此，我们仅提示以下两点，如何看待，读者尽可见仁见智：

(1) 王宠惠先生在撰写博士论文期间至少已着手准备英译《德国民法典》，已如前述。而关于鲁韦英译《德国民法典》的情况，在该英译本的翻译前言（Preface）中说，为推动美国的比较法学研究，1905年宾夕法尼亚州律师协会任命了一个特别委员会，1906年该委员会提出一项报告，建议由宾夕法尼亚州律师协会和宾夕法尼亚大学法学院合作翻译出版附有适当注释的德国民法典。委员会在该建议被接受后与Walter Loewy商定，由后者负责《民法典》和《民法典施行法》条文的翻译工作。依此可以确知，鲁韦英译《德国民法典》的工作，至早始于1906年。

(2) 王宠惠先生的英译本只记载1907年出版，未记载出版月份。鲁韦英译本记载的出版时间为1909年12月9日。前后相差足有两年以上的时间[2]。可以认为，旧金山大地震对鲁韦翻译工作的影响无疑是巨大的，但倘若没有大地震，鲁韦的英译本是否可能在1907年结束前出版，也是值得怀疑的。

当然，于此叙及此事，不过聊为趣谈，而非着意强调谁是《德国民法典》的第一个英译者。王宠惠日后成为海牙常设国际法庭的法官，自然缘于其在国际法学界所享有的声誉。而王宠惠先生之所以能蜚声国际法学界，无疑与其英译《德国民法典》有着极为重要的关系[3]。但我们大家必定也会有共识，即这一切并不是因为王宠惠先生系《德国民法典》的第一个英译者，而是因为其在《德国民法典》英译本中所表现出来的卓越学识和才华。

(五)

王宠惠先生的《德国民法典》英译本，自其出版以来一直受到法律界的肯定和推崇。于此，略陈点滴，以飨读者。

---

〔1〕 See *Michigan Law Review*, Vol. 8, No. 8, Jun., 1910, pp. 692-693.

〔2〕 英国著名的德国法专家欧内斯特·约瑟夫·舒斯特（Ernest Joseph Schuster）就王宠惠先生英译本而撰写的评论文章，发表于1907年。依此推算，王宠惠英译本的出版时间不会晚于1907年12月初。

〔3〕 参见浦薛凤："忆王宠惠博士及其英译《德国民法》"，载《传记文学》第38卷第3期。

英国著名的德国法专家欧内斯特·约瑟夫·舒斯特（Ernest Joseph Schuster），在王宠惠先生的英译本出版后不久就发表评论文章给予高度赞扬，称赞王宠惠先生的翻译表达准确，文辞易于理解，并说译者“显然是一位具有非凡天赋和极为勤勉的”学者，其才华令人“钦慕”。〔1〕

1909年12月，沃尔特·鲁韦（Walter Loewy）的《德国民法典》英译本〔2〕在美国出版，多数评论认为王宠惠先生的英译本优于鲁韦的英译本。〔3〕

德国学者弗里茨-康拉德·克吕格尔（Fritz-Konrad Krüger）在其1915年出版的《德意志帝国的政府与政治》书中，称王宠惠先生的《德国民法典》英译本是最好的。〔4〕

学者埃德温·M. 博查德（Edwin M. Borchard）在《德国的法律及法律文献指南》〔5〕，以及西蒙·L. 戈伦（Simon L. Goren）在1994年出版的《德国民法典》英译本中，都认为王宠惠先生的英译本优于鲁韦的英译本〔6〕。

---

〔1〕 全文见本书附录 Ernest Joseph Schuster, “A Chinese Commentary on the German Civil Code”；原载英国《比较立法学会杂志》1907年第8卷第247—249页（*Journal of the Society of Comparative Legislation*, Vol. 8, 1907, pp. 247-249）。中文翻译见欧内斯特·J. 舒斯特：“一位中国学者对德国民法典的译注”，陈颐译，载《华东政法学院学报》2006年第2期。

〔2〕 Walter Loewy, *The Civil Code of the German Empire*, as enacted on August 18, 1896, with the introductory statute, Boston: The Boston Book Company, 1909.

〔3〕 针对沃尔特·鲁韦《德国民法典》英译本所发表的评论文章，我们共收集到五篇，其中四篇都认为王宠惠先生的英译本更优。这四篇评论文章分别刊载于：*The American Political Science Review*, Vol. 4, No. 3, Aug., 1910, pp. 444-445; *Michigan Law Review*, Vol. 8, No. 8, Jun., 1910, pp. 692-693; *Columbia Law Review*, Vol. 10, No. 7, Nov., 1910, pp. 684-685; *The Yale Law Journal*, Vol. 19, No. 6, Apr., 1910, pp. 477-480。浦薛凤先生在文章《忆王宠惠博士及其英译〈德国民法〉》（刊于台北《传记文学》第38卷第3期）中提到“各国法学之书评，皆谓王译较优”，并说：“此次翻阅王、鲁两译本，又曾选择约五十项条文，彼此对照比较，则知王氏之英译确较高明，此因王译文字更为简洁而更为正式，合于法律条款之体裁，而在选字措辞，更为确切明白，不容曲解误会，是则书评之所以分别抑扬，王译之所以被选为参考必读课本，自非出于偶然。”

〔4〕 Fritz-Konrad Krüger, *Government and Politics of the German Empire*, New York: World Book Company, 1915, p. 307.

〔5〕 Edwin M. Borchard, *Guide to the Law and Legal Literature of Germany*, Washtington: Government Printing Office, 1912, pp. 72-73.

〔6〕 Simon L. Goren (translators), *The German Civil Code*, Fred B. Rothman & Company, 1994, Transltors' Comments and Acknowledgments, p. xxiii. See also Ian S. Forrester, Simon L. Goren, Hans-Michael Ilgen (translators), *The German Civil Code*, Fred B. Rothman & Company, 1975, Transltors' Comments and Acknowledgments, p. xxi.

浦薛凤先生回忆说，王宠惠先生的英译本，在文字上，“句斟字酌，意义明确，气韵平衡，流利自然”，且“每句每段，不特毫无洋人执笔之牵强痕迹，而且具有能文老手之高雅风格”，因而成为英、美各大学法律学院所指导的参考必读书。〔1〕

美国大学法学院直到20世纪70年代，关于《德国民法典》，仍以王宠惠先生的英译本为经典教材。美国前总统尼克松就读杜克大学法学院期间，曾读过王宠惠先生的译本。据传，尼克松在20世纪50年代（时为美国副总统）访问我国台湾地区时，因感佩王宠惠的才华，曾问及王宠惠并表示“愿拜访致敬”。〔2〕

德国著名法律学家米夏埃尔·马丁内克（Michael Martinek）教授2003年在为陈卫佐教授翻译的《德国民法典》撰写的导言中说：王宠惠译注的《德国民法典》英译本，“对于当时包括中国、美国在内的世界各国了解、学习和借鉴德国民法典是功不可没的。这个英译本不但是世界上最早的德国民法典英译本，而且在近70年的时间里（从1907年至1975年），一直是当时世界上惟一的德国民法典英文全译本。用我们今天的眼光来看，它的译文仍然十分出色，注解也不乏真知灼见，至今仍有很高的学术价值。这是中国人的骄傲”。〔3〕

另外，国外出版人 Kessinger Publishing 在2010年、Nabu Press 在

---

〔1〕 参见浦薛凤：“忆王宠惠博士及其英译《德国民法》”，载《传记文学》第38卷第3期。

〔2〕 有关记述，参见刘宝东：《出山未比在山青：王宠惠》，团结出版社2010年版，第48页；祝曙光：《法官外交家王宠惠》，福建教育出版社2015年版，第32—33页；刘昕杰：“王宠惠评传”，载《政治法学研究》2014年第1卷；高志全：“王宠惠：民国第一位法学家”，载《东莞日报》2011年9月21日第A05版。

〔3〕 引文录自陈卫佐译注：《德国民法典》，法律出版社2004年版，[德] 米夏埃尔·马丁内克：《德国民法典与中国对它的继受——陈卫佐的德国民法典新译本导言》。我们注意到，引文中“在近70年的时间里（从1907年至1975年），一直是当时世界上惟一的德国民法典英文全译本”一语，在2006年及以后各次版本修改为“在近70年的时间里（从1907年至1975年），一直是当时世界上最权威的德国民法典英文全译本”。就此，值得说明的是：①说王宠惠先生的德国民法典英译本是1907年至1975年间唯一的《德国民法典》英文全译本，自然与实际情况不符；如所周知，沃尔特·鲁韦（Walter Loewy）的《德国民法典》英文全译本于1909年在美国出版。此外，马丁内克教授以1975年为时间界限，应该是基于1975年出版了由 Ian S. Forrester, Simon L. Goren, Hans-Michael Ilgen 合译的《德国民法典》英文全译本这一事实。②了解到在1909年就有第二个《德国民法典》英文全译本后，仅将句中“惟一的”修改为“最权威的”，在我们看来也值得商榷。就《德国民法典》至1975年止未曾修正的条文而言，1975年的英译本从整体看未必优于王宠惠先生的英译本。

2011 年、Forgotten Books 在 2016 年都曾依原版重印过王宠惠先生的《德国民法典》英译本。此或许亦可作为王宠惠先生的《德国民法典》英译本"至今仍有很高的学术价值"的注脚。

（六）

本书的编校，得益于许多师友的帮助。在这里要特别感谢的是华东政法大学法律学院陈颐教授、华东政法大学外语学院朱丽芳教授和曾在美国学习的张世超同学。还要特别感谢中国政法大学出版社第四编辑部主任刘知函博士和于水莲编辑，两位老师对学术的认真、严谨和热忱以及对我本人的宽容都让我很感动。

最后，能力所限，错误难免，敬请批评指正（amicusveritatis@ 163. com）。

戴永盛

2019 年 3 月 9 日